SECURITIZATI
STRUCTURED FI
AND CAPITAL MARKE

by

STEVEN L. SCHWARCZ
Professor of Law
Duke University School of Law
Adjunct Professor of Business Administration,
The Fuqua School of Business
Founding Director, Global Capital Markets Center
Special Counsel, Kaye Scholer LLP

BRUCE A. MARKELL
Doris S. and Theodore B. Lee Professor of Law
William S. Boyd School of Law
University of Nevada Las Vegas
Of Counsel, Stutman, Treister & Glatt PC

and

LISSA LAMKIN BROOME
Wachovia Term Professor of Banking and Finance
Director, Center for Banking and Finance
University of North Carolina at Chapel Hill, School of Law

LexisNexis™

Library of Congress Cataloging-in-Publication Data

Steven L. Schwarcz
Bruce A. Markell
Lissa L. Broome
Securitization, Structured Finance and Capital Markets
Steven L. Schwarcz
Bruce A. Markell
Lissa L. Broome
ISBN# 0820548510
Library of Congress Control Number 2004101808

Editorial Offices
744 Broad Street, Newark, NJ 07102 (973) 820-2000
201 Mission St., San Francisco, CA 94105-1831 (415) 908-3200
701 East Water Street, Charlottesville, VA 22902-7587 (804) 972-7600

(Pub.3144)

DEDICATIONS

To my patient and loving family: my mother, Joyce Lamkin,
and my husband and daughter, Adam and Anna Broome

LLB

To those who are the beginning and the end, and always will be:
Ava, Amanda and Michelle

BAM

To my impatient and loving family: Susan, Daniel, and Rebekah

SLS

PREFACE

This book provides an introduction to securitization as a method of financing. In modern practice, a large variety of assets are securitized, and students who study securitization will soon realize that many asset types have developed their own terminology and special concerns. Rather than survey all the various asset types, we have attempted to provide students with background general principles common to all types of securitizations. Additional resources, for those desiring to learn more about a particular kind of securitization, may be found at www.law.unlv.edu/faculty/bam/securitization/, and at www.law.duke.edu/globalmark.

We have used publicly available materials relating to a recent auto loan securitization by Honda to illustrate many of the basic concepts related to securitization. Students may benefit from seeing the actual documents produced in this particular transaction and learning more about the specific deal from them. These documents have been collected at the UNLV website listed above and some of them are reprinted in the appendices at the back of this book.

The materials are suitable for an independent course or seminar in securitization and structured finance, and also may be used as supplementary reading or as advanced examples in courses in bankruptcy, secured transactions, trusts, corporations, securities regulation, corporate finance, tax, banking or accounting.

We thank and acknowledge the Practising Law Institute for its permission for us to excerpt material from STEVEN L. SCHWARCZ, STRUCTURED FINANCE: A GUIDE TO THE PRINCIPLES OF ASSET SECURITIZATION (PLI 3d ed. 2003). In addition, some of the other previously published work of Professor Schwarcz listed below, has been incorporated throughout this book (with permission).

Rethinking the Disclosure Paradigm in a World of Complexity, forthcoming in 2004 U. ILL. L. REV. (2004).

Securitization Post-Enron in 25 CARDOZO L. REV. ____ (forthcoming).

Commercial Trusts as Business Organizations: Unraveling the Mystery, 58 BUS. LAW. 559 (2003).

Private Ordering, 97 NW. U. L. REV. 319 (2002).

Enron and the Use and Abuse of Special Purpose Entities in Corporate Structures, 70 U. CIN. L. REV. 1309 (2002).

Private Ordering of Public Markets: The Rating Agency Paradox, 2002 U. ILL. L. REV. 1 (2002).

The Universal Language of International Securitization, 12 DUKE J. COMP. & INT'L L. 285 (2002).

The Impact of Bankruptcy Reform on "True Sale" Determination in Securitization Transactions, 7 FORDHAM J. CORP. & FIN. LAW 353 (2002).

Judgment Proofing: A Rejoinder, 52 STAN. L. REV 77 (1999).

The Inherent Irrationality of Judgment Proofing, 52 STAN. L. REV. 1 (1999).

Towards a Centralized Perfection System for Cross-Border Receivables Financing, 20 U. PENN. J. INT'L. ECON. L. 455 (1999).

The Impact on Securitization of Revised UCC Article 9, 74 CHI.-KENT L. REV. 947 (1999).

The Universal Language of Cross-Border Finance, 8 DUKE J. COMP. & INT'L L. 235 (1998).

Rethinking the Role of Recourse in the Sale of Financial Assets, 52 BUS. LAW. 159 (1996) [co-author].

Rethinking A Corporation's Obligations to Creditors, 17 CARDOZO L. REV. 647 (1996).

The Alchemy of Asset Securitization, 1 STAN. J. L., BUS. & FINANCE 133 (1994).

The Parts Are Greater Than the Whole: How Securitization of Divisible Interests Can Revolutionize Structured Finance and Open the Capital Markets to Middle-Market Companies, 1993 COLUM. BUS. L. REV. 139 (1993).

Structured Finance: The New Way to Securitize Assets, 11 CARDOZO L. REV. 607 (1990).

We are indebted to the following authors and publishers for their generosity in giving us permission to reprint excerpts from copyrighted materials:

Richard F. Broude & Bruce A. Markell, *The Priority Provisions of the UNCITRAL Convention on the Assignment of Receivables in International Trade*, 11 INT'L INSOLVENCY REV. 121 (2002).

Claire A. Hill, *Securitization: A Low-Cost Sweetener for Lemons,* 74 WASH. U.L.Q. 1061 (1996).

Lynn M. LoPucki, *The Death of Liability,* 106 YALE L.J. 1 (1996).

Lois R. Lupica, *Asset Securitization: The Unsecured Creditor's Perspective,* 76 TEX. L. REV. 595 (1998).

Bruce A. Markell, *A View from the Field: Some Observations on the Effect of International Commercial Law Reform Efforts on the Rule of Law,* 6 IND. J. GLOBAL LEGAL STUD. 497 (1999).

We thank also Willys H. Schneider and Kathleen O'Keefe, both with Kaye Scholer LLP, for their assistance with material included in Chapter 5 on tax issues. A. Bradley Ives of David L. Babson & Company Inc. also provided helpful background for Chapter 5. Any errors, of course, remain our own. Thanks to our student research assistants who helped us prepare this manuscript, including (for Professor Schwarcz) Adam Ford; (for Professor Broome) Adam Whitten, Joel Sawyer, Stephanie Patterson, and Brian Meacham; and (for Professor Markell) Carla Kok and Jin Kim. All of us send special thanks to the students to whom we have taught these materials for their patience and guidance.

Steven L. Schwarcz
Durham, NC

Bruce A. Markell
Las Vegas, NV

Lissa L. Broome
Chapel Hill, NC

SUMMARY TABLE OF CONTENTS

TABLE OF CONTENTS

Chapter 1

AN OVERVIEW OF SECURITIZATION

§ 1.01. Introduction

Securitization is a $6 trillion ($6,000,000,000,000) industry.[1] Its benefits are becoming indispensable in such diverse areas as car loans, credit card debt, student loans and home mortgages. Indeed, in 2002, the bank holding company Citigroup stated that it was engaged in 4,249 securitization transactions, structured investment vehicles and other investment funds with its own and with clients' assets totaling $926.3 billion.[2] Credit card securitizations alone account for $67 billion of that amount.[3] Although securitization may have originated in the United States, its effects are not restricted to our domestic economy; many countries are changing their laws to gain the benefits of securitization.

For purposes of law school study, securitization can be viewed as an advanced application of several of the courses traditionally taught in the later years of law school: secured transactions, tax, securities, bankruptcy and many others. It could be described, as one of us has said, as "alchemy that really works,"[4] or, as another one of us has said, as "factoring on steroids [and] a brazen attempt to avoid the automatic stay and cash collateral provisions of bankruptcy."[5] Regardless of the initial definition, it is probably safe to say that no modern transactional lawyer, anywhere in the world, can afford to be ignorant of securitization's practices and principles.

Securitization, however, is a relatively recent phenomena. The roots of securitization trace their modern origins no further back than the 1970s.[6] At that

---

1 This amount includes approximately $3.2 trillion in securitizations involving mortgaged-backed securities, and $1.6 trillion in non-mortgaged-back securities. THE BOND MARKET ASSOCIATION, OUTSTANDING VOLUME OF AGENCY MORTGAGE-BACKED SECURITIES, 1980-2002 (Reporting data as of June 30, 2003), *at* http://www.bondmarkets.com/research/mbsdat2.shtml; THE BOND MARKET ASSOCIATION, ASSET BACKED SECURITIES OUTSTANDING BY MAJOR TYPES OF CREDIT, 1995-2002 (2003), *at* http://www.bondmarkets.com/research/absos.shtml.

2 CITIGROUP, INC., 2002 ANNUAL REPORT 38 (2003).

3 *Id.* at 45-56.

4 Alchemy refers to a technique whereby medieval chemists attempted to turn base metals into gold. This phrase appears in one of the first concise overviews of securitization, Steven L. Schwarcz, *The Alchemy of Asset Securitization*, 1 STANFORD J.L. BUS & FIN. 133 (1994).

5 Bruce A. Markell, *What If Bankruptcy Reform Is Not Dead? Securitization Exclusions Could Pose Problems*, BCD WEEKLY NEWS AND COMMENT, October 9, 2001, at A3.

6 This recent heritage may account for a lack of standardized terms. When in this book we talk about securitization, we also mean to refer to practices referred to elsewhere as "asset securitization," "structured finance," or even the "disintermediation of assets."

time, financiers began to create products that have the hallmark of securitization: a financing backed by cash flows that are isolated, legally and practically, from the intended beneficiary of the financing. To give this definition more substance, a short walk through the history of securitization is helpful.

At the beginning of the twentieth century, savings and loan associations created (or, in the argot of securitization and mortgage banking, "originated") mortgages, or loans secured by the homes of the borrowers. The ability to fund these mortgages depended heavily on core deposit flows for funds to finance local housing demand. When the housing credit market collapsed during the Depression, Congress reacted by passing the National Housing Act of 1934, intended in part to create a secondary market in mortgages. To that end, the Federal National Mortgage Association (FNMA, or "Fannie Mae") was established in 1938 to provide liquidity for mortgage investment by purchasing mortgages when funds are in short supply and selling mortgages when funds are plentiful. As the nation's demand for housing increased after World War II, a capital shortage developed, and alternative capital streams were needed to finance the growing housing industry. In 1957, the Federal Home Loan Bank Board created a credit reserve system for savings and loan associations by permitting the purchase and sale of participations in interests in mortgage loans.

The first structured financing took place in 1970 when the newly-created Government National Mortgage Association (GNMA or "Ginnie Mae") began publicly trading "pass-through" securities. In a mortgage pass-through security, the investor purchases a fractional undivided interest in a pool of mortgage loans, and is entitled to share in the interest income and principal payments generated by the underlying mortgages in the pool. Mortgage lenders originate these pools of mortgages by packaging together mortgage notes with similar characteristics as to quality, term, and interest rate. These mortgage notes (and their associated mortgages) are then placed in a trust, which collects all payments from the pool of mortgages, including interest and principal payments on the mortgages. The trust then passes on such payments to investors, who, through either a government agency, a private conduit, or direct placement, have purchased certificates of ownership or participations in the pool.

A graphical representation of these types of transactions might look like the following:

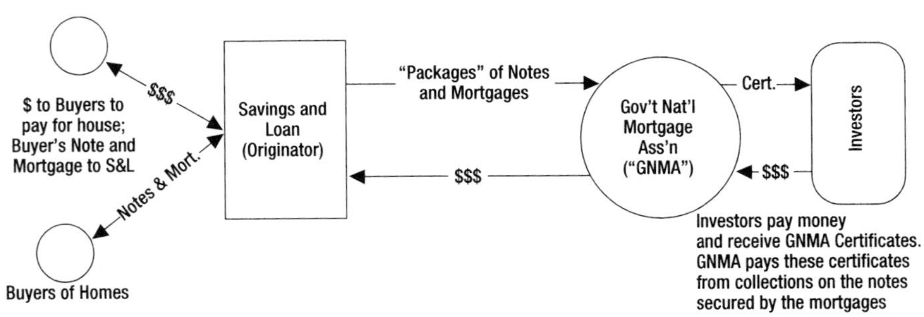

Note what happens in this structure. Originally, savings and loans "originated," kept and "serviced" the loan. Under the GNMA structure, the savings and loan can simply originate — or find — customers, and then sell off the notes and mortgages once they are signed. When this transaction is structured as a sale, the savings and loan also sells its risk (that interest rates would rise, thereby making its portfolio worth less, or that the borrower may default by failing to make payments on the mortgage when due), along with any potential reward (that if interest rates would fall, thereby making the value of the loan portfolio rise).

For a long time, home mortgages were about the only assets securitized in this way in any bulk. In recent years, however, many different types of assets have been the subject of securitization. Everyday examples would start with pools of commercial mortgage loans, and then include trade receivables, automobile loans, and credit card receivables. More exotic securitization include sports-arena revenues or even David Bowie's music royalties.

§ 1.02. Limitations on Raising Money the Old-Fashioned Way

How did securitization make the transition from a way to subsidize home mortgages to a $6 trillion dollar industry encompassing a vast array of financial assets? To understand the phenomena, you have to have at least a skeletal understanding of the traditional ways in which a company can raise money by accessing the what is called the "capital markets." In these markets, a company might raise money by selling equity securities; that is, shares or participations in the profits of a company. Shareholders are the residual owners of the firm, being paid after holders of debt, but with no necessary legal limit on the amount they may be paid. The risk that buyers of such equity interests undertake is that the company they buy into may not earn enough to pay those who hold interests senior to equity — those who lent the company money, for example — and thus equity security holders could wind up with nothing. The reward, however, is that if a business does well, the equity owners get to keep everything leftover after paying holders of debt.

This set of risks and rewards, however, may not be for everyone. Banks and other conservative institutions may very well prefer debt financing since they do not wish to incur large amounts of risk. Also, from the perspective of existing shareholders, the share of profits that a new investor would demand to contribute funds as equity may be too much — each new equity investment dilutes the ownership (and the potential profits) of the existing owners.

Debt financing comes in many different forms and flavors. The simplest method of debt financing is financing on an unsecured basis; in essence, lending money simply on the strength of the unadorned promise of the borrower to repay it. Such unsecured debt is not unheard of; most commercial paper is unsecured, and the "bonds" you hear about that are traded on national securities exchanges are also for the most part unsecured.[7] But just as some ideas may have big upside potential, so might they also have huge downside losses. When a company is not financially able to pay its debts, it might seek protection by filing for bankruptcy. When bankruptcy occurs, the general rule is that unsecured creditors share pro rata; that is, they share in proportion to the amount of their respective debts. The age of the debt (how long it has been unpaid), or even the fact that it may be represented by a judgment, is irrelevant.

One answer to the problem of unsecured debt for those interested in debt financing is to take not only the simple promise of the borrower to repay, but also to take security, or collateral, to back up that promise. The oldest form of this type of lending is the pledge, which consists of delivering the collateral to the lender to hold until the debt is repaid. The pawn shop is the modern heir to this form of lending. But some assets are valuable only if used by the debtor; an inventory of goods is useless if it cannot be sold for profit, and a car used to drive to work or deliver goods does no good parked in the lender's parking lot.

To satisfy the needs of commerce, wide-scale non-possessory secured financing evolved during the middle of the last century. Under this type of lending, a lender takes assets of the debtor as collateral, but the lender does not take possession. In lieu of the notoriety present in the changing of possession, most non-possessory security systems require some filing of a notice of the transaction, so that others will not be misled by the fact that the lender has not taken possession of the collateral. In this country, Article 9 of the Uniform Commercial Code governs these types of transactions, and that article will be discussed in Chapter 2.

The stark dichotomy of these two types of financing, however, is oversimplistic. Within each type of lending there are significant variations. One variation, at least for large companies, is provided by credit rating agencies such as Moody's Investor Service, Standard and Poor's or Fitch's Ratings.[8] These entities make their living by rating the strength of various debt offerings. You probably have heard of AAA, or "Triple A" ratings; that phrase comes from the highest rating given by Standard and Poor's or Moody's to the debt of a company.[9] And there are a plethora of these ratings: Standard and Poor's, for example, has AAA, AA, A, BBB, BB, B and so on down to C. Indeed, sometimes there are differences within these ratings; Moody's further differentiates each category

[7] Commercial paper is a debt incurred by a borrower that is evidenced by a promissory note that is repayable in 270 days or less. Bonds are debt of the borrower that is not repayable for a much longer period of time — anywhere from one year to up to twenty years.

[8] For a more detailed and extensive discussion of rating agencies, see Steven Schwarcz, *Private Ordering of Public Markets: The Rating Agency Paradox*, 2002 U. ILL. L. REV. 1 (2002).

[9] There are subtle differences in the ratings. Standard and Poor's rates debt AAA, AA, A, BBB, and so on. Fitch's Rating Service follows this format. Moody's, however, differs. The order of its ratings are Aaa, Aa, A, Baa, and so forth. In this book, we use the all capital letter approach, but intend it to be generic, and do not mean to favor one rating agency over another.

into three more areas to differentiate short-term from long-term debt; there are, for example, A-1, A-2 and A-3 debt ratings.[10]

What is the purpose of these ratings? Initially, it is to publish the perceived risk of a debt offering. Inextricably tied into the risk rating, however, is the interest rate payable on the debt offering being rated. As one might expect, to be competitive in the financial markets, AAA-rated debt obligations don't need to pay as much interest as, say, BBB-rated debt obligations. And we have a good idea on the magnitude of this difference, or spread: in the twenty-seven years between 1976 and 2002, the interest rate on AAA-rated debt obligations averaged 9.13%, while the interest rate of BBB-rated obligations averaged 10.23%; that is, there was a difference of 1.1%.[11] In the lingo of bond traders this would be a difference of 110 "basis" points, with each "basis" point being .01%. Yet another way of looking at this difference is that AAA-rated debt was 89% as costly (or about 10.7% cheaper) than BBB-rated debt.

What goes into a rating? The simple answer is that it is an assessment of the likelihood of payment, both *when* promised and *in the full amount* promised. Put more simply, a rating assesses the likelihood of *both* prompt *and* full payment. Obviously, rating agencies take the other debts of a company, as well as its prospects, into account before issuing a rating. One consequence of this calculus, and it is a consequence exploited by secured lending, is that some assets may be better indicators of repayment than the general promise of the company. If a bank takes a security interest in a debtor's fleet of trucks, as well as its unsecured promise to pay, it bargains for the right to priority — more colloquially, first call or first "dibs" — on the trucks (or their sale proceeds) should the debtor not pay its debts on time or as agreed. The study of secured transactions is the study of how to obtain this priority. As a consequence, depending on the value of the collateral and the amount of the debt, secured lending may also result in lower interest rates for borrowers.

But while secured lending may allow a lender to be first in line when a debtor liquidates all its assets, the lender still has to participate in the process of liquidation. Another way of putting this is that, at least in the United States, secured lenders are involuntary parties to a debtor's bankruptcy case. As we will see in the chapter on bankruptcy, the commencement of a bankruptcy case stays the secured lender from foreclosing, and may expose some of the lender's

---

10 A lot can turn on ratings. Many investment vehicles, such as certain mutual funds or pension funds, voluntarily restrict their holdings to only "investment grade" securities. The general definition of investment grade securities are those that are "rated in one of the four highest rating categories" of a rating agency. 12 C.F.R. § 1.2(d) (2003). In practice, this generally includes all securities which have a "BBB" or better rating.

11 Table H-15 (Selected Interest Rates), *Federal Reserve Statistical Release* (May 5, 2003), available at http://www.federalreserve.gov/releases/h15/data.htm (visited September15, 2003).

These interest rates are much lower in the first part of the 21st Century. From 2000 to 2002, the average rate on AAA-rated debt was 7.06%. The average rate on BBB-rated debt was 8.04%. The spread of .98% is close to the historic difference.

collateral to involuntary use by the debtor. When these adverse consequences are factored in, any lending directly to the borrower has to take into account the costs and hassle of a bankruptcy proceeding by the debtor.

Before linking this discussion to securitization, it is worthwhile to stop and ask: Why borrow at all? Should we all, as Shakespeare wrote, "neither a lender nor a borrower be"? The simple answer is that debt is sometimes a necessary evil. Consider a paradigm case of manufacturing. There are two phases: construction and sales. It takes money to construct, and initially that money can come from equity infusions or debt. Once construction is done, however, the goods must be sold. You have to sell what you produce to cover your cost of production, as well as reap any profit. While it would be nice to sell your wares as soon as they are built, that often is not economic reality. Moreover, while most would prefer sales to be for cash, again economic reality is different. Most business-to-business sales are on short-term credit, usually 30-day terms (not unlike your credit card debt or debt you owe to a utility: you use the service and then pay for it some 30-45 days later). During the interim — between the completion of the goods and the collection of the sales price — economic activity still continues. Employees and utilities have to be paid, materials have to be purchased to build more of whatever the firm is building. This gap has traditionally been filled by lending (either buying raw goods on 30-day credit, and thus "borrowing" from suppliers, or more formalized bank loans), or large equity investments. As set forth above, each of these have costs. And if a way exists to achieve the same result at a reduced cost, it will be chosen.

Which brings us to securitization. Securitization works because, in large part, it succeeds in providing needed cash at a cost far less than traditional means of financing. How it achieves this result is the topic of the next section.

§ 1.03. The Mechanics of a Standard Securitization

A. The Basics: Separating the Cash Flow From the Company

Securitization changes the security holder's dependence on the debtor/company for payment, by separating the source of payment from the company itself. In a typical structured financing, a company that seeks to raise cash may transfer certain of its assets to a special-purpose entity (hereinafter called the SPE),[12] which may be a trust or other similar entity that is organized in such a way that the likelihood of its bankruptcy is remote.[13] The company involved is called

[12] Sometimes these entities are referred to as special purpose vehicles (SPVs) (not to be confused with SUVs — sport utility vehicles). There is no distinction between an SPE and an SPV. We have elected to use SPE throughout this book.

[13] *See* SECURITIZATION OF FINANCIAL ASSETS, § 5.01 (Jason H.P. Kravitt ed., 2d ed. 1997).

the originator, because it usually originates or creates the income-producing assets that are the economic heart of the deal. The transfer to the SPE is intended to separate the assets from risks associated with the originator. For this reason, the originator will often structure the transfer so that it constitutes a "true sale,"[14] a sale that is sufficient under bankruptcy law to remove the assets from the originator's bankruptcy estate.

To achieve bankruptcy remoteness, the SPE's organizational structure also strictly limits its permitted business activities. The goal is to prevent creditors (other than holders of the SPE's securities) from having claims against the SPE that would enable them to file an involuntary bankruptcy petition against the SPE. Furthermore, an SPE that is owned or controlled by the originator is usually required to have one or more independent directors. The SPE must also attempt to observe all appropriate third-party formalities with the originator. These additional steps help to reduce the risk that the originator, if bankrupt, will either cause the SPE to voluntarily file for bankruptcy or persuade a bankruptcy court, in the exercise of its equitable powers, to substantively consolidate the assets and liabilities of the SPE with those of the originator.

The result is that the assets are no longer owned by the originator, but by the SPE. The assets themselves are typically intangible promises to pay the originator money some time in the future; a common example would be an originator's accounts receivable, the money owing to the originator from third parties in payment of goods or services provided to the third party by the originator. Those payment obligations generically are referred to as "receivables" or, sometimes, "financial assets."[15] The third parties obligated to pay the receivables are known as "obligors."

The SPE, and not the originator, will issue securities — usually debt or debt-like instruments — to raise cash. Those securities are intended to be payable ultimately and over time from collections on the receivables purchased by the SPE. A potential buyer of the securities therefore looks to the cash flow from the purchased receivables, and not to the credit of the originator, for repayment. The risk that these payments may not be made on time is an important factor in valuing the receivables. As long as the originator can reasonably predict the aggregate rate of default, however, it can securitize even those receivables that present some risk of uncollectibility. Therefore, a statistically large pool of receivables due from many obligors, for which payment is reasonably predictable, is generally preferable to a pool of a smaller number of receivables due from a few obligors.

---

14 *Id.* at § 5.02. The term "true sale" sometimes creates confusion because the characterization of a given transfer as a sale could refer to the accounting, usury, tax, or bankruptcy treatment of the transfer, each of which is governed by different criteria.

15 Receivables can be short term (typically due in 30 days), such as trade receivables, which represent the right to payment for goods sold or services rendered, or they can be long term, such as payments due over a period of years under loans, leases, licenses, management contracts, etc.

The separation of the originator from the receivables can enable the originator to raise funds at less expense, through securities issued by the SPE, than if it raised funds through securities it issued directly. For example, the securities issued by the SPE, depending upon the structure of the transaction, may have a higher investment rating than securities issued directly by the originator and, therefore, would bear a lower interest rate than the originator might be able to obtain on its own securities, bank lines of credit, or secured borrowings.

B. The Honda Deal: Securitization in Action

To see these principles in action, take the case of Honda Motor Company. This company, as we all know, sells cars, yet it rarely sells a new car for all cash. Most people don't have that kind of ready money to use for a new car purchase. As a consequence, consumers will often finance the purchase. Sometimes this financing comes from the purchaser's bank or credit union; other times Honda itself will finance the purchase price by entering into a contract with the car buyer under which Honda gives the buyer possession of the car in return for the buyer's promise to pay for it over five years (60 months). The buyer also gives Honda a security interest in the car pursuant to the contract.

Honda may have made a sale, but the payment of the purchase price is going to be spread over as long as five years. Since it takes far less than that time to build a car, Honda requires money now to build more cars. It could seek equity contributions, but the cost of that money and the dilution it would bring is not acceptable to shareholders. It could finance the contracts, or "factor" the receivables,[16] but since its credit rating is A-1 (and not AAA), the cost of such financing would likely be (in early 2003) around 7.2%. If it could somehow get a AAA rating on the debt, the interest rate would drop to approximately 6.5%, or a difference of approximately 70 basis points.

What difference do these 70 basis points make? Well, in Honda's case, they have approximately $1.5 billion of car contracts to finance at the time of the transaction we will study.[17] Seven-tenths of a percent of that number is approximately $10,000,000 — and that's just one year.[18]

But how can Honda obtain these savings? It is an A-rated company, not an AAA-rated company. The trick is that while Honda may be an A-rated company,

---

16 Factoring is an age-old financing technique in which receivables are sold at a discount from their face value to a finance company, called a "factor."

17 Honda tends to enter into four securitization transactions per year. The one described in the text involved 100,014 car contracts, all on a standard form, all calling for level-payments over a five-year term.

18 For the fastidious, the amount is really $10,500,000. And the total savings over the five years of the contracts would be approximately $25,000,000, since the contracts pay a little bit of principal with interest on each payment — that is, they amortize — and thus a little less interest is due each time.

it has, or can create, AAA-rated *assets*. If it can isolate car contracts from the company without great loss, and get AAA-rated financing, it makes sense to do so.

Of course, Honda could just sell the contracts outright to a third-party. Such a sale, however, presents risks that the parties may not have paid the best price; sellers will discount what they are willing to pay because the "loss" on each contract cannot be known with certainty. If, however, Honda can assure a return to a buyer or investor, the deal may be worthwhile.

C. Graphical Representation of the Honda Deal

Honda will thus structure the transaction in the following way (with explanations following this graphic):

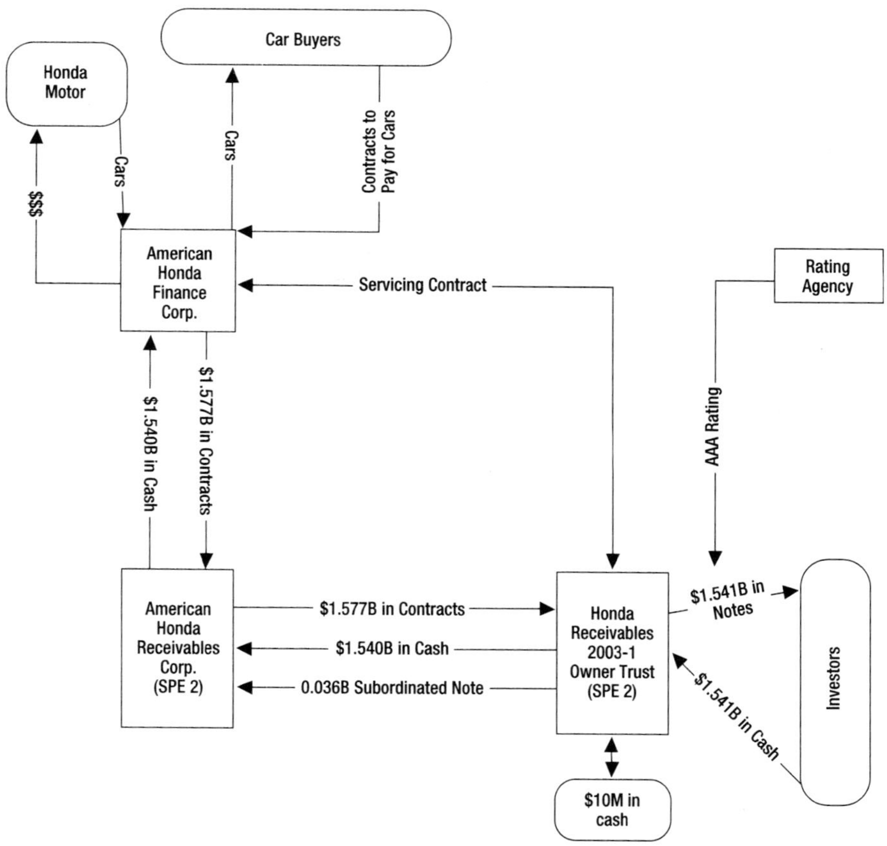

D. Explanation of the Honda Transaction in Stages

Although the schematic of the transaction may appear daunting, it can be understood by breaking down the transaction into six component parts: (1) origination; (2) sale to first SPE; (3) sale to seller; (4) seller's sale of notes to investors; (5) rating the notes; and (6) servicing the contracts on an ongoing basis.[19]

1. Origination

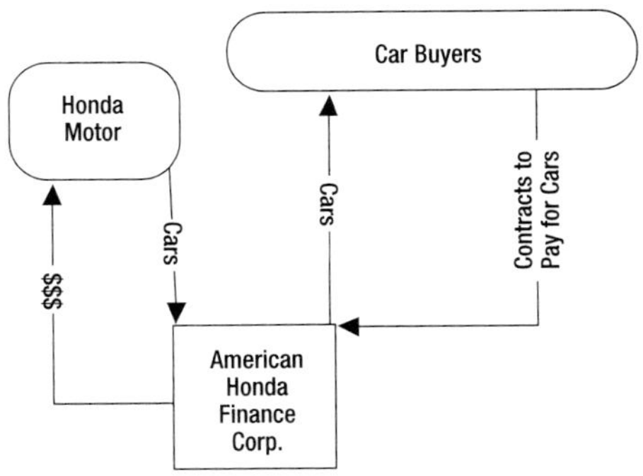

The engine that drives this securitization is the willingness and obligation of the purchasers of Honda vehicles to pay on their contracts. How do these contracts arise? Initially, in anticipation of the securitization, Honda Motor (the parent of all these entities) will supply its dealers with standard form contracts and standard loan criteria. Each time a dealer sells a car using these forms and criteria, it immediately transfers ownership of the contracts to a Honda Motor subsidiary, American Honda Finance Corp. In the securitization at issue, the parties selected some 104,014 of these financing contracts to be the basis of the securitization.

The creation of such contracts is referred to in securitization circles as "origination." That is, the Honda dealership network "originates" the contracts that will form the basis for the securitization.

---

19 The graphics that accompany each of the next six sections are nothing more than parts of the overall schematic set forth in Section 1.03.C. above.

2. First Sale of the Contracts

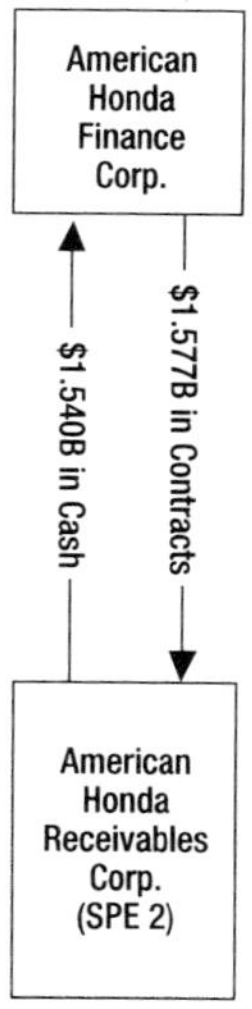

American Honda Finance, however, is still very much part of Honda Motor. Thus, if American Honda were to borrow money, and offered the contracts as collateral, banks would likely quote American Honda an interest rate close or equal to the rate Honda could obtain in the public markets with its overall A rating on its debt securities. To obtain a AAA rating on this financing, however, the assets being securitized — the consumer contracts — will have to be isolated from Honda.

As indicated above, this is done by creating a special purpose entity, or SPE, that is formed for the sole purpose of raising funds via securitization. In this transaction, the first SPE is American Honda Receivables Corp. It buys the contracts from American Honda for $1.54 billion dollars. But where does it get that money, and why does it get less money than the amount of the contracts being sold? For those answers, we look at the third stage — the second bulk sale of the 104,014 contracts to the entity issuing the securities in this transaction.

3. Second Sale of the Contracts

The second sale looks something like the following:

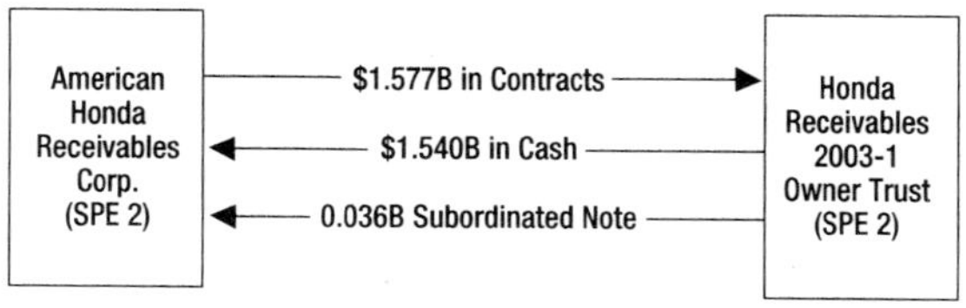

Here, a second SPE, Honda Receivables 2003-1 Owner Trust, has been created for the sole purpose of acquiring the 104,014 contracts, and issuing securities and notes backed solely by the payments related to those contracts. In the transaction sketched above, the Owner Trust buys and takes title to the $1.577 billion in automobile contracts. For that portfolio of contracts, the Owner Trust pays American Honda Receivables $1.540 billion in cash (which is the cash that American Honda Receivables will pay to American Honda Finance), and issues American Honda Receivables a subordinated note in the amount of $36 million (or, to convert that number to billions, in the amount of $.036 billion, represented by the "$.036B" in the schematic above).[20] Thus, American Honda Receivables receives a total of $1.576 billion in consideration ($1.540 billion in cash plus a $.036 billion subordinated note) for the $1.577 in auto contracts. So we are only short $10 million, or $.001 billion. To see where that money comes from, we go to stage 4, the actual sale of securities based upon the auto contracts.

4. Note Sale

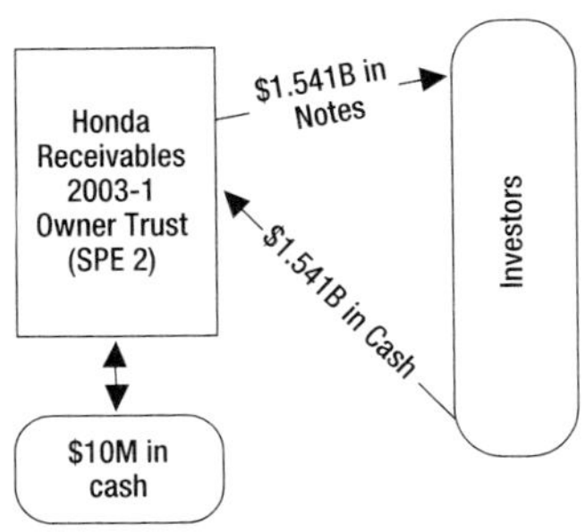

The Owner Trust was set up specifically to take title to the auto contracts, and to sell securities to the public which would be backed solely by the payments related to those contracts. The securities sold will be regular notes secured by the 104,014 auto contracts. Although the face value of those contracts is $1.577 billion, it will sell notes in the face amount of only $1.541 billion. This difference, in large part, reflects that fact that the Owner Trust has no other assets save the car contracts, and the buyers of the notes will expect some cushion in case some of the consumers stop paying their debts. In this transaction, the difference — the $36 million — has been negotiated on the basis of Honda's past record in selecting customers (the hold back is approximately 2.5% of the over-

20 Subordination in this context means that both the Owner Trust and Honda Receivables agree that the Owner Trust is not to pay anything on account of the Subordinated Note so long as there is any money due to the investors on account of their notes.

all transaction). Other originators who do not have as good a track record with respect to customer payments will have to settle for a larger cushion. Also note that the trust holds approximately $10 million as additional collateral out of the sales proceeds.

Who will buy these notes? Typically the purchasers will be mutual funds and other investment companies. For example, a search of the holdings of various mutual funds shows that funds as diverse as the Vanguard Institutional Total Bond Market Index Fund, the Canada Trust and the Standish Short Term Asset Reserve had bought notes issued by prior Honda receivable securitizations. Were you so inclined, you could invest in these mutual funds, and thus become an investor in this Honda securitization as well.

You might wonder who holds the $10 million in additional collateral and who looks out for the noteholders' interests. The answer is that the sponsors of the securtization will ensure that the notes are issued under a document called an "indenture," which will nominate an "indenture trustee," or "bond trustee." The indenture will specify the terms of the notes, the terms of their redemption, and will bind the trust to various covenants necessary to preserve the expectations of the parties. The indenture will also specify the duties of the indenture trustee, usually a banking or trust company, and these duties typically include "running the books" of the securitization, collecting any payments on the contracts (usually from the entity "servicing" the contracts — see Section III.D.6 below) and making all disbursements to the noteholders. Should there be any default, the indenture trustee is empowered by the indenture to take action on behalf of the noteholders. For these services, the indenture trustee will charge a fee, payable out of the collections and disbursements that it makes.

Thus, at the end of the day, the Owner Trust will own 104,014 customer contracts (with a collective face value of $1.577 billion) and $10 million. It will have created $1.541 billion in note obligations (which were sold to and are held by the public), and $36 million in subordinated debt (which is held by Honda Finance).

But all of this is for naught unless the rate payable to the investors is a low, AAA rate. As we saw before, to achieve that rate, the assets have to stand alone and apart from Honda. Has that occurred? And how will the investors know that it has occurred? That inquiry takes us to the fifth stage, the ratings process.

5. Note Rating

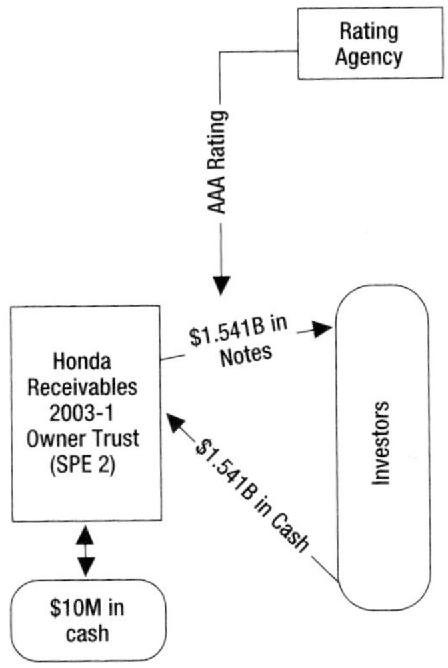

Not surprisingly, throughout this transactions, all the lawyers and other professionals involved have been communicating with the various rating companies such as Moody's and Standard and Poor's. These rating agencies review the documents against standards the agencies have developed for assessing whether, in the case of a default or other financial problems at Honda Motor, or at Honda American Finance Corp., the car payments made by the customers will continue to flow through to the investors. In large part, the agencies check the structure of the transaction against principles we will develop later in this book in the Chapter 3 on bankruptcy and the Chapter 4 on accounting. It also undertakes a substantive economic analysis of the transaction, including reviewing the economic strength of the package (in this case, the amount of cushion for the notes) and the historic performance of the parties (in this case, Honda's default and collection rates compared to other car manufacturers).

In some cases, the rating agency will request credit enhancements for the securities to be issued (although in Honda's case, they appeared not to have made such a request). These credit enhancements might include additional holdbacks (more than the 2.5% used in the Honda deal), additional collateral, letter of credit support or even guaranties of unrelated entities. These enhancements are not without some cost, and we will explore later the issues that they raise for lawyers and others.

At the conclusion of the Honda transaction, however, after paying a fee, the sponsors of the Owner Trust will receive a rating on the notes issued. If the transaction is structured to the satisfaction of the rating agency, as was the case with the Owner Trust, the notes will receive a AAA rating, and the interest payable on the notes will be at a rate consistent with other AAA-rated obligations. In the case of the Owner Trust, the blended interest rate it will pay on the notes is 1.746%.[21]

6. Servicing the Contracts and the Notes

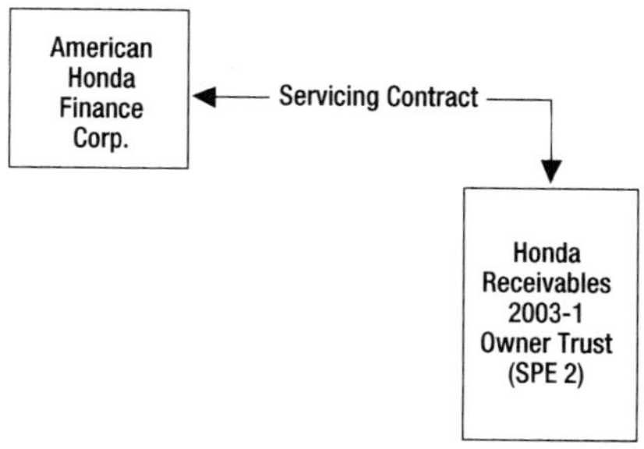

The transaction is almost complete. The consumer contracts have been bought and sold (twice), and the notes issued. But the noteholders bought their notes in anticipation that they would be receiving periodic interest. That interest is to come from payments on the consumer contracts. But the Owner Trust has few or no employees; a sophisticated organization is necessary to ensure maximum collection on these contracts. Since Honda has a keen interest in keeping its customers content (so they will buy their next car from Honda, and so that they can manage their continuing liability for warranty repairs and the like), the Owner Trust will hire a Honda unit to collect on and manage the consumer contracts; this process is generally referred to as "servicing" the contracts. In this case, the Owner Trust hired Honda American Finance Corp. to service the contracts, and thus from the consumer's perspective, nothing much has changed. The consumer still pays to Honda American; he or she doesn't much care where the money goes after that, so long as he or she gets credit for the payment. For its efforts in servicing the contracts, Honda American will receive a fee equal to one twelfth of one percent of the moneys collected. This may seem small, but if the contracts all pay in full, the $1.577 billion of collections will yield a total fee over five years of a little more than $1.3 million.

E. Concluding Overview of the Honda Securitization

At the conclusion of this transaction, has Honda improved its position? Initially, it is easy to see that Honda managed to obtain AAA-rated financing, thus doing better than if it had tried to raise the funds itself using its own

[21] This reflects that the notes are issued in four different batches, called tranches, with differing maturity dates. The first tranche is due one year after the securitization close (March, 2004), and has a 1.3% rate of interest; the second tranche is due one and one-half years (18 months) after the securitization close (September, 2005), and has a 1.46% rate of interest; the third tranche is due twenty months years after the securitization close (November, 2006), and has a 1.92% rate of interest; the fourth and final tranche is due sixty-four months after the securitization close (July, 2008), and has a 2.48% rate of interest.

credit rating. But while it gained a lower rate, it looks like it did so at the cost of losing some of its auto contracts. Recall that it sold $1.577 billion of car contracts, but received only $1.540 billion in payment. Doesn't this mean it lost the difference of $.37 billion, or $37 million?

The answer is no. Recall that the Owner Trust paid cash and a subordinated note for the contracts. The cash portion was funneled back upstream to Honda, but the subordinated note is still part of the equation downstream. After the initial transaction, Honda American Receivables Corp. owns that note. But Honda American Receivables is a wholly-owned subsidiary of Honda American Finance Corp. Thus, when Finance transferred the receivables to Receivables, it received cash as part consideration, but also saw the value of its wholly-owned subsidiary (Receivables) increase in value by the value of the note. Honda will even get the benefit, albeit remotely, from the $10 million cash holdback, as its subsidiary, Honda American Receivables Corp., is the residual beneficiary of the Owner Trust when that trust liquidates (which will typically occur when the car contracts, or most of them, are fully paid).

It is true that the note issued to Receivables Corp. and Receivable's residual interest in the Owner Trust are junior in priority to payment of the notes. Receivables Corp. will not receive a penny on these obligations until the notes issued to the investors are paid in full. But that risk is almost identical to the risk it would have assumed if the contracts had never been transferred — nonpayment of the subordinated note or the residual interest will occur only if some of Honda's customers don't pay. That risk, however, is already present before the securitization; it is the same non-payment risk Honda would have incurred if it had kept the contracts itself.

This structure thus satisfies the investors' need for high-quality, fixed-rate returns while at the same time ensuring Honda that, if more customers pay their debts that estimated, it will capture that benefit (through the subordinated note, which can then be paid).

§ 1.04. Conclusion and Questions

Securitizations are complex in form, but simple in concept. In the typical case, the originator/debtor isolates, by sale, finance or otherwise, financial assets, and then uses the proceeds to fund current operations. There are, however, atypical cases, and the efficacy of those structures requires a deeper understanding of the fundamentals of securitization, and after the following questions, the remaining chapters of this book attempt to provide that understanding.

QUESTIONS

1. Does it matter what type of assets are being securitized? In the Honda example above, the assets being securitized were car contracts, a form of "financial assets" that *also includes* accounts receivable, credit card receivables or any

other form of obligation to pay money. Would your view of securitization change if the assets subject to the securitization were not financial assets; say, inventory or mobile equipment?

2. From the standpoint of the buyer of a car, does anything change if its seller (or an affiliate of its seller) securitizes her car contract? Does she still have the same obligation to pay? Does she pay the same person at the same time every month?

3. From the standpoint of the Honda's unsecured creditors, how does Honda change after it securitizes the 104,014 car contracts? Is the change "good"?

4. In Honda's case, the discount from the face amount of the securitization was only 2.5%, given the good financial position of Honda and the good history of payment by its past customers. Would you feel any different if the discount was 10%? 20%?

Chapter 2

ARTICLE 9 OF THE UCC AND THE TRANSFER OF INTANGIBLES

§ 2.01. Introduction

We now begin our investigation of securitization in a more detailed way. In this and successive chapters, we will isolate a particular aspect of securitization, and analyze it. This process will involve looking at the myriad legal issues involved, and the consequences of various ways of resolving those issues.

The first topic is the concept of a "transfer." This concept is central to securitization; assets which are securitized are "transferred" from one entity to the next — from the originator to the special purpose entity (or "SPE") — with the expectation that such a transfer will produce particular legal results. This may sound either banal or metaphysical, but given the centrality of this concept to securitization, it is worth taking a detailed look at it.

Start by thinking of a fairly ordinary situation involving a "transfer," that of your purchase of this book. You probably went to the bookstore and saw the book on the shelf, available for purchase. You picked up the book, most likely along with others, and then proceeded to the checkstand, where you paid for the book in cash, or more likely, with a credit card. You then left the bookstore with your new purchase.

In this fairly pedestrian situation, we can ask the same question that is asked when an originator transfers assets to a SPE — when did the transfer occur? Before we get to that question, however, it might be helpful to know why and for what purpose we need to answer that question. The first purpose of asking if a "transfer" occurred might be to determine if, in taking the book out of the store, you committed criminal theft. A closely related issue might involve when the bookstore owner could bring a civil action of conversion against you for the book's value. Note here that simple possession is insufficient. Something more is needed, and we find that something more in the actions that transpired at the checkstand. If you paid for the book, and are now its owner, there is no theft and no conversion. On the other hand, if you shoplifted, there is theft and conversion.

Other, less likely but no less important, issues lurk here as well. If the book contains content that violates the copyright of someone else, the issue of when a "transfer" occurred becomes important in any action for infringement of that copyright; that is, the only proper defendants may be those who "owned" the book at some time. The concept of "transfer" may also be important to know when you could rely on the book being what it appears to be — if you get home and find the middle third of the book is blank, you likely have some action against the bookseller. Such an action might not be available if the book hasn't been transferred to you (that is, if you read today's assignment in the bookstore on the sly, only to later find out that the copy you read from was corrupted, the bookstore has no liability to you unless you "bought" the book; that is, it was "transferred" to you). Another question might be who must pay personal property taxes on the use or sale of the book, and the answer to that question as well turns on whether the book was "transferred" to you, and whether you are its "owner."

A final question is one that is central to this book. If, as you walk out of the bookstore, a sheriff walks up to you, flashes an official document entitled "levy of execution on all books of bookstore" and asks you to turn over the book, you are likely justified in telling the sheriff to look elsewhere. Why? The book is "yours"; it was "transferred" to you and you are now its sole owner. The bookstore no longer has any interest in the book, and thus neither does the bookstore's creditor who caused the sheriff to present the levy. A different result might occur if the sheriff asked you to turn over the book while you were on your way to the checkstand. At that time, it was still the bookstore's property, and as such, the book (along with all other property) was available to pay the bookstore's debts.

Let us now turn to a more analytic study of "transfer."

§ 2.02. The Concept of a "Transfer"

Both the moment of "transfer" and the durability of the transfer (that is, the quality of not being avoidable at someone else's option later) are important for securitization. Recall that securitization looks to isolate high-grade assets from lower grade assets. This "isolation" is accomplished through transfers that the law recognizes. We thus must explore the concept of a transfer to understand more completely how securitization works.

A. Transfer and Tangible Goods

Let us start the investigation of when a transfer occurs through a recent case in which the time the transfer occurred was relevant to who was responsible for collecting a tax. In the following case, Circuit City stores in Massachusetts sold electronic goods to customers, but gave them the option of picking up the items bought in another store, even if that store was in another state. The customer paid for the items at the store where the items were selected, but picked them up from a different store in a different state.

This mattered because Massachusetts levies a 5% sales tax on all goods sold; New Hampshire, one of its northern neighbors, does not have any sales tax. As a consequence, many Massachusetts residents would go to a Circuit City store in Massachusetts, select the goods they wanted at the price they liked, pay for it in Massachusetts, and then arrange to pick up the goods in New Hampshire, thereby saving themselves the 5% Massachusetts sales tax.

Well, one person's savings is another person's loss, and the Commonweath of Massachusetts sued Circuit City to collect the 5% sales tax on all such sales (which, at the time of the lawsuit, involved over $175,000). The following excerpt contains the court's analysis:

CIRCUIT CITY STORES, INC. v. COMMISSIONER OF REVENUE

439 Mass. 629, 790 N.E.2d 636 (2003)

GREANEY, J.:

. . .

Only retail sales that occur in Massachusetts are subject to the sales tax . . . . The parties agree that the statutory definition of a sale . . . applies and, thus, a sale, for purposes of this appeal, includes "any transfer of title or possession . . . of tangible personal property . . . by any means whatsoever." The focus of the parties' disagreement is when, and where, title passed from Circuit City to the customers in connection with the purchased merchandise in the alternative location sales at issue. The commissioner asserts that title passed at the cash register when Circuit City received payment for the merchandise and the customer sales receipt, representing ownership of the purchased goods, was handed to the customer. Circuit City argues that title did not pass until the purchased merchandise was physically placed in the customer's hands in New Hampshire. So far as we are aware, the concept of title in circumstances, as here, where modern inventory computer systems allow a multi-State corporation to accept full payment in one State for merchandise located in another State, while simultaneously "reserving" the merchandise (purchased "sight unseen") with the understanding that the customer will take physical possession of the merchandise at his or her convenience, has yet to be considered by an appellate court. . . .

Our tax statutes provide no explicit definition of the term "title," and so we look for guidance to the Uniform Commercial Code (UCC) . . . . Section 2-401 of the UCC instructs on the concept of title.[1] With respect to situations, as here,

---

[1] [n. 8] Although the passage of title is the material element of a sale for tax purposes, the concept of title is of small significance in determining the rights of the parties under Article 2 of the Uniform Commercial Code (UCC). See 1 W.D. Hawkland, Uniform Commercial Code Series § 2-401:1 (2001). The introductory sentence of § 2-401 of the UCC sets forth a statement of policy that the rights and obligations of parties under the UCC should be determined without dependence on the concept of title. *See* . . . § 2-401 ("Each provision of this Article with regard to the rights, obligations and remedies of the [parties] applies irrespective of title to the goods except where the provision refers to such title"). *See also* in this regard other provisions of the UCC governing rights and duties of the buyer and seller in specific situations, e.g., . . . § 2-501 (insurable interest), §§ 2-509 and 2-510 (risk of loss), § 2-709 (right to damages or price), and § 2-722 (right to sue third parties for damages to goods).

where "matters concerning title become material," § 2-401(2) provides that, "unless otherwise explicitly agreed title passes to the buyer at the time and place at which the seller completes his performance with reference to the physical delivery of the goods."[2]

The commissioner contends that delivery is made in alternative location sales "without moving the goods" and, therefore, according to § 2-401(3), title passes "at the time and place of contracting" — at the cash register in Massachusetts. . . . In our view, analysis of the passage of title under the provisions of § 2-401(2) is more straightforward. *See* Mechanics Nat'l Bank v. Gaucher, 7 Mass. App. Ct. 143, 147, 386 N.E.2d 1052 (1979) (§ 2-401[2] applies to property requiring special handling enabling buyer to take possession or where purchase price has been paid and seller holds goods for convenience of buyer).

We discern no explicit agreement between the parties concerning passage of title. Circuit City claims that testimony at the hearing with respect to its handling of alternative location sales (i.e., that Circuit City does not book the sale, credit the sale, or consider the sale to have occurred until the product is physically released to the customer) indicates an understanding between the parties that the transaction that takes place in Massachusetts constitutes, not a concluded sale, but only an order for merchandise. We disagree. The events transpiring at the cash register in Massachusetts reflect a significant degree of understanding between Circuit City and its customers that a sale, and not a mere deposit on an order, has occurred. The customer sales receipt, although not a document of title, contains a description of the item or items purchased, as well as the time and date of the sale. The record suggests that, in an ordinary case, any period of warranty relevant to the purchase begins as of this date. The purchase price reflected on the receipt represents full consideration paid for the merchandise. From the vantage point of the customer, the sales receipt represents proof of his or her right to the purchased merchandise. The fact the sale is credited to the Massachusetts store, and the commission accorded the sales associate in Massachusetts, in our view, is indicative of an intent on Circuit City's part that more than an order for merchandise takes place in Massachusetts.

The physical retention of the merchandise by Circuit City is not dispositive of "the time and place at which the seller completes his performance with reference to the physical delivery of the goods" under the UCC. . . . § 2-401(2). Section 2-503(1) describes acceptable methods of a seller's tender of delivery and states the following: "Tender of delivery requires that the seller put and hold conforming goods at the buyer's disposition and give the buyer any notification reasonably necessary to enable him to take delivery. The manner, time and place

2 [n. 9] In circumstances where "delivery is to be made without moving the goods," § 2-401(3) provides that, unless otherwise explicitly agreed: "(a) if the seller is to deliver a document of title, title passes at the time when and the place where he delivers such documents; or (b) if the goods are at the time of contracting already identified and no documents are to be delivered, title passes at the time and place of contracting."

for tender are determined by the agreement and this Article, and in particular . . . tender must be at a reasonable hour, and if it is of goods they must be kept available for the period reasonably necessary to enable the buyer to take possession . . . ."

Under common law as well, title may pass although the goods are still in the actual possession of the vendor. *See* Bristol Mfg. Co. v. Arkwright Mills, 213 Mass. 172, 176-177, 100 N.E. 55 (1912). As under the UCC, the inquiry centers, not on physical transfer of the goods, but on whether goods are placed within the actual or constructive possession of another. *See* Mitchell v. LeClair, 165 Mass. 308, 310-311, 43 N.E. 117 (1896) ("Under a contract of sale, when the goods have been . . . appropriated and set apart, the vendor has done that which by the terms of the agreement makes the whole consideration payable; and so long as he remains ready to do whatever else is to be done to give the vendee the benefit of his purchase, he is entitled to receive the agreed price without deduction on account of his retention of his lien upon the property").

Here, Circuit City performed its obligations with respect to delivery when the sale was entered as an alternative location sale into Circuit City's DPS system and the purchased merchandise was "reserved" for the customer at the designated location. It was the customer from that point on who assumed responsibility for acquiring physical receipt of the purchased merchandise. The time of such receipt was placed by Circuit City within the customer's control and packaged as a sales option offered as part of Circuit City's over-all philosophy to "wow the customer." *See* 3A R.A. Anderson, Uniform Commercial Code § 2.401.90 (3d ed. rev. 2002) (seller always obligated to deliver goods, but performance of this duty may range from merely making goods available to buyer, shipping goods to buyer, delivering goods at specified destination, making delivery of documents of title, or transferring title without delivery of goods or documents).

It is clear that, under the UCC, no title can pass under a contract for sale "prior to their identification to the contract." . . . § 2-401 (1). This was also true in common law. *See* G.E. Lothrop Theatres Co. v. Edison Elec. Illuminating Co., 290 Mass. 189, 193, 195 N.E. 305 (1935) ("title cannot pass until goods are set apart and appropriated to the contract"). We reject, however, Circuit City's argument that "identification to the contract" cannot be made in alternative location sales prior to the time that the merchandise is physically removed from inventory and the serial number is scanned in the New Hampshire store.[3] The reserve notation marked on the customer sales receipt for the purchased merchandise sufficiently reflects its status of being set aside, or identified, to

[3] [n. 13] This argument relies, in part, on Circuit City's assumption of the risk of loss on the purchased merchandise until the time that it is handed over to the customer. Section 2-509 of the UCC, however, bases risk of loss on the physical location of the goods, irrespective of whether title has already passed to the buyer. As a merchant subject to art. 2 of the UCC, Circuit City cannot transfer the risk of loss until the customer's actual receipt of the goods, even though full payment has been made and the buyer has been notified that the goods are at his disposal. *See* . . . § 2-509 (3); official comment 3 to § 2-509, 1A U.L.A. 777 (Master ed. 1989).

that particular transaction. The Circuit City district manager described the reserving system as moving merchandise to a "phantom" location to await customer pick up, and, indeed, the situation presented to the customer is just as though the merchandise actually is set aside and waiting for the customer at the pick-up counter. The purchased merchandise in the alternative location sales at issue is, by its nature, fungible. Because customers do not choose items in a store such as Circuit City by a particular serial number, but only by make and model, identification by serial number is unnecessary to the sale. . . .

[The court thus held that title passed at the cash register, and upheld the decision that Circuit City had to pay the Massachusetts tax on such sales even though the customer picked up the goods in New Hampshire.]

QUESTIONS ABOUT *CIRCUIT CITY*

1. Why is the UCC important or applicable here? *See* UCC § 2-105. Would the UCC apply to your purchase of this book? To the purchase of the copyright to this book? To the sale of the warehouse where the inventory of similar books are kept?

2. If carried to its logical extreme,

(A) What does *Circuit City* say about the consumer who picks out a wide screen TV in Boston, and then, en route to New Hampshire to pick it up, changes her mind?

(B) What does *Circuit City* say about the consumer who picks out a wide screen TV in Boston, only to find upon arrival in New Hamshire that Circuit City's creditor's have levied upon and seized all wide-screen TVs located there?

3. So when does title pass under the UCC? How much flexibility do the parties have in specifying by contract when a transfer occurs? Could Circuit City circumvent this decision by programming its computers to print out on each cash register receipt the following: "The parties expressly agree that title to the goods purchased hereby shall not transfer until physical delivery to the customer"?

B. Transfer of Intangible Personal Property at Common Law

While some securitizations involve the transfer of tangible personal property, by far the most common type of securitization requires the transfer of *intangible* personal property or, more concretely, the transfer of a promise to pay money. We saw that in Chapter 1 with respect to Honda Motor Company. It transferred its customer contracts — the intangible obligations of its customers to pay the deferred purchase price of their cars — to an SPE. These agreements, however, are more than just pieces of paper; at most they are just evidence of the contract. In other words, the customers would still be obligated to pay for their cars if Honda's storage facility where Honda stored the contracts burned to the ground.

At common law, transfers of intangible rights were often labeled "assignments," although the term "assignment" now can also mean the transfer of something less than the total ownership interest (such as an "assignment for collection," or a "collateral assignment"). Given that paper contracts (such as the Honda car purchase agreements) are at most evidence of an agreement to pay money,[4] and given that proof of ownership of an intangible right cannot be established by possession (how do you hold something that has no physical form?), the common law approached assignments of such intangible rights somewhat differently. As summarized in a case involving bank accounts (which, recall, are nothing more than the bank's intangible promise or obligation to pay money or honor checks), the law was summarized as follows:

> In sum, an assignment requires an agreement whereby the assignor agrees to transfer presently all right, title and control over the subject matter of the assignment to the assignee. Such an agreement may be manifested by conduct, writing or parol, and in particular it exists where the assignor instructs his obligor to pay the specific fund owing to him to the assignee, and the assignor either delivers that order to the assignee or notifies him of it. No agreement to assign is created, however, by either (1) an agreement between two parties that the first will pay a debt owing to the second out of a specific fund; or (2) a revocable instruction to the obligor to pay the obligation to the would-be assignee.

Miller v. Wells Fargo Bank International Corp., 406 F. Supp. 452, 474 (S.D.N.Y. 1975), *aff'd,* 540 F.2d 548 (2d Cir. 1976). *See also* Thomas W. Albrecht & Sarah J. Smith, *Corporate Loan Securitization: Selected Legal and Regulatory Issues*, 8 DUKE J. COMP. & INT'L L. 411 (1998).

Miller's test leave much to the parties. It will be their job, if they desire a true assignment, to draft the necessary documents, and give the necessary notices. But before working too hard with respect to *Miller's* common law test, we should ask whether there are any revisions or additions made by statutory law.

C. Transfer of Intangible Personal Property Under the Uniform Commercial Code

In 1999, the American Law Institute and the National Conference of Commissioners on Uniform State Laws promulgated a revised version of Article 9 of the UCC. That version has now been adopted in every state. Given the rise of securitization during the time period of its drafting, it is no surprise that revised Article 9 contains provisions that relate to securitization.

[4] Exceptions would include negotiable instruments governed by Article 3 of the Uniform Commercial Code. *See* § 3-104 (defining negotiable instrument).

This may strike you as somewhat odd; most people who have not taken a course dealing with Article 9 may think that it only deals with security interests and collateral. This impression is wrong. Its scope is much broader. Indeed, in its scope section Article 9 states that, with some exceptions, it applies to "a *sale* of accounts, chattel paper, payment intangibles, or promissory notes . . . ." UCC § 9-109(a) (emphasis supplied). Here's how this inclusion of such sales is handled by Article 9:

Steven L. Schwarcz, *The Impact on Securitization of Revised UCC Article 9*

74 CHI.-KENT L. REV. 947 (1999)

* * * What does Article 9 of the Uniform Commercial Code have to do with securitization? In its [pre-1999] form, Article 9, which generally addresse[ed] only secured transactions, nonetheless govern[ed] the sale of certain types of financial assets — accounts and chattel paper — that are commonly involved in securitization transactions. The rationale for including sales of these assets in Article 9 was that "[c]ommercial financing on the basis of accounts and chattel paper is often so conducted that the distinction between a security transfer and a sale is blurred, and a sale of such property is therefore covered . . . whether intended for security or not." This same rationale, and the significant minimization of transaction costs that the rule achieves, holds equally true today.

What has changed today, however, is that, increasingly, many other types of financial assets are sold as part of commercial financing transactions. . . . Revised Article 9 is a bold and largely successful attempt to remedy that omission and to adapt the law governing secured transactions to the realities of modern commercial and financial transactions. It accomplishes these goals in several ways.

I. Revised Article 9 Brings the Sale of Most Types of Financial Assets Within Its Scope

As a threshold matter, Revised Article 9 brings within its scope the sale not only of accounts and chattel paper, as under current law, but also of "payment intangibles" and "promissory notes." Significantly for securitization, the definition of an account is expanded from current law to include not only credit card receivables and health-care-insurance receivables but also any "right to payment . . . for property that has been or is to be . . . licensed, assigned, or otherwise disposed of," thereby covering license and franchise fee receivables. Moreover, the term payment intangible is broadly defined as "a general intangible under which the account debtor's principal obligation is a monetary obligation." This definition appears intended to cover financial assets that are not already covered by the terms account, chattel paper, and promissory notes. For example, loan participations and commercial loans not evidenced by instruments would be payment intangibles.

Accordingly, Revised Article 9 will apply to securitization transactions so long as the financial assets being sold consist of accounts (including credit card, health-care-insurance, license, and franchise fee receivables), chattel paper, promissory notes, or payment intangibles. I will refer to these types of financial assets as "covered financial assets." . . . .

One of the major controversies that arose during the Article 9 revision effort was how to perfect the sale of payment intangibles. Bankers were concerned that a perfection requirement of filing financing statements would subject them to costly new procedures when selling loan participations, a form of payment intangible. A somewhat practical solution was reached to mitigate this concern: the sale of payment intangibles would be deemed to be automatically perfected, without the need to file financing statements.[5] This solution, however, is imperfect. Buyers of payment intangibles cannot search filing records to determine whether those intangibles previously have been sold to others. Thus, an SPV in a securitization transaction cannot ascertain the priority (discussed below) of the SPV's ownership rights, other than by relying on representations of the originator. Originators that are insufficiently capitalized to back up their representations therefore may find it difficult to securitize payment intangibles.

B. Priority

Priority refers to the ranking of multiple claims against a transferred asset. In a securitization context, it means that "the SPVs and investors' claims against the transferred financial assets are superior [in ranking] to any third-party claims," including that of the originator's trustee in bankruptcy. Under [pre-1999] Article 9, priority is generally accorded to the first secured creditor to file or perfect, under a rule usually referred to as "first in time, first in right." Revised Article 9 continues that rule.[6] . . .

IV. Revised Article 9 Promotes Assignability Notwithstanding Contractual Restriction

Parties to contracts sometimes restrict the assignment of rights and obligations thereunder. These restrictions are often referred to as "anti-assignment clauses." In a securitization transaction, the parties to that contract are the originator and a third party obligated on the financial asset. Because the focus is on the originator's transfer of its rights in the financial asset to an SPV, we need only examine the obligor's ability to restrict that transfer. . . .

---

5 [n. 47] *See* § 9-309(3), 9-310(b)(2).

6 [n. 51] *See* § 9-322(a)(1) (providing that "[c]onflicting perfected security interests . . . rank according to priority in time of filing or perfection"). For an interesting critique of this rule, *see* ALAN SCHWARTZ & ROBERT E. SCOTT, COMMERCIAL TRANSACTIONS: PRINCIPLES AND POLICIES 660, 664-65 (2d ed. 1991).

Revised Article 9 . . . eliminates any argument that a transfer of financial assets in violation of an invalidated anti-assignment clause nonetheless constitutes a breach as between the obligor and the originator.[7] Second, the revision treats anti-assignment clauses in payment intangibles and promissory notes differently depending on whether the transfer in question is a sale or merely a transfer for security. Anti-assignment clauses would be ineffective in both cases from preventing perfection of the transfer of the right to payment,[8] but they would be upheld to prevent an originator from selling its underlying business relationship.[9] Thus, if the originator is a bank which has made a loan to a borrower, the bank could sell a participation in that loan — a loan participation being a payment intangible — to an SPV or other third party and could perfect that sale notwithstanding an anti-assignment clause in the underlying loan agreement; but the bank could not alter the underlying debtor-creditor relationship with its borrower. The buyer of the loan participation therefore would have no direct collection rights against the borrower. . . .

QUESTIONS ABOUT TRANSFERS, ARTICLE 9 AND SECURITIZATION

Based on the readings above, and the **selected** definitions **from Article 9** set forth below, see if you can answer the following questions about the Honda transactions outlined in chapter 1 above:

1. When America Honda Finance Corporation ("Honda"), as originator, transfers the car purchase contracts with its customers to the SPE, American Honda Receivables Corp., does Article 9 apply? Why? *See* § 9-109(a)(3). By the way, what is the correct Article 9 designation for the car contracts when they are held by Honda? Accounts? (*See* § 9-102(a)(2)). Chattel Paper? (*See* § 9-102(a)(11)). Payment Intangibles? (*See* § 9-102(a)(61)). Recall that each of the contracts not only evidences the consumer's obligation to make monthly payments, but also contain a grant by the consumer of a security interest in the car to secure the obligation to make monthly payments.

2. If Article 9 applies to the transfer, what steps under Article 9 does Honda American Finance have to undertake to ensure that the transaction is "perfected" and will not be set aside by Honda's unpaid creditors or by Honda's trustee in bankruptcy (should one be appointed)? *See* §§ 9-309(a), 9-310(a), (b).

---

7 [n. 72] *See* § 9-406(d)(2), 9-408(a)(2) (providing that a transfer in violation of an anti-assignment clause does not constitute a default).

8 [n. 73] *See id.* § 9-406(d), 9-408(a)-(b).

9 [n. 74] Revised section 9-408(d) effectively provides that, in the case of sales of payment intangibles or promissory notes and in the case of any transfer of a health-care-insurance receivable, anti-assignment clauses are ineffective to thwart perfection of the sale or other transfer but may be effective for all other purposes.

3. If Article 9 applies to the transfer, what steps under Article 9 are necessary to ensure that Honda American Finance, in addition to being perfected as set forth in problem 2, is also prior to any other creditor of Honda with respects to the payments consumers will make? *See* § 9-330(a), (b).

4. When American Honda Receivables Corp. ("Receivables") transfers the car purchase contracts it bought from Honda to Honda Receivables 2003-1 Owner Trust ("Trust"), the second SPE, does Article 9 apply? Why? Should Trust do anything different to ensure perfection and priority to the car contracts?

5. Assume that the standard form purchase contract that Honda uses has the following clause at the end: "This contract may not be assigned without the prior written consent of both parties." If Article 9 applies, does this mean that the consent of every single consumer will have to be obtained in order for either SPE to have good title to the car contracts? *See* §§ 9-406(d)(2), 9-102(a)(3) (definition of account debtor).

Selected Provisions of Revised Article 9

Section 9-109(a)(3)

Except as otherwise provided in subsections (c) and (d), this article applies to: . . .[¶](3) a sale of accounts, chattel paper, payment intangibles, or promissory notes; . . .

Section 9-102(a)

(2) "Account", except as used in "account for", means a right to payment of a monetary obligation, whether or not earned by performance, (i) for property that has been or is to be sold, leased, licensed, assigned, or otherwise disposed of, (ii) for services rendered or to be rendered, (iii) for a policy of insurance issued or to be issued, (iv) for a secondary obligation incurred or to be incurred, (v) for energy provided or to be provided, (vi) for the use or hire of a vessel under a charter or other contract, (vii) arising out of the use of a credit or charge card or information contained on or for use with the card, or (viii) as winnings in a lottery or other game of chance operated or sponsored by a State, governmental unit of a State, or person licensed or authorized to operate the game by a State or governmental unit of a State. The term includes health-care-insurance receivables. The term does not include (i) rights to payment evidenced by chattel paper or an instrument, (ii) commercial tort claims, (iii) deposit accounts, (iv) investment property, (v) letter-of-credit rights or letters of credit, or (vi) rights to payment for money or funds advanced or sold, other than rights arising out of the use of a credit or charge card or information contained on or for use with the card.

* * * * *

(11) "Chattel paper" means a record or records that evidence both a monetary obligation and a security interest in specific goods, a security interest in specific

goods and software used in the goods, a security interest in specific goods and license of software used in the goods, a lease of specific goods, or a lease of specific goods and license of software used in the goods. In this paragraph, "monetary obligation" means a monetary obligation secured by the goods or owed under a lease of the goods and includes a monetary obligation with respect to software used in the goods. . . . If a transaction is evidenced by records that include an instrument or series of instruments, the group of records taken together constitutes chattel paper.

* * * * *

(42) "General intangible" means any personal property, including things in action, other than accounts, chattel paper, commercial tort claims, deposit accounts, documents, goods, instruments, investment property, letter-of-credit rights, letters of credit, money, and oil, gas, or other minerals before extraction. The term includes payment intangibles and software.

* * * * *

(47) "Instrument" means a negotiable instrument or any other writing that evidences a right to the payment of a monetary obligation, is not itself a security agreement or lease, and is of a type that in ordinary course of business is transferred by delivery with any necessary indorsement or assignment. The term does not include (i) investment property, (ii) letters of credit, or (iii) writings that evidence a right to payment arising out of the use of a credit or charge card or information contained on or for use with the card.

* * * * *

(61) "Payment intangible" means a general intangible under which the account debtor's principal obligation is a monetary obligation.

§ 2.03. Transfers in the Form of the Creation of Security Interests Under Article 9

A. Creation of an Article 9 Security Interest

Not all transfers bestow upon the transferee the immediate right to possess the object conveyed. Transfers in this category might create "future interests" of the type that you may have studied in a property-law class, but that is not what this section is about. Rather, this section looks at transfers of property interests that provide an alternate source of repayment, often and technically referred to as transfers for purposes of security. These types of transfers arise when, for example, a person conveys or transfers an interest in property to secure or support an otherwise unsecured promise. In securitizations, many transactions include transfers for purposes of security of interests in the financial assets that are the subject of the securitization; that is, transfers of a part interest that has no right of possession until default. In the Honda case in the first chapter, for example, the noteholders received a security interest in the car contracts to secure prompt payment of the notes. In some sense, these types of transfers are no different in theory from transfers which give a bank a collateral interest in a car so that the bank will finance its purchase.

Transfers which create a security interest are fairly basic. They require two events: attachment and perfection. In a rough sense, attachment is what makes the security interest effective as between the secured party and the debtor; perfection is what makes the security interest effective against the rest of the world.

In a car purchase, you often give a bank a security interest in the car when you sign the loan documents, and it perfects the interest by inserting its name as a lienholder on the car's certificate of title. After you sign the documents and the bank notes its interest, however, the bank still can't take possession of the car. Its right to take possession only arises or matures when you default, such as by not making payments, by failing to keep insurance, or any other reason specified in the contract signed when the car was bought.

In the Honda example in Chapter 1, the car contracts were transferred absolutely to Honda American Finance, and then transferred absolutely again to Honda Receivables 2003-1 Owner Trust (the "Trust"). At that point, Trust issued notes to investors.

But the investors (and probably the rating agencies) wanted more than the simple promise of Trust to pay the notes as and when due; they wanted collateral. So the Trust secured the payment obligations represented by the notes with a security interest in its only assets, the car contracts. It did this in two steps: attachment and perfection.

As explained in more detail later, attachment occurred when the Trust signed a document denominated a trust "indenture" or something similar. This document will have been drafted by a representative of the prospective noteholders, likely a lawyer for the investment bank sponsoring the deal. It will be styled so that the Trust, as an Article 9 "debtor" will sign along with a "secured party," often entity called an "indenture trustee" or something similar.[10]

The indenture likely granted a security interest to the indenture trustee by saying something like: "Trust hereby grants a security interest to Indenture Trustee in all Honda car contracts it owns to secure payment of the Notes." This

---

[10] In the language of Article 9, the trust, as owner of the collateral (the car contracts) is the "debtor." UCC § 9-102(a)(28). The indenture trustee, even though it acts in a representative capacity for the note holders, is the "secured party." UCC § 9-102(a)(72)(E) (providing that the term "secured party" means "a trustee, indenture trustee, agent, collateral agent, or other representative in whose favor a security interest or agricultural lien is created or provided for . . .").

Many banks and trust companies have divisions or departments that offer their services, for a fee, as indenture trustees. They normally take in and account for receipts, and arrange for payments to be made on the notes. They also monitor compliance with the terms and covenants of the trust indenture.

simple sentence accomplishes "attachment" in the lingo of commercial lawyers. Upon the trust's authentication (signing) of the document, a property interest will have been created (that is, the trustee will be the transferee of a property interest), albeit a property interest in which possession is contingent upon default.[11]

One might ask why the indenture doesn't have to specify the contracts in more detail; that is, why the contracts are not specifically identified by contract number or by vehicle identification number of the car financed. Indeed, in many civil law countries, that is exactly what you would have to do. In the United States, however, Article 9 brought about the innovation of "bulk" financing of personal property. That is, the parties may specify the collateral granted by generic terms. Indeed, under Article 9 "a description of personal . . . property is sufficient, whether or not it is specific, if it reasonably identifies what is described."[12]

B. Perfection of an Article 9 Security Interest

So attachment of the security interest in the form of the grant of the security interest is relatively easy. But as noted above, there is a second step, and that second step is perfection. Revised Article 9 made this step easier than before. For perfection of an interest in chattel paper (such as the car contracts), accounts or payment intangibles, the basic method of perfection — the simple act of filing with a central authority such as a Secretary of State a one-page document called a financing statement — is all that is required.[13]

Two questions arise from the requirement of filing a financing statement — what do you file, and where do you file it? What you file is relatively easy. Revised Article 9 specifies a form (reprinted in the statute itself — see § 9-520), and that form requires relatively little information.[14] Once filled out, Section

---

11 *See* UCC § 9-203(b).

12 UCC § 9-108(a). An exception exists in that a security agreement cannot lazily state that the debtor grants a security interest in "all assets," or some similar generic specification of all the debtor's personal property. UCC § 9-108(c). Such a description, however, is perfectly permissible in a financing statement, § 9-504(2), since the function of a financing statement is to put creditors on inquiry notice, and nothing more. A security agreement, by contrast, actually operates as a transfer of rights, and thus more specification is deemed necessary to avoid confusion.

13 UCC § 9-310(a).

14 UCC § 9-516(b)..In the case of a trust as a debtor, there is some additional information to provide. Section 9-503(a)(3) states that "if the debtor is a trust or a trustee acting with respect to property held in trust, only if the financing statement: [¶] (A) provides the name specified for the trust in its organic documents or, if no name is specified, provides the name of the settlor and additional information sufficient to distinguish the debtor from other trusts having one or more of the same settlors; and [¶] (B) indicates, in the debtor's name or otherwise, that the debtor is a trust or is a trustee acting with respect to property held in trust." In Honda's case, the sponsors of the securitization will ensure that the documents creating the Trust specify its name—the "Honda Receivables 2003-1 Owner Trust." This specification of a name in its formation, or "organic" documents satisfies Section 9-503(a)(3)(A), and because the word "Trust" is part of the debtor's name, it also satisfies Section 9-503(a)(3)(B).

9-301 and 9-501, when read together, direct you to file the completed form in the state where the debtor (not the assets "designated as the collateral") is located. Section 9-307 then provides tests as to where a debtor is located. The most important innovation of Revised Article 9 is that certain entities, defined in Article 9 as "registered organizations,"[15] have set and immutable locations.

The end result of this is that if a Delaware corporation has its entire operations and all its assets in California, you do *not* file in California (where the assets are); rather, you file in Delaware, since a corporation is a "registered organization," and Section 9-307(e) states that such an entity is presumed to be located in the state in which it is incorporated.

In the Honda example, the person owning the car contracts is the Trust, and thus a financing statement with information about the trust will have to be filed in the state in which the trust is "located." With respect to organizations[16] such as the Trust, Section 9-307(b)(2) provides that a "debtor that is an organization and has only one place of business is located at its place of business." The parties structuring the securitization will thus have great flexibility in deciding where the Trust's place of business — not so helpfully defined in Section 9-307(a) as "a place where a debtor conducts its affairs" — will be.

Both American Honda Finance Corp. (the originator) and American Honda Receivables Corp. (the first SPE) are California corporations. As a consequence, two of the three financing statements (the one related to the sale from American Honda Finance to American Honda Receivables, and the one related to the sale from American Honda Receivables to the Trust) will be filed in California. Copies of these financing statements appear as Appendices 1 and 2 to this book. The third and final financing statement, the one related to the security interest granted by the Trust to the noteholders, was filed in Delaware, and a copy of it is appended as Appendix 3. Even though the Trust, in its securities filings, lists American Honda Receivables Corp.'s address as its own (indeed, the filing states that its address is "c/o American Honda Receivables Corp."), as a Delaware statutory trust it is located in Delaware, *see* 12 DEL. CODE. § 3801, *et. seq*. (2003). The trust confirmed this location by listing its Delaware trustee as the "debtor" in its UCC-1 financing statement.

---

[15] Under Section 9-102(a)(70), a "'registered organization' means an organization organized solely under the law of a single State or the United States and as to which the State or the United States must maintain a public record showing the organization to have been organized." This will include corporations, limited partnerships and limited liability companies (LLCs). It will not include partnerships or, for our purposes, trusts, since no state requires either of those types of entities to register their existence. That is, you can get a list of all California corporations from the California Secretary of State, but there is no official from whom you can obtain a list of all California partnerships or California trusts.

[16] Under the UCC, Article 1 (incorporated as to its definitions by Section 9-102(c)), specifies that an organization is nothing more than "a person other than an individual." UCC § 1-201(28). As a consequence, to the extent that a trust is a person under state law, it is an organization under the UCC.

QUESTIONS ABOUT ARTICLE 9 AND COLLATERAL IN SECURITIZATIONS

1. Trick question: In the Honda example, do the noteholders have a security interest in the cars sold pursuant to the consumer purchase contracts? If the answer to this question is "no," then just what is the nature of the noteholders' security interest, and how do they receive the benefit of the cars in the case of non-payment?

2. In the Honda example, if all entities do what they should, does it matter if the Trust does not grant a security interest in the car contracts in favor of the noteholders?

3. If you represented the noteholders, and were really nervous about getting all the assets you could as collateral, what else might the Trust have to offer?

C. Enforcement of an Article 9 Security Interest: Default

People take security interests to increase the likelihood that the debtor will perform as promised. In the Honda case, for example, the noteholders were offered security interests in the underlying car contracts to increase the probability that the Trust would make all payments as and when scheduled. If the debtor defaults, the assumption was that the secured party — the indenture trustee — could pursue the misdirected payments and recover them for the benefit of the noteholders.

This structure assumes both that enforcement of an Article 9 security interest is practical and is efficient. These assumptions are not unfounded. Especially with payment obligations such as car contracts or receivables, Article 9 is particularly effective, as the following excerpt from Section 9-607 illustrates:

(a) [**Collection and enforcement generally**.] If so agreed, and in any event after default, a secured party:

(1) may notify an account debtor or other person obligated on collateral to make payment or otherwise render performance to or for the benefit of the secured party;

(2) may take any proceeds to which the secured party is entitled under Section 9-315;

(3) may enforce the obligations of an account debtor or other person obligated on collateral and exercise the rights of the debtor with respect to the obligation of the account debtor or other person obligated on collateral to make payment or otherwise render performance to the debtor, and with respect to any property that secures the obligations of the account debtor or other person obligated on the collateral . . . .

(c) [**Commercially reasonable collection and enforcement.**] A secured party shall proceed in a commercially reasonable manner if the secured party:

(1) undertakes to collect from or enforce an obligation of an account debtor or other person obligated on collateral; and

(2) is entitled to charge back uncollected collateral or otherwise to full or limited recourse against the debtor or a secondary obligor.

With respect to securitizations, this section gives sponsors great leeway to structure transactions for the benefit of investors. Take, for example, Section 9-607(a)(1). It provides that, "after *default*, a secured party [the indenture trustee in a securitization] may notify an account debtor or other person obligated on collateral to make payment or otherwise render performance to or for the benefit of the secured party."[17] What is default? Article 9 does not define the term, but leaves it to the parties' agreement to define and shape. Thus, most well-drafted agreement will not only make missed payments a default, but will make other events that jeopardize repayment a default as well.

Thus, if the debtor (which is the Trust in the Honda case) defaults by failing to make a payment or fails to do something else the security agreement requires, the indenture trustee can request that the individual consumers pay the indenture trustee directly, instead of paying Honda's loan servicing arm.[18] And after receipt of a notice directly them to pay the indenture trustee, consumers will act at their peril (meaning they will have to pay twice) if they choose not to follow the notice and continue to pay Honda's servicing arm.[19]

This ability to require consumers to pay the trustee directly is not without some limits. Section 9-607(c) requires that this power be exercised "in a commercially reasonable manner," which presumably means that the secured party has to proceed with some care to maximize collections, although the scope of this duty has yet to be tested.

The most significant right under Section 9-607, however, may be the right to pursue payments already made to someone other than the secured party. Section 9-607(a)(2) permits the secured party to "take any proceeds to which the secured party is entitled under Section 9-315." Since the secured party has a security interest in the original account, it has a property interest in the account

---

17 UCC § 9-607(a)(1) (emphasis supplied).

18 Although that sounds potentially messy, businesses exist which can "take over" portfolios of loans and begin anew to "service" them. Those of you who have been told several times to redirect student loan payment or payments of other loans likely have been involuntary participants in this type of transition.

19 An example is *Hall Bros. Constr. Co., Inc. v. Mercantile Nat'l Bank of Indiana*, 642 N.E.2d 285 (Ind. Ct. App. 1994), in which the court affirmed an award of summary judgment in favor of bank requiring an account debtor to pay bank, when the bank had notified the account debtor under a predecessor of Section 9-607(a), and notwithstanding the notice, the account debtor still paid the debtor.

and its proceeds.[20] Section 9-315, in turn, states the secured party may trace identifiable proceeds, and provides that proceeds are identifiable for this purpose if the secured party "identifies the proceeds by a method of tracing, including application of equitable principles, that is permitted under law other than this article with respect to commingled property of the type involved."[21]

As a consequence, if the servicing agent paid someone else, the indenture trustee could attempt to trace that payment and recover it for the benefit of the noteholders. This ability to trace property distinguishes secured lending from just agreeing to prefer someone; if the debtor breaks his or her promise to prefer, the secured party can proceed against the person who was paid instead of the secured party.

---

20 *See* UCC § 9-203(f).

21 UCC § 9-315(b)(2). *See* Harris J. Diamond, Student Note, *Tracing Cash Proceeds in Insolvency Proceedings Under Revised Article 9*, 9 AM. BANKR. INST. L. REV. 385 (2001); William Stoddard, Student Note, *Tracing Principles in Revised Article 9 § 9-315(b)(2): A Matter of Careless Drafting, or an Invitation to Creative Lawyering?*, 3 NEV. L.J. 135 (2002).

Chapter 3
BANKRUPTCY AND SECURITIZATION

§ 3.01. General Overview of Bankruptcy

Securitization and bankruptcy are closely linked. Many of the structures adopted for various securitizations exist to attenuate or sever the effects of the bankruptcy of the originator from the SPE's obligation to pay investors. Although bankruptcy is a subject worthy of independent study, this chapter looks at those aspects of bankruptcy which impinge on securitization.

We start, however, with the notion that at some level, every nation must deal with bankruptcy. It is a sad fact that in every market economy, some people do not pay their debts. The legal reaction to this failure is to allow creditors, after some appropriate application to a court or administrative agency, to seize the non-paying debtor's assets. These assets are then sold and the proceeds applied to the creditor's debt. In many cases, this works fine. But a debtor's failure to pay *one* debt may be symptomatic of the debtor's inability to pay *all* debts. That general failure can lead to many creditors trying to seize the debtor's limited pool of assets. Incentives to be first — since the general rule is that the Devil takes the hindmost — abound, and sometimes the "rush to the courthouse" results in an inefficient sale or liquidation of the debtor's assets. This is especially the case if the debtor's assets are insufficient to pay all creditors in full. The consequence is that while some creditors get more than they would in an orderly liquidation (those who seized the assets first), most don't.

The historic response to this problem has been to force such debtors into a proceeding in which the debtor's assets are divided up among claimants in some form of collective setting in which all creditors and the debtor participate. Commonly referred to generically as bankruptcy, these types of proceedings have a long heritage. If a debtor's assets were insufficient to pay all creditors, for example, ancient Romans gave themselves the power to dismember and distribute a debtor's body to creditors in proportion to the amount of debts owed each.[1] Mediaeval Italians, who gave us the term "bankruptcy,"[2] remitted criminal penalties for those who could not pay all their debts if they exposed their naked bodies in public, and then banged their backsides on a public post while

---

[1] *See* 2 WILLIAM BLACKSTONE, COMMENTARIES 472 ("[Under Roman law], creditors might cut the debtor's body into pieces, and each of them take his proportionate share. . . ."). *See also* Vern Countryman, *Bankruptcy and the Individual Debtor — and a Modest Proposal to Return to the Seventeenth Century*, 32 CATH. U.L. REV. 809, 810 (1983).

[2] From the concatenation of "banca" — bench or table — and "rotta," — broken or ruptured. Merchants traded from benches or tables in a common area, and the breaking of such a bench signaled the revocation of the merchant's trading privileges or his banishment from the city.

loudly proclaiming "I am bankrupt" three times.[3] In France, those who could not pay their debts were made to wear a "Green Cap" at all times so that others would know that they had not paid their debts.[4]

Modern commerce calls for slightly different treatment. The ability, since the Nineteenth Century, to create entities such as corporations and reduce personal exposure to liability, has lead to large collections of capital that sometimes fail. To address this inevitable failure, every industrialized country and many emerging countries have statutes and systems to handle the liquidation and winding up of firms that no longer are worth keeping. These systems attempt to maximize the liqiudation proceeds of the debtor's assets, and sometimes to maximize the average returns to creditors from those proceeds. How these goals are achieved is the subject of this chapter.

A. The Basic Notion of Collective Action to Maximize Liquidation Proceeds

It is without dispute that one of the goals of bankruptcy is to increase, or even maximize, returns to creditors when their common debtor does not have enough money or assets to pay all debts in full. Historically, bankruptcy law has accomplished this by forcing all debt collection in a single proceeding, and by taking jurisdiction of all the debtor's assets in that proceeding. Once the system achieves these two actions, the system stops, or at least reigns in, individual debt collection efforts. One person, called the "trustee" in our system, is appointed to collect and liquidate the debtor's assets (often referred to as the debtor's "bankruptcy estate"), and once the estate assets are converted to money, to distribute such cash proceeds to creditors.

Why the use of trust law terms such as "trustee" and "estate"? In the English system from which we borrowed most of our debtor-creditor law, courts of equity handled both trusts and bankruptcies. With this proximity, lawyers and courts began to use the same terms for similar concepts. The debtor's assets were analogized to a trust "estate"; that is, the *res* subject to the trust. The person managing the assets was called the "trustee," just as the manager of an express trust was known as the trustee. In this scenario, creditors were analogous to the beneficiaries of the trust, and the debtor analogous to the settlor.

Notwithstanding this mixing of terms, the trustee's tasks were simple: to increase the average return to all creditors. If this required enjoining actions taken by individual creditors that might reduce the average return, the court entered such an injunction. If such actions required running the business just a little longer — to process some inventory, or to finish a project — court also

---

[3] *See* James Q. Whitman, *The Moral Menace of Roman Law and the Making of Commerce: Some Dutch Evidence*, 105 YALE L.J. 1841, 1872-73 (1996).

[4] *Id.* at 1874.

gave the trustee that power. Thus, for the good of all creditors collectively, the individual rights of particular creditors were curbed or otherwise severely limited.

A question that one might ask at this point is how does a bankruptcy case starts — who initiates it, and are there any requirements that must be shown as a condition of obtaining the relief offered by bankruptcy. The answer is that, at least in the United States, either the debtor or a combination of creditors may commence a bankruptcy case. Creditors holding an aggregate of $11,675 of unsecured claims may commence an involuntary case against a debtor, but they then have to show that the debtor was not paying its debts as they became due.[5] This is not a particularly easy showing if the debtor contests it. In stark contrast, a debtor may file a case without any showing that it is in financial distress.[6] The ability of a debtor to voluntarily file for bankruptcy has been jealously guarded by the courts, which almost uniformly hold that contracts not to file bankruptcy are unenforceable on public policy grounds.[7] As a result of the ease by which a debtor can file, and the difficulty faced by creditors in establishing the debtor's financial state, almost 98% of all bankruptcies filed in the United States are commenced voluntarily by the debtor.[8]

B. The Benefits of Reorganization

The simple model of a trustee who liquidates all assets in the most efficient manner worked best when the enterprises or debts were small, as they tended to be when owners of businesses continued to bear personal liability for all debts of the firm. When corporations appeared in the Nineteenth Century, however, changes occurred in the ways business was conducted. Especially in capital intensive industries such as transportation or manufacturing, business and enterprises took the corporate form and expanded greatly.

The new size, however, was no guaranty against failure. And fail they did. By 1915, for example, over half the railroads in this country had gone through some form of financial reorganization.[9] But traditional remedies of seizure and sale did not work well with such large concerns. Railroad ties and rails have more value in place than they do dug up and sold separately. The law side of the courts, however, did not provide any relief; their forms lead to seizure and sale, and not much else.

---

[5] 11 U.S.C. § 303(b)(1), (h).

[6] 11 U.S.C. § 301.

[7] *See Bank of China v. Huang (In re Huang)*, 275 F.3d 1173, 1177 (9th Cir. 2002) ("It is against public policy for a debtor to waive the prepetition protection of the Bankruptcy Code.").

[8] *See* Susan Block-Lieb, *Why Creditors File So Few Involuntary Petitions and Why the Number Is Not Too Small*, 57 BROOKLYN L. REV. 803 (1991).

[9] Bruce A. Markell, *Owners, Auctions, and Absolute Priority in Bankruptcy Reorganizations*, 44 STAN. L. REV. 69, 74 (1991). *See also* Paul D. Cravath, *Reorganization of Corporations*, in 1 SOME LEGAL PHASES OF CORPORATE FINANCING, REORGANIZATION AND REGULATION 153, 154 (1917).

In equity, however, creative lawyers developed the reorganization. In such a case, the form of enforcement were followed — there was a foreclosure and sale — but the result was rigged. Before the foreclosure occurred, all interested parties knew who would buy — usually the secured creditors, since they could bid in their debts at any foreclosure sale. This practice lead to shareholder interests and secured creditor interests squeezing out regular creditors, and overnight changes in ownership.

Although arguably limited by the Supreme Court in 1913,[10] this practice continued in the United States until the Depression of the 1930s. In a series of enactments during that decade, Congress codified this equity practice, and created an alternative to liquidation: reorganization.[11] The thought, and indeed the rationale, of reorganization is that some businesses are worth more if kept together, and simply given new ownership. Thus, today's reorganization statute requires the proponent of the reorganization to show that each and every creditor will receive more in reorganization than it would in liquidation.[12]

There is, of course, much more to reorganization under chapter 11 of the federal Bankruptcy Code. Reorganization occurs under the supervision of bankruptcy judges, who independently assess whether any proposed reorganization meets all the statutory requirements.[13] If the plan does pass muster, the plan is "confirmed" in an order signed by the judge. In addition to showing that creditors will get more in reorganization than in liquidation, reorganization candidates must convince the judge that, after reorganization, the reorganized debtor will be a viable economic entity; in the words of the statute, they have to show that "[c]onfirmation of the plan is not likely to be followed by the liquidation, or the need for further financial reorganization of the debtor . . . ."[14]

In addition, creditors vote by classes on the plan, and a consensual confirmation requires the affirmative vote of all classes. One aspect of consent, however, is that it need not be unanimous; a class consents to a plan of reorganization if more than half of the creditors voting approve of the plan, and those approving creditors hold at least two-thirds of the amount of debt voting. 11 U.S.C. § 1126(c). As a consequence, if a debtor had a class of creditors with ten members, and each creditor in that class held a claim of $10, it would require the affirmative vote of seven creditors for the class to approve the plan

[10] In Northern Pacific Railway Co. v. Boyd, 228 U.S. 482 (1913), the Supreme Court held that the absolute priority rule, as derived from fraudulent transfer law, rendered invalid collusive foreclosures arranged between secured creditors and shareholders.

[11] *See* Markell, *supra* note 9, at 81-84.

[12] 11 U.S.C. § 1129(a)(7). Sometimes these differences can be stark: in the WorldCom reorganization, the proponents of the plan claim that WorldCom, as reorganized, would be worth $12 billion; if liquidated, it would be worth $0.

[13] Bankruptcy judges are Article I judges, with limited powers and 14-year terms of office. 28 U.S.C. § 152.

[14] 11 U.S.C. § 1129(a)(11). There is an exception for reorganization plans which propose liquidation of the debtor following plan confirmation.

assuming that all ten creditors voted.[15] But what if only six creditors voted? You would then need only four affirmative votes (which would be more than half of the creditors, and exactly two-thirds of the amount of claims voting), since the standard only looks to creditors who actually vote. There are many more requirements, contained in Section 1129(a) of the federal Bankruptcy Code, found in title 11 of the United States Code.

From the beginning of statutory reorganization in the 1930s until 1978, however, reorganization of large firms was managed primarily by an independent trustee appointed after the bankruptcy case commenced. That created some inefficiencies; for many large debtors, the learning curve for a new manager, especially when the debtor was in financial difficulties anyway, often caused more harm than hapless management would have. In addition, in those cases of financial difficulty caused by market conditions and not management miscues, appointment of an independent trustee was seen as unneeded.

Since 1978, however, there has been no necessity of appointing a trustee. When Congress revised the Bankruptcy Code in 1978, it permitted the debtor to remain in possession of its assets, and thus was codified the notion of a "debtor in possession." A "debtor in possession," or "DIP" as it is often referred to, is a representative of the bankruptcy estate, but one with the knowledge of the business. The "DIP," however, still has all the potent tools of a bankruptcy trustee to manage the estate and raise creditors' average recovery. Among these are the automatic stay and the broad scope of "property of the estate."

C. The Automatic Stay and Estate Property

1. The Automatic Stay and Section 362

Any collective action designed to coordinate and control the actions of creditors requires an enforcement device. In many early reorganizations, the equity courts supervising the restructuring process issued injunctions against individual creditors from taking actions that would harm the overall creditor body. For example, a court might enjoin a creditor from foreclosing on some railroad track upon which that creditor held a mortgage if such a foreclosure would unduly harm the railroad's chances to reorganize. So frequent were such requests that, by degrees, such a stay was built into the Bankruptcy Code. The salient portions of the automatic stay, found in Section 362(a) of the Bankruptcy Code, read as follows:

> (a) Except as provided in subsection (b) of this section, a petition filed under section 301, 302, or 303 of this title, . . . operates as a stay, applicable to all entities, of—

---

[15] Six votes would not suffice. Although it would be more than half, it would represent votes from creditors holding only 60% of the claims, which is less than two-thirds required.

(1) the commencement or continuation, including the issuance or employment of process, of a judicial, administrative, or other action or proceeding against the debtor that was or could have been commenced before the commencement of the case under this title, or to recover a claim against the debtor that arose before the commencement of the case under this title;

(2) the enforcement, against the debtor or against property of the estate, of a judgment obtained before the commencement of the case under this title;

(3) any act to obtain possession of property of the estate or of property from the estate or to exercise control over property of the estate; . . .

(6) any act to collect, assess, or recover a claim against the debtor that arose before the commencement of the case under this title;

(7) the setoff of any debt owing to the debtor that arose before the commencement of the case under this title against any claim against the debtor . . . .

Although subject to some exceptions,[16] this language is broad, and intentionally so. Note that it differs from normal injunctions in substantial ways. Notice to creditors is *not* necessary, nor is any showing that the harm to creditors from such a stay is justified by benefits to the estate. The stay is truly "automatic."

Courts take violations of the stay seriously. Although there is currently a split among courts as to whether actions taken in violation of the stay are void or voidable, most agree that intentional violation of the stay brings with it the duty to return property taken, and to pay sanctions.

Of particular interest for securitization is Section 362(a)(3), which prohibits "any act to obtain possession of property of the estate or of property from the estate or to exercise control over property of the estate." This section, combined with Section 362(a)(6) — which essentially stops a creditor from exercising any right of setoff — effectively stops a creditor from collecting on any pre-petition claim, even if the collection is from a debt that is backed by collateral, or is directly from collateral which the creditor holds.

This cessation of payments and the bar against even requesting them is intentional, and an anathema to securitization. As we saw in Chapter 1 of this book, a high rating on debt securities takes into account not only eventual payment, as one might expect in a bankruptcy, but also prompt and timely payment, which the automatic stay completely disrupts.

---

16 Section 362(b) contains, among others, exceptions for criminal actions, 11 U.S.C. § 362(b)(1), actions taken by governments in exercise of their police powers, *id.* § 362(b)(4), and actions to enforce child support, *id.* § 362(b)(2).

As a consequence, sponsors of securitization try to distance from the originator both the assets and the liabilities involved in securitization. As indicated in the opening chapter, securtization attempts to focus lending on assets, and not their owner. To accomplish this isolation, however, attention must be paid to how bankruptcy defines the assets and debts that are protected by the automatic stay.

2. Property of the Estate and Section 541(a)

It is easy to understand why the stay protects tangible property. A trucking company cannot lose trucks at the whim of its secured creditors and hope to reorganize or liquidate in an orderly manner. Thus, many of the paragraphs of Section 362(a) refer to "property of the estate," and this property includes tangible property, such as chairs and cars. But securitization deals primarily with intangibles, property interests that you cannot touch. Such intangibles also come into the bankruptcy estate. Section 541(a)(1) of the Bankruptcy Code, which defines property of the estate for all bankruptcies, is quite broad: it brings into the estate "all legal or equitable interests of the debtor in property as of the commencement of the case."

This language thus covers not only tangible personal property, but intangible property as well. Its touchstone is property as recognized under state law. This breadth affects securitization in at least two ways: it includes rights under contracts such as those that drive securitization; and it includes that peculiar type of personal property known as "choses in action." For our purposes, choses in action include all manner of lawsuits, including those that were pending at the time of filing, and those that could arise during the administration of the estate. It includes, as well, special rights granted under the Bankruptcy Code in what are generically known as "avoidance actions."

D. Avoiding Powers and Equality of Distribution

Property of the estate not only includes the debtor's non-bankruptcy property interests, but Section 541(a)(3) of the Bankruptcy Code also brings various "avoiding powers" actions into estate property. Avoiding powers actions are statutory causes of action that further the equality of distribution principle. For example, without avoiding powers, the creditor who is paid in full one second before filing gets to keep the payment, and the creditor who would have been paid next does not. To equalize the inequalities brought about by the vagaries of filing (and by the fact that the debtor itself can file, giving the debtor strategic incentives to pay only some creditors), the estate is given the power to avoid many types of pre-bankruptcy transactions.

The most common type of avoiding powers action is the preference. Originally a device to recover payments made with the intent to prefer some, and prejudice other, creditors, the 1978 revisions to the Bankruptcy Code tried to define a preference without reference to the intent of the parties, since such intent was difficult to prove with any certainty. As it currently stands, any payment on a debt made to a non-affiliated creditor within 90 days is presumptively recoverable by the bankruptcy estate.

A highly simplified example illustrates this point. Assume that X Corp. owes Jim $500. It also owes A and B $500 each, for a grand total of $1500 in debts. X Corp. pays Jim in full with a $500 check on June 1, and X Corp. files for bankruptcy on August 1, well within the 90 day "reachback" period set forth in Section 547(b). Assume further that X Corp's assets at filing are worth only $400. Without avoiding powers, Jim will be paid in full, and A and B will share equally (since their debts were equal) in the $400 of X Corp.'s assets, giving each a $200 payment. If, however, Jim is required to return the $500 as a preference, recoveries change dramatically. X Corp.'s estate now has $900, consisting of the original $400 plus the $500 recovered from Jim. Jim, however, received a $500 claim against X Corp.'s estate when he paid back the preference, but that is not likely to pay anything close to $500. Indeed, now there are three creditors each with $500 claims, and thus they will each share equally in the $900 estate, with each receiving $300.

As a consequence of the avoidance action, the other creditors are the beneficiaries — their recovery increased from $200 to $300. Jim is a net loser; he went from payment in full of $500 to a payment of just $300. As a consequence, X Corp's other creditors are enriched at Jim's expense.

Preference law has many defenses — including a defense that the payment was made in the ordinary course of business.[17] The point, however, is that overall the preference avoidance power allows the estate to achieve a more equal distribution.

Other avoiding powers exist: the estate can avoid certain statutory liens, fraudulent transfers and most setoffs. Again, the goal of such actions is achieve a fairer distribution to creditors.

[17] The preference defenses are found in 11 U.S.C. § 547(c). Recipients of preferences, however, bear the burden of establishing their own defense, 11 U.S.C. § 547(g).

Although better left to a bankruptcy course, because one of the elements of a preference action is that any transfer actually benefit the recipient by putting it in a better position than if the transfer had not been made and creditor received a bankruptcy dividend instead, 11 U.S.C. § 547(b)(5), it is generally the case that payments on fully secured debt, and payments made from self-liquidating collateral are not preferential. This follows because in each case — a fully secured creditor or a payment from self-liquidating collateral — the payment does not improve the position of the creditor; they would be entitled to payment in full or at least the payment they received in any liquidation.

E. Cash Collateral and Use of Estate Property

Bankruptcies are not, unfortunately, over in an instant. They take time, and it is not unusual for large cases to take several years. The existence of this interim period means that the estate has to find a way to sustain itself. In most cases, if a business is the debtor, the estate will continue in its ordinary business. Under Section 363(c), such activities are permissible without court intervention, at least so long as they truly are in the ordinary course of business.

The rules are different for activities which involve property encumbered by a security interest or lien. In a sense, the debtor is only a co-owner of such property, and the property rights of the secured creditors need to be taken into account. In accordance with the general structure of the Bankruptcy Code, the estate can use such property under Section 363(e) if the secured creditor does not object. If the secured party objects, then the estate has to give the secured creditor "adequate protection" of its interest. The forms adequate protection can take are many. As listed non-exhaustively in Section 361 of the Bankruptcy Code, they include granting additional collateral, cash payments, or the protection provided by an excess of value in the collateral over the amount of the secured debt.

There are exceptions, even within this structure. Some collateral is worthy of greater protection. The Bankruptcy Code gives such extra protection to "cash collateral," that is, collateral in the form of cash or cash equivalents. Such collateral arises, for example, when collateral is sold. But some collateral — particularly important for securitization — is self-liquidating collateral. That is, collateral that in its normal course transforms from an intangible right to cash. Payments on accounts receivables, or on purchase contracts are common examples of such collateral, and such assets are important components of most securitizations.

Under Section 363(c)(4) of the Bankruptcy Code, a debtor must segregate and account for all cash collateral, and under Section 363(c)(1) may not use it unless the secured creditor consents, or unless the debtor obtains a court order (which, as set forth above, will be conditioned upon providing adequate protection for the secured creditor). As a result of these provisions, many early skirmishes in bankruptcy revolve around the ability to use cash collateral.

§ 3.02. The Potential Conflicts Between Securitization and Bankruptcy

Bankruptcy presents several possible conflicts with securitization. The first is obvious and mentioned above — if the originator's bankruptcy somehow affects the SPE, the SPE will be stayed from making payments to investors. But how does this issue get raised? Although conflicts of this type have have been avoided in many cases, cash collateral hearings present an early opportunity for conflicts.

A. The Initial Stages: The Stay and Cash Collateral Orders

For reasons explored later, not many securitizations have been tested fully in bankruptcy. One key skirmish, however, was presented in the following case.

IN RE LTV STEEL CO., INC.

37 Bankr. Ct. Dec. 137 (Bankr. N.D. Ohio 2001)

MEMORANDUM OPINION

This cause is before the Court on the emergency motion of Abbey National Treasury Services PLC ("Abbey National") for modification of an interim order entered by the Court on December 29, 2000. That order permitted LTV Steel Company, Inc., Debtor and Debtor-in-Possession in these jointly administered proceedings ("Debtor"), to use cash assets that are claimed to be cash collateral in which Abbey National has an interest. . . .

DISCUSSION

A. *Facts*

Debtor is one of the largest manufacturers of wholly-integrated steel products in the United States. . . . Debtor currently employs approximately 17,500 people in various capacities, and Debtor is also responsible for providing medical coverage and other benefits to approximately 100,000 retirees and their dependents. Debtor and 48 of its subsidiaries filed voluntary petitions for relief under Chapter 11 of Title 11, United States Code, on December 29, 2000. These cases are jointly administered.

This is not the first occasion on which Debtor has filed for relief under the Bankruptcy Code. Debtor previously filed a voluntary Chapter 11 petition in the Bankruptcy Court for the Southern District of New York on July 17, 1986. Debtor successfully emerged from Chapter 11 on June 28, 1993. Indeed, the current controversy stems from a series of financial transactions that Debtor executed after its previous reorganization. The transactions in question are known as asset-backed securitization or structured financing ("ABS"), and are generally designed to permit a debtor to borrow funds at a reduced cost in exchange for a lender securing the loan with assets that are transferred from the borrower to another entity. By structuring the transactions in this manner, the lender hopes to ensure that its collateral will be excluded from the borrower's bankruptcy estate in the event that the borrower files a bankruptcy petition.

Abbey National is a large financial institution located in the United Kingdom. Debtor and Abbey National entered into an ABS transaction in October 1994. To effectuate this agreement, Debtor created a wholly-owned subsidiary known as LTV Sales Finance Co. ("Sales Finance"). Debtor then entered into an agreement with Sales Finance which purports to sell all of Debtor's right and interest in its accounts receivables ("receivables") to Sales Finance on a continuing basis. Abbey National then agreed to loan Two Hundred Seventy Million Dollars ($270,000,000.00) to Sales Finance in exchange for Sales Finance granting Abbey National a security interest in the receivables. On the date Debtor's petition was filed, Chase Manhattan Bank ("Chase Manhattan") was Abbey National's agent for this credit facility.

In 1998, Debtor entered into another ABS financing arrangement. To that end, Debtor created LTV Steel Products, LLC ("Steel Products"), another wholly-owned subsidiary. Debtor entered into an agreement with Steel Products which purports to sell all of Debtor's right, title and interest in its inventory to Steel Products on a continuing basis. Chase Manhattan and several other banking institutions then agreed to loan Thirty Million Dollars ($30,000,000.00) to Steel Products in exchange for a security interest in Steel Products' inventory. Abbey National is not involved in this ABS facility, and it had no interest in pre-petition inventory allegedly owned by Steel Products.

Neither Sales Finance nor Steel Products is a debtor in this proceeding. Nevertheless, Debtor filed a motion with the Court on December 29, 2000 seeking an interim order permitting it to use cash collateral. This cash collateral consisted of the receivables and inventory that are ostensibly owned by Sales Finance and Steel Products. Debtors stated to the Court that it would be forced to shut it doors and cease operations if it did not receive authorization to use this cash collateral. A hearing was held on Debtor's cash collateral motion on December 29, 2000 as part of the first day hearings.

Abbey National was not present at the cash collateral hearing. However, the Court notes that Abbey National had actual notice of the hearing, first, in the form of an e-mail sent by a Chase Manhattan employee to Abbey National on December 28, 2000, and second, in the form of a telephone call made from a Chase Manhattan employee to Abbey National on December 29, 2000. Furthermore, it is clear that Debtor had given advance notice of its intention to file for bankruptcy protection to Chase Manhattan, Abbey National's agent, in the week prior to December 29, 2000. Chase Manhattan was present at the December 29, 2000 hearing.

On December 29, 2000, Debtor and Chase Manhattan reached an agreement regarding an interim order permitting Debtor to use the cash collateral. Chase Manhattan did not formally consent to the entry of this order, as it could not secure Abbey National's consent to the form of the order, but Chase Manhattan did negotiate some of the terms of the order and did not raise an objection to its entry by the Court. The Court determined that entry of the interim order was necessary to permit Debtor to continue business operations, that the interests of Abbey National and all other creditors who had an interest in the cash collateral were adequately protected by the order, and that entry of the order was in the best interests of the estate and creditors of the estate. Accordingly, the Court entered the order tendered by Debtor, the relevant provisions of which are summarized below:

1. Recognition that there is a dispute between Debtor and the secured lenders of Sales Finance and Steel Products as to whether the transactions between Debtor and those entities were true sales or disguised financing vehicles;

2. An order requiring the secured lenders to turn over to Debtor the cash proceeds of the inventory and receivables which are to be used to provide working capital for Debtor;

3. Recognition that in the event the Court determines these transactions to be true sales, the secured lenders whose cash collateral was used will be entitled to administrative expense claims against the estate;

4. Adequate protection was provided to the secured lenders in the form of senior liens on the inventory and receivables and weekly interest payments to the lenders at pre-petition non-default rates.

It is this order that Abbey National seeks to modify. Specifically, Abbey National asks the Court to modify the interim cash collateral order *nunc pro tunc* to include the following provisions:

a. The Debtors shall transfer to Sales Finance all receivables created on or after December 29, 2000 and not previously sold to Sales Finance and that would have been sold to Sales Finance were it not for the occurrence of a Liquidation Event;

b. Steel Products would continue to purchase Inventory from the Inventory Sellers and Sales Finance would continue to purchase Receivables from the Receivables Sellers, each on the same basis and on the same terms as existed prior to the Petition Date;

c. The respective Collection Accounts would be administered by the Collateral Agent in the same manner as was administered prior to the Petition Date. Therefore, notwithstanding the occurrence of any Termination Date, collection on account of the Receivables would not be required to be applied to principal payments or amortization payments (other than any payments required in connection with the maintenance by the borrowers of their respective borrowing bases);

d. Steel Products and the Collateral Agent under the Inventory Facility would continue to automatically release all liens against the Receivables purchased by Sales Finance from Steel Products;

e. All minimum borrowing base and collateral value requirements set forth in the Receivables Facility and the Inventory Facility will continue in full force and effect;

f. In all other respects, the Receivables Facility and the Inventory Facility will continue to operate as required after the occurrence of a Liquidation Event including without limitation, the reimbursement of all expenses of each Receivables Lender and Inventory Lender.

(Abbey National's Emergency Motion to Modify Interim Order at 14-16).

Abbey National argues that the interim cash collateral order should be modified because: 1) it did not receive effective notice of the December 29, 2000 hearing and was thus denied due process of law; 2) there is no basis for the Court to determine that the receivables which are Abbey National's collateral are property of Debtor's estate and 3) that even if the receivables are property of Debtor's estate, that Abbey National's interests are not adequately protected because the pre-petition receivables are diminishing at a rapid rate and will soon be depleted. Debtor argues that Abbey National did receive notice of the December 29 hearing, that Abbey National has failed to state grounds to modify the interim order pursuant to FED. R. BANKR. P. 9024, and that Abbey National's interests in the receivables are adequately protected.

B. *Issue*

There are four issues before the Court. These are: 1) the procedural basis for Abbey National's motion; 2) whether the circumstances surrounding the December 29, 2000 hearing deprived Abbey National of its right to due process; 3) whether the interim order should be modified because the cash collateral was not property of Debtor's estate; and 4) whether the interim order failed to adequately protect Abbey National's interest in the collateral.

C. *Analysis*

[The court concluded that Abbey's motion was in the nature of a request for relief from a judgment, and that it had received due process with respect to notice of the December hearing.]

3. *Whether the Receivables Are Property of Debtor's Estate*

Abbey National's next argument is that the receivables which constitute its collateral are not property of Debtor's estate, and thus this Court lacked jurisdiction to enter the interim order. We shall construe this as an argument that the interim order is void pursuant to Rule 60(b)(4).

Section 541(a) of the Bankruptcy Code provides that upon the filing of a bankruptcy petition an estate is created consisting of "all legal or equitable interests of the debtor in property as of the commencement of the case." 11 U.S.C. § 541(a)(1). The estate created by the filing of a Chapter 11 petition is very broad, and property may be included in Debtor's estate even if Debtor does not have a possessory interest in that property. *United States v. Whiting Pools, Inc.*, 462 U.S. 198, 204, 205-06, 103 S. Ct. 2309, 2313-14, 76 L. Ed. 2d 515 (1983).

Abbey National contends that the interim order is flawed because, on its face, the transaction between Debtor and Sales Finance is characterized as a true sale. Therefore, Abbey National argues, since Debtor sold its interests in the receivables to Sales Finance, Debtor no longer has an interest in the receivables and they are not property of the estate. However, Abbey National has admitted to the Court, both in its pleadings and in oral argument, that the ultimate issue of whether Debtor actually sold the receivables to Sales Finance is a fact-intensive issue that cannot be resolved without extensive discovery and an evidentiary hearing.

We find Abbey National's argument for "emergency" relief to be not well taken for several reasons. First, Abbey National's position in this regard is circular: we cannot permit Debtor to use cash collateral because it is not property of the estate, but we cannot determine if it is property of the estate until we hold an evidentiary hearing. We fail to see how we can conclude that the receivables are not property of Debtor's estate until an evidentiary hearing on that issue has been held. Because the determination of this issue must await further discovery, we decline to grant Abbey National relief from the interim order.

Furthermore, there seems to be an element of sophistry to suggest that Debtor does not retain at least an equitable interest in the property that is subject to the interim order. Debtor's business requires it to purchase, melt, mold and cast various metal products. To suggest that Debtor lacks some ownership interest in products that it creates with its own labor, as well as the proceeds to be derived from that labor, is difficult to accept. Accordingly, the Court concludes that Debtor has at least some equitable interest in the inventory and receivables, and that this interest is property of the Debtor's estate. This equitable interest is sufficient to support the entry of the interim cash collateral order.

Finally, it is readily apparent that granting Abbey National relief from the interim cash collateral order would be highly inequitable. The Court is satisfied that the entry of the interim order was necessary to enable Debtor to keep its doors open and continue to meet its obligations to its employees, retirees, customers and creditors. Allowing Abbey National to modify the order would allow Abbey National to enforce its state law rights as a secured lender to look to the collateral in satisfaction of this debt. This circumstance would put an immediate end to Debtor's business, would put thousands of people out of work, would deprive 100,000 retirees of needed medical benefits, and would have more far reaching economic effects on the geographic areas where Debtor does business. However, maintaining the current status quo permits Debtor to remain in business while it searches for substitute financing, and adequately protects and preserves Abbey National's rights. The equities of this situation highly favor Debtor. As a result, the Court declines to exercise its discretion to modify the interim order pursuant to Rule 60(b)(4).

4. Adequate Protection

The final argument Abbey National has raised in support of its motion is that its interests in the collateral are not adequately protected. Specifically, Abbey

National contends that the pre-petition receivables in which Abbey National has an interest are being depleted at a rate of Ten Million Dollars ($10,000,000.00) per day, and that the receivables will be entirely consumed in short order. Additionally, Abbey National asserts that the interim order diminished the value of Abbey National's liens. We shall treat this line of argument as one arising under Rule 60(b)(6).

Abbey National's contentions that its interest is not adequately protected can be boiled down to a simple issue. Prior to the filing of Debtor's petition, the outstanding balance on Abbey National's loan to Sales Finance was approximately Two Hundred Twenty-Four Million Eight Hundred Thousand Dollars ($224,800,000.00). This loan to Sales Finance was secured by the receivables transferred to Sales Finance, and this financing arrangement was rated AAA by Standard & Poors. However, the terms of the interim order have altered the nature of Abbey National's liens. Under the terms of the interim order, Abbey National and the other secured lenders have been granted liens on Debtor's post-petition inventory and receivables. Abbey National's loan is thus now secured by inventory and assets which do not have a AAA rating, and Abbey National must now share its liens with Debtor's other secured lenders.

We find Abbey National's arguments to be not well taken. First, we find Abbey National's contention that its collateral is being consumed at a rate of Ten Million Dollars ($10,000,000.00) per day to be disingenuous. It is true that the *pre-petition* receivables are being used by Debtor to purchase and manufacture more steel. However, Debtor's use of the *pre-petition* receivables will inevitably lead to an increase in the value of *post-petition* receivables and inventory, in which Abbey National has a security interest.

This conclusion is amply supported by the affidavit of John T. Delmore, Debtor's Assistant Controller. Mr Delmore's affidavit indicates that as of January 15, 2001, there was a sufficient equity cushion in both post-petition inventory and receivables to provide adequate protection to all of Debtor's secured lenders. The amount of the respective equity cushions equaled 39% for the receivables lenders and 179% for the inventory lenders. Furthermore, it appears that Debtor's business will continue to generate additional post-petition receivables and inventory sufficient to protect Abbey National's interest in the near future. Because we find that Abbey National's interest in cash collateral is adequately protected by an equity cushion and by the other terms of the interim order, the Court declines to exercise its discretion to modify the interim order pursuant to Rule 60(b)(6).

CONCLUSION

For the reasons stated above, . . . Abbey National's emergency motion is overruled.

QUESTIONS REGARDING *LTV*

1. According to this court, who is the owner of the receivables at issue?

2. What law did the court look to in determining who the owner of the receivables was?

3. How much did it seem to influence the bankruptcy judge that ordering the relief requested by Abbey National would "would put an immediate end to Debtor's business, would put thousands of people out of work, would deprive 100,000 retirees of needed medical benefits, and would have more far reaching economic effects on the geographic areas where Debtor does business." Under what rule of law is such information relevant?

4. If LTV does have an interest in the receivables such that their proceeds are considered cash collateral, what in the world could LTV offer as adequate protection for LTV's use of such funds? What did LTV offer?

NOTE ON *LTV*

After the difficult legal battle, LTV and Abbey settled their disagreement. As part of that settlement, Abbey rolled the receivables securitization into a debtor in possession financing (also known as "DIP Financing").[18] Under this arrangement, LTV "borrowed" the amount of the outstanding receivables from Abbey, paid them off with the proceeds, and then was left with a priority DIP Financing. The settlement also included an agreed stipulation, upon which the court entered its order, that the transactions at issue constituted "true sales," thus depriving the opinion above of any true precedential weight. If you were an unsecured creditor of LTV, would you find this arrangement helpful?

B. The End Game: Avoiding Powers and Non-Consensual Confirmation (Cramdown Again)

Bankruptcy presents other issues for securitization. Even if the initial cash collateral arrangements are finessed, there is still a significant impact that can be forced upon investors. As outlined above, the estate representative may attack financing transactions under various of the estate's avoiding powers. That concept will be explored below.

Equally worrisome, however, is the estate's so-called "cramdown" powers. Under the Bankruptcy Code, a particular treatment can be forced upon an unwilling creditor — crammed down its throat, as it were — if the proponent of the plan meets certain requirements found in the Bankruptcy Code. In partic-

18 *In re* LTV Steel Co., Inc., Case No. 00-43866, 2001 Bankr. LEXIS 635 (Bankr. N.D. Ohio, March 20, 2001).

ular, Section 1129(b) of the Bankruptcy Coder permits cramdown against a class of creditors if: (a) all other confirmation requirements except voting are met; (b) the plan does not discriminate unfairly against the non-consenting class; and (c) the plan is fair and equitable to the non-consenting class.

The key here is that the plan be "fair and equitable."[19] This is a term developed during the period of equity receiverships, and incorporated into the reorganization statutes of the 1930s, and carried through to the current Bankruptcy Code. It has several meanings. First, it means that no class can be paid more than its full claim; this ensures that all classes get their due. More importantly, however, it means that no junior class can continue to participate in the reorganization without the consent or payment in full of all senior classes. In short, debt is paid before equity.

In the century or so of cramdown jurisprudence, many different themes have emerged. One is that the value that matters is going concern value; if the reorganization leads to a continuation of the debtor in a different form, the right to participate in that reorganized debtor is tied to the value of the debtor as a going concern, not as if the business were liquidated. Another is that "payment in full" need not be payment in cash. In can be in "property," and such "property" can include a promissory note payable over many years if the present value of that note (or more precisely, the stream of payments under the note) is equal to the creditor's claim. It matters not whether the claim is secured for this concept to apply; much ink has been spilled on the issue of how to cramdown a secured creditor.

Although not many plans result in cramdown, the possibility exists, and that possibility disturbs the sensitive calculations that go into a securitization. The possibility that the form, the term or the interest rate on an obligation can unilaterally be changed later on adversely affects the pricing involved in any securitization.

A more common example from real estate lending can make the point. Many construction lenders specialize in lending to entities that construct buildings. Such lending is risky and the monitoring of the project by the lender is costly. Almost every construction loan is made only after the borrower lines up "exit" or "take-out" financing at the end of construction. There are many cases, however, in which the debtor files bankruptcy during construction, and then "crams

---

[19] This is not to trivialize the other two requirements. Meeting all the other requirements for plan confirmation often takes up an entire bankruptcy seminar, and many pages in the leading treatise on bankruptcy. *See* 7 COLLIER ON BANKRUPTCY ¶ 1129 (15th rev. ed. 2003, Alan Resnick & Henry Sommer, eds.). Unfair discrimination is, in turn, an evolving concept that likely applies primarily to a plan's treatment of claims having the same non-bankruptcy treatment. For a discussion of the concept, see Bruce A. Markell, *A New Perspective on Unfair Discrimination in Chapter 11*, 72 AM. BANKR. L.J. 227 (1998); Association of the Bar of the City of New York, *Making the Test for Unfair Discrimination More "Fair": A Proposal*, 58 BUS. LAW. 83 (2002); Bruce A. Markell, *Slouching Towards Fairness: A Reply to the ABCNY's Proposal on Unfair Discrimination*, 58 BUS. LAW. 109 (2002)

down" the construction loan by giving the creditor a long-term note with a market rate of interest, secured by the same collateral as before. In present value terms, the long-term note is worth the same as the presently-due note (that is the function of the market rate of interest; it makes the present value of the payment stream equal to the face amount of the note).

While such notes might be hypothetically equal in value, they are wildly different for loan administration purposes, and for rating purposes. In securitizations, if the possibility exists that the debtor or some other entity could invoke cramdown to change the nature of the debt without any input from a rating agency, the rating agency will not rate the investment at the high AAA rates. Thus, most securitizations are structured so that the entity liable to the investors is "bankruptcy-remote." We explore what that means below.

§ 3.03. The Major Issues: Bankruptcy Remote Entities, "True Sales," Fraudulent Transfers and Substantive Consolidation

A. Bankruptcy Remote Entities: Taking the Power to File Away From Originators

In any securitization, if the originator owns or controls the SPE, the originator may have the power to cause the SPE to file a voluntary bankruptcy petition. As we saw above, there are no legal standards that ordinarily must be met for a voluntary petition to be filed. A company would make this decision the way it would make any other significant decision. Unless restricted in its charter or bylaws, a corporation, for example, normally would make this decision by a vote of its board of directors. It is therefore important to limit, by design, the ability of the originator to cause the SPE to file a voluntary bankruptcy petition, especially since, as indicated above, agreements not to file bankruptcy are not enforceable.

The originator or sponsors accomplish the structural bar against the filing of a voluntary petition by drafting the SPE's charter, articles of incorporation, or other organizational documents to restrict the filing of a voluntary petition to a narrowly circumscribed set of circumstances. Charters of SPEs usually provide that the SPE may not place itself into bankruptcy unless a requisite number of *independent* members of the board of directors vote for bankruptcy. An independent director, for example, might be defined as a person who is not a director (other than being a director of the SPE), officer, employee, or holder of 5 percent or more of the voting securities of the originator or any of the originator's affiliates. Such an independent director theoretically would be less influenced by the originator and more likely to consider his or her fiduciary obligations when required to vote for or against the SPE's bankruptcy.[20]

---

[20] *See, e.g.,* Revlon, Inc. v. MacAndrews & Forbes Holdings, 506 A.2d 173, 179 (Del. 1986).

Sometimes, however, the independent director may just be independent of the debtor, and dependent upon others. The following case is instructive on this point.

IN RE KINGSTON SQUARE ASSOCIATES
214 B.R. 713 (Bankr. S.D.N.Y. 1997)

TINA L. BROZMAN, CHIEF JUDGE.

Introduction

Fashion has a role not only in the garment industry but in the legal one as well. One of the newest fashions in commercial real estate financing is so-called "mortgage backed securitization" coupled with the presence of corporate governance provisions known as "bankruptcy remote provisions" designed to make bankruptcy unavailable to a defaulting borrower without the affirmative consent of the mortgagee's designee on the borrower's board of directors.

Here, a group of entities owning apartment complexes was stymied by such provisions from invoking the Chapter 11 process to prevent foreclosure despite the belief of their principal that the properties had value over and above the encumbrances against them. To prevent loss of this claimed value and the potential for reorganization, the debtors' principal paid a law firm to solicit creditors to file involuntary Chapter 11 petitions. Only one trade creditor for each debtor agreed; the other petitioning creditors came from the ranks of the debtors' professionals — attorneys and various consultants. At issue is whether the petitions ought therefore be dismissed as bad faith filings, relief which the mortgagees seek.

By agreement of the parties, the only issue at trial was whether there was collusion mandating dismissal, for it was the mortgagee's contention that, standing alone, collusion in their filing warranted dismissal of these petitions. The parties have not yet tried whether there is any possibility of reorganization.

I conclude that although the debtors plainly orchestrated the filing of the involuntary petitions, they had reason to believe that reorganization was possible and did not circumvent any court-ordered or statutory restrictions on bankruptcy filings such that, absent any evidence of objective futility of the reorganization process, the cases ought not be dismissed now. However, because there is a strong suggestion in the record that the debtors' boards of directors have abdicated their fiduciary responsibilities, I am directing the appointment of chapter 11 trustees, relief for which the mortgagees asked in the alternative and as to which the Debtors have consented. The facts are drawn from the undisputed portion of the parties' pretrial order and from the evidence adduced during three days of testimony.

I.

Each of the eleven debtors (the "Debtors") is or was controlled by Morton L. Ginsberg. The Debtors represent less than one-third of the thirty-eight Ginsberg-controlled entities that were restructured in 1991 or 1993 in transactions financed by The Chase Manhattan Bank, N.A. ("Chase") and REFG Investor Two, Inc. ("REFG") (the "Movants"). All thirty-eight properties, both debtor and nondebtor, are in receivership, with foreclosure proceedings pending against them. In one case, that of Lynnewood Associates, the Movants have foreclosed upon the property. The Debtors did not contest the filing of the involuntary petitions, with the result that orders for relief have been entered in all eleven cases.

Chase and REFG seek the dismissal of the chapter 11 cases of the eleven Debtors for cause pursuant to section 1112(b) of the Bankruptcy Code. The Movants maintain that Ginsberg colluded with the petitioning creditors ("Petitioning Creditors") and their counsel, Pryor, Cashman, Sherman & Flynn ("Pryor Cashman"), to enable each Debtor to improperly avail itself of bankruptcy protection to thwart the Movants' ongoing efforts to foreclose on each of the Debtors' properties. . . .

A. The Debtors.

The eleven Debtors can be grouped readily into three categories corresponding roughly to their geographical location — Florida, The Bronx, and Metropolitan New York. [The court went on to describe the debtors related to each of these areas. In all cases, the debtors were either corporations, and Ginsberg was their president, or they were limited partnerships of which Ginsberg was the president of the corporate general partner. In all cases, each debtor owned one piece of property, usually improved real estate used as rental properties.]

None of the Debtors currently has any employees.

B. The Lenders.

Chase is the trustee for the benefit of the holders of the . . . MF Series 1991-1 [certificates]. The beneficial holder of these securities is REFG Investor One, Inc., all of whose outstanding shares are owned by an entity related to Donaldson, Lufkin & Jenrette Securities Corporation ("DLJ"). Chase is the mortgageholder for the properties of the Florida Debtors. . . .

REFG is the trustee for the benefit of the holders of the . . . MF Series 1993-2 [certificates]. All of its outstanding shares are owned by DLJ. REFG is the mortgageholder for properties of the Bronx Debtors.

The MF Series 1991-1 and Series 1993-2 certificates were underwritten by DLJ. DLJ packaged these certificates in a relatively new form of real estate financing known as "commercial mortgage backed securitization" in which debt securities would be issued to investors, with repayment secured by a pool of mortgages on various real properties. Beginning in late 1994, DLJ repurchased all the certificates for both the MF Series 1991-1 and MF Series 1993-2 from investors.

C. The MLG I and MLG II Transactions.

The Debtors became indebted to the Movants pursuant to two loan transactions. In the first, known as MLG I, Chase lent slightly more than $132 million to twenty multi-family entities including the Florida and Metropolitan New York Debtors and took back a mortgage on each property. This transaction closed on August 30, 1991. Chase holds a single blanket mortgage containing cross-collateralization and cross-default provisions for fifteen of the twenty properties. Chase holds individual mortgages on the five remaining properties.

In the second loan transaction, known appropriately enough as MLG II, REFG lent nearly $145.25 million to eighteen multi-family entities including the Bronx Debtors and took back a mortgage on each property. This transaction closed on February 11, 1993. All eighteen properties are covered by one blanket mortgage with cross-collateralization and cross-default provisions.

Integral to the MLG I and II transactions was the inclusion in the charters of each corporate Debtor or the corporate general partner of each limited partnership Debtor of a bylaw, commonly referred to as a "bankruptcy remote" or "bankruptcy proof" provision, to prevent the Debtors from seeking voluntary bankruptcy protection without the unanimous consent of the board of directors of each Debtor or of its corporate general partner and the shareholders. Each board originally consisted of Ginsberg and two others, one of whom was his designee and the other of whom was a so-called independent director.

The independent director for each board of directors is Laurence Richardson. Richardson received his law degree from the University of Virginia in 1983 and was employed as an associate at Thacher Profitt & Wood, a New York law firm, until 1986 in the residential mortgage backed securities area. After a two-year stint at E.F. Hutton beginning in 1986, Richardson worked at DLJ from February 1988 until April 1991 as a vice president. Upon his departure, he became a consultant to DLJ for the MLG I transaction as well as others. He was paid hourly for his consulting fees and received the sum of $25,000 per year for being a director for companies included in both the MLG I and II transactions.[21] Richardson's director's fees were originally paid by the management companies handling the properties and then later by the receivers. At some point, when the fees went into arrears, it was DLJ whom Richardson called to inquire about who was responsible for bringing the fees current. Richardson admits having received some of his director's fees from REFG. which at that time he did not know was a wholly-owned subsidiary of DLJ.

---

21 [n. 7] Richardson receives $10,000 per year for the MLG I properties and $15,000 for the MLG II properties. Neither Ginsberg nor Joseph Kazarnovsky, the other two directors, receives any remuneration for his services as a director. All three individuals are indemnified.

Richardson serves as an independent director for three other entities at the request of DLJ, receiving $10,000 per year per transaction. Therefore, Richardson receives the aggregate amount of $55,000 annually for serving on the various boards of directors created pursuant to DLJ-structured deals.

D. The Foreclosure Proceedings.

In 1994, the Movants issued notices of default and commenced foreclosure actions against each property, Debtor and nondebtor. With the consent of each borrower, receivers were installed at all thirty-eight properties. As of mid-1996, the Movants had obtained judgments totaling approximately $370 million and had commenced foreclosure proceedings against each of the thirty-eight properties.

Specifically with regard to the Debtors, on October 7, 1994, Chase commenced foreclosure proceedings against the Florida Debtors . . . . [The court then details the fact that all properties were in some form of receivership, that some had been foreclosed upon and not appealed and others were under appeal. In each case, involuntary bankruptcy proceedings were commenced for the express purpose of stopping the foreclosures through invocation of the automatic stay of Section 362(a) of the Bankruptcy Code.]

E. The Debtors' Financial Picture.

In the almost two years that the receivers have been in place, the Movants have advanced nearly $2 million to pay for repairs, taxes and insurance. No monies have been needed for salaries because the Debtors have no employees.

While no breakdown has been provided as to the number of apartment units for each of the Debtors, the thirty-eight Debtor and nondebtor properties in total aggregate nearly 11,200 units spread over approximately 41 garden apartment complexes. The only appraisal received into evidence, dated November 1, 1995 and prepared by Allen V. Trauben & Associates ("Trauben"), valued all the properties at $384 million. . . . If the values contained in the appraisal were found to be correct, equity may exist in the properties. However, the appraisal was admitted for the limited purpose of rebutting the charge that the friendly involuntary petitions were filed in bad faith. As noted at the outset of this decision, the parties agreed in their pretrial order not to treat reorganization prospects initially, as a result of which there is no developed record regarding valuation.

F. The Petitioning Creditors.

[The court detailed the claims of the petitioning creditors. Chief among these creditors were former lawyers for the debtors and certain real estate brokers.]

G. Pryor, Cashman, Sherman & Flynn.

Pryor Cashman represents the Petitioning Creditors. Peter D. Wolfson, Esq., a partner in that firm, testified that Edward Weisfelner, Esq. of the firm of Berlack, Israels & Liberman ("Berlack"), which Ginsberg had consulted to possibly represent the Debtor, invited him to attend a meeting on July 25, 1996 to discuss a "fairly complicated real estate transaction, that there was [sic] some Petitioning Creditors that were interested in filing an involuntary," and that Weisfelner had recommended Wolfson to them. . . . This meeting, which Wolfson described as a preliminary one that ran about 45 minutes, was attended by Wolfson, Pasternak, Ginsberg, Arthur Israel (Ginsberg's personal attorney) and Weisfelner. During this meeting, Wolfson became acquainted generally with the story of the Debtors, the MLG transactions, the foreclosure actions, and the bankruptcy remote provisions. In addition, it was related to him that involuntary petitions needed to be filed in order to salvage the Debtors, and that legal theories might exist for suit against DLJ. Wolfson advised the parties that he would require an advance of $50,000 for fees and $25,000 for expenses in the event he decided to take on the representation.

[The court then detailed the efforts undertaken by Wolfson and others to investigate the situation, to line up petitioning creditors, and to be paid. After investigation,Wolfson came to the conclusion that there was equity in the properties that would be lost if foreclosures were allowed to go forward. Ultimately, Wolfson's retainer was paid by an affiliate of Ginsberg, even though Ginsberg did not join as a petitioning creditor.]

H. Inaction by the Boards of Directors.

As each director, Kazarnovsky, Ginsberg and Richardson, testified, no meetings were held after the closing of the MLG I and II restructurings until December 16, 1996. At no other time was any meeting ever called, special or regular, to discuss the business activities of the Debtors, the defaults called by the Movants, or the commencement of the foreclosure actions. The directors conducted no business except to approve the $2.4 million loan to the Debtors to provide maintenance for the properties in June 1993. Other than this minor matter, they had little communication with each other, either by telephone or by letter, until this motion was filed. No financial reports were circulated, nor were reports or updates on the legal proceedings distributed either by counsel or by Ginsberg, as president, to the other directors.

The directors testified as to the reasons for such inactivity, even in the face of the foreclosure actions, the installation of receivers and the filing of the involuntary petitions. Both Ginsberg and Kazarnovsky believed that involving Richardson in such meetings would prove fruitless because of their belief that Richardson was simply a pawn of DLJ and would not approve any course of action that would interfere with DLJ's plans. . . . Because both Kazarnovsky and Ginsberg believed that Richardson was DLJ's agent on the board, they purposely ignored him. Significantly, the boards took no action in the face of foreclosure actions being commenced or receivers being installed. Although Ginsberg did retain counsel to contest the foreclosure proceedings in the state courts on behalf of the Debtors, there is no indication that the attorneys ever reported to anyone other than Ginsberg. Richardson learned in 1995 that the properties were being foreclosed, . . . yet he took no action and did not seek any information from anyone as to what was happening although he assumed judgments would be entered against the properties. . . . In any event, he never initiated communication with Ginsberg regarding these events nor did he ask for a directors' meeting. . . .

Richardson's overall testimony at trial was enlightening on a number of topics including his perception of his fiduciary duty as a director, the purpose of the bankruptcy proof provision and his understanding of DLJ's status. Richardson seems not to have taken any interest at all in the properties. He testified that as a director he never reviewed any documents regarding any of the Debtors including rent rolls, judgments, or state court decisions. . . . While apparently unaware of the foreclosure actions against all the properties until 1995, Richardson did acknowledge that he was certainly aware of the status of his directors' fees and made a number of inquiries of DLJ when his fees were in arrears. . . .

According to his testimony, only long after the filing of the involuntary petitions did he become aware that a director has fiduciary duty not only to a corporation's shareholders but to its creditors when the corporation becomes insolvent. Nor did he comprehend his obligations to limited partners in those entities where he was on the board of directors of the corporate general partners. Richardson candidly admitted that from his appointment as a director to the Debtors' boards in 1993 until December 1996 he believed that his duty was to the shareholders whom he identified as Ginsberg. . . . But Richardson's statement does not quite square with his later testimony when he described seeking DLJ's advice about resigning from the boards sometime in 1995. Richardson sought an answer from DLJ because he was under the impression that because DLJ had become the shareholder by virtue of its foreclosure of Ginsberg's equity interests and DLJ was now the owner of all the securities, "they became the investor who relied upon my independence to avoid a bankruptcy." In any event, Richardson had no idea until well into the midst of these cases that he had a fiduciary duty to anyone other than shareholders.

Richardson also testified that he had no knowledge of the involuntary bankruptcy proceedings until the board meetings of December 16-17 at which time he learned about the recent activity from Ginsberg and Wolfson. . . . This is an astounding statement to make in light of Richardson's filing an affidavit in this case at least two weeks earlier that was prepared by the Movants' counsel regarding the lack of board meetings during the preceding years. . . . On direct examination by Debtors' counsel, this court learned that Richardson, an attorney who has been involved in substantial financial transactions and admits to reading "carefully" formal documents presented to him, . . . somehow failed to understand or recognize the fact that a two page affidavit, drawn up with a typical bankruptcy caption and referring to "debtors" throughout, related to a bankruptcy case.[22] Richardson did not seem to question the fact that he was

22 [n. 13] "It was a very simple affidavit asking whether we had board meetings, so I just signed it. I didn't notice it had anything to do with a bankruptcy."

being asked to sign an affidavit, an action which he admits to having done "very rarely."... He failed to question what the proposed use of the affidavit was or why the Movants were seeking a sworn statement from him regarding corporate governance issues. There is no question that he read the affidavit because he suggested changes in it to Movants' counsel. . . . The average person would certainly inquire as to what was being signed; I would hazard a guess that an attorney not in the habit of executing affidavits would scrutinize such a document even more carefully.

Only after my strong suggestion, voiced during a December 5, 1996 hearing, was a directors' meeting convened. Over the course of two days, December 16 and 17, 1996, the board met telephonically and in person. The board heard from counsel representing the Petitioning Creditors and the Movants as to the legal issues involved in the various state proceedings, the instant motion, and the ramifications of voting in favor of filing voluntary petitions and authorizing the appointment of a chapter 11 trustee.

Richardson's actions at the two-day board meeting in mid-December 1996 were also somewhat peculiar. Admittedly, all the parties present were at pains to apologize for not having met sooner, and there was a need for Richardson especially to be brought up to speed regarding the overall status of both the Debtors and nondebtors. Debtors' counsel was present to advise the board and Pryor Cashman presented the Petitioning Creditors' position on the first day. At Richardson's insistence, Movants' counsel was invited into the board meeting on the second day to answer a number of questions from him. After mulling over the presentations and cursorily reviewing the papers he had been sent, Richardson refused to vote on the question as to whether the Debtors should ratify the filing of the involuntary petitions until he received answers from the parties to questions he had. . . .

Two votes were taken during the board meetings. On the first, the question of filing for bankruptcy, Richardson abstained while Ginsberg and Kazarnovsky voted in favor of ratifying the involuntary filings. Given the unanimity requirement for a bankruptcy filing, an abstention was a pocket veto. In the discussion on this issue, Richardson advised his fellow board members that he would request information from the parties before deciding on how to vote. It took him five weeks to make his request, at which time he circulated an eleven page letter to counsel for the Petitioning Creditors, the Debtors, the Highland Limited Partners and the Movants, asking extensive questions regarding the issues brought up in the documents provided to him by the parties at the directors' meetings. . . . This was a transparent stalling tactic, the effect of which was to prevent ratification of the filings. As to the second vote, the three directors voted unanimously in favor of the appointment of a chapter 11 trustee or trustees for these cases.

Finally, Richardson gave his interpretation of what the bankruptcy proof provision was all about. . . . As he read the bylaw, its purpose was to place an "independent" director on the corporate boards of directors to prevent, in the event that Ginsberg filed for personal bankruptcy, Ginsberg's filing from "suck[ing] all of these properties into that proceeding," . . . in order that, as Richardson further explained, "a creditor of Mort Ginsberg would not be able to say that somehow there was a corporate sham and therefore be able to pull these assets in." . . . . Interestingly, Richardson claims not to have known that DLJ had foreclosed on Ginsberg's equity interests, (at odds with other of his testimony) thereby making itself shareholder, but he did inquire as to whether he should resign as director after learning that DLJ had purchased all the bonds and was now foreclosing upon the properties. . . . Obviously, Richardson clearly believed that the reason for his presence, as DLJ's guardian of the properties, had been mooted because DLJ was in complete control, having installed receivers at the properties and having started to foreclose on them.

II.

The Movants argue that each of the eleven involuntary petitions was filed in bad faith and should be dismissed pursuant to section 1112(b) of the Bankruptcy Code.[23] This conclusion is said to be warranted because Ginsberg, acting on behalf of the Debtors, initiated, funded and identified seven friendly creditors to prosecute the involuntary petitions so each Debtor could obtain improper leverage against the Movants by gaining access to the bankruptcy court without violating the bankruptcy restrictions in the bylaws of the various Debtors or their corporate general partners. The Movants point out that the filing of each petition was timed either to stay a scheduled foreclosure sale or to coincide with a particular Debtor's deadline to file an appellate pleading, which resulted, the Movants claim, in the frustration of their attempts to enforce their rights against each property. The Movants dismiss the Debtors' attempts to excuse such behavior by countering that there is no such doctrine as "justifiable collusion."

The Movants have centered their case around the Second Circuit decision, Federal Deposit Ins. Corp. v. Cortez, 96 F.3d 50 (2d Cir.1996), which held that, in certain circumstances, a collusive filing of a bankruptcy case is a fraud upon the jurisdiction of the Bankruptcy Court and therefore susceptible to immediate dismissal. Because the Movants believe that the Cortez case is controlling, they did not offer initially any evidence regarding any of the Debtors' financial situations, their equity (or lack thereof) in the properties or their ability to reorganize. In other words, the Movants are of the opinion that if I were to find that collusion did occur, under Cortez I am bound to dismiss the cases. As an alternative, the Movants suggest that the facts warrant conversion of the cases to chapter 7 or appointment of a Chapter 11 trustee.

---

23 [n. 15] Section 1112(b) of the Bankruptcy Code provides in pertinent part—[O]n request of a party in interest. . . . and after notice and a hearing, the court may convert a case under this chapter to a case under Chapter 7 of this title or may dismiss a case under this chapter, whichever is in the best interest of creditors and the estate, for cause. . . .

The Debtors and Petitioning Creditors (collectively, the "Respondents") filed a joint post-trial brief in opposition to the Movants' motion. The Respondents deny that the Debtors colluded with the Petitioning Creditors to file, or orchestrate the filing of, these cases. While conceding that Ginsberg did facilitate the filing by supplying information to the Petitioning Creditors and advancing funds to their counsel, Pryor Cashman, the Respondents contend that Ginsberg acted in his individual capacity and that the Debtors took no action. They point out that any restriction contained in the Debtors' bylaws regarding the filing of voluntary petitions in bankruptcy did not extend to prevent Ginsberg or creditors of the Debtors from taking independent action such as filing an involuntary petition. In any event, the Respondents argue, the Petitioning Creditors hold valid claims against the Debtors, which the Movants never contested, and filed these cases for legitimate reasons on the careful advice of counsel, and only after counsel had performed extensive due diligence. The Respondents posit that seeking bankruptcy protection for the Debtors was the best and only method available to (i) preserve any chance of recovery on their claims (as well as those of the limited partners) before the Movants foreclosed on the assets of each Debtor, (ii) challenge the validity of the Movants' claims, and (iii) find a third party to fund a plan of reorganization or purchase the properties, which would result in a greater recovery to all parties than would be obtained from the pending foreclosures.

Moreover, the Respondents say, any aid Ginsberg gave to the Petitioning Creditors regarding the filing of the petitions was in response to the bankruptcy-remote provision contained in the bylaws of each entity that prevented the Debtors from filing voluntary petitions in bankruptcy absent a unanimous vote by the board of directors and shareholders. The Respondents argue that attempting to obtain such a vote, in light of their contention that the so-called independent director actually was beholden to DLJ, would have been an exercise in futility, a contention which subsequent events seem to have borne out. The Respondents emphasize that the bankruptcy remote provisions notwithstanding, the boards of directors had fiduciary obligations to creditors and limited partners which had to be carried out, even if to do so would have frustrated the mortgagee's efforts to foreclose. Finally, the Debtors claim that the alleged failure of the Movants to file deficiency motions in the state courts has left certain Debtors with unencumbered assets which could be used to fund a plan. . . .

III.

A. Dismissal of Involuntary Cases.

At first blush, these cases seem ripe for dismissal. The Debtors are single asset entities with no employees whose involuntary petitions were filed at the behest of their principal to circumvent what effectively were prohibitions on the filing of voluntary petitions. The petitions were filed while the Debtors were embroiled in a dispute with their secured creditor and were facing foreclosure. [Citations omitted.]

As the Movants, Chase and REFG have the burden of producing evidence that there is "cause" for relief under § 1112(b). Thereafter, if that burden is met, the Debtor must show that relief is not warranted. *In re* Lizeric Realty Corp., 188 B.R. 499, 503 (Bankr.S.D.N.Y.1995). Although the term "cause" is not defined, section 1112(b) sets forth a list, which is not exhaustive, of ten factors that can constitute cause for dismissal or conversion. *In re* Gucci, 174 B.R. 401, 409 (Bankr.S.D.N.Y.1994); *In re* Cardi Ventures, Inc., 59 B.R. 18, 21 (Bankr.S.D.N.Y.1985). As a result, within the boundaries of well-settled principles, a bankruptcy judge has wide discretion to determine if cause exists and how ultimately to dispose of the case.

Even though the Bankruptcy Code does not explicitly require that a chapter 11 petition be filed in good faith, many of the circuit courts have opined as to when a bankruptcy court may dismiss a voluntary chapter 11 petition at the inception of the case. *See*, e.g., Carolin Corp., 886 F.2d 693 (collecting cases); Little Creek Development Co., 779 F.2d at 1072 & n. 2 (collecting cases). Their theory is that if a petition is not filed in good faith, it is an abuse of judicial process or of the jurisdiction of the bankruptcy court. Carolin Corp., 886 F.2d at 699; *In re* Garsal Realty, Inc., 98 B.R. 140, 150 (Bankr. N.D.N.Y. 1989).

The inquiry into whether a bankruptcy petition was filed in good faith does not change even if the petitions under scrutiny are involuntary ones. . . .

Determining whether a petition has been filed in good faith is difficult because the very term itself, "good faith," is an amorphous notion that is largely defined by factual inquiry. *In re* Laguna Assocs., L.P., 30 F.3d 734 (6th Cir.1994); *In re* Albany Partners, Ltd., 749 F.2d 670 (11th Cir.1984). Because no single factor is determinative of good faith, I must examine the facts and circumstances of each case in light of several established guidelines or indicia, essentially conducting an "on-the-spot evaluation of the Debtor's financial condition [and] motives," Laguna Assocs., 30 F.3d at 738; Little Creek, 779 F.2d at 1072 (referring to recurring patterns of conduct and facts); *In re* Caldwell, 851 F.2d 852, 860 (6th Cir.1988). It is the totality of circumstances, rather than any single factor, that will determine whether good faith exists. Cohoes, 931 F.2d at 227; Garsal Realty, 98 B.R. at 151.

The standard in this Circuit is that a bankruptcy petition will be dismissed if both objective futility of the reorganization process and subjective bad faith in filing the petition are found. [Citations omitted.]

The Movants suggest that they do not have to meet both these tests because of the Second Circuit's recent ruling that where a debtor colludes with its creditors to seek bankruptcy protection, the ensuing bankruptcy is a fraud upon the court and must therefore be dismissed. *See* Federal Deposit Ins. Corp. v. Cortez, 96 F.3d 50 (2d Cir.1996). In other words, they argue that by virtue of the presence of collusion, the first test, looking to the case's objective futility, would be no longer relevant to my analysis. So it is to the parties' arguments that I turn.

1. The Movants' Case for Collusion

Collusion between a debtor and creditors is not a new concept in bankruptcy law, having appeared in case law since the beginning of this century. See, e.g., Blumenthal v. Strat (In re Cohn), 227 F. 843 (3d Cir.1915); Cornwall Press v. Ray Long & Richard R. Smith, Inc., 75 F.2d 276 (2d Cir.1935). Yet these early cases did not set out factors to identify collusive bankruptcy filings.

Black's Law Dictionary defines collusion as:

> a secret combination, conspiracy, or concert of action between two or more persons for a fraudulent or deceitful purpose.

Black's Law Dictionary 264 (6th ed.1990); see also *In re* New York Trap Rock Corp., 42 F.3d 747, 752 (2d Cir.1994). As this definition plainly reads, there are two components to collusion: (i) the secret acts of at least two people and (ii) the wrongful purpose. Case law from other jurisdictions recognizes this interpretation of the definition. *See* e.g., In re Winn, 49 B.R. 237, 239 (Bankr.M.D. Fla.1985). The Winn court developed a two-part test to determine whether an involuntary filing should be dismissed as collusive: first, there must appear to be concerted action between the debtor and the petitioning creditors, and second, these parties must fraudulently invoke the jurisdiction of the court. 49 B.R. at 239.

[After exhaustively reviewing the evidence, the court came to the following conclusions.] Here, the Debtors are eligible for relief and have sought to reorganize, not liquidate. Whether the Debtors can actually reorganize themselves is not possible to say at this time because no record has been made relative to the objective futility of reorganization. I do note, however, that third parties appear to exist who are interested in purchasing or investing in the Debtors' assets and in negotiating consensual plans of reorganization. . . .

I cannot overlook the lack of observance of corporate formalities by the parties in these cases. As each director, Kazarnovsky, Ginsberg and Richardson, has testified, no meetings were held after the closing of the MLG I and II restructurings. As a matter of fact, the directors had minimal communication with each other, either by telephone or by letter, until the instant motion was filed. No financial reports were circulated; no reports or updates on the legal proceedings were distributed either by counsel or by Ginsberg, as president, to the other directors. Because both Kazarnovsky and Ginsberg believed that Richardson was DLJ's agent on the board, they purposely ignored him. Significantly, the boards took no action in the face of foreclosure actions being commenced or receivers being installed.

Although Richardson learned in 1995 that the properties were being foreclosed, . . . he did nothing, failing even to seek any information from anyone as to what was happening. . . . Richardson says he was unaware in his capacity as director of his fiduciary duties to creditors and that he only learned of his duties to creditors later. . . . Basic hornbook law provides that directors occupy a fiduciary relation to the corporation and its shareholders, but the relation ordinarily does not extend to its general creditors. 3 Fletcher Cyclopedia Corporations § 849 (M. Wolf. perm. ed. 1975). Nonetheless, it is universally agreed that when a corporation approaches insolvency or actually becomes insolvent, directors' fiduciary duties expand to include general creditors. Nearly all states' law is in accord, including those states in which the Debtors or their corporate general partners are incorporated.[24] But Richardson's claim of ignorance as to the limited partners, who are plainly analogous to stockholders, proves too much to credit. Richardson is an attorney who worked on sophisticated corporate financings. It is inconceivable that he would not understand that the corporate general partners of which he was a director bore fiduciary obligations to the limited partners. (That is the stuff of a basic corporate law course in law school.) Yet he completely ignored the limited partners' plight in the face of foreclosure actions instituted by the group which placed him on the boards of directors of these and other companies and saw to it that he was paid fees, even though the consequence of foreclosure would be not to simply injure but to eliminate the limited partners' interests. Richardson's failure to carry out his fiduciary role to the creditors and the limited partners was exemplified by his failure to ratify the involuntary filings during the December 1996 board meeting. If he was the "independent" director, it was in name only. Indeed, he called DLJ to inquire about whether he ought to resign once DLJ had acquired Ginsberg's interests. In other words, he seems to have perceived his mandate as accomplished — DLJ was in control without any bankruptcy by Ginsberg.

As Kazarnovsky recalled, although Ginsberg concluded that bankruptcy was the only alternative for thwarting the foreclosures, after considering the matter, he decided to forego convening a board meeting to discuss this option for two reasons. First, he felt it would be futile because Richardson, as DLJ's designee, would never approve the idea. . . . Second, by this time, DLJ had foreclosed upon Ginsberg's equity interests and was essentially the shareholder of each Debtor. . . . He surmised that it would be highly unlikely that any petitions would be filed because, even if Richardson authorized the petitions, DLJ would not. So when the opportunity arose to test how Richardson would react when presented with the question of voting on the issue of authorizing the filing of a bankruptcy petition, Ginsberg declined to seize it and instead circumvented the corporate approval process by orchestrating the filing of these cases with the Petitioning Creditors. Whereas I cannot condone his ignoring corporate formalities, neither can I say that, standing alone, his conduct warrants dismissal of the petitions given the factual scenario.

---

24 [n. 24] The Debtors or their corporate general partners are incorporated in the following states: New York, Florida, New Jersey and Delaware. Exs. 8-15. Each of these states holds that in the event of corporate insolvency, a director has a fiduciary duty to creditors: (i) New York: Clarkson Co. Ltd. v. Shaheen, 660 F.2d 506, 512 (2d Cir.1981); (ii) Florida: Tampa Waterworks Co. v. Wood, 97 Fla. 493, 121 So. 789 (1929); (iii) New Jersey: Francis v. United Jersey Bank, 87 N.J. 15, 432 A.2d 814, 824 (1981); (iv) Delaware: Geyer v. Ingersoll Publications Co., 621 A.2d 784 (Del.Ch.1992).

The Movants continually attack Ginsberg for all the ills of these cases. It is not appropriate for me to rule now on the myriad allegations about Ginsberg's dishonesty, mismanagement and the other horribles alluded to in the various court papers. All I know is that in the face of such behavior, the Debtors and limited partners continued to keep him on as chairman of the board and president of the Debtors, and the Movants accepted his presence without taking any action against him other than to slowly and inexorably close in on each property, notwithstanding that they say they acquired his equity interests and thereby the ability to oust him. In the meantime, the Movants ignore the fact that DLJ acts as lender and shareholder, while dominating the activities of the Debtors to the extent that its board designee, who was supposed to be "independent," abdicated his fiduciary role to the Debtors, creditors and limited partners in favor of the interests of DLJ.

While I find that the Respondents did orchestrate the filing of these cases, I conclude that their intention was to circumvent the inability of the Debtors to act in the face of the pending foreclosure proceedings by taking some action to preserve value for the Debtors' estates and creditors. I cannot find, as the Movants desire, that the petitions were filed solely to delay or frustrate the Movants' remedies for it is also undisputed that the Petitioning Creditors have introduced at least one third party, and as many as two others, to make proposals to purchase the properties as a package. The Movants may feel bruised because the Respondents outmaneuvered what the Movants thought was an iron-clad provision in the corporate by-laws preventing a bankruptcy filing, but this does not mean that, without more, the petitions must be dismissed. . . .

Thus, for all the of the reasons just explained, I do not conclude that the Movants have proven that these cases were collusively filed.

B. Bankruptcy Remote Provision

Because I have not found that the Debtors and the Petitioning Creditors acted collusively in filing these cases, I need not reach the merits of the Respondents' position request that I nullify the bylaw provision containing the bankruptcy proof provision as void against public policy. In any event, given that none of the Debtors observed corporate formalities and did not prior to the involuntary filings test the directors' mettle by calling a board of directors' meeting to ascertain whether bankruptcy would be authorized, I do not believe that the issue of validity of the bankruptcy proof provision is properly before me. . . .

Conclusion

The facts presented by these cases are quite troubling. The Debtors and the Petitioning Creditors orchestrated the filing of these involuntary cases to evade what they perceived to be an insurmountable restriction against the Debtors' filing voluntary petitions. The third director has engaged in transparent stalling tactics, the effect of which is to endanger the interests of all parties other than DLJ. Allegations circulate on the periphery that Ginsberg or his subordinates may have acted improperly in managing the properties.

Because of those concerns about Ginsberg and his asserted poor history of performing on a number of other real estate loan transactions, DLJ felt justified in structuring the two loans with Ginsberg to guarantee that it could avoid a bankruptcy filing and move to foreclose on the properties swiftly in case of default regardless of whether the default was based on lack of payment or performance. DLJ thereby put itself in the awkward position of financing the original restructuring transactions, then later assuming obligations toward the creditors and limited partners by acquiring Ginsberg's equity interests, while simultaneously pursuing and enforcing state court judgment rights (through the Movants) in order to minimize its loss on the original bonds it repurchased. As a result, DLJ essentially held veto power over the acts the Debtors could take and found itself walking a tightrope between looking out for its own interests and breaching its fiduciary duties. This is too fine a line to comfortably navigate. . . .

Before the evidentiary hearings for this motion commenced, the Debtors observed that these cases cry out for a new perspective. I agree. During the December 5, 1996 hearing on that motion I hinted strongly to all the parties that I was inclined to grant the alternative relief the Movants were seeking by appointing Chapter 11 trustees. . . .

DLJ is on all sides of these cases and, because of its apparent animus towards Ginsberg, is unable or unwilling to protect interests of others to whom it has assumed obligations. Richardson has refused to authorize Chapter 11 reorganization and, through the split in its membership, the boards of directors are incapable of acting. Ginsberg is content to leave the properties in the hands of receivers, having little apparent interest in how they are being operated. Under such circumstances, appointment of a Chapter 11 trustee is the only reasonable alternative to ensure that the limited partners and creditors are protected, that the properties are not allowed to deteriorate and that Ginsberg and those creditors who are "friendly" do not stand as an impediment to what is best for these estates. As a side benefit, that relief may moot the need for an expensive trial on reorganization prospects because the trustee will have to consider possible alternatives (including dismissal, if reorganization is seen as impossible) in any event. Therefore, I am directing the Office of the United States Trustee to appoint a Chapter 11 trustee or trustees for these estates. . . .

To summarize, I hold that although the Movants have successfully demonstrated that the Debtors and Petitioning Creditors did orchestrate the filing of the eleven involuntary petitions commencing these cases, their behavior is not consonant with what is required by case law for collusion. As a result, the orchestration is not sufficient to warrant the dismissal of the cases without evidence that the Debtors have no chance at rehabilitation. The Movants, if they wish to press their motion, are to obtain a new hearing date to try this issue.

SETTLE ORDER consistent with this decision.

QUESTIONS ON *KINGSTON SQUARE*

1. What does this decision do to efforts to make an SPE bankruptcy remote? Does it signal that such efforts are ultimately futile, or that the structure of this deal was flawed?

2. If you were asked to represent an independent director such as Richardson, what would you advise that he or she do upon appointment? What would you counsel that he or she do to honor the fiduciary duties as outlined above? Come to think of it, why didn't Richardson just resign as soon as he found out about this mess? Wouldn't that have been to his benefit?

3. Is the appointment of a trustee a victory or defeat for DLJ (who now stands in the shoes of investors; note that when the deal went sour, DLJ, as sponsor, bought back the notes it had placed with various investors).

4. How do you react to *Kingston Square* if you are a rating agency? What structures would you suggest to avoid its consequences in the future?

B. "True Sale" Objections: Did the SPE Really Purchase the Securitized Assets?

Having accomplished a separation of the originator and the SPE, it is important to ensure that a court, especially a bankruptcy court, will respect the fact that ownership of the receivables has been effectively transferred to the SPE. Bankruptcy courts in particular maintain the power to "recharacterize" transactions according to their substance; that is, they are not bound by the labels the parties select. As an example, under Section 510 of the Bankruptcy Code, courts have the ability to recharacterize certain debt as equity, and subordinate its payment to that of other creditors, although such recharacterizations typically only occur with respect to debts to insiders that were structured as debt instead of equity for tax reasons.

For securitization, the issue is whether a bankruptcy court will respect sales of receivables or payment intangibles. In assessing securitizations, bankruptcy courts will examine carefully whether the transactions at issue would have been effective against creditors, and if they would have been, the courts will hold, in most cases, that they are to be respected in bankruptcy.[25] The industry shorthand for whether a bankruptcy court will uphold such transaction is that they create "true sales."[26]

---

25 An issue exists with respect to recent transactions under state statutes that have been drafted to specifically give effect to the parties' characterization of a securitization transaction. *See* Section 3.03.B.7 below for a description of such statutes.

26 The term "true sale" will have a different definition depending on the field of law for which it is operative. The three principal areas of applicability are accounting, tax, and bankruptcy.

Another way to look at this concept is that if the sale is a "true sale," then all of the debtor's property rights passed to the purchaser at the consummation of the sale, leaving nothing in the debtor that, should bankruptcy later occur, could be labeled as property of the estate. The term "true sale" is misleading, however, because a given transfer of receivables may well be a sale for certain purposes but not others.

An originator that transfers its receivables to the SPE usually will want the transfer to constitute a sale for accounting purposes. *See* Chapter 4. That way the financing is reflected on its balance sheet as a sale of assets and not as a secured loan (which would increase leverage). The originator also may want the transfer to be a sale for purposes of its indenture covenants, if such covenants restrict the originator's ability to incur debt or pledge its assets. In many cases, particularly where the indenture itself states that its interpretation is to be governed by GAAP, it may well be the case that a transfer that is an accounting sale also will be viewed as a sale under the indenture.[27]

The term "true sale" most often is used in analyzing whether the transfer of receivables effectively has removed the receivables from the originator in a way that will be honored by a bankruptcy court. Since bankruptcy law looks primarily to non-bankruptcy law for this determination, the issue is one we looked at in Chapter 2: has there been a transfer of the receivables such that the originator no longer can be said to "own" them. If the originator files for bankruptcy and the receivables are owned by the SPE, then the SPE also would own the collections on the receivables. Assuming the receivables were paid, the SPE then would have sufficient cash to pay its investors without defaulting.

If the transfer is held not to be a sale for bankruptcy purposes, then a court will find that the financing was not a "sale" but was instead a simply loan or other advance of funds by the SPE to the originator, albeit a loan or advance that is secured by the receivables.[28] The SPE would then be a creditor of the originator and have a security interest, but not an ownership interest, in the receivables. In such a case, the originator's bankruptcy would, under section 362 of the Bankruptcy Code, automatically result in a stay of all actions by creditors (including any holders of notes or other debt securities issued by the SPE) to foreclose on or otherwise obtain property of the originator.[29]

---

27 For example, the indenture covenant may restrict liens securing debt, although the term "debt" may not be defined in the indenture. Indentures often state that accounting terms used therein are to be construed in accordance with generally accepted accounting principles, or GAAP. A court therefore may use the GAAP definition of "debt."

28 *See* John Francis Hilson & Jeffrey S. Turner, Asset-Based Lending : A Practical Guide to Secured Financing § 4:6, at 4-11 (5th ed. 2002). A related issue is whether a true sale of receivables can be avoided as a "fraudulent conveyance," which is discussed in Section 3.03.B. which follows.

29 Section 362(d) provides criteria for the judge to determine whether to lift the stay. Whether the stay will be lifted depends on the facts of the given case. *See, e.g.,* 11 U.S.C. § 362(d); *In re* Comcoach Corp., 698 F.2d 571, 573–74 (2d Cir., 1983); *In re* Sweetwater, 11 Bankr. Ct. Dec. (CRR) 1220, 1227 (Bankr. 1984), *aff'd,* 57 B.R. 748 (D. Utah 1985).

If the transfer of the receivables from the originator to the SPE is recharacterized by the bankruptcy court as a secured loan rather than as a sale, the SPE may not be able to obtain payments collected on the receivables until the stay is modified. Further, under section 363 of the Bankruptcy Code, a court, after notice to creditors and the opportunity of a hearing, could order the cash collections of the receivables to be used by the originator in its business as working capital if adequate protection of the interest of the SPE in the receivables is provided by the originator or its trustee. "Adequate protection," though, does not necessarily translate into an alternative cash source of the same quality or type as originally planned.

The best recent example is the bankruptcy case of *LTV Steel Company, Inc.*, excerpted above. As we saw there, LTV challenged its pre-bankruptcy securitization facilities, arguing that the transfers to the SPEs were not true sales and, therefore, that LTV should be able to use the collections of receivables as "cash collateral" by giving adequate protection under bankruptcy law. LTV's rationale was that, without such use, it may have to cease its operations, thereby jeopardizing employee jobs and retiree benefits and adversely affecting the local economy. The bankruptcy court permitted LTV to use these collections pending resolution of the true sale issue.

For most securitizations, the available case law is sparse and does not deal directly with securitizations specifically. In analyzing the issues involved, many commentators have looked to cases involving factoring, an age old method of financing which involves the direct purchase by the "factor" of the receivable, together (usually) with notice to the person liable on the receivable to pay the factor directly. For this reason, although various courts have considered whether a given transfer of receivables constitutes a sale or a secured loan for bankruptcy purposes, the facts of the decided cases have not been representative of modern asset-securitized transactions. Other than factoring, the focus has been on cases which explore the issue of when and whether a lease of goods is really a secured transaction; indeed, Section 1-201(37) of the UCC, which defines "security interest," has been amended many times in attempts to capture crisply this distinction, without, however, much success. Accordingly, the cases are not easily harmonized, and different readers can argue as to which factors are relevant and which are entitled to the greater weight. Nonetheless, a cluster of factors can be identified that are relevant in most determinations of whether a given transfer of receivables is a sale or a secured loan. Each of these factors is indicative of whether the originator truly parted with the future economic risks and benefits of ownership of the receivables purported to be sold, and whether the SPE has taken on those risks and benefits.

1. Recourse

The most significant factor in the true sale determination appears to be the nature and extent of recourse that the transferee of the receivables has against the transferor, or in the argot of securitization, the extent of recourse that the

SPE has against the originator. As the degree of recourse increases, the likelihood that a court will find a true sale decreases. To put this in the context of the Honda case in Chapter 1, the issue would be whether the Trust had an ability to collect from Honda or any of Honda's finance subsidiaries, if the receipts from the 104,014 car contracts were insufficient to pay the notes bought by the investors. The existence of some recourse does not, however, by itself preclude characterization of the transaction as a true sale. If recourse is present, the issue is "whether the *nature* of the recourse, and the true nature of the transaction, are such that the legal rights and economic consequences of the agreement bear a great similarity to a financing transaction [i.e., a secured loan] or to a sale."[30]

For example, in the leading case of *Major's Furniture Mart v. Castle Credit Corp.*,[31] the court analyzed the recourse provisions in an accounts receivable financing agreement to determine whether the transaction should be considered a sale or a secured loan. In holding the transaction to be a secured loan, the court considered the risks that each party assumed as well as the guaranties given by Major's as to the quality and the collectibility of its accounts.[32]

Major's was required to give the following warranties: that its customers "meet the criteria set forth by Castle, that Major's perform the credit check to verify that these criteria were satisfied, and that Major's warrant that the accounts were fully enforceable legally and were 'fully and timely collectible.'"[33] Major's was also required to indemnify Castle for any losses that resulted from "a customer's failure to pay, or for any breach of warranty, and an obligation to repurchase any account after the customer was in default for more than 60 days."[34] The court concluded that "[g]uaranties of quality alone, or even guarantees of collectibility alone, might be consistent with a true sale, but Castle attempted to shift all risks to Major's, and incur none of the risks or obligations of ownership."[35] This case is illustrative of the approach courts take in determining the nature of the recourse in a particular transaction.[36]

Sometimes the originator represents and warrants that all receivables sold meet certain eligibility criteria, at the time of sale, and the originator will pro-

---

30 Major's Furniture Mart, Inc. v. Castle Credit Corp., 602 F.2d 538, 544 (3d Cir. 1979) (emphasis in original; footnotes omitted).

31 449 F. Supp 538 (E.D.P.A. 1978), *aff'd*, 602 F.2d 538 (3d Cir. 1979).

32 *Id.* at 543.

33 *Id.*

34 *Id.*

35 *Id.* To the extent that the seller of a payment stream makes representations and warranties that are not continuing representations and warranties of collectibility, but rather ones limited to the condition and characteristics of the payment streams at the time they are sold, such warranties should be no different than warranties ordinarily given by a seller of a product. *See* UCC §§ 2-312 to 2-315. Accordingly, such limited representations and warranties should not be inconsistent with treatment of the transaction as a sale.

36 *See, e.g., In re* Joseph Kanner Hat Co., 482 F.2d 937 (2d Cir. 1973).

vide an indemnity for breach of those representations and warranties. To the extent the representations and warranties are not general representations and warranties of collectibility, but rather are limited to the condition of the receivables at the time the receivables are sold, that should not differ from a warranty ordinarily given by a seller of a product.[37] Accordingly, such limited representations and warranties and indemnity should not be inconsistent with sale treatment.

2. Retained Rights and Right to Surplus

Perhaps the second most important factor indicating a secured transaction (rather than a sale) is the originator's right to redeem or repurchase transferred receivables. For example, section 9-623 of the Uniform Commercial Code (UCC) and various state mortgage statutes allow a debtor to redeem property before it is ultimately disposed of by a secured party. The absence of a right of redemption or repurchase would be a factor in favor of characterization of the receivables transaction as a true sale.

Several courts also have considered the existence of a transferor's right to any surplus collections, once the transferee has collected its investment plus an agreed yield, as indicative of a secured loan.[38] The right of the transferee of the receivables to retain all collections of transferred receivables for its own account, even after the transferee has collected its investment plus yield, would therefore be a factor in favor of characterization of the receivables transaction as a true sale.

3. Pricing Mechanism

Pricing based upon a fluctuating interest index of the type found in commercial loan agreements, such as the prime or base rate, may be indicative of a secured loan. The pricing mechanism also may be indicative of a secured loan to the extent the purchase price is retroactively adjusted to reflect actual rather than expected collections on receivables.[39]

To reduce the impact this factor might have, the SPE would purchase receivables on a discounted basis. The discount would be calculated or negotiated prior to each purchase, in part based on the SPE's then net current cost of funds and the anticipated collection and loss experience of the receivables then

---

37 *See* UCC §§ 2-312, 2-313, 2-314, 2-315.

38 *See, e.g., In re* Evergreen Valley Resort, Inc., 23 B.R. 659, 661–62 (Bankr. D. Me. 1982); *In re* Hurricane Elkhorn Coal Corp., 19 B.R. 609, 617 (Bankr. W.D. Ky. 1982), *rev'd on other grounds,* 763 F.2d 188 (6th Cir. 1985); *In re* Nixon Mach. Co., 6 B.R. 847, 854 (Bankr. E.D. Tenn. 1980).

39 *See* Home Bond Co. v. McChesney, 239 U.S. 568 (1916); Dorothy v. Commonwealth Commercial Co., 116 N.E. 143 (Ill. 1917).

to be purchased. Once a discount has been negotiated for each purchase, it would not thereafter be modified or otherwise adjusted for that purchase, regardless of differences between the actual and anticipated costs of funds and of collection experience. Such pricing would be a factor in favor of characterization of the receivables transaction as a true sale.

4. Administration and Collection of Accounts

The administration of and control over the collection of accounts receivable are factors courts sometimes cite in resolving the sale/secured loan issue. To have a true purchase, the transferee should have the authority to control the collection of the accounts.[40] Examples of such authority would include:

(1) ownership by the transferee of all the books, records, and computer tapes relating to the purchased receivables and

(2) the transferee's having the right

(a) to control the activities of any collection agent with respect to purchased receivables and at any time to appoint itself or another person as collection agent,

(b) to establish a credit and collection policy with respect to purchased receivables, and

(c) at any time to notify the obligors of the purchased receivables of the sale.

In practice, the parties often initially appoint the originator as the collection agent for the receivables transferred. That is not necessarily inconsistent with characterization as a sale if (1) the originator, as collection agent, will be acting as an agent for the SPE pursuant to established standards, much like any other agent; (2) the originator will receive a collection agent fee that represents an arm's length fee for those services; and (3) the SPE has the right at any time to appoint itself or another person as collection agent in place of the originator.

Sometimes collections of the purchased receivables are paid to the originator and commingled, or mixed, with the originator's general funds. That frequently occurs when the originator collects the receivables each day, but only remits the collections periodically (*e.g.*, monthly) to the SPE. Besides raising a potential perfection question under the UCC (see below), commingling would, if permitted by the SPE, appear to be inconsistent with the concept of a sale: the originator would be using collections that belong to the SPE. That inconsistency often can be addressed by the originator's segregating and holding the collections in trust, pending remittance to the SPE or periodic reinvestment.

[40] People v. Service Inst., Inc., 421 N.Y.S.2d 325 (Sup. Ct. 1979).

5. Other Factors

The courts have identified a variety of other factors that do not fall within the categories discussed in the preceding section, but that may be indicative of a secured loan.[41] Among the more significant of these factors are the following:

1. The originator of receivables is a debtor of the SPE on or before the purchase date;
2. The SPE's rights in the receivables can be extinguished by payments or repurchases by the originator or by payments from sources other than collections on receivables;
3. The originator is obligated to pay the SPE's costs (including attorneys' fees) incurred in collecting delinquent or uncollectible receivables;
4. The language of the documentation contains references to the transfer's being "security for" a debt; and
5. The parties' intent, as evidenced by the documentation and their actions, suggests that the parties view the transaction as a security device. Also of importance is how the parties account for the transactions on their books, records, and tax returns.

It is rare in modern commercial transactions for all the factors favoring a true bankruptcy sale to be met. There is inevitably a question of balance. Some recourse is needed to give a reasonable assurance to holders of the SPE's securities that they will be paid. It may be uneconomic for an originator to agree that the SPE obtains the entire surplus of collections once holders of the SPE's securities are paid. In each case, the parties structuring the transaction will have to balance how important it is that the transaction be a bankruptcy sale with the other commercial desires of the investors and the originator. The balance will depend, in large part, on the credit quality of the originator. It may be less important to investors to insist on a true sale for bankruptcy purposes where the originator has an investment-grade rating than where the originator is troubled or in a workout.[42]

6. Effect of 1999 Revisions to Article 9

Another factor to consider is the effort, in the 1999 revisions to Article 9, to validate certain securitization transactions by explicitly bringing them within

---

[41] *See* Hilson & Turner, *supra* note 23, at §§ 2:5 to 2:6, pp. 2-16 to 2-34.

[42] An originator sometimes may require that the receivables transfer be a loan for tax purposes so as, for example, to avoid recognition of a taxable gain that would be triggered if the transfer were treated as a tax sale. Because the bankruptcy and tax sale criteria, although not identical, are similar — and the bankruptcy courts may apply even closer scrutiny than the IRS — structuring a receivables transfer as a bankruptcy sale may well make it also a tax sale. *See* Chapter 5.

Article 9. As explored in Chapter 2 above, this effort lead to automatic perfection of some payments streams (such as payment intangibles), and clear directions with respect to filing as to other (such as instruments). This streamlining may lead courts to be more sympathetic to, and to uphold, structures which follow the lead of Revised Article 9.

7. State Law Efforts to Preempt Bankruptcy Code

The issue of whether a "true sale" has occurred is typically treated as one arising under state law. That is, a federal bankruptcy court makes a determination of what the relative rights of various debtors and creditors would be under state law, typically the UCC. This has lead some states to try to change their law of transfers to automatically validate securitization transfers.

Many states have statutes that specifically authorize securitization of some state source of revenue, such as the nationwide tobacco settlements, *see, e.g.*, N.J. STAT. ANN. § 52:18B-5, or payments for electrical power, *see, e.g.*, TEX. UTIL. CODE ANN. § 39.301 to § 39.309 (Vernon 2003).

Delaware has attempted, along with some other states, to insulate securitizations generally. In 2002, for example, Delaware added the following to Title 6 of its general statutes:

Section 2701A. Title.

This Act may be referred to as the "Asset-Backed Securities Facilitation Act".

Section 2702A. Intent.

It is intended by the General Assembly that the term "securitization transaction" shall be construed broadly.

Section 2703A. Securitization transaction.

(a) Notwithstanding any other provision of law including, but not limited to, Sections 9-506 of this title 'Debtor's right to redeem collateral' as said section existed prior to July 1, 2001, and 9-623 of the title, 'Right to redeem collateral' that became effective July 1, 2001, to the extent set forth in the transaction documents relating to a securitization transaction:

(1) Any property, assets or rights purported to be transferred, in whole or in part, in the securitization transaction shall be deemed to no longer be the property, assets or rights of the transferor;

(2) A transferor in the securitization transaction, its creditors or, in any insolvency proceeding with respect to the transferor or the transferor's property, a bankruptcy trustee, receiver, debtor, debtor in possession or similar person, to the extent the issue is governed by Delaware law, shall have no rights, legal or equitable, whatsoever to reacquire, reclaim, recover, repudiate, disaffirm, redeem or

recharacterize as property of the transferor any property, assets or rights purported to be transferred, in whole or in part, by the transferor; and

(3) In the event of a bankruptcy, receivership or other insolvency proceeding with respect to the transferor or the transferor's property, to the extent the issue is governed by Delaware law, such property, assets and rights shall not be deemed to be part of the transferor's property, assets, rights or estate.

(b) Nothing contained in this chapter shall be deemed to require any securitization transaction to be treated as a sale for federal or state tax purposes or to preclude the treatment of any securitization transaction as debt for federal or state tax purposes or to change any applicable laws relating to the perfection and priority of security or ownership interests of persons other than the transferor, hypothetical lien creditor or, in the event of a bankruptcy, receivership or other insolvency proceeding with respect to the transferor or its property, a bankruptcy trustee, receiver, debtor, debtor in possession or similar person.

It is not the purpose of this Chapter to change the tax treatment of securitizations that take place pursuant to this Chapter."

Note that the statute does not define a "securitization transaction." This form of statute has also been adopted by Alabama, ALA. CODE § 35-10A-1 to 10A-5 (2003), and in a modified form by South Dakota, which added a definition of securitization, S.D. CODIFIED LAWS § 54-1-9 (2003) ("securitization is the pooling and repackaging by a special purpose entity of assets or other credit exposures that can be sold to investors. Securitization includes transactions that create stratified credit risk positions whose performance is dependent upon an underlying pool of credit exposures, including loans and commitments.").

Two other states — North Carolina and Ohio — have adopted this basic format, but have limited the securitization to transactions engaged in by a federally-insured lender as originator.[43] Other states have tried to accomplish more or less the same goal through an amendment to their version of the UCC. Texas is a good example. Section 9.109(e) of the Texas Business and Commercial Code states:

---

[43] North Carolina, N.C. GEN. STAT. § 53-425 (2003) (defining securitization as "[t]he issuance by a special purpose entity of evidences of beneficial interest that meets one of the following criteria: [¶] a. Its most senior class at the time of issuance is rated in one of the four highest categories assigned to long-term debt or in an equivalent short-term category (within either of which there may be sub-categories or graduations indicating relative standing) by one or more nationally recognized rating organizations. [¶] b. It is sold in transactions by an issuer not involving any public offering under section 4 of the Securities Act of 1933 (15 U.S.C. 77d), as amended, or in transactions exempt from registration under the Securities Act of 1933 pursuant to Regulation S issued in accordance with the Act, or any successor regulations issued under the Act.") and Ohio, OHIO REV. CODE ANN. § 1109.75(C) (2003) ("As used in this section, "securitization" means a transfer of financial assets by a financial institution insured by the federal deposit insurance corporation (FDIC) to a special purpose entity established to issue securities supported by the financial assets to investors.").

(e) The application of this chapter to the sale of accounts, chattel paper, payment intangibles, or promissory notes is not to recharacterize that sale as a transaction to secure indebtedness but to protect purchasers of those assets by providing a notice filing system. For all purposes, in the absence of fraud or intentional misrepresentation, the parties' characterization of a transaction as a sale of such assets shall be conclusive that the transaction is a sale and is not a secured transaction and that title, legal and equitable, has passed to the party characterized as the purchaser of those assets regardless of whether the secured party has any recourse against the debtor, whether the debtor is entitled to any surplus, or any other term of the parties' agreement.

Louisiana has a similar provision, LA. REV. STAT. ANN. § 10:9-109(e).

QUESTIONS ON STATE LAWS

1. Most practitioners do not give the Delaware statute much weight in analyzing whether or not there is a "true sale" issue. Why not?

2. If you were a legislator, and were inclined to sponsor legislation of the type discussed above for all transactions, would you adopt the Delaware or the Texas approach? Why or why not?

8. An Aside and a Review: Required Legal Opinions

Complicated transactions such as securitization require many professionals to guide and assist the parties. Not surprisingly, lawyers play a large role. One way lawyers contribute is that they offer their opinion as to whether a court will respect the transaction as structured. Indeed, such a legal opinion is often required to close and fund the transaction.

What is a legal opinion? As most commonly understood, it is a binding document (usually presented in the form of a letter) in which a lawyer states an opinion of what the law is and how it will apply to a particular transaction.[44] To put the matter in clearer focus, if the lawyer is wrong, and someone (even a nonclient) has justifiably relied to his or her detriment on the inaccurate legal opinion, then the lawyer is liable for the harm caused by the reliance.[45]

---

[44] Committee on Legal Opinions, *Guidelines for the Preparation of Closing Opinions*, 57 BUS. LAW. 875 (2002); Committee on Legal Opinions, *Third-Party Legal Opinion Report, Including the Legal Opinion Accord, of the Section of Business Law, American Bar Association*, 47 BUS. LAW. 167 (1991).

[45] *See* Mehaffy, Rider, Windholz & Wilson v. Central Bank, N.A., 892 P.2d 230 (Colo. S. Ct. 1995); RESTATEMENT (THIRD) OF THE LAW GOVERNING LAWYERS §§ 51, 95 (2000).

In securitization transactions, rating agencies are significant consumers of legal opinions. Indeed, most rating agencies have published criteria for what they will, and what they will not, accept in a legal opinion. Here, for example, is what Standard & Poor's requires in legal opinions in typical securitization opinions:

SPECIFIC OPINION CRITERIA/LANGUAGE

General

- As a general matter, Standard & Poor's requires that true sale, nonconsolidation, and security interest opinions be delivered by outside counsel to any participant in a structured transaction.
- As a general matter, in connection with security interest perfection and priority opinions under state law, including certificate of title opinions, Standard & Poor's accepts an opinion of counsel not admitted to the bar of the relevant state, provided such counsel states that it bases its opinions on a review of the state's relevant statutes (opinions with respect to security interest creation should be given by counsel admitted to the bar of the relevant state).
- As a general matter, Standard & Poor's will not accept an opinion based on the *Legal Opinion Accord of the American Bar Association Section of Business Law* (1991), unless such opinion specifically identifies (by number) those sections of the Accord on which the opinion is relying. Standard & Poor's will accept an opinion stating that it should be interpreted in accordance with the *Special Report by the TriBar Opinion Committee, Opinions in the Bankruptcy Context; Rating Agency, Structured Financing and Chapter 10 Transactions*, 46 Bus. Law 717 (1991).
- As a general matter, Standard & Poor's requires "would" opinions except for nonconsolidation opinions. In this case, "should" opinions are accepted based on the fact dependent nature of nonconsolidation opinions.
- Language to the effect that the "issue is not free from doubt" or that the conclusion is "more probable than not" is not acceptable.
- The proviso "although a court may find otherwise" is not preferred but is acceptable.
- A statement that the "opinion is not a guarantee of outcome or result" is acceptable.
- Opinions requested by Standard & Poor's are expected to be given under the law of the applicable jurisdiction; an opinion given under the law of another jurisdiction with an assumption that the laws are identical is not acceptable.
- Security interest creation or perfection opinions should not contain an assumption that the description of the collateral is "reasonably" identified or

described in the security agreement or financing statements (as applicable); an assumption that the collateral is "accurately" described is acceptable. . . .

- True sale opinions should not include references to the LTV Steel bankruptcy proceedings. Standard & Poor's believes that standard opinion qualifications regarding interim orders in a bankruptcy proceeding are sufficient to address the issues raised by the LTV Steel bankruptcy proceedings.

STANDARD & POOR'S, LEGAL CRITERIA FOR STRUCTURED FINANCE TRANSACTIONS, Appendix II, at 107-08 (April 2002).

QUESTIONS ON LEGAL OPINIONS

1. You will soon be practicing. Look back at the transaction described in Chapter 1. Based upon what you know, would you be willing to give an opinion that meets the Standard & Poor's guidelines? If not, what additional information or research would you have to do?

2. Note that the fourth bullet point in Standard and Poor's guidelines requires a "would" opinion. What does that mean? The same bullet point also mentions a "should" opinion. What does that mean?

3. Does it give you any more comfort to know that it is quite likely that every one of the $6 trillion dollars worth of securitizations were issued with opinions that meet the Standard and Poor's guidelines above? Why do you think those opinions were given?

4. Is giving legal opinions part of the practice of law? What course in law school prepared you for the risks in rendering such opinions? Would you charge a standard hourly rate for giving such opinions? If you would charge a premium over hourly rates, how much of a premium would you charge?

C. Fraudulent Transfer Theories: Is Securitization a Fraud on Creditors?

1. Background on Fraudulent Transfers

The topic of fraudulent transfers is venerable and broad. In bankruptcy, the estate has the power to avoid such transfers; outside of bankruptcy, creditors have the same power. American fraudulent transfer laws date from the Statute of Elizabeth, enacted in 1571.[46] Designed as a penal statute, with the English

[46] 13 Eliz., ch. 5 (1571), *repealed by* The Law of Property Act, 15 Geo. 5, ch. 20, § 172 (1925).

Roman law had recognized as a nominate tort an action *fraus creditiorum* similar in purpose and effect to the Statute of Elizabeth. *See* 1 GARRARD GLENN, FRAUDULENT CONVEYANCES AND PREFERENCES, § 60 (Rev. ed. 1940); Max Radin, *Fraudulent Conveyances in California and the Uniform Fraudulent Conveyance Act*, 27 CALIF. L. REV. 1, 1-2, nn.1-2 (1938); Max Radin, *Fraudulent Conveyances at Roman Law*, 18 VA. L. REV. 109 (1931).

crown receiving as its penalty fully one-half of all property recovered,[47] the original Statute of Elizabeth prohibited conveyances made with the "intent to delay, hinder or defraud creditors and others of their just and lawful actions."[48]

Defrauded creditors soon turned this penal statute to their personal ends. Since such transfers were illegal, and thus presumably void, creditors reasoned that they could ignore the conveyance and follow the transferred property into the hands of the party receiving the goods.[49] In short, passage of title was ignored, and the party receiving the goods had to give them up if the debt was just.[50]

The exact language of the statute, however, seemed to require proof of "actual" fraudulent intent. Yet one who fraudulently transfers property can hardly be expected to step up and admit it. Common law lawyers and judges thus developed bridges from questionable acts commonly associated with fraud to findings of actual fraudulent intent. Called "badges of fraud,"[51] these indicia of transactions imbued with fraud developed into a sort of common law shopping list for those seeking to levy on property thought to be properly part of a debtor's estate.[52] Most badges of fraud focused on the actual intent: absconding from a jurisdiction, hiding assets and similar acts denoted a malign intent.[53]

But other badges arose which seemed more objective. Gifts by an insolvent, for example, were particularly suspect.[54] Another badge that seemed to attract creditors' efforts to expand it consisted of a transfer in which left the transferor

---

47 Parties who knowingly participated in the conveyance "incurr[ed] the penalty and forfeiture of one years value of the said lands . . . and the whole value of the said goods . . . ." 13 Eliz., ch. 5, § 2 (1571). Of this amount, "one moitie whereof" — that is, one-half — went to the crown and the other half went to the "party or parties aggrieved." *Id.* A prison term of one half year "without bail' was also provided. *Id. See also* GLENN, *supra* note 40, § 61a.

48 13 Eliz., ch. 5, § 1 (1571). The statute saw such conveyances as contributing to "the overthrow of all true and plain dealing . . . without which no commonwealth or civil society can be maintained or continued." *Id.*

49 Mannocke's Case, 3 Dyer 204b, 73 Eng. Rep. 661 (Q.B. 1571). The famous decision in Tywne's Case, 3 Coke 80b, 76 Eng. Rep. 809 (Star. Ch. 1601) did not involve a private action. Rather, it was the crown's action to receive its one-half share of the goods transferred.

50 Bethel v. Stanhope, 78 Eng. Rep. 1037, 1038 (Q.B. 1599). In 1603 Parliament followed suit and made fraudulent conveyances a part of the English bankruptcy laws. 1 Jac. 1, c. 15 (1603). In 1623 Parliament completed the process and made fraudulent transfer laws civil in nature. 21 Jac. 1, c. 19, § 7 (1623).

51 Courts initially defined "badges of fraud" as facts which are calculated to throw suspicion upon a transaction, and call for an explanation. Peebles v. Horton, 64 N.C. 374, 377 (1870); M. BIGELOW, THE LAW OF FRAUDULENT CONVEYANCES, Ch. XVII, at 515 n.2 (Knowlton, ed. 1911). *See also* Boston Trading Group, Inc. v. Burnazos, 835 F.2d 1504, 1509 (1st Cir. 1987) (badges of fraud described as "a set of objective criteria . . . use[d] as a basis for inferring fraudulent intent.").

52 The basic list is published together with Lord Coke's reporting of Tywne's Case. *See* Twyne's Case, 3 Coke 80b, 76 Eng. Rep. 809 (Star Ch. 1601).

53 The modern catalogue of the badges of fraud is listed in Section 4(b) of the UNIFORM FRAUDULENT TRANSFER ACT (UFTA).

54 *Prefatory Note to the Uniform Fraudulent Conveyance Act*, 7A U.L.A., Part II, at 2 (1999).

himself just marginally solvent, while the transferor continued in business, and continued to incur debt.[55] The rise of this new badge of fraud grew from the perceived underinclusiveness of simple insolvency. When testing insolvency, all that was required was the valuation of assets and liabilities; the result flowed from the numerical difference between the two.

Courts found such transfers on marginal insolvency to be badges of fraud — and hence permissible bridges to actual intent to defraud — if such transfers unfairly shifted the risk of liquidating assets into cash onto creditors.[56] In addition, some courts found similar unfairness if solvency after the transfer depended upon volatile or transitory factors, such as the "stability of the market."[57]

One of the first uniform acts suggested by the National Conference of Commissioners on Uniform State Laws (NCCUSL) was the Uniform Fraudulent Conveyance Act (UFCA), proposed in 1916, but not adopted until 1918.[58] This act preserved the traditional ability to set aside transactions entered into with actual intent to "hinder, delay or defraud" creditors. But it went beyond the orig-

---

55 Bohn v. Weeks, 50 Ill. App. 236, 240 (1893) (invalidating gift of $6500, when assets were $7200 to $7300, and when transferor had outstanding and overdue a $400 note); Williams v. Huges, 136 N.C. 58, 59, 48 S.E. 518, 519 (1904) (finding, as a matter of law, that assets of $11,625 were "not fully sufficient and available for the satisfaction of the [transferor's] creditors" when liabilities equaled $11,500); Black v. Sanders, 46 N.C. (1 Jones) 67, 69 (1854) (finding that retention of $7250 in assets to cover $6848 of liabilities was insufficient, basing holding on poor quality of the assets; "[n]o man would lend money upon such security"); Crumbaugh v. Kugler, 2 Ohio St. 374, 379 (1854) (retention of $48,000 of property insufficient when outstanding debts approximated $42,000; insufficiency "owing to expenses incident to sale, and the sacrifice almost universally affecting forced sales . . ."); Monroe v. Smith, 79 Pa. 459, 461 (1875); Hunters v. Waite, 44 Va. (3 Gratt.) 25, 47 (1846); Ex Parte Russell, 19 Ch. D. 588, 591, 46 L.T.R. (n.s.) 113, 115 (C.A. 1882) (finding that solvency cannot be based upon the value of "some odds and ends which can possibly be sold, and on which he puts his fancy value.").

56 *See, e.g.*, Schreyer v. Scott, 134 U.S. 405, 410 (1890) (stating that it was improper to knowingly "throw the hazards of business in which [the transferor] is about to engage upon others, instead of honestly holding his means subject to the chance of those adverse results to which all business enterprises are liable . . . ."); Mackay v. Douglas, 14 L.R.-Eq. 106, 121, 26 L.T.R. (n.s.) 721, 723 (Ch. 1872) (in which the thought process of someone who transfers assets in trust prior to going into a new business was characterized as follows: "I am going into trade; I believe I may make a great deal of money by it, but nobody knows what may happen, therefore I will make myself safe. I will make this large fortune safe by settling it on my wife and children absolutely."); ORLANDO BUMP, A TREATISE UPON CONVEYANCES MADE BY DEBTORS TO DEFRAUD CREDITORS § 258, at 297 (J. Gray rev. 4th ed. 1896).

57 Carpenter v. Roe, 10 N.Y. 227, 231 (1851) (solvency cannot depend "on the intelligence to be brought by the next steamer"); Brown v. Case, 41 Ore. 221, 229, 69 Pac. 43, 46 (1902) (solvency cannot be "contingent on stability of the market."). *See also* Izard v. Izard, 1 Bail. Eq. 228, 236-37 (S.C. 1831) ("The fluctuations in the value of property, occasioned by the mercantile condition of the country, cannot however be ranked among [those] casualties [for which the transferor need not provide].").

58 *Prefatory Note to the Uniform Fraudulent Conveyance Act*, 7A U.L.A., Part II, 2-3 (1999). The UFCA is still the law in four states — Maryland, New York, Tennessee and Wyoming — as well as the Virgin Islands. *Id.* at 1 (Supp. 2000).

inal language of the Statute of Elizabeth, codifying and distilling the cases in an attempt to produce objective tests for classifying a transfer as sufficiently "fraudulent" to allow creditors to ignore the suspect transaction and levy upon the items transferred. In short, it was the origin of constructively fraudulent transfers, and a continuation of the maxim that debtors should be just before they were generous.[59]

Many states soon adopted the UFCA.[60] Following this lead, Congress in 1938 adopted, almost verbatim, the text of the UFCA as the federal fraudulent transfer standard in the Bankruptcy Act of 1898.[61] The legislative history lauded the UFCA as incorporating the better reasoned cases under the Statute of Elizabeth.[62] Although not adopted, language stating that the federal statute should be interpreted consistently with the UFCA was suggested.[63]

The enactment of the present Bankruptcy Code in 1978 was the first major revision to the statutory text of fraudulent transfer law. The Code revised the treatment of the characterization of exchange; "reasonably equivalent value" rather than "fair consideration" became the test.[64] The financial stringency test of "unreasonably small capital," however, remained the same, and the reach of the section was expanded from conveyances to "obligations incurred."

The Uniform Fraudulent Transfer Act (UFTA), when promulgated in 1984,[65] adopted most of the Code's changes. Indeed, one of the UFTA's implied purposes

---

59 *See* Claflin v. Mess, 30 N.J. Eq. 211, 212, (1878); Black v. Sanders, 46 N.C. (1 Jones) 67, 68 (1854).

60 It was ultimately adopted by twenty-five states and the Virgin Islands. *Prefatory Note to the Uniform Fraudulent Transfer Act*, 7A U.L.A., Part II, at 268 (1999). The UFCA's influence, however, extended beyond those states which have adopted it by statute. Some states which did not enact the UFCA accepted its provisions as accurate restatements of the received learning of the Statute of Elizabeth. Molitor v. Molitor, 184 Conn. 530, 535, 440 A.2d 215, 218 (1981) (finding that the UFCA "is largely an adoption and clarification of the standards of the common law.").

61 The test was added by amendments to the 1898 Act, known generally as the Chandler Act. Act of June 22, 1938, c. 575, § 1, 52 Stat. 540, 875 (repealed 1979).

62 "We have condensed the provisions of the Uniform Fraudulent Conveyance Act, retaining its substance, and, as far as possible, its Language." NATIONAL BANKRUPTCY CONFERENCE, ANALYSIS OF H.R. 12889, 74th Cong., 2d Sess. 214 (Comm. Print 1936).

63 *Id.* at 217.

64 The two terms were intended to be equivalent with respect to the measurement of the amount of consideration. REPORT OF THE COMMISSION ON THE BANKRUPTCY LAWS OF THE UNITED STATES, H.R. DOC. NO. 137, 93d Cong., 1st Sess., Part I, at 211 (1973); Comment, *Guaranties and Section 548(a)(2) of the Bankruptcy Code*, 52 U. CHI. L. REV. 194, 198 n.18 (1985) (citing other relevant legislative history). Under the UFCA, however, "fair consideration" also included the concept of good faith. UFCA § 3. *See generally* Comment, *Good Faith and Fraudulent Conveyances*, 97 HARV. L. REV. 495 (1983). The Code and UFTA break out the concept of good faith from the concept of consideration, and make it an affirmative defense, validating the transfer or the obligation to the extent the transferee gave with good faith. 11 U.S.C. §§ 548(c) (initial transferee); 550(b) (mediate and intermediate transferees); UFTA §§ 8(a), (d) (same).

65 *Prefatory Note to the Uniform Fraudulent Transfer Act*, 7A U.L.A., Part II, at 267 (1999).

was to conform the uniform state law with the Code.[66] The UFTA, for example, adopts the reasonably equivalent value test,[67] and the Code's extension of the action to obligations.[68] It also adopts the Code's revised formulation of insolvency.[69] It has now been adopted by forty states and the District of Columbia.[70]

2. Fraudulent Transfer Law as Applied to Securitizations

The most obvious situation in which a fraudulent conveyance risk arises is where the parties structure the transaction to actually hinder, delay or defraud creditors. The recent wave of corporate scandals provides a fitting close to this topic. Enron Corp. engaged in many bankruptcy-remote and other securitization-type schemes. These transactions appear to have been put together with the intent to conceal losses or puff profits. That such transactions might very well come within the meaning of an intent to "hinder, delay or defraud" creditors standard is not far-fetched.[71]

Another situation that would raise cause for concern is if the SPE pays a purchase price that is less than the "reasonably equivalent value" of the payment stream (be it receivables or payment intangibles or something similar) it is purchasing. The risk is minimal, however, in the typical structured financing, because the purchase price for the receivables normally will be determined on an arm's length basis (although the fairness of the purchase price might be subject to greater scrutiny if the originator is a troubled company).[72]

Even transfers necessary to achieve a two-tiered structure such as the Honda example in Chapter 1, in which receivables may be transferred to a bankruptcy-remote subsidiary of the originator as a capital contribution, should generally not constitute fraudulent conveyances. It has long been held, for example, that parent support of a solvent subsidiary creates little chance of overreaching by

---

66 *See id.* at 268.

67 UFTA §§ 4(a)(2); 5(a).

68 UFTA § 4(a)(2)(i).

69 UFTA § 2. The UFTA expands upon the Code's definition, however, by creating a rebuttable presumption of insolvency if a transferor is not "generally paying its debts as they become due." *Id.* § 2(b). *See* Cook & Mendales, *The Uniform Fraudulent Transfer Act: An Introductory Critique*, 62 AM. BANKR. L.J. 87, 91-92 (1988).

70 7A U.L.A., Part II, at 9-10 (Supp. 2002).

71 *See* Jonathan Lipson, *Enron, Asset Securitization and Bankruptcy Reform: Dead or Dormant?*, 11 J. BANKR. L. & PRAC. 101 (2002).

72 In a transaction entered into before it filed for bankruptcy, Budget Group, Inc. entered into a securitization in which the discount from face value was approximately 20%. Compare this to the discount in the Honda case in chapter 1 which was 2.5%. One can wonder if the extra discount was due to Budget's bad judgment with respect to car rental customers, or whether its imminent bankruptcy figured into the discount.

the subsidiary, and ultimately inures to the benefit of the parent.[73] Nonetheless, capital contributions to companies that are not directly or indirectly majority-owned by the originator, or that are insolvent, would be subject to closer scrutiny by the courts.

D. Substantive Consolidation of SPEs with Originators

Even if the initial matters of true sale are dealt with, there remains the specter of substantive consolidation in bankruptcy. An equitable doctrine, substantive consolidation may allow a court under appropriate circumstances to consolidate the assets and liabilities of the originator and the SPE.[74] Although substantive consolidation usually arises in the context of the bankruptcy of both the originator and the SPE, a court could order a substantive consolidation even if the SPE were not in bankruptcy.[75]

Courts do not order substantive consolidation lightly. The determination that two entities should be substantively consolidated is made on a case-by-case basis, after consideration of the relevant facts of each case. Courts will take into consideration both the nature of the relationship between the entities to be consolidated and the effect of the consolidation on the creditors of each entity. The courts have identified the following among the factors to be considered for this purpose:[76]

1. The degree of difficulty in segregating and ascertaining individual liabilities and assets;
2. The presence or absence of consolidated financial statements;
3. The commingling of assets and business functions;
4. The unity of ownership and interests between the corporate entities;
5. The guaranteeing by the parent of loans of the subsidiary; and

---

[73] *See, e.g.,* Chester Airport, Inc. v. Aeroflex Corp., 237 N.Y.S.2d 752, 755 (Sup. Ct. 1962), *modified,* 238 N.Y.S.2d 715 (App. Div. 1963) (granting credit to a 51 percent subsidiary inherently brings benefit to the parent).

[74] A court also could jointly administer the bankruptcy cases of affiliated debtors. *See* FED. R. BANKR. P. 1015(b). That would *not* affect the substantive rights of debtors or creditors, but would be intended solely for administrative convenience where multiple affiliated debtors are in bankruptcy.

[75] *See, e.g.,* Sampsell v. Imperial Paper & Color Corp., 313 U.S. 215 (1941) (consolidating the assets of corporation with those of its shareholders)

[76] *See, e.g., In re* Vecco Constr. Indus., 4 Bankr. 407, 410 (Bankr. E.D. Va. 1980); *see* discussion in 2 COLLIER ON BANKRUPTCY ¶ 105.09 (15th rev. ed. 2003, Alan Resnick & Henry Sommer, eds.); Franklin v. Compton (*In re* Bonham), 229 F.3d 750 (9th Cir. 2000); Union Savings Bank v. Augie/Restivo Baking Co. Ltd. (*In re* Augie/Restivo Baking Co.), 860 F.2d 515, 516-17 (2d Cir.1988). *See also* Peter J. Lahny IV, *Asset Securitization: A Discussion of the Traditional Bankruptcy Attacks and an Analysis of the Next Potential Attack, Substantive Consolidation*, 9 AM. BANKR. INST. L. REV. 815 (2001).

6. The transfer of assets without formal observance of corporate formalities.

The presence of some or even many of these factors does not necessarily mean that a court will order a substantive consolidation. Some courts have held that because substantive consolidation is an equitable remedy, it should not be used to harm innocent holders of securities of the company (in our case, the SPE) that is the target of consolidation. Other courts, however, have permitted substantive consolidation where its benefits substantially outweigh any harm.[77]

QUESTIONS ON SUBSTANTIVE CONSOLIDATION

1. Recall that rating agencies require opinions as to whether the bankruptcy court in the originator's bankruptcy case will substantively consolidate the originator's estate with the SPE. Go back and look at the requirements for legal opinions, and add the following guideline: "Nonconsolidation opinions should not contain an assumption to the effect that the SPE is solvent (other than on the transaction's closing date)." Are you willing to give a non-consolidation opinion in the Honda transaction in Chapter 1?

2. For rating agencies and others attempting to structure transactions with certainty, how difficult to deal with are rules such as substantive consolidation? If you were given carte blanche to structure a new securitization, what would you require be present, or absent, in order for you to be absolutely certain that there was no substantive consolidation risk?

[77] Eastgroup Properties v. Southern Motel Assoc., Ltd., 935 F.2d 245 (11th Cir. 1991); *In re* Auto-train, 810 F.2d 270 (D.C. Cir. 1987).

Chapter 4
ACCOUNTING ISSUES

§ 4.01. Introduction

Numerous accounting issues arise in a securitization transaction. We will focus on three primary concerns. The first, and most critical, issue is whether the relevant transfer of financial assets will be treated as a sale or a loan for accounting purposes and hence recorded as debt on the originator's balance sheet. The second issue is whether any SPEs in the transaction that issued debt will be required to be consolidated with the originator for financial reporting purposes so that any debt issued by the SPE appears as debt on the originator's consolidated financial statements. And the third issue is whether a securitization transaction that has not resulted in the reporting of debt on the originator's balance sheet (an off-balance sheet transaction) must nevertheless be disclosed in the management discussion and analysis (MD&A) section of the originator's annual financial statements.

§ 4.02. Transfer of Financial Assets by Originator Treated as a Sale

The sale or loan determination we are making here is to decide how to record the transaction on the originator's financial statements. This is an accounting question and, interestingly enough, the accounting characterization of the transaction may differ from its characterization for other purposes, such as bankruptcy or tax. If the transfer of financial assets (such as receivables) is treated as a sale, the originator is regarded as a seller and must account for the transaction as a simple substitution of cash (the sale proceeds) for the financial assets. But if the transfer is treated as a loan, the originator is regarded as a borrower and must account for the transaction as a borrowing of cash secured by the financial assets as collateral. In such a case, the debt must be reflected as a liability on the originator's balance sheet, thereby increasing the originator's leverage. Recording this transaction as a liability for the originator could limit the originator's financing options by, for instance, violating covenants in prior borrowings by the originator relating to the type and amount of additional debt.

In September 2000, the Financial Accounting Standards Board (FASB), the representative body of independent public accountants that promulgates generally accepted accounting principles (GAAP),[1] issued its Statement of Finan-

[1] The FASB standards are officially recognized as the authoritative accounting standards by the Securities Exchange Commission and the American Institute of Certified Public Accountants.

cial Accounting Standards No. 140 (FAS 140) to address the accounting for transfers and servicing of financial assets in many securitizations.[2] Financial assets include mortgage loans (single-family, multi-family residential, and commercial property), auto loans, trade and credit card receivables, and other revolving charge accounts.[3] Securitizations of nonfinancial assets are not covered by FAS 140.[4]

The basic principle of FAS 140 is that for there to be a sale of financial assets, such as receivables, the originator must surrender control of the receivables. An originator surrenders control only if the following three requirements are satisfied:

(1) there is "presumptively" a bankruptcy true sale of such assets;

(2) the transferee is a qualifying SPE (QSPE) in which, each holder of beneficial interests in the SPE has the right to pledge or exchange those interests in the SPE; and

(3) the originator does not retain effective control over the transferred assets through the ability unilaterally to cause the SPE to return specific assets to the originator, other than through a cleanup call.[5]

FASB intends these requirements, as applied to qualifying SPEs used in securitization transactions, to create a safe harbor for securitization sale accounting based on its belief "that many securitization transactions are, in substance, sales."[6]

A. Requirements for Transfer to be a "Sale"

1. Bankruptcy "True Sale"

First, we will examine the requirements for surrender of control, and then examine the more complex issue of what SPEs meet the requirements to be designated a QSPE. The first requirement for surrender of control is that there is presumptively a bankruptcy true sale of the transferred assets. This continues an anomalous arrangement that began in FAS 125, the predecessor to FAS 140: accountants must rely, for accounting purposes, on legal advice as to whether a given transfer would or would not constitute a sale for federal bankruptcy law

---

2 In general, FAS 140 covers transfers of financial assets occurring after March 31, 2001, while FAS 125 continues to cover such transfers occurring on or before that date. FAS 140 Summary & ¶ 19.

3 FAS 140 ¶ 73; App. E ¶ 354.

4 *Id.*

5 A cleanup call is the originator's ability, toward the end of the planned life of a securitization, to purchase the remaining financial assets "if the amount of outstanding assets . . . falls to a level at which the cost of servicing . . . becomes burdensome in relation to the benefits of servicing." *Id.* Glossary ("Cleanup call").

6 *Id.* ¶ 27.

purposes.[7] The factors discussed in Chapter 3 on "true sales" under bankruptcy law are thus relevant also for the accounting characterization of the transfer as a sale rather than a loan. As a result, accountants asked to give opinions under FAS 140 will ask lawyers on the same transaction if they can rely upon the opinions lawyers give to rating agencies regarding the true sale analysis.

2. Holder of Beneficial Interests of QSPE May Pledge or Exchange Those Assets

The second requirement for surrender of control is that each holder of beneficial interests in the QSPE has the right to pledge (as collateral for a loan) or exchange those interests. This requirement mirrors the intuition that if one owns something, one can do with it as he or she pleases. FAS 140 relies, however, on a fiction. Although the focus logically should be on whether the originator has surrendered control of receivables to the SPE, *thereby giving the SPE the right to pledge or exchange those assets*, the focus instead is on the right of holders of beneficial interests of the SPE to pledge or exchange the beneficial interests. The language of FAS 140 justifies this focus by assuming that the receivables transferred to the QSPE effectively become the assets of its beneficial interest holders:

> The effect of establishing the qualifying SPE is to merge the contractual rights in the transferred assets and to allocate undivided interests in them — the beneficial interests. Therefore, the right of holders to pledge or exchange those beneficial interests is the counterpart of the right of a transferee to pledge or exchange the transferred assets themselves.[8]

This assumption is beneficial to securitization sale accounting because the right of a holder of beneficial interests to pledge or exchange those interests should be unquestioned.

3. Originator Cannot Unilaterally Cause SPE to Return Assets to It

The third requirement for surrender of control is that the originator not retain the ability to unilaterally cause the SPE to return specific assets other than through a cleanup call.[9] The notion here is that if a buyer has bought an asset from a seller, the seller should not have the right to take it back. FASB recognized, however, that "[m]any transfers of assets in securitizations empower the transferor to reclaim assets subject to certain restrictions."[10] FAS 140 there-

---

[7] *See id.* ¶ 27.

[8] *Id.* ¶ 173.

[9] *See supra* note 5.

[10] *Id.* ¶ 85.

fore permits originators (referred to as "transferors" in FAS 140) to take back some assets through "cleanup calls" and other customary removal-of-assets provisions which will be triggered only after most of the financial assets have been converted to cash and the proceeds used to pay back the SPE's investors.[11]

FAS 140 also interprets the phrase "unilaterally" in favor of sale accounting, meaning that if the originator can, acting alone, affect the financial assets being securitized, treatment as a sale may not be warranted. For example, an originator may, consistent with sale accounting, retain the right to remove defaulted receivables from the SPE — the logic being that removal then is not unilateral because it "would be allowed only after a third party's action (default [by the obligor of the receivables])."[12] An originator may not, however, consistent with sale accounting, retain the *unconditional* right to specify the transferred assets that may be removed from the QSPE.[13] Thus, the transaction will be treated as a loan rather than a sale if the originator reclaims the transferred assets at termination of the SPE either for a fixed or determinable price or because the originator holds a residual interest in those assets.[14] This might create some ambiguity as to how the originator will be able to get back any surplus value of the SPE's receivables after the securitization transaction ends. One way to accomplish this, consistent with sale accounting, may be to require the SPE, in its formative legal documents, to transfer those assets back to the originator once the transaction has ended if the return of assets provision (sometimes called a ROAP) is consistent with the requirements of FAS 140.[15]

B. Requirements for a QSPE

Even if a given securitization transaction satisfies these three requirements, sale accounting under FAS 140 further requires that the special purpose entity

---

[11] *See id.* ¶ 234.

[12] *Id.* ¶ 87.

[13] *Id.* ¶ 86.

[14] *Id.* ¶ 235.

[15] To comply with the requirements of FAS 140, the transfer may be made "only in automatic response" to certain conditions. *See id.* ¶ 35d. The transfer may be made upon the exercise by a beneficial interest holder "of a right to put that holder's beneficial interest back to the SPE" if that holder is someone other than the transferor itself, its agents, or its affiliates. *Id.* ¶ 35d(2). An automatic response may also be triggered by "[e]xercise by the transferor of a call or ROAP specified in the legal documents that established the SPE, transferred assets to the SPE, or created the beneficial interest in the transferred assets that it holds," *id.* ¶ 35d(3), or "[t]ermination of the SPE or maturity of the beneficial interest in those financial assets on a fixed or determinable date that is specified at inception." *Id.* ¶ 35d(4). Finally, an automatic response may be triggered by an event that 1) "is specified in the legal documents that established the SPE or created the beneficial interests" in the transferred assets held by the SPE; 2) "is outside the control of the transferor, its affiliates, or its agents;" *and* 3) actually causes,"or is expected at the date of transfer to cause," a decline in the fair value of the held assets "by a specified degree below the fair value of the assets" at the time of transfer to the SPE. *Id.* ¶ 35d(1).

to which the originator sold its assets be a "qualifying" SPE or QSPE. A QSPE is one in which the SPE is a trust or other legal vehicle

(a) that is "demonstrably distinct" from the originator;

(b) whose permitted activities are significantly limited and have been entirely specified in the legal documents pursuant to which it was established;

(c) that holds only "passive" receivables transferred to it and collections thereof, except that it may temporarily hold non-receivable assets obtained in connection with the collection of such receivables; and

(d) that has the right, if at all, to sell or otherwise dispose of non-cash receivables only in "automatic response" to the occurrence of certain events.[16]

1. QSPE Demonstrably Distinct from the Originator

The first characteristic of a QSPE is that the SPE be demonstrably distinct from the originator. This generally means that the originator (or its agents or affiliates) cannot unilaterally dissolve the SPE (such as through a state law controlled dissolution or other liquidation provisions), and that at least 10% of the fair value of the SPE's beneficial interests are held by unrelated third parties. It should be easy to prevent unilateral dissolution, such as by requiring that any dissolution needs the consent of the originator's beneficial interest holders. The 10% level also appears easy to achieve, as FAS 140 itself acknowledges:

> [The 10% level was chosen] because, while most common securitization SPEs have outside interests in excess of two-thirds much of the time, they do not maintain that level during ramp-up and wind-down phases or, in some cases, during seasonal variations in the level of assets [in the SPE].[17]

2. QSPE's Activities are Limited

The second characteristic of a QSPE is that its activities are significantly limited and further must be specified fully in the legal documents creating the QSPE. It is possible for the activities to change to the extent consented to by a majority of the third-party holders of the QSPE's beneficial interests.[18]

---

16 *Id.* ¶ 35.

17 *Id.* ¶ 181.

18 *See* FAS 140 ¶ 184.

3. QSPE Holds Only Passive Receivables and Collections Thereof

The third QSPE characteristic is that it may hold only passive receivables (or the collections thereon) and may only temporarily hold nonreceivable assets obtained in connection with the collection of the receivables. For instance, cars taken at foreclosure in the Honda deal would be nonreceivable assets obtained in connection with collection of the auto loans and could be held temporarily by the QSPE. The term "passive" means that the holder of the financial asset is not involved in making decisions other than those inherent in servicing.[19]

4. QSPE's Sale or Disposition of Non-Cash Receivables is Limited

The fourth characteristic of a QSPE is that the sale or other disposition of non-cash receivables be limited. Nonetheless, FASB permits a QSPE to sell or dispose of those assets in automatic response to the occurrence of certain events. These include events specified in the SPE's formative legal documents which are outside the originator's control and which cause or are expected to cause a decline in the value of those assets. Thus, a QSPE may, consistent with sale accounting, be *required* to dispose of its non-cash receivables in automatic response to an obligor default or a rating agency downgrade of the assets (or of the underlying obligor) to below a specified minimum rating;[20] but its *electing* to dispose of non-cash receivables upon the occurrence of any such events is inconsistent with sale accounting.[21] A QSPE also may sell or dispose of non-cash receivables in automatic response to the exercise by the originator of a ROAP specified in the SPE's formative legal documents, or in automatic response to the termination of the SPE or the maturity of its beneficial interests on a fixed or determinable date that is specified at the originator's inception.[22]

This addresses the problem of how the originator will get back any surplus value of the SPE's receivables after the securitization transaction ends. It may, for example, be possible to include in the SPE's formative legal documents a ROAP requiring the SPE to transfer those assets to the originator once the transaction has ended. Alternatively, the ROAP could require the SPE to transfer to the originator after the transaction ends all cash and all non-cash receivables for which the obligor is in default. This would result in the ultimate return of any surplus value since all non-cash receivables must either default or turn to cash.

---

19 *Id.* ¶ 39. *See also id.* ¶ 61 (describing servicing).

20 *Id.* ¶ 42

21 *Id.* ¶ 43.

22 *Id.* ¶ 35d.

FAS 140 therefore provides a safe harbor for the typical two-tier securitization structure. The first transfer of receivables constitutes a bankruptcy true sale to a QSPE (usually a wholly owned subsidiary of the originator). The second transfer of receivables is from the QSPE in a *non*-bankruptcy-sale (a loan transaction) to another — but not necessarily "qualifying" — SPE (usually an independent entity that is not affiliated with the originator) that issues securities to investors.[23]

§ 4.03. Accounting Consolidation

Whether the debt of the SPE that issues securities in the form of notes must be consolidated on the balance sheet of the originator is another important accounting issue. This also affects the desirability of the securitization — if consolidation is required, then the originator has to carry the securitized debt on its balance sheet, increasing the originator's leverage, and removing many of the benefits of securitization.

A. QSPEs Under FAS 140

FAS 140 also clarifies that, in a two-tier securitization (such as the Honda example in Chapter 1), the originator need not include the debt of its QSPE-subsidiary in the originator's consolidated financial statements. "A qualifying SPE [i.e., a QSPE] shall not be consolidated in the financial statements of a transferor or its affiliates."[24] Without such clarification, debt resulting from a non-bankruptcy sale transfer (i.e., the loan) from the QSPE (SPE1) to the non-QSPE (SPE2) would need to be included in the originator's consolidated financial statements, thereby indirectly defeating sale accounting. The theory of the FASB rule seems to be that in a two-tier transaction, SPE1 does not really exist and the accounting should be as if the sale of the financial assets was directly to SPE2 and that the debt issued in the capital markets by SPE2 to finance the purchase of the financial assets is to stay on SPE2's balance sheet and should not be reflected on the originator's balance sheet.

B. Non-QSPE Consolidation Under FIN 46

If an SPE is not a QSPE, as is the case of SPE2 in a typical two-tier transaction, consolidation was required on the originator's balance sheet only if the

[23] FAS 140 refers to this as a "two-step" structure. *See* FAS 140 ¶ 83. FAS 140 also would generally permit sale accounting for single-tier bankruptcy true sales from the transferor to an independent SPE. *See id.* ¶ 9. Single-tier structures, however, are infrequently used in securitization transactions.

[24] *Id.* ¶¶ 46, 199.

originator controlled the SPE through voting interests.[25] FASB's Emerging Issues Task Force (EITF) then indicated that the SEC's view was that nonconsolidation was not appropriate if the majority owner of the SPE (a third party) made only a nominal capital investment in the SPE.[26] EITF Issue 90-15 clarified that the SEC's view of "nominal" was less than 3% of the entity's assets, although 3% or more might be necessary under certain circumstances.[27] In January 2003, however, FASB issued Interpretation No. 46, Consolidation of Variable Interest Entities (FIN 46) to clarify this accounting standard. FASB declined to tackle defining an SPE and instead created new terminology for use in FIN 46. A "variable interest entity" (VIE) is an entity that does not have equity investors with voting rights or that has equity investors, but they do not provide sufficient financial resources to the VIE to support its activities. In the latter case, there is a presumption that equity equal to less than 10% of assets indicates that the equity investment is inadequate to finance the entity's activities without other support. A VIE often holds financial assets. It may include SPEs as well as other entities. FIN 46 requires consolidation of a VIE (including an SPE, but excluding an QSPE) if the originator is subject to a majority of the risk of loss from the VIE's activities or is entitled to receive a majority of the VIE's residual returns or both. These losses or returns are the "variable" interests referred to in the name "*variable* interest entity." Thus, variable interests are interests whose value fluctuates with changes in the VIE's net asset values and thus the variable interests provide a form of protection to the other investors against the risk of loss. Variable interests include things like guarantees and other credit enhancements.

The determination of whether the originator controls a majority of the variable interests requires a complex calculation based on an estimate of the present value of expected losses and expected residual returns for each variable interest holder and assigning each a probability weight. In the terminology used in FIN 46, however, an originator required to consolidate a VIE is called the primary beneficiary of the VIE. An originator is also required to disclose interests about VIEs which it is not required to consolidate, but in which it holds "significant" variable interests, as discussed further below.

1. The Effect of Enron's Collapse on Securitization Accounting

FIN 46 came about as a direct result of the collapse of Enron Corporation, which filed for bankruptcy on December 2, 2001, after once being the seventh

---

[25] FAS 95 provides that "as a general rule ownership by one company, directly or indirectly, of over fifty per cent of the outstanding voting shares of another company is a condition pointing towards consolidation."

[26] FASB, EITF Topic D-14, Transactions Involving Special Purpose Entities.

[27] FASB, EITF Issue 90-15, Impact of Nonsubstantive Lessors, Residual Value Guarantees, and Other Provisions in Leasing Transactions.

largest corporation in the United States. It now appears that Enron engaged in a range of overly complex accounting transactions, devoting much more energy to creative accounting than to making a profit to account for. Its primary motivation was to minimize financial statement losses and volatility, accelerate profits, and avoid adding debt to its balance sheet which could have hurt Enron's credit rating and thereby damaged its credibility in the energy trading business.

A common factor in many of these transactions was the use of non-consolidated SPEs to hedge certain Enron investments. In a typical transaction, Enron would transfer its own stock to an SPE in exchange for a note or cash, and also directly or indirectly guarantee the SPE's value. The SPE, in turn, would hedge the value of a particular investment on Enron's balance sheet, using the transferred Enron stock as the principal source of payment. Because of its historically rising stock price, Enron apparently judged the risk that it would have to pay on its guarantees as remote.

When Enron's stock price subsequently fell, the SPE's value also fell, triggering the Enron guarantees; these guarantee payments in turn apparently further reduced Enron stock value, triggering additional guarantees. When the value of Enron's investment and Enron's stock price simultaneously fell, the SPE lacked sufficient assets to perform its hedge. Moreover, these drops in value, or in some cases lack of sufficient third-party equity in the SPE, caused the SPEs to breach the three percent independent equity requirement for non-consolidation suggested in EITF 90-15, thereby bringing the SPEs's debt onto Enron's balance sheet.[28] FIN 46 increased this minimum independent equity requirement to ten percent of the SPE's assets.

These manipulations thrived because of a tangled web of conflicts of interest. Senior Enron executives, most notably Andrew Fastow, served as the SPEs' principals, receiving such high compensation and returns as to potentially skew their loyalty in favor of the SPEs. These and other senior Enron executives also seemed to have a somewhat casual approach towards compliance with Enron's Code of Conduct. Although the Code required disclosure to the Chairman of the Board and the CEO of Enron and a determination by the Chairman and CEO that the employee's business relationship with an entity doing business with Enron did not adversely affect Enron's interests, approval was not always sought.[29] Moreover, even where approval was obtained, the monitoring required as a condition to approval was not always properly implemented.

These abuses have given rise to a host of issues, including the central accounting issue of whether the incestuous hedging substantively transferred economic risk, thereby justifying off-balance sheet financing. The answer isn't always

---

28 *See* FASB, EITF Issue 90-15, Impact of Nonsubstantive Lessors, Residual Value Guarantees, and Other Provisions in Leasing Transactions; FASB, EITF Topic D-14, Transactions Involving Special Purpose Entities.

29 2002 Extra LEXIS 45, at *64 & n.8 (hereafter "Powers Report"). This report was issued on February, 1, 2002, and is named for William C. Powers, Jr., Chair of the Investigative Committee, as well as Dean at the University of Texas School of Law.

black and white, as suggested by the Report of Investigation by the Special Investigative Committee of the Board of Directors of Enron Corp.[30] For example, although that report states that the "'hedging' transactions did not involve substantive transfers of economic risk"[31] and thus disputes that the financial accounting was proper,[32] it inconsistently concludes that the hedges merely raise "substantial accounting questions."[33] One might even view Enron's attempt to use the "embedded" value of its own stock, increases in which could not be reflected on its balance sheet under generally accepted accounting principles, as ingenious because the stock *does* create real value for the hedging entities. Indeed, Enron even obtained independent fairness opinions from its independent auditors on at least some of these transactions.[34] In perspective, therefore, Enron and its accountants were (in many cases) making exquisitely fine judgment calls — shades of gray that, for accounting, must be rendered as black or white.

Certainly Enron can, and as we learn more will continue to, teach us many lessons. Because humans are fallible, mistakes are inevitable; and conflicts of interest make them more likely, especially where there are judgment calls. In this context, Enron illustrates that even extensive controls cannot always moderate the effect of these conflicts. Indeed, the Powers Report notes that "a conflict . . . that could be managed only through so many controls and procedures should not have been approved in the first place."[35]

C. Proposed Amendments to FAS 140

On June 10, 2003, FASB issued an exposure draft entitled "Proposed Statement of Financial Accounting Standards: Qualifying Special-Purpose Entities and Isolation of Transferred Assets, an amendment of FASB Statement No. 140" (the "FAS 140 Exposure Draft"). The comment period closed on July 31, 2003. Some of the proposed amendments are intended to clarify FAS 140, but the amendments were primarily in response to FIN 46. Certain of the amendments proposed in the Exposure Draft are intended to conform FAS 140's consolidation standards to some extent with FIN 46. The goal is to take away the "incentive to convert certain entities to qualifying SPEs to avoid consolidation."[36]

The amendments first would limit the powers of a transferor or originator to make decisions about reissuing "beneficial interests," which are the debt or

[30] *Id.*

[31] *Id.* at *22.

[32] *Id.* at *186.

[33] *Id.* at *117.

[34] *See, e.g., id.* at *112, *114.

[35] *Id.* at *222.

[36] FAS 140 Exposure Draft at *ii*.

equity securities conveying the right to receive all or a portion of the cash flows due to the SPE.[37] The rationale for this limitation is that transferors of assets to qualifying, and therefore non-consolidated, SPEs should not be allowed to retain effective control over the transferred assets.[38] As we have seen, because FAS 140 regards QSPEs as passive pass-through entities it treats assets transferred to a QSPE as effectively merged into the beneficial interests issued by the QSPE to its investors.[39] Thus, permitting the transferor/originator to control reissuance of those beneficial interests is tantamount to permitting such transferor to control the transferred assets. Therefore, under the revised rules, a QSPE may not reissue beneficial interests if any party (1) commits to deliver additional cash or other assets to fulfill the SPE's obligations to beneficial interest holders, if such party's commitments constitute more than half of all such commitments to the SPE; or (2) makes discretionary decisions about reissuing beneficial interests and also either commits to deliver additional cash or other assets to fulfill the SPE's obligations to beneficial interest holders or holds beneficial interests subordinated in any way to the most senior in priority; or (3) that holds subordinated beneficial interests commits to deliver additional cash or other assets to fulfill the SPE's obligations to beneficial interest holders.[40]

Under the rationale that originators or transferors should not be allowed to retain effective control over the transferred assets, the proposed amendments also would limit the powers of an originator or transferor to retain effective control of those assets by providing financial support, other than by holding subordinated retained interests.[41] Further, the proposed amendments provide that SPEs cannot be QSPEs if "any party involved is in a position to enhance or protect the value of its own subordinated interest by providing financial support for or making decisions about reissuing beneficial interests."[42]

The definition of QSPE would also be restricted to prohibit its entering into any agreement, other than, for example, an agreement to make discretionary servicing advances, with the transferor or its affiliates or agents that commits any of them to "deliver additional cash or other assets to the SPE or its [beneficial interest holders, *i.e.*, its investors]."[43] This prohibition includes, for example, "liquidity commitments, financial guarantees, written options," and "commitments to purchase outstanding beneficial interests directly or indirectly from the beneficial interest holders or to otherwise settle beneficial inter-

---

37 *See* FAS 140, Appendix E.

38 Exposure Draft at *ii*.

39 *See* FAS 140, ¶ 173 ("The effect of establishing the qualifying SPE is to merge the contractual rights in the transferred assets and to allocate undivided interests in them — the beneficial interests. Therefore, the right of holders to pledge or exchange those beneficial interest is the counterpart of the right of a transferee to pledge or exchange the transferred assets themselves.").

40 *See* Exposure Draft at 2 (adding new ¶¶ 35(f)(1), (f)(2), and (f)(3) to FAS 140).

41 Exposure Draft at *ii*.

42 *Id.* at *ii* & at 1.

43 Exposure Draft at 2 (adding a new ¶ 35(e) to FAS 140).

ests with their holders."[44] It also includes total return swaps.[45] The reason for this prohibition is to prevent the sorts of incestuous hedging that enabled the Enron transactions to multiply.

§ 4.04. Disclosure on Originator's Financial Statements of Off-Balance Sheet Items

Publicly traded corporations must file quarterly and annual financial statement filings with the Securities and Exchange Commission (SEC).[46] The SEC has long required that in the management discussion and analysis (MD&A) that accompanies the filings that there be a discussion of changes between equity, debt and any off-balance sheet financing arrangements. Thus, although not reflected on the balance sheet, the originator still needs to discuss any off-balance sheet transactions with nonconsolidated SPEs in the MD&A section of the originator's annual report filed with the SEC. The Sarbanes-Oxley Act of 2002 mandated that the SEC enact rules to require corporations to discuss in the MD&A "all material off-balance sheet transactions, arrangements, obligations (including contingent obligations), and other relationships of the issuer with unconsolidated entities or other persons, that may have a material current or future effect on financial condition, changes in financial condition, results of operations, liquidity, capital expenditures, capital resources, or significant components of revenues or expenses."[47]

This disclosure requirement explicitly extends to material variable interests in an unconsolidated VIE as contemplated under FIN 46. The SEC's rules issued to implement the mandate of the Sarbanes-Oxley Act require the originator to discuss its off-balance sheet arrangements in a separately captioned section of the MD&A portion of its annual report. These rules are reflected in Regulation S-K, excerpted below. Any off-balance sheet arrangement that has or is reasonably likely to have an effect on the originator's financial condition that is material to investors must be disclosed. A detailed definition of "off-balance sheet arrangements" is provided in the rules, which are designed to target means by which originators structure off-balance sheet arrangements or otherwise incur a risk of loss that is not otherwise fully transparent to investors. The nature and business purpose of off-balance sheet arrangements as well as the overall magnitude of an originator's off-balance sheet arrangements must be disclosed, along with the circumstances under which material contingent obligations or liabilities associated with the off-balance sheet arrangements could come to fruition.

---

[44] *Id.*

[45] *Id.*

[46] More about the SEC and securitizations may be found in Chapter 6.

[47] Section 401(a), 15 U.S.C. § 78m(j).

Regulation S-K

(Item 303) Management's discussion and analysis of financial condition and results of operations.
17 C.F.R. § 229.303

(a) . . .

(4) Off-balance sheet arrangements. (i) In a separately-captioned section, discuss the registrant's off-balance sheet arrangements that have or are reasonably likely to have a current or future effect on the registrant's financial condition, changes in financial condition, revenues or expenses, results of operations, liquidity, capital expenditures or capital resources that is material to investors. The disclosure shall include the items specified in paragraphs (a)(4)(i)(A), (B), (C) and (D) of this Item to the extent necessary to an understanding of such arrangements and effect and shall also include such other information that the registrant believes is necessary for such an understanding.

(A) The nature and business purpose to the registrant of such off-balance sheet arrangements;

(B) The importance to the registrant of such off-balance sheet arrangements in respect of its liquidity, capital resources, market risk support, credit risk support or other benefits;

(C) The amounts of revenues, expenses and cash flows of the registrant arising from such arrangements; the nature and amounts of any interests retained, securities issued and other indebtedness incurred by the registrant in connection with such arrangements; and the nature and amounts of any other obligations or liabilities (including contingent obligations or liabilities) of the registrant arising from such arrangements that are or are reasonably likely to become material and the triggering events or circumstances that could cause them to arise; and

(D) Any known event, demand, commitment, trend or uncertainty that will result in or is reasonably likely to result in the termination, or material reduction in availability to the registrant, of its off-balance sheet arrangements that provide material benefits to it, and the course of action that the registrant has taken or proposes to take in response to any such circumstances.

(ii) As used in this paragraph (a)(4), the term off-balance sheet arrangement means any transaction, agreement or other contractual arrangement to which an entity unconsolidated with the registrant is a party, under which the registrant has:

(A) Any obligation under a guarantee contract that has any of the characteristics identified in paragraph 3 of FASB Interpretation No. 45, Guarantor's Accounting and Disclosure Requirements for Guarantees, Including Indirect Guarantees of Indebtedness of Others (November 2002) ("FIN 45"), as may be modified or supplemented, and that is not excluded from the initial recognition and measurement provisions of FIN 45 pursuant to paragraphs 6 or 7 of that Interpretation;

(B) A retained or contingent interest in assets transferred to an unconsolidated entity or similar arrangement that serves as credit, liquidity or market risk support to such entity for such assets;

(C) Any obligation, including a contingent obligation, under a contract that would be accounted for as a derivative instrument, except that it is both indexed to the registrant's own stock and classified in stockholders' equity in the registrant's statement of financial position, and therefore excluded from the scope of FASB Statement of Financial Accounting Standards No. 133, Accounting for Derivative Instruments and Hedging Activities (June 1998), pursuant to paragraph 11(a) of that Statement, as may be modified or supplemented; or

(D) Any obligation, including a contingent obligation, arising out of a variable interest (as referenced in FASB Interpretation No. 46, Consolidation of Variable Interest Entities (January 2003), as may be modified or supplemented) in an unconsolidated entity that is held by, and material to, the registrant, where such entity provides financing, liquidity, market risk or credit risk support to, or engages in leasing, hedging or research and development services with, the registrant.

§ 4.05. The Honda Securitization

Go back to the Honda Finance example in Chapter 1. In that real-life example, Honda Finance's transfer of auto loans to Honda Receivables is likely structured as an accounting sale rather than a loan from Receivables to Finance secured by Finance's auto loans. The reason for that choice is that if the auto loans are "sold" to Honda Receivables, and the sale is reflected by a reduction of the loan assets of Honda Finance which are replaced by an increase in Finance's cash assets in the amount of the sales price, then Finance will not need to show a loan from Receivables as a liability on Finance's balance sheet (which would be offset by the loan proceeds as an addition to the Finance's assets in the form of cash).

If Honda Receivables is a QSPE as described above, then notwithstanding the fact that Receivables may be a wholly owned subsidiary of Honda Finance, its assets and liabilities will not be consolidated with those of the Finance for financial reporting purposes. Therefore, the transfer of the auto loans from Receivables to the trust can be structured as a loan by the trust to Receivables secured by the auto loans. Any liability reported as a debt on Receivable's balance sheet will not be consolidated with the balance sheet of Finance.

Even if the transaction is accounted for in this manner, it is nonetheless quite possible that Honda Finance (or its parent, Honda Motor Company) will need to discuss this off-balance sheet arrangement in the MD&A of its financial statements, including a discussion of the purpose of this off-balance sheet arrangement, the magnitude of all of the originator's off-balance sheet activities, and the risks presented to it from certain contingent obligations it may have incurred as part of its off-balance sheet arrangements, pursuant to SEC disclosure requirements arising from the Sarbanes-Oxley Act.

QUESTIONS RELATED TO ACCOUNTING

1. What are the advantages and disadvantages of permitting accounting standards to be determined by a non-governmental group composed of industry representatives?

2. Are the accounting rules regarding sale or loan characterization bright line rules or subject to reasoned interpretation? Which do you think most members of the public — or even investors — believe about the exactitude of accounting standards?

3. For a transfer to be accounted for as a sale for accounting purposes, one of the requirements is that the transfer must be a sale for bankruptcy purposes. What do the additional requirements for accounting sale treatment add to the analysis? If the standards for sale do differ between bankruptcy and accounting, how can the differences be justified by the different purposes of bankruptcy law and accounting practice?

4. What is the justification for declaring that a QSPE, even though it may have in accounting terms borrowed money secured by its receivables, not be consolidated with the originator? What would be the result if QSPEs were consolidated with the originator?

5. In the Honda transaction, can you tell from the documents included in the back of this book whether Honda Receivables is a QSPE? Where, if at all, in these documents is the accounting characterization discussed?

6. Must QSPEs be discussed in the MDA of the financial statements filed by public companies with the SEC?

7. How do the securitizations used by Enron differ from those discussed in this book, including the Honda deal?

Chapter 5

TAX ISSUES AND STRUCTURING CONSIDERATIONS

§ 5.01. The Basic Tax Issues in a Standard Securitization

This chapter provides an overview of the basic federal tax issues in a domestic securitization.[1] As we will see, tax concerns are critical in structuring the transaction, so this is a good opportunity to also describe some of the more common securitization structures.

A. Is the Transfer of the Receivables a Sale for Tax Purposes?

When an originator or a subsequent party transfer receivables in a securitization, we have seen that for commercial law, bankruptcy law and accounting reasons we need to assess the character of the securitization transaction as a sale or loan. We also have seen that each body of law employs different standards for making this assessment. We will now consider how tax law characterizes the transfer of receivables. If the transfer is a tax sale, then the seller must recognize and pay tax on any difference between the sales price and the seller's basis in the receivables (the gain on sale to the seller).[2] If the transfer is not a tax sale, then it will be considered a loan by the transferee to the transferor. A loan is not a taxable event to the transferor.

This can be confusing because the tax characterization of the asset transfer is sometimes inconsistent with the form of the transfer which, as we have seen above, may be dictated by competing regulatory, bankruptcy or accounting concerns. For example, a transfer termed a "sale" of receivables in the applicable documents might nevertheless be treated as a loan for tax purposes.[3] When the

---

[1] Cross-border tax issues — that is, the federal tax issues in a securitization that involves countries in addition to the United States and tax issues raised by non-United States law — must also be considered in an international deal. State and local tax issues vary by jurisdiction and must be separately addressed in each transaction.

[2] If the transfer is a taxable sale and there is a loss on the receivables (i.e., they are sold for less than the transferor's basis), the loss may be recognized by the transferor and offset its other income.

[3] *See, e.g.*, Commissioner v. Bollinger, 485 U.S. 340 (1988). *See also* Field Service Advisory 1355785 (Jan. 6, 1992) (IRS has advised that a securitization of credit card receivables, structured as a sale for financial and regulatory purposes, but treated as debt for tax purposes, should be characterized as a tax loan and the receivables as collateral). Courts sometimes apply more stringent rules when taxpayers attempt to ignore the form of their own transaction than when the IRS desires to ignore it. It is a basic premise of federal income tax law, however, that a transaction should be taxed in accordance with its economic substance rather than its form. Gregory v. Helvering, 293 U.S. 465 (1935).

transfer of the receivables is determined to be a "true sale" for bankruptcy purposes, it is often the case that the transaction will also be characterized as a tax sale since similar factors are relevant for finding a "true sale" and a tax sale. The basic test for a taxable sale of assets is whether the transferor has relinquished substantial incidents of ownership,[4] including the potential for appreciation as well as economic risk of a loss.

Even if the transfer of assets is a sale for tax purposes, if the transferee is a wholly owned subsidiary of the originator, any gain recognized on the tax sale may be offset by losses realized elsewhere in the consolidated enterprise. The assets may then be transferred to a second and independently owned SPE in a transaction characterized as a loan for tax purposes so that no tax would be due on the second transfer. If the first transfer of assets is a tax sale, it is also of course possible that there will be little or no gain so that the resulting income tax liability will be little or nothing.

An IRS private ruling on this subject is excerpted below. Because the ruling is private, it may not be used or cited as precedent.[5] In addition, identifying characteristics of the transaction are deleted. Nonetheless, the analysis is instructive, especially since it relates to an auto loan securitization much like the Honda deal discussed in Chapter 1. The specific issue in this ruling is whether the purchasers of the Class A Certificates engaged in a sale of assets or whether the certificate holders have merely made a loan to the issuer of the Certificates secured by the auto loan contracts.

Internal Revenue Service

Priv. Ltr. Rul. 98-39-0001 (May 29, 1998)

. . . . During the years at issue, Taxpayer sold new automobiles to its distributors, who in turn sold them to the public. Finance Sub, a wholly-owned subsidiary of Taxpayer, financed installment purchase contracts for the retail customers of the distributors. By Date 1, Finance Sub had accumulated a pool of these loans (Pool 1) . . . . On Date 1, Finance Sub securitized these loans, as described below. By Date 2, Finance Sub had accumulated another pool of loans (Pool 2) . . . . On Date 2, Finance Sub securitized these loans, as described below. This second securitization transaction was qualitatively identical to the first. Taxpayer treated each transaction as a sale on its federal income tax returns and financial statements.

YEAR 1 SECURITIZATION TRANSACTIONS

In month 1, Taxpayer formed a wholly-owned domestic subsidiary (Receivables Sub) as the first step in securitizing the loans. Finance Sub transferred Pool 1 to Receivables Sub on Date 1. Also on Date 1, Receivables Sub, Finance

4 *See, e.g.*, Gen. Couns. Mem. 39,584 (Dec. 3, 1986).

5 I.R.C. § 6110(j)(3).

Sub, and Bank 1 formed Trust 1, a grantor trust. As grantors, Receivables Sub and Finance Sub were entitled to the residual of Trust 1. Trust 1 is a bankruptcy-remote entity.

Receivables Sub transferred Pool 1 to Trust 1 on a non-recourse basis. In exchange, Trust 1 issued to Receivables Sub two classes of certificates of beneficial interest, Class A and Class B. By their terms, each certificate evidences a fractional, undivided interest in Trust 1 and its assets, the pool of loans. . . . As described below, the Class B certificates were subordinated to the Class A certificates. Receivables Sub sold most of the Class A certificates to the public and retained the Class B certificates.

Receivables Sub serviced the loans for Trust 1. As servicer, Receivables Sub was responsible for ensuring that the certificate holders timely received their principal and interest payments. Its responsibilities included collecting payments from the debtors (the purchasers of new cars who financed their purchase through Finance Sub), working with the debtors to avoid defaults, and remitting payments to the certificate holders. As servicer, Receivables Sub received [compensation based on a small percentage] of the beginning balance of the Trust each month. . . .

Taxpayer took several steps to ensure that the Class A certificate holders would timely receive their principal and interest payments. First, as stated above, the Class B certificates were subordinated to the Class A certificates and the rights of Receivables Sub as servicer. The Class B certificate holders would receive no payments on a particular distribution date, whether of interest or principal, until the Class A certificate holders were paid.

Second, Taxpayer established the Subordination Spread Account (SSA) as a reserve against possible future collection shortfalls. The SSA was not part of Trust 1, but was maintained for the benefit of the Class A certificate holders. The SSA had an initial balance . . . [and] payments otherwise intended for the Class B certificate holders would go the SSA as needed to keep the balance of the SSA [at the required level]. The required balance varied depending on the how the pool of loans performed. The fewer defaults and late payments, the less the required balance in the SSA. The more defaults and late payments on the loans, the greater the required balance. . . . Taxpayer or Receivables Sub was entitled to any funds in the SSA not needed to fund the Class A certificate holders. Thus, that part of the SSA not needed for the Class A certificate holders was part of Taxpayer's residual interest in the transaction.

Third, while the sale of the loans to Trust 1 was technically without recourse, during a limited period Finance Sub had to repurchase non-conforming loans. When it transferred the loans to Trust 1, Receivables Sub made several warranties to Trust 1. These included:

(1) the loans were free and clear of all encumbrances, liens, charges and security interests;

(2) each loan was secured by a first priority perfected security interest in the car;

(3) each loan complied with all federal and state laws, including truth-in-lending, equal credit opportunity, and disclosure laws; and

(4) no loan was more than 30 days past due.

At the end of the first or second month after the transfer to the Trust, Receivables Sub had to repurchase any loan not meeting these and other requirements. Each loan had been originated before Date 1. . . .

YEAR 3 SECURITIZATION TRANSACTION

The second securitization transaction was substantially identical to the first, except for changes in certain labels used in the various documents and the extent to which the senior trust certificates (i.e., the class held by outside investors) were overcollateralized.

Taxpayer created Trust 2 on Date 2. On Date 2, Finance Sub transferred the second pool of loans (Pool 2) to Receivables Sub. Receivables Sub then transferred Pool 2 to Trust 2. As grantors, Receivables Sub and Finance Sub were entitled to any residual funds in Trust 2. Trust 2 is a bankruptcy-remote entity. . . .

LAW AND ANALYSIS

The first issue is whether Taxpayer sold an undivided interest in the loans to the Class A certificate holders or used the loans as security in borrowing funds from the holders. If the transactions were sales, then Taxpayer must apply section 1286 of the Internal Revenue Code and recognize any gain or loss under section 1001. If the transactions were secured financings, then Taxpayer does not include the borrowed amounts in gross income. United States v. Centennial Savings Bank FSB, 499 U.S. 573, 582 (1991), 1991-2 C.B. 30.

In general, federal income tax consequences are governed by the substance of a transaction determined by the intentions of the parties to the transaction, the underlying economics, and all other relevant facts and circumstances. Gregory v. Helvering, 293 U.S. 465, 470 (1935), XIV-1 C.B. 193. The label the parties affix to a transaction does not determine its character. Helvering v. Lazarus & Co., 308 U.S. 252, 255 (1939), 1939-2 C.B. 208; Mapco Inc. v. United States, 556 F.2d 1107, 1110 (Ct. Cl. 1977).

The term "sale" is given its ordinary meaning and is generally defined as a transfer of the ownership of property for money or for a promise to pay money. Commissioner v. Brown, 380 U.S. 563, 570-71 (1965), 1965-2 C.B. 282. Whether a transaction is a sale or a financing arrangement is a question of fact, which must be ascertained from the intent of the parties as evidenced by the written agreements read in light of the attending facts and circumstances. Haggard v. Commissioner, 24 T.C. 1124, 1129 (1955), aff'd, 241 F.2d 288 (9th Cir. 1956). But see Farley Realty Co. v. Commissioner, 279 F.2d 701, 705 (2d Cir. 1960) ("[T]he parties' bona fide intentions may be ignored if the relationship the parties have created does not coincide with their intentions.").

A transaction is a sale if the benefits and burdens of ownership have passed to the purported purchaser. Highland Farms, Inc. v. Commissioner, 106 T.C. 237, 253 (1996); Grodt & McKay Realty, Inc. v. Commissioner, 77 T.C. 1221, 1237 (1981). In cases involving transfers of debt instruments, the courts have considered the following factors to be relevant in determining whether the benefits and burdens of ownership passed:

(1) whether the transaction was treated as a sale, see United Surgical Steel Co., Inc. v. Commissioner, 54 T.C. 1215, 1229-30, 1231 (1970), acq., 1971-2 C.B. 3;

(2) whether the obligors on the notes (the transferor's customers) were notified of the transfer of the notes, id.;

(3) which party serviced the notes, id.; Town & Country Food Co., Inc. v. Commissioner, 51 T.C. 1049, 1057 (1969), acq., 1969-2 C.B. xxv;

(4) whether payments to the transferee corresponded to collections on the notes, United Surgical Steel Co., 54 T.C. at 1229-30, 1231; Town & Country Food Co., 51 T.C. at 1057;

(5) whether the transferee imposed restrictions on the operations of the transferor that are consistent with a lender-borrower relationship, United Surgical Steel Co., 54 T.C. at 1230; Yancey Bros. Co. v. United States, 319 F. Supp. 441, 446 (N.D. Ga. 1970);

(6) which party had the power of disposition, American Nat'l Bank of Austin v. United States, 421 F.2d 442, 452 (5th Cir.), cert. denied, 400 U.S. 819 (1970); Rev. Rul. 82-144, 1982-2 C.B. 34;

(7) which party bore the risk of loss, Union Planters Nat'l Bank of Memphis v. United States, 426 F.2d 115, 118 (6th Cir.), cert. denied, 400 U.S. 827 (1970); Elmer v. Commissioner, 65 F.2d 568, 569 (2d Cir. 1933), aff'g 22 B.T.A. 224 (1931); Rev. Rul. 82-144; and

(8) which party had the potential for gain, United Surgical Steel Co., 54 T.C. at 1229; Town & Country Food Co., 51 T.C. at 1057; Rev. Rul. 82-144.

No single factor determines whether a sale has taken place. The facts and circumstances determine the importance of each factor. Thus, a factor-by-factor analysis is necessary to determine whether Taxpayer sold the loans.

In a typical high quality auto loan securitization transaction (as both the Taxpayer and the field agree is the case here), however, the economics dictate that only the last two factors have real significance, and only to the extent they are economically realistic. Thus, a sale has take place if the investors purchasing the Class A certificates have assumed Taxpayer's risk of loss and opportunity for profit inherent in the Trusts and their underlying loans, within economically realistic limits. If so, the cash flows due the Class A certificate holders are at the risk of the underlying cash flows of the pool. A secured financing has taken place if the cash flows due the Class A certificate holders do not depend to any real degree on the performance of the underlying debt instruments (i.e., the loans in the Pools), because then the Taxpayer would have retained the risk of loss and opportunity for gain. We conclude that the latter is the case, and thus the transactions at issue are secured financings and not sales.

Events requiring sponsors to repurchase a pooled auto loan usually occur early in the term of the loan. Curtin and Deckoff, [Asset-Backed Securities: An Attractive Addition to the Low Duration Sector of the Fixed-Income Market, 195, 208, in Lederman, ed., The Handbook of Asset-Backed Securities (NY Institute of Finance, 1990).] This indicates that this particular risk of loss is economically realistic only during the initial stages of a securitization. . . . Thus, by the time the two Trusts were formed and the Class A certificates sold to the investors, the loans in the two Trusts did not have an economically significant risk of loss of this sort that could be passed to the Class A certificate holders. This factor indicates the transaction was a secured financing, not a sale.

Arguably, extreme economic conditions could result in much higher than expected losses on the loans in the Trusts, in turn causing a severe shortfall in cash flows. If the resulting losses were great enough, the combination of the SSA, the subordination feature of the Class B certificates, and the residual cash flows might not be sufficient to cover the payments due the Class A certificate holders. This sort of catastrophic risk, however, is more theoretical than real. Haley, Securitizing Automobile Receivables, 60, 76, in Zweig, ed., The Asset Securitization Handbook (Dow Jones-Irwin 1989). Passing on only catastrophic risk to investors in a securitization, while retaining the historic risks, indicates that the transaction is a secured financing. . . .

The field claims that Taxpayer structured its deals similar to MBS [mortgage-backed securities] deals which the Service has ruled sales. The field says that characteristics common to these and the Taxpayer's deals include:

(1) the sponsor retained a clean-up call it could use when the outstanding principal balance of the mortgages in the pool dropped to 10 percent of their original balance;

(2) the sponsor retained prepayment penalties, late payment charges, and assumption fees (i.e., ancillary income) from the pooled mortgages as part of its servicing fees;

(3) the sponsor, as servicer, had to pay trustee's fees and mortgage insurance premiums out of its servicing fee;

(4) the sponsor retained the right to make advances to the MBS holders should the mortgagors pay late or default; and

(5) the sponsor retained the right to guarantee principal and interest payments on the mortgages, either itself or through a third party.

We believe none of these factors materially affects whether Taxpayer's securitizations are sales or secured financings.

First, a clean-up call is common in MBS deals, regardless of their tax classification. . . .

Second, retaining the ancillary servicing income cannot affect whether a sale or secured financing has occurred. Servicing is necessary for all securitized loans, mortgages or otherwise, regardless of whether the securitization is a sale or secured financing. Servicers routinely keep the ancillary income from servicing loans as it is one of the most profitable parts of a securitization.

Third, the servicer paying trustee expenses and mortgage insurance premiums also is common to both types of securitizations.

Fourth, the sponsor retaining the right (but not the obligation) to cover collection shortfalls cannot turn a secured financing into a sale. A legally enforceable right to force a sponsor to cover collection shortfalls cannot by itself turn a secured financing into a sale. Taxpayer put in place all the other mechanisms discussed above (over-collateralization, reserve accounts, subordination, and so forth) to ensure that the cash flows due the Class A certificate holders would not be at the risk of the cash flows of the mortgages in the Pools. The lack of a legally enforceable right to force the Taxpayer to cover collection shortfalls does not outweigh all these other factors.

Fifth, guaranteeing payments on the mortgages can be crucial in determining whether a securitization is a sale or secured financing. However, neither of Taxpayer's two securitizations have any such guarantee. This factor thus has no relevance here.

The field refers to various GAAP pronouncements as supporting its contention that Taxpayer has sold the loans. GAAP, however, cannot affect federal income tax rules unless specifically made controlling. Thor Power Tool Co. v. Comm'r, 439 U.S. 522 (1979).

Finally, the field has analyzed the how the Taxpayer's two auto loan pools have performed, and claims that the Class A certificate holders actually suffered more losses from prepayments than the Taxpayer suffered from defaults. This comparison of parts of two different risks is suspect. In any event, this hindsight analysis cannot affect whether the securitization is a sale or secured financing (as the field admits). This issue is determined at the outset of the transaction.

For the foregoing reasons, we conclude that Receivables Sub retained 100 percent ownership of Pools 1 and 2. Therefore, the transfers were secured financings. . . .

No opinion is expressed on whether the transfer of customer notes from Finance Sub to Receivables Sub is a sale or secured financing or the collateral consequences of either characterization. . . .

QUESTIONS ON THE REVENUE RULING

1. Try to diagram the securitization described in the Revenue Ruling. Use the diagram in Chapter 1 of the Honda deal as your guide.

2. What did the IRS conclude about whether the Class A certificate holders had purchased the underlying auto loans from the trust or had loaned the trust money secured by the auto loans? What factors were most important to the IRS in making this determination? What is the tax consequence of the Revenue Ruling to the Taxpayer (the originator of the auto loans)?

3. What are the forms of credit enhancement built into this deal to help assure that the Class A certificate holders will be timely and fully paid? Which of these forms of credit enhancement also appear to be present in the Honda deal described in Chapter 1?

B. Is the SPE Subject to Taxation on the Income Earned on the Receivables?

The receivables transferred by the originator to the SPE provide cash flow to the SPE that the SPE uses to pay the investors who bought securities issued by the SPE. For instance, if the receivables are interest-bearing auto loans, the interest component of the monthly payments that flow into the SPE is taxable income to the SPE, just like interest you may receive on a checking or savings account would be taxable.[6] If the SPE paid income tax on that interest income at a corporate income tax rate as high as 35% that would dramatically reduce the interest that could be paid to the investors in the securities issued by the SPE. Those investors, of course, would also be responsible for paying income tax on interest they received on their investment in the SPE. This double-taxation is to be avoided at all costs. Similarly, income received by a corporate entity is subject to taxation at the corporate level and then again at the investor level if it is returned to equity holders in the form of dividends.[7] Congress and the

[6] If the receivables are trade receivables and are not interest bearing, it is likely that they are transferred at a discount from their face value to reflect the time value of money (the receivables will not be paid until a future date) and to reflect the possibility that some of the obligors on the receivables will default on their obligation to pay. Payments in excess of the purchase price received by the SPE would also be considered income to the SPE and subject to tax, even though the receivables themselves do not specifically bear interest.

[7] The Job and Growth Tax Relief Reconciliation Act of 2003 (JGTRRA) reduces, but does not eliminate, the negative impact of double taxation of corporate income that is ultimately paid to shareholders as dividends. From 2003-2008, the tax rate on qualified dividends is reduced to 15%, and for taxpayers in the 10-15% tax bracket will be reduced to 5% through 2007 (and be 0% in 2008).

Internal Revenue Service are concerned that the interest earned on the receivables not avoid taxation entirely. Thus, if income is not taxed at the SPE level, it should be subject to taxation when received by the investors in the securities issued by the SPE. It is, therefore, common to structure the entity issuing the securities to investors so that it is not subject to an entity-level tax.

An entity that is not subject to taxation is sometimes referred to as a "pass-through" entity, meaning that the entity passes through income and expenses to others (its partners or beneficial owners) who must then pay tax on the net taxable income. A partnership, for instance, passes the income and expenses earned by the partnership through to the individual partners on a proportionate basis, and the individual partners pay income tax on their share of the partnership net income based on each partner's individual income tax rate. Similarly, a trust is an entity that typically passes through the income and expenses related to the trust assets to the beneficiaries of the trust and does not pay a separate tax at the level of the trust entity. Many SPEs are formed as trusts or treated for tax purposes as partnerships. The form of an entity for purposes of corporate law may not be the same as the characterization of the entity for tax purposes.

Sometimes an SPE is structured as an entity that is taxable as a corporation, and it may then wish to minimize its federal income tax liability by minimizing its taxable net income. A corporation's capital structure can affect its taxable net income. For instance, interest paid to creditors or debtholders (who have lent money to the corporation to finance its activities) is tax deductible, reducing the taxable net income of the corporation, while dividends paid to shareholders (the owners of the equity of a corporation) are paid out of net income after the payment of taxes and are not tax deductible. A highly leveraged corporation (one with lots of debt in relation to its equity) may be able to offset much of its income with deductions for the interest it pays to its debtholders.

C. How Are Investors Taxed on the Securities?

The third major tax issue in securitization transactions is how the investors in securities issued by the SPE will be taxed on their investment in such securities. If the securities are debt securities, the investors will be taxed in the same fashion as any other holders of debt. Interest paid on the securities will be treated as interest income. Payment of principal will be nontaxable.[8] If, on the

---

Notwithstanding this statutory reduction in the tax on dividends, the reduction is not total and is temporary. Pass-through entities will continue to provide important tax benefits to investors because not only do they totally avoid double taxation, but losses may also be passed through to investors.

[8] Original issue discount (OID), market discount, or short-term acquisition discount can arise if receivables are issued or acquired at a price less than their unpaid principal amount. The difference between principal amount and issue or acquisition price is, under certain provisions of the I.R.C., treated as equivalent to interest and taxed as ordinary income. *See* I.R.C. §§ 1271-78, 1281-83.

other hand, the securities issued by the SPE represent an ownership interest in the receivables, investors must account for their share of the SPE's income and losses and pay tax on any net taxable income.[9]

The issue of characterization of securities held by investors as debt or equity is similar, though not identical, to the sale versus loan inquiry on transfers of receivables. Characterization turns primarily on the degree of economic risk and potential upside held by the investor. A debt investment should have protection against risk of non-payment and a fixed upside. Again, the form of the investment is not conclusive. A trust certificate may be considered debt and an instrument issued pursuant to a bond indenture may be considered to be equity of the trust for tax purposes. "Thin capitalization," where the amount of capital or equity is quite small in relation to the entity's debt, generally throws doubt on characterization of securities as debt for tax purposes since the lack of capital may indicate that the purported creditor is accepting the risk of not being paid and should therefore be considered an equity owner. This factor, however, carries considerably less weight where the issuer of the purported debt securities, like a typical SPE, is a financing vehicle.[10] Accordingly, residual value or equity in an SPE of as little as 1½ to 2 percent of the SPE's assets may still permit characterization of its securities as debt, assuming the receivables (the collateral for the SPE's debt) are of high credit quality.

QUESTIONS ON TAX ISSUES

1. How does the determination of a tax sale differ from the determination of a true sale for bankruptcy purposes or a sale under generally accepted accounting principles? Should there be different standards for sale characterization depending on the purpose of the characterization?

2. Why does an SPE need to avoid entity-level taxation on its income?

§ 5.02. Securitization Structures and Types of Issuers

The best way to understand the basic tax issues just introduced is to consider them in the context of some of the more common securitization structures. Some of the structures described are the creature of Federal tax law and were designed, at least in part, to facilitate the use of securitizations as a method of lowering the cost of raising funds.

---

[9] Any tax basis remaining following prepayment or final payment of the receivable will generate a loss, and any excess of principal received over tax basis will generate a gain. Such gain, except to the extent of remaining OID, market discount, or short-term acquisition discount, will generally be capital gain to the holder if the beneficial interest is held as a capital asset. *See* I.R.C. § 1271(a).

[10] *See generally* William T. Plumb, Jr., *The Federal Income Tax Significance of Corporate Debt: A Critical Analysis and Proposal*, 26 TAX L. REV. 369, 511 (1971).

A. Securitization Structures

The structure selected for a particular securitization transaction depends on the type of assets to be securitized, what tax vehicles are available to avoid an entity-level tax on the entity issuing the securities, and the type of securities desired by investors.

1. Corporations

An SPE may be structured as a single-purpose corporation, sometimes called a "special purpose" corporation or SPC. If the SPE is a subsidiary of the originator and files consolidated tax returns with the originator, any federal income tax liability of the SPE may be offset by losses of the originator or other members of the consolidated group, alleviating some of the impact of the entity-level tax.[11] In a two-tier SPE structure, SPE1 is often a corporation that is a subsidiary of the originator. An SPE may also be structured as a corporation subject to taxation if its capital structure is such that its interest deductions fully or almost fully offset its income, minimizing the SPE's net taxable income.

2. Specific Securitization Vehicles

The federal income tax code recognizes two specific entities — REMICs and FASITs — that may be used in securitizations, neither of which is subject to an entity-level tax. Each tax structure was developed to facilitate securitizations of specific types of assets.

a) REMICs

Asset Types. We know that securitizations got their start with the pooling of mortgage loans and the issuance of securities backed by the payments received on the pooled mortgages. In 1986, Congress created Real Estate Mortgage Investment Conduits (REMICs) as a tax vehicle to facilitate the securitization of mortgage loans.[12] A REMIC is free from an entity-level tax. It may, however, hold only "qualifying assets," which include "qualified mortgages"[13]

---

[11] In addition, dividend payments can, in such case, be made tax-free to the originator, thus eliminating double taxation on the residual income remaining in the SPE after the SPE's securities are paid off. *See* Treas. Reg. § 1.1502-13.

[12] I.R.C. §§ 860D-860G.

[13] These include mortgages on residential and commercial property; stripped interests; pass-through certificates; "regular interests" in other REMICs and in FASITs, in the latter case if 95 percent or more of the value of the FASIT's assets is at all times attributable to obligations "principally secured" by interests in real property; and "qualified replacement mortgages," defined as any mortgages substituted within three months of the REMIC start-up date or substituted for defective mortgages within two years of the start-up date. I.R.C. § 860G(a)(4).

and "permitted investments."[14] "Qualified mortgages" are mortgages principally secured by real property including first and second mortgages on single-family homes, multi-family units, and commercial real estate. "Permitted investments" include passive investments that mature on or prior to the distribution dates of the REMIC's "regular" interests.[15] New assets may not be added to a REMIC after an initial three-month period, although defective mortgages may be replaced for a period of up to two years.[16] Thus, a REMIC is a passive entity. REMICs are the vehicles of choice for the issuance of mortgage-backed securities since 1992 when the taxable mortgage pool (TMP) rules became effective and essentially shut down non-REMIC mortgage securitizations[17] other than grantor trust structures discussed below.

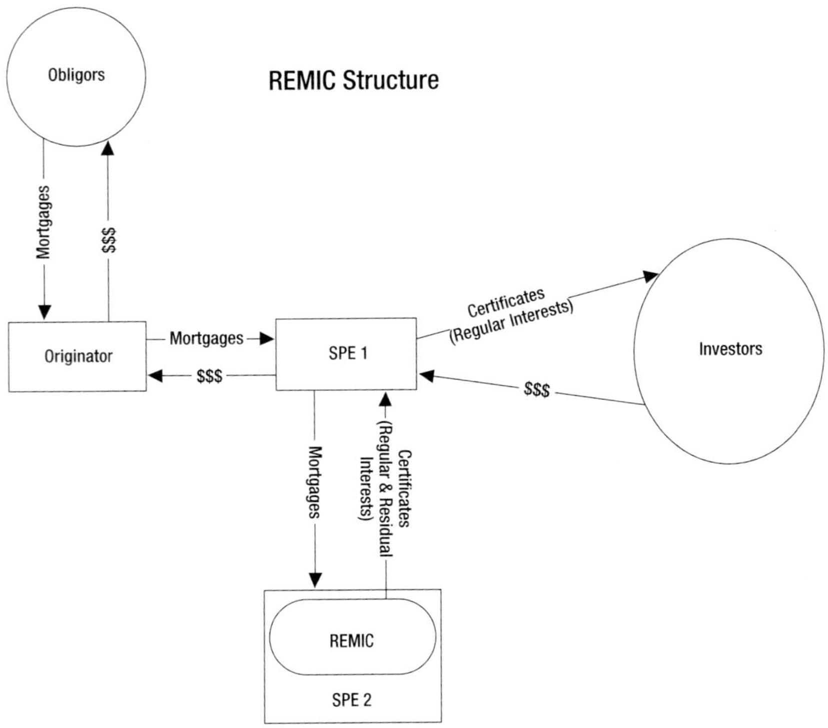

---

[14] I.R.C. § 860G(a).

[15] "Permitted investments" also include a reserve fund held by the REMIC as a credit enhancement and real property acquired in a foreclosure of a mortgage held by the REMIC so long as the real property is removed from the REMIC within three years. I.R.C. § 860G(5)-(8).

[16] *See* I.R.C. § 860G(a)(3) and (4); Treas. Reg. § 1.860G-2(b).

[17] Prior to the creation of REMICs, securitizations of mortgage-backed securities were structured as grantor trusts or collateralized mortgage obligations (CMOs). CMOs are structured as debt of special purpose corporations, while securities issued by grantor trusts are structured as pass-through (equity) interests. At that time, CMOs issued multiple classes of securities with differing maturities or sequential payment classes. Grantor trusts issued single class pass-through securities, as well

Origination. In a typical REMIC transaction, mortgages are generated by loans made by the originator to obligors secured by real estate mortgages.

First Transfer. A pool of mortgage loans is identified and transferred to an SPE in order to isolate the loans from the other operations of the originator. The SPE is also sometimes referred to as the "Depositor" of the assets into the REMIC, or, if the REMIC assets are held by a trust, the SPE may also be referred to as the "Trustor" or "Settlor." This SPE may be a subsidiary of the originator or an independent entity. If the transaction is considered a loan by the SPE to the originator secured by the mortgage loans, then there is no taxable event. If this transaction is considered a tax sale, then the originator must recognize any gain or loss on the transfer of the assets to the SPE.

Tax on Transfer of Assets to the REMIC. The transfer of mortgages to the REMIC in exchange for interests in the REMIC does not result in the recognition of gain or loss to the transferor.[18] The adjusted basis of REMIC interests received in return for a transfer of property to the REMIC is equal to the aggregate adjusted basis of the property contributed and is allocated among the interests received in proportion to their respective fair market values.[19] As the regular or residual interests are sold to investors, the SPE is required to recognize gain or loss based on the amount received in the sale in relation to its basis in the property, although if the SPE is a subsidiary of the originator any gain on the transfer may be offset by losses incurred elsewhere in the consolidated entity.

Corporate Law Structure. A REMIC can be a corporation, trust, partnership, or simply a pool of assets that has elected to be treated as a REMIC. It is important to recognize that the entity that has elected REMIC tax treatment for its REMIC assets may also hold non-REMIC assets, and that the REMIC election relates just to the REMIC assets. In the REMIC transaction diagramed here, the REMIC assets are held by a trust. The REMIC is indicated by an oval and the trust is indicated by a square that includes the oval to signify that the common law trust may also include some non-REMIC assets.

---

as interest-only (IO) and principal only (PO) strips. The IRS then ruled that grantor trusts could not be used for multi-class transactions and issued the "Sears Regulations" (so named because a subsidiary of Sears was one of the early players in the mortgage market and used grantor trust structures aggressively) to foreclose the possibility of abuse of the grantor trust structure. The Sears Regulations imposed a corporate level tax on grantor trusts that purported to issue "multiple classes of ownership interests."

The taxable mortgage pool (TMP) rules became effective in 1992 and effectively shut down non-REMIC mortgage securitizations (other than grantor trust structures) like CMOs by instituting a corporate level tax on any mortgage pooling transaction that resulted in the issuance of securities with more than one maturity. The Sears Regulations and the TMP rules have essentially forced mortgage-backed securitizations issuing multiple classes of securities to be structured as REMICs for tax purposes.

18 *See* I.R.C. § 860F(b)(1)(A).

19 *See* I.R.C. § 860F(b)(1)(B).

Entity-Level Taxation of Issuer. For tax purposes, a REMIC is treated like a trust and is not subject to taxation.[20]

Sale to the Underwriter. The SPE sells the REMIC interests to an underwriter or placement agent who will in turn sell the interests to the ultimate investors. The underwriter pays cash which is used to fund the purchase of the receivables from the originator. When these REMIC interests are sold by the SPE, it must recognize any gain or loss on the amount received in the sale in relation to its basis in the property.

Tax Treatment of REMIC Securities. The securities issued by a REMIC are sometimes referred to as "REMIC interests" and take the form of trust certificates. A REMIC must issue *at least one* "regular interest" and may issue *only one* "residual interest." Regular interests are treated as debt instruments for federal tax purposes even if they are issued in non-debt form (*i.e.*, as certificates of ownership of the underlying assets) for state law purposes to accommodate regulatory and financial accounting requirements. One or more classes of regular interests may be issued, one subordinate to another. To qualify as a regular interest, the interest must have a fixed term and unconditionally entitle the holder thereof to receive a specified principal amount.[21] Interest on regular interests generally must be based on one or more fixed rates or certain prescribed variable rates.[22] Holders of regular interests of a REMIC are taxed as are holders of any debt instruments, except that income relating to such interests must be accounted for using the accrual method of accounting, regardless of the accounting method used by the holder of the regular interest.[23]

The residual interest is treated as the equity interest in the REMIC and therefore the holder of the residual interest has tax liability for any taxable net income of the REMIC. The residual interest may, however, have a value of $0 and the REMIC can be structured to have no taxable net income. All assets, liabilities and items of income, gain, deduction, loss, and credit of a REMIC pass through to the holder of the REMIC "residual interest." The character of the income to the holder of an ownership or residual interest is the same as its character to the REMIC. Deductions passed through to a holder of an ownership or residual interest in a REMIC include a deduction for any interest accrued to holders of regular REMIC interests.

---

20 I.R.C. § 860A(a).

21 I.R.C. §§ 860G(a)(1); 860L(b)(1).

22 I.R.C. §§ 860G(a)(1)(B)(I); 860L(b)(1)(A)(ii). The permissible variable rate is generally a "qualified floating rate" as defined in Treas. Reg. § 1.1275-5(b)(1) and may, in the case of REMICs, also be a rate based on a specific (non-varying) portion of interest received by the REMIC, with respect to obligations held by it. *See* Treas. Reg. § 1.860G-1(a)(3).

23 I.R.C. §§ 860B(b); 860H(c)(3). In addition, any gain on sale of a regular REMIC interest is treated as ordinary income to the extent that prescribed rate of return exceeds any previously reported ordinary income. I.R.C. § 860B(c).

b) FASITs

Effective September 1, 1997, a new tax vehicle, a "Financial Assets Securitization Trust" (FASIT),[24] became available for the issuance of mortgage-backed and asset-backed securities. It was initially designed to extend REMIC-like tax treatment to the securitization of non-real estate assets. Thus, an entity that elects tax treatment as a FASIT is not treated as a separate taxable entity. Its sponsor (the transferor of the financial assets to the FASIT) will be treated as if it was the owner of the assets in the FASIT and as if it was the issuer of the FASIT securities. A FASIT has two forms of interests: regular interests (like debt) and a single ownership interest (like equity and comparable to a REMIC residual interest). The permitted assets of a FASIT include cash, cash equivalents, and debt instruments.

Although the FASIT structure bears many similarities to the tried and tested REMIC structure, some problematic provisions were included in the FASIT legislation. The most significant issue is that the transferor that sells asset into a FASIT must recognize taxable gain on the assets at an artificially high rate at the time of the establishment of the FASIT.[25] Any loss on the assets sold to the FASIT, however, may not be recognized by the transferor. As a result of this problem and others, the FASIT vehicle has not been used much in securitizations.

The taxation of the owners of the regular interests and the ownership interest is comparable to that for the owners of a REMIC's regular interests and residual interest.

3. Commercial Trusts

The structures used in many securitization transactions involve trusts. Although many trusts are created by solely gratuitous transfers, such as a trust set up by an individual for the benefit of a relative, "in truth, *most of the wealth that is held in trust in the United States is placed there incident to business deals,* and not in connection with gratuitous transfers."[26] Trusts created for commercial purposes — such as a securitization — may, under certain circumstances, receive the same tax treatment as trusts created by gratuitous transfers. Although the tax treatment of gratuitous trusts and commercial trusts

---

[24] I.R.C. §§ 860H-860L, enacted as part of the Small Business Job Protection Act of 1996, Pub. L. No. 104-188, § 1621, 110 Stat. 1755, 1858.

[25] I.R.C. § 860I(a)(1); 860I(d).

[26] John H. Langbein, *The Secret Life of the Trust: The Trust as an Instrument of Commerce,* 107 YALE L.J. 166 (1997) (emphasis in original).

may be the same, there are some critical differences in the two types of trusts.[27] In a typical gratuitous trust, the donor of the gift (the settlor) conveys the assets to a trustee to hold for the benefit of a beneficiary. The settlor in a gratuitous trust receives no compensation for the conveyance, whereas the settlor in a commercial trust — typically a corporation or financial institution — always receives payment for the assets conveyed to the trust. One therefore can view a commercial trust as a trust in which there is a bargained-for exchange rather than a gift. A more subtle difference is that the settlor in a gratuitous trust may or may not retain a residual interest in the trust assets, whereas the settlor in a commercial trust almost always retains a residual interest in the trust assets that remain once the business transaction is concluded. Another way of thinking about this difference is comparing the nature of the beneficiary. In a gratuitous trust, the beneficiary (an individual or entity) generally is the sole equitable owner of the trust assets, with the legal title to the trust assets retained by the trustee. In a commercial trust, the trustee also has legal title to the trust assets, but the beneficial interests of the trusts may be split up in a number of different ways. The settlor may retain a residual interest in the trust assets through its ownership of certificates issued by the trust, which mirror equity interests in a corporation in many respects. Investors also have beneficial interests in the trust assets as the holders of equity type certificates in the trust or debt-like certificates, sometimes issued as notes of the trusts.

A commercial trust can be illustrated by a typical example from structured finance. A company settles a trust by transferring financial assets to the trust in return for payment in the form of trust certificates and a bargained-for residual interest in the trust. The company then raises funds by selling the trust certificates to capital market investors, who buy the certificates expecting that the trust assets will generate sufficient cash to repay their investment plus the contractual rate of return specified in the certificates. The residual interest entitles the company to any assets remaining in the trust once the certificates are paid in full. In this way, the company does not give up more value than needed to make the deal work.

---

27 *See generally* Steven L. Schwarcz, *Commercial Trusts as Business Organizations: Unraveling the Mystery,* 58 Bus. Law. 559 (2003). Interestingly, the American Law Institute's Restatement of Trusts focuses exclusively on gratuitous trusts, noting:

> The law relating to the use of trusts as devices for conducting business and investment activities outside the express private- and charitable-trust context is not within the scope of this Restatement. Although many rules of trust law may also apply to business and investment trusts, many of these rules do not; instead other rules are drawn from other bodies of law that are specially applicable to those activities even when conducted in trust form. Thus, the business trust is a business arrangement that is best dealt with in connection with business associations; and most pooled investment vehicles are properly governed by laws applicable to investment companies and to the issuance and sale of securities.

Restatement (Third) of Trusts § 1, cmt. b. (2003).

The deal is thus an arm's length, negotiated bargain in which all parties benefit. The investors, as senior claimants of the trust, get their money back with interest. The company, as residual claimant, receives payment for the financial assets sold to the trust and is entitled to any residual value of those assets once the investors are paid in full. In economic terms, the deal is similar to a secured loan in which surplus collateral is returned to the debtor once lenders receive principal and interest.

Trusts used as SPEs in securitizations usually have three common descriptive features. First, they are relatively static entities. They usually do not operate an ongoing business but rather issue trust certificates with debt-like characteristics, repayable from cash generated by the assets acquired by the SPE. Second, any residual value of the trust assets is returned to the originator once the business transaction is consummated. The originator normally preserves this residual value by retaining a residual trust certificate. Third, trusts created pursuant to contract are not subject to entity-level taxes if their separate existence is not recognized under tax law.

A few states, including Massachusetts and Delaware, specifically recognize as a separate legal entity a "business trust" created under the state's business trust law, in which property is conveyed to a trustee and managed for the benefit of holders of certificates.[28] This state law trust structure contemplates active management while the tax code-created grantor trust (described below) does not permit management of the trust assets. Under the Delaware Business Trust Act, enacted in 1988, Delaware trust law applies to a business trust "[e]xcept to the extent otherwise provided in the governing instrument."[29] The statute specifically states that the "duties (including fiduciary duties)" of a trustee to a trust or its beneficial owner may be "restricted" by the governing instrument and any trustee "acting under a governing instrument shall not be liable to the business trust or to any such beneficial owner" for relying in good faith on the governing instrument.[30] The statute also grants a business trust broad powers to indemnify and "hold harmless" any person "from and against any and all claims and demands whatsoever."[31]

A business trust, at least under Delaware law, is therefore a state law trust that is modified by contract as is necessary to reallocate the trustee's rights and obligations in order to meet business requirements. Unlike other commercial trusts, a business trust is not a "type" of trust that satisfies a specific business purpose. Rather, a business trust is any trust that is created pursuant to a state's business trust law. Business trusts can be created as SPEs, to comply

---

[28] *See generally* Tamar Frankel, *The Delaware Business Trust Act Failure as the New Corporate Law,* 23 Cardozo L. Rev. 325 (2001); Henry Hansmann & Ugo Mattei, *The Functions of Trust Law: A Comparative Legal and Economic Analysis,* 73 N.Y.U. L. Rev. 434 (1998).

[29] Del. Code Ann. tit. 12 § 3809 (2001 & Supp. 2002).

[30] *Id.* § 3806(c).

[31] *Id.* § 3817(a).

with regulatory restrictions, or for any other purpose that commercial trusts are created. The descriptive characteristics of business trusts would be those of the type of trust created.

Once we have distinguished "commercial" trusts from gratuitous trusts, it is also important to understand some of the different types of commercial trusts that may be used in structured finance.

a) Grantor Trust

Asset Types. Grantor trusts are typically used for the securitization of a variety of non-revolving assets types, such as student loans, equipment leases, auto loans, and home mortgage loans (including second mortgages). A grantor trust must be passive, and thus its trustee may not purchase or substitute new assets or reinvest monies held by the trust. For this reason, grantor trusts cannot be used for revolving assets like credit card receivables or for pools of short-term receivables such as trade receivables since such asset pools must be managed and replenished by the trustee.

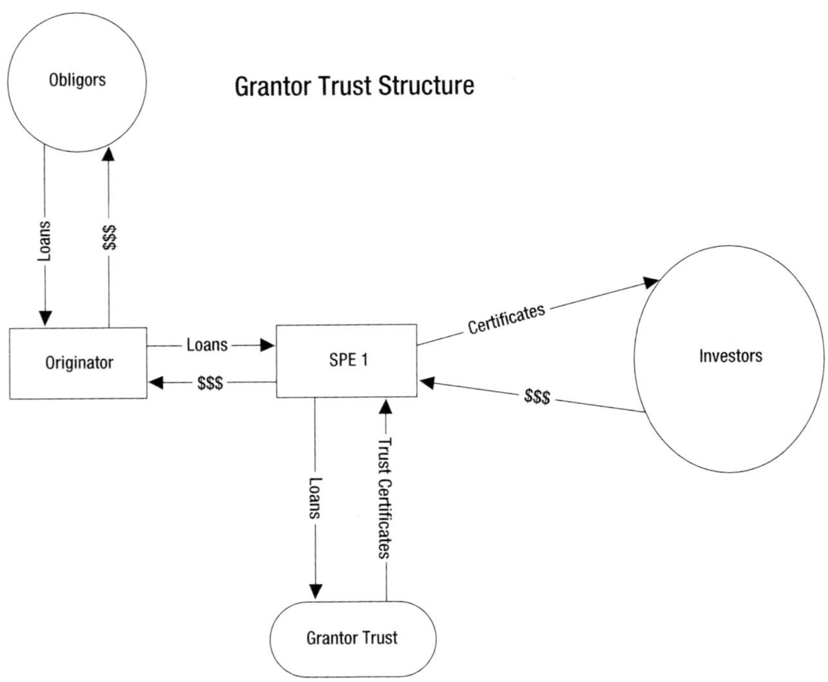

The structure for a securitization utilizing a grantor trust is virtually identical to that for a REMIC.

Origination. The assets are originated by loans or leases made by the originator to the underlying obligors.

First Transfer. A pool of loans is identified and transferred to an SPE, sometimes also called the depositor. If the transfer is structured as a loan for tax purposes, there is no taxable event upon the transfer. If the transfer is a taxable sale, then tax must be paid on any income realized from the sale of assets, although if the SPE is a subsidiary of the originator, the gain may be offset by losses elsewhere in the consolidated enterprise.

Tax on Transfer of Assets to the Grantor Trust. The transfer of the receivables by the SPE to the grantor trust in exchange for all of the pass-through certificates issued by the trust is not a taxable event.

Corporate Law Structure. The grantor trust will typically be structured as a common law trust under the law of the state of its creation.

Entity-level Taxation of Issuer. The grantor trust must meet the requirements of sections 671 through 679 of the I.R.C. to be nontaxable as an entity. The IRS has specifically recognized the ability of a trust organized for an investment purpose to be qualify as a grantor trust.

> In general, a trust for federal tax purposes is limited to a trust created simply to conserve or protect property for the trust beneficiaries. Ordinarily, the beneficiaries of the trust do no more than accept its benefits and are not its creators or voluntary planners. Certain "investment" trusts, however, are recognized as serving the traditional custodial purposes of an ordinary trust even though interests therein are voluntarily acquired by the beneficiaries. Thus, investment trusts have been treated as trusts for federal tax purposes where employed simply to hold investment assets, albeit for the benefit of voluntary investors.

T.D. 8080, 1986-1 C.F. 371.

Some of these limitations on the grantor trust structure have reduced its popularity as a securitization vehicle. One limitation is the requirement that the grantor trust be a passive entity, which acts to restrict the types of assets that may be securitized.

Sale to the Underwriter. The trust certificates are transferred to the SPE in return for its contribution of the assets to the grantor trust. When the SPE sells the certificates to the underwriter, this is treated as a sale of the underlying receivables and any gain or loss on the sale must be recognized for tax purposes.

Tax Treatment of Securities. Items of income and loss realized by the trust are passed through to the holders of the trust certificates, who pay the appropriate tax on any net income as the beneficial owners of the trust assets, thus giving rise to the common reference to the securities as "pass-through" securities. The cash collections on the receivables "pass-through" the trust to the holders of the certificates. A further limitation of the grantor trust structure is that the trust may only have multiple classes of beneficial interests where the classes are incidental to the purpose of facilitating direct investment in the assets of the trust.[32] Two classes are permitted where the sole distinction between the classes is that payments with respect to one class are subordinate to payments with respect to the other. The rationale for permitting this senior/subordinated structure is that its purpose is to facilitate direct investment in the assets of the trust. The senior class typically is sold to investors, with the transferor retaining the subordinate class as a form of overcollateralization, although the IRS has held that both the senior and subordinate classes may be sold to investors.[33] Each class of certificates represents beneficial ownership in the trust assets that is similar to an equity interest in a corporation.

b) Owner Trust

Asset Types. This structure is often used for student loans, equipment loans, and auto loans. Indeed, it is the structure used in the Honda deal. It is generally not used to securitize mortgage loans.

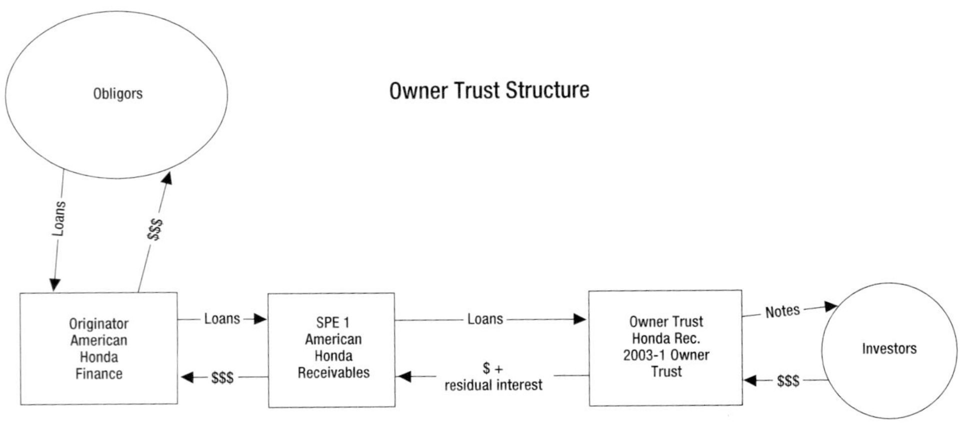

Origination. The loans are originated by an originator such as American Honda Finance from purchasers of cars from Honda Motor dealerships who elect to finance their purchase through American Honda Finance.

First Transfer. The first transfer of assets is to American Honda Receivables Corp., the SPE. American Honda Receivables is a wholly owned subsidiary of the originator, American Honda Finance, so any gain recognized on this sale of assets may be offset by losses of the consolidated enterprise.

Tax on Transfer of the Assets to the Owner Trust. Any gain on the sale of the assets when they are transferred to the Honda Receivables 2003-1 Owner Trust is taxable to the transferor, American Honda Receivables.

32 *See* Treas. Reg. §§ 301.7701-4(a), 301.7701-4(c); *see* Rev. Rul. 78-149, 1978-1 C.B. 448.

33 Rev. Rul. 92-32, 1992-1 C.B. 434.

Corporate Law Structure. An owner trust is the generic name given to a entity formed as a trust under state law, including a business trust recognized as a particular kind of trust in a few states. An owner trust is created by a depositor who transfers assets to the trust for a cash payment by the trust. The owner trust issues debt and equity securities and is considered for tax purposes to be either a grantor trust or a partnership. Often the owner trust is a Delaware of Massachusetts business trust for purposes of corporate law.

In the Honda deal, the owner trust is a Delaware business trust. The trustee of the owner trust is Bank of New York. The Bank of New York (Delaware) — a separate bank — is the trustee of the Delaware business trust. The prospectus states that the Delaware trustee is appointed only because of a requirement in the Delaware business trust statute that a trustee of the business trust be a resident of Delaware (if a natural person) or have its principal place of business in Delaware. The duties and responsibilities of the Delaware trustee in the Honda deal are specifically limited to the execution and delivery of the documents and certificates necessary to form and maintain the trust under the Delaware statute. Further, the Delaware trustee is relieved of any other management or fiduciary responsibilities.

Entity-Level Taxation of Issuer. The owner trust is not a separately recognized entity under the tax law, as is a grantor trust, REMIC or FASIT. Thus, the owner trust must either qualify as a grantor trust or be freed from an entity-level tax through the application of the "check-the-box" regulations.

Check-the-box regulations. The so-called "check-the-box" regulations, effective in 1997, permit an unincorporated entity to elect to be taxable as a partnership,[34] rather than as an entity taxable as a corporation. "The theory behind the check the box is that entity classification is already largely elective for the well-advised, and that resources currently spent by taxpayers and the IRS dealing with classification issues are better spent elsewhere."[35] These IRS regulations replaced the existing test under federal tax law to distinguish between unincorporated business entities that must be treated as corporations and are subject to an entity-level tax, and partnerships that are not. The "check-the-box" regulations permit a state law trust, and many other non-corporate entities, to simply elect to avoid an entity-level tax by choosing to be taxed as a partnership or, in the case of an entity with a single owner, simply to be ignored unless it is a "publicly traded partnership."[36]

Publicly traded partnership. A "publicly traded partnership" cannot escape entity taxation under the check-the-box rules. A partnership or other

---

[34] Treas. Reg. §§ 301.7701-2; 301.7701-3.

[35] Donald G. Carden, *Tax Legislation and Proposed Treasury Regulations Offer New Structuring Options*, *in* New Developments in Securitization 1996 77, 81-82 (Practising Law Institute 1996).

[36] Treas. Reg. §§ 301.7701-2; 301.7701-3.

entity (including a trust treated as a partnership under the check-the-box rules) that is a "publicly traded partnership" (PTP) within the meaning of Section 7704(b) of the I.R.C. and the regulations thereunder may be subject to tax as if it were a corporation. A partnership is a PTP if interests in it are traded on an "established securities market"[37] or readily tradable on a "secondary market or the substantial equivalent thereof."[38]

Interests in SPEs are typically not traded on established securities exchanges. Under applicable regulations,[39] however, interests will be *deemed* traded on the substantial equivalent of an established securities market if, taking into account all facts and circumstances, the partners are readily able to buy, sell or exchange their interests in a manner that is comparable economically to trading on an established securities market.

In order to avoid a finding of interests being traded on a secondary market or the substantial equivalent thereof, SPEs are typically structured so as to fall into a "private placement" safe harbor set forth in the PTP regulations. Under the safe harbor, a partnership will not be deemed to be a PTP so long as all interests in the partnership are issued in a transaction that is not required to be registered under the Securities Act of 1933, and so long as there are no more than 100 partners at any time during a taxable year.[40] It is therefore common to see provisions in agreements governing the operations of SPEs that limit the number of partners and provide for other restrictions on the trading of interests therein.

In the Honda deal, tax counsel is requested to issue a legal opinion that the trust is not taxable as a corporation or as a publicly traded partnership.

Tax Treatment of Notes and Certificates. Unlike a grantor trust, which issues certificates that are treated for many purposes like the equity in a corporation and convey ownership in the trust assets, an owner trust may issue beneficial interests that have debt characteristics as well as beneficial interests that have equity characteristics. Thus, an owner trust issues debt securities (notes) secured by the assets and also issues equity securities (certificates). The debt securities may have multiple maturities. The certificates may not include more than two classes if the owner trust is to be treated as a grantor trust for tax purposes. The money received from the securities issued is used to pay the SPE for the assets. The debt security holders do not own the underlying assets in this arrangement. The income and losses of the trust flow through to the owners of the equity securities issued by the trust. Note holders pay tax on the interest income they receive on the trust notes. The certificate holder is taxed on the net taxable income of the trust that passes through to it. If the cer-

---

37 *Id.* § 1.7704-1(b).

38 I.R.C. § 7704(b).

39 Treas. Reg § 1.7704-1.

40 *Id.* § 1.7704-1(h).

tificates are held by a single corporate entity, then the notes issued by the trust will be treated as if the owner of the certificates had issued them and the owner may deduct the interest on the notes in determining the net taxable income of the trust on which it owes tax. If the owner trust is characterized as a partnership on the check-the-box form, then the holders of the certificates (the equity) are treated like partners of the partnership and the holders of the notes (the debt) are treated like creditors of the partnership. If the owner trust is a grantor trust, then the equity certificate holders hold the ownership interest in the trust (in the same manner as the certificate holders of a regular grantor trust) and the holders of the debt issued by the trust are creditors of the trust.

In the Honda deal in Chapter 1, the owner trust issued four classes of notes and one class of certificates. The certificates were not part of the public offering and were to be retained by Honda Receivables. The certificates are subordinated to all four classes of notes and at the time of issuance constituted 2.25% of the initial principal balance of all the notes and the certificates. Counsel in the Honda deal is required to opine that the notes are debt of the owner trust. The offering documents also indicate that the purchaser of the notes agrees to treat the notes as debt. The certificate holders agree to teat the trust as a partnership in which the owners of the certificates are partners or, if there is only one beneficial owner of the certificates, then the certificate owner agrees to treat the trust as a disregarded entity and the certificate holder will be responsible for paying taxes on the taxable income of the trust.

c) Master Trust

Asset Types. Master trusts are often used to securitize credit cards, trade receivables and other revolving loans not secured by real estate. A master trust may be used by a company engaged in securitization that has significantly more assets than the amount of financing it currently needs. For example, a company with $50 million in trade receivables may need only $20 million of financing. Although the simplest solution would be to allocate a portion of the assets to the financing, in practice companies rarely can segregate the assets to dedicate to the financing on a cost-effective basis. They usually keep records on categories of assets, and it is difficult to obtain separate reporting for assets within a category. Some companies also may have seasonal fluctuations in financing needs so that the assets dedicated to the financing may fluctuate over time, or they may want to diversify their funding sources based on a single pool of assets.

A master trust responds to these needs. In the business transaction underlying a master trust, a company transfers specified financial assets to the SPE and the SPE transfers the assets to the trust in return for which the trust will issue at least one class of trust certificates plus a residual interest in the trust. The master trust will sell the certificates to investors which will generate the cash used to pay the SPE for the assets. In addition to cash, the SPE also receives the residual interest in the master trust. If the dollar value of the certificates is small compared to the amount of assets transferred to the trust, the amount of the residual interest may be quite substantial.

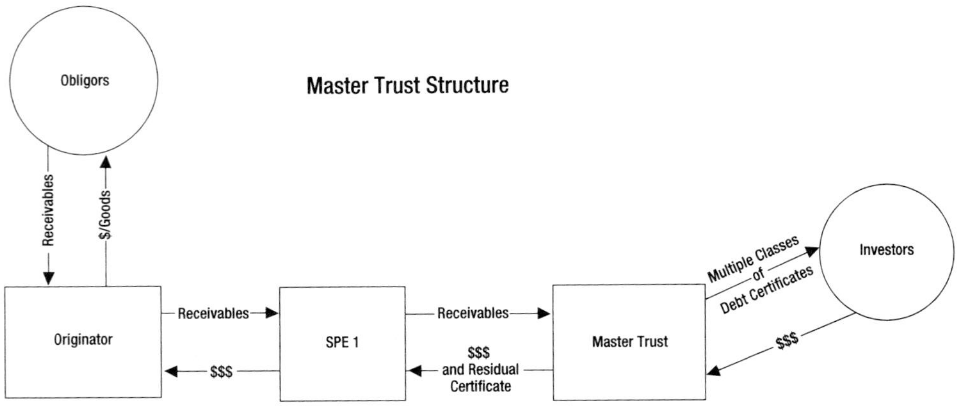

Corporate Law Structure. The master trust may be structured in a variety of ways, for instance as a limited liability company or as a business trust.

Entity-Level Taxation of Issuer. The master trust may elect partnership tax treatment under the check-the-box regulations so long as it is not considered a publicly traded partnership. Because multiple classes of securities are usually issued by a master trust (as discussed below), a master trust will not qualify for tax treatment as a grantor trust.

Tax Treatment of Securities Issued. The securities issued by the master trust are trust certificates. They are sometimes called "pass-through *debt* certificates." A master trust is flexible in that it permits more than one class of beneficial interests to be issued. If in the future the company wishes to undertake additional financing, it can notify the trustee to issue additional classes of trust certificates. Each class of certificates can have its own interest rate, events of default, covenants, maturities, and other rights, obligations and remedies. Furthermore, one or more classes of certificates can be subordinated to repayment of other classes in order to achieve an overall lower financing rate for the trust. The only limitation on the characteristics of future classes of trust certificates are contractual restrictions in the trust agreement intended to protect previously-issued certificates. This flexibility in fashioning different substantive rights and obligations for diversified classes of certificates greatly expands the range of investors who may be interested in investing, thereby increasing the total amount of financing that can be raised from the assets. Indeed, different classes of trust certificates coming from the same trust may be sold publicly as well as privately.

From a technical standpoint, master trusts combine the trust form with what are sometimes called "intercreditor agreements." Intercreditor agreements are simply contracts among multiple creditors of a debtor that allocate the respective rights, obligations, and remedies of the creditors with respect to the debtor's assets. A master trust effectively serves as an intercreditor agreement by specifying in advance many of the fundamental characteristics of the trust certificates. By defining investor rights in advance, the company controls those rights and also avoids the difficulty and expense of trying to negotiate with multiple classes of investors after trust certificates have been issued. Ultimately, master trusts are successful because they are an efficient way to diversify investor risk by permitting securities to be sold not only to multiple individual investors but also to multiple classes of investors.

4. Limited Liability Companies (LLCs)

SPEs increasingly are being formed as limited liability companies (LLCs). An LLC combines the limited liability afforded to the shareholder of a corporation with the pass-through tax treatment available to a partnership by an election of partnership tax treatment for a non-incorporated entity under the IRS check-the-box regulations. Under Delaware law, an LLC may elect a governance structure based on either a corporate or partnership model.[41] Other state statutes may not be as flexible.[42]

QUESTIONS ON SECURITIZATION STRUCTURES

1. Could any structure other than the owner trust structure have been used in the Honda deal?

2. How does the tax code facilitate securitizations? Is this sound tax policy? Is it better to create specific securitization vehicles under the Internal Revenue Code, such as REMICs or FASITs, or to more broadly adopt check-the-box regulations which permit parties to elect a particular tax characterization?

3. What special advantages does a business trust, as recognized in Delaware and Massachusetts, have from the perspective of the trustee of the trust? If there is a separate trustee who actually manages the trust (the owner trustee in the Honda Deal) is there anything to be gained from the business trust form?

---

41 Robert W. Hamilton, Corporations Including Partnerships and Limited Liability Companies 188-211(7th ed. 2001).

42 *Id.* At 192.

Chapter 6

SECURITIES LAWS AND THE INVESTMENT COMPANY ACT

We have been describing the process of securitizing financial assets (or loans or receivables). The end result of that process — as the name indicates — is the issuance of securities in the capital markets to investors that are backed by the expected payments by the obligors on the financial assets. As with any issuance of securities, careful lawyers have to explore whether the issuance of the securities requires registration under the Securities Act of 1933 (the 1933 Act).[1] Further, given the nature of most SPE's securities and structure, another issue is whether the SPE has become an "investment company" within the meaning of the Investment Company Act of 1940 (the 1940 Act).[2] We take up the 1940 Act issues first.

§ 6.01. Investment Company Act of 1940

The 1940 Act provides that any entity principally engaged in owning or holding "securities" — such as a mutual fund — must, subject to certain exemptions, register with the Securities and Exchange Commission (SEC) as an investment company. One way to think of an investment company is as a miniature stock exchange in which the investors in the company can be thought of as investors in stock traded on the exchange. The 1940 Act was promulgated as part of the comprehensive federal securities legislation enacted through the 1930s to curb a number of perceived abuses in the United States securities markets, to protect the public from being defrauded, and to ensure adequate controls and information. Unlike the 1933 Act and the non-broker-dealer sections of the Securities Exchange Act of 1934 (the 1934 Act),[3] which focus principally on the adequacy of disclosure in connection with the issuance, sale, and trading of securities, the 1940 Act is a comprehensive, *substantive* regulatory scheme. Compliance with the 1940 Act is usually very costly and burdensome.[4] Accord-

---

[1] 15 U.S.C. §§ 77a *et seq*. State "blue sky" laws may also be applicable and require that nay securities offered in a state be registered with the state. *See generally* SECURITIZATION OF FINANCIAL ASSETS § 11.02 (Jason H.P. Kravitt ed. 2d ed. 2003).

[2] 15 U.S.C. §§ 80a *et seq*.

[3] 15 U.S.C. §§ 78a *et seq*.

[4] For example, the 1940 Act imposes the following general requirements on registered investment companies:

1. restrictions on capital structure (*e.g.*, prohibitions or restrictions on the issuance of debt securities) in section 18;
2. restrictions on the composition of the board of directors or other governing body (*e.g.*, limits on the number of "interested persons" appointed) in sections 10 and 16;

ingly, registration of an SPE as an investment company is generally considered not feasible and, if possible, lawyers try to structure transactions so as to be exempt from 1940 Act registration.

Under section 3(a)(1) of the 1940 Act, an "investment company" is defined in relevant part as an issuer of securities that is either "engaged primarily . . . in the business of investing, reinvesting, or trading in securities"; or "engaged" to an extent (although not primarily) in such business, but "owns or proposes to acquire investment securities having a value exceeding 40 per centum of the value of such issuer's total assets (exclusive of Government securities and cash items) on an unconsolidated basis."[5] The term "security" is defined broadly under section 2(a)(36) of the 1940 Act to include notes, stocks, bonds, evidences of indebtedness, transferable shares, investment contracts, and "any interest or instrument commonly known as a 'security.'"[6]

Most receivables and payment streams appear to fall within the definition of the term "security" under the 1940 Act, because they are "evidences of indebtedness." Nevertheless, several exemptions from registration as an investment company may be available to an SPE. The most significant is the exemption provided by Rule 3a-7 promulgated under the 1940 Act as well as certain exemptions available under section 3(c) of the 1940 Act.

A. Section 3(c) Exemptions

Section 3(c) sets forth the 1940 Act's primary statutory exemptions. The text of the most relevant statutory exemptions is excerpted below. Section 3(c)(5)(A), for example, excludes from the definition of "investment company" entities that are "primarily engaged" in acquiring receivables that constitute "notes, drafts, acceptances, open accounts receivable, and other obligations representing part or all of the sales price of merchandise, insurance, and services."

---

3. restrictions on investment activities (*e.g.*, limits on investments in other investment companies) in section 12(d) and (e);
4. regulation of advertising (*e.g.*, filing of sales literature with the SEC) in section 24(b);
5. required shareholder votes on a number of issues (*e.g.*, approval of advisers' contracts, changes in investment policies, and appointment of auditors) in sections 13 and 15(a);
6. ongoing reporting and disclosure requirements in section 30; and
7. extensive and complicated controls on pricing of investment company shares in section 22.

5 15 U.S.C. § 80a-3.

6 15 U.S.C. § 80a-2. Under section 3(a)(2), the term "investment securities" is generally defined to include all securities except government securities, securities issued by employees' securities companies, and securities issued by majority-held subsidiaries (provided the owner is not itself an investment company). *Id.* § 80a-3(a)(2).

Many, but not all, types of receivables fall under this exclusion.[7] Included are the most common type of receivable — trade accounts receivable — since they clearly constitute the purchase price of merchandise, thereby taking advantage of the last clause of the exception.[8] Other types of receivables, however, might not come clearly within the section 3(c)(5)(A) exclusion.[9] In some of those instances, however, it has been possible to obtain a "no-action" letter[10] from the SEC, which in practice has basically the same effect as an exemption from investment company registration.

In the Days Inn of America, Inc. letter,[11] for example, the SEC staff stated that it would not recommend an enforcement action under section 3(c)(5)(A) if a wholly owned subsidiary of Days Inn acquired certain franchise fee receivables from Days Inn (through another subsidiary), privately issued and sold notes secured by those receivables, and lent the net proceeds from the note sales to Days Inn to refinance certain indebtedness of the parent company. The receivables were characterized as obligations representing part or all of the sales price of various services rendered by Days Inn to its franchisees, and on that basis were found to fall within the scope of section 3(c)(5)(A).

Even if section 3(c)(5) does not cover the receivables in question, other statutory exemptions may still be available. Section 3(c)(1), for example, provides that "[a]ny issuer whose outstanding securities (other than short-term paper) are beneficially owned by not more than one hundred persons and which is not making and does not presently propose to make a public offering of its securities" is excluded for most purposes from the definition of "investment com-

---

[7] 15 U.S.C. § 80a-3(a)(5)(A). Section 3(c)(5)(C) similarly exempts entities that are primarily engaged in "purchasing or otherwise acquiring mortgages and other liens on and interests in real estate." *Id.* § 80a-3(c)(5)(C). This was the exemption that originally was used in securitizing mortgage loans. Section 3(c)(5)(B) also exempts entities primarily engaged in making loans to manufacturers, wholesalers, retailers, and prospective purchasers of "specific merchandise, insurance, and services." *Id.* § 80a-3(c)(5)(B).

[8] *See* 1940 Act § 3(c)(5)(A), 12 U.S.C. § 80a-3(c)(5)(A)222 (sales price of merchandise).

[9] The SEC has repeatedly emphasized the legislative history of section 3(c)(5)(A), (B) (originally 1940 Act § 3(c)(6)(A), (B), 54 Stat. at 798–99), which indicates that those subsections were intended to exclude sales finance companies, factoring companies, and similar entities from the scope of the 1940 Act. In the case of section 3(c)(5)(B), the SEC staff has interpreted that exemption somewhat narrowly and has refused, for example, to issue no-action letters to companies engaged in making general working capital loans. *See, e.g.,* Alleco, Inc., SEC No-Action Letter, Ref. No. 88-165, 1988 SEC No-Act. LEXIS 921 (July 14, 1988) (section 3(c)(5)(B) does not include "a loan that does not relate to the purchase price of specific goods or services even if the loan is secured by the same kind of collateral that secures a sales financing loan").

[10] A "no-action" letter is a nonbinding response by the SEC staff to a private inquiry indicating that the staff of the SEC will not recommend to the SEC that any enforcement action be taken if a proposed transaction is carried out in a specific manner.

[11] Days Inn of America, Inc., SEC No-Action Letter, Ref. No. 88-688-CC, 1988 SEC No-Act. LEXIS 1737 (Dec. 30, 1988).

pany."[12] This so-called private investment company exemption is sometimes used in conjunction with the private offering exemption under the 1933 Act (discussed below). Also, section 3(c)(7) of the 1940 Act provides a partial exemption for "[a]ny issuer, the outstanding securities of which are owned exclusively by persons who, at the time of acquisition of such securities, are qualified purchasers [as defined in section 2(a)(51)(A)], and which is not making and does not at that time propose to make a public offering of such securities."[13]

If no statutory exemption is clearly available, sections 3(b)(2) and 6(c) of the 1940 Act permit an SPE to petition the SEC to issue an order exempting the SPE from registration on the grounds that either (1) the SPE is primarily engaged in a business other than that of investing, owning, or trading in securities (under section 3(b)(2)) or (2) an exemption is necessary or appropriate in the public interest and is consistent with the protection of investors and the other purposes of the 1940 Act (under section 6(c)).[14] Obtaining a decision on such an application can take several months, and certainly there is no guarantee that an exemptive order will ultimately be issued by the SEC. Nevertheless, there is sometimes no alternative if investment company registration is not cost-effective and another exemption cannot be found.

Investment Company Act of 1940
Section 3
15 U.S.C. § 80a-3(c)

(c) Further exemptions. Notwithstanding subsection (a) of this section, none of the following persons is an investment company within the meaning of this subchapter:

(1) Any issuer whose outstanding securities (other than short-term paper) are beneficially owned by not more than one hundred persons and which is not making and does not presently propose to make a public offering of its securities. Such issuer shall be deemed to be an investment company for purposes of the limitations set forth in subparagraphs (A)(I) and (B)(I) of section 80a-12(d)(1) of this title [15 U.S.C. §§ 80a-12(d)(1)(A)(I), (B)(I)] governing the purchase or other acquisition by such issuer of any security issued by any registered

---

12 15 U.S.C. § 80a-3(c)(1). In placing interests with institutional investors and other entities under the exemption for 100 persons or fewer set forth in section 3(c)(1), care must be taken to comply with the rule for determining beneficial ownership under section 3(c)(1)(A). Although beneficial ownership by a company is generally deemed to be ownership by only one person, it is necessary to look through the investing company and count its ultimate security holders if the company owns 10% or more of the outstanding voting securities of the SPE *and* is — or but for the section 3(c)(1) or 3(c)(7) exemptions would be — an investment company.

13 15 U.S.C. § 80a-3(c)(7).

14 *Id.* §§ 80a-3(b)(2) & 80a-6(c).

investment company and the sale of any security issued by any registered open-end investment company to any such issuer. For purposes of this paragraph:

(A) Beneficial ownership by a company shall be deemed to be beneficial ownership by one person, except that, if the company owns 10 per centum or more of the outstanding voting securities of the issuer, and is or, but for the exception provided for in this paragraph or paragraph (7), would be an investment company, the beneficial ownership shall be deemed to be that of the holders of such company's outstanding securities (other than short-term paper).

(B) Beneficial ownership by any person who acquires securities or interests in securities of an issuer described in the first sentence of this paragraph shall be deemed to be beneficial ownership by the person from whom such transfer was made, pursuant to such rules and regulations as the Commission shall prescribe as necessary or appropriate in the public interest and consistent with the protection of investors and the purposes fairly intended by the policy and provisions of this title, where the transfer was caused by legal separation, divorce, death, or other involuntary event.

. . .

(5) Any person who is not engaged in the business of issuing redeemable securities, face-amount certificates of the installment type or periodic payment plan certificates, and who is primarily engaged in one or more of the following businesses: (A) Purchasing or otherwise acquiring notes, drafts, acceptances, open accounts receivable, and other obligations representing part or all of the sales price of merchandise, insurance, and services; (B) making loans to manufacturers, wholesalers, and retailers of, and to prospective purchasers of, specified merchandise, insurance, and services; and (c) purchasing or otherwise acquiring mortgages and other liens on and interest in real estate.

. . .

(7) (A) Any issuer, the outstanding securities of which are owned exclusively by persons who, at the time of acquisition of such securities, are qualified purchasers, and which is not making and does not at that time propose to make a public offering of such securities. Securities that are owned by persons who received the securities from a qualified purchaser as a gift or bequest, or in a case in which the transfer was caused by legal separation, divorce, death, or other involuntary event, shall be deemed to be owned by a qualified purchaser, subject to such rules, regulations, and orders as the Commission may prescribe as necessary or appropriate in the public interest or for the protection of investors.

(B) Notwithstanding subparagraph (A), an issuer is within the exception provided by this paragraph if —

(i) in addition to qualified purchasers, outstanding securities of that issuer are beneficially owned by not more than 100 persons who are not qualified purchasers, if —

(I) such persons acquired any portion of the securities of such issuer on or before September 1, 1996; and

(II) at the time at which such persons initially acquired the securities of such issuer, the issuer was excepted by paragraph (1); and

(ii) prior to availing itself of the exception provided by this paragraph —

(I) such issuer has disclosed to each beneficial owner, as determined under paragraph (1), that future investors will be limited to qualified purchasers, and that ownership in such issuer is no longer limited to not more than 100 persons; and

(II) concurrently with or after such disclosure, such issuer has provided each beneficial owner, as determined under paragraph (1), with a reasonable opportunity to redeem any part or all of their interests in the issuer, notwithstanding any agreement to the contrary between the issuer and such persons, for that person's proportionate share of the issuer's net assets.

(C) Each person that elects to redeem under subparagraph (B)(ii)(II) shall receive an amount in cash equal to that person's proportionate share of the issuer's net assets, unless the issuer elects to provide such person with the option of receiving, and such person agrees to receive, all or a portion of such person's share in assets of the issuer. If the issuer elects to provide such persons with such an opportunity, disclosure concerning such opportunity shall be made in the disclosure required by subparagraph (B)(ii)(I).

(D) An issuer that is excepted under this paragraph shall nonetheless be deemed to be an investment company for purposes of the limitations set forth in subparagraphs (A)(I) and (B)(I) of section 80a-12(d)(1) of this title [15 U.S.C. §§ 80a-12(d)(1)(A)(I), (B)(I)] relating to the purchase or other acquisition by such issuer of any security issued by any registered investment company and the sale of any security issued by any registered open-end investment company to any such issuer.

(E) For purposes of determining compliance with this paragraph and paragraph (1), an issuer that is otherwise excepted under this paragraph and an issuer that is otherwise excepted under paragraph (1) shall not be treated by the Commission as being a single issuer for purposes of determining whether the outstanding securities of the issuer excepted under paragraph (1) are beneficially owned by not more than 100 persons or whether the outstanding securities of the issuer excepted under this paragraph are owned by persons that are not qualified purchasers. Nothing in this subparagraph shall be construed to establish that a person is a bona fide qualified purchaser for purposes of this paragraph or a bona fide beneficial owner for purposes of paragraph (1).

B. Rule 3a-7

One of the most widely used exemptions, however, is administrative. In 1992, the SEC adopted a new Rule 3a-7 under the 1940 Act (set forth below) that excludes from the definition of investment company SPEs meeting certain criteria,[15] and which is intended to exempt from 1940 Act registration transactions involving "virtually all assets that can be securitized."[16]

The impact of rule 3a-7 on structured finance has been profound. The rule exempts most structured financings from the definition of "investment company," thereby "remov[ing] an unnecessary and unintended barrier to the use of structured financings in all sectors of the economy."[17] The rule essentially provides an exemption from the 1940 Act for structured financings consistent with the practice in today's capital markets, as opposed to earlier exemptions (such as section 3(c)(5), discussed above) that relied on historically relevant differences in the nature of the receivables held by the SPE that are no longer meaningful.[18]

Rule 3a-7 provides, in essence, that an SPE that purchases or otherwise holds receivables (or other "eligible assets" that, by their terms, convert into cash within a finite time period)[19] will not be deemed to be an investment company if four conditions are met. The first condition is that the SPE issue securities

[15] *Exclusion from the Definition of Investment Company for Structured Financings*, Investment Company Release No. 19,105, 57 Fed. Reg. 56,248, 57,256 (Nov. 27, 1992) (codified at 17 C.F.R. § 270.3a-7) (issuers of asset-backed securities).

[16] *Exclusion from the Definition of Investment Company for Structured Financings,* Investment Co. Act Release No. 19105, 57 Fed. Reg. 56248 (1992).

[17] *Id.*

[18] Section 3(c)(5) is still meaningful, especially in instances similar to those where it has already been successfully employed as an exemption.

[19] The term "eligible assets" is broad enough to include most receivables.

whose payment depends primarily[20] on the cash flow from such receivables. The second condition is that, except as provided below, the securities issued must be nonredeemable debt securities or equity securities with debt-like characteristics ("fixed-income securities") that, in each case, are rated, at the time of their *initial* sale, as investment-grade or better[21] by at least one nationally recognized rating agency. Nonrated securities, however, may be sold to "qualified institutional buyers" and nonrated fixed-income securities may be sold to "accredited investors," as those terms are defined in rules promulgated under the 1933 Act.

The third condition is that the SPE acquire or dispose of receivables only in accordance with the terms of the agreements pursuant to which the SPE's securities are issued, and not "for the primary purpose of recognizing gains or decreasing losses resulting from market value changes"; and that such acquisitions or dispositions not result in a downgrading of the rating on the securities. These conditions apparently are intended to discourage any misuse of the exemption to permit speculation and also to avoid portfolio management practices resembling those used by mutual funds.

The fourth and final condition is that if the SPE issues securities that are not exempt from registration with the SEC under section 3(a)(3) of the 1933 Act, the SPE must appoint an independent trustee for those securities. The trustee must meet certain legal requirements referred to in the rule, and also is obligated to "take reasonable steps" to obtain a perfected security or ownership interest in the receivables that "principally generate the cash flow needed to pay" the securities.[22] In addition, the trustee must take actions necessary for the collections on the receivables to be deposited *periodically* in a segregated account maintained or controlled by the trustee for the benefit of the securities holders, but the trustee need not prevent commingling of collections during the period of time before the collections are deposited. This represents a practical compromise by the SEC to protect the collections, but in a manner intended to be consistent with industry and rating agency practice.[23]

---

20 The term "primarily" was used to clarify that a portion of the cash flows used to pay the securities could come, for example, from such sources as the disposition of assets that do not conform to a representation or warranty, and that residual interests could be paid, in part, from proceeds of the disposition of assets. *See Exclusion from the Definition of Investment Company for Structured Financings*, 57 Fed. Reg. at 56,261 nn.36, 37 and accompanying text.

21 That is, at least BBB for long-term securities or the equivalent for short-term securities.

22 Thus a perfected interest only has to be obtained in the primary cash flows and *not* in the underlying assets, such as automobiles that are the subject of securitized leases or loans. *See Exclusion from the Definition of Investment Company for Structured Financings*, 57 Fed. Reg. at 56,255 at n.82.

23 *See* 57 Fed. Reg. at 56,255. We question whether an independent trustee really is needed for the broad segment of the asset-backed securities market sold to institutional investors pursuant to the exemption available under section 4(2) of the 1933 Act.

Rule 3a-7 — Issuers of Asset-Backed Securities

17 C.F.R. § 270.3a-7

(a) Notwithstanding section 3(a) of the Act, any issuer who is engaged in the business of purchasing, or otherwise acquiring, and holding eligible assets (and in activities related or incidental thereto), and who does not issue redeemable securities will not be deemed to be an investment company;

Provided That:

(1) The issuer issues fixed-income securities or other securities which entitle their holders to receive payments that depend primarily on the cash flow from eligible assets;

(2) Securities sold by the issuer or any underwriter thereof are fixed-income securities rated, at the time of initial sale, in one of the four highest categories assigned long-term debt or in an equivalent short-term category (within either of which there may be sub-categories or gradations indicating relative standing) by at least one nationally recognized statistical rating organization that is not an affiliated person of the issuer or of any person involved in the organization or operation of the issuer, except that:

(i) Any fixed-income securities may be sold to accredited investors as defined in paragraphs (1), (2), (3), and (7) of rule 501(a) under the Securities Act of 1933 (17 CFR 230.501(a)) and any entity in which all of the equity owners come within such paragraphs; and

(ii) Any securities may be sold to qualified institutional buyers as defined in rule 144A under the Securities Act (17 CFR 230.144A) and to persons (other than any rating organization rating the issuer's securities) involved in the organization or operation of the issuer or an affiliate, as defined in rule 405 under the Securities Act (17 CFR 230.405), of such a person;

Provided, That the issuer or any underwriter thereof effecting such sale exercises reasonable care to ensure that such securities are sold and will be resold to persons specified in paragraphs (a)(2) (I) and (ii) of this section;

(3) The issuer acquires additional eligible assets, or disposes of eligible assets, only if:

(i) The assets are acquired or disposed of in accordance with the terms and conditions set forth in the agreements, indentures, or other instruments pursuant to which the issuer's securities are issued;

(ii) The acquisition or disposition of the assets does not result in a downgrading in the rating of the issuer's outstanding fixed-income securities; and

(iii) The assets are not acquired or disposed of for the primary purpose of recognizing gains or decreasing losses resulting from market value changes; and

(4) If the issuer issues any securities other than securities exempted from the Securities Act by section 3(a)(3) thereof (15 U.S.C. 77c(a)(3)), the issuer:

(i) Appoints a trustee that meets the requirements of section 26(a)(1) of the Act and that is not affiliated, as that term is defined in rule 405 under the Securities Act (17 CFR 230.405), with the issuer or with any person involved in the organization or operation of the issuer, which does not offer or provide credit or credit enhancement to the issuer, and that executes an agreement or instrument concerning the issuer's securities containing provisions to the effect set forth in section 26(a)(3) of the Act;

(ii) Takes reasonable steps to cause the trustee to have a perfected security interest or ownership interest valid against third parties in those eligible assets that principally generate the cash flow needed to pay the fixed-income security holders, provided that such assets otherwise required to be held by the trustee may be released to the extent needed at the time for the operation of the issuer; and

(iii) Takes actions necessary for the cash flows derived from eligible assets for the benefit of the holders of fixed-income securities to be deposited periodically in a segregated account that is maintained or controlled by the trustee consistent with the rating of the outstanding fixed-income securities.

(b) For purposes of this section:

(1) *Eligible assets* means financial assets, either fixed or revolving, that by their terms convert into cash within a finite time period plus any rights or other assets designed to assure the servicing or timely distribution of proceeds to security holders.

(2) *Fixed-income securities* means any securities that entitle the holder to receive:

(i) A stated principal amount; or

(ii) Interest on a principal amount (which may be a notional principal amount) calculated by reference to a fixed rate or to a standard or formula which does not reference any change in the market value or fair value of eligible assets; or

(iii) Interest on a principal amount (which may be a notional principal amount) calculated by reference to auctions among holders and prospective holders, or through remarketing of the security; or

(iv) An amount equal to specified fixed or variable portions of the interest received on the assets held by the issuer; or

(v) Any combination of amounts described in paragraphs (b)(2) (i), (ii), (iii), and (iv) of this section;

Provided, That substantially all of the payments to which the holders of such securities are entitled consist of the foregoing amounts.

QUESTIONS ON THE 1940 ACT

1. Does the Honda Receivables 2003-01 Owner Trust from Chapter 1 meet the definition of an "investment company" in the 1940 Act? Does the owner trust hold "securities" as that term is defined in the 1940 Act?

2. Assuming that the owner trust in the Honda deal is exempt from registration as an investment company, what are the possible exemptions? Which exemption did the owner trust most likely avail itself of?

3. If you wish to dig further into this topic, find the definitions of "qualified purchasers," "qualified institutional buyer," and "accredited investor" in the relevant securities statutes or rules. For what purpose is each of these three types of purchasers of securities important to the 1940 Act analysis? What are the differences between each type of purchaser? Why should the characteristics of the buyer of securities relate to the amount or type of disclosure that must be provided by the issuer of the securities?

4. Rule 3a-7 only exempts an issuer if the securities sold are rated at the time of initial sale in one of the four highest categories (*i.e.*, investment grade) by one of the rating agencies. How does this elevate the role of the rating agencies in structuring the transaction? What were the ratings of the notes in the Honda deal at the time of issuance?

5. Given that the notes in the Honda deal are registered securities, there must be an independent trustee for the securities. Who is the trustee and does the trustee meet the requirements set forth in the 1940 Act?

§ 6.02. Securities Act of 1933 and Securities Exchange Act of 1934

Even if an SPE establishes an exemption from registration under the 1940 Act, the securities it issues may still be subject to the 1933 Act and the 1934 Act to the extent that it issues nonexempt securities. The 1933 Act imposes standards of disclosure[24] and requires the filing of a registration statement with the SEC in connection with any public offering of nonexempt securities.[25] The 1934

24 1933 Act § 7, 15 U.S.C. § 77g; 1933 Act § 10, 15 U.S.C. § 77j.

25 1933 Act § 5(c), 15 U.S.C. § 883(c).

Act also imposes liability for certain types of fraudulent statements or omissions and, for certain publicly held issuers, imposes ongoing reporting requirements for financial statements.

A. Public Offerings

In considering methods of compliance with the 1933 Act, various factors must be weighed. For example, if the receivables to be acquired by the SPE have highly predictable payment streams, the originator has at least several years of collection experience, and the anticipated financing is large enough to justify the registration and related costs, an SPE may well choose to file a registration statement with the SEC and issue its securities as part of a public offering. Although such a registration can take several months to implement and is costly, registered securities issued by an SPE have the advantage of being freely issuable to and tradable by the public and therefore can be purchased by a wide range of investors.[26]

B. Section 4(2) Private Placement Exemption

If a public market is impracticable or otherwise not appropriate, the SPE may choose instead to issue its securities in a private placement under section 4(2) of the 1933 Act, which exempts from registration "transactions by an issuer not involving any public offering."[27] If the private placement is made to a relatively few large institutional investors, such as pension funds and banks, relatively little in the way of specialized disclosure documents may be required since such investors are presumed to have the sophistication and bargaining power to elicit the information necessary to make an informed investment decision.

If the private placement is to a larger number of investors, and particularly if noninstitutional investors are involved, the SPE and its sponsors might find it prudent to comply with the "safe-harbor" provisions of Regulation D promulgated by the SEC.[28] Under that rule, the SPE may, in general, sell its securities to up to thirty-five "non-accredited" investors and an unlimited number of "accredited" investors.[29] If "non-accredited" investors are included, it will generally be necessary to prepare and circulate a private offering memorandum set-

---

[26] Form S-3 (the SEC's short registration form) under the 1933 Act has also been revised to expand the benefit of rule 415 (the so-called shelf-registration rule) to offerings of investment-grade asset-backed securities. *See* 17 C.F.R. pts. 230, 239, 240, 249.

[27] 1933 Act § 4(2), 15 U.S.C. § 77d(2).

[28] 17 C.F.R. §§ 230.501–508 (2002).

[29] In addition to banks, insurance companies, and other institutional investors, the categories of accredited investors under regulation D include individuals with a net worth of $1 million or more and partnerships and corporations with total assets in excess of $5 million. 17 C.F.R. § 230.501 (a)(5), (3).

ting forth certain financial and other information required to be furnished under Regulation D.

1. Resale of Privately Placed Securities

Regardless of whether the Regulation D safe harbor is used, securities issued in a private placement will generally be deemed to be "restricted securities" and may not be resold except in compliance with the registration requirements of the 1933 Act or an exemption therefrom, such as the SEC's Rule 144[30] or Rule 144A.[31] This means that if a pension fund purchases a note or other security from an SPE, it will have to hold such security until maturity unless it wants to register that security or sell it in accordance with the restrictions (mainly in terms of time and amount) imposed by administrative regulation.

C. Exempted Securities — Section 3(a) Exemptions

Securities Act of 1933
Section 3 — Classes of Securities under this Title
15 U.S.C. § 77c

(a) Exempted securities. Except as hereinafter expressly provided, the provisions of this subchapter shall not apply to any of the following classes of securities:

. . .

(3) Any note, draft, bill of exchange, or banker's acceptance which arises out of a current transaction or the proceeds of which have been or are to be used for current transactions, and which has a maturity at the time of issuance of not exceeding nine months, exclusive of days of grace, or any renewal thereof the maturity of which is likewise limited;

. . .

Certain other exemptions may be available under the 1933 Act to an SPE that wishes to issue its securities in the public market, but wants to avoid the time

---

30 17 C.F.R. § 230.144. In general, that rule imposes, among other conditions, a one-year holding period unless the securities are resold in another private transaction (in which case the securities will generally continue to be "restricted" in the hands of the buyer). Rule 144 has broad application outside of securitization; in many cases, entrepreneurs who "take a company public" find that the shares they retain are subject to Rule 144.

31 17 C.F.R. § 230.144A. Rule 144A generally provides a nonexclusive "safe-harbor" exemption for specified resales of restricted securities to "qualified institutional buyers," provided that such buyers had more than $100 million in the aggregate owned and invested in securities on a discretionary basis (or $10 million in securities with respect to dealers). This rule is intended to increase the efficiency and liquidity of the private placement market.

and cost of filing a registration statement. If the securities are fully supported by a bank letter of credit, for example, the securities would be exempt from registration under section 3(a)(2) of the 1933 Act.[32] Under the more frequently used section 3(a)(3) "commercial paper exemption," securities having a maturity of no longer than nine months (i.e., 270 days), the proceeds of which are to be used for "current transactions," are also free from the registration requirements of the 1933 Act.[33]

In effect, the SEC has required that four criteria be satisfied in order for an issuance of commercial paper to qualify for the section 3(a)(3) exemption: such paper must (1) be of prime quality, (2) not be ordinarily purchased by the general public, (3) be used to facilitate current transactions, and (4) have a maturity of nine months or less with no automatic roll-over.[34] However, the most frequently encountered difficulty associated with the application of the section 3(a)(3) exemption is that the central requirement of a "current transaction" is not defined anywhere in the 1933 Act. The SEC has acknowledged that, with respect to financing companies (and by inference, with respect to SPEs), "current transactions . . . may properly include . . . the making of loans upon or the purchasing of . . . notes, instalment *[sic]* contracts, or other evidences of indebtedness in the usual course of business."[35] However, to obtain more certainty as to whether a proposed transaction meets the current transaction standard, it is often necessary to turn to various SEC no-action letters interpreting what is and

---

32 Unlike section 4(2), which is a "transactional" exemption applicable to all types of securities, section 3 of the 1933 Act exempts entire specified classes of securities from the registration requirement of that act. Section 3(a)(2) included among those classes " any security . . . guaranteed by any bank," with the term "bank" defined to mean "any national bank, or any banking institution organized under the laws of any State, territory, or the District of Columbia, the business of which is substantially confined to banking and is supervised by the State or territorial banking commission or similar official." That exemption is not often used in structured financings because the letter of credit typically covers only a portion of the securities.

33 The SEC, however, has adopted a more restrictive view of section 3(a)(3)'s application than a reading of the statute suggests on its face, stating:

> The legislative history of the [1933] Act makes clear that Section 3(a)(3) applies only to prime quality negotiable commercial paper of a type not ordinarily purchased by the general public, that is, paper issued to facilitate well recognized types of current operation business requirements and of a type eligible for discounting by Federal Reserve Banks.

Securities Act of 1933 Release No. 4,412, 26 Fed. Reg. 9158, 9158 (Sept. 20, 1961). Commercial paper may also be privately placed without registration under section 4(2) of the 1933 Act, but that approach is less common.

34 3 LOUIS LOSS & JOEL SELIGMAN, SECURITIES REGULATION 1211-12 (3d ed. rev. 1999).

35 Securities Act of 1933 Release No. 401, 11 Fed. Reg. 10,953, 10,953 (June 18, 1935). In a 1961 release, the SEC added that the current transaction standard "is not satisfied where the proceeds [of exempt commercial paper] are to be used for the discharge of existing indebtedness unless such indebtedness is itself exempt under Section 3(a)(3)." Securities Act of 1933 Release No. 4,412, 26 Fed. Reg. at 9158 (1961).

is not a current transaction under various circumstances.[36] Generally, the current transaction standard precludes the use of proceeds of commercial paper for permanent or fixed investments in such assets as land, buildings, or machinery; for the purchase of securities or other speculative assets; or for any fixed-capital purpose.[37] However, financing companies have been permitted to purchase or finance the following representative assets having terms not exceeding five years with the proceeds of section 3(a)(3) exempt commercial paper: consumer loans, short-term commercial loans, loans and financing leases for nonpermanent capital equipment, retail installment paper, accounts receivable and inventory loans, and home-improvement loan paper.[38] The SEC has issued hundreds of no-action letters interpreting the current transaction standard and in many cases those interpretations are in conflict or are not easily reconciled.

D. Rule 10b-5

It also should be noted that, regardless of whether an SPE issues exempt securities or issues nonexempt securities in an exempt transaction or a registered public offering, the antifraud provisions of section 10(b) of the 1934 Act and rule 10b-5 promulgated by the SEC thereunder will apply. Accordingly, an SPE and its sponsors would be liable if, in connection with the issuance and sale of its securities, they employed "any device, scheme, or artifice to defraud" or if they made "any untrue statement of a material fact or [failed] . . . to state a material fact necessary in order to make the statements made, in the light of circumstances under which they were made, not misleading."[39]

E. The Honda Deal

The Honda deal provides an example of the public offering of securities. The prospectus and prospectus supplement are important parts of the registration

[36] *See, e.g.,* Westinghouse Credit Corp., SEC No-Action Letter, 1986 SEC No-Act. LEXIS 2069 (Apr. 3, 1986) (proceeds used for equipment financing, acquisition of personal property through foreclosure, short-term commercial loans, accounts receivable loans, inventory loans, and floor plan loans all constitute current transactions); Independence Bancorp, Inc., SEC No-Action Letter, 1986 SEC No-Act. LEXIS 1902 (Feb. 11, 1986) (proceeds used for various transactions having maturities not exceeding five years all constitute current transactions); American Fletcher Mortgage Investors, SEC No-Action Letter, 1971 SEC No-Act. LEXIS 2717 (Mar. 2, 1971) (construction mortgage loans and warehousing loans with commitments for permanent takeouts in three years constitute current transactions, but development mortgage loan maturing in five years or less does not).

[37] *See* Securities Act of 1933 Release No. 4,412, 26 Fed. Reg. at 9158; LOSS & SELIGMAN, *supra* note 34, at 1215-16. However, under certain circumstances, interim financing of permanent or fixed investments may be undertaken with the proceeds of section 3(a)(3) exempt commercial paper. *See, e.g.,* Southeast Banking Corp., 1989 SEC No-Action Letter LEXIS 1157 (Nov. 21, 1989) (permissible to finance initial or remaining short-term [generally, five-year] portion of certain loans and leases).

[38] Southeast Banking Corp., *supra* note 37.

[39] Rule 10b-5, 17 C.F.R. § 240.10b-5.

statement filed with the SEC and provide lots of details about the deal for potential investors (as well as inquisitive students of securitization). The Honda Receivables 2003-1 Owner Trust is the issuer of $1.5 billion in asset-backed notes. Specifically, there are four classes of notes issued by the owner trust. Each class of note carries a different interest rate and has a different maturity date. The certificates issued by the owner trust are not being offered for sale in this document but are to be retained by American Honda Receivables. The notes are initially sold by the owner trust to the underwriters, which includes six different underwriting firms. The Form 8-K filed with the SEC contains the underwriting agreement between the underwriters and the owner trust as an exhibit. It indicates that the underwriters are obligated to purchase their proportionate share of the notes, subject to certain conditions, and then will offer the notes to the public.

QUESTIONS RELATING TO THE 1933 ACT AND THE 1934 ACT ASPECTS OF THE HONDA DEAL

1. What are the interest rates to be paid to investors in the Honda deal in each of the four classes of notes and when will each class of notes be fully paid? What are some of the likely explanations for the differences in the interest rates among the four classes of notes?

2. Why are the certificates issued by the 2003-1 Owner Trust in the Honda deal retained by Honda Receivables rather than being sold to the public?

3. The prospectus and prospectus supplement in the Honda deal both discuss various "risk factors" that investors should consider in deciding whether to purchase any of the notes issued by the owner trust. How and why do the risk factors differ between the prospectus and the prospectus supplement? Who bears the risk of default by the obligors on the auto loans?

4. Are the notes issued by the 2003-1 Owner Trust in the Honda deal exempted securities under section 3(a)(2) or 3(a)(3) of the 1933 Act? Why or why not?

Chapter 7

BANKS AND SECURITIZATION

§ 7.01. Why Banks Securitize Assets

Many banks and thrift institutions sell loans in the secondary market either to agencies such as Fannie Mae or Freddie Mac or to a special purpose entity (SPE) in a securitization. Securitizing some of its loans may be beneficial to a bank because it passes along the interest rate risk and default risk on the loans to the SPE that has purchased the loans from the bank and ultimately to the purchasers of securities issued by the SPE. The proceeds of the loan sales are often used to fund additional loans for which the bank may earn additional loan origination fees. In the short term, until the loan sale proceeds are loaned to other borrowers, the regulatory capital requirements of the bank are also reduced. Often the bank continues to service the loans even after they have been sold to the SPE, earning a fee for acting as the loan servicer.

Office of the Comptroller of the Currency Comptroller's Handbook: Asset Securitization

Nov. 1997

<www.occ.treas.gov/handbook/assetsec.pdf>

. . . . Asset securitization began with the structured financing of mortgage pools in the 1970s. For decades before that, banks were essentially portfolio lenders; they held loans until they matured or were paid off. These loans were funded principally by deposits, and sometimes by debt, which was a direct obligation of the bank (rather than a claim on specific assets).

But after World War II, depository institutions simply could not keep pace with the rising demand for housing credit. Banks, as well as other financial intermediaries sensing a market opportunity, sought ways of increasing the sources of mortgage funding. To attract investors, investment bankers eventually developed an investment vehicle that isolated defined mortgage pools, segmented the credit risk, and structured the cash flows from the underlying loans. Although it took several years to develop efficient mortgage securitization structures, loan originators quickly realized the process was readily transferable to other types of loans as well.

Since the mid 1980s, better technology and more sophisticated investors have combined to make asset securitization one of the fastest growing activities in the capital markets. The growth rate of nearly every type of securitized asset has been remarkable, as have been the increase in the types of companies using securitization and the expansion of the investor base. The business of a credit intermediary has so changed that few banks, thrifts, or finance companies can afford to view themselves exclusively as portfolio lenders.

The market for mortgage-backed securities was boosted by the government agencies that stood behind these securities. To facilitate the securitization of nonmortgage assets, businesses substituted private credit enhancements. First, they overcollateralized pools of assets; shortly thereafter, they improved third-party and structural enhancements. In 1985, securitization techniques that had been developed in the mortgage market were applied for the first time to a class of nonmortgage assets — automobile loans. A pool of assets second only to mortgages, auto loans were a good match for structured finance; their maturities, considerably shorter than those of mortgages, made the timing of cash flows more predictable, and their long statistical histories of performance gave investors confidence.

The first significant bank credit card sale came to market in 1986 with a private placement of $50 million of bank card outstandings. This transaction demonstrated to investors that, if the yields were high enough, loan pools could support asset sales with higher expected losses and administrative costs than was true within the mortgage market. Sales of this type — with no contractual obligation by the seller to provide recourse — allowed banks to receive sales treatment for accounting and regulatory purposes (easing balance sheet and capital constraints), while at the same time allowing them to retain origination and servicing fees. After the success of this initial transaction, investors grew to accept credit card receivables as collateral, and banks developed structures to normalize the cash flows.

The next growth phase of securitization will likely involve nonconsumer assets. Most retail lending is "securitizable" because cash flows are predictable. Today, formula-driven credit scoring and credit monitoring techniques are widely used for such loans, and most retail programs produce fairly homogeneous loan portfolios. Commercial financing presents a greater challenge. Because a portfolio of commercial loans is typically less homogeneous than a retail portfolio, someone seeking to invest in them must often know much more about each individual credit, and the simpler tools for measuring and managing portfolio risk are less effective. Nonetheless, investment bankers and asset originators have proven extremely innovative at structuring cash flows and credit enhancements. Evidence of this can be seen in the market for securitized commercial real estate mortgages. Commercial real estate is one of the fastest-growing types of nonconsumer assets in the securitization markets, which fund approximately 10% of commercial mortgage debt.

The evolution of securitization is not surprising given the benefits that it offers to each of the major parties in the transaction.

For Originators. Securitization improves returns on capital by converting an on-balance sheet lending business into an off-balance-sheet income stream that is less capital intensive. Depending on the type of structure used, securitization may also lower borrowing costs, release additional capital for expansion or reinvestment purposes, and improve asset/liability and credit risk management.

For Investors. Securitized assets offer a combination of attractive yields (compared with other instruments of similar quality), increasing secondary market liquidity, and generally more protection by way of collateral overages and/or guarantees by entities with high and stable credit ratings. They also offer a measure of flexibility because their payment streams can be structured to meet investors' particular requirements. Most important, structural credit enhancements and diversified asset pools free investors of the need to obtain a detailed understanding of the underlying loans. This has been the single largest factor in the growth of the structured finance market.

For Borrowers. Borrowers benefit from the increasing availability of credit on terms that lenders may not have provided had they kept the loans on their balance sheets. For example, because a market exists for mortgage-backed securities, lenders can now extend fixed rate debt, which many consumers prefer over variable rate debt, without overexposing themselves to interest rate risk. Credit card lenders can originate very large loan pools for a diverse customer base at lower rates than if they had to fund the loans on their balance sheet. Nationwide competition among credit originators, coupled with strong investor appetite for the securities, has significantly expanded both the availability of credit and the pool of cardholders over the past decade.

Federal Reserve Board
Trading and Capital-Markets Activities Manual

Section 3020.1
March 1999
<www.federalreserve.gov/boarddocs/supmanual/trading/trading.pdf>

. . . . Banking organizations have long been involved in asset-backed securities (ABS), both as investors and as major participants in the securitization process. In recent years, banks have both increased their participation in the long-established residential mortgage-backed securities market and expanded their activities in securitizing other types of assets, such as credit card receivables, automobile loans, boat loans, commercial real estate loans, student loans, nonperforming loans, and lease receivables.

While the objectives of securitization may vary from institution to institution, several benefits can be derived from securitized transactions. First, the sale of assets may reduce regulatory costs by reducing both risk-based capital requirements and the reserves held against the deposits used to fund the sold assets. Second, securitization provides originators with an additional source of funding or liquidity since the process of securitization converts an illiquid asset into a security with greater marketability. Securitized issues often require a credit enhancement, which results in a higher credit rating than what would normally be obtainable by the institution itself. Consequently, securitized issues may provide the institution with a cheaper form of funding. Third, securitization may be used to reduce interest-rate risk by improving the institution's asset/liability mix. This is especially true if the institution has a large investment in fixed-rate, low-yield assets. Finally, the ability to sell these securities worldwide diversifies the institution's funding base, which reduces the bank's dependence on local economies. . . .

QUESTIONS

1. Are banks more likely to be engaged in securitization of loans than nonfinancial companies?

2. What are the benefits for banks of securitizing loans?

§ 7.02. The Statutory Authority for Bank Asset Securitization

SECURITIES INDUSTRY ASS'N v. CLARKE

885 F.2d 1034 (2d Cir. 1989), *cert. denied*, 493 U.S. 1070 (1990)

MESKILL, CIRCUIT JUDGE.

. . .

A. Mortgage Pass-Through Certificates

Mortgage pass-through certificates are used by banks as a mechanism for selling mortgage loans. A number of mortgage loans previously originated by a bank are placed in a pool. The bank then transfers the pool to a trust. In exchange for the pool, the trustee transfers to the bank pass-through certificates. These certificates represent fractional undivided interests in the pool of mortgage loans. The certificates may then be sold publicly or privately.

After sale of the certificates, the mortgage loans are often serviced by the originator-bank. In such a case, the bank collects the loan payments and "passes through" the principal and interest on a pro rata basis to the certificate holders. In doing so, the bank may deduct service or other fees.

Use of this mechanism has important benefits for banks, benefits that have resulted in its increasing popularity and use. Because residential mortgage loans typically are of long duration, banks traditionally have bought and sold the loans to facilitate management of their assets and liabilities. Use of the pass-through certificate mechanism makes the sale of these loans easier. Individual loans do not have to be sold separately, and buyers may find it more efficient and less risky to purchase interests in a pool of mortgages instead of single mortgages.

B. The January 23, 1987 Offering of SPN Bank

A Prospectus and Prospectus Supplement dated January 23, 1987 described the offering of approximately $194 million of Security Pacific Mortgage Pass-Through Certificates, Series 1987-B.

The Prospectus provided for the creation of a pool consisting of conventional, fixed-rate residential mortgage loans. "Each Mortgage Loan [would] be selected by [SPN Bank] for inclusion in the Mortgage Pool from among those originated by [SPN Bank] in the ordinary course of [SPN Bank's] lending activities as carried on in its offices in California." Certain characteristics of the mortgages to be selected were specified.

The Prospectus provided that, at the time of issuance of the series, "[SPN Bank] will assign the Mortgage Loans in the Mortgage Pool evidenced by that series to the Trustee. . . . The Trustee will, concurrently with such assignment, authenticate and deliver Certificates evidencing such series to [SPN Bank] in exchange for the Mortgage Loans." The freely transferable certificates would represent fractional undivided interests in the Trust Fund.

Limited credit support for the issue was to be provided either by (1) an irrevocable letter of credit issued by SPN Bank, (2) a limited guaranty issued by an entity other than SPN Bank, or (3) third-party mortgage insurance purchased by SPN Bank in its role as servicer of the mortgage loans. If SPN Bank provided its own letter of credit, the coverage was to be no more than ten percent of the initial aggregate principal balance of the mortgage pool. Any risk of delinquency or default not covered by these mechanisms of credit support would be borne by the certificate holders. . . .

C. SIA's Challenge to SPN Bank's Offering

SIA is a national trade association. . . . SIA stated [in a letter to the Comptroller] its belief that SPN Bank's participation in the transaction constituted a violation of the Glass-Steagall Act. The letter asked the Comptroller to review the transaction and "declare the bank's involvement in it to be contrary to the Glass-Steagall Act.". . .

DISCUSSION

. . .

E. The Comptroller Correctly Determined That SPN Bank's Sale of the Certificates Was Within the "Business of Banking" and Therefore Did Not Violate the Glass-Steagall Act

The Comptroller correctly concluded that SPN Bank has the express power under the national banking laws to sell its mortgage loans. In 1982, Congress amended 12 U.S.C. § 371(a) to provide that "[a]ny national banking association may make, arrange, purchase or sell loans or extensions of credit secured by liens on interests in real estate, subject to such terms, conditions, and limitations as may be prescribed by the Comptroller of the Currency by order, rule, or regulation." Legislative history indicates that the amendment was intended to "simplif[y] the real estate lending authority of national banks by deleting rigid statutory requirements. Section 403 [which amended 12 U.S.C. § 371] is intended to provide national banks with the ability to engage in more creative and flexible financing, and to become stronger participants in the home financing market." S.Rep. No. 536, 97th Cong., 2nd Sess. 27 (1982), reprinted in 1982 U.S.Code Cong. & Admin.News 3054, 3081; see also id. at 60, 1982 U.S. Code Cong. & Admin. News at 3114. . . .

In determining that the use of mortgage pass-through certificates to sell mortgage loans fell within SPN Bank's "incidental powers" under 12 U.S.C. § 24 (Seventh), the Comptroller turned to the test adopted in *Arnold Tours [v. Camp]*, 472 F.2d [427] at 432 [(1st Cir. 1972)]. There, the First Circuit framed the inquiry as follows: in order to be authorized under section 16's "incidental powers" provision, a national bank's activity must be "convenient [and] useful in connection with the performance of one of the bank's established activities pursuant to its express powers under the National Bank Act." Id.

Although he applied the test of *Arnold Tours*, the Comptroller argued that that test is unnecessarily restrictive of the powers of national banks. . . . We have no need to address the Comptroller's position that the *Arnold Tours* test is overly restrictive, as we believe that the proper test is no more restrictive than *Arnold Tours* and we agree with the Comptroller that SPN Bank's activities here satisfied even the *Arnold Tours* test.

We have little difficulty concluding that SPN Bank's use of the pass-through certificate mechanism is "convenient [and] useful in connection with the performance of" its power to sell its mortgage loans. See *Arnold Tours*, 472 F.2d at 432. Indeed, SIA does not appear to argue otherwise. The pass-through certificate mechanism permits the bank to offer purchasers an interest in a pool of mortgage loans, rather than just single mortgage loans. The popularity of the mechanism confirms what seems apparent, that many investors who might be wary of the risk of investing in a single mortgage loan will be willing to invest in a pool of loans. With the increased marketability that pass-through certificates make possible comes increased liquidity, an important benefit as banks face the task of funding long term mortgage loans with short term deposits. We thus conclude that the Comptroller's view that SPN Bank's "incidental powers" authorized its activity in the transaction at issue here was reasonable.

The Comptroller properly recognized that once he determined that SPN Bank's activity was authorized under section 16 [12 U.S.C. § 24 (Seventh), he did not need to analyze the transaction under section 21 [12 U.S.C. § 378(a)(1)].[1] "[S]ection 21 cannot be read to prohibit what section 16 permits. . . . Therefore, if we find that the [Comptroller] acted reasonably in concluding that section 16 permits [SPN Bank's] activities, that is the end of our analysis." See Securities

---

[1] [Eds.] Sections 16 and 21 of the Glass-Steagall Act were its principal provisions separating commercial and investment banking.

Industry Ass'n v. Board of Governors, 807 F.2d 1052, 1057 (D.C.Cir. 1986), cert. denied, 483 U.S. 1005 (1987) (*Bankers Trust II*). This is so because section 21 "was not intended to require banks to abandon an accepted banking practice that was subjected to regulation under § 16." *ICI,* 450 U.S. at 63; see also *Bankers Trust I*, 468 U.S. at 149 ("§ 16 and § 21 seek to draw the same line"). . . .

The Gramm-Leach-Bliley Act of 1999 (GLBA) permits bank holding companies that meet the requirements of 12 U.S.C. § 1843(l)(1) to file for a designation as a financial holding company that may engage in "financial in nature activities,"[2] including "[i]ssuing or selling instruments representing interests in pools of assets permissible for a bank to hold directly." 12 U.S.C. § 1843(k)(4)(B).

§ 7.03. Insolvency of Bank Originator

Insolvent banks are dealt with or "resolved" by the Federal Deposit Insurance Corporation (FDIC) under the provisions of the Federal Deposit Insurance Act (FDIA) rather than under the Federal Bankruptcy Code. 11 U.S.C. § 109(b). The FDIC is appointed as receiver of the insolvent bank and also acts as insurer of the claims of depositors against the bank for an amount up to $100,000 per depositor. Thus, issues relating to property of the estate of the insolvent bank are governed by the FDIA and its accompanying regulations, rather than by the analysis discussed in the chapter on bankruptcy.

Federal Deposit Insurance Corporation

Treatment by the Federal Deposit Insurance Corporation as Conservator or Receiver of Financial Assets Transferred by an Insured Depository Institution in Connection With a Securitization or Participation
65 Fed. Reg. 49189 (Aug. 11, 2000)

. . . Pursuant to 12 U.S.C. 1821(e)(1), the FDIC, when acting as conservator or receiver of any insured depository institution, has the power to disaffirm or repudiate any contract or lease (i) to which the institution is a party; (ii) the performance of which the conservator or receiver, in the conservator's or receiver's discretion, determines to be burdensome; and (iii) the disaffirmance or repudiation of which the conservator or receiver determines, in the conservator's or receiver's discretion, will promote the orderly administration of the institution's affairs. Repudiation of a contract relieves the FDIC from performing any unperformed obligations remaining under the contract. Repudiation also entitles the other party to the contract to a claim for damages, which are limited by

[2] To qualify as a financial holding company, a bank holding company must be well-capitalized, well-managed and its depository institution subsidiaries must have satisfactory or better Community Reinvestment Act (CRA) ratings. 12 U.S.C. § 1843(*l*).

statute to actual direct compensatory damages determined as of the date of the appointment of the receiver or conservator. *See* 12 U.S.C. 1821(e)(3). In addition, pursuant to 12 U.S.C. 1821(d)(9), 1821(n)(4)(I), and 1823(e), no agreement that tends to diminish or defeat the FDIC's interest in an asset acquired from an insured depository institution is enforceable against the FDIC unless such agreement meets certain requirements. One of those requirements is that the agreement be executed by the depository institution and by any person claiming an adverse interest thereunder contemporaneously with the acquisition of the asset by the institution. This is referred to as the "contemporaneous" requirement.

Under generally accepted accounting principles, a transfer of financial assets is accounted for as a sale if the transferor surrenders control over the assets. One of the conditions for determining whether the transferor has surrendered control is that the assets have been isolated from the transferor, i.e., put presumptively beyond the reach of the transferor and its creditors, even in bankruptcy or receivership. This is known as the "legal isolation" condition.

Whether the legal isolation condition has been met is determined primarily from a legal perspective. This determination involves considerations of the kind of receivership into which the transferor may be placed and the powers of the receiver to reach assets that were transferred prior to its appointment. If the available evidence provides reasonable assurance that the transferred assets would be beyond the reach of the powers of a bankruptcy trustee or receiver for the transferor, then a determination that the transferred assets have been legally isolated is appropriate.

Where the transferor is an insured depository institution for which the FDIC may be appointed as conservator or receiver, the issue arises whether financial assets transferred by the institution in connection with a securitization or in the form of a participation would be put beyond the reach of the FDIC as conservator or receiver for the institution in light of (i) the statutory authority of the FDIC to repudiate contracts to which such institution is a party and (ii) the provisions of sections 11(d)(9), 11(n)(4)(I), and 13(e) of the Federal Deposit Insurance Act regarding the enforceability of agreements against the FDIC. The specific issues are whether the FDIC might, in the exercise of its authority to repudiate contracts, avoid a transfer of financial assets in connection with a securitization or in the form of a participation, and recover such assets; and whether the FDIC might challenge the enforceability of an agreement executed in relation to a transfer of financial assets in connection with a securitization or a participation by asserting the "contemporaneous" requirement with respect to such an agreement.

The final rule resolves these issues by clarifying the powers of the FDIC as conservator or receiver with respect to financial assets transferred by an insured depository institution in connection with a securitization or in the form of a participation. The FDIC believes that this clarification should provide sufficient assurance to determine that the legal isolation condition is met. . . .

[12 C.F.R.] Sec. 360.6 Treatment by the Federal Deposit Insurance Corporation as Conservator or Receiver of Financial Assets Transferred in Connection With a Securitization or Participation.

(a) Definitions. (1) Beneficial interest means debt or equity (or mixed) interests or obligations of any type issued by a special purpose entity that entitle their holders to receive payments that depend primarily on the cash flow from financial assets owned by the special purpose entity.

(2) Financial asset means cash or a contract or instrument that conveys to one entity a contractual right to receive cash or another financial instrument from another entity.

(3) Participation means the transfer or assignment of an undivided interest in all or part of a loan or a lease from a seller, known as the "lead", to a buyer, known as the "participant", without recourse to the lead, pursuant to an agreement between the lead and the participant. Without recourse means that the participation is not subject to any agreement that requires the lead to repurchase the participant's interest or to otherwise compensate the participant due to a default on the underlying obligation.

(4) Securitization means the issuance by a special purpose entity of beneficial interests:

(i) The most senior class of which at time of issuance is rated in one of the four highest categories assigned to long-term debt or in an equivalent short-term category (within either of which there may be sub-categories or gradations indicating relative standing) by one or more nationally recognized statistical rating organizations, or

(ii) Which are sold in transactions by an issuer not involving any public offering for purposes of section 4 of the Securities Act of 1933 (15 U.S.C. 77d), as amended, or in transactions exempt from registration under such Act pursuant to Regulation S thereunder (or any successor regulation).

(5) Special purpose entity means a trust, corporation, or other entity demonstrably distinct from the insured depository institution that is primarily engaged in acquiring and holding (or transferring to another special purpose entity) financial assets, and in activities related or incidental thereto, in connection with the issuance by such special purpose entity (or by another special purpose entity that acquires financial assets directly or indirectly from such special purpose entity) of beneficial interests.

(b) The FDIC shall not, by exercise of its authority to disaffirm or repudiate contracts under 12 U.S.C. 1821(e), reclaim, recover, or recharacterize as property of the institution or the receivership any financial assets transferred by an insured depository institution in connection with a securitization or participation, provided that such transfer meets all conditions for sale accounting treatment under generally accepted accounting principles, other than the "legal isolation" condition as it applies to institutions for which the FDIC may be appointed as conservator or receiver, which is addressed by this section.

(c) Paragraph (b) of this section shall not apply unless the insured depository institution received adequate consideration for the transfer of financial assets at the time of the transfer, and the documentation effecting the transfer of financial assets reflects the intent of the parties to treat the transaction as a sale, and not as a secured borrowing, for accounting purposes.

(d) Paragraph (b) of this section shall not be construed as waiving, limiting, or otherwise affecting the power of the FDIC, as conservator or receiver, to disaffirm or repudiate any agreement imposing continuing obligations or duties upon the insured depository institution in conservatorship or receivership.

(e) Paragraph (b) of this section shall not be construed as waiving, limiting or otherwise affecting the rights or powers of the FDIC to take any action or to exercise any power not specifically limited by this section, including, but not limited to, any rights, powers or remedies of the FDIC regarding transfers taken in contemplation of the institution's insolvency or with the intent to hinder, delay, or defraud the institution or the creditors of such institution, or that is a fraudulent transfer under applicable law.

(f) The FDIC shall not seek to avoid an otherwise legally enforceable securitization agreement or participation agreement executed by an insured depository institution solely because such agreement does not meet the "contemporaneous" requirement of sections 11(d)(9), 11(n)(4)(I), and 13(e) of the Federal Deposit Insurance Act (12 U.S.C. 1821(d)(9), (n)(4)(I), 1823(e)).

(g) This section may be repealed or amended by the FDIC upon 30 days notice and opportunity for comment provided in the Federal Register, but any such repeal or amendment shall not apply to any transfers of financial assets made in connection with a securitization or participation that was in effect before such repeal or modification.

QUESTIONS

1. How does the FDIC's test for the legal isolation of assets in the case of an insolvent bank originator differ from the true sale determination in the case of an insolvent nonbank corporation under general principles of bankruptcy law?

2. How does the FDIC rely on rating agencies? What other system of rules does the FDIC rely on?

§ 7.04. Bank Investment in Securities Issued in a Securitization

The ability of banks to invest in securities is generally limited by 12 U.S.C. § 24(Seventh) (for national banks) and 12 U.S.C. § 335 (for state banks that are members of the Federal Reserve System). Those statutes and the regulations adopted pursuant to them permit banks to own without limitation "Type I" securities. Included within the Type I designation are pass-through mortgage-backed securities issued by Ginnie Mae, Fannie Mae, or Freddie Mac.[3] Pursuant to the Riegle Community Development and Regulatory Improvement Act of 1994, banks may also purchase without limitation commercial and residential mortgage-backed securities (so-called "Type IV" securities) and securities backed by pools of small business loans so long as the securities purchased are rated in one of the top two rating categories.[4] For securities backed by pools of small business loans that do not meet the rating requirement, there is an investment limit of 25% of the bank's capital and surplus for any one issuer. "Type V" securities are other securities based on pools of loans other than those covered by the Type IV designation. Thus, Type V securities include securities backed by auto loans, credit card loans, home equity loans, and other nonmortgage assets. A bank may buy investment grade rated Type V securities so long as the bank's investment in securities of any one issuer does not exceed 25% of the bank's capital and surplus.[5]

QUESTION

If a bank wished to purchase the notes issued in the Honda securitization, could it? Would there be any limitations on the amount of the notes the bank could purchase?

§ 7.05. Capital Calculation

Although banks are highly leveraged enterprises that fund most of their operations with funds borrowed from depositors, they are subject to regulatory minimum capital requirements. As a general matter, the amount of required capital is based on the value of assets adjusted for perceived risk. When a bank sells assets to an SPE, it is usually not required to maintain capital against the assets sold, although retained interests, direct and implicit recourse, and some credit enhancements may present capital issues.

---

[3] Federal Reserve System, Trading and Capital-Markets Activities Manual § 4110.1 (April 2003).

[4] *Id.* § 4105.1.

[5] *Id.*

Federal Reserve System
Trading and Capital-Markets Activities Manual

Section 2110.1

<www.federalreserve.gov/boarddocs/supmanual/trading/trading.pdf>

. . . [T]he baseline for capital-adequacy assessment is an organization's risk-based capital ratio (the ratio of qualifying capital to assets and off-balance sheet items that have been "risk weighted" according to their perceived credit risk). Supervisors also focus on the tier 1 leverage ratio to help assess capital adequacy.[6]. . .

RISK-BASED CAPITAL MEASURE

The principal objectives of the risk-based capital measure are to (1) make regulatory capital requirements generally sensitive to differences in risk profiles among banking organizations; (2) factor off-balance-sheet exposures into the assessment of capital adequacy; (3) minimize disincentives to holding liquid, low-risk assets; and (4) achieve greater consistency in the evaluation of the capital adequacy of major banks throughout the world. The risk-based capital measure focuses primarily on the credit risk associated with the nature of banking organizations' on — and off-balance-sheet exposures and on the type and quality of their capital. It provides a definition of capital and a framework for calculating risk-weighted assets by assigning assets and off-balance-sheet items to broad categories of credit risk. A banking organization's risk-based capital ratio is calculated by dividing its qualifying capital by its risk-weighted assets. The risk-based capital measure sets forth minimum supervisory capital standards that apply to all banking organizations on a consolidated basis.

Definition of Capital

The risk-based capital ratio focuses principally on broad categories of credit risk. For most banking organizations, the ratio does not incorporate other risk factors that may affect the organization's financial condition. These factors may include overall interest-rate exposure; liquidity, funding, and market risks; the quality and level of earnings; investment or loan portfolio concentrations; the effectiveness of loan and investment policies; the quality of assets; and management's ability to monitor and control financial and operating risks. An overall assessment of capital adequacy must take into account these other factors and may differ significantly from conclusions that might be drawn solely from the level of an organization's risk-based capital ratio.

For risk-based capital purposes, a banking organization's capital consists of two major components: core capital elements (tier 1 capital) and supplementary

---

6 [Eds.] The leverage ratio is calculated by dividing a bank's capital by its assets. Generally, the leverage ratio must be 3% or greater. 12 C.F.R. § 3.6 (national banks); 12 C.F.R. pt. 225 (state member banks); 12 C.F.R. pt. 325 (state nonmember banks). The leverage ratio requirement increases if the bank is rated less highly by regulators on other factors during its regular examination.

capital elements (tier 2 capital). Core capital elements include common equity including capital stock, surplus, and undivided profits; qualifying noncumulative perpetual preferred stock (or, for bank holding companies, cumulative perpetual preferred stock, the aggregate of which may not exceed 25 percent of tier 1 capital); and minority interest in the equity accounts of consolidated subsidiaries. Tier 1 capital is generally defined as the sum of core capital elements less goodwill, unrealized holding losses in the available-for-sale equity portfolio, and other intangible assets that do not qualify within capital, as well as any other investments in subsidiaries that the Federal Reserve determines should be deducted from tier 1 capital. Tier 1 capital represents the highest form of capital, namely permanent equity. Tier 2 capital consists of a limited amount of the allowance for loan and lease losses, perpetual preferred stock that does not qualify as tier 1 capital, mandatory convertible securities and other hybrid capital instruments, long-term preferred stock with an original term of 20 years or more, and limited amounts of term subordinated debt, intermediate-term preferred stock, and unrealized holding gains on qualifying equity securities. . . .

Risk-Weighted Assets

Each asset and off-balance-sheet item is assigned to one of four broad risk categories based on the obligor or, if relevant, the guarantor or type of collateral. The risk categories are zero, 20, 50, and 100 percent. The standard risk category, which includes the majority of items, is 100 percent. The appropriate dollar value of the amount in each category is multiplied by the risk weight associated with that category. The weighted values are added together and the resulting sum is the organization's risk-weighted assets, the denominator of the risk-based capital ratio.

Off-balance-sheet items are incorporated into the risk-based capital ratio by first being converted into a "credit-equivalent" amount. To accomplish this, the face amount of the item is multiplied by a credit conversion factor (zero, 20, 50, or 100 percent). The credit-equivalent amount is then assigned to a risk category in the same manner as on-balance-sheet items. . . .

As the Federal Reserve indicated in the excerpt above, off-balance sheet items must be considered in a bank's capital calculation. For instance, bank standby letters of credit are contingent liabilities and hence not reported as debt on a bank's balance sheet. They function much like a bank guarantee of debt and carry a 100% credit conversion factor for capital purposes. Performance bonds or commercial letters of credit related to a particular transaction have a 50% conversion factor, as do unused portions of loan commitments with an original maturity of longer than one year. Short-term trade-related and self-liquidating obligations, such as those represented by a documentary letter of credit, have a 20% conversion factor.

The notion of risk-adjusted capital was pioneered by the Bank for International Settlements (BIS) and its Basel Committee, a panel of central bankers from the major industrialized countries who recognized the need for uniform international capital standards. The Basel Accord of 1988 forms the backbone of the capital ratios required for U.S. banks today and is also used by regulators in over one hundred other countries to measure capital adequacy.

The Accord contemplates two different capital ratios for a bank to be considered "adequately capitalized" — a ratio of Tier 1 capital to risk-adjusted assets and other off-balance sheet items of at least 4%, and a total capital ratio of at least 8%. A "well-capitalized" bank has Tier 1 risk-adjusted ratio of at least 6% and a total capital risk-adjusted ratio of at least 10%.

The Basel Committee is currently considering a revision of the 1988 Accord to recognize the development of enhanced risk measurement techniques and to respond to criticism leveled against it. Critics noted that the 1988 Accord does not consider operational risk and does not measure or account for portfolio risk. Further, the risk-weighting categories employed are crude at best. For instance, all commercial loans — including those to blue chip companies as well as those to risky start-up ventures — carry the same risk weighting even though the former are less risky than the latter.

In response to such criticism, the Committee issued a preliminary proposal to amend the Accord in 1999 (the "First Consultative Paper"). The amendments to the 1988 Accord are generally referred to as "Basel II." After receiving comments on that proposal, a massive revised version was issued in January 2001 (the "Second Consultative Paper"). To properly consider all comments on the proposal the Basel Committee announced that it was postponing its timeline for finalizing the proposal from 2004 to 2005, and in April 2003 the "Third Consultative Paper" was issued.

The new Accord is based on three pillars — a minimum regulatory capital charge, supervisory review, and market discipline. The Basel Committee has attempted to respond to the criticism of the risk-adjusted capital calculation by making the minimum regulatory capital charge more risk sensitive. For instance, rather than weight all corporate loans equally at 100%, the new Accord proposes that corporate loans receive a weighting of 20%, 50%, 100% or 150%, depending on the external credit rating (if any) of the corporate borrower. Borrowers without external credit ratings would be subject to the 100% risk weighting. Critics have noted that unrated borrowers may well be more risky than those that have received a low credit rating.

An alternative to the traditional risk weighting of loans is based on an institution's internal rating of risk. Especially in the case of large, complex banking organizations, the Basel Committee believes that sophisticated internal risk models may be an acceptable (and perhaps even a superior) alternative risk measurement system to the one described above. The internal-ratings based (IRB) approach is described in two forms — a simpler, foundation format and a more advanced framework. The advanced approach provides an individual institution with much greater flexibility in measuring its risk. Some observers believe that allowing an institution to assess its own risk — even when subject to review by the appropriate regulator — is akin to asking the fox to guard the henhouse. In addition, the new Accord proposes to consider how credit risk mitigation techniques, such as guarantees, credit derivatives, and collateralized credit exposures, should factor into an IRB approach.

Basic capital issues are how much capital a bank must hold for securities in which it has invested that were issued in a securitization transaction and whether capital must be held against assets transferred to a SPE for the purposes of securitizing those assets. The Federal Reserve's Trading and Capital-Market Activities Manual provides that:

> a 100 percent risk weighting is assigned for corporate issues and a 20 percent rating for state or municipal issues. Under risk-based capital regulations, a transfer of assets is a "true sale" as long as the banking organization (1) retains no risk of loss and (2) has no obligation to any party for the payment of principal or interest on the assets transferred. Unless these conditions are met, the banking organization is deemed to have sold the assets with recourse; thus, capital generally must be held against the entire risk-weighted amount of the assets sold [subject to certain exceptions.][7]

An additional area of concern for bank regulators is how to assess capital against interests retained by banks in a securitization. This issue gained notoriety as the result of several highly publicized bank failures where the failed banks retained significant interests in securitizations. The resulting new regulatory treatment is described below and replaces a prior Interagency Guidance on Asset Securitization Activities.[8]

---

[7] Federal Reserve System, Trading and Capital-Markets Activities Manual § 4.105.1 (April 2003).

[8] Interagency Guide on Asset Securitization Activities, Board of Governors of the Federal Reserve System, SR 99-37 (SUP), Dec. 13, 1999.

Joint Final Rule of the OCC, FRB, FDIC, and OTS Risk-Based Capital Guidelines; Capital Adequacy Guidelines; Capital Maintenance; Capital Treatment of Recourse, Direct Credit Substitutes and Residual Interests in Asset Securitizations

66 Fed. Reg. 59614 (Nov. 29, 2001) (codified at 12 C.F.R. pt. 3 (OCC), pt. 567 (OTS), pts. 208 & 225 (FRB), pt. 325 (FDIC))

. . .

II. Background

A. Asset Securitization

Asset securitization is the process by which loans or other credit exposures are pooled and reconstituted into securities, with one or more classes or positions, that may then be sold. Securitization[9] provides an efficient mechanism for banking organizations to buy and sell loan assets or credit exposures and thereby to increase the organization's liquidity.

Securitizations typically carve up the risk of credit losses from the underlying assets and distribute it to different parties. The "first dollar," or most subordinate, loss position is first to absorb credit losses; the most "senior" investor position is last to absorb losses; and there may be one or more loss positions in between ("second dollar" loss positions). Each loss position functions as a credit enhancement for the more senior positions in the structure.

For residential mortgages sold through certain Federally-sponsored mortgage programs, a Federal government agency or Federal government-sponsored enterprise (GSE) guarantees the securities sold to investors and may assume the credit risk on the underlying mortgages. However, many of today's asset securitization programs involve assets that are not Federally supported in any way. Sellers of these privately securitized assets therefore often provide other forms of credit enhancement — that is, they take first or second dollar loss positions — to reduce investors' credit risk.

A seller may provide this credit enhancement itself through recourse arrangements. The agencies use the term "recourse" to refer to the credit risk that a

---

[9] [n. 7] For purposes of this discussion, references to "securitization" also include structured finance transactions or programs and synthetic transactions that generally create stratified credit risk positions, which may or may not be in the form of a security, whose performance is dependent upon a pool of loans or other credit exposures. Synthetic transactions bundle credit risks associated with on-balance sheet assets and off-balance sheet items and resell them into the market. For examples of synthetic securitization structures, see Banking Bulletin 99-43, November 15, 1999 (OCC); SR Letter 99-32, Capital Treatment for Synthetic CLOs, November 17, 1999 (Board).

banking organization retains in connection with the transfer of its assets. Banking organizations have long provided recourse in connection with sales of whole loans or loan participations; today, recourse arrangements frequently are also associated with asset securitization programs. Depending on the type of securitization transaction, the sponsor of a securitization may provide a portion of the total credit enhancement internally, as part of the securitization structure, through the use of excess spread accounts, overcollateralization, retained subordinated interests, or other similar on-balance sheet assets. When these or other on-balance sheet internal enhancements are provided, the enhancements are "residual interests" for regulatory capital purposes. Such residual interests are a form of recourse.

A seller may also arrange for a third party to provide credit enhancement[10] in an asset securitization. If the third-party enhancement is provided by another banking organization, that organization assumes some portion of the assets' credit risk. In this final rule, all forms of third-party enhancements, i.e., all arrangements in which a banking organization assumes credit risk from third-party assets or other claims that it has not transferred, are referred to as "direct credit substitutes."[11] The economic substance of a banking organization's credit risk from providing a direct credit substitute can be identical to its credit risk from retaining recourse on assets it has transferred.

Many asset securitizations use a combination of recourse and third-party enhancements to protect investors from credit risk. When third-party enhancements are not provided, the selling banking organization ordinarily retains virtually all of the credit risk on the assets transferred.

B. Risk Management Exposure Arising From Securitization Activities

While asset securitization can enhance both credit availability and a banking organization's profitability, managing the risks associated with this activity can pose significant challenges. The risks involved, while not new to banking organizations, may be less obvious and more complex than the risks of traditional lending. Specifically, securitization can involve credit, liquidity, operational, legal, and reputational risks in concentrations and forms that may not be fully recognized by management or adequately incorporated into a banking organization's risk management systems.

The capital treatment required by the final rule provides one important way of addressing the credit risk presented by securitization activities. However, a banking organization's compliance with capital standards should be complemented by effective risk management strategies. The agencies expect that banking organizations will identify, measure, monitor and control the risks of their

10 [n. 8] As used in this final rule, the terms "credit enhancement" and "enhancement" refer to both recourse arrangements, including residual interests, and direct credit substitutes.

11 [n. 9] For purposes of this rule, purchased credit-enhancing interest-only strips are also "residual interests."

securitization activities (including synthetic securitizations using credit derivatives) and explicitly incorporate the full range of risks into their risk management systems. Management is responsible for having adequate policies and procedures in place to ensure that the economic substance of their risks is fully recognized and appropriately managed. Banking organizations should be able to measure and manage their risk exposure from risk positions in the securitizations, either retained or acquired, and should be able to assess the credit quality of any retained residual portfolio. The formality and sophistication with which the risks of these activities are incorporated into a banking organization's risk management system should be commensurate with the nature and volume of its securitization activities. Banking organizations with significant securitization activities, no matter what the size of their on-balance sheet assets, are expected to have more advanced and formal approaches to manage the risks. . . .

III. Description of the Final Rule: Treatment of Recourse, Residual Interests and Direct Credit Substitutes

This final rule amends the agencies' regulatory capital standards as follows:

- It defines the terms "recourse," "residual interest" and related terms and revises the definition of "direct credit substitute";
- It provides more consistent risk-based capital treatment for recourse obligations and direct credit substitutes;
- It varies the capital requirements for positions in securitization transactions according to their relative risk exposure, using credit ratings from rating agencies to measure the level of risk;
- It permits the limited use of a banking organization's qualifying internal risk rating system to determine the capital requirement for certain unrated direct credit substitutes;
- It permits the limited use of a rating agency's review of the credit risk of positions in structured programs and qualifying software to determine the capital requirement for certain unrated direct credit substitutes and recourse exposures (but not residual interests);
- It requires a banking organization to deduct credit-enhancing interest-only strips, whether retained or purchased, that are in excess of 25% of Tier 1 capital from Tier 1 capital and from assets (concentration limit);
- It requires a banking organization to maintain risk-based capital in an amount equal to the face amount of a residual interest that does not qualify for the ratings-based approach (including credit-enhancing interest-only strips that have not been deducted from Tier 1 capital) (dollar-for-dollar capital); and

- It permits each agency to modify a stated risk-weight, credit conversion factor or credit equivalent amount, if warranted, on a case-by-case basis.

The agencies intend to apply this final rule to the substance, rather than the form, of a securitization transaction. Regulatory capital will be assessed based on the risks inherent in a position within a securitization, regardless of its characterization.

A. *The General Approach Taken in the Final Rule*

. . .

3. Capital Charge for Residual Interests

The final rule imposes a "dollar-for-dollar" capital charge on residual interests and a concentration limit on a subset of residual interests — credit-enhancing I/O strips. Under the combined approach, credit-enhancing I/O strips are limited to 25% of Tier 1 capital. Everything above that amount will be deducted from Tier 1 capital. Generally, all other residual interests that do not qualify for the ratings-based approach (including any credit-enhancing I/O strips that were not deducted from Tier 1 capital) are subject to a dollar-for-dollar capital charge. In no event will this combined capital charge exceed the face amount of a banking organization's residual interests.

. . .

7. Clean-Up Calls

The final rule clarifies the agencies' longstanding interpretations on the use of clean-up calls in a securitization. A clean-up call is an option that permits a servicer or its affiliate (which may be the originator) to take investors out of their positions in a securitization before all of the transferred loans have been repaid. The servicer accomplishes this by repurchasing the remaining loans in the pool once the pool balance has fallen below some specified level. This option in a securitization raises longstanding agency concerns that a banking organization may implicitly assume a credit-enhancing position by exercising the option when the credit quality of the securitized loans is deteriorating. An excessively large clean-up call facilitates a securitization servicer's ability to take investors out of a pool to protect them from absorbing credit losses and, thus, may indicate that the servicer has retained or assumed the credit risk on the underlying pool of loans.

As a result, clean-up calls are treated generally as recourse and direct credit substitutes. However, because clean-up calls can also serve an administrative function in the operation of a securitization, the agencies have included a limited exemption for these options. Under the final rule, an agreement that permits a banking organization that is a servicer or an affiliate of the servicer to elect to purchase loans in a pool is not recourse or a direct credit substitute if the agreement permits the banking organization to purchase the remaining loans in a pool when the balance of those loans is equal to or less than 10 percent of the original pool balance. However, an agreement that permits the remaining loans to be repurchased when their balance is greater than 10 percent of the original pool balance is considered to be recourse or a direct credit substitute. The exemption from recourse or direct credit substitute treatment for a clean-up call of 10 percent or less recognizes the real market need to be able to call a transaction when the costs of keeping it outstanding are burdensome. However, to minimize the potential for using such a feature as a means of providing support for a troubled portfolio, a banking organization that exercises a clean-up call should not repurchase any loans in the pool that are 30 days or more past due. Alternatively, the banking organization should repurchase the loans at the lower of their estimated fair value or their par value plus accrued interest. Regardless of the size of the clean-up call, the agencies will closely scrutinize any transaction where the banking organization repurchases deteriorating assets for an amount greater than a reasonable estimate of their fair value and will take action accordingly. . . .

The agencies have also released Interagency Questions and Answers on the Capital Treatment of Recourse, Direct Credit Substitutes, and Residual Interests in Securitizations.[12]

Typically, bank regulators have viewed the capital adequacy rules and the requirement that banks account for securitizations according to GAAP accounting principles to be adequate to reflect the risks retained by the bank in a securitization transaction in which it is the originator. In December 2001, however, shock waves reverberated throughout the securitization community as Enron, an energy trading firm, declared bankruptcy and came under intense criticism for its use of off-balance sheet SPEs to conceal losses and debt.[13] One of the shocks was felt by PNC Financial Group, which was directed by the Federal Reserve Board to restate its financial reports for 2001 by placing on its balance sheet certain low-quality assets previously transferred to several off-balance sheet SPEs.[14] The FRB appears to have taken this action because of its concern that given certain contractual guarantees and other financial support provisions, PNC had not really transferred to the SPE the credit risks associated with the loans, even though the transactions may have technically qualified as a sale for purposes of GAAP. Some observers raised concerns that the FRB was rewriting GAAP for bank regulatory purposes. At a minimum, it seems that the FRB's actions indicated its intention to look more to the economic substance of the transaction than the form of the transaction. This uncertainty came at the

---

[12] Interagency Questions and Answers on the Capital Treatment of Recourse, Direct Credit Substitutes, and Residual Interests in Asset Securitizations, OCC 2002-22 (May 23, 2002).

[13] *See* Steven L. Schwarcz, *The Uses and Abuses of Special Purpose Entities in Corporate Structures*, 70 U. CINN. L. REV. 1309 (2002)..

[14] *See* Joyita R. Basu, Note, *Accounting for and Disclosure of Special Purpose Entities by Financial Holding Companies: Lessons from PNC Financial Services*, 7 N.C. BANKING INST. 177 (2003).

same time that the Financial Accounting Standards Board (FASB) announced that it would be reviewing and revising GAAP with respect to when an SPE should be consolidated with the originator of the assets for financial reporting purposes — an effort that ultimately resulted in FIN 46. See Chapter 4 on accounting considerations.

Following the FRB's actions in PNC Financial Corporation, the banking regulatory agencies issued an Interagency Guidance on Implicit Recourse. An excerpt is set forth below.

Interagency Guidance on Implicit Recourse in Asset Securitizations

FIL-52-2002 (May 24, 2002)

. . . Generally, the contractual retention of credit risk by a banking organization associated with assets it has sold constitutes recourse. Accordingly, the capital adequacy guidelines require the organization to hold risk-based capital against the entire outstanding amount of those assets securitized. . . .

In contrast to contractual recourse exposures, implicit recourse is a more subtle form of exposure. Implicit recourse arises from an institution providing post-sale support to a securitization in excess of any contractual obligation. Despite differences in how contractual and implicit recourse exposures originate, both types of credit enhancements expose an institution to the risk of loss arising from deterioration in the credit quality of the underlying assets of the securitization. Banking organizations deemed to be providing implicit recourse are generally required to hold capital against the entire outstanding amount of assets sold, as though they remained on the books, for risk-based capital purposes.

Banking organizations typically have provided implicit recourse in situations where the originating organization perceived that the failure to provide this support, even though not contractually required, would damage its future access to the asset-backed securities market. An originating banking organization can provide implicit recourse in a variety of ways. The ultimate determination as to whether implicit recourse exists depends on the facts. However, as discussed in detail later in this document, the following actions point to a finding of implicit recourse:

- Selling assets to a securitization trust or other special purpose entity (SPE) at a discount from the price specified in the securitization documents, which is typically par value;
- Purchasing assets from a trust or other SPE at an amount greater than fair value;
- Exchanging performing assets for nonperforming assets in a trust or other SPE; and
- Funding credit enhancements beyond contractual requirements.

By providing implicit recourse, a banking organization signals to the market that the risks inherent in the securitized assets are still held by the organization and, in effect, have not been transferred. Accordingly, supervisors must be attentive to banking organizations that provide implicit support given the risk these actions pose to the organizations' financial condition. Increased attention should be given to situations where a banking organization is more likely to provide implicit support.

Particular attention should be paid to revolving securitizations, such as those used for credit card lines and home equity lines of credit, where receivables generated by the lines are sold into the securitization. Typically, these securitizations provide that, when certain performance criteria hit specified thresholds, no new receivables can be sold into the securitization, and the principal on the bonds issued will begin to pay out. Such an event, known as an early amortization event, is intended to protect investors from further deterioration in the underlying asset pool. Once an early amortization event occurs, the banking organization could have difficulties using securitization as a continuing source of funding and, at the same time, have to fund the new receivables generated by the lines of credit on its balance sheet. Thus, banking organizations have an incentive to avoid early amortization by providing implicit support to the securitization. . . .

A key factor in each scenario and regulatory determination is the potential risk of loss to which the banking organization's earnings and capital may be exposed as a result of the banking organization's actions. . . .

[The remainder of the Guidance provides numerous examples, including the following:]

After the establishment of a master trust for a pool of credit card receivables, the receivables in the trust begin to experience adverse performance. A combination of lower-than-expected yields and higher-than-anticipated chargeoffs on the pool causes spreads to compress significantly (although not to zero). The banking organization's internally generated forecasts indicate that spreads will likely become negative in the near future. Management takes action to support the trust by purchasing the low-quality (delinquent) receivables from the trust at par although their market value is less than par. The receivables purchased from the trust represent approximately one-third of the trust's total receivables. This action improves the overall performance of the trust and avoids a potential early amortization event.

Issue

Does the purchase of low-quality receivables from a trust at par constitute implicit recourse for regulatory capital purposes?

Regulatory Determination

Yes, this activity constitutes implicit recourse because the purchase of low quality receivables at an above-market price exposes the banking organization's earnings and capital to potential future losses from assets that had previously been sold. Accordingly, the banking organization is required to hold risk-based capital for the remaining assets in the trust as if they were retained on the balance sheet, as well as for the assets that were repurchased. . . .

An Interagency Guidance (excerpted below) has declared that it is an unsafe and unsound practice for a banking organization to include covenants in securitization documents triggering early amortization of the securities issued in the securitization related to supervisory actions. Such supervisory triggers might include downgrading of a banking organization's composite examination rating (the CAMEL rating), a determination by the banking regulator that the banking organization is no longer "well-capitalized," or the imposition of any type of written enforcement action against the banking organization by its regulator.

Interagency Advisory on the Unsafe and Unsound Use of Covenants Tied to Supervisory Actions in Securitization Documents

OCC 2002-21 (May 23, 2002)

. . . . Revolving securitizations such as securitizations of credit cards, commercial loans (CLOs), and home equity lines of credit often use early amortization as a way of protecting investors from deterioration in asset quality. Early amortization events and servicer default triggers are typically defined in the prospectus, pooling and servicing agreement, or insurance agreement if a third-party insurance company guarantees the transaction. Early amortization triggers accelerate the repayment of the principal of the securities issued by the trust ahead of their scheduled maturity. The purpose of early amortization is to protect investors from prolonged exposure to a pool of receivables whose performance has deteriorated.

Typically, early amortization events are tied to quantitative economic triggers such as a minimum level of excess spread,[15] a level of delinquencies on the underlying receivables, or the minimum amount of seller's interest in the pooled receivables. If an early amortization event occurs, investors may lose confidence in the stability of the banking organization's asset-backed securities, limiting the ability of the organization to raise new funds through securitization. At the same time, the organization is continuing to book on balance sheet new receivables that need to be funded. A banking organization heavily reliant upon securitization and lacking alternative sources of funding that is faced with these circumstances will experience liquidity challenges. Covenants that require the transfer of servicing to a third party can result in the loss of earnings, inef-

[15] [n. 3] "Excess spread is generally defined as finance charge collections minus certificate interest, servicing fees, and charge-offs allocated to the series." Standard & Poor's Structured Finance Credit Card Criteria, p. 20.

ficiencies associated with unused servicer capacity, and loss of customer confidence.

The agencies are concerned about the negative safety and soundness implications of covenants that link supervisory actions or thresholds to the trigger of early amortization or the transfer of servicing. Triggers related to supervisory actions can result in a banking organization experiencing an early amortization event at a time when its ability to access other funding sources is limited, thereby resulting in liquidity problems. Such triggers also could potentially inhibit supervisors from taking actions intended to cure problems at a troubled organization because those actions activate a trigger that could cause a worsening of the condition or failure of the organization. Moreover, triggers premised upon the action of banking supervisors could result in an early amortization event when the supervisory action is linked to events that have limited or no relevance to the performance of the securitized assets. Such events may include an adverse change in the issuing organization's supervisory composite rating or regulatory capital status, or a supervisory concern related to compliance with consumer lending laws and the Community Reinvestment Act.

The banking agencies are also concerned that covenants related to supervisory actions may obligate banking organization management to disclose confidential examination information. Management and board members are reminded that information contained within examination reports is confidential. Disclosure of such information by a banking organization's directors, officers, employees, attorneys, auditors, or independent auditors, without explicit authorization by the institution's primary regulator, is a violation of the agencies' regulations.

Banking organization management and boards of directors should ensure that covenants related to supervisory actions or thresholds are not included in securitization documents. Effective immediately, the use of covenants that provide for the early termination of the transaction or compel the transfer of servicing due, directly or indirectly, to the occurrence of a supervisory action or event will, under appropriate circumstances, be criticized as an unsafe and unsound banking practice. The agencies may also take other supervisory or enforcement actions such as requiring additional capital, denying capital relief under low-level recourse exposure provisions for risk-based capital (regardless of GAAP treatment), or other supervisory response at the discretion of the primary supervisor.

QUESTIONS

1. If a bank owned notes issued in the Honda securitization, how would the bank calculate the minimum required capital it would be required to hold against the Honda notes?

2. If a bank securitizes some of its loans, how is it likely to stay involved in the securitization process? Some residual interests retained by banks (and other originators) in securitizations have been referred to as "toxic waste." Do you think that characterization is apt?

Chapter 8

INTERNATIONAL AND CROSS-BORDER ISSUES IN SECURITIZATION

§ 8.01. Introduction

Cross-border securitization involves the interaction of multiple legal systems with, at least to the American-trained lawyer, strange terms and sometimes even stranger rules. A complete mastery of these alien rules and terms is not necessary to be an effective securitization lawyer. Instead, what is needed is a grasp of the fundamental legal principles of cross-border finance, in order to ask the right questions of local counsel and understand the response and its implications. It is, effectively, like learning a new language, but one that has remarkable similarities to our own.

Securitization has an increasingly international focus, in part because companies that wish to raise funds from the capital markets may not be located in countries with established capital markets. In order to access capital market funding, those companies will have to structure deals that cross their national borders.

§ 8.02. Differences in Foreign Markets

The first step in any potential cross-border financing is to determine its jurisdictional framework, including the jurisdictions of the company seeking financing — in our case, the originator — and of the source of that financing. A French company seeking a loan from a French bank located in Paris is not engaged in a cross-border financing; it is a French financing and French law applies. But if a French company wants financing from a United States bank, or from United States (or London or Singapore) capital markets, it is a cross-border financing — requiring examination of the laws of the jurisdictions whose borders have been crossed and the manner in which those laws work (or, more often, fail to work) together.[1]

In any cross-border financing, it is critical to understand the primary differences between and among different legal systems. Most American-trained

[1] The theme of knowing how to ask the right questions of local counsel presumes, of course, that there is a manageable number of jurisdictions in which local counsel will be needed. In some cases, many different jurisdictions have potential connections to the transaction. Resolving those conflicts of laws, to try to reduce the number of local counsel, is the subject of a considerable literature which is beyond the scope of this chapter. *See, e.g.*, EUGENE F. SCOLES & PETER HAY LIPSTEIN, CONFLICT OF LAWS (2000); FRIEDRICH K. JUENGER, CHOICE OF LAW AND MULTISTATE JUSTICE (1993); LAWRENCE COLLINS, ESSAYS IN INTERNATIONAL LITIGATION AND THE CONFLICT OF LAWS (1994).

lawyers, for example, are familiar and comfortable with the common law system. To them, the legal systems of Canada and the United Kingdom may not seem terribly strange. But most of the rest of the world follows a civil law tradition which traces back to Roman times. The difference is critical, for creative common law lawyers helped develop securitization using principles familiar to the common law; transporting securitization to a different legal system requires being able to understand and adapt these fundamental principles. Understanding the differences can be especially critical when a securitization is organized under commonlaw principles, but relies on receivables or other financial assets which were created under a civil regime.

A. Choice of Law Issues

1. Developed Law vs. Undeveloped (or Absence of) Law

In common law countries, the history of commercial law is in part the history of pushing public courts to accept private norms; the law merchant (*lex mercatoria*), now partially incorporated into Section 1-103(b) of the Uniform Commercial Code, was an effort to standardize commercial terms and practices across international borders. In the Eighteenth Century, Lord Mansfield would often convene an advisory jury of merchants knowledgeable in the subject matter of the case before him.[2] Standardization of commercial law across borders through the law merchant brings more certainty to transborder transactions, which helps increase cross-border economic activity that benefits the economies involved. Such standardization often requires many countries, particularly developing ones, to engage in commercial law reform. Often the IMF and World Bank encourage countries to engage in such legal reforms.[3]

---

[2] See Task Force of the A.B.A. Subcommittee on General Provisions, Sales, Bulk Transfers, and Documents of Title, Committee on the Uniform Commercial Code, *An Appraisal of the March 1, 1990, Preliminary Report of the Uniform Commercial Code Article 2 Study Group*, 16 DEL. J. CORP. L. 981, 1284 (1991).

[3] The websites of both the World Bank (www.worldbank.org) and the International Monetary Fund (www.imf.org) contain examples of numerous initiatives designed to modernize the commercial law of developing countries.

Indeed, the norms of international commerce tend to adopt English as the preferred language for international contracts because of its near universality and its adoption by major trading countries such as the United Kingdom and the United States. A good example of this can be found in the October 1998 issue of the *International Business Lawyer*, which was devoted to a symposium entitled *Same Words, Different Meanings: English Legalese in Non-English Contracts*. 26 INT'L BUS. LAW. 1 (1998). Notwithstanding this move towards standardization, lawyers in civil law countries often plead with their common law cousins to be sensitive to the potential differences in law, and the different assumptions different laws make. *See, e.g.,* Vladimíra Glatzová, *When Is a Warranty Not a Warranty? Common Law Versus Civil Law*, 26 INT'L BUS. LAW. 453 (1998).

Nowhere is this drive for certainty and standardization better seen than in securitization. Securitization initially evolved in a common law environment. It relies on common law recognition of the ability to transfer in bulk present and future receivables for a present consideration. These common law notions may not, however, be universally recognized, as shown in the following excerpt.

Bruce A. Markell, *A View from the Field: Some Observations on the Effect of International Commercial Law Reform Efforts on the Rule of Law*

6 IND. J. GLOBAL LEGAL STUD. 497, 502-05 (1999)

. . . A short story illustrates these differences, even among so-called developed countries. I have represented the International Bar Association at the UNCITRAL receivables convention working group sessions. My status as an American law professor is known. During the discussions, the group was grappling with the thorny issue of proceeds. The draft convention, at least in English, specified the conditions under which a secured party would get proceeds of receivables; that is, when the secured party could claim the payments made in satisfaction of the receivables transferred. Under United States securitization law, proceeds play an important role. When a secured party's collateral is sold or parted with by its debtor, the proceeds concept automatically gives the secured party a property interest in the goods or property received in exchange, without the necessity of any writing or other action by the parties.

When examining the relevant provision, in each of the seven official languages of the United Nations, the discussion seemed to be at cross-purposes. In an effort to simplify the matter, so I assume, the chair of the working group asked me (without notice) to explain the concept of proceeds to the whole group. Fighting back the fears that used to accompany being called on in law school, I gave what I thought was a short explanation along the above lines. When I was finished, there was a short silence, followed by the chair's instruction to the interpreters not to translate the word "proceeds" when uttered by a delegate, and simply to use the English word, presumably because what I had explained was not picked up by common translations of the word. I use this example not to illustrate that legal terms sometimes do not translate well. Rather, given the centrality of the proceeds concept to financial tools such as securitization, the example shows that even when the United Nations gets countries to talk about harmonization of commercial law, the process of commercial law reform is not easy, even among developed States.

The reaction of global capital markets to such continuing differences in commercial law regimes is not hard to predict. Uncertainty in application of commercial law confronts investors with increased costs, perhaps chilling investments the host nation desperately needs. Commercial law reform, in keeping with international harmonization, signals not only legal and economic certainty, but also commitment to the rule of law more generally. Such signals attract global capital and produce benefits for the domestic economy.

The flow of these benefits, and how different legal systems can choke it off, is illustrated by the following transaction. When visiting Indonesia to study the feasibility of a personal property security law I was a member of a team that interviewed many lenders and debtors. We sought, among other things, to learn how goods were actually being financed in the absence of a formal personal property security system. One of the lenders we visited had been in the business of lending funds to enable Indonesians to purchase motorcycles. In the year prior to the current Asian crisis, they had financed over 400,000 motorcycles through a simple title retention system. For each loan, they investigated the creditworthiness of the borrower by checking not only publicly available sources, but also by sending an agent to interview the proposed borrower's family, neighbors, and local vendors. When the loan was made, no payment book or other system of isolated payment was used. Rather, the company employed 4000 agents to make 11,000 individual collections per day. The interest rate on such loans? Thirty-six to thirty-eight percent. As this business grew, global capital markets took note. A securitization was proposed. Many legal obstacles were met, including the uncertainty that Indonesian law would recognize the bulk transfer of so many receivables and whether the various currencies involved could be traded at the level needed to hedge the risks involved. But the deal was done. And the effective rate for the investment secured by these high-yield receivables? We were told it was seven to eight percent.

The vast difference in interest rates before and after securitization is a crude measure of the cost to a country such as Indonesia of having legal systems (and, quite frankly, political instability) at odds with those that built and which drive global capital markets. Even with certainty of text and norms, however, there remains other, equally daunting, impediments confronting the spread of the rule of law through harmonization of commercial law.

2. Civil Law vs. Common Law

It is not an exaggeration to say that civil law and common law approaches to taking security or collateral to ensure the repayment of obligations differ radically, or even contradict, each other at significant points. The civil law, for example, generally has not looked expansively on the assignment of intangibles such as receivables.[4] In particular, the laws of many civil law countries do not permit assigning receivables in bulk[5] or the assignment of receivables not yet

[4] *See, e.g.*, Spiros Bazinas, *Multi-Jurisdictional Receivables Financing: UNCITRAL's Impact on Securitization and Cross-Border Perfection*, 12 DUKE J. COMP. & INT'L L. 365 (2002); Bruce A. Markell, *UNCITRAL's Receivables Convention: The First Step But Not the Last*, 12 DUKE J. COMP. & INT'L L. 401 (2002).

[5] That is, an assignment that does not specify the debtor or other facets of the debt. A typical bulk assignment could read: "X transfers all receivables owed to it on this date to Y."

in existence.[6] Moreover, the civil law may not recognize a transfer unless the person obligated on the receivable (the debtor) receives notice of the transfer. Furthermore, a transfer for security of a right to payment will be invalidated if the underlying contract contains an anti-assignment clause.[7]

Under current practices, these restrictions can limit the financing opportunities available to many companies. The costs associated with describing every receivable definitively upon its creation and so notifying the debtor, may significantly impact the cost of credit, by multiplying the administrative work necessary to ensure an effective transfer. This can be detrimental to credit, in that it would require the borrower and debtor to create new agreements each time a receivable, or batch of receivables, arose, thus greatly increasing administrative costs. This is unfortunate since receivables are a very desirable form of credit, and with the emergence of companies based upon information technology, may be one of the few types of collateral that financing institutions will be willing to lend against.

If capital markets are intended to be the source of financing, one *also* must consider the local regulatory restrictions on the use of those markets. For example, United States capital markets are a significant source of securitization financing because they have a broad investor base and efficient pricing. However, as set forth in Chapter 6, the issuance of securities to investors in these markets may require disclosure and regulation, particularly if the securities are issued without restrictions on trading (so-called "public" offerings). In contrast, offshore or Euromarkets may be more flexible, but may have a more limited investor base. Issuers of securities sometimes can avoid regulation entirely by combining markets — for example, using United States capital markets for a private placement of subordinated debt to support a public offering of senior debt securities conducted offshore.

B. Structuring the Transaction

Often a financing transaction — particularly a securitization — can be structured as a loan or a sale.[8] In many jurisdictions, a secured lender's remedies may be so strong that a sale structure provides only a marginal advantage. If struc-

---

6 This would occur if the grant were something like "X transfers to Y all receivables now owed or hereafter arising."

7 *See generally* John H. Merryman, The Civil Law Tradition: Europe, Latin America and East Asia 1169 (1994); Philip R. Wood, Comparative Law of Security and Guarantees 4-5 (1995); Ulrich Drobnig, *Secured Credit in International Insolvency Proceedings*, 33 Tex. Int'l L.J. 53, 60 (1998); Richard Walsh, *Pacific Rim Collateral Security Laws: What Happens When the Project Goes Wrong?*, 4 Stan. J.L. Bus. & Fin. 115, 124-25 (1999).

8 For an article analyzing whether particular securitization transactions should be viewed as loans or sales, see Peter Pantaleo et al., *Rethinking the Role of Recourse in the Sale of Financial Assets*, 52 Bus. Law. 159 (1996).

tured as a loan, its form is relatively simple. In the United Kingdom, for example, secured creditors' rights are considered to be sufficiently strong that some securitizations are structured as "whole-business" securitizations, in which all of the assets of a business may be taken as security for a loan which is in turn securitized. This structure works only because of the conclusion that the holder of the type of security involved — a floating charge — can dispossess a bankruptcy trustee and administer the defaulting debtor's assets for the benefit of the holders of the floating charge.[9]

On the other hand, in some jurisdictions the commercial laws governing loans secured by receivables may be so unsophisticated compared to the laws governing the sale of receivables that a sale is a more prudent structure. Or it may be the that local law protects the originator's assets against creditor enforcement, as with the automatic stay under United States bankruptcy law.[10] In such cases, investors may prefer a sale structure. When deciding how to structure the transaction, the essential question is the extent to which the investors providing the financing will be repaid in the event of the local law equivalent of a bankruptcy case.

A related question is how the originator must account for the transaction on its balance sheet. If the transaction is a loan, the originator would account for it as debt. But if the transaction is accomplished through a sale, the originator may be able to avoid booking a debt ("off balance sheet" financing). The ultimate accounting treatment, however, would be subject to the accounting principles that prevail in the originator's jurisdiction.[11]

C. Commercial Finance Issues

The next section examines how the SPE and its investors stand as against the originator's creditors. These questions typically are addressed by laws that

---

9 *See* Benedicte Pfister, *Whole Business Securitizations: A Unique Opportunity for UK Assets* (Moody's Investor Service, International Structured Finance Special Report, Oct. 19, 2000) (describing how whole business securitizations have been used in the United Kingdom to securitize businesses such as hotels, pubs, theme parks and airports).

10 *See* 11 U.S.C. § 362, discussed in Chapter 3. A secured creditor could not foreclose on its collateral without court permission, which is rarely given. European countries increasingly have been adopting bankruptcy laws that include a stay of action by creditors against a bankrupt company in order to facilitate the company's rehabilitation. *See generally* Eberhard Schollmeyer, *The New European Convention on International Insolvency*, 13 BANKR. DEV. J. 421 (1997).

11 Accounting principles vary widely between different systems; in the United States, "Generally Accepted Accounting Principles" (GAAP) are used for reporting purposes. For other purposes, as in tax or corporate law, deviations from GAAP are permitted. How substantial the differences between jurisdictions can be is best illustrated by an example. When Daimler-Benz, the German automaker, wanted to have a listing on the New York Stock Exchange it did not want to file financial information according to United States GAAP. When it eventually did file, it showed a loss of DM 949 million instead of a profit of DM 168 million it had shown under German accounting rules. *See* David Waller, *Daimler-Benz Pierces Accounting Mystique*, FIN. TIMES, Sept. 23, 1993, at 24.

seek to allocate priority to collateral or to ensure equality of distribution, or to preserve the integrity, of a debtor's estate.

1. Perfection and Priority

As discussed in Chapter 2, the term "perfection" often is used to refer to protection of a transferee's interest in transferred assets from the transferor's creditors.[12] For assets that are physically located in a particular jurisdiction, the law of that jurisdiction, or sometimes of the transferor's jurisdiction, usually governs perfection. In a securitization transaction, perfection means protecting the SPE's interest in the transferred receivables from claims of the originator's creditors. Because receivables are intangible, and therefore not physically located in any particular jurisdiction, the law of the originator's jurisdiction intuitively would be expected to, and usually does, govern perfection. But that is not universally the case.

Some jurisdictions have a filing or other public notice system for perfection.[13] Other legal systems may require notification of obligors, which may be unacceptable and expensive.[14] Often, the local perfection procedures may be unclear or impractical, in which case investors are forced to rely on the originator's representations, warranties, and covenants that the assets transferred to the SPE are, and will remain, unencumbered by third parties.

Priority refers to the ranking of multiple claims against a transferred asset. In a securitization context, it means that the SPE's and investors' claims against the transferred receivables are superior to any third-party claims. In a jurisdiction that requires perfection by filing, priority is normally accomplished by being the first to file against the assets.[15] If the originator is located in a jurisdiction that does not have a filing or other registration system to indicate priority, the investors again may have to rely on the originator's representations, warranties, and covenants. This, of course, creates a much greater risk of fraud than where a public filing system is used.

---

[12] Or from the transferor's bankruptcy representative. In some jurisdictions, the concept of perfection is not well recognized. Once an asset is transferred, the transferor is simply deemed no longer to have an interest in the asset.

[13] The purpose of filing is "to place third parties on notice of the transfer" of the asset. In the United States this is usually done by filing a UCC-1 financing statement.

[14] Besides the obvious costs involved in having to notify all the obligors of, for example, trade receivables, it sometimes may also be culturally unacceptable to do so because notification might be seen as a signal that the company is in financial difficulties. "This is a problem practitioners often run into. . . . But it is a problem that is not documented in the literature." Petrina R. Dawson, *Rating Games with Contingent Transfer: A Structured Finance Illusion*, 8 DUKE J. COMP. & INT'L L. 381, 399 n.102 (1998).

[15] See the authorities cited in note 7, *supra*. Sometimes referred to as "first-in-time, first-in-right," this generally gives priority to the first person to file against the asset. Priority is ascertained by searching the filing records to determine whether other parties have prior filings against the relevant collateral or assets. *See, e.g.*, UCC § 9-323.

If the transaction involves receivables that will be created at a future date, one also must ask if the local law permits the transfer of an asset not then in existence.[16] Bankruptcy or insolvency laws[17] also may restrict an originator's ability to transfer its future assets.[18]

Without a system for making transfers of receivables publicly ascertainable, receivables financings are discouraged because assignees will not be able to determine their priority at the time of the transfer.

2. Commingling

Another risk is that cash proceeds of assets pledged or sold to an SPE may be mixed, or "commingled," with the originator's own funds. This risk to some extent reflects common sense: if the originator is freely permitted to use collections, a court may find the originator's control inconsistent with the SPE's claim that it has a perfected interest in the collections. Local law may ameliorate this risk somewhat.[19] Commingling also can be prevented by using lockboxes, or by segregating cash flows. Control over cash flows — such as requiring obligors to make payments into a trust account located in the United States — also may mitigate the perfection risk.[20] If these approaches are not available, one should ascertain whether proceeds are traceable, and ask local counsel whether traced proceeds are protected.[21]

---

16 As indicated by the authorities cited in note 7, many civil law jurisdictions provide that a pledge or assignment can only be made when an asset exists. This is based on the civil law view that a pledge is a real right "as opposed to a personal right; it gives the creditor a right to seize and sell assets and get a privilege on the proceeds of the sale." Michael H. Rubin & McGinchey Stafford Lang, *Recent Developments In Security Devices, With an Emphasis on Louisiana Law*, SB21 ALI-ABA 571, 588 (199x).

17 Such as 11 U.S.C. § 552. *See* Steven L. Schwarcz, *Protecting Rights, Preventing Windfalls: A Model for Harmonizing State and Federal Laws on Floating Liens*, 75 N.C. L. REV. 403, 434 (1997) (analyzing United States bankruptcy law restrictions on floating liens, and arguing those restrictions should not apply to securitization transactions).

18 In a collateral context, a lien on future arising assets is often referred to as a "floating lien." *See* UCC § 9-204, cmt. 2, and one of the express purposes of Article 9 in the United States is the validation of such floating liens. UCC § 9-205, cmt. 2.

19 *See, e.g.*, UCC § 9-315(b) (providing a formula that limits to some extent the degree to which a perfected security interest will be lost by commingling).

20 In many civil law countries, however, bailment, custody, and other trust concepts are not always recognized with respect to commingled cash, as civil law countries generally do not recognize trust concepts. *See generally* Donovan W. M. Waters, *The Institution of the Trust in Civil and Common Law*, 252 RECUEIL DES COURS 113 (1995); Justin P. Thorens, *The Common Law Trust and the Civil Law Lawyer*, *in* COMPARATIVE AND PRIVATE INTERNATIONAL LAW: ESSAYS IN HONOR OF JOHN HENRY MERRYMAN ON HIS 70TH BIRTHDAY 309-15 (David S. Clark ed., 1990).

21 Another potential concern is that the method of perfection may refer to the original collateral, but not the proceeds. If the anticipated form of the proceeds is known (e.g., cash), that concern can be alleviated by also describing the proceeds.

D. Contractual and Legal Restrictions

After determining or selecting the applicable law, the next issue is to determine whether applicable contractual or legal restrictions regarding the applicable financial assets will affect the financing. With respect to contractual restrictions, there are two principal types of restrictions. First, there may be restrictions in the contract (anti-assignment clauses) pursuant to which collateral or receivables are originated. For example, a lease or license contract may prohibit the lessor's (or licensor's) assignment of rights to payment received thereunder. Under United States law, certain restrictions on the assignment of receivables, such as accounts receivable, are unenforceable,[22] but the laws of other jurisdictions may, and do, differ.

The second type of contractual restrictions can arise through negative pledge or similar covenants contained in the originator's financing documents.[23] Sometimes financings must be restructured to get around a restrictive covenant. This takes creativity and an understanding of how the covenant is to be interpreted. For example, would a covenant restricting a secured loan also restrict a sale? The answer can be ambiguous if, under the governing law, the line between a sale and a secured loan is unclear. Furthermore, the governing law is not always obvious. For example, the covenant may be contained in a financing document stated to be governed by English law, but the covenant may prohibit liens on assets of a company located in Mexico. To determine whether English law or Mexican law governs the interpretation of whether the financing in question violates the covenant by creating a lien, counsel in both jurisdictions must be consulted. Sometimes even then the answer may be unclear.

E. Enforcement Issues

1. Private Enforcement Issues

In an international context, it is not enough to have theoretical rights under the law. The critical question is whether one can enforce those rights, recognizing that the legal system granting the rights may not be the same as the one in which enforcement occurs, and that foreigners may not be viewed favorably when enforcing rights against local citizens. In some developing economies,

---

22 *See* UCC § 9-401(b)("An agreement between the debtor and secured party which prohibits a transfer of the debtor's rights in collateral or makes the transfer a default does not prevent the transfer from taking effect.").

23 These financing documents typically were put into place for other financings, not the financing being structured. For example, "negative pledge clauses" prohibit or limit the creation of secured debt. On the issue of negative pledge clauses, see generally Thomas C. Mitchell, *The Negative Pledge Clause and the Classification of Financing Devices: A Question of Perspective* (pts. 1 & 2), 60 AM. BANKR. L.J. 153, 263 (1986).

bribery and graft combine to produce decision at odds with the written law.[24] In light of these problems, investors will want the originator to submit to their jurisdiction, or at least the jurisdiction of the SPE. Of course, investors must determine whether those jurisdictions would enforce such an arrangement. Submission to jurisdiction could entail, for example, appointing an agent of the originator in the investors' (or SPE's) jurisdiction to accept service of legal process, usually referred to as a "process agent."

If investors can obtain jurisdiction over the originator in their own (or the SPE's) jurisdiction, it may not matter that the originator has no significant assets outside of its home jurisdiction. Investors would simply sue where the originator has submitted to jurisdiction, obtain a judgment, and take the judgment to the originator's home jurisdiction to be enforced.[25] However, counsel in the home jurisdiction should be consulted in advance to verify whether such a judgment would be recognized and what, if any, defenses could be raised to its enforcement.

2. Enforcement Issues Related to Sovereignty of Parties

Another potential problem is that the originator itself could be immune from suit under its local law, particularly if it has sovereign or quasi-sovereign ownership.[26] Requiring the originator to waive sovereign immunity may be a solution to this problem. In the United States, for example, such a waiver is enforceable under the United States Foreign Sovereign Immunities Act of 1976, as amended.[27] This, however, only means that United States courts will respect the waiver of sovereign immunity. One still must ask local counsel whether the waiver will be respected in the originator's jurisdiction.

---

[24] *IBRA Critisizes Jakarta Commercial Court*, THE JAKARTA POST, May 19, 2000 (reporting that the state restructuring agency, IBRA, was voicing "concerns against 'funny' verdicts" that seemed to go "beyond human logic," and indicating that "informed source[s] said the cost of fighting bankruptcy at the Jakarta Commercial Court ranged between $20,000 and $40,000.")

[25] While arbitral awards are governed by the United Nations' Convention for the Recognition and Enforcement of Foreign Arbitral Awards, no such treaty exists for the enforcement of foreign judgments. Countries often recognize foreign judgments on the basis of reciprocity. In the United States, this varies from state to state; however, several states have adopted the Uniform Foreign Money Recognition Act and the Uniform Enforcement of Foreign Judgment Act. *See generally* Shirley Sostre-Oquendo, *Recognition and Enforcement of Foreign Judgments in the United States and Canada in the Free Trade Era*, 1992 DET. C.L. REV. 1019. In other countries similar laws exist. *See, e.g.*, INTRODUCTION TO THE LAW AND LEGAL SYSTEM OF KOREA 1152 (Sang Hyun Song ed., 1983).

[26] Sovereign immunity is traditionally a concept of public international law. Under this concept the sovereign, historically the monarch, today the state and its officials, cannot be sued unless they consent. While it was considered to be absolute in the beginning, over time certain recognized exemptions have developed. *See* MALCOM N. SHAW, INTERNATIONAL LAW 491-522 (4th ed. 1997). The most important exemption under the United States Foreign Sovereign Immunity Act is the "commercial activity exemption." *See* 28 U.S.C. § 1603(d). A similar example can be found in the United Kingdom in § 3(3) of its State Immunity Act of 1978.

[27] *See* 28 U.S.C. §§ 1602 *et seq.*

Other sovereign risks include currency exchange controls — the risk that the originator's home jurisdiction may limit the export or private use of United States dollars or other relevant foreign currency.[28] This risk might be mitigated by issuing securities denominated in local currency (rather than United States dollars).[29] Risk mitigation can also be attained if the originator has significant assets outside its home jurisdiction or offshore obligors on receivables,[30] or by arranging local currency swaps for United States dollars (discussed below in Section IV). One should also inquire whether the originator's home jurisdiction has ever imposed, or is likely to impose, debt moratoria of the type that would restrict the originator from paying its debts to foreigners.[31] Finally, inquiry should be made as to whether the SPE must be licensed in that jurisdiction to enforce its rights against the originator.

QUESTIONS

1. You are the general counsel for an investment company. Your company has been asked to buy debt instruments backed by the present and future revenues of a hydroelectric dam to be built in a foreign country. The debt instruments are part of a securitization of the future revenues of the power sales the dam will generate. What questions do you ask on behalf of your investors?

2. Same facts as Question 1. From a purely legal standpoint, does it matter to you if the dam is to be built in a civil law or a common law country? A developing or an industrialized nation?

3. One aspect of Revised Article 9 (adopted in all United States jurisdictions since 2001) is that taking a perfected security interest in a bank account is as

---

[28] Currency control has occurred before in several places, for example Brazil, Nigeria, China, Romania, South Africa, Venezuela and, at least de facto, in Mexico. *See, e.g.*, Scott McMurray, *Soybean Futures Prices are Expected to Plunge on Reforms Unveiled by the President of Brazil*, WALL ST. J., Mar. 19, 1990, at C12; Thomas Petzinger Jr. & Peter Truell, *U.K. Audit Points to Larger BCCI Role by Two Top United States Cable-TV Executives*, WALL ST. J., Jan. 17, 1992, at A4; *Trade Conference in Beijing Attracts United States Businessmen*, WALL ST. J., June 21, 1988; *Romania Revives Currency Curb*, WALL ST. J., Feb. 27, 1992, at A8; Ken Wells, *United States Investment in South Africa Quickens*, WALL ST. J., Oct. 6, 1994, at A15; *Observer: Caracas Chestnut*, FIN. TIMES, July 25, 1994, at 15; David Asman, *The Americas: Complex Models Won't Stop Mexico's Peso From Tumbling*, WALL ST. J., Feb. 17, 1995, at A11.

[29] However, exchange controls could limit the export of the local currency. Furthermore, investors may not want to invest in securities denominated in a local currency.

[30] That way, enforcement against those assets or obligors will not, de facto, be subject to the local laws of the company's country.

[31] Debt moratoria have happened before, for example in the Philippines, South Africa and Russia. *See* Julia Leung, *Filipinos Plan Again to Issue Overseas Bonds*, WALL ST. J., Oct. 30, 1992, at B4B; Neil Behrmann, *South Africa Hopes to Reschedule Debt as Total Declines*, WALL ST. J., June 11, 1993; Terence Roth & Tim Carrington, *Moscow Stops Paying Bank Debt Principal*, WALL ST. J., Dec. 5, 1991, at A3. Political risk insurance sometimes may be available to cover specific risks, although it is very expensive. *See* Claire A. Hill, *How Investors React to Political Risk*, 8 DUKE J. COMP. & INT'L L. 283 (1998).

easy as placing the words "I grant a security interest in bank account xxx to secure all debt to bank" in the contract between the bank and the customer. *See* UCC §§ 9-203(b)(3)(D); 9-104. How does this fact enter into any structuring decisions with regard to a proposed cross-border securitization?

§ 8.03. UNCITRAL's Receivables Convention[32]

Starting in 1995, and ending with final approval the United Nations General Assembly in 2002, the United Nations Commission on International Trade Law (known by its acronym, "UNCITRAL") has produced an international convention that is designed to overcome many of the obstacles noted in Section II above.[33] As drafted, UNCITRAL's Convention on the Assignment of Receivables in International Trade (the "Convention")[34] is an ambitious document. As stated in its preamble, one of the goals of the Convention is to "promote the availability of capital and credit at more affordable rates and thus facilitate the development of international trade."[35] It seeks to achieve this aim by regularizing the process by which a lender or other financier secures a borrower's repayment obligation with receivables. In this regard, the Convention seeks to standardize the law of transfer by, among other things, permitting the assignment of receivables in bulk, as well as the assignment of future receivables.[36] The Convention also provides guidance on when the debtor on a receivable must pay the assignee,[37] and when such payment discharges the debtor's obligation on the receivable.[38]

A law that desires or aims to be attractive to securitization investors, however, needs to address priority upon default or insolvency of any one of the participants. Indeed, such provisions are critical; the interest rate and willingness to

---

32 This section borrows heavily and is based upon Richard F. Broude & Bruce A. Markell, *The Priority Provisions of the UNCITRAL Convention on the Assignment of Receivables in International Trade*, 11 INT'L INSOLVENCY REV. 121 (2002).

33 Although at the end of 2003 only three countries have signed the Convention, one of those is the United States (although Senate ratification is necessary for the Convention to be effective). Many more countries are said to be seriously considering its adoption. The Convention will come into force six months after the fifth nation approves of the Convention. Art. 45, ¶ 1.

34 The full Commission approved the text at its thirty-fourth session in July, 2001. *Report of the United Nations Commission on International Trade Law on its thirty-fourth session* (Vienna, 25 June — 13 July 2001), United Nations document A/56/17, at 38-39 (July 27, 2001) [hereinafter, the "*Report*"]. The text became final and official upon adoption by the United Nations General Assembly at its 85th plenary meeting on December 12, 2001. Resolution 56/81, General Assembly of the United Nations (New York, December 12, 2001), United Nations document A/RES/56/81, at 1-2 (January 15, 2002) [hereinafter, as the "*Resolution*"]. Both the *Report* and the *Resolution* contain identical versions of the *Convention's* text. *Report, supra* at 82-98; *Resolution, supra* at 2-22.

35 *Convention*, Preamble, 5th ¶, *reprinted in Resolution*, supra note 34, at 3.

36 Art. 8.

37 Art. 17, ¶ 2.

38 Art. 15, ¶ 6.

invest depend on its ability to assess and quantify the risk of default. The Convention handles priority through a combination of carefully selected definitions and through special provisions related to the potential insolvency of the assignor,[39] found in Section III of Chapter 4, consisting of Articles 22-25. This chapter looks at the relevant definitions and then at the articles devoted specifically to priority.

A. Definitions

The Convention begins with definitions. For purposes of examining the priority provisions, the most relevant definitions are those of a receivable, an assignment, location and of priority itself. Also important are the definitions of the parties involved.

1. Parties

The Convention anticipates that assignment of receivables will occur in transactions consisting of three parties. The person who owes the obligation encompassed by the receivable is the "debtor,"[40] and it is upon the credit of the debtor that most transactions covered by the Convention will depend. Either alone or in bulk, the ability of debtors to pay, and the timeliness of their payments, provide the safety and collateral that are prerequisites to the lending of funds.

The debtor obviously owes its obligation to someone. Under the Convention, that someone is called the assignor.[41] In a credit transaction, it is the assignor who borrows the money secured by the monetary obligations owed to it by the assignor's debtors.[42]

The final member of the triad is the financier, the person supplying credit to the assignor on the strength of the receivables assigned. Under the Convention,

---

[39] The Convention is primarily concerned with the insolvency of the assignor, and does not have much, if any, application to the potential insolvency of the the assignee or debtor. *Note by the Secretariat, Receivables Financing: Commentary to the draft Convention on Assignment in Receivables Financing (Part II)*, at ¶ 106, UNCITRAL Document A/CN.9/WG.II/WP.106 (September 16, 1999) [hereinafter, "WP106"].

[40] Art. 2(a). The full text of Article 2(a) bears repeating, since it contains many key terms:

> (a) "Assignment" means the transfer by agreement from one person ("assignor") to another person ("assignee") of all or part of or an undivided interest in the assignor's contractual right to payment of a monetary sum ("receivable") from a third person ("the debtor"). The creation of rights in receivables as security for indebtedness or other obligation is deemed to be a transfer;[. . . .]

[41] *Id.*

[42] The full definition of assignor is set forth in note 40.

this person is called the assignee,[43] a term indicating that it receives some interest, or is assigned some interest, in the receivable from the assignor.[44]

2. Basic Terms: "Assignment" and "Receivable"

The Convention also carefully defines its most basic terms: assignment and receivable. An assignment:

> means the transfer by agreement from one person ("assignor") to another person ("assignee") of all or part of or an undivided interest in the assignor's contractual right to payment of a monetary sum ("receivable") from a third person ("the debtor").[45]

This is a fairly straightforward definition. It includes a partial assignment, as in the transfer of an undivided part interest. It also includes an assignment for purposes of security.[46] As long as there is some agreed transfer of some interest in the underlying contract right, it will qualify as an assignment.

The definition of receivable is similarly straightforward, and contained in the definition quoted above. It is a "contractual right to payment of a monetary sum."[47] Notice first that to be covered by the Convention, the receivable must be contractually based; initial efforts to bring within the Convention non-contractual rights to pay money (such as court judgments and some types of obligations owed by governmental entities) were abandoned in favor of a narrower scope.

What is left, however, is still quite broad. Given the generic and global definition, it is easier to state what types of payment obligations are excluded than are covered, and that is the province of Article 4. Specifically excluded are the rights and obligations of any person under the law governing negotiable instruments.[48] Also excluded are assignments "made . . . (b) [a]s part of the sale or change in the ownership or legal status of the business out of which the assigned receivables arose."[49]

---

[43] The full definition of assignee is set forth in note 40.

[44] Financing practice in the United States and Canada uses different terms. Under American and Canadian practice, the debtor is an "account debtor"; the assignor is a "debtor"; and the assignee is a "secured party".

[45] Art. 2(a).

[46] This is made explicit by the last sentence of Article 2(a): "The creation of rights in receivables as security for indebtedness or other obligation is deemed to be a transfer."

[47] Art. 2(a).

[48] Art. 4, ¶ 3.

[49] Art. 4, ¶ 1(b).

Finally, the Convention excludes assignments made "[t]o an individual for his or her personal, family or household purposes,"[50] Note that this exclusion, which refers to the nature of the assignment and not to the nature of the receivable, does *not* take consumer receivables out of the Convention. To the contrary, if a consumer receivable is assigned for something other than "personal, family or household purposes," as in the securitization of credit card receivables, it is covered by the Convention so long as the other requirements, such as internationality, are present.

3. Priority

Priority under the Convention "means the right of a person in preference to the right of another person . . . ."[51] This definition is very simple — it includes priority of payment, such as arises from contractual subordination or from a simple statutory priority. It does not necessarily mean, however, priority based upon having a superior and senior interest in property; the definition only includes such determinations "to the extent relevant for [the] purpose" of determining the right of preference.[52] Put another way, when the Convention uses the term priority, it does not necessarily refer to a priority *in rem*,[53] but may include

---

[50] Art. 4, ¶ 1(a). This type of assignment is unlikely to occur in numbers that would be significant.

[51] Art. 5(g). The definition goes on to state that "to the extent relevant for such purpose, [the term "priority"] includes the determination whether the right is a personal or a property right, whether or not it is a security right for indebtedness or other obligation and whether any requirements necessary to render the right effective against a competing claimant have been satisfied." *Id.*

[52] Art. 5(g). These references were made to ensure that the Convention will only determine the relative rights of the assignee, the assignor and any competing claimant; there is no intent to change or alter the rights of non-parties. *See Report, supra* note 34, at ¶ 149.

> "Competing claimant," in turn, is defined as any other assignee of the receivable (whether or not the Convention applies to the assignment under which that assignee makes claim); a creditor of the assignor, or the assignor's insolvency administrator. Art. 5(m).

[53] In an earlier draft, the determination of a right as *in rem* or *in personam* was left undecided. As explained in the proposed commentary:

> The *in rem* nature of the right in proceeds is an issue that is distinct from the issue of priority. A claimant with priority in accordance with the law applicable under the draft Convention will obtain payment first and will prevail over another claimant (other than a claimant with a super-priority, non consensual right; see draft article 25 (5)) whether that other claimant has a right *in rem* or *ad personam* . . . . However, the *in rem* nature of the right of a claimant with respect to proceeds may be decisive in the case of insolvency. If the claimant with priority has a right *in rem* with respect to proceeds, that claimant will be able to separate the proceeds from the insolvency estate (if an outright assignment is involved) or be treated as a secured creditor and receive payment before unsecured creditors (if an assignment by way of security is involved). If, on the other hand, a claimant with priority has a right *ad personam*, it will receive payment proportionately with other unsecured creditors, if there is any balance left after payment of any creditors with special privileges and security rights.

WP106, *supra* note 39, at ¶ 95.

a reference to such *in rem* rights if such reference is required in order to determine the answer to any particular inquiry.

Priority also is a concept applied after the assignment is deemed valid between the assignor and the assignee under appropriate law.[54] This determination often involves matters upon which the Convention is silent intentionally, such as a writing requirement, or a requirement that particular language be used to effectuate a transfer.[55] Such matters are left to the law outside the Convention, and the Convention supplies no guidance on what law should supply the rules for such formal requirements — whether they should be the laws of the forum state, the laws of the debtor's location or the laws of the assignor's location.[56]

4. Location

The defined term location serves two distinct purposes in the Convention. Initially, the location of the parties determines the applicability of the Convention. Only if at least two of the three basic parties are in different "locations" does the Convention apply.[57] That is, the Convention applies to the domestic assignment of international receivables (a situation arising when the debtor is located in a state different from the assignor), as well as to the international assignment of domestic receivables (a situation arising when the assignee is located in a different state from the assignor).[58]

A second and, for purposes of securitization, more important use of location is in the fixing of priority systems. The next part of this Section examines this use (and also sets forth the specific definitions).

---

54 WP106, *supra* note 39, at ¶ 72.

55 Indeed, the Commission at its approval session deleted the following provision from the text of the Convention:

> An assignment is valid as to form if it meets the form requirements, if any form requirements exist, of either the law of the State in which the assignor is located or any other law applicable by virtue of the rules of private international law.

Report, supra note 34, at ¶ 162.

56 Although early drafts of the Convention included a section on formal requisites to an assignment, the final draft of the Convention deals with form only in Article 27, which is in the Convention's optional conflicts of law Chapter. *Report, supra* note 34, at ¶ 163.

Chapter V, containing the autonomous choice of law rules, is optional by virtue of Article 39, which permits a signatory to opt-out of Chapter V by special declaration.

57 Art. 1(a). The Convention also applies to a wholly-domestic receivable (all three parties are in one state) if, at one time, two of the three parties were in different states; that is, once the Convention applies to a receivable, subsequent assignments will not affect that jurisdiction. Art. 1(b).

58 *See* Art. 3 (defining internationality of receivables).

B. Priority Provisions — Direct Application of the Convention

The Convention, and its priority rules, directly apply only if the assignor is located in a state which has ratified the Convention.[59] The principal priority provisions of the Convention themselves are found in Section III of Chapter IV of the Convention, consisting of Articles 22 through 25. The main approach, however, is evident in Article 22, which states:

Article 22
Law applicable to competing rights

With the exception of matters that are settled elsewhere in this Convention and subject to articles 23 and 24, *the law of the State in which the assignor is located governs the priority of the right of an assignee* in the assigned receivable over the right of a competing claimant.[60]

As indicated in this text, Article 22 and the Convention do not adopt a single substantive rule of priority. That approach was attempted initially, but abandoned in part due to the perception that it would lead to a document that would be unacceptable to many, and that the necessary (but perhaps not optimal) levels of certainty and simplicity could be attained through a choice of law rule.[61]

In its stead, the Convention adopts a single choice of law rule, so that parties will at least have a unique pointer to a specific state as the source of priority rules governing the assignment.

This makes location critical, since Article 22's pointer is to the state where the assignor is located. In this regard, the Convention adopts the following definition of location in Article 5(h):

(h) A person is located in the State in which it has its place of business. If the assignor or the assignee has a place of business in more than one State, the place of business is that place where the central administration of the assignor or the assignee is exercised. If the debtor has a place of business in more than one State, the place of business is that which has the closest relationship to the original contract. If a person does not have a place of business, reference is to be made to the habitual residence of that person;[62]

---

[59] Art. 1, ¶ 1(a). The priority rules of the Convention might apply, however, even if the Convention does not directly apply if the jurisdiction in which the priority contest with respect to an assignment has adopted the Convention, and has not opted out of Chapter V. See discussion in text regarding Chapter V and its effects.

[60] Art. 22 (emphasis supplied).

[61] *Report of the Working Group on International Contract Practices on the Work of its Twenty-Seventh Session* (Vienna, 20 - 31 October 1997), ¶ 22, UNCITRAL Document A/CN.9/445 (November 21, 1997).

[62] Art. 5(h). There was a proposal to define the location of a bank, and its branches, separately, but it ultimately did not prevail. *Report, supra* note 34, at ¶¶ 150-53.

Thus, one looks not to the place of formal location (as would be the case if the Convention had chosen the place of incorporation as location), but to the substance of where the assignor has its place of central administration. Note that this is not the same as the "centre of main interests" adopted in UNCITRAL's Model Law on Cross-Border Insolvency. Under Article 16(3) of that document: "In the absence of proof to the contrary, the debtor's registered office, or habitual residence in the case of an individual, is presumed to be the centre of the debtor's main interests."

As a consequence, under the Model Law there is a presumption of location, and the burden of going forward with evidence as to location falls only upon those who wish to challenge the presumption. With respect to receivables, however, the Convention adopts a different approach. It does not adopt a presumption, instead relying on a functional definition: an assignor or assignee is located at the "place where the central administration of the assignor or the assignee is exercised."[63] Without the benefit of a presumption such as given by the Model Law, the Convention will affect the burden of going forward with the evidence, placing it on the party initiating litigation seeking or challenging priority in all cases.

In most cases, this will not be problematic. The parties will look to where decisions are made, where assets are found, and where business is booked. If these indicia do not uniquely point to one state, financiers will be left in no worse a situation than they are at present, and will endeavor to ensure that their interest is valid in each jurisdiction in which the assignor is possibly located.

Once the assignor's location is identified, the Convention supplies rules to resolve disputes among competing assignees, among the assignor's creditors and the assignee, and between the assignor's insolvency administrator and the assignee.[64] It does this by defining these three classes of claimants as "competing claimants," in Article 5(m).[65] In short, effort was made to ensure that,

---

63 Art. 5(h).

64 The Convention borrows the definitions of "insolvency administrator" from the Cross-Border Model Law. Under the Convention, an "insolvency proceeding" is defined in Article 5(f) as:

> a collective judicial or administrative proceeding, including an interim proceeding, in which the assets and affairs of the assignor are subject to control or supervision by a court or other competent authority for the purpose of reorganization or liquidation;

In turn, an "insolvency administrator" is defined in Article 5(e) of the Convention as:

> a person or body, including one appointed on an interim basis, authorized in an insolvency proceeding to administer the reorganization or liquidation of the assignor's assets or affairs;

65 Article 5(m) provides:

(m) "Competing claimant" means:

(i) Another assignee of the same receivable from the same assignor, including a person who, by operation of law, claims a right in the assigned receivable as a result of its right in other property of the assignor, even if that receivable is not an international receivable and the assignment to that assignee is not an international assignment;

(ii) A creditor of the assignor; or

(iii) The insolvency administrator.

assuming universal adoption of the Convention, a court in the debtor's location would cause the debtor to pay an amount owing on a receivable to the assignor *even if* the domestic, non-Convention law of the debtor's location would not so provide. This result would obtain even if the law of the debtor's location does not adopt the priority rule so applied (as would occur if an assignor were located in a state adopting a priority system based on registration, and the debtor were in a state which maintained a priority system based upon temporal priority of assignment only). This result should also be obtained regardless of whom the competing claimant is — be it another assignee, an unrelated creditor of the assignor or the assignor's insolvency administrator.

The law thus selected not only provides the substantive rules on priority, but, through the application of that forum's rule on priority, will also select any rules on whether the assignee has *in personam* or *in rem* rights (or both) to any proceeds of the receivables.[66] In this context, the Convention defines proceeds as:

> whatever is received in respect of an assigned receivable, whether in total or partial payment or other satisfaction of the receivable. The term includes whatever is received in respect of proceeds. The term does not include returned goods.[67]

The Convention also contains special rules on proceeds, but these also attempt to reflect the inquiry back to the law of the forum state, and are discussed later.[68]

In its most basic form, the Convention thus attempts to require a court subject to the Convention to determine all substantive disputes regarding the priority of an assignment of receivables, and the disposition of any proceeds, under the law of the assignor's location.[69]

---

[66] Art. 24, ¶ 1. The dual nature of this rule is facilitated by its incorporation through use of the term "proceeds," which decidedly is ambiguous as to whether an *in rem* or an *in personam* right is involved. See Art. 5(g).

[67] Art. 5(j). Note that this definition includes proceeds of proceeds, which will cause courts to engage in various forms of tracing to give effect to the definition.

[68] Art. 24, ¶ 1. This rule, and the special rule for proceeds held by the assignor when the proceeds are intentionally segregated, are discussed below.

[69] This follows directly if the state in which the assignor is located has adopted the Convention. Art. 1, ¶ 1(a). This follows indirectly if the dispute in litigated in a state, most likely that of the debtor, which has adopted the Convention and has not excluded application of Chapter V. *See* Art. 30, ¶ 1.

C. Priority Provisions — Indirect Application Through the Conflicts of Laws Provisions of the Convention

The priority rules of the Convention might apply, however, even if the Convention does not directly apply if the jurisdiction in which the priority contest occurs with respect to an assignment has adopted the Convention. This is because the conflicts of laws rules contained in Chapter V contain the same priority rules as does Chapter IV. In particular, Article 30 of the Convention states that:

Article 30
Law applicable to priority

1. The law of the State in which the assignor is located governs the priority of the right of an assignee in the assigned receivable over the right of a competing claimant.

2. The rules of the law of either the forum State or any other State that are mandatory irrespective of the law otherwise applicable may not prevent the application of a provision of the law of the State in which the assignor is located.

3. Notwithstanding paragraph 2 of this article, in an insolvency proceeding commenced in a State other than the State in which the assignor is located, any preferential right that arises, by operation of law, under the law of the forum State and is given priority over the rights of an assignee in insolvency proceedings under the law of that State may be given priority notwithstanding paragraph 1 of this article.

Thus, if a state where a debtor is located has adopted the Convention, but the assignor's state has not, a court sitting in the debtor's state will be directed by Chapter V in general, and Article 30 in particular, to the law of the assignor's location to resolve any priority contest. This is the same rule as adopted in Chapter IV for receivables as to which the Convention directly applies. Put another way, by altering a state's conflict of laws rules for all cross-border transactions in receivables, the Convention directs courts in the states which adopt it to apply the law of the assignor's state to resolve priority, regardless of whether the Convention formally applies to the particular transaction.

By way of example, if the debtor is located in the state in which the litigation is brought, and that state has adopted the Convention including Chapter V, then the forum court is arguably bound by Article 30 of the Convention. That article directs the court, notwithstanding the inapplicability of the Convention to the particular receivable, to apply the law of the assignor to resolve the priority dispute. In this sense, Chapter V indirectly extends the Convention to cases in which the forum state, but not the state in which the assignor is located, has adopted the Convention.

D. Exceptions: Public Policy and Governmental Priorities

As simple as the basic choice of law rules are, there are some exceptions. First, the Convention deals with the obvious objection that application of another jurisdiction's priority rules may be contrary to the forum state's public policy. Article 23, ¶ 1 addresses this, and sets a high standard to be met before a forum state's public policy can be used to frustrate application of the law of the assignor. It states:

> The application of a provision of the law of the State in which the assignor is located may be refused only if the application of that provision is manifestly contrary to the public policy of the forum State.[70]

This public policy, however, is restricted. It is limited to international public policy,[71] the application of which could result in setting aside a priority rule of the law applicable but not in the positive application of a priority rule reflecting the public policy of the forum State. As noted in the proposed commentary:

> For a priority rule to be set aside under [Art. 23, ¶ 1], it must be "manifestly contrary" to the public policy of the forum State. The notion of "manifestly contrary" is used in international texts (including article 6 of the UNCITRAL Model Law on Cross-Border Insolvency, article 16 of the Rome Convention and article 18 of the Inter-American Convention on the Law Applicable to International Contracts) as a qualification of public policy. The purpose of such a qualification is to emphasize that public policy exceptions should be interpreted restrictively and [Art. 23, ¶ 1] should be invoked only in exceptional circumstances concerning matters of fundamental importance for the forum State. Otherwise, the certainty achieved by draft article [22] could be seriously compromised, a result that would have a negative impact on the availability and the cost of credit on the basis of receivables.[72]

---

[70] Art. 23, ¶ 1.

[71] The *Report* notes that:

> It was widely felt that the word "manifestly" was necessary to ensure that public policy exceptions would be interpreted restrictively and paragraph 1 would be invoked only in exceptional circumstances concerning matters of fundamental importance for the forum State.

Report, supra note 34, at ¶ 39. The restrictive scope of the language is made clear in the proposed commentary:

> The public policy meant in paragraph (3) [now paragraph (1)] is the international public policy of the forum State. Recourse to such public policy has only a negative effect in the sense that it may defeat the application of a provision of the law applicable under draft article 25 [now 23] which is manifestly contrary to the public policy of the forum State (*e.g.*, a rule giving priority to a foreign State for taxes).

WP106, *supra* note 39, at ¶ 89.

[72] WP106, *supra* note 39, at ¶ 90.

In some cases, however, there may be significant governmental objectives frustrated by the application of non-forum law. Tax claims of the forum state and wage claims for workers in the forum state are but two of the possible classes of claims that might deserve different treatment. This different treatment is adopted in Article 23(3), which states:

> [I]n an insolvency proceeding commenced in a State other than the State in which the assignor is located, any preferential right that arises, by operation of law, under the law of the forum State and is given priority over the rights of an assignee in insolvency proceedings under the law of that State may be given priority notwithstanding Article 22. A State may deposit at any time a declaration identifying any such preferential right.[73]

An illustration of this is as follows. Assume that both Canada and the United States are parties to the Convention. Assume further than an insolvency proceeding with respect to an assignor located in the United States is commenced in Canada, and that the assignor owes a priority tax debt to the government of Canada. Assume that this debt is of the type that would have priority over assignees with *in rem* rights in receivables (as is the case with a floating, but not a fixed, charge). This tax claim, however, would not enjoy such a superior position in the United States; while recognized, it would simply be a priority unsecured debt, and would be paid out of non-collateral.[74] Finally, assume that the assignor's Canadian assets are equal to the tax debt and that the assignor's debt to the assignee is the same as the tax claim, so that depending on priority issues, payment of either the tax claimant or the assignee would effectively preclude payment to the other.

A quick reading of Article 23 would initially indicate that the Canadian insolvency court should not accord the tax debt any priority, because the Convention says that the law of the assignor's location supplies the rules of priority, and United States law would not accord priority. Under Article 23(3), however, a Canadian insolvency court may, even if contrary to United States law, apply Canadian law to give the debt priority in the Canadian proceeding. As a consequence, the Canadian court could subordinate or defeat the competing claims of the financier/assignee to the tax claimants.[75]

E. Exceptions: Certain Types of Proceeds

The critical exception to the Convention's private international law solution to priority is contained in Article 24. In that Article, the Convention creates some

---

73 Art. 23(3).

74 11 U.S.C. § 507(a)(8). Under the United States bankruptcy law, a foreign government is recognized as a "governmental unit" and thus is entitled to priority treatment for all tax claims on the same basis as domestic tax claims.

75 *See* Report, *supra* note 34, at ¶ 39.

special substantive rules regarding proceeds to apply whenever courts are bound to apply the Convention. Article 24 is divided into three paragraphs, the first two of which deal directly with priority.[76] Article 24, ¶ 1 deals with priority as to proceeds received by the assignee, such as payments made directly by debtors to the assignee such as a factor or invoice discounter. The Convention allows the assignee to keep such payments to the extent that the assignee would, under the law applicable in the location of the assignor, have priority with respect to the receivable that generated the proceeds. Specifically, the Convention states:

> If proceeds are received by the assignee, the assignee is entitled to retain those proceeds to the extent that the assignee's right in the assigned receivable had priority over the right of a competing claimant in the assigned receivable.[77]

By way of illustration, assume that assignor X owes money to creditor Y. Debtor Z owes money to X. Y and Z are both located in the same state (Gondor); X is located in a different country (Fillmore), as is assignee A . A lends funds to X, and takes as collateral the receivable owed X by Z, in the process taking all steps necessary under Fillmore law to perfect its security interest. A notifies Z of the assignment, and notifies Z to pay A directly; Z does.

Even if Gondor has a rule that states that A would hold all payments by Z in trust for Y (if, for example, Y belonged to a privileged class of creditors, such as those defrauded by X), Article 24, ¶ 1 allows A to keep the proceeds so long as Fillmore has adopted the Convention, and A has taken all actions necessary under Fillmore law to perfect A's security interest. Of course, the forum state would have to be bound, either because it is a Convention state or otherwise, to apply the Convention.

The second paragraph of Article 24 provides for a more critical change. It applies in situations in which the assignor has received proceeds of a receivable, and governs the relative rights between the assignor and assignee when such a circumstance occurs. Article 24, ¶ 2 states:

> If proceeds are received by the assignor, the right of the assignee in those proceeds has priority over the right of a competing claimant in those proceeds to the same extent as the assignee's right had priority over the right in the assigned receivable of that claimant if:
>
> (a) The assignor has received the proceeds under instructions from the assignee to hold the proceeds for the benefit of the assignee; and

---

[76] The third paragraph protects the rights of setoff, such a bank might have, if the proceeds can be traced to an asset (a bank account or another receivable) against which setoff can be exercised. As a consequence, if a receivable is paid by check, and the check deposited into a bank account, the account will be proceeds, but the bank may have, under applicable law, a setoff right should the assignor owe it any obligation. *See Report, supra* note 34, at ¶ 43.

[77] Art. 24, ¶ 1.

(b) The proceeds are held by the assignor for the benefit of the assignee separately and are reasonably identifiable from the assets of the assignor, such as in the case of a separate deposit or securities account containing only proceeds consisting of cash or securities.[78]

This section focuses on a counterfactual: it awards priority based on what that priority *would have been* had the payment *not* been made. This special priority, however, arises in only one specific situation. To obtain the benefit of this special rule, (a) the assignee must have taken all necessary steps to perfect its interest in the original receivable under the law of the state in which the assignor is located; (b) the assignor must be instructed to hold the proceeds for the benefit of the assignee (as if the assignor had been told to segregate or hold the proceeds in trust); *and* (c) the assignee must be able to trace and identify the proceeds in the possession of the assignor, such as when the parties have made arrangements for a separate bank account to hold all collections with respect to assigned receivables, and that account is in the name of the assignor.

Thus, if an assignee would have had priority over an insolvency administrator with respect to an uncollected receivable, that priority will extend to a collected receivable to the extent that the assignee has instructed the assignor to hold the proceeds for the benefit of the assignee,[79] if the receipts are being held in a segregated account.[80]

F. Model Priority Provisions

Although the Convention does not adopt a single *substantive* rule of priority (except as to some forms of proceeds), the working group recognized that many legal systems do not have well-developed rules for sorting out priorities in receivables. To that end, Article 42 of the Convention permits states as they adopt the Convention to select from among five different priority systems set

---

[78] Art. 24, ¶ 2.

[79] It is not clear whether the instruction to hold the proceeds for the benefit of the assignee needs to be specific to the particular collection, or may be a generic instructions contained, for example, in the original documents of assignment. Given the goals of the Convention, which are laid out in the text at note 34 *supra*, the latter would seem to be the better interpretation.

[80] The report makes clear that Article 24, ¶ 2 is a safe harbor that parties may opt into by structuring their transactions in accordance with the requirements of the rest of Article 24. As the *Report* states:

> It was widely felt that draft article [24] introduced a special rule applicable only where parties chose to structure their transactions in a certain way so as to take advantage of the protection afforded by draft article [24]. It was stated that such a rule, which was not unlike special national legislation, could benefit parties to securitization or confidential invoice discounting transactions, which were common practice all over the world and on the basis of which parties were able to obtain more credit and at a more affordable cost.

WP106, *supra* note 39, at ¶ 4.

forth in the Annex to the Convention.[81] Adoption of any one of these options then sets the priority rules that are to be used in connection with determining the law of the assignor's location under Article 22.[82] A state may also choose not to make such a declaration.

In any event, the Convention anticipates that at least some Contracting States will adopt a system of registration of notice of security interests in receivables, and to that end looks to establish such a registry.[83] To induce use of the registry, a state could adopt the Convention, not make a declaration under Article 42, but still use the registry.[84]

G. The Convention and Securitization

If widely adopted, the Convention will facilitate cross-border securitization. It seeks to overcome the seemingly inevitable contradiction of local laws not by changing them all to one standard, but rather providing a universal pointer to the law that will determine priority and which will enforce rights upon default. This is second-level certainty, but certainty of a sort nonetheless. Until such time as there truly is a universal "law merchant," the Convention should provide sufficient certainty to allow expansion of securitization in those countries which adopt it, which in turn will enable the Convention to achieve its aims of making more credit available at lower prices to all economies.

QUESTIONS

1. How well does UNCITRAL's convention handle questions regarding priority of receivables?

2. Assume the convention is in effect, and that you are responsible for the legal architecture of a securitization of credit card receivables from Sri Lanka. If Sri Lanka has not adopted the convention, but the jurisdictions of the SPE and the debtor (the credit card issuer) have, what effect does this have on your structuring decisions?

3. You are asked for advice on how to structure a securitization of consumer receivables in Sweden, a country which has adopted the UNCITRAL convention (and which convention is in force). Your local counsel tells you that the non-Convention law of Sweden strictly enforces anti-assignment clauses in contracts, and would view a securitization as a prohibited assignment. You are also told that the receivables to be securitized will likely have such anti-assignment clauses. Sweden, a civil law country, adopted the Convention without change,

---

[81] Art. 42, ¶ 1.

[82] Art. 42, ¶ 2.

[83] Convention, Annex, Section II. *See also Report, supra* note 34, at ¶¶ 100-03.

[84] Art. 42(4).

and the adopting statute did not refer to the general law of assignments. Does the non-Convention law of Sweden on assignments give you cause for concern?

§ 8.04. Exchange Rate Risk and Other Risks Related to Foreign Currency Exchange

Currency exchange issues loom large in cross-border finance. The problem is that the currency in which investors invest may be different than the currency received to repay them. For example, if investors buy United States dollar-denominated securities to enable an SPE to purchase a portfolio of Japanese yen-denominated receivables, the investors would be taking the added risk that, when the receivables pay, the dollar-to-yen exchange rate would yield insufficient dollars to repay them.[85] Investors generally prefer the exchange rate risk to be "hedged"[86] through "swaps" and other derivative products.

A "derivative" product means a contract that creates future rights and obligations regarding an asset that underlies a larger transaction.[87] Derivative products can be broken down into forward contracts and options. In an option, one party pays for the right (but not the obligation) to buy an asset at a future date for a negotiated price. A forward contract is a contractual obligation to buy (or, from the seller's standpoint, to sell) an asset, such as foreign currency, at a specified price at a future settlement date. A swap is an array of forward contracts — a forward contract covering each date that settlement is to be made.[88]

---

85 Of course, investors could convert the yen to dollars on the spot market. "A spot transaction involves the immediate purchase of, payment for, and delivery of a fixed amount of a currency. Such transactions are said to occur on the spot market. AMA MANAGEMENT HANDBOOK 6-43 (John J. Hampton ed., 3d ed. 1994) at 6-43. But fluctuating exchange rates put investors at risk that a weakened yen would yield insufficient dollars.

86 "Hedging, using the futures market, is the process of neutralizing or significantly reducing financial risks . . . . There are two fundamental reasons for hedging. The first is to reduce risk . . . . The second is the ability to separate the timing decision from market opportunities." *See id.* at 6-32.

87 See, *e.g.*, Joseph L. Motes III, Note, *A Primer on the Trade and Regulation of Derivative Instruments*, 49 SMU L. REV. 579, 583-84 (1996). A great deal of derivative documentation is standardized worldwide through use of so-called "ISDA forms" developed by the International Swaps and Derivatives Association.

88 *See* Motes, *supra* note 87, at 590. The actual underlying swapped assets are rarely exchanged. Rather, one party to the swap makes a payment to the other based on the net valuation of the swapped assets on the future settlement date. *See* JOHN F. MARSHALL & KENNETH R. KAPNER, THE SWAPS MARKET 32 (2d ed. 1993) ("The underlying assets may or may not be exchanged and are referred to as notionals."). The asset could be foreign currencies in the case of currency swaps in cross-border finance transactions, or might be oil in the case of a swap involving a company that needs oil at a future date and wants to fix the price. Swaps are therefore akin to gambles on future asset values. Indeed, there is ongoing controversy as to whether derivative products can be abused, particularly where investors borrow on leverage to purchase derivative products for speculation. In a non-leveraged context, however, the use of derivatives to hedge currency (or interest rate) risks in cross-border transactions is not only prudent but essential for minimizing the risk to investors.

Currency hedging is accomplished by entering into a swap with a third party (called a swap counterparty[89]) to exchange the relevant currencies at the future settlement dates. The parties contractually agree in advance to the exchange rate that will be deemed to apply on those settlement dates to ensure that the currency conversion will yield sufficient dollars to repay investors.[90]

Investors, of course, will want to be comfortable that the counterparty will be able to perform its swap obligations on each settlement date if the net value of the swap at that date runs against the counterparty.[91] If, therefore, there is a realistic risk that the counterparty may be unable to perform, the investors may attempt to minimize performance risk by requiring the counterparty to collateralize its future obligations or obtain a third-party guaranty, not unlike a lender requiring assurance of future performance from a borrower. The performance risk also can be minimized by requiring the counterparty to make daily or other periodic adjustment payments of the changing net value of the swap, thereby reducing the risk that the counterparty will be unable to pay the net amount due at a future date. This is referred to as "marking to market."[92]

The terms of the swap agreement also may be relevant. For example, any conditions precedent to effectiveness may need to be satisfied at the closing when the investors provide financing. Also, the SPE may be subject to taxes if it gains the advantage of the swap.

§ 8.05. Tax Issues

Tax issues in cross-border securitizations will include those relevant in purely domestic transactions, discussed in Chapter 5, as well as certain additional issues. Issues common to both United States and cross-border transactions (*e.g.*, sale vs. loan of receivables or entity-level tax on SPE) may have to be determined under foreign as well as (or instead of) United States law, depending on the location of the originator, the receivables and the SPE. Additional tax issues, unique to cross-border situations, are described below.

---

89 Counterparties are often financial institutions, or their affiliates, that deal in derivative products (swap dealers).

90 Thus, if the investors expect to receive payment in Japanese yen and, based on the anticipated amount of yen, need an exchange rate of 126.29 yen per United States dollar to be fully repaid in dollars, a swap counterparty would be sought who is willing to exchange dollars for yen at that rate on the future settlement dates. If on a settlement date the exchange rate has changed to 130 yen per dollar, the investors would be protected because the swap counterparty has taken the currency exchange risk. But the swap party would profit on the exchange if the exchange rate has become 125 yen per dollar.

91 That is, if the exchange rate has changed to make the value of the currency that the counterparty has agreed to sell higher than the price it agreed to accept for the sale.

92 For a description of the mark-to-market methodology, see THE HANDBOOK OF CURRENCY AND INTEREST RATE RISK MANAGEMENT 25-29 (Robert J. Schwartz & Clifford W. Smith Jr. eds., 1990). Forward contracts that include periodic marking to market are called "futures contracts."

A. Withholding Tax

Payments in a securitization transaction of amounts treated as interest for income tax purposes may be subject to United States or foreign withholding taxes, and the cost thereof must be factored into the particular transaction. This can occur, for example, if there is a tax sale of receivables with obligors in one country paying interest on the underlying receivables to an SPE or investors in another country; if a transaction between the originator in one country and an SPE or ultimate investor in another country is treated as a tax loan; or if an SPE in one country raises money by issuing debt to investors in another country.

Many countries, including the United States (at a statutory rate of 30 percent), impose a withholding tax on the gross amount of interest paid to certain foreign persons not otherwise engaged in business in the country from which the interest is paid.[93] The amount is withheld by the payor on behalf of the payee and paid over to the appropriate taxing authority.[94] Frequently, this withholding tax is reduced or eliminated pursuant to the applicable terms of an income tax treaty between the country of the payee and that of the payor, but this will not always be the case. If not eliminated, it will be necessary to determine which party will bear the cost of the tax. In most cases, this cost will be borne by the borrower, by means of an indemnity and "gross-up" provision under which the borrower is required to pay the lender an extra amount so as to compensate, on an after-tax basis, for the tax withheld. Establishing an SPE in a tax haven jurisdiction or in a jurisdiction with a wide tax treaty network sometimes may minimize withholding tax costs.

Bilateral tax treaties (between the originator's and the SPE's jurisdictions), where they exist, can reduce or eliminate withholding taxes. For example, such tax treaties exist between the United States and most major European countries, and also among European Union countries.

---

93 I.R.C. §§ 1441, 1442. There is a statutory exemption from United States withholding tax for "portfolio interest." I.R.C. §§ 871(h); 881(c). "Portfolio interest" does not, however, include interest received by a bank on an extension of credit made pursuant to a loan agreement entered into in the ordinary course of its trade or business (I.R.C. § 881(c)(3)(A)), interest received by parties owning 10 percent or more of the interests in a debtor corporation or partnership (I.R.C. §§ 871(h)(3)(B); 881(c)(3)(B)), or certain "contingent" interest, determined by reference to cash flow, income, change in value of property or distributions made by a debtor or related person (I.R.C. § 871(h)(4)). The portfolio interest exemption will be available in certain securitization transactions.

94 The IRS has issued regulations which, to some degree, simplify the responsibilities of withholding agents and the means of identifying entitlement to exemptions from withholding tax. *See, e.g.,* Treas. Reg. § 1.1441-1(e) (discussing withholding agent's reliance on beneficial owner withholding certificates, intermediary withholding certificates, qualified intermediary withholding certificates and certain presumptions available to withholding agents for purposes of treating a payee as foreign or domestic).

B. Taxation of the SPE and Its Shareholders

As noted above, it sometimes may be desirable to form an SPE involved in a cross-border securitization in a tax haven jurisdiction. This will both minimize withholding tax on any interest payments made *by* the SPE and avoid mainstream tax on net income of the SPE, assuming it is an entity subject to such tax. Use of a tax haven can, however, also increase the potential withholding tax burden on any interest payments to be made *to* the SPE, either by the underlying obligors on the receivables or by the originator, because tax havens are not typically parties to tax treaties that would eliminate withholding taxes.

It is also important to ensure that the SPE will not be subject to any mainstream income tax in a jurisdiction other than that in which it is actually resident. For example, if the SPE owns receivables of obligors in another jurisdiction and the originator services the receivables in that other jurisdiction on behalf of the SPE, the question arises whether the SPE will be deemed "doing business" or to have a "permanent establishment" in that jurisdiction. Either finding could subject the SPE to mainstream income tax in that jurisdiction. Generally, however, the SPE will not be subjected to such tax if the servicer is performing purely ministerial functions and has no power to bind the SPE in any way (*e.g.*, by virtue of being able to agree to changes in the terms of the receivables).

With respect to the United States, a corporation will not be deemed engaged in a trade or business therein if it only effects transactions in stocks or securities for its own account; this is because there is a statutory safe harbor against being treated as so engaged if activities are limited to investment for one's own account.[95] If, however, an SPE is buying many different obligations (including loans and loan participations) over a period of time, an issue arises as to whether the SPE would be viewed as engaged in some part of financing business; such a finding would remove the SPE from the protection of the investment safe harbor. To minimize this risk, certain guidelines should be observed, including, for example, restricting the SPE to buying loans in the secondary market rather than originating loans; not permitting the SPE to buy revolving facilities, which raise an issue of origination; not permitting negotiation of specific terms of loans; and/or prohibiting an SPE from receiving amounts denominated as fees that could be construed as having been received in return for performance of services.

If the SPE is a foreign corporation with United States shareholders, account must also be taken of certain so-called "anti-avoidance" provisions of the Internal Revenue Code. These include the Subpart F rules on "controlled foreign corporations" (or "CFCs"), *i.e.,* foreign corporations controlled by United States shareholders, and the "foreign personal holding company" and "passive foreign investment company" (or "PFIC") rules.

---

[95] I.R.C. § 864(b)(2)(A).

Under the Subpart F rules,[96] certain earnings (including passive interest and dividend income) of United States-controlled foreign corporations may be treated as taxable to the United States shareholders even if not actually distributed. In addition, deemed dividends can result if a CFC's assets serve, either directly or indirectly, to secure a United States shareholder's debt; or if the debt is purchased or guaranteed by the CFC; or if two-thirds or more of the CFC's stock is used to secure the debt.[97] Thus, for example, if an SPE is a CFC and it buys receivables from a related United States originator in a tax loan transaction, Subpart F issues could arise.

Under the foreign personal holding company rules, passive income of a closely held SPE can be imputed to United States shareholders. This arises, however, only if the SPE is controlled, directly or indirectly, by five or fewer United States individuals.[98]

Under the PFIC rules, any United States shareholder of an SPE that is a PFIC (*i.e.,* that has primarily passive income), whether or not the United States shareholders are in control, may be liable for an interest charge on dividend distributions from the SPE, unless an election is made either to recognize as dividends the SPE earnings on a current basis or, in the case of regularly traded PFIC stock, to take into account each year, under a "mark-to-market" regime, the built-in gain or loss attributable to the difference between the stock's current value and the shareholder's adjusted tax basis therein.[99]

C. Other Cross-Border Tax Issues

Other tax issues that may arise in cross-border securitizations include generation of currency gains or losses under I.R.C. § 988, to the extent, for example, that a United States party to the transaction is entitled to receive (or required to pay) currency other than United States dollars; potential withholding tax on swap payments;[100] and potential transfer price adjustments

---

96 *See* I.R.C. § 951-964.

97 I.R.C. § 956(d); Treas. Reg. § 1.956-2(c).

98 *See* I.R.C. § 551-558.

99 *See* I.R.C. § 1291-1298. Under the "mark-to-market" election, a PFIC shareholder's adjusted basis in the PFIC stock will be increased by any amount previously included in income as a result of the election and decreased by any amounts allowed as a deduction thereby. *See* I.R.C. § 1296(b).

100 For United States purposes, although Treas. Reg. § 1.863-7 provides that swap payments to foreign counterparties do not generally constitute United States source income (and thus are not subject to United States withholding tax), non-periodic payments made to United States counterparties pursuant to a swap agreement may give rise to United States source interest income. Under Treas. Reg. § 1.446-3(g)(4), a "significant" non-periodic payment is treated as a loan to the United States counterparty and the time value component associated with such loan must be recognized as United States source interest for all purposes of the Code. Although "significant" for these purposes is not defined, an example in the regulations provides that a non-periodic payment is significant if it exceeds 40 percent of the present value of the fixed payments under the swap agree-

under I.R.C. section 482, where sales or other transfers take place between affiliated parties in different jurisdictions. Transfer pricing issues could arise, for example, if there are multiple SPEs in different jurisdictions or if receivables being sold arise from sales between United States and non-United States affiliates.

§ 8.06. Rating Agency Issues

It is increasingly common in cross-border financial transactions, and especially in securitizations, for investors to rely to a large extent on rating agencies for comfort as to the structure of the transaction and for informational diligence on the underlying collateral or other assets.[101] As we have discussed with domestic securitizations, rating agencies are private companies[102] whose business is assessing the risks associated with the full and timely payment of debt securities.[103] The significance of the rating depends entirely on the reputation among investors of the particular rating agency. For rating debt securities issued in securitization transactions, the most respected and trusted agencies are Standard & Poor's, Moody's Investors Service and Fitch Ratings,[104] all founded in the United States but now having offices and providing ratings to investors worldwide.[105]

---

ment. *See* Treas. Reg. § 1.446-3(g)(6) Ex. 3. Thus, if a swap agreement provides for a significant non-periodic payment and the foreign counterparty cannot claim the benefits of the portfolio interest exemption or an applicable income tax treaty, the United States source interest income arising from the significant non-periodic payment will be subject to United States withholding tax at a rate of 30 percent. *See, also,* Treas. Reg. § 1441-4(a)(3) (a withholding agent that pays amounts attributable to a notional principal contract described in Treas. Reg. 1.863-7(a) or 1.988-2(e) shall have no obligation to withhold on amounts paid under the terms thereof, (but not including any amount treated as interest under Treas. Reg. § 1.446-3(g)) regardless of whether a withholding certificate is provided, but income will generally be treated as effectively connected with the conduct of a United States trade or business unless agent can rely on a withholding certificate to the contrary).

101 For a discussion of rating agencies, see Steven L. Schwarcz, *Private Ordering of Public Markets: The Rating Agency Paradox*, 2002 U. Ill. L. Rev. 1 (2002).

102 Rating agencies are neither governmental agencies nor are they presently regulated in the United States. The only minimal form of governmental control is in the context of designating a rating agency a "nationally recognized statistical rating organization" (NRSRO). For a description of the informal process of designation, see Amy K. Rhodes, *The Role of the SEC in the Regulation of the Rating Agencies: Well-Placed Reliance or Free-Market Interference?*, 20 Seton Hall Legis. J. 293, 323 (1996).

103 What is rated is both the likelihood of payment *and* the timeliness of payment on the securities. *See* Salomon B. Samson & Gail I. Hessol, *Ultimate Recovery in Ratings: A Conceptual Framework*, S&P CreditWeek, Nov. 6, 1996, at 25. Equity securities are not rated because they have neither a specified maturity date nor a contractually-fixed principal amount.

104 In the United States, Fitch IBCA, Duff & Phelps operates as Fitch, Inc.

105 Rating agencies make their rating determinations based solely on information provided by the issuer of securities. Hence, a rating agency, whatever its reputation, cannot provide a rating that is more reliable than that information. Ratings do not, for example, cover the risk of fraud.

Rating agencies view their ratings as worldwide standards, and not as relative risk standards within countries. Thus, a BBB rating on securities is intended to convey the same level of risk irrespective of the jurisdiction in which the securities are issued.[106] The existence and almost universal acceptance of ratings make it much easier for investors in the capital markets to assess the safety of a given issuance of securities. In a securitization context, this facilitates the ability of an SPE to issue securities, and of investors in those securities to resell them to other investors. However, the almost universal demand by investors for ratings makes rating agencies to a large extent gatekeepers of the types of securities that investors will buy. This can slow down experimentation with potentially innovative securitization structures, although the rating agencies have shown great flexibility by devoting resources to individual countries, and developing structures within each country that play to that country's legal and cultural strengths, such as the "whole business" securitizations of the United Kingdom.

QUESTIONS

1. Are the currency, tax and rating issues legal issues, or economic issues regarding pricing?

2. From a tax standpoint, what issues are most relevant to structuring the securitization, if you know that most of the investors will be subject to Untied States law? Do these concerns lessen or increase if the investor base is truly multi-national?

106 Interview with Petrina Dawson, Managing Director and Associate General Counsel, Standard & Poor's Ratings Group (Mar. 11, 1998).

Chapter 9
THE ECONOMICS OF SECURITIZATION

The articles excerpted below contain a debate between proponents and critics of securitization as to whether it is a financing technique resembling alchemy or a technique that disadvantages unsecured creditors of the originator in a zero-sum game. As you read these excerpts, keep your own list of the arguments made in support of and against the economic efficiency of securitization.

§ 9.01. The Debate

Steven L. Schwarcz, *The Alchemy of Asset Securitization*
1 STAN. J.L. BUS. & FIN. 133 (1994)

. . . . Securitization is most valuable when the cost of funds, reflected in the interest rate that is necessary to entice investors to purchase the SPV's securities, is less than the cost of the originator's other, direct sources of funding. The SPV's lower cost of funds is passed on to the originator through a higher selling price for the originator's receivables. The goal of securitization, therefore, is to obtain low cost capital market funding by separating all or a portion of an originator's receivables from the risks associated with the originator. . . .

A securitization transaction can provide obvious cost savings by permitting an originator whose debt securities are rated less than investment grade or whose securities are unrated to obtain funding through an SPV whose debt securities have an investment grade rating. Even an originator with an investment grade rating may derive benefit from securitization if the SPV can issue debt securities with a higher investment grade rating and, as a result, significantly decrease the originator's interest costs. . . .

Asset securitization does, however, afford companies with acceptable risk levels the possibility of real cost savings. To determine whether an originator will achieve an overall cost savings from securitization, one must assess the interest savings possible (as discussed above) against the costs of the securitization transaction. A company considering securitization should compare (i) the expected differential between interest payable on non-securitized financing and interest payable on securities issued by an applicable SPV with (ii) the expected difference in transaction costs between the alternative funding options. Whether or not the originator will achieve a cost savings partially depends on the way in which the originator structures the securitization because . . . transaction costs can vary over a wide range. . . .

The indirect benefits of securitization will often more than compensate for its indirect costs. One of the most important indirect benefits is that asset securitization provides a source of off balance sheet funding. Because a securitization is usually viewed, for accounting purposes, as a sale of assets and not as financing, the originator does not record the transaction as a liability on its balance sheet. Such off balance sheet funding thus raises capital without increasing the originator's leverage or debt-to-equity ratio on its financial statements.

Another benefit of asset securitization is that it may represent an additional and untapped source of financing for an originator. Sometimes originators will find that investor appetite for their securities has become temporarily sated. In other words, the amount of originator risk exposure that the capital markets are prepared to accept may be less than the amount of capital market financing desired by the originator. In these cases, securitization permits the originator to obtain additional capital market funding through an SPV. This change in form is not an attempt to mislead investors. Investors are often prepared to accept the more limited risks associated with the SPV, namely the default risk of the receivables, as compared to the greater risk associated with the originator as a whole. As a result, by providing an additional source of capital market funding, securitization can be beneficial even to investment grade originators.

Certain securitizations may also result in a lower weighted average interest rate to the originator through the use of a "senior/subordinate" securities structure at the SPV level. Sophisticated investors provide the equivalent of "credit enhancement" to the SPV by purchasing subordinated securities. The originator thereby allocates certain repayment risks to these investors, who are in the business of assessing and accepting such risks and who consequently are willing to accept a higher level of risk than the average investor. The interest rate on these subordinated securities would be higher than the interest rate on the non-subordinated (or senior) securities to compensate for the greater risk. Nonetheless, this combination of senior and subordinated securities will still be of benefit to the originator if, as is usually the case, the resulting blended interest rate on the combined securities is lower than the rate that would have been applicable if only one class of securities had been issued.

The senior/subordinate structure can also be used to expand the universe of parties available to provide credit enhancement. An entity providing external credit enhancement in the form of a guarantee or its equivalent is usually required to have a credit rating at least equal to that of the securities being guaranteed. However, the number of highly rated credit enhancers — including banks — is relatively small. Moreover, because of high capital reserve requirements, third party credit enhancement provided by regulated institutions such as banks has become very expensive. But investors in subordinated securities have no rating requirement. The credit enhancement comes from their initial cash investment in the SPV's subordinated securities. Because the proceeds of the SPV's subordinated securities are used to purchase receivables and thereby further overcollateralize the SPV's senior securities, the subordinated securities supplement the means by which the senior securities are paid. . . .

A "zero-sum game" is one in which one person's benefit exactly offsets another person's loss, so that the net payoff of the entire game is zero. Is securitization a zero-sum game, or does it create a genuine cost reduction for parties?

Only an empirical study would fully answer this question. Such a study is not only beyond the scope of this article, but difficult to envision given that the corporate finance world rarely lends itself to controlled experiments. Nonetheless, a common sense analysis indicates that securitization can create a net cost savings.

This article has shown that, despite its transaction costs, securitization can be less expensive than alternative funding sources because it enables originators to obtain low cost capital market funding. Even investment grade originators who already have direct access to capital market funding may prefer securitization because of its indirect benefits, such as the provision of off balance sheet funding. Although indirect benefits are harder to quantify, many companies that use securitization are investment grade. This fact is significant when one considers that profit maximizing companies generally do not engage in activities whose benefits are illusory.

These observations leave unanswered, however, the question whether securitization enables originators to realize a gain at the expense of others, such as the originator's unsecured general creditors. For example, some critics have argued that unsecured creditors are harmed by securitization because it reduces the amount of the originator's unencumbered assets available for debt repayment. This argument is flawed, however; securitization merely replaces one type of asset, receivables, with another type, cash. The unsecured creditor has the same amount of unencumbered assets to levy against after the securitization as it did before the securitization.

Other critics have argued that securitization could hurt creditors because the cash received is unlikely to stay within the originator. The originator, they say, may speculate or fraudulently transfer the cash. Given that the originator will have already sold its receivables, the originator will have to wait until new receivables are created and mature for its cash flow to regenerate. This dissipation of cash may eventually result in a liquidity crisis unless the securitization can be repeated or refinanced.

One cannot assume wasteful behavior simply because an originator sells its receivables for cash. In fact, given the scrutiny imposed by rating agencies and other independent parties such as credit enhancers, securitization may present fewer opportunities for self-dealing than other financing methods. Nonetheless, securitization, just like any other sale of assets by an originator, may become suspect if implemented when an originator is on the brink of bankruptcy. An originator, for example, may be seeking to convert receivables into cash to make preferential payments to certain creditors or even to fraudulently hide assets. The potential for such suspect actions, however, is not unique to securitization transactions. The same issues would arise, for example, if on the eve of bankruptcy an originator sold, or borrowed money by encumbering, a factory or equipment and similarly sought to dissipate the sale or loan proceeds. Such questionable uses of proceeds are more appropriately addressed by preference and fraudulent conveyance laws, which seek to ensure equality of distribution of a debtor's estate.

The Delaware Supreme Court recently put debtors on notice that near-bankrupt corporations must be mindful of their responsibilities to act in their creditors' interests and not to their detriment. In *Credit Lyonnais Bank v. Pathe Communications*,[1] the court noted that a board of directors of a corporation in the "vicinity of insolvency" owes a fiduciary duty not only to its shareholders but also to its creditors. This ruling gives greater assurance that a troubled corporation will not speculate with the cash received from a securitization to the detriment of creditors.

The question nonetheless remains: does securitization genuinely reduce net financing costs? A possible method of testing this hypothesis is to examine it in light of the principle of "exposure conservation." This principle states that:

> Secured creditors will charge lower interest rates because security reduces their risks, but unsecured creditors will raise their interest rates in response because security reduces the assets on which they can levy, and so increases their risks. The interest rate reductions are precisely matched by interest rate increases; hence, the firm makes no net gain from granting security.[2]

If one assumes, *arguendo,* that the principle of exposure conservation means that unsecured creditors will raise their rates in response to a debtor's securitization, just as they would in response to a debtor's secured financing, the principle would indicate that the rise in unsecured interest rates should precisely match the rate reduction granted by the secured creditor in return for taking collateral. As a result, the originator would realize no net gain.

The principle of exposure conservation assumes that interest rates do not vary with the source of financing. A securitization, however, provides a new source of financing — the capital markets, whose rates are systematically lower than the rates at which small or medium size firms commonly borrow. Prior to engaging in a securitization, an originator is financing itself through secured and unsecured loans. After the securitization, the originator raises funds by accessing the capital markets through the SPV.

---

1 [n. 51] No. 12150, 1991 LEXIS 215, at *108 (Del. Ch. Dec. 30, 1991).

2 [n. 53] Alan Schwartz, *The Continuing Puzzle of Secured Debt*, 37 VAND. L. REV. 1051,1054 (1984) (emphasis deleted); *cf.* Franco Modigliani & Merton Miller, *The Cost of Capital, Corporation Finance and the Theory of Investment*, 48 AM. ECON. REV. 261 (1958). In a perfect universe, every savings achieved by changing one part of a company's capital structure will result in offsetting costs to other parts of the capital structure, including by taking advantage of third parties. Securitization achieves a net cost savings because the universe is imperfect.

The transformation from secured financing to capital market funding with its comparatively lower interest rate thus can reduce net financing costs.[3] So long as the added transaction costs are less than the interest saved by using securitization instead of secured financing, the principle of exposure conservation supports the proposition that securitization creates a net gain. The following examples help to illustrate this point.

An originator with $100 million of unsecured debt, bearing an interest rate of x percent, plans to repay $50 million of this unsecured debt with the proceeds of a new $50 million issuance of secured debt. The principle of exposure conservation states that the interest rate on the secured debt will be reduced to x — y percent, but this reduction in rate will be matched by an interest rate increase on the remaining unsecured debt to x + y percent. This analysis assumes that the unsecured creditors are free to adjust to a market rate. Therefore, according to the theory, the originator makes no net gain from granting security.

If this originator repaid the $50 million of the unsecured debt from the proceeds of a securitization, instead of from the issuance of secured debt, the interest rate on the remaining unsecured debt would again rise to x + y percent.[4] However, because capital market rates are generally lower than secured financing rates, . . . the interest rate on the securitized debt will reduce to x – y – z percent (where z percent represents the rate differential between capital market and secured financing rates).

If securitization bore no transaction costs, the originator would save exactly z percent of $50 million in annual interest costs by refinancing through a securitization rather than secured financing. The originator's actual cost saving, however, would be at least partially offset by transaction costs. But as long as

---

[3] [n. 54] . . . [T]he interest rate on commercial paper was consistently lower than that of the bank prime loan rate over the last three years. . . . 80 FED. RES. BULL., A25, A26, Domestic Financial Statistics (Nov. 1994).

[4] [n. 55] The increase in the unsecured borrowing rate is assumed to be the same whether triggered by secured financing or securitization. In practice, however, such rate increase will be less for securitization because, as previously discussed, securitization merely replaces receivables with cash and therefore does not reduce the assets on which unsecured creditors can levy. Furthermore, securitization does not affect a company's leverage ratio for financial reporting purposes. A precise comparison of the differences that may affect unsecured creditors between securitization and secured financing is subtle and depends on the structure of the transaction. For example, in a securitization, any excess receivables sold may or may not be available to repay unsecured creditors once the securitized debt is paid, while in a secured financing excess collateral may be used to repay unsecured creditors once the secured debt is paid. On the other hand, in a securitization if the receivables sold are insufficient to pay the securitized debt the holders of such debt will have no claim against the originator's remaining assets. In a secured financing if the collateral is insufficient to pay the secured debt, the holders of such debt generally may assert an unsecured claim against the originator's remaining assets, and such unsecured claim will be *pari passu* with the originator's other unsecured claims. *See* 11 U.S.C. § 506(a) (1988). Accordingly, the author believes that the assumption used in this article as to the increase in the unsecured borrowing rate may be overly conservative; therefore, the actual net cost saving enjoyed by the originator may be even greater than portrayed.

an originator's interest and transaction costs for a securitization are less than the costs of a secured financing, securitization will create a net cost savings by providing access to lower cost capital market funding.

But why should the capital markets be prepared to fund securitization transactions at a lower rate than secured financing? At least one explanation is that securitization serves as a means of reducing "monitoring costs," a theory originally presented by Jackson and Kronman in the secured financing arena.[5] Because the interest rate on the loan is determined when the loan is made, a borrower may take actions that increase the loan's riskiness after the loan is made. Jackson and Kronman argue that a creditor will incur certain monitoring costs as a result to ensure that the borrower's actions do not increase the riskiness of the loan. In this regard, a secured creditor should have lower monitoring costs than an unsecured creditor because the secured creditor needs to monitor the borrower's actions only in regard to the collateral backing its loan and can disregard how the borrower acts generally.

Subsequent commentators have argued, however, that secured financing may not reduce, and indeed may increase, the need to monitor the borrower's financial condition. The reason is that if the borrower enters bankruptcy, an automatic stay will freeze the secured creditor's ability to exercise remedies against the collateral and thereby impair the secured creditor's collateral position. As a result, the secured creditor has a significant interest in ensuring the continued viability of the borrower and will incur monitoring costs to further that interest in addition to the costs of monitoring the collateral.

In a securitization, on the other hand, the originator's receivables are sold to a bankruptcy remote SPV in a "true sale." Consequently, a bankruptcy of the originator would not adversely affect the ability of investors to receive payment on their asset-backed securities. Because a bankruptcy remote structure separates the source of payment of the SPV's securities from the risks associated with the originator, the need to monitor the originator's financial condition is largely eliminated. Although the risks associated with servicing and collecting the receivables still necessitate some monitoring, these risks can be borne by providers of credit enhancement or investors in subordinated securities, parties who are in the business of precisely assessing and absorbing such risks.

Securitization, thus, creates genuine cost reductions. By eliminating the risk of bankruptcy to investors, many different types of companies can better utilize their most valuable asset, their receivables, by accessing low cost capital market funding. . . .

In many cases, securitization not only reduces an originator's direct financing costs but also provides significant indirect benefits. Securitization entails real costs, however, and therefore should only be used after comparison with

---

5 [n. 56] Thomas H. Jackson & Anthony T. Kronman, *Secured Financing and Priorities Among Creditors*, 88 YALE L.J. 1143 (1979).

alternative sources of funding. Because securitization has only been applied to a portion of its potential market opportunities, it promises to be a financing technique that will continue to grow. Securitization, in short, brings to financial technology what the sought-after philosopher's stone promised to bring to base metals — the ability to turn them into gold!

Claire A. Hill, *Securitization: A Low-Cost Sweetener for Lemons*

74 WASH. U. L.Q. 1061 (1996)

. . . . Generally, a securitization security can command a higher price either because of its higher quality, greater access to financing sources ("liquidity"), or both. Unsurprisingly, higher quality securities command higher prices than lower quality securities. And more liquid securities — that is, securities more cheaply and readily saleable to more investors — command higher prices than less liquid securities.

Quality and liquidity are related. A security will only be liquid if its quality is readily known; similarly, a security will only command the "high quality" price if its quality is readily known to be high. Thus, there is significant overlap between what must be done to make a security high quality, and what must be done to make it liquid.

Securitization, its proponents claim, offers a better — cheaper — way of achieving higher quality and liquidity. Implicit in this claim is that higher quality is achieved without a commensurate decrease in the quality of the remainder of the firm. Securitization must, somehow, make the sum of the firm's more and less valuable parts greater than the whole.[6]

I now explore the cost reductions and other benefits securitization could offer. I first consider benefits which contribute both to higher quality and to liquidity.

Firms engaging in financing transactions, like firms engaging in most any transaction, suffer from the well-known "lemons" problem. The borrower (in this case, the seller of the receivables) knows more about the firm than the lender (in this case, the buyer of pool securities) does, and has an incentive to exaggerate the firm's quality. The lender knows this, and offers the borrower only a "lemons" price based on her worst-case estimate. The borrower can get the lender to offer more only if the borrower can convince the lender that the borrower is not a "lemon." Some firms have more severe lemons problems than others: The financial community — that is, the community of prospective financiers

---

[6] [n. 115] Benston has difficulty seeing how securitization makes the parts worth more than the whole. He also notes that given securitization's costliness, it would have to offer a large increment of value to avoid being negative-sum. *See* [George J.] Benston, *The Future of Asset Securitization: The Benefits and Costs of Breaking up the Bank,* 5 J. APPLIED CORP. FIN. 71 (1992) . . . .

— has insufficient information to appraise such firms' prospects or their potential liabilities, and cannot learn more without incurring considerable expense.

Of course, implicit in the lemons problem is a violation of the Modigliani and Miller assumption of complete and costless access to information.[7] Securitization may offer a lower cost solution to the lemons problem. The subject matter of the conveyance consists of securities backed by receivables. Thus, information is needed both about the securities and the receivables. And . . . information is also needed about the firm selling the receivables. Securitization offers a low cost, credible way for such information to be produced and provided to investors.

Securitization may help firms learn and demonstrate more easily that their receivables are not "lemons." Securitization permits economies of scale and scope in the acquisition and dissemination of information about a firm's receivables. Firms, knowing they will be securitizing their receivables, can work with specialist appraisers (rating agencies and insurers) to develop receivables that are more easily appraised. Prospectively, receivables can be standardized, as to terms, documentation, and underwriting criteria. . . .

I have identified several benefits securitization may offer. One is to reduce information costs. Securitization may inspire the development and use of lower cost appraisal techniques for some of a firm's receivables. Securitization also may inspire a firm to create a capital structure consisting of securities that lend themselves to lower cost appraisal. Lower cost appraisal could lead to more efficient risk bearing; someone better situated to appraise a risk may be better at bearing it. Indeed, securitization may reduce aggregate information costs for all of a firm's financiers in a variety of ways. Securitization helps to extract, from a mass of hard-to-quantify risks, some particular risks that can be more easily quantified. And a firm's selection of securitization may be a low-cost signal of its quality.

Securitization also may increase a firm's cash inflows in several ways. Securitization permits specialization in receivables origination and servicing. It also may inspire more efficient receivables origination and management, and lead to reductions in agency costs. Securitization also may increase a firm's cash inflows by reducing regulatory costs. It may reduce costs of complying with applicable regulatory regimes, or help make available certain regulatory subsidies. Moreover, it may reduce bankruptcy costs by moving some assets (receivables) from the firm to a more bankruptcy-remote location. Securitization also may permit a firm to select differently labelled treatments for tax and other purposes, and select either a debt or an equity tax regime for the transaction, whichever is more favorable. Finally, securitization also may reduce transaction costs associated with the assembly of a particular portfolio or make possible the assembly of a theretofore impossible portfolio.

---

[7] [Eds.] Franco Modigliani & Merton H. Miller, *The Cost of Capital, Corporation Finance and the Theory of Investment,* 48 AM. ECON. REV. 261 (1958).

Of these benefits, two seem largest: information cost reductions and regulatory cost reductions. Securitization may offer significant reductions in information costs. However, this benefit seems larger for some firms, particularly lemons firms, than for others.

The magnitude of securitization's regulatory cost reduction benefit also varies markedly among transactions. For some transactions, the benefit is extremely large; for others, it may be quite small. The largest regulatory cost reduction benefits occur only under regimes applicable to particular firms or transactions. The benefits of more generally applicable regulatory cost reductions are likely to be smaller. Bankruptcy cost reductions, for instance, should be of some benefit, but mostly to firms whose financial condition is middling — sufficiently good that the transaction structure is viable without costly safeguards, but not so good that the prospect of bankruptcy is exceedingly remote. Tax savings, too, should be fairly small. Generally, all securitization does is make less costly a firm's choice of financing structures by allowing it to choose among the previously available tax treatments.

Securitization's other benefits seem smaller. Nonfinancing firms should benefit more from better origination and servicing of their receivables. They may not have had sufficient resources or incentive to put into place the mechanisms the securitization transaction structure requires. By contrast, financing firms likely will have had both the resources and incentive to originate and service their receivables efficiently, even absent securitization. Some financing firms may benefit from being able to specialize in receivables origination — if others really are much better risk bearers, then this benefit might be fairly sizeable. And specialization in receivables servicing may enable more efficient, and cheaper, servicing. Another benefit securitization may offer also follows from carving up tasks and assigning them to specialists: those specialists may compete with each other to help structure transactions that use their expertise yet more efficiently. All firms may benefit from securitization's ability to assist investors in assembling investment portfolios. However, securitization's contribution is simply to offer a new type of security, somewhat different from the securities previously available. The increment of additional value added should not be significant.

Some of the foregoing benefits rely on differences between investors. For instance, the regulatory constraints on purchases of lower quality securities, and the regulatory subsidies for purchases of securitization securities, apply only to certain subsets of investors. Similarly, some specialization benefits rely on the existence of investors with different skills and expertise. However, many other benefits do not rely on investor differences. For instance, specialization of third parties likely benefits all investors: if receivables can be appraised and monitored more cheaply by a rating agency and insurer, investor differences should not appreciably affect the availability of this benefit. Most importantly, however, the information cost reducing effect responsible for sweetening lemons firms does not rely on investor differences. While some investors may be better situated than others to appraise lemons firms, securitization's solution to the lemons problem is to extract from such firms the risks more readily appraised by nonspecialists (or, more precisely, specialists in appraising nonfirm-specific assets). . . .

Lois R. Lupica, *Asset Securitization: The Unsecured Creditor's Perspective*

76 TEX. L. REV. 595 (1998)

. . . . One of the most frequently cited advantages to securitization is that it provides a firm with financing at a less expensive effective interest rate than the firm could obtain through a direct secured lending arrangement. . . . [T]his lower effective financing rate can be attributed, in large part, to securitization's prototypical bankruptcy-remote structure, in which the assets transferred are removed from the purview of the originator's trustee in bankruptcy. Indeed, neither academic commentators nor transaction participants have offered an apology for the fact that the financial advantages gained by an originator from the movement of these assets beyond the reach of its general creditors are among the driving forces behind the proliferation of the number and types of originators securitizing assets.

Once the bankruptcy risk is effectively eliminated from the transaction, the sale of the assets can return a relatively high price to the originator. This price is analogous to the lower interest rate charged by secured creditors who have identified and earmarked a secondary source of repayment in the event of a debtor default (commonly known as collateral), as compared to the higher interest rate charged by unsecured creditors who have no such payment back-up arrangement. In a secured lending context, in the event of a debtor's liquidation, it is the secured creditors who have priority of payment over the unsecured creditors, precisely because of the presence of the earmarked collateral.

This priority arrangement forms the basis for one of the fundamental premises of Article 9 and the Bankruptcy Code; in the event of a debtor's liquidation, secured lenders get paid from their collateral (or its equivalent in value) before unsecured creditors. Unsecured creditors must be satisfied with a pro rata share of whatever is left over. Notwithstanding the endurance of this accepted commercial practice, whether secured creditors ought to continue to have priority over the subordinated claims of general unsecured creditors has been and continues to be a topic of dispute among academics and commercial practitioners.[8] . . . .

The essence of this discussion is the question of whether secured credit is efficient and whether secured claims' priority status in bankruptcy results in an

---

8 [n. 124] *See generally Symposium on the Revision of Article 9 of the Uniform Commercial Code,* 80 VA. L. REV. 1783 (1994) . . . .

inequitable outcome. Implicit in this question is the issue of whether secured creditors are realizing gains at the expense of unsecured creditors in a way that challenges accepted principles of efficiency and equity.

In their seminal article written in 1979, Professors Thomas H. Jackson and Anthony T. Kronman argued that the legal rules allowing creditors to take security for loans are economically efficient.[9] They rest their conclusion on two arguments. First, they argued that unsecured creditors are compensated for their subordinated status by being paid an interest rate premium. Second, they contended that even in the absence of a legal regime providing for secured credit, creditors would establish a parallel priority scheme because of the market advantages inherently available for riskier unsecured loans.

Professor Alan Schwartz challenged this conclusion and its underlying assumptions in a 1981 article.[10] Professor Schwartz took issue with the conclusion of secured credit's efficiency and outlined the difficulties with the "conventional efficiency story" offered to explain secured debt. He suggested that the savings gained by debtors borrowing from some creditors on a secured basis are offset by the premiums demanded by unsecured creditors for their heightened risk of noncollection. He further questioned whether one can conclude that security is efficient without identifying a reduction in social cost and explored the issue of whether the aggregate benefits of security equal or exceed its aggregate costs. Unable either to identify the reduced costs or to effectively quantify benefits of a system of security, Schwartz concluded that the efficiency of secured debt was unproven.

Since the publication of Professor Schwartz's article, many academics have addressed the efficiency of secured transactions. Some have concluded that secured credit's efficiency is unproven, or at least problematic, and others have sought to substantiate their contention of efficiency by cataloging a roster of justifications for its continued existence. The justifications offered for the persistence of secured credit include the potential for secured credit to (1) protect against asset wasting or dissipation, (2) signal that a debtor with secured credit is a good credit risk, (3) reduce the total costs of monitoring the debtor's business behavior, and (4) generally increase the availability of credit.

The claim of securitization's efficiency is less substantiated than the same claim with respect to secured credit. Although many of the same justifications for secured credit's continued existence have been used to justify and explain the increasing number of securitization transactions, these justifications do not fully or accurately explain securitization's place in the credit market.

---

[9] [n. 126] *See* Thomas H. Jackson & Anthony T. Kronman, *Secured Financing and Priorities Among Creditors,* 88 YALE L.J. 1143, 1157 (1979).

[10] [n. 129] *See* [Alan] Schwartz, [*Security Interests and Bankruptcy Priorities: A Review of Current Theories,* 10 J. LEGAL STUD. 1 (1981)].

Challenges to the Efficiency of Securitization

1. Securitization's Efficiency Is Unproven. — On its face, securitization appears to be a creative, albeit complex, way of reducing a firm's effective interest rate while offering it positive strategic advantages. In a hypothetical vacuum where the only parties' interests to be considered are those of the originator and the ABS [asset-backed securities] investors, the fact that an increasing number of firms are securitizing assets to meet the market's "insatiable" demand for ABS suggests that the economic benefits exceed the costs for these parties. This conclusion assumes that parties are acting with sufficient rationality to accurately assess the costs and benefits to them.

When securitization's third-party distributional effects are taken into account, a firm may be securitizing assets even when the transaction results in economic inefficiencies. When firm managers pursue investments and financing strategies that increase expected creditor losses more than such strategies increase expected shareholder return, such investments are inefficient. The dissonance between what decisions are good for the firm, versus what is good for the firm's creditors, results in an inefficient enrichment of shareholders at the expense of creditors.

To illustrate, suppose a firm has $100 in assets and $100 in liabilities. Upon liquidation, the firm's creditors would get paid in full and its shareholders would be left with nothing. The firm knows of an investment opportunity that will cost $100 and will return $200 if successful, but zero if unsuccessful. There is a one-in-two chance of success or failure.

Should the firm make this investment? From the creditors' perspective, it should not. If the investment succeeds, the firm creditors will get no more than $100, but if the investment does not succeed, the creditors will be left with nothing. However, from the standpoint of the firm (that is, its shareholders), it should make the investment. If the investment loses, it is the creditors that bear the loss. Because the firm is insolvent anyway, the shareholders lose nothing if the firm loses its investment, but if the investment pays off, it is they, not the creditors, who reap the benefit.

Furthermore, an originator's ability to divert value from its unsecured creditors to its ABS investors results in costs to unsecured creditors who fail to adjust to and adapt their behaviors to their heightened post-securitization risk. To the extent a creditor can understand and predict the effect securitization will have on its chance of repayment, both in the absence of and in bankruptcy, it can negotiate terms to reflect this risk. If the originator did not bargain with its unsecured creditors prior to the securitization, either because the creditors are involuntary or otherwise nonadjusting,[11] a transfer of value from the creditor

---

11 [n. 145] . . . . Nonadjusting creditors include tort claimants; government tax and regulatory agencies; creditors with claims so small it is not practical to seek information about the debtor on an ongoing basis or adjust lending terms accordingly; and unsecured creditors who extent credit on fixed terms, foreclosing the opportunity for adjustments in the future. *See* [Lucian Arye Bebchuk &

to the firm's shareholders will result. As is the case with secured credit, it is primarily these nonadjusting creditors that are subject to the greatest economic costs when a firm securitizes. Securitization may result in a transfer of value from these nonadjusting creditors, and to the extent there is no corresponding adjustment in the cost of unsecured credit, the shareholders of the securitizing firm have captured such value.

Even if one can assume perfect information and consent on the part of unsecured creditors and other third parties with claims against securitizing originators, the conclusion that securitization is an efficient way for a firm to finance its operations and thus ought to be encouraged remains unproven.

2. Securitization's Justifications. — In the absence of bankruptcy, secured credit results in a number of benefits to a debtor and its other creditors that support and enhance the efficient outcome of the secured credit transaction. These benefits relate to a secured party's ability to control what has been referred to as "debtor misbehavior" and have been used to justify secured credit's prominent position in our commercial economy. These justifications include the potential for secured credit resulting in: (1) protection against asset wasting or dissipation, (2) the provision of a signal that a debtor with secured credit is a good credit risk, (3) a reduction in the total costs of monitoring the debtor's business behavior, and (4) a general increase in the availability of credit. These controls on a debtor's post-financing behavior, however, are not available to a firm's unsecured creditors when the firm engages in a securitization.

a. Securitization prevents a debtor from wasting assets. — When an asset transfer is characterized as a transfer of collateral for a loan (and thus a transfer made in connection with a secured financing), the originator with title to the assets pledges them to a lender as collateral, but retains an ownership interest in them. In such a case, the debtor who enjoys the secured credit extended by its lender no longer has the freedom to do what it wants with its encumbered assets, notwithstanding its retention of title to them. The debtor is commonly precluded by agreement from giving away, selling, or wasting these assets.

In contrast, the objective of a securitizing originator is to remove, through a sale, certain assets of the originator from its ownership and control. Once removed, neither contract nor statute requires the originator to preserve these assets or their value, and upon their sale, the securitized assets become the property of the purchaser. The originator is not required or motivated to preserve the consideration received from the asset sale; as stated above, it is free to spend this cash any way it chooses — or to simply squander it.

In addition, asset purchasers, in contrast to lenders, have no interest in contractually prohibiting an originator from inefficient decisionmaking — which may include both imprudent business decisions and the wasting of non-securi-

---

Jesse M. Fried, *The Uneasy Case for the Priority of Secured Claims in Bankruptcy,* 105 YALE L.J. 857,] at 870 [(1996)].

tized assets. Lenders may, and indeed often do, outline a set of behaviors foreclosed to the debtor because of their potential for adverse distributional consequences. These behaviors may include restrictions against encumbrances on the transfer of certain assets, restrictions on certain investment activity, restrictions on the creation of certain security interests, and even a prohibition against a change in the debtor's business policies, practices, or type of industry. These restrictions serve as a check on a borrower's post-credit extension behavior and protect the interests of the borrower's unsecured creditors. Post-securitization, there is no party with sufficient interest in the originator to control any aspect of its ongoing behavior.

Moreover, a further objective of a securitizing originator is to remove its securitized assets from its potential bankruptcy estate. Indeed, that is what a bankruptcy-remote transactional structure is designed to do — transfer the assets to an entity that is not required to participate in the debtor's bankruptcy. The fundamental difference in a bankruptcy context between a secured financing and a securitization is that a secured creditor, by statute, is a necessary party to the debtor's bankruptcy, whereas securitization participants (meaning the SPC [also referred to as an SPE or SPE] as asset transferee and the ABS investors) have as their goal the establishment of a remote position from the bankrupt originator. In such a case, if the asset transfer is upheld by the court, the asset transferee (the SPC) is not subject to the reach of the automatic stay, and the payment source of the ABS (the securitized assets) is effectively separated from the bankruptcy estate of the originator.

b. Securitization provides a signal to third parties with respect to the credit risk of the originator. — Another justification commonly offered for secured debt is that it provides a signal to unsecured creditors of debtor's prospects. According to this "signaling" explanation, secured credit allows unsecured creditors to extend credit at a reduced interest rate because such debtor is a better risk than other debtors without secured credit.

Whatever the merits of this explanation for secured credit, the signal broadcasted when an entity securitizes its assets should not be read the same way as the secured credit signal. As stated previously, the current market of originators is largely comprised of firms with low credit ratings, those with little or no borrowing track records, and entities with a lack of exposure to a diversity of investors. Indeed, it is because of these qualities that many of the newest securitization market originators have turned to structured finance. If the market demands (and rating agencies and investors do) that the originators securitize only their highest quality assets, then the prevailing signal to unsecured creditors is not that the originator is a good risk — and therefore unsecured creditors should charge a discounted interest rate — but that the originator's highest quality assets have been sold — with only "junk" remaining from which the unsecured creditors can satisfy their claims.

Moreover, unsecured creditors may not have access to sufficient information to read the broadcasted signal; the adequacy of disclosure of the quality of securitized assets has been called into question in recent years. In response to the market's concerns, the SEC is considering revising its disclosure standards for certain ABS issuances. The securitization signal is a difficult one to read and, as such, the interest rates charged by the unsecured creditors are not an accurate reflection of the risks being borne.

c. Securitization reduces monitoring costs to creditors. — Theorists posit two distinct models of monitoring by secured creditors: (1) secured creditors monitor the assets encumbered by the security interest, or (2) they monitor the debtor's entire business to determine the probability of default. Monitoring may serve either as a private good, having no direct effect upon the firm's other creditors, or it may result in a public good, where the other creditors of the debtor (and often the unsecured creditors) reap the benefit of the monitor's diligence. Monitoring may have positive consequences for creditors: the monitor takes on the role of a "joint venturer" of the debtor, attuning its radar to the issue of creditor repayment. Alternatively, monitoring may inflict negative externalities on interested third parties. For example, a creditor's monitoring of a debtor may allow the creditor to detect an imminent default more quickly and thereby give that creditor the advance information and opportunity to seize the debtor's assets first.

If purchasers of securitized assets monitor at all, they do so in the form of short-term private monitoring. The asset purchaser's concern in the course of its pre-securitization diligence is with the quality of the assets sold and the corresponding credit enhancement. Beyond this initial diligence, there is no reason for ongoing monitoring of the originator's business behavior.

In contrast, one of the primary concerns of unsecured creditors is the debtor's post-credit-extension behavior. They want to ensure that the debtor refrains from engaging in any behavior riskier than the behavior engaged in when their initial bargain was struck. If the securitized assets are moved from the originator's purview to a bankruptcy-remote entity, ultimate purchasers of the ABS have no continuing incentive to monitor the debtor for risky behavior. As a result, the originator's unsecured creditors are left with one of two alternatives: (1) to maintain their lending relationship with the debtor in the absence of monitoring, or (2) to monitor the debtor themselves.

A debtor-creditor relationship in the absence of monitoring is a risky one; the less information available to the creditor, the higher the risk that the creditor will be unable to preempt a catastrophic event that leads to default. Furthermore, monitoring by an unsecured creditor is expensive and should result in a higher interest rate charged for the credit; correspondingly, a relationship in the absence of monitoring should require higher interest costs. Because, however, unsecured creditors of securitizing firms are not operating in a world of perfect information, they may not know or understand the extent to which the debtor is being monitored and, as such, they may find themselves in either a position of bearing higher risk or higher expenses than if their debtor used its assets as collateral for a secured loan.

d. Securitization results in a general increase in the availability of credit (and is this a good thing?) — Securitization, with its focus on the quality of the assets to be securitized and not the general credit quality of the originator, may, in some circumstances, make credit more available to an increasing number and variety of entities. Securitization may be the only way for a particular originator to raise money. As a result, securitization may benefit a securitizing entity's unsecured creditors by increasing the overall liquidity of the borrowing party. If securitization results in the improvement of the financial health of the originator and thus signals the continuation of the originator, securitization should give comfort to those unsecured creditors who rely on the cash flow of their debtor's business — the so-called "cash-flow surfers." Once the originator's assets are sold (securitized), the originator is "awash with cash." Arguably, the unsecured then have a far better chance of getting paid.

This justification, however, rests upon a fundamental assumption: that the cash that results from the liquidated assets is used to pay unsecured creditors. Although the originator may choose to channel the cash resulting from this increase in liquidity to repay unsecured creditors, it may instead spend the cash on inventory that fails to turn over, or on projects that do not succeed or do not increase the firm's profitability. What an originator chooses to do with an increase in its liquidity is determinative of whether such an increase is a benefit or a detriment to its unsecured creditors. Because investors have no incentive to monitor an originator once the asset transfer is complete, there are even fewer controls on a firm's post-securitization behavior than there are on a firm's post-secured-credit behavior.

This justification for securitization raises the question of whether the common welfare is improved by the enhancement of a firm's ability to raise cash in the public markets, even though that firm has an unproven credit performance or low credit rating. Arguably, firms that have been unable to establish a borrowing track record based upon the traditional credit profile have one or more indicia that flag them as a credit risk. Firms that are a high credit risk are significantly more likely to end up in bankruptcy. If securitization enables these high-risk firms to transfer their highest quality assets to a third party and provides no corresponding controls on the consideration for this transfer, upon bankruptcy, the unsecured creditors are left with a smaller residual pool of assets to share.

Furthermore, as a greater number of financially marginal parties enter the securitization market, an increasing number of poorly structured transactions occur because of haste, volume, or simple ineptitude. To the extent there is a heightened risk factor for the unsecured creditors of originators with "well structured" securitization transactions, there is an even greater risk for an unsecured creditor of an originator with a structured financing destined to collapse.

The high volume of ABS issuances in recent years has led at least one commentator to observe that investors have been so eager to invest in them that they have not diligently required that the assets or the company behind them "prove their reliability." If the securitized assets are not of high quality or if they do not have sufficient credit enhancement or if the deal is structured so that the originator is to absorb the first loss up to a specified level, the originator's remaining assets will be further drained, leaving even fewer assets in its residual pool.

The implicit assumption supporting each of these justifications for secured credit, as well as for the proliferation of securitization transactions, is that unsecured creditors consented to their status. This implied consent suggests that unsecured creditors (1) have agreed to whatever consequences the law attaches to their credit extension, and (2) have contracted with perfect information.

This "bargain model" of secured credit was originally articulated by Professor Thomas Jackson. His theory "views bankruptcy as a system designed to mirror the agreement one would expect the creditors to form among themselves were they able to negotiate such an agreement from an ex ante position."[12] The bargain model is based on the idea that the pre-bankruptcy position of creditors should be altered in bankruptcy only when such an alteration maximizes the net repayment of assets as a collective. To the extent that the failure of a debtor's business is anticipated by the creditors' pre-bankruptcy bargain, allowances and adjustments were made at the time of the bargain. It is the job of the bankruptcy laws to provide the omitted terms of the bargain for those parties who had no opportunity to participate in the bankruptcy process — the unsecured creditors.

Professor Lynn LoPucki forcefully challenged the assumption of consent in a recent article advocating the reordering of the priority scheme for certain specified creditors.[13] In *The Unsecured Creditor's Bargain*, LoPucki contends that secured debt facilitates the exploitation of involuntary creditors, as well as voluntary but uninformed creditors, by imposing on them a bargain to which they have provided no "meaningful consent." He argues that involuntary creditors, such as tort victims and environmental claimholders, have no opportunity to negotiate their subordinate status and therefore cannot charge an interest rate that offsets their heightened risk of non-payment in the event of a debtor's insolvency. He further argues that uninformed voluntary creditors (those participants in the credit markets who miscalculate their likelihood of recovery from an insolvent debtor) also fail to negotiate an interest rate premium. LoPucki proposes that security interests be subordinated to the claims of these voluntary uninformed and involuntary unsecured creditors.

---

12 [n. 188] *See* [Thomas H.] Jackson, [Bankruptcy, Non-Bankruptcy Entitlement, and the Creditor's Bargain, 91 YALE L.J. 857,] 860 [(1982)].

13 [n. 192] *See* [Lynn M.] LoPucki, [*The Unsecured Creditor's Bargain,* 80 VA. L. REV. 1887 (1994)].

The bargain model, when used to explain an unsecured creditor's subordinate position after its debtor securitizes its valuable assets, is likewise based upon false assumptions. Neither involuntary nor voluntary uninformed unsecured creditors have the information or the opportunity to make *ex ante* adjustments in their bargain to reflect their actual risk. The interest rate charged does not reflect the heightened risk they are subject to because of the asset securitization.

Furthermore, although most voluntary uninformed unsecured creditors are probably aware that their debtor has the option to incur secured debt, they are less likely to be familiar enough with the structural intricacies of securitization transactions to ask the right questions and understand the implications of securitization. Because of the complex nature of securitization, even these unsecured creditors may not know how to evaluate a firm with a securitized portfolio. They may not be equipped to effectively analyze the extent to which risk is retained by the securitizing firm or to understand how to quantify the firm's loss and prepayment assumptions. Securitization documentation is considerably more complex than the documents customarily prepared in connection with secured lending, and the party conducting the diligence must be alert to the issues of hidden liabilities, unacceptable operational constraints, and the various economic, operational, and reporting obligations incurred.

Finally, the unsecured creditor must be prepared to respond to any representations, warranties, and covenants found in the securitization documentation that unduly restrict the firm's future ability to operate in a way that benefits the creditor. The creditor should also be wary of any alteration in assumptions made at the time of the securitization that adversely affects it. The unsecured creditor needs to know whether the transaction will interfere with its contractual relationship with the debtor-originator and, if so, whether the parties can make a correction in a previously negotiated interest rate. It is not at all clear, however, that the information sought by even the most tenacious unsecured creditor will be discoverable or comprehensible. As such, it is unrealistic to assume that full information and consent have informed the interest rate charged by these largely uninformed or involuntary unsecured creditors.

To illustrate the extent to which unsecured creditors are excluded from the pre-bankruptcy bargaining process, suppose the securitizing firm is a consumer retailer and the receivables securitized are credit card accounts. The consumer goods customer's purchases that result in accounts receivable are purchased with service contracts or repair or replacement warranties, and these customers are entitled to their money back or an exchange if the goods are defective.

If a portion of these credit card accounts are sold (securitized), and therefore not available to satisfy the warranty claims of the originator's customers, the purchase risks of the customers are increased and their unsecured claims against the firm will be more difficult to satisfy. As a result, consumers who purchase goods from firms that securitize a portion of their assets are more likely to become unpaid unsecured creditors than consumers who purchase from firms that have only secured credit. As such, the securitizing firms should charge these consumers/potential unsecured creditors lower prices.

If the consumers/potential unsecured creditors are unaware of the retailer's securitization, the prices they are willing to pay for the goods of securitizing firms will be unaffected by the securitization. The consumers (and other unsecured creditors with claims against this retailer) will consequently pay higher prices than they should pay and the securitizing firm will enjoy the transactional inefficiency surplus, at the expense of the unknowing or involuntary unsecured claimants.

If a securitizing firm ultimately declares bankruptcy, uninformed and involuntary unsecured creditors may find themselves in an even less advantageous position. Unless the integrity of the transaction's structure is challenged, a securitizing firm is transferring assets out of its potential bankruptcy estate and consequently, in the event of a bankruptcy, these assets are not available to the firm's unsecured creditors. As such, the asset purchasers are not motivated to aid the firm in preserving the value of the estate. Not surprisingly, the securitizing firm's unsecured creditors are assuming a risk of nonpayment, as a result of the securitization, that is arguably greater than the risk unsecured creditors experience when their debtor borrows money on a secured basis.

In contrast, in a secured lending arrangement, if the debtor enters bankruptcy, the collateralized assets remain in the debtor's estate and the debtor gets the benefit (the upside potential) of any increase in value of a collateralized asset during the pendency of the bankruptcy proceeding. The secured creditor is required to participate in the debtor's bankruptcy and is motivated to encourage the preservation of the estate; in the event of a decrease in the value of the collateral, the estate may be the pool from which it receives a portion of its recovery. The secured creditor may not just walk away from the debtor in bankruptcy with its collateral — it is constrained by the automatic stay imposed at the time of the bankruptcy filing, and the debtor has use of the collateral during the pendency of the bankruptcy if the stay is not lifted. Thus, the relationship established between the debtor and the secured lender survives the debtor's bankruptcy, which has the potential to benefit the unsecured creditors.

Because of the different relationship ABS purchasers have with their financing seeking originator, the interest rates charged the securitizing originator by its unsecured creditors should be higher than those charged to debtors whose other funding comes from secured credit. If the unsecured interest rate does indeed reflect the risk differential, then one can conclude that securitization, pursuant to the analysis laid out by Jackson and Kronman, is indeed efficient. This analysis, however, rests upon the fundamental assumption of perfect information and fully informed consent by the unsecured creditors. This assumption, subject to considerable challenge when applied to secured credit, is even less reliable when a firm with unsecured creditors is securitizing assets.

The best that may be concluded in the absence of empirical evidence is that the justifications for securitization are unpersuasive and unproven. Securitized transactions may be efficient, or they may be inefficient, with unsecured creditors subject to effects which are in many circumstances more detrimental than those effects they are subject to when their borrower uses its assets as collateral for a secured loan.

Unsecured creditors of securitizing originators may be exposed to the further risk that a bankruptcy court, in scrutinizing a structured finance transaction, will reverse the asset transfer in the exercise of its equitable discretion. The ensuing litigation will be expensive, time consuming, and, until there has been a full resolution of this issue, will lead to even greater uncertainty in the credit markets. . . .

It has been said that the "majority of innovations on Wall Street die young." An innovation that falls within an exception to this maxim is asset securitization, whose market has been increasing in volume every year since the first issuance in the mid-1980s. It is clear that a great many people are making a great deal of money from the billions of dollars of ABS that are brought to market every year. It is equally clear that there remain unanswered questions with respect to the economic and social efficiency of structured finance transactions.

The most modest conclusion that may be drawn is that structured finance's efficiency is unproven. A bolder assertion, and one this Article predicts will be supported by empirical evidence, is that securitization is inefficient. When value is diverted from nonadjusting creditors to parties with greater knowledge, resources, and opportunity to bargain *ex ante* for greater leverage to encourage voluntary repayment (and in the event of bankruptcy, to guarantee priority repayment), then this value represents a distributional inefficiency. Moreover, unsecured creditors of securitizing originators do not receive the benefits of protection from the phenomenon of debtor misbehavior that they receive when their debtor uses its assets as security for credit. In the absence of such protections, unsecured creditors are more vulnerable to the risk of nonpayment as well as the risk of debtor's bankruptcy.

Presumably, even if the efficiency of securitization is ever proven to unanimous satisfaction, the distributional consequences of some parties being preferred over others will result in inequities. Such consequences will continue to fuel the flame of commercial law scholars, practitioners, bankruptcy trustees, and eventually courts and legislatures concerned about "stronger" market participants benefitting at the expense of their weaker counterparts — the unsecured creditors. If this prediction is realized at a time when the volume and type of securitizing originators in bankruptcy mirrors the profile of the newest securitization transaction originators, the ABS market will be subject to a drastic adjustment. Investors will lose the value of their investments as the previously transferred assets are returned to the originator's bankruptcy estate.

Empirical data is needed to conclusively demonstrate the harm experienced by the unsecured creditors of securitizing originators. Such a study would track dollar values with respect to securitization's benefits and its costs to third parties. This empirical examination will have to be conducted over time to observe and quantify the market effects of widespread originator bankruptcies.

Lynn M. LoPucki, *The Death of Liability*

106 Yale L.J. 1 (1996)

. . . . Asset securitization is both a substitute for borrowing and a powerful new strategy for judgment proofing. . . . [T]he asset-securitization strategy puts ownership of the company's valuable assets in an entity separate from the one that is at risk for liability. The advantage of the asset-securitization strategy . . . is virtual elimination of the risk that the courts will disregard the entity that holds the assets. Though the bankruptcy-remote vehicle is created pursuant to the debtor's plan, it is not only separately incorporated but is at all times controlled by arms-length investors. The terms of the transaction between the debtor and the bankruptcy-remote vehicle have real economic consequences for both. What is perhaps more important, by the time the issues are litigated, the bankruptcy-remote vehicle may be publicly held, with hundreds or thousands of innocent investors. Considering that even the most provocative division of a company into separate asset-holding and liability-incurring entities — one with one hundred percent congruity of ownership — is likely to be honored by the courts, it seems unlikely that the courts will consolidate the bankruptcy-remote vehicles created in asset securitizations, which typically have no congruity of ownership with the debtor.

Today, asset securitization is used primarily with regard to obligations owing to the debtor, including accounts receivable, mortgages, student loans, credit card receivables, and commercial loans. But practitioner-commentators stress that any income-producing asset can be securitized . . . . Transaction costs are probably the only limit on what may be the subject of securitization. By selling any asset to a bankruptcy-remote entity and leasing it back, the debtor can transform it into an "income-producing" asset that can then be securitized. Even a debtor's bank account, which is both an account and an income-producing asset, might be included.

Through asset securitization, a company potentially could divest itself of all of its assets, yet continue to use all of those assets in the continued operation of its business. To grasp the enormous potential, assume that, through a series of asset securitizations, Exxon Corporation disposes of all of its assets. As the cash from these transactions becomes available, Exxon distributes the cash to its shareholders in the form of dividends, leaving the company with neither assets nor liabilities. (I will refer to this judgment-proof Exxon as "Zero-Asset Exxon.") Because Exxon contracts to continue use of each asset even as Exxon sells it, the operations of Zero-Asset Exxon remain exactly as they were when it was a multibillion dollar company. But as a result of the asset-securitization transactions and the distribution of the proceeds, Zero-Asset Exxon is now judgment proof.

Even in this extreme application, the courts are unlikely to disregard the asset-securitization transactions. Pursuant to the principle of transferability, the transactions are effective until avoided through litigation so that innocent parties who rely on the transactions in the interim are protected. An argument might be made that a particular securitization is avoidable because it was made "with actual intent to hinder, delay, or defraud any creditor of the debtor." But to recover from the bankruptcy-remote entity, the judgment creditor would have to prove that the bankruptcy-remote entity did not receive the transfer "in good faith and for a reasonably equivalent value." That seems highly unlikely with regard to an arms-length transaction in which the buyer paid the full fair market value of the property. To attack this judgment-proof structure would require extensive litigation. A judgment creditor of Zero-Asset Exxon who levied on assets used in the company's business would be levying on assets owned by some bankruptcy-remote vehicle. By that wrongful levy, the judgment creditor would incur liability to the bankruptcy-remote entity for conversion.

As an alternative source of recovery, judgment creditors of Zero-Asset Exxon could pursue the proceeds of the asset-securitization transaction that were used to pay dividends. To do that, the creditors would sue the shareholders who received the dividends under a theory that the dividends were a fraudulent transfer. As a practical matter, however, the dividends would be unrecoverable. First, they may have been paid out to tens of thousands of shareholders, each of whom would be liable for only the amount that shareholder received. Second, the statute of limitations on the most likely theory of recovery would run four years after the transfer, so that four years after Exxon became a zero-asset company, its judgment-proof structure would for all practical purposes become legally unassailable.

One might suppose that the problem lies with fraudulent transfer law for failing to provide an appropriate remedy. But in fact the problem runs much deeper. First, fraudulent transfer law is limited by the principle of transferability; allowing easy avoidance of transfers would disrupt markets by clouding nearly all transfers and forcing expensive and time — consuming investigations by would-be subsequent transferees. Second, the Zero-Asset Exxon structure could be achieved without Zero-Asset Exxon making any transfer at all. Exxon could form a new company, Zero-Asset Exxon, to which Exxon rents all of its assets. Because the new company would start with only nominal assets, it would be judgment proof. The new company could not be faulted for fraudulent transfer because it would not have made any transfer. This demonstrates that the fault lies not with fraudulent transfer law but with the more fundamental principle of enforcement only against property of the debtor.

The schemes in the preceding examples show the structure of the future that judgment proofing will produce. There will be entities that own things and entities that do things. Those that own things — the bankruptcy-remote vehicles — will not do anything, lest they expose their assets to liability. Those that do things — the operating companies — will not own anything, lest their judgment creditors have something to attach.

From the fact that few large corporations have become entirely judgment proof, a purely economic analysis might conclude that the costs of judgment proofing exceed the benefits. But, to force a simple idea into the complex language of economic analysis, the costs of judgment proofing may be culturally determined. That is, judgment proofing may be costly solely because it conflicts with cultural norms. Reliance on such structures might bring consumer boycotts, management insecurity, and judicial hostility.

Asset securitization has not been restrained by cultural norms against judgment proofing because it has not been recognized as a judgment-proofing technique. Yet it is. Asset securitization is booming because investors are willing to pay more for securitized assets than for securitized businesses. In an article aptly titled *The Alchemy of Asset Securitization*, Professor Schwarcz attempts to explain why.[14] He begins by acknowledging the troublesome principle of "exposure conservation." Finance theory tells us that selling securities that allocate the risks and returns from a business enterprise does not change the total risks and returns. Slicing the rights in different ways may add to the value of one type of security, but only by detracting from the value of another. Securitization renders investments liquid at lower transaction costs, so it is certainly plausible that securitization may add value. But that cannot explain why asset securitization would be chosen over business securitization. Schwarcz considers several possible explanations for the market's preference for securitized assets over securitized businesses and ultimately selects the one most often mentioned by others: Asset securitization, unlike business securitization, "eliminates the risk of bankruptcy to investors."

What risk of bankruptcy is eliminated by asset securitization? That depends on the form in which the investment would have been made if it had not been made through asset securitization. From Schwarcz's description, it would appear that asset securitization is being substituted principally for unsecured bank lending and unsecured issues of public debt. Such debt is a liability, and in bankruptcy it shares pro rata with other kinds of liability claims. The owners of securitized assets, by contrast, keep their assets when the debtor files bankruptcy; they need not share with the holders of liability. In other words, debtors are substituting asset securitization, a judgment-proof financial structure, for unsecured debt, a non-judgment-proof structure. That a debtor's cost of funds obtained by asset securitization is lower than the cost of funds obtained by unsecured borrowing may be just the market's way of saying that it prefers judgment-proof companies because they are "efficient" liability avoiders.

14 [Eds.] This article is excerpted earlier in this chapter.

Another way of stating essentially the same argument is to note that stocks and bonds are the most junior claims against the assets of a company. They are defeated by anyone with a direct claim against the assets. The claims of third-party owners, such as those created in asset securitization, are the most senior claims. That the market will pay more for senior claims against the same assets than it will pay for junior claims against them suggests that priority matters. Perhaps the principal advantage of third-party ownership of assets over mere ownership of the company is that third-party owners of assets have priority over liability claims while stockholders do not.

Asset securitization may be the silver bullet capable of killing liability. In the few skirmishes in which asset-securitization structures have been challenged in bankruptcy, they have been upheld. Though the effect ultimately may be to defeat liability interests, this outcome should not be surprising. Liability is in disrepute. Asset securitization, by contrast, is widely regarded as an engine of the U.S. economy. Commentators all seem to agree that the savings available through asset securitization depend on the insulation of the securitized asset from bankruptcy — in essence, from liability. For the courts to strike down routine asset securitizations simply because they render the debtors judgment proof would eliminate the central advantage of asset securitization over the more traditional issuance of public debt. . . .

Steven L. Schwarcz, *The Inherent Irrationality of Judgment Proofing*

52 STAN. L. REV. 1 (1999)

. . . . LoPucki's central assertion is that the advent of securitization and other innovative business transactions is causing the death of liability.[15] However, by focusing on the structuring of business transactions, he ignores the important differences between arm's length and non-arm's length transactions. Different motivations, perspectives, and costs are inherent in each. In an arm's length judgment proofing transaction, each company will seek independent gain, whereas in a non-arm's length structure, judgment proofing only needs to benefit the controlling company. My analysis therefore addresses arm's length and non-arm's length transactions separately. . . .

To provide a context for the analysis, consider companies F1 and F2, which are unrelated. F1 is about to sell its assets to F2 and lease them back — a sale-leaseback being the threshold transaction in which F1 converts its ordinary assets into securitizable income-producing assets (in the form of leases) while still being able to use the original assets. F1, however, would have an immediate and significant disincentive against engaging in this threshold transaction: It would be taxed on the sale income.

---

[15] [Eds.] LoPucki's article is excerpted above.

If F1 nonetheless engages in the sale-leaseback, the lease theoretically can be securitized. Securitization has been alleged to be the most dangerous threat to liability. But a close analysis shows that allegation to be unfounded. Formalistically, only the buyer of the original assets, F2, can lease those assets back to F1, and therefore only F2 will hold leases which can be securitized. Thus, F1, the very company that is in danger of becoming judgment-proofed by securitization, would not technically be a party to the securitization transaction. More substantively, securitization is merely a way of allowing F2 to finance the purchase of F1's assets, with F1 receiving the sale proceeds. Judgment proofing only could result from F1's disposition of those sale proceeds for less than their value. That disposition, if it occurred, would be independent of the securitization transaction.

Even an argument that securitization indirectly facilitates judgment proofing by enabling F2 to finance the purchase of F1's assets would fail because F2 could finance the purchase of those assets through traditional techniques, such as bank borrowing. The possibility that securitization or other financing techniques might be misused should not undermine their overall legitimacy. In any event, the likelihood that F2 would be able to obtain securitization or other financing on the strength of a lease to F1 is extremely remote. Few investors or bank lenders would be willing to take the risk that future rentals of a judgment proof lessee would be paid.

The alarming description of Exxon's ability to judgment proof itself through securitization vividly demonstrates my point. Recall the claim that

> by selling any asset to a bankruptcy-remote entity and leasing it back, the debtor can transform it into an "income-producing" asset that can then be securitized.
>
> . . . To grasp the enormous potential, assume that, through a series of asset securitizations, Exxon Corporation disposes of all of its assets. . . . Because Exxon contracts to continue use of each asset even as Exxon sells it, the operations of Zero-Asset Exxon remain exactly as they were when it was a multibillion dollar company.[16]

Exxon first sells its assets to the bankruptcy-remote entity and receives a cash purchase price, and the entity then leases those assets back to Exxon, with the lease becoming the income-producing asset. But the bankruptcy-remote entity alone owns that income-producing asset. Exxon merely is a lessee. Therefore, on a formalistic level, only the entity, and not Exxon, could sell that asset in a securitization transaction.

More substantively, Exxon's creditors would not have to worry about a securitization transaction. In the unlikely event that the bankruptcy-remote entity is able to finance the purchase of Exxon's assets, the funds raised would be

---

16 [n. 62] [Lynn M. LoPucki, The Death of Liability, 106 YALE L.J. 1], at 25-26 (footnotes omitted).

paid to Exxon as the purchase price. Hence, Exxon's hard assets are merely replaced by cash. Because Exxon's creditors are only interested in repayment of their claims, they should be satisfied with the cash. Only a subsequent disposition of that cash, unrelated to the securitization, would cause judgment proofing. Securitization itself is not a judgment proofing technique.

Next consider the parent-subsidiary ownership strategy. (This strategy is not technically arm's length; however, I include it in this discussion because it is one of the transactional structures referenced by LoPucki.) Although the strategy "is in wide use among the largest companies in America," there is no evidence that it causes judgment proofing. However, there is significant evidence that parent-subsidiary ownership allows a manufacturing company to obtain lower-cost financing, thereby arguably benefitting its involuntary creditors by lowering the company's overall debt burden. LoPucki apparently draws an incorrect conclusion from the parent-subsidiary ownership strategy because he assumes, without basis, that Operations (the parent) "distributes any proceeds beyond its immediate cash needs to its shareholders." Not only does that assumption not reflect business reality, it illustrates the failure to distinguish between structuring an arm's length transaction and the completely unrelated step of paying dividends.

Finally, examine LoPucki's "essential structure" of judgment proofing. If a company wishes to judgment proof itself, it would have to transfer its assets. It is possible to divide potential recipients of the transfer into three categories: the company's creditors, the company's owners (its shareholders), and third parties other than creditors and owners. A transfer of assets to creditors would be the antithesis of judgment proofing. A transfer of assets to shareholders could cause judgment proofing, but the payment of such dividends is not necessarily dependent on the essential structure. A transfer of assets to unrelated third parties should not cause judgment proofing because no rational company will give away its assets without demanding equivalent value in return. Thus, in an arm's length context, none of these transfers causes judgment proofing.

The failure to recognize that structuring an arm's length transaction does not cause judgment proofing stems from a failure to trace cash flows. . . .

Steven L. Schwarcz, *Securitization Post-Enron*
25 CARDOZO L. REV. ___ (forthcoming)

. . . . "When an economist says that [something] is efficient, nine times out of ten he means Kaldor-Hicks efficient."[17] Securitization transactions therefore would be efficient if the aggregate benefit to the SPV's investors and the originator exceeds any net harm to the originator's unsecured creditors.

[17] [n. 77] [RICHARD A. POSNER, ECONOMIC ANALYSIS OF LAW] § 1.02, AT 14. . . .

For purposes of analysis, call the originator's benefit X, the SPV-investors' benefit Y, and any net harm to unsecured creditors Z. A securitization transaction would be efficient where X + Y equals or exceeds Z. Because commercial parties usually will not voluntarily engage in transactions unless they expect material gains, X + Y would be expected to be material. If, therefore, Z is likely to be nonmaterial, X + Y would be expected to exceed Z for most securitization transactions, making securitization efficient. I next argue that Z is not only likely to be nonmaterial, but also to be zero or even negative.

Z is likely to be zero or negative because securitization transactions do not, in the aggregate, result in net harm but instead, as shown below, create net *value* for unsecured creditors. My argument has three steps. First, because securitization provides the originator with new money, unsecured creditors are not harmed, absent the originator investing or otherwise using that money in a manner that reduced its value ("overinvestment"). Second, even though overinvestment sometimes occurs, it only harms unsecured creditors where the originator becomes insolvent; that harm should be more than offset by the originator's lower interest-cost burden (thereby preserving value to pay unsecured creditors) and the fact that securitization provides liquidity to companies that need liquidity but are unable to borrow, thereby enhancing creditor recovery. Third, both empirical evidence and the relative rarity of covenants restricting securitization transactions demonstrate that unsecured creditors themselves view securitization as providing net value.

1. *Absent Overinvestment, Unsecured Creditors Are Not Harmed:* Securitization always provides the originator with new money in the form of cash received for the sale of financial assets. Thus it merely substitutes for one type of asset, financial assets, another type, cash. As a result, absent overinvestment, unsecured creditors have the same amount of unencumbered assets to levy against after as before the securitization.

For example, assume an originator has assets worth $U and unsecured claims of $V. The originator proposes to raise $W of new money in a securitization, by selling $W + x face-amount of financial assets to an SPV — x representing the necessary overcollateralization. Before the securitization, the unsecured creditors would be paid their $V of claims from the $U of assets. After giving effect to the securitization, the originator's assets would be $U — (W + x) + W, which equals $U — x. Although this might appear to be a reduction in value equal to x, in fact it is not: x merely reflects that valuation of the face amount of financial assets sold must take into account the time value of money — collections on those financial assets being due at future dates — and the risk that those assets may default.

Therefore, before the securitization, the $V of unsecured creditor claims can be paid from the $U face amount of assets, whose real value (discounting for time value of money and risk of default) equals $U — x. After the securitization, the $V of unsecured creditor claims likewise can be paid from $U — x of assets. The unsecured creditors have not been harmed.

In fact, the sale of financial assets may actually *benefit* the originator and its creditors by transferring the risk on those assets. Unlike a secured loan, where any collateral shortfall gives rise to an unsecured deficiency claim in that amount, in a securitization the SPV and its investors only have recourse against the financial assets purchased, and not against the originator or its other assets. Accordingly, the SPV and its investors — and not the originator or its unsecured creditors — bear the risk that those financial assets may be insufficient to repay the investors. If it turns out in retrospect that x was too small — meaning that the discount from face value of the financial assets sold, taking into account time value of money and risk of default, should have been greater than x, only the SPV and its investors take that risk. On the other hand, if, in retrospect, x is too big, most securitization deals permit the originator, at deal's end, to recover the surplus value from the SPV.

2. *Any Harm from Overinvestment Should be More than Offset:* The foregoing analysis concedes that overinvestment of securitization proceeds can, and undoubtedly sometimes does, occur. I next show, however, that the risk of overinvestment does not make securitization inefficient.

This risk first must be placed into perspective. Overinvestment is a normal — though minimal — business risk of any financing, not just securitization. In fact, given the scrutiny imposed by rating agencies, securitization may present fewer opportunities for intentional overinvestment than other financing methods. It is nonetheless possible that securitization may become suspect if implemented — even though this use of securitization is rare — when the originator is on the brink of insolvency. That potential for dissipating cash proceeds is not, however, unique to securitization. The same concern would arise, for example, if an insolvent company sold, or borrowed money by encumbering, a factory or equipment. But questionable uses of proceeds are already, and more appropriately, addressed by preference and fraudulent conveyance laws.

To the limited extent overinvestment occurs, it only harms unsecured creditors if the company — in our case, the originator — becomes insolvent. This is because unsecured creditors of a solvent company are eventually repaid. Because securitization is rarely used for originators on the brink of insolvency and, as discussed, the risk of overinvestment itself is minimal, there should be few cases where unsecured creditors are harmed by overinvestment of securitization proceeds.

Furthermore, viewing securitization transactions in the aggregate, any harm to unsecured creditors in those few cases should be more than offset by securitization's benefits. There are two such benefits that indirectly profit unsecured creditors: securitized debt has a lower interest-rate cost than corporate debt, so the cost differential is available to pay unsecured creditors; and securitization can be used to provide needed liquidity to viable companies unable to borrow, keeping them out of bankruptcy (and thus enhancing creditor recovery). Consider each such benefit in turn.

Securitized debt has a lower interest-rate cost than corporate debt because it provides a new source of financing, the capital markets, whose rates are systematically lower than the rates at which many companies commonly borrow. . . . If, therefore, an originator funds a portion of its financing needs through securitization, the interest-cost saving would be available to pay the originator's unsecured creditors.

Securitization also can be used to provide needed liquidity to otherwise viable companies unable to borrow. Because lack of liquidity is perhaps the leading cause of business bankruptcies, increasing liquidity is likely to decrease bankruptcies. That, in turn, increases unsecured creditor value. To understand why, consider the expected value of unsecured claims with, and without, the availability of liquidity from securitization.

The expected value of those claims equals the probability of the originator's bankruptcy multiplied by the amount of its unsecured creditors' recovery in bankruptcy, plus the probability of the originator staying out of bankruptcy multiplied by the amount of its unsecured creditors' recovery outside of bankruptcy. For purposes of illustration, assume a hypothetical originator, faced with a 10% risk of bankruptcy unless it obtains liquidity, with $1 million of assets and $1 million of unsecured claims. Assuming a 75% bankruptcy valuation of the assets, the expected value of the originator's unsecured claims, absent liquidity, is equal to (0.1 x $750,000) + (0.9 x $1,000,000) = $975,000. However, to the extent securitization — by providing liquidity — reduces the risk of bankruptcy, the expected value of the originator's unsecured claims will increase. For example, if securitization reduces the originator's risk of bankruptcy merely from 10% to 9%, the expected value of those claims would increase to (0.09 x $750,000) + (0.91 x $1,000,000) = $977,500. If securitization reduces the originator's risk of bankruptcy to 5%, the expected value of those claims would increase to as much as (0.05 x $750,000) + (0.95 x $1,000,000) = $987,500. And, of course, to the extent securitization reduces the originator's risk of bankruptcy below 5%, the expected value of the originator's unsecured claims would increase even more.

This result — that securitization, by providing liquidity, reduces the risk of bankruptcy thereby increasing the expected value of an originator's unsecured claims — obtains irrespective of the starting numbers. . . . The greater the reduction in the risk of bankruptcy, the higher the increase. . . .

Indeed, the only way securitization can reduce the expected value of unsecured claims is by increasing the risk that originators will go bankrupt. That should not generally happen. The availability of liquidity usually decreases, not increases, the risk of bankruptcy. Furthermore, investors will not invest where the originator, notwithstanding the securitization, is likely to go bankrupt. Originators at risk of going bankrupt are able to utilize securitization only if the liquidity thereby provided makes their bankruptcy unlikely. Thus, securitization should always increase, or have a neutral impact on, the expected value of unsecured claims.

This is, of course, a very powerful result. In comparison, secured debt, unlike securitization, has a more ambiguous impact on the expected value of unsecured creditor claims. The dramatic difference in the impact of these two forms of financing on those claims is due to the fact that secured debt is, *to the full extent of such debt*, a claim that, in bankruptcy, has priority over the originator's unsecured creditors; whereas the proceeds of such debt constitute an asset that, in bankruptcy, potentially loses a portion of its value. In contrast, securitization does not create debt but merely substitutes assets — cash in return for financial assets. Unsecured creditors are thus not subordinated to anyone in their recovery.

For these reasons, unsecured creditors as a class generally should benefit from securitization, notwithstanding possible harm to creditors in individual cases. As shown below, unsecured creditors themselves believe that securitization is beneficial.

3. *Unsecured Creditors Themselves View Securitization as Providing Net Value:* Both empirical evidence and the widespread exclusion of securitization transactions from negative-pledge, asset-sale, and similar covenants demonstrate that unsecured creditors themselves view securitization as providing net value. First consider covenants.

To protect their interests, unsecured creditors traditionally impose these types of restricting covenants on borrowing companies, usually by including the covenants in loan agreements. These covenants almost always include negative-pledge covenants, which restrict the company's ability to incur secured debt. In contrast, secured creditors rarely impose covenants restricting the company's ability to enter into securitization transactions:

> We often have to navigate our way through restrictive covenants in both secured and unsecured debt indentures in connection with trade receivables securitizations. As you indicated, these restrictions are often contained in sections dealing with restrictions on liens and sale of assets. We also encounter the restriction in the context of restrictions on the formation of subsidiaries (which, of course, are needed to allow the company to realize the residual value of the receivables) or requirements that cause newly-formed subsidiaries to become guarantors of the secured or unsecured debt (obviously, not permitted in securitization transactions). *Having said all that, I believe that your premise that securitization transactions are more favored by other lenders in [sic] basically correct. This can be seen through the development over the last several years of general exceptions from the negative covenants for securitization transactions. Moreover, some indentures will permit securitization transactions as long as the proceeds realized in connection therewith are reinvested in the business of company.*[18]

[18] [n. 131] E-mail from Henry G. Morriello, securitization partner, Kaye Scholer LLP, to the author (Feb. 3, 2003; emphasis added) (on file with author). . . .

I recognize, of course, that the absence of restrictions on securitization transactions is not dispositive evidence of securitization's efficiency. The scarceness of those restrictions might be explained, for example, by a greater desire on the part of originators themselves to preserve the option to engage in securitization transactions, and therefore to more vehemently oppose the imposition of covenants restricting securitization than covenants restricting secured lending. Nonetheless, the absence of those restrictions at least indicates that unsecured creditors are not overtly threatened by securitization transactions.

Moreover, empirical evidence supports the stronger claim — that unsecured creditors view securitization as providing net value. This can be confirmed by observing how the prices of unsecured debt are affected by securitization. To this end, my research assistant, DongJu Song, and I examined the data on public bond prices, because these data are at least somewhat available. A drop in bond prices following a securitization suggests that investors believe the securitization will hurt bondholders, whereas an increase in bond prices suggests the opposite.

We randomly selected several thousand securitization debt issues listed as outstanding in the 1999 Mergent Bond Record. From that set, we identified to the extent publicly ascertainable the originator of each such securitization. We then excluded originators that, at the time of the relevant securitization, were distressed or otherwise appeared to be subject to exogenous factors that might influence bond prices. From that subset, we next attempted to examine each such originator's public bond prices for the 24-hour period prior to and after the announcement of the securitization. Using all of the available data services — Datastream, Bloomberg, Lexis, Dow Jones News Retrieval Service, Westlaw, Moody's, Standard & Poor's, the *Wall Street Journal*, and the Internet — we were able to locate originator bond data for 145 securitization transactions issued between 1994 and 1999. We were unable to obtain bond data for all of the originators because some did not have bonds outstanding during the relevant period and most of the bond-price information services limit their archived data to bonds rated investment grade or better.

Subject to these limitations, the data from the bond test suggest that bondholders believe they will benefit from securitization. The average price change for the bonds of these 145 transactions, adjusting for the effect of general corporate bond market performance, was an eight-cent, or 0.089% increase in bond price, with statistical significance of 88.27%. This means that our sample demonstrates an 88% probability that the effect of a securitization transaction on the originators' unsecured creditors is positive.

These data, the relative rarity of covenants restricting securitization transactions, and the fact that securitization provides the originator with sale proceeds equal to the value of the assets sold and any harm from overinvestment of those proceeds should be more than offset, indicate that securitization creates net value for unsecured creditors. As a result, Z, the net harm to unsecured creditors, should be zero if not negative — and thus certainly non-material. Accordingly, X + Y will equal or exceed Z, making securitization Kaldor-Hicks efficient. . . .

4. *Securitization is Efficient Notwithstanding its Impact on Non-Adjusting Creditors:* This article so far has not explicitly addressed securitization's efficiency in light of its impact on unsecured creditors that cannot adjust their interest rates to compensate for problems ("non — adjusting creditors"). Non-adjusting creditors include involuntary creditors, such as tort creditors, as well as voluntary creditors that, for whatever reason — e.g., they extend credit on fixed terms or, like some trade creditors, their claims are so small that it is impractical to monitor — cannot adjust their interest rates. There is a perceived uneasiness that securitization may harm non-adjusting creditors without any offsetting compensation, and that such uncompensated harm might make securitization inefficient or unfair. I discuss the matter of unfairness . . . below. This [p]art . . . focuses on the issue of efficiency.

There are at least three explanations why, notwithstanding possible harm to non-adjusting creditors, securitization is efficient. First, Kaldor-Hicks efficiency is a function of aggregate benefit and harm, not harm to any particular sub-class (such as non-adjusting creditors). Thus, a transaction can be efficient even though non-adjusting creditors are harmed. My analysis shows that securitization is efficient even though unsecured creditors — a class which includes non-adjusting creditors — may be harmed. Thus, securitization is efficient even though non-adjusting creditors may be harmed.

The second explanation why securitization is efficient follows from the work of Professor Robert Scott in the secured-lending context, which should have similar application here. Scott has argued that the efficiency effects of non-adjustment turn on whether subsequent positive-value projects would be financed without secured credit.[19] In our context, the parallel argument would be that the efficiency effects of non-adjustment turn on whether subsequent positive-value projects would be financed without securitization. Although an empirical question, it appears that securitization is, indeed, sometimes the only method of financing positive-value projects. To that extent, any adverse impact of non-adjustment would be mitigated.

Scott notes, however, that even if some positive-value projects can only be financed with secured credit — or, in our context, with securitization — the ultimate question is, "[w]hat are the relative value of these two offsetting effects."[20] In other words, does the value of financing those positive-value projects sufficiently offset any harm to non-adjusting creditors? In the secured lending context, he answers, "[a]t this point we do not have a clue."[21] In the securitization

19 [n. 151] Robert C. Scott, *The Truth About Secured Financing*, 82 CORNELL L. REV. 1436, 1443 (1997).

20 [n. 153] [*Id.*], at 1461.

21 [n. 154] *Id.*

context, though, we have more than a clue. The net harm to non-adjusting creditors is likely to be zero or negative. Thus, few, if any additional positive-value projects — and, as mentioned, there may be many such projects — would be needed to offset the harm.

The third explanation why securitization is efficient is the most straightforward: as shown . . . below (and already implicitly shown in the discussion above), non-adjusting creditors, as a class, are not actually harmed by securitization.

The foregoing analysis has shown that securitization is efficient under the Kaldor-Hicks model of efficiency. But that model only requires that the aggregate benefit to the parties to the securitization — the originator and the SPV's investors — exceeds any net harm to the originator's unsecured creditors. Kaldor-Hicks efficiency alone does not ensure that securitization is fair to unsecured creditors.

My analysis, however, implicitly demonstrates that securitization is indeed fair to, and does not prejudice, unsecured creditors as a class. Although individual unsecured creditors certainly could, and undoubtedly will, sometimes be harmed by securitization transactions, I have shown that Z, the net harm to unsecured creditors as a class, is not only non-material but also likely to be zero or negative. This is because securitization transactions, in the aggregate, create net value for unsecured creditors. Even though unsecured creditors sometimes will be harmed where an originator that goes bankrupt overinvests the securitization proceeds, that harm should be more than offset in the aggregate by the lower interest-cost burden on originators and the liquidity provided to originators that are unable to borrow.

Thus unsecured creditors *as a class* benefit from, and thus are not harmed by, securitization. Absent favoritism or prejudice, fairness must be judged by reference to a class, not its individual members.

Nonetheless, my article must respond to perceived uneasiness that securitization would be unfair to the extent that it harms non-adjusting creditors. My analysis, however, already *implicitly* demonstrates that securitization does not harm non-adjusting creditors as a class. This is because the claims of unsecured creditors are *pari passu*, and nothing in my analysis turns on unsecured creditors being voluntary or involuntary or having the ability to adjust their interest rates to offset harm. Therefore, by showing that securitization has a positive, or at worst neutral, impact on repayment of the undifferentiated class of creditors holding unsecured claims, the analysis necessarily shows that securitization has that same positive or at worst neutral impact on repayment of the subclass of non-adjusting creditors.

Furthermore, the [earlier] conclusions . . . which confirm this analysis by examining the experience of voluntary creditors, should apply equally to involuntary and other non-adjusting creditors. . . . [E]mpirical data on bond-market pricing as well as the relative rarity of contractual covenants restricting securitization . . . show that unsecured creditors themselves view securitization as providing net value. Although any decision to (or not to) impose contractual covenants also should reflect the views of non-adjusting creditors. That is because the creditors studied, having decided *ex ante* not to impose such covenants, are unable to adjust their rates in the event of a future securitization. Therefore, *except as discussed in the next paragraph,* they will not be "adjusting" creditors who can raise their interest rates to compensate for possible securitization risk. Their favorable views of securitization thus should reflect the views of non-adjusting creditors, with whom they are *pari passu.*

The only counter-argument is that unsecured credit unprotected by covenants restricting securitization may be priced *ex ante* at high interest rates to offset later securitization risk. That argument is weak, however, since most unsecured credit lacks the protection of these covenants. Moreover, . . . empirical data on bond-market pricing belie that argument. If the bonds were priced *ex ante* to offset future securitization risk, the effect of a subsequent securitization on bond pricing would be neutral. The data, however, show a price increase.

The empirical data on bond-market pricing likewise confirm my analysis. Although those data result from voluntary purchases and sales, bonds are usually fixed-rate instruments and thus investors in the bonds are not "adjusting" creditors except to the extent they buy at a discount (buying at a discount being the economic equivalent of raising the bonds' interest rate). However, whereas buying at a discount lowers bond prices, the empirical data show that securitization instead has the effect of *raising* bond prices. This suggests that voluntary bond investors are effectively non-adjusting creditors insofar as securitization is concerned. Their favorable views of securitization therefore, as before, should reflect the views of non-adjusting creditors, with whom their claims are *pari passu.*

This conclusion stands to reason: securitization benefits unsecured creditors as a class; the claims of non-adjusting creditors are *pari passu* with the claims of all other unsecured creditors; therefore non-adjusting creditors are benefitted or at least not materially harmed by securitization, the same as other unsecured creditors. Nonetheless, one might ask how this conclusion comports with the Modigliani & Miller theorem, that in a perfect universe any savings achieved by changing one part of a company's capital structure will result in offsetting costs to other parts of the capital structure. At least part of the answer is that the universe in which securitization operations is *not* perfect. Its imperfections include, among other things, information asymmetry and intermediation costs. An answer also is provided by recent scholarship, which finds that "incentives for asset securitization . . . involve forces purely internal to the contractual parties." This finding "responds to normative criticism of [securitization] by those who see it simply as a means of responding to external factors, like the possibility of involuntary creditors." . . .

QUESTIONS ON EFFICIENCY

1. Should an originator's unsecured creditors bargain for covenants to protect themselves in the event the originator subsequently enters into a securtization transaction? What should such covenants include? Why might unsecured creditors not bargain for such a covenant? Is the argument that unsecured creditors do not insert securitization covenants because they are unfamiliar with or do not expect a securitization to take place persuasive in the light of the volume of securitization transactions that take place today?

2. According to securitization's critics, who suffers more from a securitization, voluntary contractual unsecured creditors of the originator, or the originator's nonadjusting creditors? Why do securitization proponents believe that securitization are efficient notwithstanding their potential impact on nonadjusting creditors?

3. Both securitzation's proponents (Professor Schwarcz in the *Alchemy* excerpt) and critics (Professor Lupica) claim that empirical work is necessary to prove securitization's efficiency or inefficiency and each claim that such empirical work will support their position on the debate. What empirical work would test the proposition of securitization's efficiency? How practical would it be to accomplish such work? Does Professor Schwarcz's empirical work discussed in *Securitization Post-Enron* settle the debate?

4. Professor LoPucki argues that securitization proceeds could be used, as in the case of Zero-Asset, Exxon to pay dividends to the originator's shareholders at the expense of the claims of the originator's unsecured creditors. Does Professor Schwarcz answer that claim in *Securitization Post-Enron* by his assertion that unsecured creditors of the originator are in fact benefitted by the originator's securitization?

5. Compare the arguments of Professors Schwarcz, Hill and Lupica on whether creditor monitoring will increase or decrease after a securitization and whether a securitization is a positive or negative signal regarding the credit risk of the originator. Is each viewing the issue from the same perspective or do they differ between whether they are concerned about the originator and its creditors, or the SPE and its creditors?

Appendix 1

[redacted]

0305960552

FILED
SACRAMENTO, CA
FEB 27, 2003 AT 1604
KEVIN SHELLEY
SECRETARY OF STATE

UCC FINANCING STATEMENT

FOLLOW INSTRUCTIONS (front and back) CAREFULLY

A. NAME & PHONE OF CONTACT AT FILER [optional]

B. SEND ACKNOWLEDGMENT TO: (Name and Address)

Please return copy to:
CT CORPORATION SYSTEM
Attn: John Ryan
915 L Street, Suite 1440
Sacramento, CA 95814

THE ABOVE SPACE IS FOR FILING OFFICE USE ONLY

1. DEBTOR'S EXACT FULL LEGAL NAME - insert only one debtor name (1a or 1b) - do not abbreviate or combine names

1a. ORGANIZATION'S NAME America Honda Finance Corporation					
OR 1b. INDIVIDUAL'S LAST NAME	FIRST NAME	MIDDLE NAME		SUFFIX	
1c. MAILING ADDRESS 700 Van Ness Avenue, Building 300	CITY Torrence	STATE CA	POSTAL CODE 90501-1485	COUNTRY USA	
1d. SEE INSTRUCTIONS 95-3472715	ADD'L INFO RE ORGANIZATION DEBTOR	1e. TYPE OF ORGANIZATION Corporation	1f. JURISDICTION OF ORGANIZATION California	1g. ORGANIZATIONAL ID #, if any CA0951492	☐ NONE

2. ADDITIONAL DEBTOR'S EXACT FULL LEGAL NAME - insert only one debtor name (2a or 2b) - do not abbreviate or combine names

2a. ORGANIZATION'S NAME					
OR 2b. INDIVIDUAL'S LAST NAME	FIRST NAME	MIDDLE NAME		SUFFIX	
2c. MAILING ADDRESS	CITY	STATE	POSTAL CODE	COUNTRY	
2d. SEE INSTRUCTIONS	ADD'L INFO RE ORGANIZATION DEBTOR	2e. TYPE OF ORGANIZATION	2f. JURISDICTION OF ORGANIZATION	2g. ORGANIZATIONAL ID #, if any	☐ NONE

3. SECURED PARTY'S NAME (or NAME of TOTAL ASSIGNEE of ASSIGNOR S/P) - insert only one secured party name (3a or 3b)

3a. ORGANIZATION'S NAME American Honda Receivables Corporation				
OR 3b. INDIVIDUAL'S LAST NAME	FIRST NAME	MIDDLE NAME		SUFFIX
3c. MAILING ADDRESS 700 Van Ness Avenue, Building 300	CITY Torrence	STATE CA	POSTAL CODE 90501-1485	COUNTRY USA

4. This FINANCING STATEMENT covers the following collateral:

See Schedule A attached hereto and made a part hereof

5. ALTERNATIVE DESIGNATION [if applicable]: ☐ LESSEE/LESSOR ☐ CONSIGNEE/CONSIGNOR ☐ BAILEE/BAILOR ☐ SELLER/BUYER ☐ AG. LIEN ☐ NON-UCC FILING

6. ☐ This FINANCING STATEMENT is to be filed [for record] (or recorded) in the REAL ESTATE RECORDS. Attach Addendum [if applicable]

7. Check to REQUEST SEARCH REPORT(S) on Debtor(s) [ADDITIONAL FEE] [optional] ☐ All Debtors ☐ Debtor 1 ☐ Debtor 2

8. OPTIONAL FILER REFERENCE DATA

File with SOS-CA

FILING OFFICE COPY — UCC FINANCING STATEMENT (FORM UCC1) (REV. 05/22/02)

DB DRAFT OF FEBRUARY 20, 2003

SCHEDULE A

to Financing Statement on Form UCC-1

TRANSFEROR/DEBTOR: American Honda Finance Corporation ("AHC")

TRANSFEREE/SECURED PARTY: American Honda Receivables Corp. ("AHRC")

This filing covers all right, title and interest of the Transferor in, to and under and to the following:

a. the receivables consisting of retail installment sale contracts secured by new or used Honda and Acura motor vehicles, together with all accessions thereto (the "Financed Vehicles") listed in Schedule A to the Receivables Purchase Agreement, dated as of February 1, 2003 (the "Agreement"), between AHFC and AHRC, and all proceeds thereof and payments thereunder (the "Receivables"), and all monies due thereon or paid thereunder or in respect thereof (including proceeds of Receivables which AHFC or AHRC is required or has elected to purchase) on or after February 1, 2003;

b. the security interests in the Financed Vehicles;

c. any proceeds of any physical damage insurance policies covering the Financed Vehicles and in any proceeds of any credit life or credit disability insurance policies relating to the Receivables or the Obligors;

d. any proceeds of recourse rights against the dealer of motor vehicles who sold a Financed Vehicle and who originated and assigned the Receivable relating to such Financed Vehicle to AHFC, and any successor to such dealer;

e. the right to realize upon any property (including the right to receive future liquidation proceeds) that shall have secured a Receivable an have been repossessed by or on behalf of the Issuer; and

f. the proceeds of any and all the foregoing.

Definitions:

"Financed Vehicle" means, with respect to any retail installment sale or conditional sale contract, the related new or used Honda or Acura motor vehicle, together with all accessions thereto securing the related Obligor's indebtedness under such retail installment sale or conditional sale contract.

"Issuer" means Honda Auto Receivables 2003-1 Owner Trust, a Delaware statutory trust.

Appendix 2

[redacted]

0305960543

FILED
SACRAMENTO, CA
FEB 27, 2003 AT 1604
KEVIN SHELLEY
SECRETARY OF STATE

UCC FINANCING STATEMENT

FOLLOW INSTRUCTIONS (front and back) CAREFULLY

A. NAME & PHONE OF CONTACT AT FILER [optional]

B. SEND ACKNOWLEDGMENT TO: (Name and Address)

Please return copy to:
CT CORPORATION SYSTEM
Attn: John Ryan
915 L Street, Suite 1440
Sacramento, CA 95814

THE ABOVE SPACE IS FOR FILING OFFICE USE ONLY

1. DEBTOR'S EXACT FULL LEGAL NAME - insert only one debtor name (1a or 1b) - do not abbreviate or combine names

1a. ORGANIZATION'S NAME: America Honda Receivables Corp.						
OR 1b. INDIVIDUAL'S LAST NAME		FIRST NAME	MIDDLE NAME		SUFFIX	
1c. MAILING ADDRESS: 700 Van Ness Avenue, Building 300		CITY: Torrence	STATE: CA	POSTAL CODE: 90501-1485	COUNTRY: USA	
1d. SEE INSTRUCTIONS: 33-0525098	ADD'L INFO RE ORGANIZATION DEBTOR	1e. TYPE OF ORGANIZATION: Corporation	1f. JURISDICTION OF ORGANIZATION: California	1g. ORGANIZATIONAL ID #, if any: CI837226		☐ NONE

2. ADDITIONAL DEBTOR'S EXACT FULL LEGAL NAME - insert only one debtor name (2a or 2b) - do not abbreviate or combine names

2a. ORGANIZATION'S NAME						
OR 2b. INDIVIDUAL'S LAST NAME		FIRST NAME	MIDDLE NAME		SUFFIX	
2c. MAILING ADDRESS		CITY	STATE	POSTAL CODE	COUNTRY	
2d. SEE INSTRUCTIONS	ADD'L INFO RE ORGANIZATION DEBTOR	2e. TYPE OF ORGANIZATION	2f. JURISDICTION OF ORGANIZATION	2g. ORGANIZATIONAL ID #, if any		☐ NONE

3. SECURED PARTY'S NAME (or NAME of TOTAL ASSIGNEE of ASSIGNOR S/P) - insert only one secured party name (3a or 3b)

3a. ORGANIZATION'S NAME: American Honda Receivables 2003-1 Owner Trust					
OR 3b. INDIVIDUAL'S LAST NAME	FIRST NAME	MIDDLE NAME		SUFFIX	
3c. MAILING ADDRESS: The Bank of New York (Delaware) as Delaware Trustee: White Clay Center Route 273	CITY: Newark	STATE: DE	POSTAL CODE: 19711	COUNTRY: USA	

4. This FINANCING STATEMENT covers the following collateral:

See Schedule A attached hereto and made a part hereof

5. ALTERNATIVE DESIGNATION [if applicable]: ☐ LESSEE/LESSOR ☐ CONSIGNEE/CONSIGNOR ☐ BAILEE/BAILOR ☐ SELLER/BUYER ☐ AG. LIEN ☐ NON-UCC FILING

6. ☐ This FINANCING STATEMENT is to be filed [for record] (or recorded) in the REAL ESTATE RECORDS. Attach Addendum [if applicable]

7. Check to REQUEST SEARCH REPORT(S) on Debtor(s) [ADDITIONAL FEE] [optional] ☐ All Debtors ☐ Debtor 1 ☐ Debtor 2

8. OPTIONAL FILER REFERENCE DATA

File with SOS-CA

FILING OFFICE COPY — UCC FINANCING STATEMENT (FORM UCC1) (REV. 05/22/02)

SCHEDULE A
to Financing Statement on Form UCC-1

TRANSFEROR/DEBTOR: American Honda Receivables Corp. ("AHRC")

TRANSFEREE/SECURED PARTY: Honda Auto Receivables 2003-1 Owner Trust (the "Issuer")

This filing covers all right, title and interest of the Transferor in, to and under and to the following:

a. the receivables consisting of retail installment sale contracts secured by new or used Honda and Acura motor vehicles, together with all accessions thereto (the "Financed Vehicles") listed in Schedule A to the Sale and Servicing Agreement, dated as of February 1, 2003 (the "Agreement"), among American Honda Finance Corporation ("AHFC"), and all proceeds thereof and payments thereunder (the "Receivables"), AHRC and the Issuer and all proceeds thereof and payments thereunder (the "Receivables"), and all monies due thereon or paid thereunder or in respect thereof (including proceeds of Receivables which AHFC or AHRC is required or has elected to purchase) on or after February 1, 2003;

b. the security interests in the Financed Vehicles;

c. any proceeds of any physical damage insurance policies covering the Financed Vehicles and in any proceeds of any credit life or credit disability insurance policies relating to the Receivables or the Obligors;

d. any proceeds of recourse rights against the dealer of motor vehicles who sold a Financed Vehicle and who originated and assigned the Receivable relating to such Financed Vehicle to AHFC, and any successor to such dealer;

e. the Receivables Purchase Agreement, dated as of February 1, 2003, between AHFC and AHRC, as purchaser, but not the obligations of AHRC thereunder;

f. the right to realize upon any property (including the right to receive future liquidation proceeds) that shall have secured a Receivable an have been repossessed by or on behalf of the Issuer; and

g. all funds, and all investment property, from time to time carried in or credited to the accounts designated in the Agreement as the Collection Account, the Note Distribution Account, the Payahead Account, the Yield Supplement Account and the Reserve Fund, including the initial deposit made into the Yield Supplement Account and Reserve Fund, and in all investment income and proceeds thereof.

h. any (i) irrevocable letter of credit naming the Indenture Trustee as beneficiary or (ii) surety bond, insurance policy or deposit of cash or securities, in either case, securing obligations of the AHFC or any replacement servicer with respect to the Receivables; and

i. the proceeds of any and all the foregoing.

<u>Definitions:</u>

"<u>Accounts</u>" means the Collection Account, the Note Distribution Account, the Payahead Account, the Yield Supplement Account and the Reserve Fund.

"<u>Collection Account</u>" means the account designated as such in, and established and maintained pursuant to the Agreement.

"Financed Vehicle" means, with respect to any retail installment sale or conditional sale contract, the related new or used Honda or Acura motor vehicle, together with all accessions thereto securing the related Obligor's indebtedness under such retail installment sale or conditional sale contract.

"Indenture" means the indenture, dated as of February 1, 2003 between the Issuer and the Indenture Trustee.

"Indenture Trustee" means the Person acting as Indenture Trustee under the Indenture, its successors in interest and any successor trustee under the Indenture.

"Insurance Policy" means, with respect to a Receivable, an insurance policy covering physical damage, credit life, credit disability, theft, mechanical breakdown or any similar event relating to the related Financed Vehicle or Obligor.

"Note Distribution Account" means the account designated as such in, and established and maintained pursuant to the Agreement.

"Obligor" means the purchaser or co-purchasers of the related Financed Vehicle purchased in part or in whole by the execution and delivery of a retail installment contract or any other Person who owes or may be liable for payments under such retail installment contract.

"Payahead Account" means the account designed as such in, and established and maintained pursuant to the Agreement.

"Receivable" means any retail installment sale contract executed by an Obligor in respect of a Financed Vehicle, and all proceeds thereof and payments thereunder, which Receivables shall be identified in a Schedule or Receivables.

"Receivables Purchase Agreement" means the receivables purchase agreement, dated as of February 1, 2003, between AHFC and the Seller, as amended or supplemented from time to time.

"Reserve Fund" means the account designated as such, and established and maintained pursuant to the agreement.

"Schedule of Receivables" means the schedule of Receivables attached as Schedule A to the Agreement, as it may be amended from time to time.

"Trust" means the Issuer.

"Trust Agreement" means the trust agreement, dated as of January 21, 2003, as amended and restated, on February 25, 2003, among the Depositor, the Owner Trustee and the Delaware Trustee.

"Yield Supplement Account" means the account designated as such in, and established and maintained pursuant to the Agreement.

Copies of Schedule A listing the Receivables and the Sale and Servicing Agreement and related documents transferring the Receivables from American Honda Finance Corporation to American Honda Receivables Corp. and from American Honda Receivables Corp. to the Issuer are available upon request by contacting JPMorgan Chase Bank, 4 New York Plaza, 6th Floor, New York, New York 1004, attention: Honda Auto Receivables 2003-1 Owner Trust.

THE TRANSACTIONS PROVIDED FOR IN THE AGREEMENT ARE INTENDED BY EACH OF THE PARTIES THERETO ONLY AS A SALE. THIS FINANCING STATEMENT IS FILED FOR PROTECTION PURPOSES ONLY AND IS NOT TO BE CONSTRUED AS

EVIDENCE OF THE EXISTENCE OF ANY INDEBTEDNESS OR OTHER OBLIGATION OF AMERICAN HONDA RECEIVABLES CORP.

The security interest described herein has been collaterally assigned by Honda Auto Receivables 2003-1 Owner Trust to the Indenture Trustee to secure the obligations of Honda Auto Receivables 2003-1 Owner Trust under the Indenture. Upon release of the Indenture, the Identure Trustee shall execute and file an assignment of this financing statement back to Honda Auto Receivables 2003-1 Owner Trust.

Appendix 3

UCC FINANCING STATEMENT

FOLLOW INSTRUCTIONS (front and back) CAREFULLY

A. NAME & PHONE OF CONTACT AT FILER [optional]

B. SEND ACKNOWLEDGMENT TO: (Name and Address)

Please return copy to:
CT CORPORATION SYSTEM
Attn: Alan WInston
1350 Trost Blvd., Suite 100
Walnut Creek, CA 94597-2152
(800) 874-8820

DELAWARE DEPARTMENT OF STATE
U.C.C. FILING SECTION
FILED 12:22 PM 02/27/2003
INITIAL FILING NUM: 3048836 4
AMENDMENT NUMBER: 0000000
SRV: 030129194

THE ABOVE SPACE IS FOR FILING OFFICE USE ONLY

1. DEBTOR'S EXACT FULL LEGAL NAME - insert only one debtor name (1a or 1b) - do not abbreviate or combine names

1a. ORGANIZATION'S NAME			
Honda Auto Receivables 2003-1 Owner Trust			
OR 1b. INDIVIDUAL'S LAST NAME	FIRST NAME	MIDDLE NAME	SUFFIX

1c. MAILING ADDRESS	CITY	STATE	POSTAL CODE	COUNTRY
The Bank of New York (Delaware) as Delaware Trustee: White Clay Center Route 273	Newark	DE	19711	USA

1d. SEE INSTRUCTIONS	ADD'L INFO RE ORGANIZATION DEBTOR	1e. TYPE OF ORGANIZATION	1f. JURISDICTION OF ORGANIZATION	1g. ORGANIZATIONAL ID #, if any
		Statutory Trust	Delaware	3616683 ☐ NONE

2. ADDITIONAL DEBTOR'S EXACT FULL LEGAL NAME - insert only one debtor name (2a or 2b) - do not abbreviate or combine names

2a. ORGANIZATION'S NAME			
OR 2b. INDIVIDUAL'S LAST NAME	FIRST NAME	MIDDLE NAME	SUFFIX

2c. MAILING ADDRESS	CITY	STATE	POSTAL CODE	COUNTRY

2d. SEE INSTRUCTIONS	ADD'L INFO RE ORGANIZATION DEBTOR	2e. TYPE OF ORGANIZATION	2f. JURISDICTION OF ORGANIZATION	2g. ORGANIZATIONAL ID #, if any
				☐ NONE

3. SECURED PARTY'S NAME (or NAME of TOTAL ASSIGNEE of ASSIGNOR S/P) - insert only one secured party name (3a or 3b)

3a. ORGANIZATION'S NAME			
American Honda Receivables 2003-1 Owner Trust			
OR 3b. INDIVIDUAL'S LAST NAME	FIRST NAME	MIDDLE NAME	SUFFIX

3c. MAILING ADDRESS	CITY	STATE	POSTAL CODE	COUNTRY
4 New York Plaza, 5th Floor	New York	NY	10004	USA

4. This FINANCING STATEMENT covers the following collateral:

See Schedule A attached hereto and made a part hereof

5. ALTERNATIVE DESIGNATION [if applicable]: ☐ LESSEE/LESSOR ☐ CONSIGNEE/CONSIGNOR ☐ BAILEE/BAILOR ☐ SELLER/BUYER ☐ AG. LIEN ☐ NON-UCC FILING

6. ☐ This FINANCING STATEMENT is to be filed [for record] (or recorded) in the REAL ESTATE RECORDS. Attach Addendum [if applicable]

7. Check to REQUEST SEARCH REPORT(S) on Debtor(s) [ADDITIONAL FEE] [optional] ☐ All Debtors ☐ Debtor 1 ☐ Debtor 2

8. OPTIONAL FILER REFERENCE DATA

File with SOS--DE

FILING OFFICE COPY — UCC FINANCING STATEMENT (FORM UCC1) (REV. 05/22/02)

SCHEDULE A
to Financing Statement on Form UCC-1

DEBTOR:	Honda Auto Receivables 2003-1 Owner Trust (the "Issuer")
SECURED PARTY:	JPMorgan Chase Bank, as Indenture Trustee pursuant to the Indenture, dated as of February 1, 2003 (the "Indenture"), between Honda Auto Receivables 2003-1 Owner Trust and JPMorgan Chase Bank (the "Indenture Trustee").

This filing covers all right, title and interest of the Debtor in, to and under and to the following:

a. the receivables consisting of retail installment sale contracts secured by new or used Honda and Acura motor vehicles, together with all accessions thereto (the "Financed Vehicles") listed in Schedule A to the Sale and Servicing Agreement, dated as of February 1, 2003 (the "Agreement"), among American Honda Finance Corporation ("AHFC"), American Honda Receivables Corp. ("AHRC") and Honda Auto Receivables 2003-1 Owner Trust, and all proceeds thereof and payments thereunder (the "Receivables"), and all monies due thereon or paid thereunder or in respect thereof (including proceeds of Receivables which AHFC or AHRC is required or has elected to purchase) on or after February 1, 2003;

b. the security interests in the Financed Vehicles;

c. any proceeds of any physical damage insurance policies covering the Financed Vehicles and in any proceeds of any credit life or credit disability insurance policies relating to the Receivables or the Obligors;

d. any proceeds of recourse rights against the dealer of motor vehicles who sold a Financed Vehicle and who originated and assigned the Receivable relating to such Financed Vehicle to AHFC, and any successor to such dealer;

e. the right to realize upon any property (including the right to receive future liquidation proceeds) that shall have secured a Receivable relating to such Finance Vehicle to AHFC, and any successor to such dealer;

f. all funds, and all investment property, from time to time carried in or credited to the accounts designated in the Agreement as the Collection Account, the Note Distribution Account, the Payahead Account, the Yield Supplement Account and the Reserve Fund, including the initial deposit made into the Yield Supplement Account and Reserve Fund, and in all investment income and proceeds thereof.

g. the rights of AHRC under the Receivables Purchase Agreement, dated as of February 1, 2003, between AHFC and AHRC, as purchaser, and the rights of the Issuer under the Agreement;

h. any (i) irrevocable letter of credit naming the Indenture Trustee as beneficiary or (ii) surety bond, insurance policy or deposit of cash or securities, in either case, securing obligations of the AHFC or any replacement servicer with respect to the Receivables; and

i. all payments on or under and all proceeds of every kind and nature whatsoever in respect of any or all of the foregoing, including all proceeds of the conversion thereof, voluntary or involuntary, into cash or other liquid property, all cash proceeds, accounts, accounts receivable, notes, drafts, acceptances, chattel paper, checks, deposit accounts, insurance proceeds, condemnation awards, rights to payment of any and every kind and other forms of obligations and receivables, instruments and other property which at any time constitute all or part of or are included in the proceeds of any of the foregoing.

Definitions:

"Accounts" means the Collection Account, the Note Distribution Account, the Payahead Account, the Yield Supplement Account and the Reserve Fund.

"Collection Account" means the account designated as such in, and established and maintained pursuant to the Agreement.

"Financed Vehicle" means, with respect to any retail installment sale or conditional sale contract, the related new or used Honda or Acura motor vehicle, together with all accessions thereto securing the related Obligor's indebtedness under such retail installment sale or conditional sale contract.

"Indenture" means the indenture, dated as of February 1, 2003 between the Issuer and the Indenture Trustee.

"Indenture Trustee" means the Person acting as Indenture Trustee under the Indenture, its successors in interest and any successor trustee under the Indenture.

"Insurance Policy" means, with respect to a Receivable, an insurance policy covering physical damage, credit life, credit disability, theft, mechanical breakdown or any similar event relating to the related Financed Vehicle or Obligor.

"Note Distribution Account" means the account designated as such in, and established and maintained pursuant to the Agreement.

"Obligor" means the purchaser or co-purchasers of the related Financed Vehicle purchased in part or in whole by the execution and delivery of a retail installment contract or any other Person who owes or may be liable for payments under such retail installment contract.

"Payahead Account" means the account designed as such in, and established and maintained pursuant to the Agreement.

"Receivable" means any retail installment sale contract executed by an Obligor in respect of a Financed Vehicle, and all proceeds thereof and payments thereunder, which Receivables shall be identified in a Schedule or Receivables.

"Receivables Purchase Agreement" means the receivables purchase agreement, dated as of February 1, 2003, between AHFC and the Seller, as amended or supplemented from time to time.

"Reserve Fund" means the account designated as such, and established and maintained pursuant to the agreement.

"Schedule of Receivables" means the schedule of Receivables attached as Schedule A to the Agreement, as it may be amended from time to time.

"Trust" means the Issuer.

"Trust Agreement" means the trust agreement, dated as of January 21, 2003, as amended and restated, on February 25, 2003, among the Depositor, the Owner Trustee and the Delaware Trustee.

"Yield Supplement Account" means the account designated as such in, and established and maintained pursuant to the Agreement.

Copies of Schedule A listing the Receivables of the Agreement and related documents transferring the Receivables from American Honda Finance Corporation to American Honda Receivables Corp. and from American Honda Receivables Corp. to the Issuer are available upon request by contacing JPMorgan Chase Bank, 4 New York Plaza, 6th Floor, New York, New York 1004, attention: Honda Auto Receivables 2003-1 Owner Trust.

Appendix 4

Appendix 4

PROSPECTUS

HONDA AUTO RECEIVABLES TRUSTS
ASSET BACKED NOTES
ASSET BACKED CERTIFICATES
AMERICAN HONDA RECEIVABLES CORP., SELLER
AMERICAN HONDA FINANCE CORPORATION, SERVICER

THE TRUSTS:

1. A new trust will be formed to issue each series of securities and a particular trust may issue multiple series of securities;
2. Each trust will consist of:

- a pool of retail installment sale contracts secured by new or used Honda or Acura motor vehicles; and
- other assets specified in the applicable prospectus supplement.

THE SECURITIES:

1. will be asset-backed securities sold periodically in one or more series;
2. will be paid only from the assets of the related trust and any form of credit enhancement;
3. will be issued as part of a designated series that may include one or more classes; and
4. will consist of:

- notes (which will be treated as indebtedness of the trust) and/or
- certificates (which will represent an undivided ownership interest in the trust).

YOU SHOULD REVIEW CAREFULLY THE FACTORS SET FORTH UNDER "RISK FACTORS" BEGINNING ON PAGE 12 OF THIS PROSPECTUS.

NEITHER THE SECURITIES AND EXCHANGE COMMISSION NOR ANY STATE SECURITIES COMMISSION HAS APPROVED OR DISAPPROVED THE SECURITIES OR DETERMINED THAT THIS PROSPECTUS OR THE APPLICABLE PROSPECTUS SUPPLEMENT IS ACCURATE OR COMPLETE. ANY REPRESENTATION TO THE CONTRARY IS A CRIMINAL OFFENSE.

The amounts, prices and terms of each offering of securities will be determined at the time of sale and will be described in a prospectus supplement that will be attached to this prospectus.

This prospectus may be used to offer and sell any series of securities only if accompanied by the prospectus supplement for that series.

The date of this prospectus is February 19, 2003.

[Table of Contents Omitted]

IMPORTANT NOTICE ABOUT INFORMATION PRESENTED IN THIS PROSPECTUS AND THE ACCOMPANYING PROSPECTUS SUPPLEMENT

We provide information to you about the securities in two separate documents that progressively provide varying levels of detail:

- This prospectus, which provides general information, some of which may not apply to a particular series of securities including your series, and
- The accompanying prospectus supplement, which will describe the specific terms of the offered securities.

We have started with several introductory sections describing the trust and the securities in abbreviated form, followed by a more complete description of the terms. The introductory sections are:

- Summary of Terms — which gives a brief introduction to the securities to be offered, and
- Risk Factors — which describes briefly some of the risks to investors of a purchase of the securities.

You can find a listing of the pages where capitalized terms used in this prospectus are defined under the caption "Index of Terms" beginning on page 91 in this prospectus.

Whenever we use words like "intends," "anticipates" or "expects" or similar words in this prospectus, we are making a forward-looking statement, or a projection of what we think will happen in the future. Forward-looking statements are inherently subject to a variety of circumstances, many of which are beyond our control and could cause actual results to differ materially from what we anticipate. Any forward-looking statements in this prospectus speak only as of the date of this prospectus. We do not assume any responsibility to update or review any forward-looking statement contained in this prospectus to reflect any change in our expectation about the subject of that forward-looking statement or to reflect any change in events, conditions or circumstances on which we have based any forward-looking statement.

IF THE TERMS OF A PARTICULAR SERIES OF SECURITIES VARY BETWEEN THIS PROSPECTUS AND THE PROSPECTUS SUPPLEMENT, YOU SHOULD RELY ON THE INFORMATION IN THE PROSPECTUS SUPPLEMENT. . . . .

[List of Terms and Risk Factors Omitted; See Prospectus Supplement, eds.]

FORMATION OF THE TRUSTS

American Honda Receivables Corp. (the "Seller") will establish each trust (each, a "Trust") pursuant to a Trust Agreement (as amended and supplemented from time to time, the "Trust Agreement") or a Pooling and Servicing Agreement (as amended from time to time, the "Pooling and Servicing Agreement"), as applicable.

The terms of each series of notes or certificates issued by each Trust and additional information concerning the assets of each Trust and any applicable credit or cash flow enhancement will be set forth in a supplement to this prospectus (a "prospectus supplement"). The notes and certificates are collectively referred to in this prospectus as the "Securities."

PROPERTY OF THE TRUSTS

The property of each Trust will consist of a pool (each, a "Receivables Pool") of retail installment sale contracts originated on or after the date indicated in the applicable prospectus supplement between Honda and Acura dealers (the "Dealers") and retail purchasers (the "Obligors"). These contracts are referred to as the "Receivables" and evidence the indirect financing made available by American Honda Finance Corporation ("AHFC") to the Obligors. The Receivables will be secured by new or used Honda and Acura motor vehicles (the "Financed Vehicles") and all principal and interest payments made on or after the applicable cutoff date (each, a "Cutoff Date") and other property, all as specified in the applicable prospectus supplement. "New" vehicles may include "demonstration" vehicles, which are not titled in some states and may be classified as new vehicles in those states.

The Receivables will be originated by Dealers in accordance with AHFC's requirements under agreements with Dealers governing the assignment of the Receivables to AHFC (the "Dealer Agreements"). AHFC will purchase the Receivables of each Receivables Pool in the ordinary course of business pursuant to the Dealer Agreements.

On or before the date of the initial issuance of any series of Securities (each, a "Closing Date"), AHFC will sell the Receivables comprising the related Receivables Pool to the Seller, and the Seller will sell those Receivables to the Trust pursuant to, if the Trust is to be treated other than as a grantor trust for federal income tax purposes, the related Sale and Servicing Agreement among the Seller, the Servicer and the Trust (as amended and supplemented from time to time, the "Sale and Servicing Agreement") or, if the Trust is to be treated as a grantor trust for federal income tax purposes, the related Pooling and Servicing Agreement. AHFC will continue to service the Receivables.

In addition to the Receivables, the property of each Trust will also include the following:

1. amounts that may be held in separate trust accounts established and maintained by the Servicer with the Trustee pursuant to the related Sale and Servicing Agreement or Pooling and Servicing Agreement;
2. security interests in the Financed Vehicles and any related property;
3. the rights to proceeds from claims on physical damage, credit life and disability insurance policies covering the Financed Vehicles or the Obligors;
4. AHFC's right to receive payments from Dealers obligated to repurchase Receivables from AHFC which do not meet specified representations made by the Dealers;
5. the Seller's right under, as applicable, the Sale and Servicing Agreement, the Pooling and Servicing Agreement, the Purchase Agreement and the Yield Supplement Agreement, if any;
6. the Seller's right to realize upon any property (including the right to receive future net liquidation proceeds) that secured a Receivable; and
7. all proceeds of the foregoing.

Various forms of credit and cash flow enhancement may be used to benefit holders of the related Securities, including a Reserve Fund. In limited circumstances, a Trust will also have access to the funds in a Yield Supplement Account.

THE RECEIVABLES

AHFC will purchase the Receivables from the Dealers in the ordinary course of business in accordance with AHFC's underwriting standards. The Receivables to be held by each Trust will be randomly selected from those motor vehicle retail installment sale contracts in AHFC's portfolio that meet several criteria. The Seller will not use selection procedures adverse to Securityholders when selecting the Receivables from qualifying retail installment sale contracts. These criteria provide that each Receivable:

1. was originated in the United States and the Obligor is not a federal, state or local governmental entity;
2. provides for level monthly payments which provide interest at the annual percentage rate ("APR") and fully amortize the amount financed over an original term to maturity no greater than the number of months specified in the applicable prospectus supplement;
3. is attributable to the purchase of a new or used Honda or Acura motor vehicle and is secured by that vehicle; and
4. satisfies the other criteria, if any, set forth in the applicable prospectus supplement.

Each Receivable will provide for the allocation of payments (each, a "Scheduled Payment") according to (i) the simple interest method ("Simple Interest Receivables"), (ii) the "actuarial" method ("Actuarial Receivables") or (iii) the "sum of periodic balances" or "sum of monthly payments" method ("Rule of 78s Receivables" and, together with the Actuarial Receivables, the "Precomputed Receivables").

Simple Interest Receivables. Payments on Simple Interest Receivables will be applied first to interest accrued through the date immediately preceding the date of payment and then to unpaid principal. Accordingly, if an Obligor pays an installment before its due date, the portion of the payment allocable to interest for the payment period will be less than if the payment had been made on the due date, the portion of the payment applied to reduce the principal balance will be correspondingly greater, and the principal balance will be amortized more rapidly than scheduled. Conversely, if an Obligor pays an installment after its due date, the portion of the payment allocable to interest for the payment period will be greater than if the payment had been made on the due date, the portion of the payment applied to reduce the principal balance will be correspondingly less, and the principal balance will be amortized more slowly than scheduled, in which case a larger portion of the principal balance may be due on the final scheduled payment date. No adjustment to the scheduled monthly payments is made in the event of early or late payments, although in the case of late payments the Obligor may be subject to a late charge.

Actuarial Receivables. An Actuarial Receivable provides for amortization of the contract over a series of fixed level monthly installments. Each scheduled payment is deemed to consist of an amount of interest equal to 1/12 of the stated APR of the Receivable multiplied by the scheduled principal balance of the Receivable and an amount of principal equal to the remainder of the Scheduled Payment. No adjustment to the scheduled monthly payments is made in the event of early or late payments, although in the case of late payments the Obligor may be subject to a late charge.

Rule of 78s Receivables. A Rule of 78s Receivable provides for the payment by the Obligor of a specified total amount of payments, payable in monthly installments on the related due date, which total represents the principal amount financed and finance charges in an amount calculated on the basis of the related APR for the term of that Receivable. The rate at which the amount of finance charges is earned and, correspondingly, the amount of each Scheduled Payment allocated to reduction of the outstanding principal balance of a Rule of 78s Receivable are calculated in accordance with the Rule of 78s. Under the Rule of 78s, the portion of each payment allocable to interest is higher during the early months of the term of a Rule of 78s Receivable and lower during later months than that under a constant yield method for allocating payments between interest and principal. Notwithstanding the foregoing, all payments received by the Servicer on or in respect of the Rule of 78s Receivables will be allocated pursuant to the related Transfer and Servicing Agreement, as the case may be, on an actuarial basis. No adjustment is made in the event of early or late payments, although in the case of late payments the Obligor may be subject to a late charge.

In the event of a prepayment in full (voluntarily or by acceleration) of a Precomputed Receivable, a "rebate" will be made to the Obligor of that portion of the total amount of payments under the Receivable allocable to "unearned" interest charges. In the event of the prepayment in full (voluntarily or by acceleration) of a Simple Interest Receivable, a "rebate" will not be made to the Obligor, but the Obligor will be required to pay interest only to the date immediately preceding the date of prepayment. The amount of a rebate under a Precomputed Receivable will always be less than or equal to the remaining scheduled payments of interest that would have been due under a Simple Interest Receivable for which all remaining payments were made on schedule. Payments to Securityholders will not be affected by rebates under the Rule of 78s Receivables because pursuant to the related Transfer and Servicing Agreement the payments will be determined using the actuarial method.

Unless otherwise provided in the related prospectus supplement, each Trust will account for the Rule of 78s Receivables as if those Receivables were Actuarial Receivables. Amounts received upon prepayment in full of a Rule of 78s Receivable in excess of the then outstanding principal balance of the Receivable and accrued interest thereon (calculated pursuant to the actuarial method) will not be paid to the Noteholders or passed through to the Certificateholders of the applicable series but will be deemed to be an excess amount and released to the Seller or otherwise applied as set forth in the related prospectus supplement.

Additional information with respect to each Receivables Pool will be set forth in the related prospectus supplement, including, to the extent appropriate, the composition, the distribution by APR and by the states of origination, the portion of the Receivables Pool consisting of Precomputed Receivables and of Simple Interest Receivables and the portion of the Receivables Pool secured by new and used vehicles.

UNDERWRITING OF MOTOR VEHICLE LOANS

AHFC purchases retail installment sale contracts secured by new or used Honda and Acura motor vehicles from approximately 1,270 Dealers, as of December 31, 2001, located throughout the United States. These contracts are underwritten using AHFC's standard underwriting procedures. The Receivables are originated by Dealers in accordance with AHFC's requirements under existing Dealer Agreements and will be purchased in accordance with AHFC's underwriting procedures which emphasize, among other factors, the applicant's willingness and ability to pay and the value of the vehicle to be financed.

AHFC requires that applications received from Dealers be signed by the applicant and contain, among other information, the applicant's name, address, social security number, residential status, source and amount of monthly income and amount of monthly rent or mortgage payment. Upon receipt of the above information, AHFC obtains a credit report from an independent credit bureau reporting agency. AHFC reviews the credit report to determine the applicant's current credit status and past credit performance. AHFC considers both negative factors including past due credit, repossessions, loans charged off by other lenders and previous bankruptcy and also positive factors such as amount of credit and favorable payment history.

AHFC's credit decision is influenced by, among other things, a credit scoring system and other considerations. The credit scoring process considers residence and employment stability, credit bureau information, application and contract information. The credit scoring process also takes into account income requirements and the ratio of income to total debt. AHFC makes its final credit decision based upon the degree of credit risk perceived and the amount of credit requested.

AHFC's retail installment sale contract requires that Obligors maintain specific levels and types of insurance coverage to protect the Financed Vehicle against loss. At the time of purchase, an Obligor signs a statement which indicates that he or she either has or will have the necessary insurance, and which shows the name and address of the insurance company along with a description of the type of coverage. AHFC generally requires Obligors to provide it with evidence of compliance with the foregoing insurance requirements; however, AHFC performs no ongoing verification of insurance coverage. AHFC will not be obligated to make payments to a Trust for any loss when third party insurance has not been maintained.

The amount of a retail installment sale contract secured by a new or used Honda or Acura motor vehicle generally will not exceed 120% of the dealer invoice cost of the related vehicle plus select accessories at the dealer cost, sales tax, title and registration fees, insurance premiums for credit life and credit disability insurance and certain fees for extended service contract or, in the case of used motor vehicles, the NADA average trade-in value (as adjusted for higher/lower mileage).

SERVICING OF THE RECEIVABLES

AHFC considers a retail installment sale contract to be past due or delinquent for servicing and enforcement of collection purposes when the Obligor fails to make at least 90% of a Scheduled Payment on a cumulative basis (after giving effect to any past due payments) by the related due date; any portion of a Scheduled Payment not paid on the related due date automatically becomes due with the next scheduled payment. AHFC mails a computer generated delinquency notice to the Obligor on the eleventh and twenty-first days of delinquency. If the delinquent receivable cannot be brought current or completely collected within 60 days, AHFC generally attempts to repossess the vehicle. AHFC holds repossessed vehicles in inventory to comply with any applicable statutory requirements for reinstatement and then sells those vehicles (generally within 60 days after repossession). AHFC's Marketing Department handles motor vehicle sales for AHFC, including the sale of repossessed vehicles. AHFC consigns the repossessed vehicles to a local auction or to an independent transport company for transport to another auction location. Each motor vehicle undergoes an auction condition report, which is sent to AHFC. Each auction site is expected to sell the motor vehicle within 60 days of taking the motor vehicle into inventory. Any deficiencies remaining after repossession and sale of the vehicle or after the full charge-off of the receivable are pursued by or on behalf of AHFC to the extent practicable and legally permitted. We refer you to "Certain Legal Aspects of the Receivables — Deficiency Judgments and Excess Proceeds." AHFC attempts to contact Obligors and establish and monitor repayment schedules until the deficiencies are either paid in full or become impractical to pursue.

USE OF PROCEEDS

Each Trust will use the net proceeds from the sale of the Securities of a given series to purchase Receivables from the Seller and to fund any related Reserve Fund or other accounts of the Trust. The Seller will purchase Receivables from AHFC from the net proceeds it receives from any Trust.

THE TRUSTEE

The trustee for each Trust (the "Trustee") or the trustee under any Indenture pursuant to which notes are issued (the "Indenture Trustee") will be specified in the applicable prospectus supplement. The Trustee's or the Indenture Trustee's liability in connection with the issuance and sale of the related Securities is limited solely to the express obligations of that Trustee or Indenture Trustee set forth in the related Trust Agreement, Pooling and Servicing Agreement, Sale and Servicing Agreement or Indenture, as applicable. A Trustee or Indenture Trustee may resign at any time, in which event the Servicer, or its successor, will be obligated to appoint a successor thereto. The Administrator of a Trust that is not a grantor trust may also remove a Trustee or Indenture Trustee that becomes insolvent or otherwise ceases to be eligible to continue in that capacity under the related Trust Agreement, Sale and Servicing Agreement or Indenture, as applicable. The Servicer for a Trust that is a grantor trust may remove a Trustee that becomes insolvent or otherwise ceases to be eligible to continue in that capacity under the related Pooling and Servicing Agreement. In those circumstances, the Servicer or, in the case of a series that includes notes, the Administrator, as the case may be, will be obligated to appoint a successor thereto. Any resignation or removal of a Trustee or Indenture Trustee and appointment of a successor trustee will not become effective until acceptance of the appointment by the successor.

THE SELLER

The Seller is a wholly owned, limited purpose finance subsidiary of AHFC and was incorporated in the State of California in August 1992. The Seller's principal executive offices are located at 700 Van Ness Avenue, Torrance, California 90501 and its telephone number is (310) 781-6131.

The Seller was organized primarily for the purpose of acquiring retail installment sale contracts similar to the Receivables and associated rights from AHFC, causing the issuance of securities similar to the Securities and engaging in related transactions. The Seller's articles of incorporation limit the activities of the Seller to the foregoing purposes and to any activities incidental to and necessary for those purposes.

THE SERVICER

American Honda Finance Corporation (sometimes referred to herein as the "Servicer") was incorporated in the State of California in February 1980. AHFC's principal executive offices are located at 700 Van Ness Avenue, Torrance, California 90501. Its telephone number is (310) 781-4100. AHFC and its Canadian subsidiary, Honda Canada Finance, Inc. ("HCFI"), provide wholesale and retail financing to authorized dealers in the United States and Canada for the following:

(1) Honda and Acura automobiles, minivans and sport utility vehicles;

(2) Honda motorcycles (including scooters and all terrain vehicles); and

(3) Honda power equipment including lawn and utility tractors, lawnmowers, snow throwers, water pumps, portable outboard motors, outboard marine engines and generators. Receivables related to these assets are not included as assets of the Trust.

AHFC and HCFI also offer retail leasing for Honda and Acura motor vehicles or Honda motorcycles throughout the United States and Canada. AHFC (and through its wholly owned subsidiary, American Honda Service Contract Corporation, in Florida) administers the sale of vehicle service contracts throughout the United States for American Honda Motor Co., Inc. ("AHMC"), a California corporation.

AHFC has the following wholly owned special purpose finance subsidiaries:

- American Honda Receivables Corp., a California corporation,
- American Honda Receivables Corp. II, a California corporation,
- Honda Titling Inc., a Delaware corporation, and
- Honda Funding Inc., a Delaware corporation.

AHFC is a wholly owned subsidiary of AHMC. AHMC is a wholly owned subsidiary of Honda Motor Co., Ltd., a Japanese corporation which is a worldwide manufacturer and distributor of motor vehicles, motorcycles and power equipment. AHMC is the sole authorized distributor in the United States of the following:

(1) Honda and Acura motor vehicles and Honda motorcycles;

(2) Honda power equipment; and

(3) Honda and Acura parts and accessories.

WHERE YOU CAN FIND MORE INFORMATION ABOUT YOUR SECURITIES

The Trust — The Trustee will provide to securityholders ("Securityholders") (which shall be Cede & Co. ("Cede") as the nominee of DTC unless Definitive Securities are issued under the limited circumstances described in this prospectus) unaudited monthly and annual reports concerning the Receivables and other specified matters. We refer you to "Description of the Transfer and Servicing Agreements — Statements to Securityholders" and " — Evidence as to Compliance" in this prospectus. Copies of these reports may be obtained at no charge at the offices specified in the applicable prospectus supplement.

The Seller — AHRC, as Seller of the Receivables, has filed with the Securities and Exchange Commission (the "SEC") a registration statement on Form S-3 under the Securities Act of 1933 (the "Securities Act") of which this prospectus forms a part. The registration statement is available for inspection without charge at the public reference facilities maintained at the principal office of the SEC at Judiciary Plaza, 450 Fifth Street, N.W., Washington, D.C. 20549, and at the regional offices of the SEC at Citicorp Center, 500 West Madison Street, Suite 1400, Chicago, Illinois 60661, and Seven World Trade Center, Suite 1300, New York, New York 10048. You may obtain information on the operation of the SEC's public reference rooms by calling the SEC at (800) SEC-0330. You may obtain copies of SEC filings at prescribed rates by writing to the Public Reference Section of the SEC at Judiciary Plaza, 450 Fifth Street, N.W., Washington, D.C. 20549. The SEC also maintains a website (http:// www.sec.gov) that contains reports, registration statements, proxy and information statements and other information regarding issuers that file electronically with the SEC.

Copies of the operative agreements relating to the Securities will also be filed with the SEC.

DELINQUENCIES, REPOSSESSIONS AND NET LOSSES

Information concerning AHFC's experience pertaining to delinquencies, repossessions and net losses on its portfolio of new and used retail motor vehicle receivables (including receivables previously sold that AHFC continues to service) will be set forth in each prospectus supplement. There can be no assurance that the delinquency, repossession and net loss experience on any Receivables Pool will be comparable to prior experience or to the information in any prospectus supplement.

WEIGHTED AVERAGE LIFE OF THE SECURITIES

The weighted average life of the Securities of any series will generally be influenced by the rate at which the principal balances of the related Receivables are paid, which payment may be in the form of scheduled amortization or prepayments. For this purpose, the term "prepayments" includes prepayments in full, partial prepayments (including those related to rebates of extended warranty contract costs and insurance premiums), liquidations due to default as well as receipts of proceeds from physical damage, credit life and disability insurance policies and repurchases or purchases by the Seller or AHFC, as the case may be, of particular Receivables for administrative reason or for breaches of representations and warranties. The term "weighted average life" means the average amount of time during which each dollar of principal of a Receivable is outstanding.

All of the Receivables will be prepayable at any time without penalty to the Obligor. However, partial prepayments on the Precomputed Receivables made by Obligors will not be paid on the Payment Date following the Collection Period in which they were received but will be retained and applied towards payments due in later Collection Periods. If prepayments in full are received on the Precomputed Receivables or if full or partial prepayments are received on the Simple Interest Receivables, the actual weighted average life of the Receivables may be shorter than the scheduled weighted average life of the Receivables set forth in the related prospectus supplement. The rate of prepayment of motor vehicle retail installment sale contracts are influenced by a variety of economic, social and other factors, including the fact that an Obligor generally may not sell or transfer the Financed Vehicle securing a Receivable without the consent of the Servicer.

No prediction can be made as to the rate of prepayment on the Receivables in either stable or changing interest rate environments. AHFC maintains limited records of the historical prepayment experience of the motor vehicle retail installment sale contracts included in its portfolio. However, no assurance can be given that prepayments on the Receivables will conform to historical experience and no prediction can be made as to the actual prepayment experience on the Receivables. The rate of prepayment on the Receivables may also be influenced by the structure of the related contract. In addition, under some circumstances, the Seller or Servicer will be obligated to repurchase Receivables from a given Trust pursuant to the related Sale and Servicing Agreement or Pooling and Servicing Agreement as a result of breaches of particular representations and warranties or covenants. We refer you to "Description of the Transfer and Servicing Agreements — Sale and Assignment of Receivables" and " — Servicing Procedures". We also refer you to "Description of the Transfer and Servicing Agreements — Termination" Regarding the Servicer's Option to Purchase the Receivables from a Given Trust. Any reinvestment risk resulting from the rate of prepayments of the Receivables and the payment of prepayments to Securityholders will be borne entirely by the Securityholders. In addition, early retirement of the Securities may be effected by the exercise of the option of the Servicer, or any successor to the Servicer, to purchase all of the Receivables remaining in the Trust when the Pool Balance is 10% or less of the Pool Balance as of the Cutoff Date.

In addition, pursuant to agreements between AHFC and the Dealers, each Dealer is obligated to repurchase from AHFC contracts which do not meet particular representations and warranties made by that Dealer (these Dealer repurchase obligations are referred to in this prospectus as "Dealer Recourse"). These representations and warranties relate primarily to the origination of the retail installment sale contracts and the perfection of the security interests in the related Financed Vehicles, and do not typically relate to the creditworthiness of the related Obligors or the collectability of the contracts. Although the Dealer Agreements with respect to the Receivables will not be assigned to the Trustee, the related Sale and Servicing Agreement or Pooling and Servicing Agreement will require that AHFC deposit any recovery in respect of any Receivable pursuant to any Dealer Recourse in the related Collection Account. The sales by the Dealers of retail installment sale contracts to AHFC do not generally provide for recourse against the Dealers for unpaid amounts in the event of a default by an Obligor thereunder, other than in connection with the breach of the foregoing representations and warranties. We refer you to "Description of the Transfer and Servicing Agreements — Sale and Assignment of Receivables" and " — Servicing Procedures."

In light of the above considerations, there can be no assurance as to the amount of principal payments to be made on the Securities of a given series on each Payment Date, since the amount of principal payments will depend, in part, on the amount of principal collected on the related Receivables Pool during the applicable Collection Period. No prediction can be made as to the actual prepayment experience on the Receivables, and any reinvestment risks resulting from a faster or slower rate of prepayment of Receivables will be borne entirely by the Securityholders of a given series. We refer you to "Risk Factors — You May Experience Reduced Returns on Your Investment Resulting from Prepayments, Repurchases or Early Termination of the Trust" in this prospectus.

The applicable prospectus supplement may set forth additional information regarding the maturity and prepayment considerations applicable to the particular Receivables Pool and the related series of Securities.

POOL FACTORS AND TRADING INFORMATION

The "Note Pool Factor" for each class of notes will be a seven-digit decimal which the Servicer will compute prior to each payment with respect to that class of notes. The Note Pool Factor represents the remaining outstanding principal amount of that class of notes, as of the close of business on the last day of the applicable Collection Period, as a fraction of the initial outstanding principal amount of that class of notes. The "Certificate Pool Factor" for each class of certificates will be a seven-digit decimal which the Servicer will compute prior to each payment with respect to that class of certificates indicating the remaining Certificate Balance of that class of certificates, as of the close of business on the last day of the applicable Collection Period, as a fraction of the Original Certificate Balance of that class of certificates. The "Certificate Balance" for any class of certificates as of any Payment Date will equal the Original Certificate Balance of that class, as reduced by all amounts distributed on or prior to that Payment Date on that class of certificates and allocable to principal. The "Original Certificate Balance" for each class of certificates will be stated in the applicable prospectus supplement.

Each Note Pool Factor and each Certificate Pool Factor will initially be 1.0000000 and thereafter will decline to reflect reductions in the outstanding principal amount of the applicable class of notes, or the reduction of the Certificate Balance of the applicable class of certificates, as the case may be. A Noteholder's portion of the aggregate outstanding principal amount of the related class of notes is the product of (1) the original denomination of that

Noteholder's note and (2) the applicable Note Pool Factor. A Certificateholder's portion of the aggregate outstanding Certificate Balance for the related class of certificates is the product of (1) the original denomination of that Certificateholder's certificate and (2) the applicable Certificate Pool Factor.

The Securityholders will receive monthly reports concerning payments received on the Receivables, the Pool Balance, each Certificate Pool Factor or Note Pool Factor, as applicable, and various other items of information.

THE NOTES

GENERAL

With respect to each Trust that issues notes, one or more classes (each, a "class") of notes of the related series will be issued pursuant to the terms of an indenture (the "Indenture"). A form of the Indenture has been filed as an exhibit to the registration statement of which this prospectus is a part. The following summary does not purport to be complete and is subject to, and is qualified in its entirety by reference to, all the provisions of the notes and the Indenture.

Each class of notes will initially be represented by one or more notes, in each case registered in the name of the nominee of DTC, except as set forth below. Notes will be available for purchase in the denominations specified in the applicable prospectus supplement in book-entry form only. The Seller has been informed by DTC that DTC's nominee will be Cede, unless another nominee is specified in the applicable prospectus supplement. Accordingly, that nominee is expected to be the holder of record of the notes (a "Noteholder") of each class. No Noteholder will be entitled to receive a physical certificate representing a note until Definitive Notes are issued under the limited circumstances described in this prospectus or in the applicable prospectus supplement. All references in this prospectus and in the applicable prospectus supplement to actions by Noteholders refer to actions taken by DTC upon instructions from its participating organizations and all references in this prospectus and in the applicable prospectus supplement to payments, notices, reports and statements to Noteholders refer to payments, notices, reports and statements to DTC or its nominee, as the registered holder of the notes, for distribution to Noteholders in accordance with DTC's procedures. We refer you to "Certain Information Regarding the Securities — Book-Entry Registration" and " — Definitive Securities."

PRINCIPAL AND INTEREST ON THE NOTES

The applicable prospectus supplement will describe the timing and priority of payment, seniority, allocations of losses, interest rate (the "Interest Rate") and amount of or method of determining payments of principal and interest on each class of notes of a given series. The rights of holders of any class of notes to receive payments of principal and interest may be senior or subordinate to the rights of holders of any other class or classes of notes of that series. Payments of interest on a class of notes will generally be made prior to payments of principal on the class. A series may include one or more classes of notes (the "Strip

Notes") entitled to (1) principal payments with disproportionate, nominal or no interest payments or (2) interest payments with disproportionate, nominal or no principal payments. Each class of notes may have a different Interest Rate, which may be a fixed, variable or adjustable Interest Rate (and which may be zero for some classes of Strip Notes), or any combination of the foregoing. The applicable prospectus supplement will specify the Interest Rate for each class of notes of a given series or the method for determining the Interest Rate. We refer you to "Certain Information Regarding the Securities — Fixed Rate Securities" and " — Floating Rate Securities." One or more classes of notes of a series may be redeemable in whole or in part, including as a result of the Servicer exercising its option to purchase the related Receivables Pool or other early termination of the related trust.

One or more classes of notes of a given series may have fixed principal payment schedules, in the manner and to the extent set forth in the applicable prospectus supplement. Noteholders of those notes would be entitled to receive as payments of principal on any given Payment Date the amounts set forth on that schedule with respect to those notes.

To the extent provided in the related prospectus supplement, payments of interest to Noteholders of two or more classes within a series may have the same priority. Under some circumstances, on any Payment Date the amount available for those payments could be less than the amount of interest payable on the notes. If this is the case, each class of Noteholders will receive its ratable share (based upon the aggregate amount of interest due to that class of Noteholders) of the aggregate amount of interest available for payment on the notes. We refer you to "Description of the Transfer and Servicing Agreements — Distributions on the Securities" and " — Credit and Cash Flow Enhancement."

If a series of notes includes two or more classes of notes, the sequential order and priority of payment in respect of principal and interest, and any schedule or formula or other provisions, of each of those classes will be set forth in the applicable prospectus supplement. Payments of principal and interest within any class of notes will be made on a pro rata basis among all the Noteholders of that class.

THE INDENTURE

Modification of Indenture. If a Trust has issued notes pursuant to an Indenture, the Trust and the Indenture Trustee may, with the consent of the holders of a majority of the outstanding notes of the related series (or relevant class or classes of notes of the series), execute a supplemental indenture to add provisions to, change in any manner or eliminate any provisions of, the related Indenture, or modify (except as provided below) in any manner the rights of the related Noteholders.

Without the consent of the holder of each outstanding affected note, no supplemental indenture will:

1. change (A) the due date of any installment of principal of or interest on that note or reduce the principal amount of that note, (B) the Interest Rate for that note or the redemption price for that note, (C) provisions of the Indenture relating to the application of collections on, or proceeds of a sale of, the Trust Estate to payments of principal and interest on the note, or (D) any place of payment where or the coin or currency in which that note or any interest on that note is payable;
2. impair the right to institute suit for the enforcement of specified provisions of the related Indenture regarding payment;
3. reduce the percentage of the aggregate amount of the outstanding notes of a series of notes, the consent of the holders of which is required for any supplemental indenture or any waiver of compliance with specified provisions of the related Indenture or of specified defaults and their consequences as provided for in that Indenture;
4. modify or alter the provisions of the related Indenture regarding the voting of notes held by the applicable Trust, any other obligor on those notes, the Seller or an affiliate of any of them;
5. reduce the percentage of the aggregate outstanding amount of notes, the consent of the holders of which is required to direct the related Indenture Trustee to sell or liquidate the Receivables if the proceeds of that sale would be insufficient to pay the principal amount of and accrued but unpaid interest on the outstanding notes of that series;
6. reduce the percentage of the aggregate principal amount of notes required to amend the sections of the related Indenture that specify the applicable percentage of aggregate principal amount of the notes of a series necessary to amend the Indenture or other specified agreements; or
7. permit the creation of any lien ranking prior to or on a parity with the lien of the related Indenture with respect to any of the collateral for that note or, except as otherwise permitted or contemplated in the Indenture, terminate the lien of that Indenture on any of the collateral or deprive the holder of any note of the security afforded by the lien of the Indenture.

The Trust and the applicable Indenture Trustee may also enter into supplemental indentures, without obtaining the consent of the Noteholders of the related series, for the purpose of, among other things, adding any provisions to or changing in any manner or eliminating any of the provisions of the related Indenture or of modifying in any manner the rights of those Noteholders; provided that that action will not adversely affect in any material respect the interest of any of those Noteholders.

Events of Default; Rights Upon Event of Default. With respect to the notes of a given series in the related prospectus supplement, "Events of Default" under the related Indenture will consist of:

1. a default for five days or more in the payment of any interest on any of the notes when the same becomes due and payable;

2. a default in the payment of the principal of or any installment of the principal of any of the notes when the same becomes due and payable;
3. a default in the observance or performance of any covenant or agreement of the applicable Trust made in the related Indenture and the continuation of the default for a period of 30 days after notice is given to that Trust by the applicable Indenture Trustee or to that Trust and the applicable Indenture Trustee by the holders of at least 25% in principal amount of the notes then outstanding acting together as a single class;
4. any representation or warranty made by the applicable Trust in the related Indenture or in any certificate delivered pursuant thereto or in connection therewith having been incorrect in a material respect as of the time made, and the breach not having been cured within 30 days after written notice is given to that Trust by the applicable Indenture Trustee or to that Trust and the applicable Indenture Trustee by the holders of at least 25% in principal amount of the notes then outstanding acting together as a single class;
5. particular events of bankruptcy, insolvency, receivership or liquidation of the applicable Trust; or
6. other events, if any, set forth in the related prospectus supplement.

However, the amount of principal required to be paid to Noteholders of an affected series under the related Indenture will generally be limited to amounts available to be deposited in the Collection Account. Therefore, the failure to pay any principal on any class of notes generally will not result in the occurrence of an Event of Default until the final scheduled Payment Date for that class of notes. The failure to pay interest to holders of a subordinated class of notes on a particular Payment Date will generally not constitute an Event of Default. In addition, as described below, following the occurrence of an Event of Default (other than the Events of Default described in (1) and (2) above) and acceleration of the maturity of the notes, the Indenture Trustee is not required to sell the assets of the Trust, and the Indenture Trustee may sell the assets of the Trust only after meeting requirements specified in the Indenture. Under those circumstances, even if the maturity of the notes has been accelerated, there may not be any funds to pay the principal owed on the notes.

If an Event of Default should occur and be continuing with respect to the notes of any series, the related Indenture Trustee or holders of a majority in principal amount of the most senior notes then outstanding (or relevant class or classes of notes) may declare the notes to be immediately due and payable. This declaration may, under specified circumstances, be rescinded by the holders of a majority in principal amount of the most senior notes then outstanding (or relevant class or classes of notes).

If the notes of any series are due and payable following an Event of Default with respect thereto, the related Indenture Trustee may (1) institute proceedings to collect amounts due or foreclose on Trust property, (2) exercise remedies as a secured party, (3) sell the assets of the related trust, or (4) elect to have the applicable Trust maintain possession of those Receivables and continue to apply collections on those Receivables as if there had been no declaration of acceleration. Unless otherwise specified in the applicable prospectus supplement, however, the Indenture Trustee is prohibited from selling the assets of the related trust following an Event of Default (other than a default in the payment of any principal on any note of a particular series or a default for five days or more in the payment of any interest on the most senior notes of a particular series), unless:

1. the holders of the notes of the related series then outstanding (or relevant class or classes of notes) consent to the sale; or
2. the proceeds of the sale are sufficient to pay in full the principal of and the accrued interest on all outstanding notes of the related series at the date of the sale; or
3. the Indenture Trustee determines that the Trust Estate will not continue to provide sufficient funds to make all payments on the outstanding notes of the related series as those payments would have become due if the obligations had not been declared due and payable, and the Indenture Trustee obtains the consent of the holders of 66 2/3% of the aggregate outstanding amount of the most senior notes then of the related series outstanding (or relevant class or classes of notes).

Subject to the provisions of the applicable Indenture relating to the duties of the related Indenture Trustee, if an Event of Default occurs and is continuing with respect to a series of notes, the Indenture Trustee will be under no obligation to exercise any of the rights or powers under the Indenture at the request or direction of any of the holders of the notes, if the Indenture Trustee reasonably believes it will not be adequately indemnified against the costs, expenses and liabilities that might be incurred by it in complying with the request. Subject to the provisions for indemnification and other limitations contained in the related Indenture, the holders of a majority of the aggregate principal amount of the most senior notes of the related series then outstanding (or relevant class or classes of notes of the series) will have the right to direct the time, method and place of conducting any proceeding or any remedy available to the applicable Indenture Trustee, and the holders of at least 51% of the aggregate principal amount of the most senior notes of the related series then outstanding (or relevant class or classes of notes) may, in some cases, waive a default, except a default in the deposit of collections or other required amounts, any required payment from amounts held in any trust account in respect of amounts due on the notes, payment of principal or interest or a default in respect of a covenant or provision of the Indenture which cannot be modified without the waiver or consent of all the holders of the outstanding notes of the related series.

Unless otherwise specified in the related prospectus supplement, no holder of a note of any series will have the right to institute any proceeding with respect to the related Indenture, unless:

1. the holder of a note or notes previously has given to the applicable Indenture Trustee written notice of a continuing Event of Default;

2. the Event of Default arises from the Servicer's failure to remit payments when due or the holders of not less than 25% of the aggregate principal amount of the most senior notes of the related series then outstanding (or relevant class or classes of notes) have requested in writing that the Indenture Trustee institute the proceeding in its own name as Indenture Trustee;
3. the holder or holders of notes have offered the Indenture Trustee reasonable indemnity; and
4. the Indenture Trustee has for 60 days failed to institute a proceeding;

In addition, each Indenture Trustee and the related Noteholders, by accepting the related notes, will covenant that they will not at any time institute against the applicable Trust any bankruptcy, reorganization or other proceeding under any federal or state bankruptcy or similar law.

With respect to any Trust, neither the related Indenture Trustee nor the related Trustee in its individual capacity, nor any holder of a certificate representing an ownership interest in that Trust nor any of their respective owners, beneficiaries, agents, officers, directors, employees, affiliates, successors or assigns will, in the absence of an express agreement to the contrary, be personally liable for the payment of the principal of or interest on the related notes or for the agreements of that Trust contained in the applicable Indenture.

Particular Covenants. Each Indenture will provide that the related Trust may not consolidate with or merge into any other entity, unless, among other things,

1. the entity formed by or surviving the consolidation or merger is organized under the laws of the United States or any state;
2. that entity expressly assumes the Trust's obligation to make due and punctual payments upon the notes of the related series and the performance or observance of every agreement and covenant of the Trust under the Indenture;
3. no Event of Default shall have occurred and be continuing immediately after the merger or consolidation;
4. each rating agency delivers a letter to the Indenture Trustee to the effect that the consideration or merger will not result in a qualification, reduction or withdrawal of its then current rating on any class of notes;
5. that Trust has received an opinion of counsel to the effect that the consolidation or merger would have no material adverse tax consequence to the Trust or to any related Noteholder or Certificateholder;
6. the parties take any action necessary to maintain the lien and security interest created by the Indenture; and
7. the Indenture Trustee has received an officer's certificate and an opinion of counsel stating that the consolidation or merger comply with the terms of the Indenture and all conditions precedent provided in the Indenture have been complied with.

Each Trust will not, among other things,

- except as expressly permitted by the applicable Indenture, the applicable Transfer and Servicing Agreements or other specified documents with respect to that Trust (collectively, the "Related Documents"), sell, transfer, exchange or otherwise dispose of any of the assets of the Trust unless directed to do so by the Indenture Trustee;
- claim any credit on or make any deduction from the principal of and interest payable on the notes of the related series (other than amounts withheld under the Code or applicable state law) or assert any claim against any present or former holder of those notes because of the payment of taxes levied or assessed upon the Trust;
- except as expressly permitted by the Related Documents, dissolve or liquidate in whole or in part;
- permit the validity or effectiveness of the related Indenture to be impaired or permit any person to be released from any covenants or obligations with respect to the notes under the Indenture except as may be expressly permitted by the Indenture;
- permit any lien or other encumbrance to be created on or extend to or otherwise arise upon or burden the assets of the Trust or any part thereof, or any interest in the assets of the Trust or the proceeds of those assets; or
- assume or incur any indebtedness other than the related notes or as expressly permitted by the related Indenture or the Related Documents.

No Trust may engage in any activity other than as specified in this prospectus or in the applicable prospectus supplement.

Annual Compliance Statement. Each Trust will be required to file annually with the related Indenture Trustee a written statement as to the fulfillment of its obligations under the related Indenture.

Indenture Trustee's Annual Report. The Indenture Trustee for each Trust will be required to mail each year to all related Noteholders a brief report relating to its eligibility and qualification to continue as Indenture Trustee under the related Indenture, any amounts advanced by it under the Indenture, the amount, interest rate and maturity date of specified indebtedness owing by the Trust to the applicable Indenture Trustee in its individual capacity, the property and funds physically held by the Indenture Trustee and any action taken by it that materially affects the related notes and that has not been previously reported.

Satisfaction and Discharge of Indenture. An Indenture will be discharged with respect to the collateral securing the related notes upon the delivery to the related Indenture Trustee for cancellation of all of those notes or, with specified limitations, upon deposit with the Indenture Trustee of funds sufficient for the payment in full of all the notes.

THE CERTIFICATES

GENERAL

With respect to each Trust that issues certificates, one or more classes of certificates of the related series will be issued pursuant to the terms of a Trust Agreement or a Pooling and Servicing Agreement, a form of each of which has been filed as an exhibit to the Registration Statement of which this prospectus forms a part. The following summary does not purport to be complete and is subject to, and is qualified in its entirety by reference to, all the provisions of the certificates and the Trust Agreement or Pooling and Servicing Agreement, as applicable.

Except for the certificates, if any, of a given series purchased by the Seller, each class of certificates will initially be represented by one or more certificates registered in the name of the nominee for DTC, except as set forth below. Except for the certificates, if any, of a given series purchased by the Seller, the certificates will be available for purchase in the denominations specified in the applicable prospectus supplement in book-entry form only. The Seller has been informed by DTC that DTC's nominee will be Cede, unless another nominee is specified in the applicable prospectus supplement. Accordingly, that nominee is expected to be the holder of record of the certificates (a "Certificateholder") of any series that are not purchased by the Seller. No Certificateholder (other than a Trust) will be entitled to receive a physical certificate representing a certificate until Definitive Certificates are issued under the limited circumstances described in this prospectus or in the applicable prospectus supplement. All references in this prospectus and in the applicable prospectus supplement to actions by Certificateholders refer to actions taken by DTC upon instructions from DTC Participants and all references in this prospectus and in the applicable prospectus supplement to distributions, notices, reports and statements to Certificateholders refer to distributions, notices, reports and statements given, made or sent to DTC or its nominee, as the case may be, as the registered holder of the certificates, for distribution to Certificateholders in accordance with DTC's procedures with respect thereto. We refer you to "Certain Information Regarding the Securities — Book-Entry Registration" and " — Definitive Securities." Any certificates of a given series owned by the Seller or its affiliates will be entitled to equal and proportionate benefits under the applicable Trust Agreement, except that those certificates will be deemed not to be outstanding for the purpose of determining whether the requisite percentage of Certificateholders have given any request, demand, authorization, direction, notice, consent or other action under the Related Documents (other than the commencement by the related Trust of a voluntary proceeding in bankruptcy as described under "Description of the Transfer and Servicing Agreements- — Insolvency Event").

PAYMENTS OF PRINCIPAL AND INTEREST

The timing and priority of payments, seniority, allocations of losses, pass through rate (the "Pass Through Rate") and amount of or method of determining payments with respect to principal and interest of each class of certificates will be described in the applicable prospectus supplement. Payments of interest on those certificates will be made on the dates specified in the applicable prospectus supplement (each, a "Payment Date"). To the extent provided in the applicable prospectus supplement, a series may include one or more classes of certificates (the "Strip Certificates") entitled to (1) payments in respect of principal with disproportionate, nominal or no interest payments or (2) interest payments with disproportionate, nominal or no payments in respect of principal. Each class of certificates may have a different Pass Through Rate, which may be a fixed, variable or adjustable Pass Through Rate (and which may be zero for some classes of Strip Certificates) or any combination of the foregoing. The applicable prospectus supplement will specify the Pass Through Rate for each class of certificates of a given series or the method for determining the Pass Through Rate. We also refer you to "Certain Information Regarding the Securities — Fixed Rate Securities" and " — Floating Rate Securities." Payments in respect of the certificates of a given series that includes notes may be subordinate to payments in respect of the notes of that series as more fully described in the applicable prospectus supplement. The rights of holders of any class of certificates to receive payments of principal and interest may also be senior or subordinate to the rights of holders of any other class or classes of certificates of that series as more fully described in the applicable prospectus supplement. Payments in respect of principal of and interest on any class of certificates will be made on a pro rata basis among all the Certificateholders of that class.

In the case of a series of certificates that includes two or more classes of certificates, the timing, sequential order, priority of payment or amount of payments in respect of interest and principal, and any schedule or formula or applicable other provisions, of each class shall be as set forth in the applicable prospectus supplement.

If and as provided in the applicable prospectus supplement, amounts remaining on deposit in the Collection Account after all required payments to the related Securityholders have been made may be released to the Seller, AHFC or one or more third party credit or liquidity enhancement providers.

CERTAIN INFORMATION REGARDING THE SECURITIES

FIXED RATE SECURITIES

Any class of Securities (other than some classes of Strip Notes or Strip Certificates) may bear interest at a fixed rate per annum ("Fixed Rate Securities") or at a variable or adjustable rate per annum ("Floating Rate Securities"), as more fully described below and in the applicable prospectus supplement. Each class of Fixed Rate Securities will bear interest at the applicable per annum Interest Rate or Pass Through Rate, as the case may be, specified in the applicable prospectus supplement. Interest on each class of Fixed Rate Securities will be computed on the basis of a 360-day year consisting of twelve 30-day months or other day count basis as is specified in the applicable prospectus supplement. We refer you to "The Notes — Principal and Interest on the Notes" and "The Certificates — Payments of Principal and Interest."

FLOATING RATE SECURITIES

Interest Rate Basis. Each class of Floating Rate Securities will bear interest during each applicable Interest Period at a rate per annum determined by reference to an interest rate basis (the "Base Rate"), plus or minus the Spread, if any, or multiplied by the Spread Multiplier, if any, in each case as specified in the applicable prospectus supplement. The "Spread" is the number of basis points to be added to or subtracted from the related Base Rate applicable to the Floating Rate Securities. The "Spread Multiplier" is the percentage of the related Base Rate applicable to the Floating Rate Securities by which that Base Rate will be multiplied to determine the applicable interest rate on those Floating Rate Securities. The applicable prospectus supplement will designate one of the following Base Rates as applicable to a particular Floating Rate Security:

- LIBOR (a "LIBOR Security");
- the Commercial Paper Rate (a "Commercial Paper Rate Security");
- the Treasury Rate (a "Treasury Rate Security");
- the Federal Funds Rate (a "Federal Funds Rate Security");
- the CD Rate (a "CD Rate Security"); or
- any other Base Rate that is set forth in the applicable prospectus supplement.

"Business Day" as used in this prospectus means, unless otherwise specified in the applicable prospectus supplement:

1. for United States dollar denominated Securities for which Libor is not an applicable Interest Rate Basis:

- any day other than a Saturday or Sunday, that is neither a legal holiday nor a day on which commercial banks are authorized or required by law, regulation or executive order to close in The City of New York (a "New York Business Day");

2. for United States dollar denominated Securities for which Libor is an applicable Interest Rate Basis:

- a day that is both (1) a day on which commercial banks are open for business, including dealings in the designated Index Currency (as defined below) in London (a "London Business Day") and (2) a New York Business Day;

3. for non-United States dollar denominated Securities (other than Securities denominated in euro) for which Libor is not an applicable Interest Rate Basis:

- a day that is both (1) a day other than a day on which commercial banks are authorized or required by law, regulation or executive order to close in the

Principal Financial Center (as defined below) of the country issuing the Specified Currency (as defined below) (a "Principal Financial Center Business Day") and (2) a New York Business Day;

4. for non-United States dollar denominated Securities (other than Securities denominated in euro) for which Libor is an applicable Interest Rate Basis:

- a day that is all of (1) a Principal Financial Center Business Day; (2) a New York Business Day; and (3) a London Business Day;

5. for euro denominated Securities for which Libor is not an applicable Interest Rate Basis:

- a day that is both (1) a day on which the Trans-European Automated Realtime Gross Settlement Express Transfer (TARGET) System is open (a "TARGET Business Day") and (2) a New York Business Day;

6. for euro denominated Securities for which Libor is an applicable Interest Rate Basis:

- a day that is all of (1) a TARGET Business Day; (2) a New York Business Day; and (3) a London Business Day.

"Principal Financial Center" means, unless otherwise specified in the applicable prospectus supplement:

- the capital city of the country issuing the Specified Currency except that with respect to United States dollars, Australian dollars, Canadian dollars, Deutsche marks, Dutch guilders, South African rand and Swiss francs, the Principal Financial Center will be The City of New York, Sydney and Melbourne, Toronto, Frankfurt, Amsterdam, Johannesburg and Zurich, respectively; or
- the capital city of the country to which the Index Currency relates, except that with respect to United States dollars, Canadian dollars, Deutsche marks, Dutch guilders, Portuguese escudos, South African rand and Swiss francs, the Principal Financial Center will be the The City of New York, Toronto, Frankfurt, Amersterdam, London, Johannesburg and Zurich, respectively.

"Specified Currency" means the currency in which a particular Security is denominated (or, if the currency is no longer legal tender for the payment of public and private debts, any other currency of the relevant country which is then legal tender for the payment of such debts).

"Index Currency" means the currency specified in the applicable prospectus supplement as the currency for which LIBOR will be calculated. If no currency is specified in the applicable prospectus supplement, the Index Currency will be United States dollars.

Interest Reset Dates. Each applicable prospectus supplement will specify whether the rate of interest on the related Floating Rate Securities will be reset daily, weekly, monthly, quarterly, semiannually, annually or some other specified period (each, an "Interest Reset Period") and the dates on which that Interest Rate will be reset (each, an "Interest Reset Date"). Unless otherwise specified in the applicable prospectus supplement, the Interest Reset Date will be, in the case of Floating Rate Securities which reset:

(1) daily, each Business Day;

(2) weekly, the Wednesday of each week (with the exception of weekly reset Treasury Rate Securities which will reset the Tuesday of each week except as described below);

(3) monthly, the third Wednesday of each month;

(4) quarterly, the third Wednesday of March, June, September and December of each year;

(5) semiannually, the third Wednesday of the two months specified in the applicable prospectus supplement;

(6) annually, the third Wednesday of the month specified in the applicable prospectus supplement; or

(7) any other Interest Reset Date set forth in the applicable prospectus supplement.

Unless otherwise specified in the related prospectus supplement, if any Interest Reset Date for any Floating Rate Security would otherwise be a day that is not a Business Day, the applicable Interest Reset Date will be postponed to the next succeeding day that is a Business Day, except that in the case of a Floating Rate Security as to which LIBOR is an applicable Base Rate, if that Business Day falls in the next succeeding calendar month, that Interest Reset Date will be the immediately preceding Business Day. In addition, in the case of a Floating Rate Security for which the Treasury Rate is an applicable Interest Rate Basis, if the Interest Determination Date would otherwise fall on an Interest Reset Date, then the applicable Interest Reset Date will be postponed to the next succeeding Business Day.

Except as set forth above or in the applicable prospectus supplement, the interest rate in effect on each date will be:

- if the date is an Interest Reset Date, the interest rate determined on the related Interest Determination Date, as defined below, immediately preceding that Interest Reset Date, or
- if the day is not an Interest Reset Date, the interest rate determined on the related Interest Determination Date immediately preceding the most recent Interest Reset Date.

Interest Payments. The interest Payment Dates will be specified in the applicable prospectus supplement. Unless otherwise specified in the related prospectus supplement, if any Payment Date for a Floating Rate Security (other than the final Payment Date) would otherwise be a day that is not a Business Day, that Payment Date will be the next succeeding day that is a Business Day except that in the case of a Floating Rate Security as to which LIBOR is the applicable Base Rate, if the Business Day falls in the next succeeding calendar month, the applicable Payment Date will be the immediately preceding Business

Day. If the final Payment Date of a Floating Rate Security falls on a day that is not a Business Day, the payment of principal, premium, if any, and interest will be made on the next succeeding Business Day, and no interest on that payment shall accrue for the period from and after that scheduled Payment Date.

Each Floating Rate Security will accrue interest on an "Actual/360" basis, an "Actual/Actual" basis, or a "30/360" basis, in each case as specified in the applicable prospectus supplement. For Floating Rate Securities calculated on an Actual/360 basis and Actual/Actual basis, accrued interest for each Interest Period will be calculated by multiplying:

(1) the face amount of the Floating Rate Security;

(2) the applicable interest rate; and

(3) the actual number of days in the related Interest Period, and dividing the resulting product by 360 or 365, as applicable (or, with respect to an Actual/Actual basis Floating Rate Security, if any portion of the related Interest Period falls in a leap year, the product of (1) and (2) above will be multiplied by the sum of (x) the actual number of days in that portion of that Interest Period falling in a leap year divided by 366 and (y) the actual number of days in that portion of that Interest Period falling in a non-leap year divided by 365).

For Floating Rate Securities calculated on a 30/360 basis, accrued interest for an Interest Period will be computed on the basis of a 360-day year consisting of twelve 30-day months, irrespective of how many days are actually in that Interest Period. With respect to any Floating Rate Security that accrues interest on a 30/360 basis, if any Payment Date, including the related final Payment Date, falls on a day that is not a Business Day, the related payment of principal or interest will be made on the next succeeding Business Day as if made on the date that payment was due, and no interest will accrue on the amount so payable for the period from and after that Payment Date.

The "Interest Period" with respect to any class of Floating Rate Securities will be set forth in the applicable prospectus supplement.

Interest Determination Dates. The interest rate applicable to each Interest Reset Period beginning on the Interest Reset Date with respect to that Interest Reset Period will be the rate determined on the applicable "Interest Determination Date," as follows unless otherwise specified in the applicable prospectus supplement:

- The Interest Determination Date for the CD Rate, the Commercial Paper Rate and the Federal Funds Rate will be the second Business Day preceding each Interest Reset Date for the related Floating Rate Security;
- The Interest Determination Date for LIBOR will be the second London Banking Day preceding each Interest Reset Date;
- The Interest Determination Date for the Treasury Rate will be the day in the week in which the related Interest Reset Date falls on which day Treasury Bills, as defined below, are normally auctioned. Treasury Bills are normally

sold at auction on Monday of each week, unless that day is a legal holiday, in which case the auction is normally held on the following Tuesday, except that the auction may be held on the preceding Friday; provided, however, that if an auction is held on the Friday of the week preceding the related Interest Reset Date, the related Interest Determination Date will be that preceding Friday; and provided further, that if an auction falls on any Interest Reset Date, then the related Interest Reset Date will instead be the first Business Day following that auction.

As used in this prospectus, "London Banking Day" means any day on which commercial banks are open for business (including dealings in designated Index Currency) in London.

Maximum and Minimum Interest Rates. As specified in the applicable prospectus supplement, Floating Rate Securities of a given class may also have either or both of the following (in each case expressed as a rate per annum):

(1) a maximum limitation, or ceiling, on the rate at which interest may accrue during any Interest Period, which may be an available funds cap rate, and (2) a minimum limitation, or floor, on the rate at which interest may accrue during any Interest Period. In addition to any maximum interest rate that may be applicable to any class of Floating Rate Securities, the interest rate applicable to any class of Floating Rate Securities will in no event be higher than the maximum rate permitted by applicable law, as the same may be modified by United States law of general application.

Calculation Agent. Each Trust with respect to which a class of Floating Rate Securities will be issued will appoint, and enter into agreements with, a calculation agent (each, a "Calculation Agent") to calculate Interest Rates on each class of Floating Rate Securities. The applicable prospectus supplement will set forth the identity of the Calculation Agent for each class of Floating Rate Securities of a given series, which may be the related Trustee or Indenture Trustee with respect to that series. All determinations of interest by the Calculation Agent shall, in the absence of manifest error, be conclusive for all purposes and binding on the holders of Floating Rate Securities of a given class. All percentages resulting from any calculation on Floating Rate Securities will be rounded to the nearest one hundred-thousandth of a percentage point, with five one millionths of a percentage point rounded upwards (e.g., 9.876545% (or .09876545) would be rounded to 9.87655% (or .0987655)), and all dollar amounts used in or resulting from that calculation on Floating Rate Securities will be rounded to the nearest cent (with one-half cent being rounded upwards).

Calculation Date. Unless specified otherwise in the applicable prospectus supplement, the "Calculation Date," if applicable, pertaining to any Interest Determination Date, will be the earlier of:

- the thirteenth calendar day after the applicable Interest Determination Date, or, if that day is not a Business Day, the next succeeding Business Day, or
- the Business Day preceding the applicable Interest Payment Date or final scheduled Payment Date, as the case may be.

Index Maturity means the period to maturity of the instrument or obligation with respect to which the Base Rate will be calculated.

CD Rate Securities. Each CD Rate Security will bear interest at the rates calculated with reference to the CD Rate and the Spread or Spread Multiplier, if any, specified in that CD Rate Security and in the applicable prospectus supplement.

Unless otherwise specified in the applicable prospectus supplement, "CD Rate" means the rate on the applicable Interest Determination Date for negotiable United States dollar certificates of deposit having the Index Maturity designated in the applicable prospectus supplement as published in H.15(519) (as defined below) under the heading "CDs (secondary market)."

The following procedures will be followed if the CD Rate cannot be determined as described above:

(1) If the rate referred to above is not published prior to 3:00 P.M., New York City time, on the related Calculation Date, then the CD Rate on the applicable Interest Determination Date will be the rate for negotiable United States dollar certificates of deposit of the Index Maturity designated in the applicable prospectus supplement as published in H.15 Daily Update (as defined below), or other recognized electronic source used for the purpose of displaying the applicable rate, under the heading "CDs (secondary market)."

(2) If the rate referred to in clause (1) above is not so published by 3:00 P.M., New York City time, on the related Calculation Date, then the CD Rate for the applicable Interest Determination Date will be the rate calculated by the Calculation Agent as the arithmetic mean of the secondary market offered rates as of 10:00 A.M., New York City time, on the applicable Interest Determination Date of three leading nonbank dealers in negotiable United States dollar certificates of deposit in The City of New York selected by the Calculation Agent for negotiable United States dollar certificates of deposit of major United States money market banks for negotiable certificates of deposit with a remaining maturity closest to the Index Maturity designated in the applicable prospectus supplement in an amount that is representative for a single transaction in that market at that time.

(3) If the dealers selected by the Calculation Agent are not quoting as set forth in clause (2) above, the CD Rate on the applicable Interest Determination Date will be the rate in effect on the applicable Interest Determination Date.

"H.15(519)" means the weekly statistical release designated as H.15(519) or any successor publication, published by the Board of Governors of the Federal Reserve System.

"H.15 Daily Update" means the daily update of H.15(519), available through the world-wide-web site of the Board of Governors of the Federal Reserve System at http://www.bog.frb.fed.us/releases/ h15/update, or any successor site or publication.

Commercial Paper Rate Securities. Each Commercial Paper Rate Security will bear interest at the rates calculated with reference to the Commercial Paper Rate and the Spread or Spread Multiplier, if any, specified in that Commercial Paper Rate Security and in the applicable prospectus supplement.

Unless otherwise provided in the applicable prospectus supplement, "Commercial Paper Rate" means the Money Market Yield (as defined below) on the applicable Interest Determination Date of the rate for commercial paper having the Index Maturity specified in the applicable prospectus supplement, as published in H.15(519) under the heading "Commercial Paper — Nonfinancial".

The following procedures will be followed if the Commercial Paper Rate cannot be determined as described above:

(1) If the rate referred to above is not published by 3:00 P.M., New York City time, on the related Calculation Date, then the Commercial Paper Rate will be the Money Market Yield on the applicable Interest Determination Date of the rate for commercial paper having the Index Maturity specified in the applicable prospectus supplement published in H.15 Daily Update, or other recognized electronic source for the purpose of displaying the applicable rate under the heading "Commercial Paper — Nonfinancial."

(2) If by 3:00 P.M. New York City time, on the related Calculation Date, the Commercial Paper Rate is not yet published in either H.15(519) or H.15 Daily Update, then the Commercial Paper Rate for the applicable Interest Determination Date will be calculated by the Calculation Agent as the Money Market Yield of the arithmetic mean of the offered rates at approximately 11:00 A.M., New York City time, on the applicable Interest Determination Date of three leading dealers of United States commercial paper in The City of New York selected by the Calculation Agent for commercial paper having the Index Maturity specified in the applicable prospectus supplement placed for industrial issuers whose bond rating is "Aa" or the equivalent, by a nationally recognized securities rating organization.

(3) If the dealers selected by the Calculation Agent are not quoting as mentioned in clause (2) above, the Commercial Paper Rate determined on the applicable Interest Determination Date will be the rate in effect on the applicable Interest Determination Date.

"Money Market Yield" means a yield (expressed as a percentage rounded upwards to the nearest one hundred-thousandth of a percentage point) calculated in accordance with the following formula:

D x 360 Money Market Yield = ——— — — x 100 360 — (D x M)

where "D" refers to the applicable per annum rate for commercial paper quoted on a bank discount basis and expressed as a decimal, and "M" refers to the actual number of days in the Interest Period for which interest is being calculated.

Federal Funds Rate Securities. Each Federal Funds Rate Security will bear interest at the rates calculated with reference to the Federal Funds Rate and the

Spread or Spread Multiplier, if any, specified in that Federal Funds Rate Security and in the applicable prospectus supplement.

Unless otherwise provided in the applicable prospectus supplement, "Federal Funds Rate" means the rate on the applicable Interest Determination Date for United States dollar federal funds as published in H.15(519) under the heading "Federal Funds (Effective)" as displayed on Bridge Telerate, Inc. or any successor service on page 120 or any other page as may replace the applicable page on the service ("Telerate Page 120").

The following procedures will be followed if the Federal Funds Rate cannot be determined as described above:

(1) If the rate referred above does not appear on Telerate Page 120 or is not published prior to 3:00 P.M., New York City time, on the related Calculation Date, the Federal Funds Rate for the applicable Interest Determination Date will be the rate on the applicable Interest Determination Date for United States dollar federal funds published in H.15 Daily Update, or other recognized electronic source for the purpose of displaying the applicable rate under the heading "Federal Funds (Effective)."

(2) If the Federal Funds Rate is not so published by 3:00 P.M., New York City time, on the related Calculation Date, the Federal Funds Rate for the applicable Interest Determination Date will be calculated by the Calculation Agent as the arithmetic mean of the rates for the last transaction in overnight United States dollar federal funds arranged by three leading brokers of United States dollar federal funds transactions in The City of New York selected by the Calculation Agent before 9:00 A.M., New York City time, on the applicable Interest Determination Date

(3) If brokers so selected by the Calculation Agent are not quoting as mentioned in clause (2) above, the Federal Funds Rate for the applicable Interest Determination Date will be the Federal Funds Rate in effect on the applicable Interest Determination Date.

LIBOR Securities. Each LIBOR Security will bear interest at the rates calculated with reference to LIBOR and the Spread or Spread Multiplier, if any, specified in that LIBOR Security and in the applicable prospectus supplement.

Unless otherwise provided in the applicable prospectus supplement, "LIBOR" means:

1. if "LIBOR Telerate" is specified in the applicable prospectus supplement, or if neither "LIBOR Reuters" nor "LIBOR Telerate" is specified in the applicable prospectus supplement as the method for calculating LIBOR, LIBOR will be the rate for deposits in the Index Currency having the Index Maturity designated in the applicable prospectus supplement, commencing on the second London Banking Day immediately following the applicable Interest Determination Date that appears on the Designated LIBOR Page specified in the applicable prospectus supplement as of 11:00 A.M. London time, on the applicable Interest Determination Date, or

2. If "LIBOR Rueters" is specified in the applicable prospectus supplement, LIBOR will be the arithmetic mean of the offered rates for deposits in the Index Currency having the Index Maturity designated in the applicable prospectus supplement, commencing on the second London Banking Day immediately following the applicable Interest Determination Date, that appear on the Designated LIBOR Page specified in the applicable prospectus supplement as of 11:00 A.M. London time on the applicable Interest Determination Date, if at least two offered rates appear (except as provided in the following sentence). If the Designated LIBOR Page by its terms provides for only a single rate, then the single rate will be used.

The following procedures will be followed if LIBOR cannot be determined as described above:

1. With respect to an Interest Determination Date on which fewer than two offered rates appear, or no rate appears, as the case may be, on the applicable Designated LIBOR Page, LIBOR for the applicable Interest Determination Date will be the rate calculated by the Calculation Agent as the arithmetic mean of at least two quotations obtained by the Calculation Agent after requesting the principal London offices of each of four major reference banks in the London interbank market, as selected by the Calculation Agent, to provide the Calculation Agent with their offered quotations for deposits in the Index Currency for the period of the Index Maturity designated in the applicable prospectus supplement, commencing on the second London Banking Day immediately following the applicable Interest Determination Date, to prime banks in the London interbank market at approximately 11:00 A.M., London time, on the applicable Interest Determination Date and in a principal amount that is representative for a single transaction in the applicable Index Currency in that market at that time. If at least two quotations are provided, LIBOR determined on the applicable Interest Determination Date will be the arithmetic mean of those quotations.
2. If fewer than two quotations referred to in clause (1) above are provided, LIBOR determined on the applicable Interest Determination Date will be rate calculated by the Calculation Agent as the arithmetic mean of the rates quoted at approximately 11:00 A.M. (or another time specified in the applicable prospectus supplement), in the applicable Principal Financial Center, on the applicable Interest Determination Date, by three major banks, in that Principal Financial Center selected by the Calculation Agent for loans in the Index Currency to leading European banks, having the Index Maturity designated in the applicable prospectus supplement and in a principal amount that is representative for a single transaction in the Index Currency in that market at that time.
3. If the banks so selected by the Calculation Agent are not quoting as mentioned in clause (2) above, LIBOR for the applicable Interest Determination Date will be LIBOR in effect on the applicable Interest Determination Date.

"Designated LIBOR Page" means either:

- if "LIBOR Telerate" is designated in the applicable prospectus supplement or neither "LIBOR Reuters" nor "LIBOR Telerate" is specified in the applicable prospectus supplement as the method for calculating LIBOR, the display on Bridge Telerate, Inc., or any successor service on the page designated in the applicable prospectus supplement or any page as may replace the designated page on that service for the purpose of displaying the London interbank rates of major banks for the applicable Index Currency.
- if "LIBOR Reuters" is designated in the applicable prospectus supplement, the display on Reuters Monitor Money Rates Service or any successor service on the page designated in the applicable prospectus supplement or any page that may replace that designated page on that service for the purpose of displaying London interbank rates of major banks for the applicable Index Currency, or

Treasury Rate Securities. Each Treasury Rate Security will bear interest calculated with reference to the Treasury Rate and the Spread or Spread Multiplier, if any, specified in the Treasury Rate Security and in the applicable prospectus supplement.

Unless otherwise provided in the applicable prospectus supplement, "Treasury Rate" means the rate from the auction held on the applicable Interest Determination Date ("Auction") of direct obligations of the United States ("Treasury Bills") having the Index Maturity specified in the applicable prospectus supplement, under the heading "Investment Rate" on the display on Bridge Telerate, Inc., or any successor service on page 56 or any other page as may replace page 56 of that service ("Telerate Page 56") or page 57 or any other page as may replace page 57 of that service ("Telerate Page 57").

The following procedures will be followed if the Treasury Rate cannot be determined as described above:

1. If the rate described above is not so published by 3:00 P.M., New York City time, on the related Calculation Date, the Treasury Rate for the applicable Interest Determination Date will be the Bond Equivalent Yield (as defined below) of the rate for the applicable Treasury Bills as published in H.15 Daily Update, or other recognized electronic source used for the purpose of displaying the applicable rate, under the caption "U.S. Government Securities/Treasury Bills/Auction High."
2. If the rate described in clause (1) above is not so published by 3:00 P.M., New York City time, on the related Calculation Date, the Treasury Rate for the applicable Interest Determination Date will be the Bond Equivalent Yield of the auction rate of the applicable Treasury Bills announced by the United States Department of the Treasury.
3. If the rate described in clause (2) above is not announced by the United States Department of the Treasury, or if the Auction is not held, the Treasury Rate for the applicable Interest Determination Date will be the Bond Equiv-

alent Yield of the rate on the applicable Interest Determination Date of Treasury Bills having the Index Maturity specified in the applicable prospectus supplement published in H.15(519) under the caption "U.S. Government Securities/Treasury Bills/ Secondary Market."

4. If the rate described in clause (3) above is not so published by 3:00 P.M., New York City time, on the related Calculation Date, the Treasury Rate for the applicable Interest Determination Date will be the rate on the applicable Interest Determination Date of the applicable Treasury Bills as published in H.15 Daily Update, or other recognized electronic source used for the purpose of displaying the applicable rate, under the caption "U.S. Government Securities/ Treasury Bills/ Secondary Market."
5. If the rate described in clause (4) above is not so published by 3:00 P.M., New York City time, on the related Calculation Date, the Treasury Rate for the applicable Interest Determination Date will be the rate for the applicable Interest Determination Date calculated by the Calculation Agent as the Bond Equivalent Yield of the arithmetic mean of the secondary market bid rates, as of approximately 3:30 P.M., New York City time, on the applicable Interest Determination Date, of three primary United States government securities dealers, selected by the Calculation Agent, for the issue of Treasury Bills with a remaining maturity closest to the Index Maturity specified in the applicable prospectus supplement.
6. If the dealers selected by the Calculation Agent are not quoting as described in clause(s) above, the Treasury Rate for the applicable Interest Determination Date will be the rate in effect on the applicable Interest Determination Date.

"Bond Equivalent Yield" means a yield calculated in accordance with the following formula and expressed as a percentage:

D x N Bond Equivalent Yield = — — — — — - - — x 100 360 — (D x M)

where "D" refers to the applicable per annum rate for Treasury Bills quoted on a bank discount basis, "N" refers to 365 or 366, as the case may be, and "M" refers to the actual number of days in the interest period for which interest is being calculated.

INDEXED SECURITIES

To the extent specified in any prospectus supplement, any class of Securities of a given series may consist of Securities ("Indexed Securities") in which the principal amount payable on the final scheduled Payment Date for that class (the "Indexed Principal Amount") and/or the interest payable on any Payment Date is determined by reference to a measure (the "Index") which will be related to (1) the exchange rates of one or more currencies; (2) the price or prices of specified commodities; (3) specified stocks, which may be based on U.S. or foreign stocks, on specified dates specified in the applicable prospectus supplement; or (4) another price, interest rate, exchange rate or other financial index or indices as are described in the applicable prospectus supplement. Holders of Indexed

Securities may receive a principal amount on the related final scheduled Payment Date that is greater than or less than the face amount of the Indexed Securities depending upon the relative value on the related final scheduled Payment Date of the specified indexed item. The applicable prospectus supplement will also contain information as to the method for determining the principal amount payable on the related final scheduled Payment Date, if any, and, where applicable, historical information with respect to the specific indexed item or items and special tax considerations associated with investment in Indexed Securities. Notwithstanding anything to the contrary in this prospectus, for purposes of determining the rights of a holder of a Security indexed as to principal in respect of voting for or against amendments to the related Trust Agreement, Indenture, or other related agreements, as the case may be, and modifications and the waiver of rights under those agreements, the principal amount of that Indexed Security shall be deemed to be the face amount thereof upon issuance less any payments allocated to principal of that Indexed Security.

If the determination of the Indexed Principal Amount of an Indexed Security is based on an Index calculated or announced by a third party and that third party either suspends the calculation or announcement of that Index or changes the basis upon which that Index is calculated (other than changes consistent with policies in effect at the time that Indexed Security was issued and permitted changes described in the applicable prospectus supplement), then that Index shall be calculated for purposes of that Indexed Security by an independent calculation agent named in the applicable prospectus supplement on the same basis, and subject to the same conditions and controls, as applied to the original third party. If for any reason that Index cannot be calculated on the same basis and subject to the same conditions and controls as applied to the original third party, then the Indexed Principal Amount of that Indexed Security shall be calculated in the manner set forth in the applicable prospectus supplement. Any determination of that independent calculation agent shall, in the absence of manifest error, be binding on all parties.

The applicable prospectus supplement will describe whether the principal amount of the related Indexed Security, if any, that would be payable upon redemption or repayment prior to the applicable final scheduled Payment Date will be the face amount of that Indexed Security, the Indexed Principal Amount of that Indexed Security at the time of redemption or repayment or another amount described in that prospectus supplement.

INTEREST RATE SWAPS

The Trust may also include a derivative arrangement for the payment of interest on the Securities of a series or any class of Securities. A derivative arrangement may include a guaranteed rate agreement, a maturity liquidity facility, a tax protection agreement, an interest rate cap or floor agreement, an interest rate or currency swap agreement or any other similar arrangement. The type of derivative arrangement, if any, for a series of Securities or class of Securities will be described in the applicable prospectus supplement.

VARIABLE FUNDING NOTE

The applicable prospectus supplement for a Trust may provide that the Trust issue one or more series of Securities having particular maturity dates and at the same time the Trust may issue amortizing floating notes, known as "variable funding notes", which relate to those particular maturity dates. These Securities may have a balance that may (1) decrease based on the amortization of the related Receivables or (2) increase based on principal collections used to purchase additional Receivables.

Interest Rate Flexibility For a Variable Funding Note. The prospectus supplement may provide that the Securities issued in connection with a variable funding note may have different rates of interest which may be fixed or floating. The related prospectus supplement will specify the interest rate for each series or class of Securities and the method, if any, for determining subsequent changes to the interest rate.

PRO-RATA PAY/SUBORDINATE SECURITIES

The applicable prospectus supplement for a Trust may provide that one or more classes of Securities will be payable on an interest only or principal only basis. In addition, the Securities may include two or more classes that differ as to timing, sequential order, priority of payment, interest rate or amount of distributions of principal or interest or both. Distributions of principal or interest or both on any class of Securities may be made upon the occurrence of specified events, in accordance with a schedule or formula, or on the basis of collections from designated assets of the Trust. A series may include one or more classes of Securities, as to which accrued interest will not be distributed but rather will be added to the principal or specified balance of the Security on each Payment Date.

REVOLVING PERIOD

The applicable prospectus supplement for a Trust may provide that all or a portion of the principal collected on the Receivables may be applied by the Trustee to the acquisition of subsequent Receivables during a specified period rather than used to distribute payments of principal to Securityholders during that period. These Securities would then possess an interest only period, also commonly referred to as a "revolving period", which will be followed by an "amortization period", during which principal would be paid. Any interest only or revolving period may terminate prior to the end of the specified period and result in earlier than expected principal repayment of the Securities.

BOOK-ENTRY REGISTRATION

Each class of Securities offered by this prospectus will be represented by one or more certificates registered in the name of Cede, as nominee of The Depository Trust Company ("DTC"). Securityholders may hold beneficial interests in Securities through DTC (in the United States) or Clearstream Banking, societe anonyme (referred to herein as "Clearstream, Luxembourg") or Euroclear Bank S.A./NV as operator of the Euroclear System ("Euroclear") (in Europe or Asia) directly if they are participants of those systems, or indirectly through organizations which are participants in those systems. Clearstream, Luxembourg and Euroclear will hold omnibus positions on behalf of their participants (referred to herein as "Clearstream, Luxembourg Participants" and "Euroclear Participants", respectively) through customers' securities accounts in their respective names on the books of their respective depositaries (collectively, the "Depositaries") which in turn will hold those positions in customers' securities accounts in the Depositaries' names on the books of DTC.

No Securityholder will be entitled to receive a certificate representing that person's interest in the Securities, except as set forth below. Unless and until Securities of a class are issued in fully registered certificated form under the limited circumstances described below, all references in this prospectus to actions by Noteholders, Certificateholders or Securityholders shall refer to actions taken by DTC upon instructions from DTC Participants (as defined below), and all references in this prospectus to distributions, notices, reports and statements to Noteholders, Certificateholders or Securityholders shall refer to distributions, notices, reports and statements to Cede, as the registered holder of the Securities, for distribution to Securityholders in accordance with DTC procedures. Therefore, it is anticipated that the only Noteholder, Certificateholder or Securityholder will be Cede, as nominee of DTC. Securityholders will not be recognized by the related Trustee as Noteholders, Certificateholders or Securityholders as those terms will be used in the relevant agreements, and Securityholders will only be permitted to exercise the rights of holders of Securities of the related class indirectly through DTC and DTC Participants, as further described below.

Transfers between DTC Participants will occur in accordance with DTC rules. Transfers between Clearstream, Luxembourg Participants and Euroclear Participants will occur in accordance with their applicable rules and operating procedures.

Cross-market transfers between persons holding directly or indirectly through DTC, on the one hand, and directly or indirectly through Clearstream, Luxembourg Participants or Euroclear Participants, on the other, will be effected in DTC in accordance with DTC rules on behalf of the relevant European international clearing system by its Depositary. However, each of these cross-market transactions will require delivery of instructions to the relevant European international clearing system by the counterparty in that system in accordance with that system's rules and procedures and within that system's established deadlines (European time). The relevant European international clearing system will, if the transaction meets its settlement requirements, deliver instructions to its Depositary to take action to effect final settlement on its behalf by delivering or receiving securities in DTC, and making or receiving payment in accordance with normal procedures for same-day funds settlement applicable to

DTC. Clearstream, Luxembourg Participants and Euroclear Participants may not deliver instructions directly to their respective Depositaries.

Because of time-zone differences, credits of securities received in Clearstream, Luxembourg or Euroclear as a result of a transaction with a DTC Participant will be made during subsequent securities settlement processing and dated the business day following the DTC settlement date. Those credits or any transactions in those securities settled during that processing will be reported to the relevant Euroclear Participant or Clearstream, Luxembourg Participant on that business day. Cash received in Clearstream, Luxembourg or Euroclear as a result of sales of Securities by or through a Clearstream, Luxembourg Participant or a Euroclear Participant to a DTC Participant will be received with value on the DTC settlement date but will be available in the relevant Clearstream, Luxembourg or Euroclear cash account only as of the business day following settlement in DTC.

DTC is a limited purpose trust company organized under the laws of the State of New York, a "banking organization" within the meaning of the New York Banking Law, a member of the Federal Reserve System, a "clearing corporation" within the meaning of the New York Uniform Commercial Code and a "clearing agency" registered pursuant to Section 17A of the Exchange Act of 1934. DTC was created to hold securities for its participating members ("DTC Participants") and to facilitate the clearance and settlement of securities transactions between DTC Participants through electronic book-entries, thereby eliminating the need for physical movement of certificates. DTC Participants include securities brokers and dealers, banks, trust companies and clearing corporations which may include underwriters, agents or dealers with respect to the Securities of any class or series. Indirect access to the DTC system also is available to others such as banks, brokers, dealers and trust companies that clear through or maintain a custodial relationship with a DTC Participant, either directly or indirectly (the "Indirect DTC Participants"). The rules applicable to DTC and DTC Participants are on file with the SEC.

Securityholders that are not DTC Participants or Indirect DTC Participants but desire to purchase, sell or otherwise transfer ownership of, or other interests in, Securities may do so only through DTC Participants and Indirect DTC Participants. DTC Participants will receive a credit for the Securities on DTC's records. The ownership interest of each Securityholder will in turn be recorded on respective records of the DTC Participants and Indirect DTC Participants. Securityholders will not receive written confirmation from DTC of their purchase, but Securityholders are expected to receive written confirmations providing details of the transaction, as well as periodic statements of their holdings, from the DTC Participant or Indirect DTC Participant through which the Securityholder entered into the transaction. Transfers of ownership interests in the Securities of any class will be accomplished by entries made on the books of DTC Participants acting on behalf of Securityholders.

To facilitate subsequent transfers, all Securities deposited by DTC Participants with DTC will be registered in the name of Cede, as nominee of DTC. The deposit of Securities with DTC and their registration in the name of Cede will effect no change in beneficial ownership. DTC will have no knowledge of the actual Securityholders and its records will reflect only the identity of the DTC Participants to whose accounts those Securities are credited, which may or may not be the Securityholders. DTC Participants and Indirect DTC Participants will remain responsible for keeping account of their holdings on behalf of their customers. While the Securities of a series are held in book-entry form, Securityholders will not have access to the list of Securityholders of that series, which may impede the ability of Securityholders to communicate with each other.

Conveyance of notices and other communications by DTC to DTC Participants, by DTC Participants to Indirect DTC Participants and by DTC Participants and Indirect DTC Participants to Securityholders will be governed by arrangements among them, subject to any statutory or regulatory requirements that may be in effect from time to time.

Under the rules, regulations and procedures creating and affecting DTC and its operations, DTC is required to make book-entry transfers among DTC Participants on whose behalf it acts with respect to the Securities and is required to receive and transmit payments of principal of and interest on the Securities. DTC Participants and Indirect DTC Participants with which Securityholders have accounts with respect to the Securities similarly are required to make book-entry transfers and receive and transmit those payments on behalf of their respective Securityholders.

DTC's practice is to credit DTC Participants' accounts on each Payment Date in accordance with their respective holdings shown on its records, unless DTC has reason to believe that it will not receive payment on that Payment Date. Payments by DTC Participants and Indirect DTC Participants to Securityholders will be governed by standing instructions and customary practices, as is the case with securities held for the accounts of customers in bearer form or registered in "street name", and will be the responsibility of that DTC Participant and not of DTC, the related Indenture Trustee or Trustee (or any paying agent appointed by the Indenture Trustee or Trustee), the Seller or the Servicer, subject to any statutory or regulatory requirements that may be in effect from time to time. Payment of principal of and interest on each class of Securities to DTC will be the responsibility of the related Indenture Trustee or Trustee (or any paying agent), disbursement of those payments to DTC Participants will be the responsibility of DTC and disbursement of those payments to the related Securityholders will be the responsibility of DTC Participants and Indirect DTC Participants. DTC will forward those payments to its DTC Participants which thereafter will forward them to Indirect DTC Participants or Securityholders.

Because DTC can only act on behalf of DTC Participants, who in turn act on behalf of Indirect DTC Participants and some other banks, a Securityholder may be limited in its ability to pledge Securities to persons or entities that do not participate in the DTC system, or otherwise take actions with respect to those Securities due to the lack of a physical certificate for those Securities.

DTC has advised the Seller that it will take any action permitted to be taken by a Securityholder only at the direction of one or more DTC Participants to whose account with DTC the Securities are credited. Additionally, DTC has advised the Seller that it will take those actions with respect to specified percentages of the Securityholders' interest only at the direction of and on behalf of DTC Participants whose holdings include undivided interests that satisfy those specified percentages. DTC may take conflicting actions with respect to other undivided interests to the extent that those actions are taken on behalf of DTC Participants whose holdings include those undivided interests.

Neither DTC nor Cede will consent or vote with respect to the Securities. Under its usual procedures, DTC will mail an "Omnibus Proxy" to the related Indenture Trustee or Trustee as soon as possible after any applicable record date for that consent or vote. The Omnibus Proxy will assign Cede's consenting or voting rights to those DTC Participants to whose accounts the related Securities are credited on that record date (which record date will be identified in a listing attached to the Omnibus Proxy).

Clearstream, Luxembourg has advised us that it is organized under the laws of the Grand Duchy of Luxembourg as a professional depositary. Clearstream, Luxembourg holds securities for Clearstream, Luxembourg Participants and facilitates the clearance and settlement of securities transactions between Clearstream, Luxembourg Participants through electronic book-entry changes in Clearstream accounts of Clearstream, Luxembourg Participants or between a Clearstream account and a Euroclear account, thereby eliminating the need for physical movement of certificates. For transactions between a Clearstream, Luxembourg participant and a participant of another securities settlement system, Clearstream, Luxembourg generally adjusts to the settlement rules of the other securities settlement system. Transactions may be settled by Clearstream, Luxembourg in numerous currencies, including United States dollars. Clearstream, Luxembourg provides to Clearstream, Luxembourg Participants, among other things, services for safekeeping, administration, clearance and settlement of internationally traded securities and securities lending and borrowing. Clearstream, Luxembourg also deals with domestic securities markets in several countries through established depository and custodial relationships. As a professional depositary, Clearstream, Luxembourg is subject to regulation by the Luxembourg Commission de Surveillance du Secteur Financier, "CSSF". Clearstream, Luxembourg Participants are world-wide financial institutions including underwriters, securities brokers and dealers, banks, trust companies and clearing corporations. Indirect access to Clearstream, Luxembourg is available to other institutions that clear through or maintain a custodial relationship with a Clearstream, Luxembourg Participant. Clearstream, Luxembourg has established an electronic bridge with Euroclear to facilitate settlement of trades between Clearstream, Luxembourg and Euroclear.

Euroclear was created in 1968 to hold securities for Euroclear Participants and to clear and settle transactions between Euroclear Participants through simultaneous electronic book-entry delivery against payment, thereby eliminating the need for physical movement of certificates and any risk from lack of simultaneous transfers of securities and cash. Transactions may now be settled in numerous currencies, including United States dollars. Euroclear provides various other services, including securities lending and borrowing, and interfaces with domestic markets in several countries. Euroclear is operated by Euroclear Bank S.A./NV (the "Euroclear Operator"), under contract with Euroclear Clearance System S.C., a Belgian cooperative corporation (the "Cooperative"). All operations are conducted by the Euroclear Operator, and all Euroclear securities clearance accounts and Euroclear cash accounts are accounts with the Euroclear Operator, not the Cooperative. The Cooperative establishes policy for Euroclear on behalf of Euroclear Participants. Euroclear Participants include banks (including central banks), securities brokers and dealers and other professional financial intermediaries and may include any underwriters, agents or dealers with respect to any class or series of Securities offered by this prospectus. Indirect access to Euroclear is also available to other firms that clear through or maintain a custodial relationship with a Euroclear Participant, either directly or indirectly.

The Euroclear Operator has advised us that it is licensed by the Belgian Banking and Finance Commission to carry out banking activities on a global basis. As a Belgian bank, it is regulated and examined by the Belgian Banking Commission.

Securities clearance accounts and cash accounts with the Euroclear Operator are governed by the Terms and Conditions Governing Use of Euroclear and the related Operating Procedures of the Euroclear System and applicable Belgian law (collectively, the "Terms and Conditions"). The Terms and Conditions govern transfers of securities and cash within Euroclear, withdrawals of securities and cash from Euroclear and receipts of payments with respect to securities in Euroclear. All securities in Euroclear are held on a fungible basis without attribution of specific certificates to specific securities clearance accounts. The Euroclear Operator acts under the Terms and Conditions only on behalf of Euroclear Participants and has no record of or relationship with persons holding through Euroclear Participants.

Payments with respect to Securities held through Clearstream, Luxembourg or Euroclear will be credited to the cash accounts of Clearstream, Luxembourg Participants or Euroclear Participants in accordance with the relevant system's rules and procedures, to the extent received by its Depositary. Those payments will be subject to tax withholding in accordance with relevant United States tax laws and regulations. We refer you to "Material Income Tax Consequences." Clearstream, Luxembourg or the Euroclear Operator, as the case may be, will take any other action permitted to be taken by a Securityholder on behalf of a Clearstream, Luxembourg Participant or Euroclear Participant only in accordance with its relevant rules and procedures and subject to its Depositary's ability to effect those actions on its behalf through DTC.

DTC, Clearstream, Luxembourg and Euroclear are under no obligation to perform or continue to perform the foregoing procedures and such procedures may be discontinued at any time.

DEFINITIVE SECURITIES

The notes, if any, and the certificates of a given series will be issued in fully registered, certificated form ("Definitive Notes" and "Definitive Certificates", respectively, and collectively referred to in this prospectus as "Definitive Securities") to Noteholders or Certificateholders or their respective nominees, rather than to DTC or its nominee, only if:

1. DTC is no longer willing or able to discharge properly its responsibilities as depository with respect to those Securities and the Seller, the Administrator or the Trustee is unable to locate a qualified successor (and if it is the Seller or the Administrator that has made that determination, the Seller or that Administrator so notifies the applicable Trustee in writing);
2. the Seller or the Administrator or the Trustee, as applicable, at its option, elects to terminate the book-entry system through DTC; or
3. after the occurrence of an Event of Default or a Servicer Default with respect to those Securities, holders representing at least a majority of the outstanding principal amount of the notes or the certificates, as the case may be, of that series, acting together as a single class, advise the applicable Trustee through DTC in writing that the continuation of a book-entry system through DTC (or a successor thereto) with respect to those notes or certificates is no longer in the best interests of the holders of those Securities.

Upon the occurrence of any event described in the immediately preceding paragraph, the applicable Trustee or Indenture Trustee will be required to notify all applicable Securityholders of a given series through DTC Participants of the availability of Definitive Securities. Upon surrender by DTC of the Definitive Certificates representing the corresponding Securities and receipt of instructions for re-registration, the applicable Trustee or Indenture Trustee will reissue those Securities as Definitive Securities to those Securityholders.

Payments of principal of, and interest on, the Definitive Securities will thereafter be made by the applicable Trustee or Indenture Trustee in accordance with the procedures set forth in the related Indenture or the related Trust Agreement or Pooling and Servicing Agreement, as applicable, directly to holders of Definitive Securities in whose names the Definitive Securities were registered at the close of business on the applicable record date specified for those Securities in the applicable prospectus supplement. Those payments will be made by check mailed to the address of that holder as it appears on the register maintained by the applicable Trustee or Indenture Trustee. The final payment on any Definitive Security, however, will be made only upon presentation and surrender of that Definitive Security at the office or agency specified in the notice of final payment to the applicable Securityholders. The applicable Trustee or the Indenture Trustee will provide notice to the applicable Securityholders not less than 15 nor more than 30 days prior to the date on which final payment is expected to occur.

Definitive Securities will be transferable and exchangeable at the offices of the applicable Trustee or of a registrar named in a notice delivered to holders of Definitive Securities. No service charge will be imposed for any registration of transfer or exchange, but the applicable Trustee may require payment of a sum sufficient to cover any tax or other governmental charge imposed in connection therewith.

DESCRIPTION OF THE TRANSFER AND SERVICING AGREEMENTS

The following summary describes material terms of each Sale and Servicing Agreement or Pooling and Servicing Agreement pursuant to which a Trust will purchase Receivables from the Seller and the Servicer will agree to service those Receivables, each Trust Agreement (or in the case of a grantor trust, the Pooling and Servicing Agreement) pursuant to which a Trust will be created and certificates will be issued and each Administration Agreement pursuant to which AHFC will undertake specified administrative duties with respect to a Trust that issues notes (collectively, the "Transfer and Servicing Agreements"). Forms of the Transfer and Servicing Agreements have been filed as exhibits to the registration statement of which this prospectus forms a part. The provisions of any of the Transfer and Servicing Agreements may differ from those described in this prospectus and, if so, will be described in the applicable prospectus supplement. This summary does not purport to be complete and is subject to, and qualified in its entirety by reference to, all the provisions of the Transfer and Servicing Agreements.

SALE AND ASSIGNMENT OF RECEIVABLES

On or prior to the Closing Date specified with respect to any given Trust in the applicable prospectus supplement, AHFC will sell and assign to the Seller, without recourse, pursuant to a Purchase Agreement (the "Purchase Agreement"), its entire interest in the Receivables comprising the related Receivables Pool, including the security interests in the Financed Vehicles. On the Closing Date, the Seller will transfer and assign to the applicable Trustee on behalf of the Trust, without recourse, pursuant to a Sale and Servicing Agreement or a Pooling and Servicing Agreement, as applicable, its entire interest in the Receivables comprising the related Receivables Pool, including its security interests in the related Financed Vehicles. Each Receivable will be identified in a schedule appearing as an exhibit to the related Sale and Servicing Agreement or Pooling and Servicing Agreement (a "Schedule of Receivables"), but the existence and characteristics of the related Receivables will not be verified by the related Trustee. The applicable Trustee will, concurrently with the transfer and assignment, on behalf of the Trust, execute and deliver the related notes and/or certificates. The net proceeds received from the sale of the certificates and the notes of a given series will be applied to the purchase of the related Receivables from the Seller and, to the extent specified in the applicable prospectus supplement, to make any required initial deposit into the Reserve Fund and the Yield Supplement Account, if any. The Seller will initially retain the most subordinated class of Securities of the related series.

AHFC, pursuant to a Purchase Agreement, and the Seller, pursuant to a Sale and Servicing Agreement or a Pooling and Servicing Agreement, will represent and warrant, among other things, that:

1. the information provided in the related Schedule of Receivables is true and correct in all material respects;
2. at the time of origination of each Receivable, the related Obligor on each Receivable is required to maintain physical damage insurance covering the Financed Vehicle in accordance with AHFC's normal requirements;
3. as of the applicable Closing Date, each of those Receivables is or will be secured by a first priority perfected security interest in favor of AHFC in the Financed Vehicle;
4. to the best of its knowledge, as of the applicable Closing Date, the related Receivables are free and clear of all security interests, liens, charges and encumbrances and no offsets, defenses or counterclaims have been asserted or threatened;
5. each related Receivable, at the time it was originated, complied and, as of the applicable Closing Date, complies in all material respects with applicable federal and state laws, including, consumer credit, truth — in-lending, equal credit opportunity and disclosure laws; and
6. any other representations and warranties that may be set forth in the applicable prospectus supplement are true and correct in all material respects.

Unless otherwise provided for in the related prospectus supplement, as of the last day of the second (or, if the Seller so elects, the first) Collection Period following the discovery by or notice to the Seller of a breach of any representation or warranty of the Seller that materially and adversely affects the interests of the related Securityholders in any Receivable, the Seller, unless the breach is cured, will repurchase that Receivable (a "Warranty Receivable") from that Trust and, pursuant to the related Purchase Agreement, AHFC will purchase that Warranty Receivable from the Seller, at a price equal to the Warranty Purchase Payment for that Receivable. The "Warranty Purchase Payment" for (1) a Precomputed Receivable will be equal to (a) the sum of (i) all remaining Scheduled Payments, (ii) all past due Scheduled Payments for which an Advance has not been made, (iii) all outstanding Advances made by the Servicer in respect of the Precomputed Receivable and (iv) an amount equal to any reimbursements of outstanding Advances made to the Servicer with respect to the Precomputed Receivable from collections made on or in respect of other Receivables, minus (b) the sum of (i) of all Payments Ahead in respect to such Warranty Receivable held by the Servicer or on deposit in the Payahead Account, (ii) the rebate, calculated on an actuarial basis, that would be payable to the Obligor on the Precomputed Receivable were the Obligor to prepay the Precomputed Receivable in full on that day (a "Rebate") and (iii) any proceeds of the liquidation of the Precomputed Receivable previously received (to the extent applied to reduce the Principal Balance of the Precomputed Receivable) and (2) a Simple Interest Receivable, will be equal to its unpaid principal balance, plus interest thereon at a rate equal to the APR to the last day of the Collection Period relating to the repurchase. This repurchase obligation will constitute the sole remedy available to the Securityholders or the Trust for any uncured breach by the Seller. The obligation of the Seller to repurchase a Receivable will not be conditioned on performance by AHFC of its obligation to purchase that Receivable from the Seller pursuant to the related Purchase Agreement.

Pursuant to each Sale and Servicing Agreement or Pooling and Servicing Agreement, the Seller and each Trust will designate the Servicer as custodian to maintain possession as that Trust's agent of the related retail installment sale contracts and any other documents relating to the Receivables. To assure uniform quality in servicing both the Receivables and the Servicer's own portfolio of motor vehicle retail installment sale contracts, as well as to facilitate servicing and reduce administrative costs, the documents evidencing the Receivables will not be physically segregated from other motor vehicle retail installment sale contracts of the Servicer, or those which the Servicer services for others, or marked to reflect the transfer to the related Trust as long as AHFC is servicing the Receivables. However, Uniform Commercial Code ("UCC") financing statements reflecting the sale and assignment of the Receivables by AHFC to the Seller and by the Seller to the applicable Trust will be filed, and the respective accounting records and computer files of AHFC and the Seller will reflect that sale and assignment. Because the Receivables will remain in the Servicer's possession and will not be stamped or otherwise marked to reflect the assignment to the Trustee, if a subsequent purchaser were able to take physical possession of the Receivables without knowledge of the assignment, the Trust's interest in the Receivables could be defeated. In addition, in some cases, the Trustee's security interest in collections that have been received by the Servicer but not yet remitted to the related Collection Account could be defeated. We refer you to "Certain Legal Aspects of the Receivables — Security Interests" in this prospectus.

ACCOUNTS

With respect to each Trust that issues notes, the Servicer will establish and maintain with the related Trustee or Indenture Trustee one or more accounts (each, a "Collection Account"), in the name of the Trustee or Indenture Trustee on behalf of the related Securityholders, into which payments made on or with respect to the related Receivables and amounts released from any Yield Supplement Account, Reserve Fund or other form of credit enhancement will be deposited for payment to the related Securityholders. With respect to each Trust that does not issue notes, the Servicer will also establish and maintain a

Collection Account and any other Account in the name of the related Trustee on behalf of the related Certificateholders.

If so provided in the related prospectus supplement, the Servicer will establish for each series of Securities an additional account (the "Payahead Account"), in the name of the related Trustee or, if that Trust issues notes, the Indenture Trustee, into which, to the extent required by the Sale and Servicing Agreement or Pooling and Servicing Agreement, early payments by or on behalf of Obligors on Precomputed Receivables ("Payments Ahead") will be deposited until the time as the related payment becomes due. Until that time as Payments Ahead are transferred from the Payahead Account to a Collection Account, they will not constitute collected interest or collected principal and will not be available for payment to the applicable Noteholders or Certificateholders. The Payahead Account will initially be maintained with the applicable Indenture Trustee or Trustee.

Any other accounts to be established with respect to a Trust, including any Yield Supplement Account or any Reserve Fund, will be described in the applicable prospectus supplement.

For any series of Securities, funds in the related Collection Account, any Yield Supplement Account, the Reserve Fund and other accounts that may be identified in the applicable prospectus supplement (collectively, the "Accounts") will be invested as provided in the related Sale and Servicing Agreement or Pooling and Servicing Agreement in Eligible Investments. "Eligible Investments" are generally limited to investments acceptable to the rating agencies rating the Securities as being consistent with the rating of those Securities (including obligations of the Servicer and its affiliates, to the extent consistent with that rating). Except as described below or in the related prospectus supplement, Eligible Investments are limited to obligations or securities that mature on or before the next Payment Date for that series. However, to the extent permitted by the rating agencies, funds in any Account (other than the Collection Account) may be invested in obligations or securities that will not mature prior to the next Payment Date with respect to those certificates or notes and will not be sold to meet any shortfalls. Thus, the amount of cash in any Reserve Fund or the Yield Supplement Account at any time may be less than the balance of the Reserve Fund or the Yield Supplement Account, as the case may be. If the amount required to be withdrawn from any Reserve Fund or the Yield Supplement Account to cover shortfalls in collections on the related Receivables (as provided in the applicable prospectus supplement) exceeds the amount of cash in the Reserve Fund or the Yield Supplement Account, as the case may be, a temporary shortfall in the amounts paid to the related Noteholders or Certificateholders could result, which could, in turn, increase the average life of the notes or the certificates of that series. Investment earnings on funds deposited in the Accounts, net of losses and investment expenses, shall be released to the Servicer or the Seller on each Payment Date and shall be the property of the Servicer or the Seller, as the case may be.

For each Trust, the Accounts will be maintained with the related Indenture Trustee or the Trustee so long as it is an "Eligible Institution," which is a depository institution or trust company,

1. the short-term unsecured debt obligations of which have a rating of "P-1" by Moody's Investors Service, Inc. ("Moody's") and a rating of "A-1+" by Standard & Poor's Ratings Services, a division of The McGraw Hill Companies, Inc. ("Standard & Poor's") (the "Required Deposit Rating"); or
2. having corporate trust powers and organized under the laws of the United States, any state thereof, the District of Columbia or the Commonwealth of Puerto Rico which has a long-term deposit rating from (A) Moody's of at least "Baa3" or (B) Standard & Poor's of at least "BBB-" (or such lower rating as either rating agency shall approve in writing).

If the related Indenture Trustee or the Trustee, as the case may be, ceases to be an Eligible Institution, then the Servicer shall, with the assistance of the Indenture Trustee or the Trustee as may be necessary, cause each Account to be moved to an Eligible Institution.

SERVICING PROCEDURES

The Servicer will make reasonable efforts to collect all payments due with respect to the Receivables held by any Trust and will, consistent with the related Sale and Servicing Agreement or Pooling and Servicing Agreement, follow the collection procedures it follows with respect to comparable motor vehicle retail installment sale contracts it services for itself and others.

The Servicer will be authorized to grant certain rebates, adjustments or extensions with respect to a Receivable. However, if any modification of a Receivable extends the maturity of a Receivable beyond the final scheduled maturity date set forth in the applicable prospectus supplement (the "Final Scheduled Maturity Date") the Servicer will be obligated to purchase the Receivable as described below.

In addition, the Servicer will covenant that, except as otherwise contemplated in the related agreement (including the provisions in the immediately two preceding paragraphs):

1. it will not release any Financed Vehicle from the security interest granted in the related Receivable;
2. it will do nothing to impair the rights of the Securityholders in the Receivables;
3. it will not alter the APR of any Receivable;
4. it will not modify the number of payments under a Receivable or the maturity of a Receivable beyond the Final Scheduled Maturity Date unless it is making advances corresponding to reduction in Scheduled Payments as described above; and
5. it will not alter the amount financed under a Receivable.

The Servicer or the Trustee shall inform the other party and the Indenture Trustee promptly upon the discovery of any breach by the Servicer of the above obligations that would materially and adversely affect any Receivable. Unless the breach is cured by the last day of the second Collection Period following the discovery (or, if the Servicer so elects, the last day of the first Collection Period following the discovery), the Servicer is required to purchase any Receivable materially and adversely affected by the breach (an "Administrative Receivable") from the Trust at a price equal to the Administrative Purchase Payment for that Receivable. The "Administrative Purchase Payment" (1) for a Precomputed Receivable, will be equal to (a) the sum of (i) all remaining Scheduled Payments (plus any applicable yield maintenance payments), (ii) an amount equal to any reimbursements of Advances made by the Servicer with respect to the Precomputed Receivable from collections on or in respect of other Receivables and (iii) all past due Scheduled Payments for which an Advance has not been made, minus (b) all Payments Ahead in respect of the Precomputed Receivable held by the Servicer or on deposit in the Payahead Account and (2) for a Simple Interest Receivable, will be equal to its unpaid Principal Balance, plus interest thereon at a rate equal to the sum of the Interest Rate or Pass Through Rate specified in the related Sale and Servicing Agreement or Pooling and Servicing Agreement and the Servicing Fee Rate to the last day of the Collection Period relating to that purchase. Upon the purchase of any Administrative Receivable, the Servicer will for all purposes of the related Sale and Servicing Agreement or the Pooling and Servicing Agreement, as applicable, be deemed to have released all claims for the reimbursement of outstanding Advances made in respect of that Administrative Receivable. This purchase obligation will constitute the sole remedy available to the Certificateholders or the Trustee for any uncured breach by the Servicer.

If the Servicer determines that eventual payment in full of a Receivable is unlikely, the Servicer will follow its normal practices and procedures to recover all amounts due upon that Receivable, including repossessing and disposing of the related Financed Vehicle at a public or private sale, or taking any other action permitted by applicable law. We refer you to "Certain Legal Aspects of the Receivables."

INSURANCE ON FINANCED VEHICLES

Each Receivable requires the related Obligor to maintain specific levels and types of insurance coverage to protect the Financed Vehicle against losses. AHFC requires evidence of insurance coverage by the Obligors at the time of origination of the Receivables, but performs no verification of continued coverage after origination. AHFC will not be obligated to make payments to the Trust for any loss as to which third party insurance has not been maintained, except to the extent of its obligations under the related Purchase Agreement. Since the Obligors may select their own insurers to provide the requisite coverage, the specific terms of their policies may vary. AHFC will not be required to monitor the maintenance of insurance. A failure by an Obligor to maintain physical damage insurance will constitute a default under the related Receivable. We refer you to "The Receivables — Underwriting of Motor Vehicle Loans". In the event that the Obligor fails to maintain any required insurance and this failure results in a shortfall in amounts to be distributed to Noteholders which is not covered by amounts on deposit in the Reserve Fund or by subordination of payments on the certificates to the extent described in this prospectus, the Securityholders could suffer a loss on their investment.

COLLECTIONS

With respect to each Trust, the Servicer will deposit all payments on Receivables received from Obligors and all proceeds of Receivables collected during the collection period specified in the applicable prospectus supplement (each, a "Collection Period") into the Collection Account not later than two Business Days after receipt. However, so long as AHFC is the Servicer, if each condition to making monthly deposits as may be required by the related Sale and Servicing Agreement or Pooling and Servicing Agreement (including, the satisfaction of specified ratings criteria by AHFC and the absence of any Servicer Default) is satisfied, the Servicer may retain these amounts until the Business Day immediately preceding the related Payment Date. The Servicer will be entitled to withhold, or to be reimbursed from amounts otherwise payable into or on deposit in the Collection Account, amounts previously deposited in the Collection Account but later determined to have resulted from mistaken deposits or postings. Except in some circumstances described in the related Sale and Servicing Agreement or Pooling and Servicing Agreement, pending deposit into the Collection Account, collections may be employed by the Servicer at its own risk and for its own benefit and will not be segregated from its own funds.

The Servicer or the Seller, as the case may be, will remit the aggregate Warranty Purchase Payments and Administrative Purchase Payments of Receivables to be purchased from the Trust to the Collection Account on the Business Day immediately preceding the related Payment Date.

If the Servicer were unable to remit the funds as described above, Securityholders might incur a loss. To the extent set forth in the applicable prospectus supplement, the Servicer may, in order to satisfy the requirements described above, obtain a letter of credit or other security for the benefit of the related Trust to secure timely remittances of collections on the related Receivables and payment of the aggregate Warranty Purchase Payments and Administrative Purchase Payments with respect to Receivables required to be repurchased by the Seller or the Servicer, as applicable.

Collections on or in respect of a Receivable made during a Collection Period (including Warranty Purchase Payments and Administrative Purchase Payments) which are not late fees, extension fees or certain other similar fees or charges will be applied first to any outstanding Advances made by the Servicer with respect to the Receivable, and then to the related Scheduled Payment. Any collections on or in respect of a Receivable remaining after those applications will be considered an "Excess Payment". Excess Payments constituting a prepayment in full of Precomputed Receivables and any Excess Payments relating to Simple Interest Receivables will be applied as a prepayment in respect of the Receivable (each, a "Prepayment"). All other Excess Payments in respect of Precomputed Receivables will be held by the Servicer (or if the Servicer has not satisfied particular requirements, deposited in the Payahead Account), as a Payment Ahead.

ADVANCES

Unless otherwise provided in the related prospectus supplement, if the Scheduled Payment due on a Precomputed Receivable (other than an Administrative Receivable or a Warranty Receivable) is not received in full by the end of the month in which it is due, whether as the result of any extension granted to the Obligor or otherwise, the amount of Payments Ahead, if any, not previously applied with respect to the Precomputed Receivable, shall be applied by the Servicer to the extent of the shortfall and the Payments Ahead shall be reduced accordingly. If any shortfall remains, the Servicer will make an advance to the Trust in an amount equal to the shortfall (each, a "Precomputed Advance"). The Servicer will not be obligated to make a Precomputed Advance to the extent that it determines, in its sole discretion, that the Precomputed Advance will not be recovered from subsequent collections on or in respect of the related Precomputed Receivable. All Precomputed Advances shall be reimbursable to the Servicer, without interest, if and when a payment relating to a Receivable with respect to which a Precomputed Advance has previously been made is subsequently received (other than from Administrative Purchase Payments). Upon the determination by the Servicer that reimbursement from the preceding source is unlikely, it will be entitled to recover unreimbursed Precomputed Advances from collections on or in respect of other Precomputed Receivables.

In addition, if the Scheduled Payment on a Simple Interest Receivable (other than an Administrative Receivable or a Warranty Receivable) is not received in full by the end of the month in which it is due, the Servicer shall, subject to the limitations set forth below, advance to the Trust in an amount with respect to the Simple Interest Receivable equal to the product of the Principal Balance of the Simple Interest Receivable as of the first day of the related Collection Period and one-twelfth of its APR minus the amount of interest actually received on the Simple Interest Receivable during the related Collection Period (each, a "Simple Interest Advance", and together with the Precomputed Advances, the "Advances"). If a calculation results in a negative number, an amount equal to such negative amount shall be paid to the Servicer in reimbursement of outstanding Simple Interest Advances. In addition, in the event that a Simple Interest Receivable becomes a liquidated Receivable, the amount of accrued and unpaid interest thereon (but not including interest for the current Collection Period) shall, up to the amount of all outstanding Simple Interest Advances in respect thereof, be withdrawn from the related Collection Account and paid to the Servicer in reimbursement of the outstanding Simple Interest Advances. No advances of principal will be made with respect to Simple Interest Receivables. The Servicer will not be obligated to make a Simple Interest Advance (other than in respect of an interest shortfall arising from the prepayment of a Simple Interest Receivable) to the extent that it determines, in its sole discretion, that Simple Interest Advance will not be recovered from subsequent collections on or in respect of the related Simple Interest Receivable.

The Servicer will make all Advances by depositing into the related Collection Account an amount equal to the aggregate of the Precomputed Advances and Simple Interest Advances due in respect of a Collection Period on the Business Day immediately preceding the related Payment Date.

SERVICING COMPENSATION

Unless otherwise provided in the applicable prospectus supplement, the Servicer will be entitled to receive a basic servicing fee for each Collection Period in an amount equal to a specified percent per annum (as set forth in the applicable prospectus supplement, the "Servicing Fee Rate") of the Pool Balance as of the first day of the related Collection Period (the "Base Servicing Fee"). The Base Servicing Fee (together with any portion of the Base Servicing Fee that remains unpaid from prior Payment Dates) will be paid solely to the extent of amounts available for that purpose as set forth in the applicable prospectus supplement. However, the Base Servicing Fee will be paid prior to the payment of available amounts to the Noteholders or the Certificateholders of the given series.

Unless otherwise provided in the applicable prospectus supplement, the Servicer will also be entitled to collect and retain any late fees, prepayment charges and other administrative fees or similar charges allowed by applicable law with respect to the related Receivables and any interest earned during a Collection Period from the investment of monies in the Collection Account as additional servicing compensation (the "Supplemental Servicing Fee" and, together with the Base Servicing Fee, the "Total Servicing Fee"). Payments by or on behalf of Obligors will be allocated to scheduled payments and late fees and other charges in accordance with the Servicer's normal practices and procedures. In addition, the Servicer will be entitled to reimbursement from any given Trust for specified liabilities. The Servicer will be paid the Base Servicing Fee for each Collection Period on the Payment Date related to that Collection Period prior to the payment of interest on any class of notes or certificates. However, if each rating agency for a series of notes or certificates confirms that it will not reduce the rating of any class of notes or certificates in that series, as the case may be, the Base Servicing Fee in respect of a Collection Period (together with any portion of the Base Servicing Fee that remains unpaid from the prior Payment Dates) will be paid at the beginning of that Collection Period out of collections of interest on the related Receivables.

The Total Servicing Fee will compensate the Servicer for performing the functions of a third party servicer of motor vehicle receivables as an agent for the beneficial owner of those Receivables, including collecting and posting all payments, responding to inquiries of Obligors on the Receivables, investigating delinquencies, sending payment statements to Obligors, reporting tax information to Obligors, paying costs of collections and policing the collateral. The Total Servicing Fee also will compensate the Servicer for administering the particular Receivables Pool, including making Advances, accounting for collections and furnishing monthly statements to the related Trustee and Indenture Trustee with respect to payments. The Total Servicing Fee also will reimburse the Servicer for specified taxes, the fees of the related Trustee and Indenture Trustee, if any, accounting fees, outside auditor fees, data processing costs and other costs incurred in connection with administering the applicable Receivables Pool.

The "Pool Balance" will equal the aggregate Principal Balance of the Receivables. The "Principal Balance" of a Receivable as of any date will equal the original principal balance of the Receivable minus the sum of (i) in the case of a Precomputed Receivable, that portion of all Scheduled Payments due on or prior to that date allocable to principal, computed in accordance with the actuarial method, (ii) in the case of a Simple Interest Receivable, that portion of all Scheduled Payments actually received on or prior to that date allocable to principal, (iii) any Warranty Purchase Payment or Administrative Purchase Payment with respect to the Receivable allocable to principal (to the extent not included in clauses (i) and (ii) above and (iv) any Prepayments or other payments applied to reduce the unpaid principal balance of the Receivable (to the extent not included in clauses (i), (ii) and (iii) above).

YIELD SUPPLEMENT ACCOUNT; YIELD SUPPLEMENT AGREEMENT

Yield Supplement Account. A "Yield Supplement Account" may be established with respect to any class or series of Securities. The terms relating to any of Yield Supplement Account will be set forth in the applicable prospectus supplement. Each Yield Supplement Account will be designed to hold funds to be applied by the related Trustee or, if that Trust issues notes, the related Indenture Trustee, to provide payments to Securityholders in respect of Receivables that have APRs less than the sum of the Pass Through Rate or Interest Rate specified in the applicable prospectus supplement plus the Servicing Fee Rate specified in the applicable prospectus supplement (the "Required Rate"). Unless otherwise specified in the applicable prospectus supplement, each Yield Supplement Account will be maintained with the same entity with which the related Collection Account is maintained and will be created on the related Closing Date with an initial deposit in an amount and by the Seller or other person specified in the applicable prospectus supplement.

On each Payment Date, the related Trustee or Indenture Trustee will transfer to the Collection Account from monies on deposit in the Yield Supplement Account an amount specified in the applicable prospectus supplement (the "Yield Supplement Deposit") in respect of the Receivables having APRs less than the Required Rate for that Payment Date. Unless otherwise specified in the applicable prospectus supplement, amounts on deposit on any Payment Date in the Yield Supplement Account in excess of the "Required Yield Supplement Amount" specified in the applicable prospectus supplement, after giving effect to all payments to be made on that Payment Date, will be released to the Seller. The Seller or other person specified in the applicable prospectus supplement will not have any obligation after the related Closing Date to deposit any amounts into the Yield Supplement Account after the related Closing Date even if the amount on deposit in that account is less than the Required Yield Supplement Amount for any Payment Date. Monies on deposit in the Yield Supplement Account may be invested in Eligible Investments under the circumstances and in the manner described in the related Pooling and Servicing Agreement or Trust Agreement.

DISTRIBUTIONS ON THE SECURITIES

With respect to each series of Securities, beginning on the Payment Date specified in the applicable prospectus supplement, payments of principal of and interest (or, where applicable, of principal or interest only) on each class of those Securities entitled thereto will be made by the applicable Indenture Trustee to the Noteholders and by the applicable Trustee to the Certificateholders of that series. The timing, calculation, allocation, order, source, priorities of and requirements for all payments to each class of Noteholders and all payments to each class of Certificateholders of that series will be set forth in the applicable prospectus supplement.

With respect to each Trust, on each Payment Date, collections on the related Receivables will be withdrawn from the related Collection Account and will be paid to the Noteholders and/or Certificateholders to the extent provided in the applicable prospectus supplement. Credit enhancement, such as a Reserve Fund, may be available to cover any shortfalls in the amount available for payment to the Securityholders on that date to the extent specified in the applicable prospectus supplement. As more fully described in the applicable prospectus supplement,

1. payments of principal of a class of Securities of a given series will be subordinate to payments of interest on that class;
2. payments in respect of one or more classes of certificates of that series may be subordinate to payments in respect of notes, if any, of that series or other classes of certificates of that series; and
3. payments in respect of one or more classes of notes of that series may be subordinated to payments in respect of other classes of notes of that series.

CREDIT AND CASH FLOW ENHANCEMENT

The amounts and types of credit and cash flow enhancement arrangements and the applicable provider, with respect to each class of Securities of a given series, if any, will be set forth in the applicable prospectus supplement. If and to the extent provided in the applicable prospectus supplement, credit and cash flow enhancement may be in the form of subordination of one or more classes of Securities, Reserve Funds, over-collateralization, letters of credit, credit or liquidity facilities, surety bonds, guaranteed investment contracts, swaps or other interest rate protection agreements, repurchase obligations, yield supplement agreements, other agreements with respect to third party payments or other support, cash deposits or other arrangements that may be described in the applicable prospectus supplement or any combination of the foregoing. If specified in the applicable prospectus supplement, credit or cash flow enhancement for a class of Securities may cover one or more other classes of Securities of the same series, and credit or cash flow enhancement for a series of Securities may cover one or more other series of Securities.

The presence of a Reserve Fund and other forms of credit enhancement for the benefit of any class or series of Securities is intended to enhance the likelihood of receipt by the Securityholders of that class or series of the full amount of principal and interest due on those Securities and to decrease the likelihood that that Securityholders will experience losses. Credit or cash flow enhancement for a class or series of Securities will not provide protection against all risks of loss and will not guarantee repayment of the entire principal of and interest on those Securities. If losses occur which exceed the amount covered by any credit enhancement or which are not covered by any credit enhancement, Securityholders of any class or series will bear their allocable share of deficiencies, as described in the applicable prospectus supplement. In addition, if a form of credit enhancement covers more than one class or series of Securities, Securityholders of any of that class or series will be subject to the risk that that credit enhancement will be exhausted by the claims of Securityholders of other classes or series.

Reserve Fund. If provided in the applicable prospectus supplement, pursuant to the related Sale and Servicing Agreement or Pooling and Servicing Agreement, the Seller or a third party will establish for a series or class of Securities an account, as specified in the applicable prospectus supplement, which may be designated as a "Reserve Fund" (the "Reserve Fund"), which will be maintained with the related Trustee or Indenture Trustee, as applicable. Unless otherwise specified in the prospectus supplement, the Reserve Fund will be funded by an initial deposit by the Seller or a third party on the Closing Date in the amount set forth in the applicable prospectus supplement (the "Reserve Fund Initial Deposit"). To the extent provided in the applicable prospectus supplement, the amount on deposit in the Reserve Fund will be increased on each Payment Date thereafter up to the Specified Reserve Fund Balance (as defined in the applicable prospectus supplement) by the deposit in the Reserve Fund of the amount of collections on the related Receivables remaining on each Payment Date after all specified payments on that date are made. The applicable prospectus supplement will describe the circumstances and manner under which payments may be made out of the Reserve Fund, either to holders of the Securities covered by that prospectus supplement or to the Seller or a third party. Monies on deposit in the Reserve Fund may be invested in Eligible Investments under the circumstances and in the manner described in the related Sale and Servicing Agreement or the Pooling and Servicing Agreement.

Surety Bond. The prospectus supplement may provide that the Trust enter into agreements with an insurer such that the insurer may guarantee payments of principal and/or interest on the Securities. If, on the date so specified in the prospectus supplement, the amount on deposit in the Collection Account after giving effect to all amounts deposited to or payable from a Payahead Account, a prefunding account or a capitalized interest agreement with respect to the related Payment Date, is less than the sum of the Base Servicing Fee, and amounts due to Securityholders on the related Payment Date, the Trustee by delivering a notice to the insurer shall demand payment under the surety bond in an amount equal to the deficiency. The applicable prospectus supplement will describe the circumstances and manner under which payments may be made under the surety bond, either to Securityholders, or the Trustee or the Indenture Trustee, as the case may be.

Pre-Funding Feature. A Trust may enter into an agreement with the Seller, in which the Seller will sell additional Receivables to the Trust after the Closing Date. The transfer of Receivables to the Trust after the Closing Date is known as a pre-funding feature. Any subsequent Receivables will be required to conform to the requirements described in the related prospectus supplement. If a pre-funding feature is used, the Trustee will be required to deposit all or a portion of the proceeds of the sale of the Securities of the series in a segregated account. The subsequent Receivables will be transferred to the Trust in exchange for money released from that segregated account. Any transfer of Receivables must occur within a specified period, not to exceed one year. If a Trust elects federal income tax treatment as a grantor trust, the pre-funding period will be limited to three months. If all of the monies originally deposited in the segregated account are not used by the end of the specified period, all remaining monies will be applied as a mandatory prepayment of a designated class or classes of Securities.

Cash Collateral Account. The prospectus supplement may provide that upon the occurrence of an event of default by the Servicer, a segregated cash collateral account may be established as security for the Servicer's obligations under the Sale and Servicing Agreement or the Pool and Servicing Agreement, as the case may be.

NET DEPOSITS

As an administrative convenience, as long as specified conditions are satisfied, the Servicer will be permitted to make the deposit of collections, aggregate Advances and Administrative Purchase Payments for any Trust for or with respect to the related Collection Period net of payments to be made to the Servicer with respect to that Collection Period. The Servicer may cause to be made a single, net transfer to the Collection Account. The Servicer, however, will account to the Trustee, any Indenture Trustee, the Noteholders, if any, and the Certificateholders with respect to each Trust as if all deposits, payments and transfers were made individually. With respect to any Trust that issues both certificates and notes, if the related Payment Dates are not the same for all classes of Securities, all distributions, deposits or other remittances made on a Payment Date will be treated as having been distributed, deposited or remitted on the same Payment Date for the applicable Collection Period for purposes of determining other amounts required to be distributed, deposited or otherwise remitted on a Payment Date.

STATEMENTS TO TRUSTEES AND THE TRUST

On or prior to each Payment Date (each, a "Determination Date" to be specified in the applicable prospectus supplement), the Servicer will provide to the applicable Indenture Trustee, if any, and the applicable Trustee a statement setting forth with respect to a series of Securities substantially the same information that is required to be provided in the periodic reports provided to Securityholders of that series described under " — Statements to Securityholders" below.

STATEMENTS TO SECURITYHOLDERS

With respect to each series of Securities that includes notes, on or prior to each Payment Date, the Servicer will prepare and provide to the related Indenture Trustee a statement to be delivered to the related Noteholders on that Payment Date. In addition, on or prior to each Payment Date, the Servicer will prepare and provide to the related Trustee of each Trust, a statement to be delivered to the Certificateholders. Each statement to be delivered to Securityholders will include (to the extent applicable) the following information (and any other information so specified in the applicable prospectus supplement) as to the notes of that series and as to the certificates of that series with respect to that Payment Date:

1. the amount of the payment allocable to the principal amount of each class of those notes and to the Certificate Balance of each class of those certificates;
2. the amount of the payment allocable to interest on each class of Securities of that series;
3. the amount of the distribution allocable to the Yield Supplement Deposit, if any;
4. the Pool Balance as of the close of business on the last day of the related Collection Period after giving effect to payments allocated to principal reported under clause (1) above;
5. the amount of the total Servicing Fee paid to the Servicer with respect to the related Collection Period;
6. the Interest Rate or Pass Through Rate for the Interest Period relating to the succeeding Payment Date for any class of notes or certificates of that series with variable or adjustable rates;
7. the Noteholders' Interest Carryover Shortfall, the Noteholders' Principal Carryover Shortfall, the Certificateholders' Interest Carryover Shortfall and the Certificateholders' Principal Carryover Shortfall (each as defined in

the applicable prospectus supplement), if any, in each case as applicable to each class of Securities;

8. the Note Pool Factor for each class of those notes, and the Certificate Balance and the Certificate Pool Factor for each class of those certificates, each after giving effect to all payments reported under clause (1) above on that date;
9. the amount of non-recoverable Advances on that Payment Date;
10. the balance of any related Reserve Fund on that date, after giving effect to changes thereto on that date and the amount of those changes;
11. the amount of Trust fees and expenses;
12. the Available Amounts, as that term is defined in the prospectus supplement;
13. the amount available under the Servicer's letter of credit, surety bond or insurance policy (the "Servicer Letter of Credit") as provided in the Sale and Servicing Agreement, if any, and the amount as a percentage of the Pool Balance as of the last day of that Collection Period; and
14. payments to and from third party credit enhancement providers, if any.

Each amount set forth in subclauses (1), (2), (5) and (7) above will be expressed in the aggregate and as a dollar amount per $1,000 of the original principal amount of each class of notes or the Original Certificate Balance of each class of certificates, as the case may be.

Copies of the statements may be obtained by the Securityholders by delivering a request in writing addressed to the applicable Trustee at its address set forth in the applicable prospectus supplement.

Within the prescribed period of time for tax reporting purposes after the end of each calendar year during the term of each Trust, the applicable Trustee will mail to each person who at any time during that calendar year has been a Securityholder with respect to that Trust and received any payment a statement containing information for the purposes of that Securityholder's preparation of federal income tax returns. We refer you to "Material Income Tax Consequences."

EVIDENCE AS TO COMPLIANCE

Each Sale and Servicing Agreement and Pooling and Servicing Agreement will provide that a firm of independent public accountants will furnish to the related Trust and Indenture Trustee or Trustee, as applicable, annually a statement as to compliance in all material respects by the Servicer during the preceding twelve months (or, in the case of the first statement, from the applicable Closing Date, which may be longer than twelve months) with specified standards relating to the servicing of the applicable Receivables.

Each Sale and Servicing Agreement and Pooling and Servicing Agreement will also provide for delivery to the related Trust and Indenture Trustee or Trustee, as applicable, substantially simultaneously with the delivery of those accountants' statement referred to above, of a certificate signed by an officer of the Servicer stating that the Servicer has fulfilled its obligations under the Sale and Servicing Agreement or Pooling and Servicing Agreement, as applicable, throughout the preceding twelve months (or, in the case of the first certificate, from the Closing Date) in all material respects or, if there has been a default in the fulfillment of any obligation, describing each default. The Servicer has agreed to give each Indenture Trustee and each Trustee notice of specified Servicer Defaults under the related Sale and Servicing Agreement or Pooling and Servicing Agreement, as applicable.

Copies of the statements and certificates may be obtained by Securityholders by a request in writing addressed to the applicable Trustee.

CERTAIN MATTERS REGARDING THE SERVICER

Each Sale and Servicing Agreement and Pooling and Servicing Agreement will provide that AHFC may not resign from its obligations and duties as Servicer under those documents, except upon AHFC's determination that its performance of those duties is no longer permissible under applicable law. No resignation will become effective until the related Indenture Trustee or Trustee, as applicable, or a successor servicer has assumed AHFC's servicing obligations and duties under the related Sale and Servicing Agreement or Pooling and Servicing Agreement.

Each Sale and Servicing Agreement and Pooling and Servicing Agreement will further provide that neither the Servicer nor any of its directors, officers, employees or agents will be under any liability to the related Trust or the related Noteholders or Certificateholders for taking any action or for refraining from taking any action pursuant to the related Sale and Servicing Agreement or Pooling and Servicing Agreement or for errors in judgment; except that neither the Servicer nor any person will be protected against any liability that would otherwise be imposed by reason of willful misfeasance, bad faith or negligence in the performance of the Servicer's duties under that document or by reason of reckless disregard of its obligations and duties under that document. In addition, each Sale and Servicing Agreement and Pooling and Servicing Agreement will provide that the Servicer is not obligated to appear in, prosecute or defend any legal action that is not incidental to the Servicer's servicing responsibilities under the related Sale and Servicing Agreement or Pooling and Servicing Agreement and that, in its opinion, may cause it to incur any expense or liability. The Servicer may, however, undertake any reasonable action that it may deem necessary or desirable in respect of the related Sale and Servicing Agreement or Pooling and Servicing Agreement, the rights and duties of the parties thereto and the interests of the Securityholders under the applicable agreement. In that event, the legal expenses and costs of that action and any liability resulting therefrom will be expenses, costs and liabilities of the Servicer, and the Servicer will not be entitled to be reimbursed therefor.

Under the circumstances specified in each Sale and Servicing Agreement and Pooling and Servicing Agreement, any entity into which the Servicer may be merged or consolidated, or any entity resulting from any merger or consolidation to which the Servicer is a party, or any entity succeeding to all or substantially all of the business of the Servicer will be the successor of the Servicer under the related Sale and Servicing Agreement or Pooling and Servicing Agreement.

SERVICER DEFAULT

Except as otherwise provided in the related prospectus supplement, "Servicer Default" under each Sale and Servicing Agreement and Pooling and Servicing Agreement will consist of the following:

1. any failure by the Servicer to deposit in or credit to any Account any required payment or make the required payments therefrom and that failure continues unremedied for three Business Days after discovery thereof by the Servicer or after the giving of written notice of the failure to (a) the Servicer by the Trustee or the Indenture Trustee, as applicable or

   (b) the Servicer and the Trustee or the Indenture Trustee, as applicable, of written notice of the failure from not less than 25% of the voting interests of the most senior class of Securities then outstanding;

2. any failure by the Servicer (or the Seller, as long as AHFC is the Servicer) to duly observe or perform in any material respect any other covenants or agreements in the Sale and Servicing Agreement or the Pooling and Servicing Agreement, which failure materially and adversely affects the rights of the Securityholders, and which failure continues unremedied for 90 days after the giving of written notice of the failure to (a) the Servicer or the Seller, as the case may be, by the Trustee or the Indenture Trustee, as applicable, or (b) the Servicer or the Seller, as the case may be, and the Trustee or the Indenture Trustee by the holders of not less than 25% of the voting interests of the most senior class of Securities then outstanding; and

3. the occurrence of events of insolvency, readjustment of debt, marshalling of assets and liabilities or similar proceedings with respect to the Seller (as long as AHFC is the Servicer) Servicer indicating its insolvency, reorganization pursuant to bankruptcy proceedings or inability to pay its obligations (any of these events with respect to the Servicer being an "Insolvency Event").

RIGHTS UPON SERVICER DEFAULT

In the case of any Trust that has issued notes, unless otherwise provided in the related prospectus supplement, so long as a Servicer Default under a Sale and Servicing Agreement remains unremedied, the related Indenture Trustee or holders of notes of the related series evidencing not less than 25% of the principal amount of the most senior class of notes then outstanding may terminate all the rights and obligations of the Servicer under the Sale and Servicing Agreement, and at that time the Indenture Trustee or a successor servicer appointed by the Indenture Trustee will succeed to all the responsibilities, duties and liabilities of the Servicer under the Sale and Servicing Agreement and will be entitled to similar compensation arrangements. In the case of any Trust that has not issued notes, or the notes have been discharged in accordance with their terms, unless otherwise provided in the related prospectus supplement, as long as a Servicer Default under the related Sale and Servicing Agreement or Pool and Servicing Agreement remains unremedied, the related Trustee or holders of certificates of the related series evidencing not less than 25% of the principal amount of the certificates then outstanding (but excluding for purposes of that calculation and action all certificates held by the Seller, the Servicer or any of their affiliates), acting together as a single class, may terminate all the rights and obligations of the Servicer under the related Sale and Servicing Agreement or Pooling and Servicing Agreement, and at that time the Trustee or a successor servicer appointed by the Trustee will succeed to all the responsibilities, duties and liabilities of the Servicer in its capacity under the Sale and Servicing Agreement and will be entitled to similar compensation arrangements.

However, if a bankruptcy trustee or similar official has been appointed for the Servicer, and no Servicer Default other than the appointment of a bankruptcy trustee or similar official has occurred, that bankruptcy trustee or official may have the power to prevent that Indenture Trustee, those Noteholders, that Trustee or those Certificateholders, as applicable, from effecting a transfer of servicing as described above. If that Indenture Trustee or Trustee is unwilling or unable to so act, it may appoint, or petition a court of competent jurisdiction for the appointment of, a successor servicer with a net worth of at least $50,000,000 and whose regular business includes the servicing of motor vehicle and motorcycle receivables. The related Indenture Trustee or the Trustee, or any person appointed as successor servicer, will be the successor in all respects to the predecessor Servicer under the related Sale and Servicing Agreement or Pooling and Servicing Agreement and all references in the related Sale and Servicing Agreement or Pooling and Servicing Agreement to the Servicer shall apply to that successor servicer. The related Indenture Trustee or Trustee may make arrangements for compensation to be paid, but the compensation for the successor servicer may not be greater than the Base Servicing Fee under the related Sale and Servicing Agreement or Pooling and Servicing Agreement. Notwithstanding termination, the Servicer will be entitled to payment of specified amounts payable to it prior to the termination for services it rendered prior to the termination. Upon payment in full of the principal of and interest on the notes, the Certificateholders will succeed to the rights of the Noteholders with respect to removal of the Servicer.

WAIVER OF PAST DEFAULTS

With respect to each Trust that has issued notes, unless otherwise provided in the applicable prospectus supplement, (1) the holders of not less than a majority of the most senior class of Securities then outstanding or (2) in the case of any Servicer Default that does not adversely affect the related Indenture Trustee or the related Noteholders, the holders of certificates of that series (or relevant class or classes of certificates of the series) evidencing a majority of the aggregate Certificate Balance of those certificates then outstanding (but excluding for purposes of calculation and action all certificates held by the Seller, the Servicer or any of their affiliates), may, on behalf of all those Noteholders or Certificateholders, waive any default by the Servicer in the performance of its obligations under the related Sale and Servicing Agreement and its consequences, except a Servicer Default in making any required deposits to the related Collection Account in accordance with that Sale and Servicing Agreement. With respect to each Trust that has not issued notes, holders of certificates of that series evidencing a majority of the aggregate Certificate Balance of those certificates then outstanding (or relevant class or classes of certificates but excluding for purposes of calculation and action all certificates held by the Seller, the Servicer or any of their affiliates), may, on behalf of all those Certificateholders, waive any default by the Servicer in the performance of its obligations under the related Pooling and Servicing Agreement, except a Servicer Default in making any required deposits to the related Account in accordance with the related Pooling and Servicing Agreement. No waiver will impair those Noteholders' or Certificateholders' rights with respect to subsequent defaults.

AMENDMENT

Unless otherwise provided in the related prospectus supplement, each of the Transfer and Servicing Agreements may be amended by the parties to the related Agreements, without the consent of the related Noteholders or Certificateholders (a) to cure any ambiguity, correct or supplement any provision in the related Transfer and Servicing Agreement that may be inconsistent with any other provision in that agreement, or make any other provisions with respect to matters or questions arising under that agreement that are not inconsistent with the provisions of that agreement or (b) to change the formula for amounts required to be on deposit in a Reserve Fund, the remittance schedule for deposits to Accounts and the requirements to allow the Servicer to remit funds monthly provided that the amendment will not materially and adversely affect the interest of any Noteholder or certificateholder, in the case of amendments pursuant to clause (a) above, as evidenced by an opinion of counsel and in the case of amendments pursuant to clause (b) above, letters from the rating agencies that the amendment will not result in a downgrade of any notes.

Each of the Transfer and Servicing Agreements may also be amended by the parties to the related Agreement thereto with the consent of:

1. the holders of notes evidencing a majority of the principal amount of the then outstanding notes, if any, of the related series (or relevant class or classes of notes of the series); or
2. in the case of any amendment that does not adversely affect the related Indenture Trustee or the related Noteholders, the holders of the certificates of that series evidencing a majority of the outstanding Certificate Balance (or relevant class or classes of certificates of the series, but excluding for purposes of calculation and action all certificates held by the Seller, the Servicer or any

of their affiliates), for the purpose of adding any provisions to or changing in any manner or eliminating any of the provisions of the related Transfer and Servicing Agreement or of modifying in any manner the rights of those Noteholders or Certificateholders.

No amendment of a Transfer and Servicing Agreement, however, shall:

(A) increase or reduce in any manner the amount of, or accelerate or delay the timing of, collections of payments on the related Receivables or distributions that are required to be made for the benefit of those Noteholders or Certificateholders without the consent of each of the "adversely affected" Noteholder or Certificateholder; or

(B) reduce the aforesaid percentage of the principal amount of the then outstanding notes or certificates of that series which is required to consent to any amendment, without the consent of the holders of all the then outstanding notes or certificates of each affected class.

LIST OF SECURITYHOLDERS

Three or more holders of the certificates of any class in a series or one or more holders of those certificates of that class evidencing not less than 51% of the Certificate Balance of those certificates may, by written request to the related Trustee, obtain access to the list of all Certificateholders maintained by that Trustee for the purpose of communicating with other Certificateholders with respect to their rights under the related Trust Agreement or Pooling and Servicing Agreement or under those certificates.

No Transfer and Servicing Agreement will provide for the holding of annual or other meetings of Securityholders.

INSOLVENCY EVENT

Each Trust Agreement will provide that the related Trustee does not have the power to commence a voluntary proceeding in bankruptcy with respect to the related Trust without the unanimous prior approval of all Certificateholders (including the Seller) of that Trust and the delivery to that Trustee by each Certificateholder (including the Seller) of a certificate certifying that that Certificateholder reasonably believes that that Trust is insolvent.

PAYMENT OF NOTES

Upon the payment in full of all outstanding notes of a given series and the satisfaction and discharge of the related Indenture, the related Trustee will succeed to all the rights of the Indenture Trustee, and the Certificateholders of that series will succeed to all the rights of the Noteholders of that series, under the related Sale and Servicing Agreement, except as otherwise provided in the Sale and Servicing Agreement.

TERMINATION

The respective obligations of the Seller, the Servicer, AHFC (so long as AHFC has rights or obligations under the related Transfer and Servicing Agreement), the related Trustee and the related Indenture Trustee, as the case may be, pursuant to a Transfer and Servicing Agreement will terminate upon the earlier of:

- the maturity or other liquidation of the last Receivable and the disposition of any amounts received upon liquidation of any remaining Receivables;
- the payment to Securityholders of all amounts required to be paid to them pursuant to the related agreement; or
- the election by the Servicer to purchase the corpus of the Trust as described below.

The Trustee will give written notice of termination to each Securityholder of record. The final distribution to any Securityholder will be made only upon surrender and cancellation of that holder's Security at any office or agency of the Trustee specified in the notice of termination. Any funds remaining in the Trust, after the Trustee has taken measures to locate a Securityholder set forth in the related Transfer and Servicing Agreement and those measures have failed, will be distributed, subject to applicable law, to the Seller.

Unless otherwise provided in the applicable prospectus supplement, in order to avoid excessive administrative expense, the Servicer will have the option to purchase from each Trust, as of the end of any applicable Collection Period, if the then outstanding Pool Balance with respect to the Receivables held by that Trust is 10% or less of the Pool Balance as of the related Cutoff Date, the corpus of the Trust at a price equal to the aggregate Administrative Purchase Payments for the Receivables (including Receivables that became defaulted receivables in the Collection Period preceding the Payment Date on which that purchase is effected) (less liquidation expenses). The related Trustee and related Indenture Trustee, if any, will give written notice of termination to each Securityholder.

Upon termination of any Trust, the assets of that Trust will be liquidated and the proceeds from any liquidation (and amounts held in related Accounts) will be applied to pay the notes and the certificates of the related series in full, to the extent of amounts available.

As more fully described in the applicable prospectus supplement, any outstanding notes of the related series will be redeemed concurrently with any of the events specified above and the subsequent payment to the related Certificateholders of all amounts required to be paid to them pursuant to the applicable Trust Agreement or Pooling and Servicing Agreement will effect early retirement of the certificates of that series.

ADMINISTRATION AGREEMENT

AHFC, in its capacity as administrator (the "Administrator"), will enter into an agreement (as amended and supplemented from time to time, an "Administration Agreement") with each Trust that issues notes and the related Indenture Trustee pursuant to which the Administrator will agree, to the extent provided in that Administration Agreement, to provide the notices and to perform other administrative obligations required by the related Indenture. As compensation for the performance of the Administrator's obligations under the applicable Administration Agreement and as reimbursement for its expenses related thereto, the Administrator will be entitled to a monthly administration fee in an amount that may be set forth in the applicable prospectus supplement (the "Administration Fee"), which fee will be paid by the Servicer.

CERTAIN LEGAL ASPECTS OF THE RECEIVABLES

GENERAL

The transfer of the Receivables to the applicable Trustee, the perfection of the security interests in the Receivables and the enforcement of rights to realize on the Financed Vehicles as collateral for the Receivables are subject to a number of federal and state laws, including the UCC as in effect in various states. The Servicer and the Seller will take the action described below to perfect the rights of the applicable Trustee in the Receivables. If another party purchases (including the taking of a security interest in) the Receivables for new value in the ordinary course of its business, without actual knowledge of the Trust's interest, and takes possession of the Receivables, that purchaser would acquire an interest in the Receivables superior to the interest of the Trust.

SECURITY INTERESTS

General. In states in which retail installment sale contracts such as the Receivables evidence the credit sale of motor vehicles by dealers to obligors, the contracts also constitute personal property security agreements and include grants of security interests in the vehicles under the applicable UCC. Perfection of security interests in financed motor vehicles is generally governed by the motor vehicle registration laws of the state in which the vehicle is located. In most states, a security interest in a motor vehicle is perfected by obtaining possession of the certificate of title to the motor vehicle or notation of the secured party's lien on the motor vehicle's certificate of title.

All retail installment sale contracts acquired by AHFC from Dealers name AHFC as obligee or assignee and as the secured party. AHFC also takes all actions necessary under the laws of the state in which the related Financed Vehicle is located to perfect its security interest in that Financed Vehicle, including, where applicable, having a notation of its lien recorded on the related certificate of title and obtaining possession of that certificate of title. Because AHFC continues to service the contracts as Servicer under the Sale and Servicing Agreement or the Pooling and Servicing Agreement, as applicable, the Obligors on the contracts will not be notified of the sale from AHFC to the Seller or the sale from the Seller to the related Trust.

Perfection. Pursuant to the related Purchase Agreement, AHFC will sell and assign its security interest in the Financed Vehicles to the Seller and, with respect to each Trust, pursuant to the related Sale and Servicing Agreement or Pooling and Servicing Agreement, as applicable, the Seller will assign its security interest in the Financed Vehicles to that Trust. However, because of the administrative burden and expense, none of AHFC, the Seller or the related Trustee will amend any certificate of title to identify that Trust as the new secured party on that certificate of title relating to a Financed Vehicle. However, UCC financing statements with respect to the transfer to the Seller of AHFC's security interest in the Financed Vehicles and the transfer to the Trustee of the Seller's security interest in the Financed Vehicles will be filed. In addition, the Servicer will continue to hold any certificates of title relating to the Financed Vehicles in its possession as custodian for that Trust pursuant to the related Sale and Servicing Agreement or Pooling and Servicing Agreement. We refer you to "Description of the Transfer and Servicing Agreements — Sales and Assignment of Receivables."

In most states, an assignment such as that under each Purchase Agreement or each Sale and Servicing Agreement or Pooling and Servicing Agreement is an effective conveyance of a security interest without amendment of any lien noted on a motor vehicle's certificate of title, and the assignee succeeds to the assignor's rights as secured party. Although re-registration of the motor vehicle is not necessary to convey a perfected security interest in the Financed Vehicles to the Trust, because the Trust will not be listed as lienholder on the certificates of title, the security interest of that Trust in the vehicle could be defeated through fraud or negligence. In those states, in the absence of fraud or forgery by the motor vehicle owner or the Servicer or administrative error by state or local agencies, the notation of AHFC's lien on the certificates of title will be sufficient to protect that Trust against the rights of subsequent purchasers of a Financed Vehicle or subsequent lenders who take a security interest in a Financed Vehicle. In each Purchase Agreement, AHFC will represent and warrant, and in each Sale and Servicing Agreement or Pooling and Servicing Agreement, the Seller will represent and warrant, that it has taken all action necessary to obtain a perfected security interest in each Financed Vehicle. If there are any Financed Vehicles as to which AHFC failed to obtain and assign to the Seller a perfected security interest, the security interest of the Seller would be subordinate to, among others, subsequent purchasers of the Financed Vehicles and holders of perfected security interests in the Financed Vehicles. To the extent that failure has a material and adverse effect on the Trust's interest in the related Receivables, however, it would constitute a breach of the warranties of AHFC under the related Purchase Agreement or the Seller under the related Sale and Servicing Agreement or Pooling and Servicing Agreement. Accordingly, pursuant to the related Sale and Servicing Agreement or Pooling and Servicing Agreement, the Seller would be required to repurchase the related Receivable from the Trust and, pursuant to the related Purchase Agreement, AHFC would be required to purchase that Receivable from the Seller, in each case unless the breach was cured. Pursuant to each Sale and Servicing Agreement and Pooling and Servicing Agreement, the Seller will assign to the related Trust its rights to cause AHFC to purchase that Receivable under the related Purchase Agreement. We refer you to "Description of the Transfer and Servicing Agreements — Sale and Assignment of Receivables" and "Risk Factors — Interests of Other Persons in the Receivables and Financed Vehicles Could be Superior to the Trust's Interest, which May Result in Reduced Payments on Your Securities."

Continuity of Perfection. Under the laws of most states, the perfected security interest in a motor vehicle would continue for four months after the motor vehicle is moved to a state that is different from the one in which it is initially registered and thereafter until the owner re-registers the motor vehicle in the new state. A majority of states generally require surrender of a certificate of title to re-register a motor vehicle. In those states (such as California) that require a secured party to hold possession of the certificate of title to maintain perfection of the security interest, the secured party would learn of the re-registration through the request from the obligor under the related installment sales contract to surrender possession of the certificate of title. In the case of motor vehicles registered in states providing for the notation of a lien on the certificate of title but not possession by the secured party (such as Texas), the secured party would receive notice of surrender from the state of re-registration if the security interest is noted on the certificate of title. Thus, the secured party would have the opportunity to re-perfect its security interest in the vehicle in the state of relocation. However, these procedural safeguards will not protect the secured party if through fraud, forgery or administrative error, the debtor somehow procures a new certificate of title that does not list the secured party's lien. Additionally, in states that do not require a certificate of title for registration of a motor vehicle, re-registration could defeat perfection. In the ordinary course of servicing the Receivables, AHFC will take steps to effect re-perfection upon receipt of notice of re-registration or information from the Obligor as to relocation. Similarly, when an Obligor sells a Financed Vehicle, AHFC must surrender possession of the certificate of title or will receive notice as a result of its lien noted on the certificate of title and accordingly will have an opportunity to require satisfaction of the related Receivable before release of the lien. Under each Sale and Servicing Agreement and Pooling and Servicing Agreement, the Servicer will be obligated to take appropriate steps, at the Servicer's expense, to maintain perfection of security interests in the Financed Vehicles and will be obligated to purchase the related Receivable if it fails to do so and that failure has a material and adverse effect on the Trust's interest in the Receivable.

Priority of Liens Arising by Operation of Law. Under the laws of most states (including California), liens for repairs performed on a motor vehicle and liens for unpaid taxes take priority over even a perfected security interest in a Financed Vehicle. The Code also grants priority to specified federal tax liens over the lien of a secured party. The laws of some states and federal law permit the confiscation of motor vehicles by governmental authorities under some circumstances if used in unlawful activities, which may result in the loss of a secured party's perfected security interest in the confiscated vehicle. AHFC will represent and warrant to the Seller in each Purchase Agreement, and the Seller will represent and warrant to the Trust in each Sale and Servicing Agreement and Pooling and Servicing Agreement, that, as of the related Closing Date, each security interest in a Financed Vehicle is prior to all other present liens (other than tax liens and other liens that arise by operation of law) upon and security interests in that Financed Vehicle. However, liens for repairs or taxes could arise, or the confiscation of a Financed Vehicle could occur, at any time during the term of a Receivable. No notice will be given to the Trustee, any Indenture Trustee, any Noteholders or any Certificateholders in respect of a given Trust if a lien arises or confiscation occurs that would not give rise to the Seller's repurchase obligation under the related Sale and Servicing Agreement or Pooling and Servicing Agreement or AHFC's repurchase obligation under the related Purchase Agreement.

REPOSSESSION

In the event of default by an obligor, the holder of the related retail installment sale contract has all the remedies of a secured party under the UCC, except where specifically limited by other state laws. Among the UCC remedies, the secured party has the right to perform repossession by self-help means, unless it would constitute a breach of the peace or is otherwise limited by applicable state law. Unless a motor vehicle financed by AHFC is voluntarily surrendered, self-help repossession is the method employed by AHFC in most states and is accomplished simply by retaking possession of the Financed Vehicle. In cases where an obligor objects or raises a defense to repossession, or if otherwise required by applicable state law, a court order must be obtained from the appropriate state court, and that vehicle must then be recovered in accordance with that order. In some jurisdictions, the secured party is required to notify that obligor of the default and the intent to repossess the collateral and to give that obligor a time period within which to cure the default prior to repossession. In some states, an obligor has the right to reinstate its contract and recover the collateral by paying the delinquent installments and other amounts due.

NOTICE OF SALE; REDEMPTION RIGHTS

In the event of default by an obligor under a retail installment sale contract, some jurisdictions require that the obligor be notified of the default and be given a time period within which to cure the default prior to repossession. Generally, this right of cure may only be exercised on a limited number of occasions during the term of the related contract.

The UCC and other state laws require the secured party to provide an obligor with reasonable notice of the date, time and place of any public sale and/or the date after which any private sale of the collateral may be held. In most states, an obligor has the right to redeem the collateral prior to actual sale by paying the secured party the unpaid principal balance of the obligation, accrued interest on the obligation plus reasonable expenses for repossessing, holding and preparing the collateral for disposition and arranging for its sale, plus, in some jurisdictions, reasonable attorneys' fees. In some states, an obligor has the right to redeem the collateral prior to actual sale by payment of delinquent installments or the unpaid balance.

DEFICIENCY JUDGMENTS AND EXCESS PROCEEDS

The proceeds of resale of motor vehicles generally will be applied first to the expenses of resale and repossession and then to the satisfaction of the indebtedness. While some states impose prohibitions or limitations on deficiency judgments if the net proceeds from resale do not cover the full amount of the indebtedness, a deficiency judgment can be sought in those states that do not prohibit or limit those judgments. In addition to the notice requirement described above, the UCC requires that every aspect of the sale or other disposition, including the method, manner, time, place and terms, be "commercially reasonable." Generally, courts have held that when a sale is not "commercially reasonable," the secured party loses its right to a deficiency judgment. However, the deficiency judgment would be a personal judgment against the obligor for the shortfall, and a defaulting obligor can be expected to have very little capital or sources of income available following repossession. Therefore, in many cases, it may not be useful to seek a deficiency judgment or, if one is obtained, it may be settled at a significant discount or be uncollectible. In addition, the UCC permits the obligor or other interested party to recover for any loss caused by noncompliance with the provisions of the UCC. Also, prior to a sale, the UCC permits the obligor or other interested person to prohibit the secured party from disposing of the collateral if it is established that the secured party is not proceeding in accordance with the "default" provisions under the UCC.

Occasionally, after resale of a repossessed vehicle and payment of all expenses and indebtedness, there is a surplus of funds. In that case, the UCC requires the creditor to remit the surplus to any holder of a subordinate lien with respect to that vehicle or if no lienholder exists, the UCC requires the creditor to remit the surplus to the obligor.

CERTAIN BANKRUPTCY CONSIDERATIONS

In structuring the transactions contemplated by this prospectus, the Seller has taken steps that are intended to make it unlikely that the voluntary or involuntary application for relief by AHFC, under the United States Bankruptcy Code or similar applicable state laws (collectively, "Insolvency Laws"), will result in consolidation of the assets and liabilities of the Seller with those of AHFC. These steps include the creation of the Seller as a wholly owned, limited purpose subsidiary pursuant to articles of incorporation and bylaws containing limitations (including restrictions on the nature of the Seller's business and on its ability to commence a voluntary case or proceeding under any Insolvency Law without the unanimous affirmative vote of all of its directors). In addition, to the extent that the Seller granted a security interest in the Receivables to the Trust, and that interest was validly perfected before the bankruptcy or insolvency of AHFC and was not taken or granted in contemplation of insolvency or with the intent to hinder, delay or defraud AHFC or its creditors, that security interest should not be subject to avoidance, and payments to the Trust with respect to the Receivables should not be subject to recovery by a creditor or trustee in bankruptcy of AHFC.

However, delays in payments on the Securities and possible reductions in the amount of those payments could occur if:

(A) a court were to conclude that the assets and liabilities of the Seller should be consolidated with those of AHFC in the event of the application of applicable Insolvency Laws to AHFC;

(B) a filing were made under any Insolvency Law by or against the Seller; or

(C) an attempt were to be made to litigate any of the foregoing issues.

On each Closing Date, counsel to the Seller will give an opinion to the effect that, based on a reasoned analysis of analogous case law (although there is no precedent based on directly similar facts), and, subject to facts, assumptions and qualifications specified in the opinion and applying the principles set forth in the opinion, in the event of a voluntary or involuntary bankruptcy case in respect of AHFC under Title 11 of the United States Bankruptcy Code at a time when AHFC was insolvent, the property of the Seller would not properly be substantively consolidated with the property of the estate of AHFC. Among other things, that opinion will assume that each of the Seller and AHFC will follow specified procedures in the conduct of its affairs, including maintaining records and books of account separate from those of the other, refraining from commingling its assets with those of the other, and refraining from holding itself out as having agreed to pay, or being liable for, the debts of the other. The Seller and AHFC intend to follow these and other procedures related to maintaining their separate corporate identities. However, there can be no assurance that a court would not conclude that the assets and liabilities of the Seller should be consolidated with those of AHFC.

AHFC will warrant in each Purchase Agreement that the sale of the related Receivables by it to the Seller is a valid sale. Notwithstanding the foregoing, if AHFC were to become a debtor in a bankruptcy case, a court could take the position that the sale of Receivables to the Seller should instead be treated as a pledge of those Receivables to secure a borrowing of AHFC. If a court were to reach such conclusions, or a filing were made under any Insolvency Law by or against the Seller, or if an attempt were made to litigate any of the foregoing issues, delays in payments on the certificates (and possible reductions in the amount of payments) could occur. In addition, if the transfer of Receivables to the Seller is treated as a pledge instead of a sale, a tax or government lien on the property of AHFC arising before the transfer of a Receivable to the Seller may have priority over the Seller's interest in that Receivable. Also, while AHFC is the Servicer, cash collections on the Receivables may be commingled with general funds of AHFC and, in the event of a bankruptcy of AHFC, a court may conclude that the Trust does not have a perfected interest in those collections.

AHFC and the Seller will treat the transactions described in this prospectus as a sale of the Receivables to the Seller, so that the automatic stay provisions of the United States Bankruptcy Code should not apply to the Receivables if AHFC were to become a debtor in a bankruptcy case.

CONSUMER PROTECTION LAWS

Numerous federal and state consumer protection laws and related regulations impose substantial requirements upon lenders and servicers involved in consumer finance. These laws include the Truth-in-Lending Act, the Equal Credit Opportunity Act, the Federal Trade Commission Act, the Fair Credit Billing Act, the Fair Credit Reporting Act, the Fair Debt Collection Practices Act, the Magnuson-Moss Warranty Act, the Federal Reserve Board's Regulations B and Z, the Soldiers' and Sailors' Civil Relief Act of 1940, the Texas Consumer Credit Code, state adoptions of the National Consumer Act and of the Uniform Consumer Credit Code and state motor vehicle retail installment sales acts and other similar laws. Also, state laws impose finance charge ceilings and other restrictions on consumer transactions and require contract disclosures in addition to those required under federal law. These requirements impose specific statutory liabilities upon creditors who fail to comply with their provisions. In some cases, this liability could affect an assignee's ability to enforce consumer finance contracts such as the Receivables.

The so-called "Holder-in-Due-Course" Rule of the Federal Trade Commission (the "FTC Rule"), the provisions of which are generally duplicated by the Uniform Consumer Credit Code, other statutes or the common law in some states, has the effect of subjecting a seller (and specified creditors and their assignees) in a consumer credit transaction to all claims and defenses that the obligor in the transaction could assert against the seller of the goods. Liability under the FTC Rule is limited to the amounts paid by the obligor under the contract, and the holder of the contract may also be unable to collect any balance remaining due under that contract from the obligor. The FTC Rule is generally duplicated by the Uniform Consumer Credit Code, other state statutes or the common law in certain states.

Most of the Receivables will be subject to the requirements of the FTC Rule. Accordingly, each Trust, as holder of the related Receivables, will be subject to any claims or defenses that the purchaser of the applicable Financed Vehicle may assert against the seller of the related Financed Vehicle. As to each Obligor, these claims are limited to a maximum liability equal to the amounts paid by the Obligor on the related Receivable. Under most state motor vehicle dealer licensing laws, sellers of motor vehicles are required to be licensed to sell motor vehicles at retail sale. Furthermore, federal odometer regulations promulgated under the Motor Vehicle Information and Cost Savings Act require that all sellers of new and used vehicles furnish a written statement signed by the seller certifying the accuracy of the odometer reading. If the seller is not properly licensed or if a written odometer disclosure statement was not provided to the purchaser of the related Financed Vehicle, an obligor may be able to assert a defense against the seller of the vehicle. If an Obligor were successful in asserting any of those claims or defenses, that claim or defense would constitute a breach of the Seller's representations and warranties under the related Sale and Servicing Agreement or Pooling and Servicing Agreement and a breach of AHFC's warranties under the related Purchase Agreement and would, if the breach materially and adversely affects the Receivable or the interests of the Securityholders, create an obligation of the Seller and AHFC, respectively, to repurchase the Receivable unless the breach is cured. We refer you to "Description of the Transfer and Servicing Agreements — Sale and Assignment of Receivables."

Courts have applied general equitable principles to secured parties pursuing repossession and litigation involving deficiency balances. These equitable principles may have the effect of relieving an obligor from some or all of the legal consequences of a default.

In several cases, consumers have asserted that the self-help remedies of secured parties under the UCC and related laws violate the due process protections provided under the 14th Amendment to the Constitution of the United States. Courts have generally upheld the notice provisions of the UCC and related laws as reasonable or have found that the repossession and resale by the creditor do not involve sufficient state action to afford constitutional protection to borrowers.

From time to time, AHFC has been involved in litigation under consumer protection laws. In addition, substantially all of the motor vehicle contracts originated by AHFC in California after 1990 (the "California Contracts") provided that the contract may be rescinded by the related Dealer if the Dealer is unable to assign the contract to a lender within ten days of the date of the contract. As of the date of this prospectus, the ten-day rescission period had run in respect of all of the California Contracts in which the rescission provision appears. Although there is authority, which is not binding upon any court, providing that a conditional sale contract containing such a provision does not comply with California law and would render the contract unenforceable, to the Seller's and AHFC's knowledge, the issue has not been presented before any California court. On the Closing Date, the Seller will receive an opinion of counsel to the effect that all of the California Contracts are enforceable under California law and applicable federal laws.

AHFC and the Seller will represent and warrant under each Purchase Agreement and each Sale and Servicing Agreement and Pooling and Servicing Agreement, as applicable, that each Receivable complies with all requirements of law in all material respects. Accordingly, if an Obligor has a claim against a Trust for violation of any law and that claim materially and adversely affects that Trust's interest in a Receivable, that violation would constitute a breach of the representations and warranties of AHFC under the Purchase Agreement and the Seller under the related Sale and Servicing Agreement or Pooling and

Servicing Agreement and would create an obligation of AHFC and the Seller to repurchase the Receivable unless the breach is cured. We refer you to "Description of the Transfer and Servicing Agreements — Sale and Assignment of Receivables."

FORFEITURE FOR DRUG, RICO AND MONEY LAUNDERING VIOLATIONS

Federal law provides that property purchased or improved with assets derived from criminal activity or otherwise tainted, or used in the commission of certain offenses can be seized and ordered forfeited to the United States of America. The offenses which can trigger such a seizure and forfeiture include, among others, violations of the Racketeer Influenced and Corrupt Organizations Act, the Bank Secrecy Act, the anti money laundering laws and regulations, including the USA Patriot Act of 2001 and the regulations issued pursuant to that Act, as well as the narcotic drug laws. In many instances, the United States may seize the property even before a conviction occurs.

OTHER LIMITATIONS

In addition to the laws limiting or prohibiting deficiency judgments, numerous other statutory provisions, including federal bankruptcy laws and related state laws, may interfere with or affect the ability of a secured party to realize upon collateral or to enforce a deficiency judgment. For example, in a Chapter 13 proceeding under the federal bankruptcy law, a court may prevent a creditor from repossessing a motor vehicle and, as part of the rehabilitation plan, reduce the amount of the secured indebtedness to the market value of the vehicle at the time of bankruptcy (as determined by the court), leaving the creditor as a general unsecured creditor for the remainder of the indebtedness. A bankruptcy court may also reduce the monthly payments due under a contract or change the rate of interest and time of repayment of the indebtedness.

Under the terms of the Soldiers' and Sailors' Relief Act of 1940 (the "Relief Act"), an Obligor who enters the military service after the origination of that Obligor's Receivable (including an Obligor who is a member of the National Guard or is in reserve status at the time of the origination of the Obligor's Receivable and is later called to active duty) may not be charged interest above an annual rate of 6% during the period of that Obligor's active duty status, unless a court orders otherwise upon application of the lender. In addition, some states, including California, allow members of its national guard to extend payments on any contract obligation if called into active service by the Governor for a period exceeding 7 days. It is possible that the foregoing could have an effect on the ability of the Servicer to collect the full amount of interest owing on some of the Receivables. In addition, both the Relief Act and the laws of some states, including California, New York and New Jersey, imposes limitations that would impair the ability of the Servicer to repossess the released Financed Vehicle during the Obligor's period of active duty status. Thus, if that Receivable goes into default, there may be delays and losses occasioned by the inability to exercise the Trust's rights with respect to the Receivable and the related Financed Vehicle in a timely fashion.

Any shortfall pursuant to either of the two preceding paragraphs, to the extent not covered by amounts payable to the Securityholders from amounts on deposit in the related Reserve Fund or from coverage provided under any other credit enhancement mechanism, could result in losses to the Securityholders.

MATERIAL INCOME TAX CONSEQUENCES

The following general discussion of the anticipated material federal income tax consequences of the purchase, ownership and disposition of the notes and the certificates of any series, to the extent it relates to matters of law or legal conclusions with respect thereto, represents the opinion of tax counsel to each Trust with respect to the related series on the material matters associated with those consequences, subject to the qualifications set forth in this prospectus. "Tax Counsel" with respect to each Trust will be specified in the applicable prospectus supplement. The summary does not purport to deal with federal income tax consequences applicable to all categories of investors, some of which may be subject to special rules. For example, it does not discuss the tax treatment of Noteholders or Certificateholders that are insurance companies, regulated investment companies or dealers in securities. Moreover, there are no cases or Internal Revenue Service ("IRS") rulings on similar transactions involving both debt and equity interests issued by a trust with terms similar to those of the notes and the certificates. As a result, the IRS may disagree with all or a part of the discussion below. It is suggested that prospective investors consult their own tax advisors in determining the federal, state, local, foreign and any other tax consequences to them of the purchase, ownership and disposition of the notes and the certificates.

The following summary is based upon current provisions of the Internal Revenue Code of 1986, as amended (the "Code"), the Treasury regulations promulgated under the Code and judicial or ruling authority, all of which are subject to change, which change may be retroactive. Each Trust will be provided with an opinion of Tax Counsel regarding the federal income tax matters discussed below. An opinion of Tax Counsel, however, is not binding on the IRS or the courts. No ruling on any of the issues discussed below will be sought from the IRS. For purposes of the following summary, references to the Trust, the notes, the certificates and related terms, parties and documents shall be deemed to refer to each Trust and the notes, certificates and related terms, parties and documents applicable to that Trust. The federal income tax consequences to Certificateholders will vary depending on whether the Trust is treated as a partnership (or a "disregarded entity," in the event that there is a single beneficial owner of the Certificates) or a grantor trust under the Code. The prospectus supplement for each series of certificates will specify whether the Trust will be treated as a partnership (or a disregarded entity) or a grantor trust.

TAX TREATMENT OF OWNER TRUSTS

TAX CHARACTERIZATION OF THE TRUST

The following general discussion of the anticipated federal income tax consequences of the purchase, ownership and disposition of the notes and the certificates of a Trust nominally referred to as an "owner trust" in the applicable prospectus supplement (an "Owner Trust"), to the extent it relates to matters of law or legal conclusions with respect thereto, represents the opinion of Tax Counsel to each Owner Trust with respect to the related series on the material matters associated with those consequences, subject to the qualifications set forth in this prospectus. In addition, Tax Counsel has prepared or reviewed the statements in this prospectus under the heading "Material Income Tax Consequences — Tax Treatment of Owner Trusts," and is of the opinion that those statements are correct in all material respects. Those statements are intended as an explanatory discussion of the related tax matters affecting investors generally, but do not purport to furnish information in the level of detail or with the attention to an investor's specific tax circumstances that would be provided by an investor's own tax advisor. Accordingly, it is suggested that each investor consult its own tax advisor with regard to the tax consequences to it of investing in notes or certificates.

Tax Counsel will deliver its opinion that an Owner Trust will not be an association (or publicly traded partnership) taxable as a corporation for federal income tax purposes. This opinion will be based on the assumption that the terms of the Related Documents will be complied with, and on Tax Counsel's conclusion that the nature of the income of the Trust will exempt it from the rule that some publicly traded partnerships are taxable as corporations.

If the Owner Trust were taxable as a corporation for federal income tax purposes, the Trust would be subject to corporate income tax on its taxable income. The Trust's taxable income would include all its income on the Receivables, possibly reduced by its interest expense on the notes. Any corporate income tax could materially reduce cash available to make payments on the notes and the certificates, and Certificateholders could be liable for any tax of this type that is not paid by the Trust.

TAX CONSEQUENCES TO OWNERS OF THE NOTES

Treatment of the Notes as Indebtedness. The Seller and any Noteholders will agree, and the beneficial owners of the notes (the "Note Owners") will agree by their purchase of notes, to treat the notes as debt for federal income tax purposes. Except as otherwise provided in the related prospectus supplement, Tax Counsel will deliver its opinion that the notes will be classified as debt for federal income tax purposes. The discussion below assumes this characterization of the notes is correct.

OID, Indexed Securities, Etc. The discussion below assumes that all payments on the notes are denominated in U.S. dollars, and that the notes are not Indexed

Securities or Strip Notes (as defined in this prospectus). Moreover, the discussion assumes that the interest formula for the notes meets the requirements for "qualified stated interest" under Treasury regulations (the "OID regulations") relating to original issue discount ("OID"), and that any OID on the notes (i.e., any excess of the principal amount of the notes over their issue price) does not exceed a de minimis amount (i.e., 1/4% of their principal amount multiplied by the number of full years included in determining their term), all within the meaning of the OID regulations. In determining whether any OID on the notes is de minimis, the Seller expects to use a reasonable assumption regarding prepayments (a "Prepayment Assumption") to determine the weighted average maturity of the notes. If these conditions are not satisfied with respect to any given series of notes, additional tax considerations with respect to those notes will be disclosed in the applicable prospectus supplement.

Interest Income on the Notes. Based on the above assumptions, except as discussed in the following paragraph, the notes will not be considered issued with OID. The stated interest on the notes will be taxable to a Note Owner as ordinary interest income when received or accrued in accordance with that Note Owner's method of tax accounting. Under the OID regulations, the Note Owner of a note issued with a de minimis amount of OID must include that OID in income, on a pro rata basis, as principal payments are made on the note. A purchaser who buys a note for more or less than its principal amount will generally be subject, respectively, to the premium amortization or market discount rules of the Code.

The Note Owner of a note that has a fixed maturity date of not more than one year from the issue date of that Note (a "Short-Term Note") may be subject to special rules. An accrual basis Note Owner of a Short-Term Note (and some cash method Note Owners, including regulated investment companies, as set forth in Section 1281 of the Code) generally would be required to report interest income as interest accrues on a straight-line basis or under a constant yield method over the term of each interest period. Other cash basis Note Owners of a Short-Term Note would, in general, be required to report interest income as interest is paid (or, if earlier, upon the taxable disposition of the Short-Term Note). However, a cash basis Note Owner of a Short-Term Note reporting interest income as it is paid may be required to defer a portion of any interest expense otherwise deductible on indebtedness incurred to purchase or carry the Short-Term Note until the taxable disposition of the Short-Term Note. A cash basis Note Owner that is not required to report interest income as it accrues under Section 1281 may elect to accrue interest income on all nongovernment debt obligations with a term of one year or less, in which case the Note Owner would not be subject to the interest expense deferral rule referred to in the preceding sentence. Certain special rules apply if a Short-Term Note is purchased for more or less than its principal amount.

Sale or Other Disposition. If a Note Owner sells a note, the Note Owner will recognize gain or loss in an amount equal to the difference between the amount realized on the sale and the Note Owner's adjusted tax basis in the note. The adjusted tax basis of a note to a particular Note Owner will equal the Note Owner's cost for the note, increased by any market discount, acquisition discount, OID and gain previously included in income by that Note Owner with respect to the note and decreased by the amount of bond premium, if any, previously amortized and by the amount of payments of principal and OID previously received by that Note Owner with respect to that note. Any gain or loss, and any gain or loss recognized on a prepayment of the notes, will be capital gain or loss if the note was held as a capital asset, except for gain representing accrued interest and accrued market discount not previously included in income. Capital losses generally may be used only to offset capital gains.

Foreign Owners. Interest paid (or accrued) to a Note Owner who is not a U.S. Person (a "Foreign Owner") generally will be considered "portfolio interest," and generally will not be subject to United States federal income tax and withholding tax if the interest is not effectively connected with the conduct of a trade or business within the United States by the Foreign Owner and:

1. the Foreign Owner is not actually or constructively a "10 percent shareholder" of the Trust or the Seller (including a holder of 10% of the outstanding certificates issued by the Trust) or a "controlled foreign corporation" with respect to which the Trust or the Seller is a "related person" within the meaning of the Code;
2. the Foreign Owner is not a bank receiving interest described in Section 881(c)(3)(A) of the Code;
3. the interest is not contingent interest described in Section 871(h)(4) of the Code; and
4. the Foreign Owner does not bear specified relationships to any Certificateholder.

To qualify for the exemption from taxation, the Foreign Owner must provide the applicable Trustee or other person who is otherwise required to withhold U.S. tax with respect to the notes with an appropriate statement (on Form W-8BEN or a similar form), signed under penalty of perjury, certifying that the Note Owner is a Foreign Owner and providing the Foreign Owner's name and address. If a note is held through a securities clearing organization or other financial institution, the organization or may provide the relevant signed statement to the withholding agent; in that case, however, the signed statement must be accompanied by a Form W-8BEN or substitute form provided by the Foreign Owner and the Foreign Owner must notify the financial institution acting on its behalf of any changes to the information on the Form W-8BEN (or substitute form) within 30 days of that change. If interest paid to a Foreign Owner is not considered portfolio interest, then it will be subject to United States federal income and withholding tax at a rate of 30 percent, unless reduced or eliminated pursuant to an applicable tax treaty. In order to claim the benefit of any applicable tax treaty, the Foreign Owner must provide the applicable Trustee or other person who is required to withhold U.S. tax with respect to the notes with an appropriate statement (on Form W-8BEN or a similar form), signed under penalties of perjury, certifying that the Foreign Owner is entitled to benefits under the treaty.

Any capital gain realized on the sale, redemption, retirement or other taxable disposition of a Note by a Foreign Owner will be exempt from United States federal income and withholding tax, provided that (1) the gain is not effectively connected with the conduct of a trade or business in the United States by the Foreign Owner and (2) in the case of an individual Foreign Owner, the Foreign Owner is not present in the United States for 183 days or more during the taxable year of disposition.

As used in this prospectus, a "U.S. Person" means:

1. a citizen or resident of the United States;
2. a corporation or partnership (including an entity treated as a corporation or partnership for United States federal income tax purpose) created or organized under the laws of the United States, any state thereof, or the District of Columbia;
3. an estate, the income of which from sources outside the United States is includible in gross income for federal income tax purposes regardless of its connection with the conduct of a trade or business within the United States; or
4. a trust if (a) a court within the U.S. is able to exercise primary supervision over the administration of the trust and one or more United States persons have authority to control all substantial decisions of the trust or (b) such trust was in existence on August 20, 1996 and is eligible to elect, and has made a valid election, to be treated as a U.S. Person despite not meeting the requirements of clause (a).

Backup Withholding. Each Note Owner (other than an exempt Note Owner such as a corporation, tax-exempt organization, qualified pension and profit — sharing trust, individual retirement account or nonresident alien who provides certification as to status as a nonresident) will be required to provide, under penalties of perjury, a certificate (on Form W-9) providing the Note Owner's name, address, correct federal taxpayer identification number and a statement that the Note Owner is not subject to backup withholding. Should a nonexempt Note Owner fail to provide the required certification, amounts otherwise payable to the Note Owner may be subject to backup withholding tax, and the Trust will be required to withhold and remit the withheld amount to the IRS. Any such amount withheld would be credited against the Note Owner's federal income tax liability.

Possible Alternative Treatments of the Notes. If, contrary to the opinion of Tax Counsel, the IRS successfully asserted that one or more of the notes did not represent debt for federal income tax purposes, the notes might be treated as equity interests in the Trust. If so treated, the Trust might be taxable as a corporation with the adverse consequences described above (and the taxable corporation would not be able to reduce its taxable income by deductions for interest expense on notes recharacterized as equity). Alternatively, and most likely in the view of Tax Counsel, the Trust might be treated as a publicly traded partnership that would not be taxable as a corporation because it would meet specified qualifying income tests. Nonetheless, treatment of the notes as equity interests in a publicly traded partnership could have adverse tax consequences to some Note Owners. For example, income to some tax-exempt entities (including pension funds) may be "unrelated business taxable income," income to Foreign Owners may be subject to U.S. tax and cause Foreign Owners to be subject to U.S. tax return filing and withholding requirements, and individual Note Owners might be subject to some limitations on their ability to deduct their share of trust expenses.

TAX CONSEQUENCES TO OWNERS OF THE CERTIFICATES

Treatment of the Trust as a Partnership. The Seller and the Servicer will agree, and the beneficial owners of the certificates (the "Certificate Owners") will agree by their purchase of certificates, to treat the Owner Trust as a partnership (or as an entity disregarded as separate from the Certificate Owner in the event that there is a single Certificate Owner) for purposes of federal and state income tax, franchise tax and any other tax measured in whole or in part by income. If the Owner Trust is treated as a partnership, the assets of the partnership would be the assets held by the Trust, the partners of the partnership would be the Certificate Owners (including the Seller in its capacity as recipient of payments from the Reserve Fund), and the notes would be debt of the partnership. However, the proper characterization of the arrangement involving the Trust, the certificates, the notes, the Seller and the Servicer is not clear because there is no authority on transactions closely comparable to that contemplated in this prospectus.

A variety of alternative characterizations are possible. For example, because the certificates have features characteristic of debt, the certificates might be considered debt of the Seller or the Trust. Any characterization of this type generally would not result in materially adverse tax consequences to Certificate Owners as compared to the consequences from treatment of the certificates as equity in a partnership, described below. The following discussion assumes that the certificates represent equity interests in a partnership.

Indexed Securities, Etc. The following discussion assumes that all payments on the certificates are denominated in U.S. dollars, none of the certificates are Indexed Securities or Strip Certificates, and that a series of Securities includes a single class of certificates. If these conditions are not satisfied with respect to any given series of certificates, additional tax considerations with respect to those certificates will be disclosed in the applicable prospectus supplement.

Partnership Taxation. As a partnership, the Owner Trust will not be subject to federal income tax. Rather, each Certificate Owner will be required to separately take into account that Owner's allocated share of income, gains, losses, deductions and credits of the Owner Trust. The Trust's income will consist primarily of interest and finance charges earned on the Receivables (including appropriate adjustments for market discount, OID and bond premium) and any gain upon collection or disposition of Receivables. The Trust's deductions will consist primarily of interest accruing with respect to the notes, servicing and other fees, and losses or deductions upon collection or disposition of Receivables.

The tax items of a partnership are allocable to the partners in accordance with the Code, Treasury regulations and the partnership agreement (here, the Trust Agreement and related documents). In the Trust Agreement, the Certificate Owners will agree that the yield on a certificate is intended to qualify as a "guaranteed payment" and not as a distributive share of partnership income. A guaranteed payment would be treated by a Certificate Owner as ordinary income, but may not be treated as interest income. The Trust Agreement will provide that, to the extent that the treatment of the yield on a Certificate as a guaranteed payment is not respected, the Certificate Owners of each class of certificates will be allocated taxable income of the Trust for each month equal to the sum of:

1. the interest that accrues on the certificates in accordance with their terms for that month, including interest accruing at the Pass Through Rate for that month and interest on amounts previously due on the certificates but not yet paid;
2. any Trust income attributable to discount on the Receivables that corresponds to any excess of the principal amount of the certificates over their initial issue price;
3. prepayment premium payable to the Certificate Owners for that month; and
4. any other amounts of income payable to the Certificate Owners for that month.

That allocation will be reduced by any amortization by the Trust of premium on Receivables that corresponds to any excess of the initial issue price of certificates over their initial principal amount. All remaining taxable income of the Trust will be allocated to the Seller. Except as provided below, losses and deductions generally will be allocated to the Certificate Owners only to the extent the Certificate Owners are reasonably expected to bear the economic burden of those losses or deductions. Any losses allocated to Certificate Owners could be characterized as capital losses, and the Certificate Owners generally would only be able to deduct those losses against capital gain income, and deductions would be subject to the limitations set forth below. Accordingly, a Certificate Owner's taxable income from the Trust could exceed the cash it is entitled to receive from the Trust.

Based on the economic arrangement of the parties, this approach for allocating Trust income and loss should be permissible under applicable Treasury regulations, although no assurance can be given that the IRS would not require a greater amount of income to be allocated to Certificate Owners. Moreover, even under the foregoing method of allocation, Certificate Owners may be allocated income equal to the entire Pass Through Rate plus the other items described above even though the Trust might not have sufficient cash to make current cash payments of that amount. Thus, cash basis Certificate Owners will, in effect, be required to report income from the certificates on the accrual basis and Certificate Owners may become liable for taxes on Trust income even if they have not received cash from the Trust to pay those taxes. In addition, because tax allocations and tax reporting will be done on a uniform basis for all Certificate Owners but Certificate Owners may be purchasing certificates at different times and at different prices, Certificate Owners may be required to report on their tax returns taxable income that is greater or less than the amount reported to them by the Trust.

For each taxable year of the Certificate Owner, the Certificate Owner will be required to report items of income, loss and deduction allocated to them by the Owner Trust for the Trust's taxable year that ends on or before the last day of that taxable year of the Certificate Owner. The Code prescribes rules for determining the taxable year of the Trust. It is likely that, under these rules, the taxable year of the Trust will be the calendar year. However, in the event that all of the Certificate Owners possessing a 5 percent or greater interest in the equity or profits of the Trust share a taxable year that is other than the calendar year, the Trust could be required to use that year as its taxable year.

A significant portion of the taxable income allocated to a Certificate Owner that is a pension, profit sharing or employee benefit plan or other tax-exempt entity (including an individual retirement account) generally will constitute "unrelated business taxable income" taxable to that Certificate Owner under the Code.

An individual taxpayer's share of expenses of the Owner Trust (including fees to the Servicer but not interest expense) would be miscellaneous itemized deductions. Those deductions might be disallowed to the individual in whole or in part and might result in that Certificate Owner being taxed on an amount of income that exceeds the amount of cash actually paid to that Certificate Owner over the life of the Trust.

The Owner Trust intends to make all tax calculations relating to income and allocations to Certificate Owners on an aggregate basis. If the IRS were to require that those calculations be made separately for each Receivable, the Trust might be required to incur additional expense but it is believed that there would not be a material adverse effect on Certificate Owners.

Discount and Premium. It is believed that the Receivables were not issued with OID, and, therefore, the Owner Trust should not have OID income. However, the purchase price paid by the Trust for the Receivables may be greater or less than the remaining principal balance of the Receivables at the time of purchase. If so, the Receivables will have been acquired at a premium or discount, as the case may be. (As indicated above, the Trust will make this calculation on an aggregate basis, but might be required to recompute it on a Receivable-by-Receivable basis.)

If the Owner Trust acquires the Receivables at a market discount or premium, the Trust will elect to include that discount in income currently as it accrues over the life of the Receivables or to offset the premium against interest income on the Receivables. As indicated above, a portion of the market discount income or premium deduction may be allocated to Certificate Owners.

Section 708 Termination. Under Section 708 of the Code, the Owner Trust will be deemed to terminate for federal income tax purposes if 50% or more of the capital and profits interests in the Trust are sold or exchanged within a 12-month period. If that termination occurs, the Trust will be considered to transfer all of it assets and liabilities to a new partnership in exchange for an interest in the new partnership, after which the Trust would be deemed to distribute interests in the new partnership to Certificate Owners (including the purchasing partner who caused the termination) in liquidation of the terminated partnership. The Trust will not comply with technical requirements that might apply when a constructive termination occurs. As a result, the Trust may be subject to tax penalties and may incur additional expenses if it is required to comply with those requirements. Furthermore, the Trust might not be able to comply due to lack of data.

Disposition of Certificates. Generally, capital gain or loss will be recognized on a sale of certificates in an amount equal to the difference between the amount realized and the seller's tax basis in the certificates sold. A Certificate Owner's tax basis in a certificate will generally equal the Certificate Owner's cost increased by the Certificate Owner's share of Trust income (includible in income) and decreased by any payments received with respect to that certificate. In addition, both the tax basis in the certificates and the amount realized on a sale of a certificate would include the Certificate Owner's share of the notes and other liabilities of the Trust. A Certificate Owner acquiring certificates at different prices may be required to maintain a single aggregate adjusted tax basis in those certificates, and, upon sale or other disposition of some of the certificates, allocate a portion of that aggregate tax basis to the certificates sold (rather than maintaining a separate tax basis in each certificate for purposes of computing gain or loss on a sale of that certificate).

Any gain on the sale of a certificate attributable to the holder's share of unrecognized accrued market discount on the Receivables would generally be treated as ordinary income to the holder and would give rise to special tax reporting requirements. The Owner Trust does not expect to have any other assets that would give rise to those special reporting requirements. Thus, to avoid those special reporting requirements, the Trust will elect to include market discount in income as it accrues.

If a Certificate Owner is required to recognize an aggregate amount of income (not including income attributable to disallowed itemized deductions described above) over the life of the certificates that exceeds the aggregate cash payments with respect thereto, the excess will generally give rise to a capital loss upon the retirement of the certificates.

Allocations Between Transferors and Transferees. In general, the Owner Trust's taxable income and losses will be determined monthly and the tax items for a particular calendar month will be apportioned among the Certificate Owners in proportion to the principal amount of certificates owned by them as of the close of the last day of that month. As a result, a Certificate Owner purchasing certificates may be allocated tax items (which will affect its tax liability and tax basis) attributable to periods before the Certificate Owner actually owned the certificates.

The use of a monthly convention may not be permitted by existing regulations. If a monthly convention is not allowed (or only applies to transfers of less than all of the partner's interest), taxable income or losses of the Owner Trust might be reallocated among the Certificate Owners. The Seller is authorized to revise the Owner Trust's method of allocation between transferors and transferees to conform to a method permitted by future regulations.

Section 754 Election. In the event that a Certificate Owner sells its certificates at a profit (loss), the purchasing Certificate Owner will generally have a higher (or lower) basis in the certificates than the selling Certificate Owner had. The tax basis of the Owner Trust's assets will not be adjusted to reflect that higher (or lower) basis unless the Trust were to file an election under Section 754 of the Code. In order to avoid the administrative complexities that would be involved in keeping accurate accounting records, as well as potentially onerous information reporting requirements, the Owner Trust will not make that election. As a result, Certificate Owners might be allocated a greater or lesser amount of Trust income than would be appropriate based on their own purchase price for certificates.

Administrative Matters. The Trustee is required to keep or have kept complete and accurate books of the Owner Trust. These books will be maintained for financial reporting and tax purposes on an accrual basis and the fiscal year of the Trust will be set forth in the applicable prospectus supplement. The Trustee will file a partnership information return (IRS Form 1065) with the IRS for each taxable year of the Trust during which the Owner Trust is treated as a partnership for federal income tax purposes, and for each such taxable year will report each Certificate Owner's allocable share of items of Trust income and expense to holders and the IRS on Schedule K-1. The Trust will provide the Schedule K-1 information to nominees that fail to provide the Trust with the information statement described below and those nominees will be required to forward that information to the Certificate Owners. Generally, Certificate Owners must file tax returns that are consistent with the information return filed by the Trust or be subject to penalties unless the Certificate Owner timely notifies the IRS of all those inconsistencies.

Under Section 6031 of the Code, any person that holds certificates as a nominee at any time during a calendar year is required to furnish the Trust with a statement containing specified information on the nominee, the Certificate Owners and the certificates so held. The information includes (1) the name, address and taxpayer identification number of the nominee and (2) as to each Certificate Owner (x) the name, address and identification number of that person, (y) whether that person is a U.S. person, a tax-exempt entity or a foreign government, an international organization, or any wholly-owned agency or instrumentality of any of the foregoing, and (z) specified information on certificates that were held, bought or sold on behalf of that person throughout the year. In addition, brokers and financial institutions that hold certificates through a nominee are required to furnish directly to the Trust information as to themselves and their ownership of certificates. A clearing agency registered under Section 17A of the Exchange Act is not required to furnish any information statement of this type to the Trust. The information referred to above for any calendar year must be furnished to the Trust on or before the following January 31. Nominees, brokers and financial institutions that fail to provide the Trust with the information described above may be subject to penalties.

The Seller will be designated as the tax matters partner in the related Trust Agreement, and as such is designated to receive notice on behalf of, and to provide notice to those Certificate Owners not receiving notice from, the IRS, and to represent the Certificate Owners in certain disputes with the IRS. The Code provides for administrative examination of a partnership as if the partnership were a separate and distinct taxpayer. Generally, the statute of limitations for partnership items does not expire before three years after the date on which the partnership information return is filed. Any adverse determination following an audit of the return of the Trust by the appropriate taxing authorities could result in an adjustment of the returns of the Certificate Owners, and, under some circumstances, a Certificate Owner may be precluded from separately litigating a proposed adjustment to the items of the Trust. As the tax matters partner, the Seller may enter into a binding settlement on behalf of all Certificate Owners with a less than 1 percent interest in the Trust (except for any group of those Certificate Owners with an aggregate interest of 5 percent or more in Trust profits that elects to form a notice group or Certificate Owners who otherwise notify the IRS that the Seller is not authorized to settle on their behalf). In the absence of a proceeding at the Trust level, a Certificate Owner under some circumstances may pursue a claim for credit or refund on his own behalf by filing a request for administrative adjustment of a Trust item. It is suggested that each Certificate Owner consult its own tax advisor with respect to the impact of these procedures on its particular case. An adjustment could also result in an audit of a Certificate Owner's returns and adjustments of items not related to the income and losses of the Trust.

Tax Consequences to Foreign Certificate Owners. It is not clear whether the Trust would be considered to be engaged in a trade or business in the United States for purposes of federal withholding taxes with respect to Certificate Owners who are not U.S. Persons ("Foreign Certificate Owners") because there is no clear authority dealing with that issue under facts substantially similar to those described in this prospectus. Although it is not expected that the Owner Trust would be engaged in a trade or business in the United States for those purposes, the Trust will withhold as if it were so engaged in order to protect the Trust from possible adverse consequences of a failure to withhold. The Trust expects to withhold on the portion of its taxable income that is allocable to Foreign Certificate Owners pursuant to Section 1446 of the Code, as if that income were effectively connected to a U.S. trade or business, at a rate of 35% for Foreign Certificate Owners that are taxable as corporations and the highest individual tax rate for all other Foreign Certificate Owners. Subsequent adoption of Treasury regulations or the issuance of other administrative pronouncements may require the Trust to change its withholding procedures. In determining a holder's withholding status, the Trust may rely on IRS Form W-8BEN (or any applicable successor form), IRS Form W-9 or the holder's certification of nonforeign status signed under penalties of perjury.

Each Foreign Certificate Owner might be required to file a U.S. individual or corporate income tax return (including, in the case of a corporation, the branch profits tax) on its share of the Trust's income. Each Foreign Certificate Owner must obtain a taxpayer identification number from the IRS and submit that number to the Trust on Form W-8BEN (or any applicable successor form) in order to assure appropriate crediting of the taxes withheld. A Foreign Certificate Owner generally would be entitled to file with the IRS a claim for refund with respect to taxes withheld by the Trust, taking the position that no taxes were due because the Trust was not engaged in a U.S. trade or business.

However, interest payments made (or accrued) to a Foreign Certificate Owner generally will be considered guaranteed payments to the extent those payments are determined without regard to the income of the Trust. If these interest payments are properly characterized as guaranteed payments, then the interest will not be considered "portfolio interest," in which case Certificate Owners would be subject to United States federal income tax and withholding tax at a rate of 30 percent, unless reduced or eliminated pursuant to an applicable treaty. In that case, a Foreign Certificate Owner would only be entitled to claim a refund for that portion of the taxes, if any, in excess of the taxes that should be withheld with respect to the guaranteed payments.

Backup Withholding. Payments made on the certificates and proceeds from the sale of the certificates will be subject to a backup withholding tax if, in general, the Certificate Owner fails to comply with specified identification procedures, unless the holder is an exempt recipient under applicable provisions of the Code. We refer you to " — Tax Consequences to Owners of the Notes — Backup Withholding" above.

TAX TREATMENT OF GRANTOR TRUSTS

Tax Characterization of the Trust as a Grantor Trust. The following general discussion of the anticipated federal income tax consequences of the purchase, ownership and disposition of the certificates of a Trust nominally referred to as a "grantor trust" in the applicable prospectus supplement (a "Grantor Trust"), to the extent it relates to matters of law or legal conclusions with respect thereto, represents the opinion of Tax Counsel to each Grantor Trust with respect to the related series on the material matters associated with those consequences, subject to the qualifications set forth in this prospectus. In addition, Tax Counsel has prepared or reviewed the statements in this prospectus under the heading "Material Income Tax Consequences — Tax Treatment of Grantor Trusts," and is of the opinion that those statements are correct in all material respects. Those statements are intended as an explanatory discussion of the possible effects of the classification of any Trust as a grantor trust for federal income tax purposes on investors generally and of related tax matters affecting investors generally, but do not purport to furnish information in the level of detail or with the attention to an investor's specific tax circumstances that would be provided by an investor's own tax advisor. Accordingly, it is suggested that each investor consult its own tax advisors with regard to the tax consequences to it of investing in certificates of a Grantor Trust ("Grantor Trust Certificates").

Tax Counsel will deliver its opinion that the Grantor Trust will not be classified as an association taxable as a corporation and that the Trust will be classified as a grantor trust under subpart E, Part I of subchapter J of Chapter 1 of Subtitle A of the Code. In this case, beneficial owners of Grantor Trust Certificates (referred to as "Grantor Trust Certificateholders") could be considered to own either (1) an undivided interest in a single debt obligation held by the Grantor Trust and having a principal amount equal to the total stated principal amount of the Receivables and an interest rate equal to the relevant Pass Through Rate or (2) an interest in each of the Receivables and any other Trust property.

The determination of whether the economic substance of a property transfer is a sale or a loan secured by the transferred property has been made by the IRS and the courts on the basis of numerous factors designed to determine whether the transferor has relinquished (and the transferee has obtained) substantial incidents of ownership in the property. Among those factors, the primary factors examined are whether the transferee has the opportunity to gain if the property increases in value, and has the risk of loss if the property decreases in value.

The relevant pooling and servicing agreement will express the intent of the Seller to sell, and the Grantor Trust Certificateholders to purchase, the Receivables, and the Seller and each Grantor Trust Certificateholder, by accepting a beneficial interest in a Grantor Trust Certificate, will agree to treat the Grantor Trust Certificates as ownership interests in the Receivables and any other Trust property.

Treatment as Debt Obligation. If a Grantor Trust Certificateholder was considered to own an undivided interest in a single debt obligation, the principles described under " — Tax Treatment of Owner Trusts — Tax Consequences to Owners of the Notes" would apply. Each Grantor Trust Certificateholder, rather than reporting its share of the interest accrued on each Receivable, would, in general, be required to include in income interest accrued or received on the principal amount of the Grantor Trust Certificates at the relevant Pass Through Rate in accordance with its usual method of accounting.

The Grantor Trust Certificates would be subject to OID rules, described below under " — Stripped Bonds and Stripped Coupons" and " — Original Issue Discount." In determining whether any OID on the Grantor Trust Certificates is de minimis, the Seller expects to use a reasonable Prepayment Assumption to determine the weighted average life of the Grantor Trust Certificates. OID includible in income for any accrual period (generally, the period between payment dates) would generally be calculated using a Prepayment Assumption and an anticipated yield established as of the date of initial sale of the Grantor Trust Certificates, and would increase or decrease to reflect prepayments at a faster or slower rate than anticipated. The Grantor Trust Certificates would also be subject to the market discount provisions of the Code to the extent that a Grantor Trust Certificateholder purchased those certificates at a discount from the initial issue price (as adjusted to reflect prior accruals of OID).

The remainder of the discussion in this prospectus assumes that a Grantor Trust Certificateholder will be treated as owning an interest in each Receivable (and the proceeds therefrom), any right to receive Yield Supplement Deposits and any other Trust property, although for administrative convenience, the Servicer will report information on an aggregate basis (as though all of the Receivables and the Yield Supplement Agreement were a single obligation). The amount and, in some instances, character, of the income reported to a Grantor Trust Certificateholder may differ under this method for a particular period from that which would be reported if income were reported on a precise asset-by-asset basis.

Characterization. Each Grantor Trust Certificateholder will be treated as the owner of a pro rata undivided interest in the interest and principal portions of the Trust represented by the Grantor Trust Certificates and will be considered the equitable owner of a pro rata undivided interest in each of the Receivables in the Trust, any right to receive Yield Supplement Deposits, and any other Trust property. Any amounts received by a Grantor Trust Certificateholder in lieu of amounts due with respect to any Receivable because of a default or delinquency in payment will be treated for federal income tax purposes as having the same character as the payments they replace.

For federal income tax purposes, the Seller will be treated as having retained a fixed portion of the interest due on each Receivable having an annual percentage rate in excess of the sum of the applicable Pass Through Rate and the Servicing Rate (each, a "High Yield Receivable") equal to the difference between (1) the annual percentage rate of the Receivable and (2) the sum of the applicable Pass Through Rate and the Servicing Rate (the "Retained Yield"). The Retained Yield will be treated as "stripped coupons" within the meaning of Section 1286 of the Code, and the Stripped Receivables will be treated as "stripped bonds." We refer you to " — Stripped Bonds and Stripped Coupons" below. Accordingly, each Grantor Trust Certificateholder will be treated as owning its pro rata percentage interest in (1) payments received under any Yield Supplement Agreement, and (2) the principal of, and interest payable on, each Receivable (minus the Retained Yield on the High Yield Receivables).

Those Receivables that bear interest at a rate which is less than or equal to the sum of the applicable Pass Through Rate and the Servicing Rate (the "Low Yield Receivables") will not be treated as stripped bonds. Instead, Yield Supplement Deposits will be payable to eliminate the difference between the actual yield on each Low Yield Receivable and the yield the Receivable would have had if its interest rate had equaled the sum of the applicable Pass Through Rate and the Servicing Rate. We refer you to " — Yield Supplement Deposits" below.

Each Grantor Trust Certificateholder will be required to report on its federal income tax return in accordance with that Grantor Trust Certificateholder's method of accounting its pro rata share of the entire income from the Receivables in the Trust represented by Grantor Trust Certificates, including interest, OID (if any), prepayment fees, assumption fees, any gain recognized upon an assumption, late payment charges received by the Servicer and any gain recognized upon collection or disposition of the Receivables (but not including any portion of the Retained Yield). A Grantor Trust Certificateholder will also be required to report under its usual method of accounting any payments received under any Yield Supplement Agreement to the extent that these payments are treated as income. Under Sections 162 or 212, each Grantor Trust Certificateholder will be entitled to deduct its pro rata share of Base Servicing Fees, prepayment fees, assumption fees, any loss recognized upon an assumption and late payment charges retained by the Servicer, provided that those amounts are reasonable compensation for services rendered to the Trust. Grantor Trust Certificateholders that are individuals, estates or trusts will be entitled to deduct their share of expenses only to the extent those expenses plus all other Section 212 expenses exceed two percent of its adjusted gross income. In addition, Grantor Trust Certificateholders who are individuals may be subject to additional deduction limitations based on adjusted gross income.

A Grantor Trust Certificateholder using the cash method of accounting must take into account its pro rata share of income and deductions as and when collected by or paid to the Servicer. A Grantor Trust Certificateholder using an accrual method of accounting must take into account its pro rata share of income and deductions as they become due or are paid to the Servicer, whichever is earlier. Because (1) interest accrues on the Receivables over differing monthly periods and is paid in arrears and (2) interest collected on a Receivable generally is paid to Certificateholders in the following month, the amount of interest accruing to a Grantor Trust Certificateholder during any calendar month will not equal the interest distributed in that month. The actual amount of discount on a Receivable will be includible in income as principal payments are received on the Receivables. If the Base Servicing Fees paid to the Servicer are deemed to exceed reasonable servicing compensation, the amount of that excess could be considered as an ownership interest retained by the Servicer (or any person to whom the Servicer assigned for value all or a portion of the Base Servicing Fees) in a portion of the interest payments on the Receivables. The Receivables would then be subject to the "stripped bond" and "stripped coupons" rules of the Code discussed below.

Discount and Premium. In determining whether a Grantor Trust Certificateholder has purchased its interest in the Receivables (or any Receivable) held by the related Trust at a discount or premium and whether the Receivables (or any

Receivable) have OID, market discount, or amortizable premium, a portion of the purchase price of a Certificate should be allocated to the Grantor Trust Certificateholder's undivided interest in accrued but unpaid interest, amounts collected at the time of purchase but not distributed, and rights to receive Yield Supplement Deposits. As a result, the portion of the purchase price allocable to a Grantor Trust Certificateholder's undivided interest in the Receivables (or any Receivable) will be increased or decreased, as applicable, and the potential OID, market discount, or amortizable premium on the Receivables (or any Receivable) could be increased or decreased accordingly.

Premium. A Grantor Trust Certificateholder that acquires an interest in Receivables at a premium over the "stated redemption price at maturity" of the Receivables may elect to amortize that premium under a constant interest method. Amortizable bond premium will be treated as an offset to interest income on that Grantor Trust Certificate. The basis for that Grantor Trust Certificate will be reduced to the extent that amortizable premium is applied to offset interest payments. It is not clear whether a reasonable prepayment assumption should be used in computing amortization of premium allowable under Section 171. With some exceptions, a Grantor Trust Certificateholder that makes this election for a Grantor Trust Certificate that is acquired at a premium will be deemed to have made an election to amortize bond premium with respect to all debt instruments having amortizable bond premium that the Grantor Trust Certificateholder holds during the year of the election or thereafter. Absent an election to amortize bond premium, the premium will be deductible as an ordinary loss upon disposition of the Certificate or pro rata as principal is paid on the Receivables.

If a premium is not subject to amortization using a reasonable prepayment assumption, the holder of a Grantor Trust Certificate acquired at a premium should recognize a loss if a Receivable prepays in full, equal to the difference between the portion of the prepaid principal amount of that Receivable that is allocable to the Grantor Trust Certificate and the portion of the adjusted basis of the Grantor Trust Certificate that is allocable to that Receivable. If a reasonable prepayment assumption is used to amortize that premium, it appears that that loss would be available, if at all, only if prepayments have occurred at a rate faster than the reasonable assumed prepayment rate. It is not clear whether any other adjustments would be required to reflect differences between an assumed prepayment rate and the actual rate of prepayments.

Stripped Bonds and Stripped Coupons. Although the tax treatment of stripped bonds is not entirely clear, based on guidance from the IRS, each purchaser of a Grantor Trust Certificate will be treated as the purchaser of a stripped bond (to the extent that the Receivables consist of High Yield Receivables) which generally should be treated as a single debt instrument issued on the day it is purchased for purposes of calculating any original issue discount. Generally, under applicable Treasury regulations (the "Section 1286 Treasury Regulations"), if the discount on a stripped bond is larger than a de minimis amount (as calculated for purposes of the OID rules of the Code), that stripped bond will be considered to have been issued with OID. We refer you to " — Original Issue Discount" below. Based on the preamble to the Section 1286 Treasury Regulations, Tax Counsel is of the opinion that, although the matter is not entirely clear, the interest income on the certificates at the sum of the Pass Through Rate and the portion of the Servicing Rate that does not constitute excess servicing will be treated as "qualified stated interest" within the meaning of the Section 1286 Treasury Regulations. The Trustee will treat that income in this manner for tax information reporting purposes. In this case, the amount of OID on a High Yield Receivable will equal the amount by which the purchase price of a High Yield Receivable is less than the portion of the remaining principal balance of the Receivable allocable to the interest acquired.

Original Issue Discount. The IRS has stated in published rulings that, in circumstances similar to those described in this prospectus, the special rules of the Code relating to OID will be applicable to a Grantor Trust Certificateholder's interest in those Receivables meeting the conditions necessary for these rules to apply. Generally, a Grantor Trust Certificateholder that acquires an undivided interest in a Receivable issued or acquired with OID must include in gross income the sum of the "daily portions," as defined below, of the OID on that Receivable for each day on which it owns a Grantor Trust Certificate, including the date of purchase but excluding the date of disposition. In the case of an original Grantor Trust Certificateholder, the daily portions of OID with respect to a Receivable generally would be determined as follows. A calculation will be made of the portion of OID that accrues on the Receivable during each successive monthly accrual period (or shorter period in respect of the date of original issue or the final Payment Date). This will be done, in the case of each full monthly accrual period, by adding (1) the present value of all remaining payments to be received on the Receivable under the Prepayment Assumption used in respect of the Receivables and (2) any payments received during that accrual period, and subtracting from that total the "adjusted issue price" of the Receivable at the beginning of that accrual period. No representation is made that the Receivables will prepay at any prepayment assumption. The "adjusted issue price" of a Receivable at the beginning of the first accrual period is the amount of the purchase price paid by the Grantor Trust Certificateholder for the Grantor Trust Certificate that is allocable to the Receivable, and the "adjusted issue price" of a Receivable at the beginning of a subsequent accrual period is the "adjusted issue price" at the beginning of the immediately preceding accrual period plus the amount of OID allocable to that accrual period and reduced by the amount of any payment on the Receivable (other than "qualified stated interest") made at the end of or during that accrual period. The OID accruing during that accrual period will then be divided by the number of days in the period to determine the daily portion of OID for each day in the period. With respect to an initial accrual period shorter than a full monthly accrual period, the daily portions of OID must be determined according to a reasonable method, provided that that method is consistent with the method used to determine the yield to maturity of the Receivables.

If the amount of OID is de minimis under the rule set forth above, a High Yield Receivable would not be treated as having OID. The actual amount of discount on a High Yield Receivable would be includible in income as principal payments are received on the Receivable, in the proportion that each principal payment bears to the total principal amount of the Receivable.

With respect to the Receivables, the method of calculating OID as described above will cause the accrual of OID to either increase or decrease (but never below zero) in any given accrual period to reflect the fact that prepayments are occurring at a faster or slower rate than the prepayment assumption used in respect of the Receivables. Subsequent purchasers that purchase Receivables at more than a de minimis discount should consult their tax advisors with respect to the proper method to accrue that OID.

Yield Supplement Deposits. The proper Federal income tax characterization of the Yield Supplement Deposits is not clear. Moreover, the sum of the income and deductions properly reportable by a Grantor Trust Certificateholder in any taxable year may not equal the amounts that would be reportable if a Grantor Trust Certificateholder held instead of an interest in the Receivables and in the Yield Supplement Agreement either (1) a debt instrument bearing interest at the applicable Pass Through Rate or (2) an interest in a trust holding Receivables each of which bears interest at a rate at least equal to the sum of the Pass Through Rate plus the Servicing Rate. It is likely that the right to receive Yield Supplement Deposits will be treated as a separate asset purchased by each Grantor Trust Certificateholder, in which case a portion of each Grantor Trust Certificateholder's purchase price or other tax basis in the Grantor Trust Certificate equal to the fair market value of the right to receive the Yield Supplement Deposits should be allocated to the right to receive payments of Yield Supplement Deposits. The right to receive Yield Supplement Deposits may be treated as a loan made by a Grantor Trust Certificateholder to the Seller in an amount equal to the present value, discounted at a rate equal to the sum of the applicable Pass Through Rate and the Servicing Rate, of the projected Yield Supplement Deposits. In that event, a portion of the Yield Supplement Deposits generally representing a yield equal to the applicable Pass Through Rate plus the Servicing Rate on such discounted value should be treated as interest includible in income as accrued or received, and the remainder should be treated as a return of the principal amount of the deemed loan. Alternatively, it is possible that the entire amount of each Yield Supplement Deposit should be included in income as accrued or received, in which event a Grantor Trust Certificateholder should also be entitled to amortize the portion of its purchase price allocable to its right to receive Yield Supplement Deposits. The method of calculating that amortization is unclear, and could result in the inclusion of greater amounts of income than a Grantor Trust Certificateholder's actual yield on a Receivable. Alternatively, it is possible that the Yield Supplement Deposits could be treated as payments adjusting the purchase price of the Low Yield Receivables, rather than as a separate asset. In that event, a Grantor Trust Certificateholder could be treated as having purchased each Low Yield Receivable at a discount (which may consist of imputed interest, market discount, or both) that, combined with the actual coupon rate of the Receivable, produces a yield equal to the sum of the applicable Pass Through Rate and the Servicing Rate. It is not clear whether, and to what extent, the amounts includible in income or amortizable under any of these methods would be adjusted to take account of prepayments on the Receivables. Moreover, it is possible that the IRS might contend that none of the above methods is appropriate, and that income with respect to the Yield Supplement Agreement should be reported by a Grantor Trust Certificateholder in some other manner. In addition, to the extent that the amounts payable pursuant to Yield Supplement Agreement decline during any period by reason of prepayments on the Receivables, it is possible that a portion of the amount amortizable by the Grantor Trust Certificateholder during that period would be treated as a capital loss (which would not offset ordinary income), rather than as an ordinary deduction. It is suggested that Grantor Trust Certificateholders consult their tax advisors regarding the appropriate method of accounting for income attributable to the Yield Supplement Agreement.

Market Discount. A Grantor Trust Certificateholder that acquires an undivided interest in Receivables may be subject to the market discount rules of Sections 1276 through 1278 to the extent an undivided interest in a Receivable is considered to have been purchased at a "market discount." Generally, the amount of market discount is equal to the excess of the portion of the principal amount of that Receivable allocable to that Grantor Trust Certificateholder's undivided interest in the Receivable over that holder's tax basis in that interest. Market discount with respect to a Receivable will be considered to be zero if the amount allocable to the Receivable is less than 0.25% of the Receivable's stated redemption price at maturity multiplied by the weighted average maturity remaining after the date of purchase. Treasury regulations implementing the market discount rules have not yet been issued; therefore, it is suggested that investors consult their own tax advisors regarding the application of these rules and the advisability of making any of the elections allowed under Code Sections 1276 through 1278.

The Code provides that any principal payment (whether a scheduled payment or a prepayment) or any gain on disposition of a market discount bond shall be treated as ordinary income to the extent that it does not exceed the accrued market discount at the time of that payment. The amount of accrued market discount for purposes of determining the tax treatment of subsequent principal payments or dispositions of the market discount bond is to be reduced by the amount so treated as ordinary income.

The Code also grants the Treasury Department authority to issue regulations providing for the computation of accrued market discount on debt instruments, the principal of which is payable in more than one installment. While the Treasury Department has not yet issued regulations, rules described in the relevant legislative history will apply. Under those rules, the holder of a market discount bond may elect to accrue market discount either on the basis of a constant interest rate or according to one of the following methods. If a Grantor Trust Certificate is issued with respect to which there is OID, the amount of market discount that accrues during any accrual period would be equal to the product of (1) the total remaining market discount and (2) a fraction, the numerator of which is the OID accruing during the period and the denominator of which is the total remaining OID at the beginning of the accrual period. If a Grantor Trust Certificate is issued with respect to which there is no OID, the amount of market discount that accrues during a period is equal to the product of (1) the total remaining market discount and (2) a fraction, the numerator of which is the amount of stated interest paid during the accrual period and the denominator of which is the total amount of stated interest remaining to be paid at the beginning of the accrual period. For purposes of calculating market discount under any of the above methods in the case of instruments (such as the Grantor Trust Certificates) that provide for payments that may be accelerated by reason of prepayments of other obligations securing those instruments, the same prepayment assumption applicable to calculating the accrual of OID will apply. Because the regulations described above have not been issued, it is impossible to predict what effect those regulations might have on the tax treatment of a Grantor Trust Certificate purchased at a discount or premium in the secondary market.

A Grantor Trust Certificateholder who acquired a Grantor Trust Certificate at a market discount also may be required to defer a portion of its interest deductions for the taxable year attributable to any indebtedness incurred or continued to purchase or carry that Grantor Trust Certificate purchased with market discount. For these purposes, the de minimis rule referred to above applies. Any deferred interest expense would not exceed the market discount that accrues during that taxable year and is, in general, allowed as a deduction not later than the year in which the market discount is includible in income. If that holder elects to include market discount in income currently as it accrues on all market discount instruments acquired by the holder in that taxable year or thereafter, the interest deferral rule described above will not apply.

Election to Treat All Interest as OID. The OID regulations permit a Grantor Trust Certificateholder to elect to accrue all interest, discount (including de minimis market or original issue discount) and premium in income as interest, based on a constant yield method. If that election were to be made with respect to a Grantor Trust Certificate with market discount, the Grantor Trust Certificateholder would be deemed to have made an election to include in income currently market discount with respect to all other debt instruments having market discount that that Grantor Trust Certificateholder acquires during the year of the election or thereafter. Similarly, a Grantor Trust Certificateholder that makes this election for a Grantor Trust Certificate that is acquired at a premium will be deemed to have made an election to amortize bond premium with respect to all debt instruments having amortizable bond premium that that Grantor Trust Certificateholder owns or acquires. We refer you to " — Premium" above. The election to accrue interest discount and premium on a constant yield method with respect to a grantor trust certificate is irrevocable except with the approval of the IRS.

Sale or Exchange of a Grantor Trust Certificate. Sale or exchange of a Grantor Trust Certificate prior to its maturity will result in gain or loss equal to the difference, if any, between the amount received and the owner's adjusted basis in the Grantor Trust Certificate. The adjusted basis generally will equal the seller's purchase price for the Grantor Trust Certificate, increased by any market discount, OID and gain previously included in the seller's gross income with respect to the Grantor Trust Certificate, and reduced by the amount of any premium, if any, previously amortized and by the amount of any payments of principal and OID on the Grantor Trust Certificate previously received by the seller. That gain or loss will be capital gain or loss to an owner for which a Grantor Trust Certificate is a "capital asset" within the meaning of Section 1221, and will be long-term or short-term depending on whether the Grantor Trust Certificate has been owned for the long-term capital gain holding period (currently more than one year).

A Grantor Trust Certificate will be an "evidence of indebtedness" within the meaning of Section 582(c)(1), so that gain or loss recognized from the sale of a Grantor Trust Certificate by a bank or a thrift institution to which that section applies will be treated as ordinary income or loss.

Foreign Persons. Generally, interest or OID paid by the person required to withhold tax under Section 1441 or 1442 to (1) a Grantor Trust Certificateholder that is not a U.S. Person (as defined under " — Tax Treatment of Owner Trusts — Tax Consequences to Owners of the Notes — Foreign Owners") (a "Foreign Grantor Trust Certificateholder") or (2) a person holding on behalf of a Foreign Grantor Trust Certificateholder, as well as accrued OID recognized by the Foreign Grantor Trust Certificateholder on the sale or exchange of that Grantor Trust Certificate, will not be subject to withholding to the extent that a Grantor Trust Certificate evidences ownership in Receivables issued after July 18, 1984 by natural persons, if that Foreign Grantor Trust Certificateholder complies with specified identification requirements (including delivery of a statement, signed by the Foreign Grantor Trust Certificateholder under penalties of perjury, certifying that that Foreign Grantor Trust Certificateholder is not a U.S. Person and providing the name and address of that Foreign Grantor Trust Certificateholder). Additional restrictions apply to Receivables where the obligor is not a natural person in order to qualify for the exemption from withholding.

Although it is not entirely clear, it is likely that amounts received by a Foreign Grantor Trust Certificateholder that are attributable to payments of Yield Supplement Deposits received pursuant to any Yield Supplement Agreement generally would not be subject to withholding tax. It is suggested that Foreign Grantor Trust Certificateholders consult their tax advisors regarding the withholding tax consequences of amounts received on the Grantor Trust Certificates that are attributable to payments of Yield Supplement Deposits received pursuant to any Yield Supplement Agreement.

Information Reporting and Backup Withholding. The Servicer will furnish or make available, within a reasonable time after the end of each calendar year, to each person who was a Grantor Trust Certificateholder at any time during that year, that information as may be deemed necessary or desirable to assist Grantor Trust Certificateholders in preparing their federal income tax returns, or to enable holders to make that information available to beneficial owners or financial intermediaries that hold Grantor Trust Certificates as nominees on behalf of beneficial owners. If a holder, beneficial owner, financial intermediary or other recipient of a payment on behalf of a beneficial owner fails to supply a certified taxpayer identification number or if the Secretary of the Treasury determines that that person has not reported all interest and dividend income required to be shown on its federal income tax return, backup withholding may be required with respect to any payments. Any amounts deducted and withheld from a payment to a recipient would be allowed as a credit against that recipient's federal income tax liability. . . .

MATERIAL STATE TAX CONSEQUENCES WITH RESPECT TO OWNER TRUSTS

The activities to be undertaken by the Servicer in servicing and collecting the Receivables will take place in California. The State of California imposes a state individual income tax and a corporate franchise tax on corporations, partnerships and other entities doing business in the State of California. This discussion relates only to Owner Trusts and is based upon present provisions of California statutes and the regulations promulgated under those statutes, and applicable judicial or ruling authority, all of which are subject to change, which change may be retroactive.

Because of the variation in each state's tax laws based in whole or in part upon income, it is impossible to predict tax consequences to holders of notes and certificates in all of the state taxing jurisdictions in which they are already subject to tax. It is suggested that Note Owners and Certificate Owners consult their own tax advisors with respect to state tax consequences arising out of the purchase, ownership and disposition of notes and certificates.

For purposes of the following summary, references to the Trust, the notes, the certificates and related terms, parties and documents shall be deemed to refer to each Owner Trust and the notes, certificates and related terms, parties and documents applicable to that Trust.

Tax Consequences with Respect to the Notes. It is expected that Tax Counsel will advise each Owner Trust that issues notes that, assuming the notes will be treated as debt for federal income tax purposes, the notes will be treated as debt for California income and franchise tax purposes. Accordingly, Note Owners not otherwise subject to taxation in California would not become subject to taxation in California solely because of a holder's ownership of notes. However, a Note Owner already subject to California's income tax or franchise tax could be required to pay additional California tax as a result of the Note Owner's ownership or disposition of notes.

Tax Consequences with Respect to the Certificates Issued by an Owner Trust. Based on regulations issued by the Franchise Tax Board with respect to the California tax characterization of an owner trust as a partnership and not as an association taxable as a corporation or other taxable entity, Tax Counsel will opine that an Owner Trust will not be an association (or publicly traded partnership) taxable as a corporation for California income and franchise tax purposes. In that case, the resulting constructive partnership should not be treated as doing business in California but rather should be viewed as a passive holder of investments and, as a result, should not be subject to the California franchise tax (which, if applicable, could possibly result in reduced payments to Certificate Owners).

Under current law, Certificate Owners that are nonresidents of California and are not otherwise subject to California income tax may be subject to California income tax on the income from the constructive partnership. In any event, classification of the arrangement as a "partnership" would not cause a Certificate Owner not otherwise subject to taxation in California to pay California tax on income beyond that derived from the certificates.

It is not clear whether the Trust would be considered to be engaged in a trade or business in the United States for purposes of California withholding taxes with respect to Certificate Owners that are Foreign Owners because there is no clear authority dealing with that issue under facts substantially similar to those described in this prospectus. Although it is not expected that the Trust would be engaged in a trade or business in the United States for those purposes, the Trust will withhold on amounts paid to Certificate Owners that are Foreign Owners as if it were so engaged in order to protect the Trust from possible adverse consequences of a failure to withhold. The Trust expects to withhold on the portion of its taxable income from California sources that is allocable to Certificate Owners that are Foreign Owners pursuant to Section 18666 of California's Revenue and Taxation Code, as if that income were effectively connected to a U.S. trade or business, at the maximum appropriate rate.

If the certificates are instead treated as ownership interests in an association taxable as a corporation or a "publicly traded partnership" taxable as a corporation, then the hypothetical entity should not be subject to the California franchise tax (which, if applicable, could result in reduced payments to Certificate Owners). A Certificate Owner not otherwise subject to tax in California would not become subject to California tax as a result of its mere ownership of that interest.

MATERIAL STATE TAX CONSEQUENCES WITH RESPECT TO GRANTOR TRUSTS

It is expected that Tax Counsel will advise each Grantor Trust that the Trust will be treated as a grantor trust for California tax purposes, and that, for California tax purposes, Grantor Trust Certificateholders could be considered to own either (1) an undivided interest in a single debt obligation held by the Trust and having a principal amount equal to the total stated principal amount of the Receivables and an interest rate equal to the related Pass Through Rate or (2) an interest in each of the Receivables and any other Trust assets.

It is suggested that Grantor Trust Certificateholders consult their tax advisors regarding the state tax consequences associated with the purchase, ownership and disposition of the Grantor Trust Certificates.

The federal and state tax discussions set forth above are included for general information only and may not be applicable depending upon your particular tax situation. it is suggested that you consult your tax advisor with respect to the tax consequences to you of the purchase, ownership and disposition of notes and certificates, including the tax consequences under state, local, foreign and other tax laws and the possible effects of changes in federal or other tax laws.

ERISA CONSIDERATIONS

Section 406 of the Employee Retirement Income Security Act of 1974, as amended ("ERISA") and Section 4975 of the Code prohibit a pension, profit-sharing or other employee benefit plan, as well as individual retirement accounts and some types of Keogh Plans (each a "Benefit Plan"), from engaging in transactions involving "plan assets" with persons that are "parties in interest" under ERISA or "disqualified persons" under the Code with respect to that Benefit Plan. ERISA also imposes duties on persons who are fiduciaries of Benefit Plans subject to ERISA and prohibits specified transactions between a Benefit Plan and parties in interest with respect to those Benefit Plans. Under ERISA, any person who exercises any authority or control with respect to the management or disposition of the assets of a Benefit Plan is considered to be a fiduciary of that Benefit Plan (subject to exceptions not here relevant). A violation of these "prohibited transaction" rules may result in an excise tax or other penalties and liabilities under ERISA and the Code for those persons. Certain exemptions from the prohibited transaction rules could be applicable to the purchase and holding of Securities by a Benefit Plan depending on the type and circumstances of the plan fiduciary making the decision to acquire the Securities. Potentially available exemption would include, without limitation, Prohibited Transaction Class Exemption ("PTCE") 90-1, which exempts certain transactions involving insurance company pooled separate accounts; PTCE 95-60, which exempts certain transactions involving insurance company general accounts; PTCE 91-38, which exempts certain transactions involving bank collective investment funds; PTCE 84-14, which exempts certain transactions effected on behalf of a plan by a "qualified professional asset manager"; and PTCE 96-23, which exempts certain transactions effected on behalf of a plan by an "in-house asset manager." Insurance company general accounts should also discuss with their legal counsel the availability of exemptive relief under Section 401(c) of ERISA. A purchaser of Securities should be aware, however, that even if the conditions specified in one or more exemptions are met, the scope of the relief provided by the applicable exemption or exemptions might not cover all acts that might be construed as prohibited transactions.

Some transactions involving a Trust might be deemed to constitute prohibited transactions under ERISA and the Code with respect to a Benefit Plan that purchased notes or certificates if assets of the Trust were deemed to be assets of the Benefit Plan. Under a regulation issued by the United States Department of Labor (the "Plan Assets Regulation"), the assets of a Trust would be treated as plan assets of a Benefit Plan for the purposes of ERISA and the Code only if the Benefit Plan acquired an "equity interest" in the Trust and none of the exceptions contained in the Plan Assets Regulation was applicable. An equity interest is defined under the Plan Assets Regulation as an interest other than an instrument which is treated as indebtedness under applicable local law and which has no substantial equity features. The likely treatment in this context of notes and certificates of a given series will be discussed in the applicable prospectus supplement.

Employee benefit plans that are governmental plans (as defined in Section 3(32) of ERISA) and some church plans (as defined in Section 3(33) of ERISA) are not subject to ERISA requirements nor to Section 4975 of the Code. However, governmental plans may be subject to state or local laws that impose similar requirements. In addition, governmental plans and church plans that are "qualified" under Section 401(a) of the Code are subject to restrictions with respect to prohibited transactions under Section 503(a)(1)(B) of the Code, the sanction for violation being loss of "qualified" status.

Due to the complexities of the "prohibited transaction" rules and the penalties imposed upon persons involved in prohibited transactions, it is important that the fiduciary of any Benefit Plan considering the purchase of Securities consult with its tax and/or legal advisors regarding whether the assets of the related Trust would be considered plan assets, the possibility of exemptive relief from the prohibited transaction rules and other issues and their potential consequences.

UNDERWRITING

On the terms and conditions set forth in an underwriting agreement with respect to the notes, if any, of a given series and an underwriting agreement with respect to the certificates of that series (collectively, the "Underwriting Agreements"), the Seller will agree to cause the related Trust to sell to the underwriters named in the Underwriting Agreements (the "Underwriters") and in the applicable prospectus supplement, and each of those Underwriters will severally agree to purchase, the principal amount of each class of notes and certificates, as the case may be, of the related series set forth in the Underwriting Agreements and in the applicable prospectus supplement.

In each of the Underwriting Agreements with respect to any given series of Securities, the several Underwriters will agree, subject to the terms and conditions set forth in the Underwriting Agreements, to purchase all the notes and certificates, as the case may be, described in the Underwriting Agreements which are offered by this prospectus and by the applicable prospectus supplement if any of those notes and certificates, as the case may be, are purchased.

Each prospectus supplement will either (1) set forth the price at which each class of notes and certificates, as the case may be, being offered by that prospectus supplement will be offered to the public and any concessions that may be offered to some dealers participating in the offering of those notes and certificates or (2) specify that the related notes and certificates, as the case may be, are to be resold by the underwriters in negotiated transactions at varying prices to be determined at the time of that sale. After the initial public offering of those notes and certificates, those public offering prices and those concessions may be changed.

Each Underwriting Agreement will provide that AHFC and the Seller will indemnify the Underwriters against specified civil liabilities, including liabilities under the Securities Act, or contribute to payments the several Underwriters may be required to make in respect thereof.

Each Trust may, from time to time, invest the funds in its Accounts in Eligible Investments acquired from the Underwriters or from the Seller.

Pursuant to each Underwriting Agreement with respect to a given series of Securities, the closing of the sale of any class of Securities subject to that Underwriting Agreement will be conditioned on the closing of the sale of all other classes of Securities of that series.

The place and time of delivery for the Securities in respect of which this prospectus is delivered will be set forth in the applicable prospectus supplement.

LEGAL OPINIONS

Certain legal matters relating to the Securities of any series will be passed upon for the related Trust, the Seller and the Servicer by counsel specified in the applicable prospectus supplement. In addition, certain United States federal and California state tax and other matters will be passed upon for the related Trust by counsel specified in the applicable prospectus supplement. Certain legal matters will be passed upon for the Underwriters by counsel specified in the applicable prospectus supplement. . . . .

NO DEALER, SALESPERSON OR OTHER PERSON HAS BEEN AUTHORIZED TO GIVE ANY INFORMATION OR TO MAKE ANY REPRESENTATIONS OTHER THAN THOSE CONTAINED IN OR INCORPORATED BY REFERENCE IN THIS PROSPECTUS AND, IF GIVEN OR MADE, SUCH INFORMATION OR REPRESENTATIONS MUST NOT BE RELIED UPON AS HAVING BEEN AUTHORIZED BY THE SELLER OR ANY UNDERWRITER. NEITHER THE DELIVERY OF THIS PROSPECTUS NOR ANY SALE MADE HEREUNDER SHALL UNDER ANY CIRCUMSTANCE CREATE AN IMPLICATION THAT THERE HAS BEEN NO CHANGE IN THE AFFAIRS OF THE SELLER OR THE RECEIVABLES SINCE THE DATE THEREOF. THIS PROSPECTUS DOES NOT CONSTITUTE AN OFFER OR SOLICITATION BY ANYONE IN ANY STATE IN WHICH SUCH OFFER OR SOLICITATION IS NOT AUTHORIZED OR IN WHICH THE PERSON MAKING SUCH

OFFER OR SOLICITATION IS NOT QUALIFIED TO DO SO OR TO ANYONE TO WHOM IT IS UNLAWFUL TO MAKE SUCH OFFER OR SOLICITATION.

AMERICAN HONDA
RECEIVABLES CORP.
SELLER
AMERICAN HONDA
FINANCE CORPORATION
SERVICER

UNTIL MAY 20, 2003 (90 DAYS AFTER THE DATE OF THIS PROSPECTUS), ALL DEALERS EFFECTING TRANSACTIONS IN THE NOTES, WHETHER OR NOT PARTICIPATING IN THIS DISTRIBUTION, MAY BE REQUIRED TO DELIVER A PROSPECTUS. THIS DELIVERY REQUIREMENT IS IN ADDITION TO THE OBLIGATION OF DEALERS TO DELIVER A PROSPECTUS WHEN ACTING AS UNDERWRITERS AND WITH RESPECT TO THEIR UNSOLD ALLOTMENTS OR SUBSCRIPTIONS.

HONDA AUTO RECEIVABLES
2003-1 OWNER TRUST
$376,000,000
1.30% ASSET BACKED NOTES, CLASS A-1
$462,000,000
1.46% ASSET BACKED NOTES, CLASS A-2
$386,000,000
1.92% ASSET BACKED NOTES, CLASS A-3
$317,700,000
2.48% ASSET BACKED NOTES, CLASS A-4

PROSPECTUS SUPPLEMENT
JOINT BOOKRUNNERS
BANC ONE CAPITAL MARKETS, INC.
DEUTSCHE BANK SECURITIES
CO-MANAGERS
BANC OF AMERICA SECURITIES LLC
BARCLAYS CAPITAL
CREDIT SUISSE FIRST BOSTON
SALOMON SMITH BARNEY

End of Filing

Appendix 5

Appendix 5

FILED PURSUANT TO RULE 424(B)(5)
REGISTRATION FILE NO.: 333-71022

PROSPECTUS SUPPLEMENT
(TO PROSPECTUS DATED FEBRUARY 19, 2003)

HONDA AUTO RECEIVABLES 2003-1 OWNER TRUST
ISSUER

AMERICAN HONDA RECEIVABLES CORP.,
SELLER

AMERICAN HONDA FINANCE CORPORATION,
SERVICER

$1,541,700,000 ASSET BACKED NOTES

- The trust will issue four classes of notes and a class of certificates.
- The notes are backed by a pledge of the trust's assets. The trust's assets include fixed rate motor vehicle retail installment sales contracts secured by new and used automobiles and light-duty trucks.
- Only the notes described on the following table are being offered by this prospectus supplement and the accompanying prospectus.

YOU SHOULD REVIEW CAREFULLY THE FACTORS SET FORTH UNDER "RISK FACTORS" BEGINNING ON PAGE XXX OF THIS PROSPECTUS SUPPLEMENT AND PAGE XXX IN THE ACCOMPANYING PROSPECTUS.

This prospectus supplement does not contain complete information about the offering of the securities. No one may use this prospectus supplement to offer and sell the securities unless it is accompanied by the prospectus. If any statements in this prospectus supplement conflict with statements in the prospectus, the statements in this prospectus supplement will control.

The securities are asset backed securities issued by the trust. The securities are not obligations of American Honda Receivables Corp., American Honda Finance Corporation, or any of their respective affiliates. Neither the securities nor the receivables are insured or guaranteed by any government agency.

NEITHER THE SEC NOR ANY STATE SECURITIES COMMISSION HAS APPROVED OR DISAPPROVED THE SECURITIES OR DETERMINED THAT THIS PROSPECTUS SUPPLEMENT OR THE PROSPECTUS IS ACCURATE OR COMPLETE. ANY REPRESENTATION TO THE CONTRARY IS A CRIMINAL OFFENSE.

	Initial Principal Amount	Interest Rate(1)	Accrual Method(1)	First Interest Payment Date	Final Scheduled Payment Date
Class A-1 Notes	$376,000,000	1.30%	Actual/360	March 18, 2003	March 18, 2004
Class A-2 Notes	$462,000,000	1.46%	30/360	March 18, 2003	September 19, 2005
Class A-3 Notes	$386,000,000	1.92%	30/360	March 18, 2003	November 20, 2006
Class A-4 Notes	$317,700,000	2.48%	30/360	March 18, 2003	July 18, 2008

(1) Interest generally will accrue on the Class A-1 Notes from (and including) the previous payment date to (but excluding) the related payment date, and on the Class A-2, Class A-3 and Class A-4 Notes from (and including) the 18th day of each month to (but excluding) the 18th day of the succeeding month.

The terms of the offering are as follows:

	Initial Public Offering Price(1)	Underwriting Discount	Proceeds to Seller(2)
Per Class A-1 Note	100.00000%	0.125%	99.87500%
Per Class A-2 Note	99.99427%	0.175%	99.81927%
Per Class A-3 Note	99.99166%	0.220%	99.77166%
Per Class A-4 Note	99.98802%	0.250%	99.73802%
Total	$ 1,541,603,274.54	$ 2,921,590.00	$ 1,538,681,324.54

(1) Plus accrued interest, if any, from February 25, 2003.

(2) Before deducting expenses payable by the seller, estimated to be $700,000. The notes will bedelivered in book-entry form only on or about February 25, 2003.

- We will not list the notes on any national securities exchange or on any automated quotation system of any registered securities association such as NASDAQ.

JOINT BOOKRUNNERS

**BANC ONE CAPITAL MARKETS, INC. DEUTSCHE
BANK SECURITIES
CO-MANAGERS**

**BANC OF AMERICA SECURITIES LLC
BARCLAYS CAPITAL
CREDIT SUISSE FIRST BOSTON
SALOMON SMITH BARNEY**

**THE DATE OF THIS PROSPECTUS SUPPLEMENT
IS FEBRUARY 19, 2003.**

TABLE OF CONTENTS

*[Eds. — Page numbers added.]

IMPORTANT NOTICE ABOUT INFORMATION PRESENTED IN THIS PROSPECTUS SUPPLEMENT AND THE ACCOMPANYING PROSPECTUS

Information about the securities is provided in two separate documents that progressively provide increasing levels of detail: (1) the accompanying prospectus, which provides general information, some of which may not apply to a particular class of securities, including your class; and (2) this prospectus supplement, which describes the specific terms of your class of securities.

IF THE DESCRIPTION OF THE TERMS OF YOUR SECURITIES VARIES BETWEEN THIS PROSPECTUS SUPPLEMENT AND THE ACCOMPANYING PROSPECTUS, YOU SHOULD RELY ON THE INFORMATION IN THIS PROSPECTUS SUPPLEMENT.

Cross-references are included in this prospectus supplement and in the accompanying prospectus which direct you to more detailed descriptions of a particular topic. You can also find references to key topics in the Table of Contents on page XXX in this prospectus supplement and the Table of Contents on page XXX in the accompanying prospectus.

You can find a listing of the pages where capitalized terms used in this prospectus supplement are defined under the caption “Index of Terms” beginning on page XXX in this prospectus supplement and under the caption “Index of Terms” beginning on page XXX in the accompanying prospectus. . . .

SUMMARY OF TERMS

The following summary contains a brief description of the notes. You will find a detailed description of the terms of the offering of the notes following this summary. You should carefully read this entire document and the accompanying prospectus to understand all of the terms of the offering of the notes. You should consider both documents when making your investment decision.

RELEVANT PARTIES

ISSUER/TRUST	Honda Auto Receivables 2003-1 Owner Trust.
SELLER	American Honda Receivables Corp.
SERVICER	American Honda Finance Corporation.
INDENTURE TRUSTEE	JPMorgan Chase Bank.
OWNER TRUSTEE	The Bank of New York.
DELAWARE TRUSTEE	The Bank of New York (Delaware).

RELEVANT AGREEMENTS

INDENTURE	The indenture is between the issuer and the indenture trustee. The indenture provides for the terms relating to the notes.
TRUST AGREEMENT	The trust agreement is among the seller, the owner trustee and the Delaware trustee. The trust agreement governs the creation of the trust and provides for the terms relating to the certificates.
SALE AND SERVICING AGREEMENT	The sale and servicing agreement is among the trust, the servicer and the seller. The sale and servicing agreement governs the transfer of the receivables by the seller to the trust and the servicing of the receivables by the servicer.
ADMINISTRATION AGREEMENT	The administration agreement is among American Honda Finance Corporation, as administrator, the owner trustee and the indenture trustee. The administration agreement governs the provision of reports by the administrator and the performance by the administrator of other administrative duties for the trust.
PURCHASE AGREEMENT	The purchase agreement is between American Honda Finance Corporation and the seller. The purchase agreement governs the sale of the receivables by American Honda Finance Corporation to the seller.

RELEVANT DATES

CLOSING DATE	Expected to be February 25, 2003.
CUTOFF DATE	February 1, 2003.
PAYMENT DATES	The trust will pay interest and principal on the securities on the 18th day of each month. If the 18th day of the month is not a business day, payments on the securities will be made on the next business day. The date that any payment is made is called a payment date. The first payment date is March 18, 2003.
FINAL SCHEDULED PAYMENT DATES	The final principal payment for each class of securities is scheduled to be made on the

applicable final scheduled payment date specified on the front cover of this prospectus supplement.

RECORD DATE

So long as the securities are in book-entry form, the trust will make payments on the securities to the holders of record on the day immediately preceding the payment date. If the securities are issued in definitive form, the record date will be the last day of the month preceding the payment date.

DESCRIPTION OF THE SECURITIES

OFFERED NOTES

The offered notes consist of the class A-1 notes, the class A-2 notes, the class A-3 notes and the class A-4 notes, as described on the cover page.

SECURITIES NOT OFFERED

The trust will also issue $35,577,657.84 initial principal amount of certificates. The trust is not offering the certificates. The certificates will represent fractional undivided interests in the trust. Payments of interest on and principal of the certificates are subordinated to the payments of interest on and principal of the notes as described herein. The certificates are not being offered by this prospectus supplement and initially will be retained by the seller. Any information in this prospectus supplement regarding the certificates is intended only to give you a better understanding of the notes.

RECEIVABLES

The trust's main source of funds for making payments on the notes will be collections on its motor vehicle retail installment sale contracts, also known as the receivables.

The principal balance of the receivables on February 1, 2003, referred to as the "cutoff date," was $1,557,277,657.84. As of the cutoff date, the receivables had the following characteristics:

- number of receivables 104,014
- average principal balance $15,164.09
- weighted average annual percentage rate 5.55%

- weighted average remaining term to maturity 50.82 months
- weighted average original term to maturity $7.35 months

Approximately 99.89% of the receivables owned by the trust are classified as simple interest receivables. These receivables are described in more detail in "The Receivables" in the accompanying prospectus. We refer you to "The Receivables" in this prospectus supplement for more information on the receivables.

TERMS OF THE NOTES

In general, noteholders are entitled to receive payments of interest and principal from the trust only to the extent that collections from trust assets and funds resulting from credit enhancements are sufficient to make those payments. Interest and principal collections from trust assets will be divided among the various classes of securities in specified proportions. The trust will pay interest and principal to noteholders of record as of the preceding record date.

INTEREST

The interest rate for each class of notes is set forth on the front cover of this prospectus supplement. The class A-1 notes will accrue interest on an actual/360 basis from (and including) the previous payment date to (but excluding) the related payment date, except that the first interest accrual period will be from (and including) the closing date to (but excluding) March 18, 2003. This means that the interest due on each payment date will be the product of: (i) the outstanding principal balance of the class A-1 notes, (ii) the related interest rate, and (iii) the actual number of days since the previous payment date (or, in the case of the first payment date, since the closing date) divided by 360.

The class A-2, class A-3 and class A-4 notes will accrue interest on a 30/360 basis from (and including) the 18th day of each calendar month to (but excluding) the 18th day of the succeeding calendar month except that the first interest accrual period will be from (and including) the closing date to (but excluding) March 18, 2003. This means that the interest due on each payment date will be the product of: (i) the outstanding principal balance of the related class of notes, (ii) the applicable interest rate, and (iii) 30 (or, in the case of the first payment date, 23) divided by 360.

If noteholders of any class do not receive all interest owed to them on a payment date, the trust will make payments of interest on later payment dates to make up the shortfall together with interest on those amounts, to the extent funds from specified sources are available to cover the shortfall.

PRINCIPAL

- Amounts allocated to the notes: Principal on the notes will be payable generally in an amount equal to the noteholders' percentage of the sum of the following amounts referred to asthe "principal distributable amount":

1. principal collections on the receivables during the prior calendar month;
2. any prepayments (full or partial) on the receivables allocable to principal received during the prior calendar month;
3. the principal balance of each receivable which the seller or the servicer purchased with respect to the prior calendar month; and
4. the principal balance of receivables that became defaulted receivables during the prior calendar month.

Principal payments on the notes as described above will be made from all available amounts after the servicing fee, non-recoverable advances and trust fees and expenses have been paid and after payment of interest on the notes.

- The noteholders' percentage will equal 100% until the principal amount of the class A-1 notes has been paid in full. After the principal amount of the class A-1 notes has been paid in full, the noteholders' percentage will equal the percentage equivalent of a fraction the numerator of which is the sum of the initial aggregate principal amounts of the class A-2, class A-3 and class A-4 notes and the denominator of which is the sum of the initial aggregate principal amounts of the class A-2, class A-3 and class A-4 notes and the initial aggregate principal amount of the certificates. After the class A-1, class A-2, class A-3 and class A-4 notes have been paid in full, the noteholders' percentage shall be zero.

- Order of payment among classes: No principal payments will be made (1) on the class A-2 notes until the class A-1 notes have been paid in full; (2) on the class A-3 notes until the class A-1 and the class A-2 notes have been paid in full; and (3) on the class A-4 notes until the class A-1 notes, the class A-2 notes and the class A-3 notes have been paid in full. However, upon the acceleration of the notes following an event of default, the noteholders' percentage will be 100% until the notes have been paid in full. Principal payments will be made first to the holders of the class A-1 notes until they have been paid in full. After the class A-1 notes have been paid in full, principal payments will be made to the class A- 2 notes, the class A-3 notes and the class A-4 notes on a pro rata basis based on the outstanding principal balance of those classes of notes. After all classes of notes have been paid in full, principal payments will be made on the certificates until the certificates have been paid in full.
- Final scheduled payment dates: The trust must pay the outstanding principal balance of each class of notes by its final scheduled payment date as specified on the cover page of this prospectus supplement.

We refer you to "Payments on the Notes — Calculation of Available Amounts" in this prospectus supplement for more detailed information regarding payments of principal on the notes.

OPTIONAL REDEMPTION

The servicer may cause the trust to redeem any outstanding securities when the outstanding aggregate principal balance of the receivables declines to 10% or less of the initial aggregate principal balance of the receivables as of the cutoff date.

We refer you to "Description of the Transfer and Servicing Agreements — Optional Purchase" in this prospectus supplement for more detailed information.

CREDIT ENHANCEMENT

Credit enhancement is intended to protect you against losses and delays in payments on your securities by absorbing losses on the receivables and other shortfalls in cash flows. The credit enhancement for the notes will include the certificates, the reserve fund and the subordination of the seller's right to receive excess interest.

CERTIFICATES

The certificates have an initial principal balance of $35,577,657.84 and represent approximately 2.25% of the initial principal balance of all the notes and the certificates.

The certificates will be subordinated in priority of payment to all classes of notes. The certificates will not receive any interest or principal distributions on any payment date until all of the principal and interest owing on the notes on that payment date have been paid in full and the reserve fund has been funded to its required level.

RESERVE FUND

On each payment date, the trust will use funds in the reserve fund to cover shortfalls in payments of interest and principal required to be paid on the notes.

On the closing date, the seller will cause to be deposited $7,886,388.29 into the reserve fund, which is 0.50% of the initial aggregate principal balance of the receivables as of the cutoff date. On each payment date, after making required payments to the servicer and to the holders of the notes, the trust will make a deposit into the reserve fund to the extent necessary to maintain the amount on deposit in the reserve fund at a specified balance. For more detailed information about the reserve fund, we refer you to "Credit Enhancement — Reserve Fund" in this prospectus supplement.

EXCESS INTEREST

The seller is entitled to receive payments of interest collected on the receivables which are not used by the trust to make other required payments. The seller's right to receive this excess interest is subordinated to the payment of servicing and trust fees, the payment of principal and interest on the notes, the funding of the reserve fund and the payment of principal and interest on the certificates.

YIELD SUPPLEMENT ACCOUNT

On the closing date, the seller will cause to be deposited $267,720.61 into the yield supplement account. Neither the seller nor the servicer will make any additional deposits to the yield supplement account after the closing date. On or before each payment date, the indenture trustee will withdraw from funds on deposit in the yield supplement account and deposit in the collection account the aggregate amount by which (1) one month's interest on the principal balance of each discount receivable (other than a discount receivable that is a defaulted receivable) at a rate equal to the time weighted average note rate plus 1.00% (the servicing rate) exceeds (2) one month's interest on the principal balance of each such discount receivable at the annual percentage rate of that receivable. In addition, the indenture trustee will withdraw from the yield supplement account and deposit in the collection account amounts on deposit in the yield supplement account in excess of the amount required to be on deposit therein. Discount receivables are those receivables that have interest rates which are less than the sum of the time weighted average note rate and 1.00%.

For detailed information about the yield supplement account, we refer you to "Description of the Transfer and Servicing Agreement — Yield Supplement Account" in this prospectus supplement.

TAX STATUS

Subject to important considerations described in this prospectus supplement and the accompanying prospectus, Dewey Ballantine LLP, tax counsel to the trust, will deliver its opinion that:

1. the notes will be characterized as debt for tax purposes; and
2. the trust will not be characterized as an association (or a publicly traded partnership) taxable as a corporation for federal income and California income and franchise tax purposes.

If you purchase the notes, you will agree to treat the notes as debt. The seller and any subsequent purchaser of the certificates will agree to treat the trust (1) as a partnership in which the owners of the certificates are partners or (2) if there is only one beneficial owner of the certificates, as a "disregarded entity," for federal income and California income and franchise tax purposes.

We refer you to "Material Income Tax Consequences" in this prospectus supplement and "Material Income Tax Consequences — Tax Treatment of Owner Trusts" in the accompanying prospectus.

ERISA CONSIDERATIONS

The notes may be purchased by employee benefit plans and individual retirement accounts, subject to those considerations discussed under "ERISA Considerations" in this prospectus supplement and in the accompanying prospectus.

We refer you to "ERISA Considerations" in this prospectus supplement and in the accompanying prospectus. If you are a benefit plan fiduciary considering the purchase of the notes you should, among other things, consult with your counsel in determining whether all required conditions have been satisfied.

ELIGIBILITY FOR PURCHASE BY MONEY MARKET FUNDS

The class A-1 notes will be eligible for purchase by money market funds under Rule 2a-7 under the Investment Company Act of 1940, as amended. A money market fund should consult its legal advisers regarding the eligibility of such notes under Rule 2a-7 and whether an investment in such notes satisfies such fund's investment policies and objectives.

RATINGS

It is a condition to the issuance of the securities that the securities will receive the following ratings from Standard & Poor's Ratings Services, a division of The McGraw-Hill Companies, Inc., Moody's Investors Service, Inc. and Fitch Ratings:

CLASS	STANDARD & POOR'S	MOODY'S	FITCH
A-1	A-1+	P-1	F1+
A-2	AAA	Aaa	AAA
A-3	AAA	Aaa	AAA
A-4	AAA	Aaa	AAA

RISK FACTORS

You should consider the following risk factors (and the factors set forth under "Risk Factors" in the accompanying prospectus) in deciding whether to purchase the securities of any class.

The assets of the trust are the only source of funds for payments on the securities. The securities are not obligations of, and will not be insured or guaranteed by, any governmental agency or the seller, the servicer, any trustee or any of their affiliates. You must rely solely on payments on the receivables and amounts on deposit in the reserve fund and the yield supplement account for payments on the notes. Although funds in the reserve fund will be available to cover shortfalls in payments of interest and principal on each payment date, the amounts deposited in the reserve fund and the yield supplement account will be limited. No additional deposits will be made into the yield supplement account after the deposit on the closing date. If the entire reserve fund and the yield supplement account have been used, the trust will depend solely on current collections on the receivables to make payments on the notes. Any excess amounts released from the reserve fund to the seller will no longer be available to securityholders on any later payment date. We refer you to "Credit Enhancement — Reserve Fund" in this prospectus supplement.

Payment defaults or the insolvency or dissolution of the seller may result in prepayment of the securities, which may result in losses. If the trust fails to pay principal of the notes when due, or fails to pay interest on the notes within five days of the due date, the indenture trustee or the holders of a majority of the notes outstanding may declare the entire amount of the notes to be due immediately. If this happens, the indenture trustee may sell the assets of the trust and prepay the notes if certain conditions are met, as set forth in the prospectus under "The Notes — Indenture — Events of Default; Rights Upon Events of Default." In the event that the indenture trustee sells the receivables under adverse market conditions, proceeds from the sale of the receivables may not be sufficient to repay all of the notes and you may suffer a loss.

Classes of notes that receive principal payments before other classes will be repaid more rapidly than the other classes. In addition, because principal of each class of notes will be paid sequentially, classes of notes that have higher sequential numerical class designation will be outstanding longer and therefore will be exposed to the risk of losses on the receivables during periods after other classes have been receiving most or all amounts payable on their notes, and after which a disproportionate amount of credit enhancement may have been applied and not replenished. As a result, the yields of the class A-2, class A-3 and class A-4 notes will be relatively more sensitive to losses on the receivables and the timing of such losses. If the actual rate and amount of losses exceed your expectations, and if amounts in the reserve fund are insufficient to cover the resulting shortfalls, the yield to maturity on your notes may be lower than anticipated, and you could suffer a loss. Classes of notes that receive payments earlier than expected are exposed to greater reinvestment risk and classes of notes that receive principal later than expected are exposed to greater risk of loss. In either case, the yields on your notes could be materially and adversely affected.

Upon the occurrence of an event of default and acceleration of the notes, principal payments will be made first on the class A-1 notes until the class A-1 notes have been paid in full, and thereafter on the class A-2 notes, class A-3 notes and class A-4 notes pro rata based on the amount outstanding under each such class. Consequently, even after an event of default and acceleration of all the notes, the class A-2 noteholders, class A-3 noteholders and class A-4 noteholders will not receive payments on principal until the class A-1 notes have been paid in full.

Economic conditions in the states where obligors reside may affect delinquencies, losses and prepayments on the receivables. The following economic conditions may affect payments on the receivables:

- unemployment,
- interest rates,
- inflation rates, and
- consumer perceptions of the economy.

If a large number of obligors are located in a particular state, the occurrence of these conditions in that state could increase the delinquency, credit loss or repossession experience of the receivables. If there is a concentration of obligors and receivables in particular states, any adverse economic conditions in those states may affect the performance of the securities more than if this concentration did not exist.

As of the cutoff date, American Honda Finance Corporation's records indicate that the billing addresses of the originating dealers of the receivables were concentrated in the following states:

STATE	PERCENTAGE OF INITIAL POOL BALANCE
California	17.34%
Texas	7.82%
Florida	6.05%
New Jersey	5.79%
New York	5.62%
Pennsylvania	5.18%

No other state, by billing address, constituted more than 5.00% of the aggregate principal balance of the receivables as of the cutoff date.

For a discussion of the breakdown of the receivables by state, we refer you to "The Receivables" in this prospectus supplement.

Extreme weather conditions, such as the flooding that occurred in June 2001 and

July 2002 in the State of Texas could cause substantial business disruptions, economic losses, unemployment and an economic downturn. As a result, the related obligors' ability to make timely payments could be adversely affected. The trust's ability to make payments on the notes could be adversely affected if the related obligors were unable to make timely payments.

In the first half of 2001, California experienced energy shortages that resulted in unpredictable rolling blackouts and higher energy costs. This potential crisis could someday spread to other states and affect the entire nation. These higher energy costs could reduce the amount of money that the affected obligors have available to make monthly payments. Higher energy costs and blackouts could also cause business disruptions, which could cause unemployment and an economic downturn. Such obligors could potentially become delinquent in making monthly payments or default if they were unable to make payments due to increased energy bills or unemployment. The trust's ability to make payments on the notes could be adversely affected if the related obligors were unable to make timely payments.

The Soldiers' and Sailors' Civil Relief Act of 1940, or the Relief Act, provides relief to obligors who enter active military service and to obligors in reserve status who are called to active duty after the origination of their receivables. The response of the United States to the terrorist attacks on September 11, 2001 has included rescue efforts and may involve military operations that will increase the number of citizens who are in active military service, including persons in reserve status who have been called or will be called to active duty. The Relief Act provides, generally, that an obligor who is covered by the Relief Act may not be charged interest on the related receivable in excess of 6% per annum during the period of the obligor's active duty. These shortfalls are not required to be paid by the obligor at any future time. The servicer is not required to advance these shortfalls as delinquent payments, and such shortfalls are not covered by any form of credit enhancement on the notes. In the event that there are not sufficient available funds to off-set interest shortfalls on the receivables due to the application of the Relief Act or similar legislation or regulations, a noteholders' interest carryover shortfall will result. Such noteholders' interest carryover shortfalls will be paid in subsequent periods, to the extent of available funds, before payments of principal are made on the notes and might result in extending the anticipated maturity of your class of notes or possibly result in a loss in the absence of sufficient credit enhancement. The Relief Act also limits the ability of the servicer to repossess the financed vehicle securing a receivable during the related obligor's period of active duty and, in some cases, may require the servicer to extend the maturity of the receivable, lower the monthly payments and readjust the payment schedule for a period of time after the completion of the obligor's military service. As a result, there may be delays in payment and increased losses on the receivables. Those delays and increased losses will be borne primarily by the certificates, but if such losses are greater than anticipated, you may suffer a loss. We do not know how many receivables have been or may be affected by the application of the Relief Act.

If an obligor on a simple interest contract makes a payment on the contract ahead of schedule (for example, because the obligor intends to go on vacation), the weighted average life of the securities could be affected. This is because the additional scheduled payments will be treated as a principal prepayment and applied to reduce the principal balance of the related receivable and the obligor will generally not be required to make any scheduled payments during the period for which it was paid-ahead. During this paid-ahead period, interest will continue to accrue on the principal balance of the contract, as reduced by the application of the additional scheduled payments, but the obligor's contract would not be considered delinquent during this period. While the servicer may be required to make interest advances during this period, no principal advances will be made. Furthermore, when the obligor resumes the required payments, the payments so paid may be insufficient to cover the interest that has accrued since the last payment by that obligor. This situation will continue until the regularly scheduled payments are once again sufficient to cover all accrued interest and to reduce the principal balance of the receivable.

The payment by the trust of the paid-ahead principal amount on the notes will generally shorten the weighted average life of the notes. However, depending on the length of time during which a paid-ahead simple interest receivable is not amortizing as described above, the weighted average life of the notes may be extended. In addition, to the extent the servicer makes advances on a paid-ahead simple interest receivable which subsequently goes into default, because liquidation proceeds for this receivable will be applied first to reimburse the servicer for its advances, the loss on this receivable may be larger than would have been the case had advances not been made.

AHFC's portfolio of retail installment sale contracts has historically included simple interest receivables which have been paid-ahead by one or more scheduled monthly payments. There can be no assurance as to the number of receivables in the trust which may become paid-ahead simple interest receivables as described above or the number or the principal amount of the scheduled payments which may be paid-ahead.

You may receive payment of principal on your notes earlier than you expected. If that happens, you may not be able to reinvest the principal you receive at a rate as high as the rate on your notes. Prepayments on the receivables will shorten the life of the notes to an extent that cannot be predicted. Prepayments may occur for a number of reasons. Some prepayments may be caused by the obligors under the receivables. For example, obligors may:

- make early payments, since receivables will generally be prepayable at any time without penalty;
- default, resulting in the repossession and sale of the financed vehicle; or
- damage the vehicle or become unable to pay due to death or disability, resulting in payments to the trust under any existing physical damage, credit life or other insurance.

Some prepayments may be caused by the seller or the servicer. For example, the seller will make representations and warranties regarding the receivables, and the servicer will agree to take or refrain from taking certain actions with respect to the receivables. If the seller or the servicer breaches a representation or warranty and the breach is material and cannot be remedied, it will be required to purchase the affected receivables from the trust. This will result, in effect, in the prepayment of the purchased receivables. In addition, the servicer has the option to purchase the receivables from the trust when the total outstanding principal balance of the receivables is 10% or less of the total outstanding principal balance of the receivables as of the cutoff date.

The rate of prepayments on the receivables may be influenced by a variety of economic, social and other factors. The seller has limited historical experience with respect to prepayments. For these reasons, the seller cannot predict the actual prepayment rates for the receivables. The seller, however, believes that the actual rate of prepayments will result in the weighted average life of the receivables being shorter than the period from the closing date to the final scheduled maturity date for the related class of notes. If this is the case, the weighted average life of each class of notes will be correspondingly shorter.

A security rating is not a recommendation to buy, sell or hold securities. Similar ratings on different types of securities do not necessarily mean the same thing. You should analyze the significance of each rating independently from any other rating. A rating agency may change its rating of the notes after the notes are issued if that rating agency believes that circumstances have changed. Any subsequent change in a rating will likely affect the price that a subsequent purchaser would be willing to pay for the notes and your ability to resell your notes.

The notes are not a suitable investment for any investor that requires a regular or predictable schedule of payments or payment on specific dates. The notes are complex investments that should be considered only by sophisticated investors. We suggest that only investors who, either alone or with their financial, tax and legal advisors, have the expertise to analyze the prepayment, reinvestment and default risks, the tax consequences of an investment and the interaction of these factors should consider investing in the notes.

During the months of November and December 2003, the servicer expects to implement a new computer system designed to improve operating efficiency and minimize the disruption of operations. The implementation of this system should be completed on or before December 31, 2003. The servicer has employed various testing procedures over the last nine months to ensure that the new computer system will function as designed. The servicer will perform comprehensive additional tests over the next several months in its continued efforts to ensure that the new computer system will function as intended. In addition to the security features in its current computer system, the servicer has engaged an experienced data conversion team to protect the integrity of the data stored on the servicer's system during the implementation period. However, it is not possible to determine with complete certainty that all problems potentially affecting the receivables have been identified or corrected. As a result, some or all the following consequences are possible:

- Operational inconveniences and inefficiencies may divert resources from normal collection activities;
- Serious system failures may require significant efforts by the servicer to prevent or alleviate material business disruptions;
- Any system failures could disrupt normal collection activities and could result in delays in payment or credit losses on the receivables; and
- Other unforeseen circumstances may interfere with servicing operations and adversely affect collections on the receivables.

If any such delays in payment or credit losses on the receivables included in the trust are greater than you anticipated, the yield on your class of notes could be adversely affected and, if any losses exceed the available credit enhancement, you may suffer a loss.

THE TRUST

GENERAL

The Honda Auto Receivables 2003-1 Owner Trust (the "Trust") is a Delaware statutory trust that was formed pursuant to the trust agreement (the "Trust Agreement") among American Honda Receivables Corp., as seller (the "Seller"), The Bank of New York, as owner trustee (the "Owner Trustee") and The Bank of New York (Delaware), as Delaware Trustee. After its formation, the Trust will not engage in any activity other than:

1. acquiring, holding and managing the Receivables and the other assets of the Trust and proceeds from those assets;
2. issuing the notes and the certificates;
3. making payments on the notes and the certificates; and
4. engaging in other activities that are necessary, suitable or convenient to accomplish the foregoing or are incidental to or connected with those activities.

On the Closing Date, the Trust will be capitalized with an amount equal to the certificate balance of $35,577,657.84 (the "Initial Certificate Balance"), excluding amounts deposited in the Reserve Fund. The certificates will be retained by the Seller. The equity of the Trust, together with the net proceeds from the sale of the notes, will be used by the Trust to purchase the Receivables from the Seller pursuant to the sale and servicing agreement among the Issuer, the Servicer and the Seller (the "Sale and Servicing Agreement") and to fund the Reserve Fund and the Yield Supplement Account.

American Honda Finance Corporation ("AHFC") will be appointed to act as the servicer of the Receivables (in that capacity, the "Servicer"). The Servicer will service the Receivables pursuant to the Sale and Servicing Agreement, the Administration Agreement and the Trust Agreement and will be compensated for those services as described under "Description of the Transfer and Servicing Agreements — Servicing Compensation" in this prospectus supplement and "Description of the Transfer and Servicing Agreements — Servicing Compensation" in the accompanying prospectus.

Pursuant to agreements between AHFC and the Dealers, each Dealer will repurchase from AHFC those contracts that do not meet specified representations and warranties made by the Dealer. These Dealer repurchase obligations are referred to in this prospectus supplement as "Dealer Recourse." Those representations and warranties relate primarily to the origination of the contracts and the perfection of the security interests in the related financed vehicles, and do not relate to the creditworthiness of the related Obligors or the collectability of those contracts. Although the Dealer Agreements with respect to the Receivables will not be assigned to the Issuer, the Sale and Servicing Agreement will require that any recovery by AHFC in respect of any Receivable pursuant to any Dealer Recourse be deposited in the Collection Account to satisfy AHFC's repurchase obligations under the Sale and Servicing Agreement. The sales by the Dealers of retail installment sale contracts to AHFC do not generally provide for recourse against the Dealers for unpaid amounts in the event of a default by an Obligor, other than in connection with the breach of the foregoing representations and warranties.

Each certificate represents a fractional undivided ownership interest in the Trust. The Trust property includes the Receivables and monies due or received under the Receivables on or after the Cutoff Date. The Reserve Fund will be maintained by the Indenture Trustee for the benefit of the Noteholders and the Yield Supplement Account will be maintained for the benefit of the Noteholders and the Certificateholders.

The Trust will be located in the State of Delaware and administered in New York, New York, in care of The Bank of New York, as Owner Trustee, at the address set forth below under "The Owner Trustee, the Delaware Trustee and the Indenture Trustee."

CAPITALIZATION OF THE TRUST

The following table illustrates the capitalization of the Trust as of the Closing Date, as if the issuance and sale of the notes and issuance of the certificates had taken place on that date:

Class A-1 Notes	$ 376,000,000.00
Class A-2 Notes	$ 462,000,000.00
Class A-3 Notes	$ 386,000,000.00
Class A-4 Notes	$ 317,700,000.00
Certificates	$ 35,577,657.84
Total	$1,577,277,657.84

In addition, the audited balance sheet of the Trust has been attached as Annex B to this prospectus supplement.

THE OWNER TRUSTEE, THE DELAWARE TRUSTEE AND THE INDENTURE TRUSTEE

The Bank of New York is the Owner Trustee under the Trust Agreement. The principal executive offices of The Bank of New York are located at 101 Barclay

Street, 8th Floor West, New York, New York 10286. The Seller and its affiliates may maintain normal commercial banking relations with the Owner Trustee and its affiliates.

The Bank of New York (Delaware) is the Delaware trustee (the "Delaware Trustee") under the Trust Agreement. The principal executive offices of the Delaware Trustee are located at White Clay Center Route 273, Newark, Delaware 19711.

JPMorgan Chase Bank is the indenture trustee under the Indenture (the "Indenture Trustee" and, together with the Owner Trustee and the Delaware Trustee, the "Trustees"). JPMorgan Chase Bank is a New York banking corporation and its corporate trust offices are located at 4 New York Plaza, 6th Floor, New York, New York 10004. The Seller and its affiliates may maintain normal commercial banking relations with the Indenture Trustee and its affiliates.

THE RECEIVABLES

The property of the Trust will consist of a pool of retail installment sale contracts (the "Receivables") originated on or after June 12, 1998, between Honda and Acura dealers (the "Dealers") and retail purchasers (the "Obligors"). The Receivables were originated by Dealers in accordance with AHFC's requirements under agreements with Dealers governing the assignment of the Receivables to AHFC. The Receivables evidence the indirect financing made available by AHFC to the Obligors. The Receivables are secured by new or used Honda and Acura motor vehicles (the "Financed Vehicles") and all principal and interest payments made on or after February 1, 2003 (the "Cutoff Date") and other property specified in the Receivables.

AHFC purchased the Receivables from the Dealers in the ordinary course of business in accordance with AHFC's underwriting standards. On or before the date of the initial issuance of the securities (the "Closing Date"), AHFC will sell the Receivables to the Seller. The Seller will, in turn, sell the Receivables to the Trust on the Closing Date pursuant to the Sale and Servicing Agreement. AHFC will continue to service the Receivables. The Receivables to be held by the Trust will be selected from those motor vehicle retail installment sale contracts in AHFC's portfolio that meet several criteria. These criteria provide that each Receivable:

1. was originated in the United States and the Obligor is not a federal, state or local governmental entity;
2. has a contractual Annual Percentage Rate ("APR") ranging from 1.90% to 15.39%;
3. provides for level monthly payments that fully amortize the amount financed over its original term except that the payment in the first or last month during the life of the Receivable may be minimally different from the level payment;

4. has a remaining term to maturity of not less than 6 months and not more than 59 months;
5. is less than 30 days past due;
6. was originated on or after June 12, 1998 and on or prior to October 30, 2002;
7. has been entered into by an Obligor that was not in bankruptcy proceedings or is bankrupt or insolvent (according to the records of AHFC); and
8. is secured by a Financed Vehicle that has not been repossessed (according to the records of AHFC).

No selection procedures believed to be adverse to the Securityholders will be utilized in selecting the Receivables from qualifying retail installment sale contracts. Except as described in item (2) above, the Receivables were not selected on the basis of their APRs.

The composition, distribution by APR and state of the Receivables as of the Cutoff Date are as set forth in the following tables. Approximately 99.89% and 0.11% of the Receivables (based on the Pool Balance as of the Cutoff Date) constitute Simple Interest Receivables and Precomputed Receivables, respectively. We refer you to "The Receivables" in the accompanying prospectus for a further description of the characteristics of Simple Interest Receivables and Precomputed Receivables.

COMPOSITION OF THE RECEIVABLES

Aggregate Principal Balance	$1,577,277,657.84
Number of Receivables	104,014
Average Principal Balance	$15,164.09
Average Original Amount Financed	$17,285.58
Range of Original Amount Financed	$2,013.32 to $81,062.46
Weighted Average APR(1)	5.55%
Range of APRs	1.90% to 15.39%
Weighted Average Original Term to Maturity(1)	57.35 months
Range of Original Terms to Maturity	12 months to 60 months
Weighted Average Remaining Term to Maturity(1)	50.82 months
Range of Remaining Terms to Maturity	6 months to 59 months
Percentage by Principal Balance of Receivables of New Motor Vehicles	8.16%

(1) Weighted by Principal Balance as of the Cutoff Date.

Percentage by Principal Balance of Receivables of Used Motor Vehicles 11.84%

Percentage by Principal Balance of Receivables Financed through Honda Dealers 93.04%

Percentage by Principal Balance of Receivables Financed through Acura Dealers 6.96%

DISTRIBUTION OF THE RECEIVABLES BY APR

(Percentages may not add to 100.00% due to rounding)

RANGE OF APRS (%)	NUMBER OF RECEIVABLES	PERCENTAGE OF AGGREGATE NUMBER OF RECEIVABLES	INITIAL POOL BALANCE	PERCENTAGE OF INITIAL POOL BALANCE
1.01 — 2.00	2,103	2.02%	$ 19,520,390.08	1.24%
2.01 — 3.00	4,504	4.33	46,645,308.64	2.96
3.01 — 4.00	5,735	5.51	93,208,880.05	5.91
4.01 — 5.00	53,019	50.97	834,614,559.04	52.91
5.01 — 6.00	16,081	15.46	241,153,691.76 1	5.29
6.01 — 7.00	8,171	7.86	129,112,549.12	8.19
7.01 — 8.00	4,000	3.85	61,553,066.50	3.90
8.01 — 9.00	3,060	2.94	44,716,841.86	2.84
9.01 — 10.00	2,581	2.48	38,793,944.52	2.46
10.01 — 11.00	3,460	3.33	53,619,264.30	3.40
11.01 — 12.00	884	0.85	10,030,329.14	0.64
12.01 — 13.00	339	0.33	3,675,584.62	0.23
13.01 — 14.00	60	0.06	516,247.63	0.03
14.01 — 15.00	15	0.01	104,135.23	0.01
15.01 — 16.00	2	0.00	12,865.35	0.00
TOTAL:	104,014	100.00%	$ 1,577,277,657.84	00.00%

DISTRIBUTION OF RECEIVABLES BY STATE(1) BASED ON THE ADDRESSES OF THE ORIGINATING DEALERS

(Percentages may not add to 100.00% due to rounding)

STATE	NUMBER OF RECEIVABLES	PERCENTAGE OF AGGREGATE NUMBER OF RECEIVABLES	INITIAL POOL BALANCE	PERCENTAGE OF INITIAL POOL BALANCE
Alabama	1,640	1.58%	$ 26,171,506.59	1.66%
Alaska	48	0.05	755,864.48	0.05
Arizona	1,892	1.82	29,836,810.13	1.89
Arkansas	631	0.61	9,830,482.91	0.62
California	18,376	17.67	273,462,943.60	17.34
Colorado	1,261	1.21	19,431,259.50	1.23
Connecticut	1,993	1.92	27,883,239.03	1.77
Delaware	625	0.60	8,939,357.76	0.57
Florida	6,066	5.83	95,477,126.90	6.05
Georgia	3,610	3.47	59,075,692.28	3.75
Hawaii	381	0.37	6,163,756.15	0.39
Idaho	164	0.16	2,562,101.39	0.16
Illinois	3,587	3.45	53,736,913.99	3.41
Indiana	1,125	1.08	16,582,724.14	1.05
Iowa	541	0.52	7,890,185.15	0.50
Kansas	575	0.55	8,812,096.15	0.56
Kentucky	789	0.76	11,618,557.85	0.74
Louisiana	1,556	1.50	24,797,915.62	1.57
Maryland	4,778	4.59	75,586,041.57	4.79
Massachusetts	2,549	2.45	33,962,271.99	2.15
Michigan	1,686	1.62	24,936,773.69	1.58
Minnesota	945	0.91	13,929,251.89	0.88
Mississippi	478	0.46	7,769,062.50	0.49
Missouri	1,583	1.52	23,961,585.32	1.52
Montana	128	0.12	1,825,345.87	0.12
Nebraska	326	0.31	4,770,425.23	0.30
Nevada	472	0.45	7,893,243.24	0.50
New Hampshire	607	0.58	8,159,562.50	0.52
New Jersey	6,228	5.99	91,287,810.69	5.79
New Mexico	384	0.37	6,114,274.32	0.39
New York	6,149	5.91	88,690,798.27	5.62

(1) Based solely on the addresses of the originating dealers.

North Carolina	3,260	3.13	50,171,900.58	3.18
North Dakota	119	0.11	1,877,571.33	0.12
Ohio	3,391	3.26	48,302,105.38	3.06
Oklahoma	878	0.84	13,533,290.63	0.86
Oregon	964	0.93	13,766,129.51	0.87
Pennsylvania	5,615	5.40	81,722,127.75	5.18
Rhode Island	328	0.32	4,578,717.77	0.29
South Carolina	1,564	1.50	24,318,581.64	1.54
South Dakota	141	0.14	2,050,831.63	0.13
Tennessee	2,275	2.19	37,210,441.29	2.36
Texas	7,490	7.20	123,394,243.67	7.82
Utah	478	0.46	7,354,243.58	0.47
Vermont	142	0.14	1,681,813.67	0.11
Virginia	3,219	3.09	50,539,272.63	3.20
Washington	1,639	1.58	25,462,564.11	1.61
West Virginia	290	0.28	4,505,330.45	0.29
Wisconsin	998	0.96	14,202,831.67	0.90
Wyoming	50	0.05	690,679.85	0.04
TOTAL:	104,014	100.00%	$ 1,577,277,657.84	100.00%

MATURITY AND PREPAYMENT CONSIDERATIONS

Information regarding maturity and prepayment considerations with respect to the securities is set forth under “Weighted Average Life of the Securities” in the accompanying prospectus and “Risk Factors — You may experience reduced returns on your investment resulting from prepayments, repurchases or early termination of the trust” in the accompanying prospectus. Except as otherwise provided in this prospectus supplement, no principal payments will be made on the class A-2 notes until the class A-1 notes have been paid in full; no principal payments will be made on the class A-3 notes until the class A-1 and class A-2 notes have been paid in full; and no principal payments will be made on the class A-4 notes until the class A-1, class A-2 and class A-3 notes have been paid in full. In addition, no principal payments will be made on the certificates until the class A-1 notes have been paid in full. We refer you to “Payments on the Notes” in this prospectus supplement.

Because the rate of payment of principal of each class of notes depends primarily on the rate of payment (including prepayments) of the principal balance of the Receivables, final payment of any class of notes could occur significantly earlier or later than their respective final scheduled Payment Dates set forth on the front cover (each, a “Final Scheduled Payment Date”) in this prospectus supplement. Securityholders will bear the risk of being able to reinvest principal payments on the securities at yields at least equal to the yield on their respective classes of notes. No assurance can be made as to the rate of prepayments on the Receivables in either stable or changing interest rate environments. Notwithstanding anything to the contrary, it is expected that the final payment of principal on the class A-1 notes will occur no later than March 18, 2004.

Although the Receivables have different APRs, disproportionate rates of prepayments of Receivables with APRs greater than or less than the Required Rate will generally not affect your yield. However, higher rates of prepayments of Receivables with higher APRs will decrease the amount available to cover delinquencies and defaults on the Receivables and may decrease the amounts available to be deposited in the Reserve Fund.

DELINQUENCIES, REPOSSESSIONS AND LOAN LOSS INFORMATION

Set forth below is information concerning AHFC's experience with respect to its entire portfolio of new and used Honda and Acura motor vehicle retail installment sale contracts, which includes contracts sold by but still being serviced by AHFC. Credit losses are an expected cost of extending credit and are considered in AHFC's rate-setting process. AHFC's strategy is to minimize credit losses while providing financing support for the sale of new or used Honda and Acura motor vehicles.

AHFC establishes an allowance for expected credit losses and deducts amounts reflecting charge — offs against such allowance. For retail financing, the account balance related to a retail installment sale contract is charged against the allowance for credit losses when the contract has been delinquent for 120 days, unless AHFC has repossessed the collateral associated with the contract. In these cases, the account balances are not charged against the allowance for credit losses until AHFC has either sold the repossessed motor vehicle or held it in repossession inventory for more than 90 days. AHFC credits any recoveries from charge-offs related to a retail installment sale contract to the allowance.

Delinquency, repossession and loss experience may be influenced by a variety of economic, social and geographic conditions and other factors beyond the control of AHFC. There is no assurance that AHFC's delinquency, repossession and loss experience with respect to its retail installment sale contracts, or the experience of the Trust with respect to the Receivables, will be similar to that set forth below.

There can be no assurance that the behavior of the Receivables included in the Trust will be comparable to AHFC's experience shown in the following tables. The percentages in the tables below have not been adjusted to eliminate the effect of the growth of AHFC's portfolio. Accordingly, the delinquency, repossession and net loss percentages would be expected to be higher than those shown if a group of receivables were isolated at a period in time and the delinquency, repossession and net loss data showed the activity only for that isolated group over the periods indicated.

In the table below, the period of delinquency for the years ended March 31, 1999 and 1998 was based on the number of days more than 40% of a scheduled payment on a cumulative basis was contractually past due. The period of delinquency for the reporting periods beginning with the fiscal year ended March 31, 2000, is based on the number of days more than 10% of a scheduled payment on a cumulative basis is contractually past due. If the period of delinquency used by AHFC for prior reporting periods was based on the number of days more than 10% of a scheduled payment on a cumulative basis was contractually past due, then its historical delinquency experience may have been materially higher in each of the prior years presented below.

DELINQUENCY EXPERIENCE(1)(5)
(DOLLARS IN THOUSANDS)

	AT DECEMBER 31,	AT MARCH 31,				
	2002	2002	2001	2000	1999	1998
Principal Amount Outstanding(2)	$ 13,864,417	$ 11,247,959	$ 8,108,877	$ 5,961,674	$ 4,011,174	$ 2,929,360
Delinquencies(3)						
30-59 Days	$ 192,623	$ 73,754	$ 57,434	$ 46,299	$ 30,781	$ 29,330
60-89 Days	35,003	10,932	8,560	6,693	4,847	4,400
90 Days or More	11,293	4,814	2,745	2,463	1,576	1,699
Repossessions(4)	31,991	24,623	12,027	8,300	7,968	7,438
Total Delinquencies and Repossessions	$ 270,910	$ 114,124	$ 80,766	$ 63,755	$ 45,173	$ 42,867
Total Delinquencies and Repossessions as a Percentage of Principal Amount Outstanding	1.95%	1.01%	1.00%	1.07%	1.13%	1.46%

(1) Includes contracts that have been sold but are still being serviced by AHFC.

(2) Remaining principal balance and unearned finance charges for all outstanding contracts.

(3) For the fiscal years ended March 31, 1999 and 1998, the period of delinquency was based upon the number of days more than 40% of the scheduled payment was contractually past due. For the reporting periods beginning with the fiscal year ended March 31, 2000, the period of delinquency is based on the number of days more than 10% of the scheduled payment is contractually past due.

(4) Amounts shown represent the outstanding principal balance for contracts for which the related vehicle had been repossessed and not yet liquidated.

(5) Totals may not add exactly due to rounding.

	FOR THE NINE MONTHS ENDED DECEMBER 31, 2002
Principal Amount Outstanding(2)	$13,864,417
Average Principal Amount Outstanding(3)	$12,844,730
Number of Contracts Outstanding	1,137,393
Average Number of Contracts Outstanding(3)	1,064,602
Number of Repossessions	6,552
Number of Repossessions as a Percentage of the Average Number of Contracts Outstanding	0.82%(7)
Gross Charge-Offs(4)	$ 56,838
Recoveries(5)	$ 15,713
Net Losses	$ 41,126
Net Losses as a Percentage of Average Principal Amount Outstanding	0.43%(7)

NET CREDIT LOSS AND REPOSSESSION EXPERIENCE(1)(6)
(DOLLARS IN THOUSANDS)
FOR THE YEAR ENDED MARCH 31,

	2002	2001	2000	1999	1998
Principal Amount Outstanding(2)	$11,247,959	$8,108,877	$5,961,674	$4,011,174	$2,929,360
Average Principal Amount Outstanding(3)	$10,080,855	$7,314,872	$5,146,609	$3,727,024	$2,675,524
Number of Contracts Outstanding	965,964	729,029	544,143	388,012	278,261
Average Number of Contracts Outstanding(3)	873,496	654,200	478,517	351,693	252,723
Number of Repossessions	5,736	4,131	3,092	2,968	3,576
Number of Repossessions as a Percentage of the Average Number of Contracts Outstanding	0.66%	0.63%	0.65%	0.84%	1.42%
Gross Charge-Offs(4)	$ 45,967	$ 28,443	$ 24,626	$ 25,119	$ 32,598
Recoveries(5)	14,988	12,383	10,043	10,719	8,245
Net Losses	$ 30,979	$ 16,060	$ 14,583	$ 14,399	$ 24,353
Net Losses as a Percentage of Average Principal Amount Outstanding	0.31%	0.22%	0.28%	0.39%	0.91%

(1) Includes contracts that have been sold but are still being serviced by AHFC.

(2) Remaining principal balance and unearned finance charges for all outstanding contracts.

(3) Average of the loan balance or number of contracts, as the case may be, is calculated for a period by dividing the total monthly amounts by the number of months in the period.

(4) Amount charged-off is the remaining principal balance, excluding any expenses associated with collection, repossession or disposition of the related vehicle, plus earned but not yet received finance charges, net of any proceeds collected prior to charge-off.

(5) Proceeds received on previously charged-off contracts.

(6) Totals may not add exactly due to rounding.

(7) Annualized.

WEIGHTED AVERAGE LIFE OF THE NOTES

Prepayments on motor vehicle receivables can be measured relative to a payment standard or model. The model used in this prospectus supplement, the Absolute Prepayment Model ("ABS"), represents an assumed rate of prepayment each month relative to the original number of receivables in a pool of receivables. ABS further assumes that all the receivables in question are the same size and amortize at the same rate and that each receivable in each month of its life will either be paid as scheduled or be paid in full. For example, in a pool of receivables originally containing 10,000 receivables, a 1% ABS rate means that 1% of the receivables, or 100 receivables, prepay each month. ABS does not purport to be an historical description of prepayment experience or a prediction of the anticipated rate of prepayment of any pool of receivables, including the Receivables.

As the rate of the payment of principal of each class of notes will depend on the rate of payment (including prepayments) of the principal balance of the Receivables, final payment of any class of notes could occur significantly earlier than the respective Final Scheduled Payment Dates. Reinvestment risk associated with early payment of the notes of any class will be borne exclusively by the holders of such notes.

The tables captioned "Percentage of Initial Class A Note Principal at Various ABS Percentages" (the "ABS Tables") have been prepared on the basis of the characteristics of the Receivables described under "The Receivables Pool". The ABS Tables assume that (1) the Receivables prepay in full at the specified constant percentage of ABS monthly, with no defaults, losses or repurchases, (2) each scheduled monthly payment on each Receivable is scheduled to be made and is made on the last day of each month and each month has 30 days, (3) payments are made on the notes on each Payment Date (and each such date is assumed to be the 18th day of each applicable month), (4) the balance in the Reserve Fund on each Payment Date is the required amount described under "Credit Enhancement — Reserve Fund" and (5) except as indicated in the ABS Tables, the Servicer does not exercise its option to purchase the Receivables on the earliest Payment Date on which such option may be exercised. The hypothetical pools each have a cut-off date of February 1, 2003. The ABS Tables indicate the projected weighted average life of each class of notes and sets forth the percentage of the initial principal amount of each class of notes that is projected to be outstanding after each of the Payment Dates shown at various constant ABS percentages.

The ABS Tables also assume that the Receivables have been aggregated into hypothetical pools with all of the receivables within each such pool having the following characteristics and that the level scheduled monthly payment for each of the pools (which is based on the aggregate principal balance, APR, original term to maturity and remaining term to maturity as of the assumed cutoff date) will be such that each pool will be fully amortized by the end of its remaining term to maturity.

POOL	AGGREGATE PRINCIPAL BALANCE	APR	REMAINING TERM TO MATURITY (IN MONTHS)	ORIGINAL TERM TO MATURITY (IN MONTHS)
1	$ 24,987.50	8.405%	6	60
2	$ 6,548,619.26	8.407%	10	59
3	$ 2,720,114.70	5.623%	16	37
4	$ 25,560,325.00	2.853%	20	26
5	$ 55,080,371.09	3.622%	28	37
6	$ 48,221,255.83	5.265%	32	39
7	$ 40,593,689.54	6.154%	40	51
8	$ 187,865,070.61	6.466%	46	57
9	$ 435,109,186.95	5.752%	52	60
10	$ 775,554,037.36	5.394%	56	60
TOTAL	$1,577,277,657.84			

The actual characteristics and performance of the Receivables will differ from the assumptions used in constructing the ABS Tables. The assumptions used are hypothetical and have been provided only to give a general sense of how the principal cash flows might behave under varying prepayment scenarios. For example, it is very unlikely that the Receivables will prepay at a constant level of ABS until maturity or that all of the Receivables will prepay at the same level of ABS. Moreover, the diverse terms of receivables within each of the hypothetical pools could produce slower or faster principal distributions than indicated in the ABS Table at the various constant percentages of ABS specified, even if the original and remaining terms to maturity of the Receivables are as assumed. Any difference between such assumptions and the actual characteristics and performance of the Receivables, or actual prepayment experience, will affect the percentages of initial amounts outstanding over time and the weighted average life of each class of notes.

PERCENTAGE OF INITIAL CLASS A-1 NOTE PRINCIPAL AT VARIOUS ABS PERCENTAGES

PAYMENT DATE	0.50%	1.00%	1.30%	1.50%	1.70%	2.00%
Closing Date	100.00%	100.00%	100.00%	100.00%	100.00%	100.00%
March, 2003	90.03	87.74	86.28	85.25	84.15	81.13
April, 2003	80.11	75.62	72.75	70.74	68.59	64.33
May, 2003	70.24	63.64	59.42	56.47	53.34	47.86
June, 2003	60.41	51.80	46.30	42.45	38.38	31.71
July, 2003	50.63	40.09	33.37	28.67	23.73	15.90
August, 2003	40.89	28.53	20.64	15.15	9.38	0.42
September, 2003	31.21	17.11	8.12	1.87	0.00	0.00
October, 2003	21.58	5.83	0.00	0.00	0.00	0.00
November, 2003	11.99	0.00	0.00	0.00	0.00	0.00
December, 2003	2.46	0.00	0.00	0.00	0.00	0.00
January, 2004	0.00	0.00	0.00	0.00	0.00	0.00
Weighted Average Life (years) (1)(2)	0.45	0.37	0.34	0.31	0.30	0.27
Weighted Average Life (years) (1)(3)	0.45	0.37	0.34	0.31	0.30	0.27

(1) The weighted average life of a Note is determined by (x) multiplying the amount of each principal payment on a Note by the number of years from the date of issuance of the Note to the related Payment Date, (y) adding the results and (z) dividing the sum by the original principal amount of the Note.

(2) This calculation assumes that the Servicer does not exercise its option to purchase the Receivables.

(3) This calculation assumes that the Servicer exercises its option to purchase the Receivables.

This Table has been prepared based on the assumptions herein (including the assumptions regarding the characteristics and performance of the Receivables, which will differ from the actual characteristics and performance thereof) and should be read in conjunction therewith.

PERCENTAGE OF INITIAL CLASS A-2 NOTE PRINCIPAL AT VARIOUS ABS PERCENTAGES

PAYMENT DATE	0.50%	1.00%	1.30%	1.50%	1.70%	2.00%
Closing Date	100.00%	100.00%	100.00%	100.00%	100.00%	100.00%
March, 2003	100.00	100.00	100.00	100.00	100.00	100.00
April, 2003	100.00	100.00	100.00	100.00	100.00	100.00
May, 2003	100.00	100.00	100.00	100.00	100.00	100.00
June, 2003	100.00	100.00	100.00	100.00	100.00	100.00
July, 2003	100.00	100.00	100.00	100.00	100.00	100.00
August, 2003	100.00	100.00	100.00	100.00	100.00	100.00
September, 2003	100.00	100.00	100.00	100.00	96.32	88.37
October, 2003	100.00	100.00	96.69	91.19	85.48	76.67
November, 2003	100.00	95.81	87.13	81.11	74.88	65.24
December, 2003	100.00	87.13	77.73	71.23	64.53	54.09
January, 2004	94.58	78.67	68.58	61.60	54.41	43.20
February, 2004	87.26	70.33	59.59	52.17	44.52	32.59
March, 2004	79.98	62.10	50.76	42.92	34.85	22.25
April, 2004	72.74	53.99	42.09	33.87	25.40	12.20
May, 2004	65.53	45.98	33.58	25.01	16.18	2.42
June, 2004	58.37	38.09	25.23	16.35	7.19	0.00
July, 2004	51.28	30.35	17.07	7.90	0.00	0.00
August, 2004	44.24	22.72	9.08	0.00	0.00	0.00
September, 2004	37.23	15.21	1.24	0.00	0.00	0.00
October, 2004	30.26	7.81	0.00	0.00	0.00	0.00
November, 2004	23.58	0.75	0.00	0.00	0.00	0.00
December, 2004	16.94	0.00	0.00	0.00	0.00	0.00
January, 2005	10.34	0.00	0.00	0.00	0.00	0.00
February, 2005	3.79	0.00	0.00	0.00	0.00	0.00
March, 2005	0.00	0.00	0.00	0.00	0.00	0.00
Weighted Average Life (years) (1)(2)	1.46	1.24	1.12	1.05	0.98	0.89
Weighted Average Life (years) (1)(3)	1.46	1.24	1.12	1.05	0.98	0.89

(1) The weighted average life of a Note is determined by (x) multiplying the amount of each principal payment on a Note by the number of years from the date of issuance of the Note to the related Payment Date, (y) adding the results and (z) dividing the sum by the original principal amount of the Note.

(2) This calculation assumes that the Servicer does not exercise its option to purchase the Receivables.

(3) This calculation assumes that the Servicer exercises its option to purchase the Receivables.

This Table has been prepared based on the assumptions herein (including the assumptions regarding the characteristics and performance of the Receivables, which will differ from the actual characteristics and performance thereof) and should be read in conjunction therewith.

PERCENTAGE OF INITIAL CLASS A-3 NOTE PRINCIPAL AT VARIOUS ABS PERCENTAGES

PAYMENT DATE	0.50%	1.00%	1.30%	1.50%	1.70%	2.00%
Closing Date	100.00%	100.00%	100.00%	100.00%	100.00%	100.00%
March, 2003	100.00	100.00	100.00	100.00	100.00	100.00
April, 2003	100.00	100.00	100.00	100.00	100.00	100.00
May, 2003	100.00	100.00	100.00	100.00	100.00	100.00
June, 2003	100.00	100.00	100.00	100.00	100.00	100.00
July, 2003	100.00	100.00	100.00	100.00	100.00	100.00
August, 2003	100.00	100.00	100.00	100.00	100.00	100.00
September, 2003	100.00	100.00	100.00	100.00	100.00	100.00
October, 2003	100.00	100.00	100.00	100.00	100.00	100.00
November, 2003	100.00	100.00	100.00	100.00	100.00	100.00
December, 2003	100.00	100.00	100.00	100.00	100.00	100.00
January, 2004	100.00	100.00	100.00	100.00	100.00	100.00
February, 2004	100.00	100.00	100.00	100.00	100.00	100.00
March, 2004	100.00	100.00	100.00	100.00	100.00	100.00
April, 2004	100.00	100.00	100.00	100.00	100.00	100.00
May, 2004	100.00	100.00	100.00	100.00	100.00	100.00
June, 2004	100.00	100.00	100.00	100.00	100.00	91.53
July, 2004	100.00	100.00	100.00	100.00	98.14	80.52
August, 2004	100.00	100.00	100.00	99.58	87.96	69.85
September, 2004	100.00	100.00	100.00	89.94	78.05	59.52
October, 2004	100.00	100.00	92.31	80.54	68.42	49.54
November, 2004	100.00	100.00	83.57	71.60	59.27	40.07
December, 2004	100.00	92.57	75.01	62.88	50.39	30.94
January, 2005	100.00	84.39	66.65	54.40	41.79	22.14
February, 2005	100.00	76.34	58.48	46.15	33.45	13.68
March, 2005	96.73	68.43	50.51	38.14	25.40	5.57
April, 2005	88.98	60.67	42.74	30.36	17.62	0.00
May, 2005	81.27	53.04	35.17	22.83	10.13	0.00
June, 2005	73.62	45.55	27.79	15.53	2.92	0.00
July, 2005	66.45	38.56	20.91	8.74	0.00	0.00

August, 2005	59.33	31.71	14.23	2.17	0.00	0.00
September, 2005	52.26	24.98	7.73	0.00	0.00	0.00
October, 2005	45.23	18.40	1.42	0.00	0.00	0.00
November, 2005	38.59	12.21	0.00	0.00	0.00	0.00
December, 2005	32.00	6.15	0.00	0.00	0.00	0.00
January, 2006	25.45	0.22	0.00	0.00	0.00	0.00
February, 2006	18.95	0.00	0.00	0.00	0.00	0.00
March, 2006	12.49	0.00	0.00	0.00	0.00	0.00
April, 2006	6.08	0.00	0.00	0.00	0.00	0.00
May, 2006	0.00	0.00	0.00	0.00	0.00	0.00
Weighted Average Life (years) (1)(2)	2.65	2.32	2.13	2.00	1.88	1.70
Weighted Average Life (years) (1)(3)	2.65	2.32	2.13	2.00	1.88	1.70

(1) The weighted average life of a Note is determined by (x) multiplying the amount of each principal payment on a Note by the number of years from the date of issuance of the Note to the related Payment Date, (y) adding the results and (z) dividing the sum by the original principal amount of the Note.

(2) This calculation assumes that the Servicer does not exercise its option to purchase the Receivables.

(3) This calculation assumes that the Servicer exercises its option to purchase the Receivables.

This Table has been prepared based on the assumptions herein (including the assumptions regarding the characteristics and performance of the Receivables, which will differ from the actual characteristics and performance thereof) and should be read in conjunction therewith.

PERCENTAGE OF INITIAL CLASS A-4 NOTE PRINCIPAL AT VARIOUS ABS PERCENTAGES

PAYMENT DATE	0.50%	1.00%	1.30%	1.50%	1.70%	2.00%
Closing Date	100.00%	100.00%	100.00%	100.00%	100.00%	100.00%
March, 2003	100.00	100.00	100.00	100.00	100.00	100.00
April, 2003	100.00	100.00	100.00	100.00	100.00	100.00
May, 2003	100.00	100.00	100.00	100.00	100.00	100.00
June, 2003	100.00	100.00	100.00	100.00	100.00	100.00
July, 2003	100.00	100.00	100.00	100.00	100.00	100.00
August, 2003	100.00	100.00	100.00	100.00	100.00	100.00
September, 2003	100.00	100.00	100.00	100.00	100.00	100.00
October, 2003	100.00	100.00	100.00	100.00	100.00	100.00
November, 2003	100.00	100.00	100.00	100.00	100.00	100.00
December, 2003	100.00	100.00	100.00	100.00	100.00	100.00
January, 2004	100.00	100.00	100.00	100.00	100.00	100.00

February, 2004	100.00	100.00	100.00	100.00	100.00	100.00
March, 2004	100.00	100.00	100.00	100.00	100.00	100.00
April, 2004	100.00	100.00	100.00	100.00	100.00	100.00
May, 2004	100.00	100.00	100.00	100.00	100.00	100.00
June, 2004	100.00	100.00	100.00	100.00	100.00	100.00
July, 2004	100.00	100.00	100.00	100.00	100.00	100.00
August, 2004	100.00	100.00	100.00	100.00	100.00	100.00
September, 2004	100.00	100.00	100.00	100.00	100.00	100.00
October, 2004	100.00	100.00	100.00	100.00	100.00	100.00
November, 2004	100.00	100.00	100.00	100.00	100.00	100.00
December, 2004	100.00	100.00	100.00	100.00	100.00	100.00
January, 2005	100.00	100.00	100.00	100.00	100.00	100.00
February, 2005	100.00	100.00	100.00	100.00	100.00	100.00
March, 2005	100.00	100.00	100.00	100.00	100.00	100.00
April, 2005	100.00	100.00	100.00	100.00	100.00	97.32
May, 2005	100.00	100.00	100.00	100.00	100.00	88.29
June, 2005	100.00	100.00	100.00	100.00	100.00	79.69
July, 2005	100.00	100.00	100.00	100.00	95.39	71.70
August, 2005	100.00	100.00	100.00	100.00	87.56	64.11
September, 2005	100.00	100.00	100.00	94.93	80.05	56.91
October, 2005	100.00	100.00	100.00	87.50	72.88	50.13
November, 2005	100.00	100.00	94.56	80.58	66.21	43.86*
December, 2005	100.00	100.00	87.62	73.93	59.86	37.98
January, 2006	100.00	100.00	80.90	67.55	53.83	32.50
February, 2006	100.00	93.23	74.41	61.44	48.11*	27.40
March, 2006	100.00	86.35	68.15	55.60	42.72	22.71
April, 2006	100.00	79.63	62.11	50.05	37.65	18.41
May, 2006	99.66	73.08	56.31	44.76*	32.91	14.51
June, 2006	91.99	66.69	50.74	39.76	28.50	11.24
July, 2006	84.64	60.65	45.54*	35.14	24.47	8.28
August, 2006	77.36	54.77	40.56	30.78	20.75	5.64
September, 2006	70.13	49.06	35.81	26.70	17.36	3.94
October, 2006	62.95	43.51*	31.29	22.90	14.30	2.43
November, 2006	55.84	38.12	27.00	19.37	11.56	1.12
December, 2006	48.78	32.90	22.95	16.13	9.15	0.00
January, 2007	42.85*	28.51	19.54	13.38	7.09	0.00
February, 2007	36.96%	24.26%	16.32%	10.88%	5.31%	0.00%
March, 2007	31.13	20.16	13.30	8.61	3.81	0.00
April, 2007	25.34	16.19	10.48	6.57	2.58	0.00

May, 2007	19.61	12.37	7.86	4.78	1.65	0.00
June, 2007	13.93	8.69	5.44	3.23	0.98	0.00
July, 2007	10.40	6.38	3.89	2.20	0.47	0.00
August, 2007	6.90	4.17	2.47	1.32	0.14	0.00
September, 2007	3.43	2.04	1.17	0.58	0.00	0.00
October, 2007	0.00	0.00	0.00	0.00	0.00	0.00
Weighted Average Life (years) (1)(2)	3.88	3.65	3.45	3.28	3.08	2.76
Weighted Average Life (years) (1)(3)	3.72	3.45	3.21	3.04	2.83	2.57
*Month of Optional Purchase (3)	Jan-07	Oct-06	Jul-06	May-06	Feb-06	Nov-05

(1) The weighted average life of a Note is determined by (x) multiplying the amount of each principal payment on a Note by the number of years from the date of issuance of the Note to the related Payment Date, (y) adding the results and (z) dividing the sum by the original principal amount of the Note.

(2) This calculation assumes that the Servicer does not exercise its option to purchase the Receivables.

(3) This calculation assumes that the Servicer exercises its option to purchase the Receivables.

This Table has been prepared based on the assumptions herein (including the assumptions regarding the characteristics and performance of the Receivables, which will differ from the actual characteristics and performance thereof) and should be read in conjunction therewith.

NOTE FACTORS

The "Note Pool Factor" with respect to any class of notes will be a seven-digit decimal indicating the principal amount of that class of notes as of the close of business on the Payment Date in that month as a fraction of the respective principal amount thereof as of the Closing Date. The Servicer will compute the Note Pool Factor each month for each class of notes. Each Note Pool Factor will initially be 1.0000000 and thereafter will decline to reflect reductions in the principal amount of each class of notes. The portion of the principal amount of any class of notes for a given month allocable to a Noteholder can be determined by multiplying the original denomination of the holder's note by the related Note Pool Factor for that month.

Pursuant to the Transfer and Servicing Agreements, the Securityholders will receive monthly reports concerning the payments received on the Receivables, the Pool Balance, the related Note Pool Factors and various other items of information pertaining to the Trust. Securityholders of record during each calendar year will be furnished information by the Indenture Trustee or the Owner Trustee, as appropriate, for tax reporting purposes not later than the latest date permitted by law. We refer you to "Description of the Transfer and Servicing Agreements — Statements to Securityholders" in the accompanying prospectus.

USE OF PROCEEDS

The Seller will use the net proceeds from the sale of the Securities to purchase the Receivables from AHFC pursuant to the Purchase Agreement and to fund the Reserve Fund and the Yield Supplement Account.

THE SELLER AND THE SERVICER

Information regarding the Seller and the Servicer is set forth under the captions "The Seller" and "The Servicer" in the accompanying prospectus.

THE NOTES

GENERAL

The notes will be issued pursuant to the terms of the Indenture, a form of which has been filed as an exhibit to the registration statement. A copy of the final signed Indenture will be filed with the Securities and Exchange Commission (the "SEC") following the issuance of the Securities. The following summary describes material terms of the notes and the Indenture. The summary does not purport to be complete and is subject to, and is qualified in its entirety by reference to, all the provisions of the notes and the Indenture. Where particular provisions or terms used in the Indenture are referred to, the actual provisions (including definitions of terms) are incorporated by reference as part of the summary. The following summary supplements, and to the extent inconsistent therewith replaces, the description of the general terms and provisions of the notes of any given series and the related Indenture set forth in the accompanying prospectus, to which description reference is hereby made.

PAYMENTS OF INTEREST

Each class of notes will constitute Fixed Rate Securities, as that term is defined under "Certain Information Regarding the Securities — Fixed Rate Securities" in the accompanying prospectus. Interest on the principal balances of the classes of the notes will accrue at the respective per annum interest rates set forth on the cover of this prospectus supplement (each, an "Interest Rate") and will be due and payable to the Noteholders monthly on the 18th of each month (or, if that date is not a Business Day, on the next succeeding Business Day) (a "Payment Date") commencing March 18, 2003.

Interest on the outstanding principal amount of class A-1 notes will accrue at the related Interest Rate from and including the most recent Payment Date on which interest has been paid (or from and including the Closing Date with respect to the first Payment Date) to but excluding the current Payment Date. Interest on the class A-2, class A-3 and class A-4 notes will accrue at the related Interest Rate from and including the 18th day of the month (or from and including the Closing Date with respect to the first Payment Date) to and excluding the 18th day of the following calendar month.

Interest on the class A-1 notes will be calculated on the basis of the actual number of days in the related Interest Period divided by 360, and interest on the class A-2, class A-3 notes and the class A-4 notes will be calculated on the basis of a 360-day year consisting of twelve 30-day months. Interest accrued but not paid on any Payment Date will be due on the next Payment Date, together with interest on that amount at the applicable Interest Rate (to the extent lawful). Interest payments on the notes will generally be made from Available Amounts and from amounts on deposit in the Reserve Fund, after the Servicing Fee, non-recoverable Advances and all accrued and unpaid Trustees' fees, and any amounts due to the Trustees for reimbursement of expenses or in respect of indemnification and other administrative fees of the Trust ("Trust Fees and Expenses") have been paid; provided, however, that until the notes have been paid in full, the annual amount paid to the Trustees out of the Available Amounts allocation described herein shall not exceed $100,000. We refer you to "Credit Enhancement — Reserve Fund" and "Payments on the Notes" in this prospectus supplement.

Interest payments to holders of the class A-1 notes, the class A-2 notes, the class A-3 notes and the class A-4 notes (collectively, the "Notes") will have the same priority. Under specified circumstances, the amount available for interest payments could be less than the amount of interest payable on the notes on any Payment Date, in which case the holders of the Notes will receive their ratable share (based upon the aggregate amount of interest due to that class) of the aggregate amount available to be distributed in respect of interest on the notes.

PAYMENTS OF PRINCIPAL

Until the notes have been paid in full, principal payments to Noteholders will be made on each Payment Date in the amount and order of priority described in this prospectus supplement under "Payments on the Notes — Payment of Distributable Amounts." On each Payment Date, principal of the notes will be payable generally in an amount equal to the Noteholders' Percentage of the Principal Distributable Amount. Principal payments on the notes will be made from Available Amounts after the Servicing Fee, non-recoverable Advances and Trust Fees and Expenses have been paid and after the Noteholders' Interest Distributable Amount has been distributed. Notwithstanding the foregoing, if amounts actually allocated to the Noteholders on any Payment Date is less than the Noteholders' Distributable Amount, funds will be withdrawn from the Reserve Fund so that an amount equal to the Noteholders' Distributable Amount may be allocated to the Noteholders.

Principal payments will be allocated among the notes so that no principal payments will be made on:

1. the class A-2 notes until the class A-1 notes have been paid in full;
2. the class A-3 notes until the class A-1 notes and class A-2 notes have been paid in full; and

3. the class A-4 notes until the class A-1 notes, class A-2 notes and class A-3 notes have been paid in full.

Notwithstanding the foregoing, on each Payment Date after the acceleration of the notes following an Event of Default, the notes will receive 100% of the Principal Distributable Amount until the notes are paid in full. That Principal Distributable Amount will be paid first to holders of record of each of the class A-1 notes until the class A-1 notes have been paid in full. After the class A-1 notes have been paid in full principal payments will be made to the class A-2 notes, the class A-3 notes and the class A-4 notes (together with the holders of the class A-1 notes, the "Noteholders") on a pro rata basis based on the principal balance of that class of outstanding notes. Beginning on the Payment Date on which the Notes have been paid in full, the remainder of the Principal Distributable Amount, if any, and on each subsequent Payment Date, 100% of the Principal Distributable Amount, will be paid to the holders of record of the certificates (the "Certificateholders") until the certificates have been paid in full.

The actual Payment Date on which the outstanding principal amount of any class of notes is paid may be significantly earlier than its Final Scheduled Payment Date based on a variety of factors, including the factors described under "Weighted Average Life of the Securities" in the accompanying prospectus.

If the principal amount of a class of notes has not been paid in full on or prior to its Final Scheduled Payment Date, the Noteholders' Principal Distributable Amount for that Payment Date will, to the extent the remaining Available Amounts are sufficient, include an amount sufficient to reduce the unpaid principal amount of that class of notes to zero on that Payment Date. We refer you to "Payment on the Notes — Payment of Distributable Amounts" in this prospectus supplement.

EVENTS OF DEFAULT; RIGHTS UPON EVENT OF DEFAULT.

Upon an Event of Default under the Indenture, the Noteholders will have the rights set forth in the prospectus under "The Notes — Indenture — Events of Default; Rights Upon Event of Default." The Indenture Trustee may sell the Receivables subject to certain conditions set forth in the Indenture following an Event of Default, including a default in the payment of any principal on any note or a default for five days or more in the payment of any interest on any note. In the case of an Event of Default not involving any such default in payment, the Indenture Trustee is prohibited from selling the Receivables unless one of the conditions set forth in the accompanying prospectus under "The Notes — Indenture — Events of Default and — Rights Upon Event of Default" has been satisfied.

NOTICES

Noteholders will be notified in writing by the Indenture Trustee of any Event of Default, Servicer Default or termination of, or appointment of a successor to, the

Servicer promptly upon a Responsible Officer (as defined in the Transfer and Servicing Agreements) obtaining actual knowledge of these events.

If notes are issued other than in book-entry form, those notices will be mailed to the addresses of Noteholders as they appear in the register maintained by the Indenture Trustee prior to mailing. Those notices will be deemed to have been given on the date of that publication or mailing.

GOVERNING LAW

The Indenture and the notes are governed by and shall be construed in accordance with the laws of the State of California applicable to agreements made in and to be performed wholly within that jurisdiction.

THE CERTIFICATES

GENERAL

The certificates will be issued pursuant to the terms of the Trust Agreement, a form of which has been filed as an exhibit to the registration statement. A copy of the final signed Trust Agreement will be filed with the SEC following the issuance of the securities. The certificates will evidence undivided ownership interests in the Trust created pursuant to the Trust Agreement.

The following summary describes material terms of the certificates and the Trust Agreement. The summary does not purport to be complete and is subject to, and qualified in its entirety by reference to, all the provisions of the certificates and the Trust Agreement. The following summary supplements, and to the extent inconsistent therewith replaces, the description of the general terms and provisions of the certificates of any given series and the related Trust Agreement set forth in the accompanying prospectus, to which description reference is hereby made.

PAYMENTS OF INTEREST

Interest on the Certificate Balance will accrue during each Interest Period at 2.48% per annum (the "Pass Through Rate") and will be payable to the Certificateholders on the related Payment Date.

The certificates will constitute Fixed Rate Securities, as that term is defined under "Certain Information Regarding the Securities — Fixed Rate Securities" in the accompanying prospectus. Interest due on a Payment Date will accrue during the related Interest Period and will be calculated on the basis of a 360-day year consisting of twelve 30-day months. Interest distributions with respect to the certificates generally will be made from Available Amounts after:

1. payment of the Servicing Fee;
2. payment of accrued and unpaid Trust Fees and Expenses to the Trustees; provided that, until the Notes have been paid in full, the annual amount paid to the Trustees out of the Available Amount allocation described herein shall not exceed $100,000;

3. distribution of the Noteholders' Distributable Amounts to the Noteholders; and
4. depositing of funds in the Reserve Fund so that the amount on deposit in the Reserve Fund equals the Specified Reserve Fund Balance.

We refer you to "Payments on the Notes — Payment of Distributable Amounts" in this prospectus supplement.

Interest payments due for any Payment Date but not paid on that Payment Date will be due on the next Payment Date increased by an amount equal to interest accrued on that amount at the Pass Through Rate (to the extent lawful).

PAYMENTS OF PRINCIPAL

No principal payments will be made on the certificates until the class A-1 notes have been paid in full. Thereafter, principal payments of the certificates will be made on each Payment Date from Available Amounts after payments of certain fees and expenses, the Noteholders' Interest Distributable Amount, the Noteholders' Percentage of the Principal Distributable Amount, payment, if any, to the Reserve Fund and payment of interest on the certificates.

Notwithstanding the foregoing, on each Payment Date after the acceleration of the notes following an Event of Default, the certificates will not receive any of the Principal Distributable Amount until the notes have been paid in full.

NOTICES

Certificateholders will be notified in writing by the Owner Trustee of any Event of Default, Servicer Default or termination of, or appointment of a successor to, the Servicer promptly upon specified officer of the Owner Trustee obtaining actual knowledge of these events. Except for the monthly and annual reports to Certificateholders described this prospectus supplement, the Owner Trustee is not obligated under the Trust Agreement to forward any other notices to the Certificateholders. There are no provisions in the Trust Agreement for the regular or special meetings of Certificateholders.

GOVERNING LAW

The Trust Agreement and the certificates are governed by and shall be construed in accordance with the laws of the State of Delaware applicable to agreements made in and to be performed wholly within that jurisdiction.

PAYMENTS ON THE NOTES

On or before the 13th calendar day of each month (or, if the 13th day is not a Business Day, the next succeeding Business Day (each a "Determination Date"), the Servicer will inform the Owner Trustee and the Indenture Trustee of, among other things, the amount of funds collected on or in respect of the Receivables, the amount of Advances to be made by and reimbursed to the Servicer and the Servicing Fee and other servicing compensation payable to the Servicer, in each case with respect to the immediately preceding Collection Period. On or prior to each Payment Date, the Servicer will also determine the following:

1. Available Amounts;
2. Noteholders' Interest Distributable Amount;
3. Certificateholders' Interest Distributable Amount;
4. Principal Distributable Amount;
5. Yield Supplement Withdrawal Amount, if any; and
6. based on the available funds and other amounts available for payment on the related Payment Date as described below, the amount to be distributed to the Noteholders and Certificateholders.

The Indenture Trustee or the Issuer, as the case may be, will make payments to the Noteholders and Certificateholders out of the amounts on deposit in the Collection Account. The amounts to be distributed to the Noteholders and Certificateholders will be determined in the manner described below.

CALCULATION OF AVAILABLE AMOUNTS

The amount of funds available for distribution on a Payment Date (the "Available Amounts") will generally equal the sum of the following amounts (without duplication) received or allocated by the Servicer on or in respect of the Receivables during the related Collection Period (which in the case of Precomputed Receivables shall be computed in accordance with the actuarial method and in the case of the Simple Interest Receivables shall be calculated in accordance with the simple interest method):

1. all collections on or in respect of the Receivables other than Defaulted Receivables;
2. all amounts realized on Defaulted Receivables from whatever sources (including, without limitation, proceeds of any insurance policy), net of expenses incurred by the Servicer in accordance with its customary servicing procedures and amounts required by law to be refunded to the related Obligor ("Net Liquidation Proceeds");
3. all Advances made by the Servicer;
4. all Warranty Purchase Payments with respect to Warranty Receivables repurchased by the Seller in respect of that Collection Period;
5. all Administrative Purchase Payments with respect to Administrative Receivables purchased by the Servicer in respect of that Collection Period; and
6. any Yield Supplement Withdrawal Amounts.

Available Amounts on any Payment Date will exclude the following amounts:

1. amounts received on a particular Receivable (other than a Defaulted Receivable) to the extent that the Servicer has previously made an unreimbursed Advance in respect of that Receivable; and

2. Net Liquidation Proceeds with respect to a particular Receivable to the extent of unreimbursed Advances in respect of that Receivable.

A "Defaulted Receivable" is a Receivable (other than an Administrative Receivable or a Warranty Receivable) as to which, (a) all or part of a scheduled payment is 120 days or more than 120 days past due and the Servicer has not repossessed the related Financed Vehicle or (b) the Servicer has, in accordance with its customary servicing procedures, determined that eventual payment in full is unlikely and has either repossessed and liquidated the related Financed Vehicle or repossessed and held the related Financed Vehicle and held in its repossession inventory for 90 days, whichever occurs first.

PAYMENT OF DISTRIBUTABLE AMOUNTS

Prior to each Payment Date, the Servicer will calculate the amount to be distributed to the Noteholders and Certificateholders. On each Payment Date, the Servicer will allocate amounts on deposit in the Collection Account with respect to the related Collection Period as described below and will instruct the Indenture Trustee to make the following payments and distributions from amounts on deposit in the Collection Account in the following amounts and order of priority:

1. to the Servicer, the Servicing Fee, including any unpaid Servicing Fees with respect to one or more prior Collection Periods, and non-recoverable Advances;
2. to the Indenture Trustee, the Delaware Trustee and the Owner Trustee, any accrued and unpaid Trust Fees and Expenses, in each case to the extent such fees and expenses have not been previously paid by the Servicer, in its capacity as administrator under the related administration agreement; provided that, until the Notes have been paid in full, the annual amount paid to the Trustees out of the Available Amount allocation described in this clause (2) shall not exceed $100,000;
3. to the Noteholders, the Noteholders' Interest Distributable Amount, from Available Amounts;
4. to the Noteholders, the Noteholders' Principal Distributable Amount, from Available Amounts;
5. to the Reserve Fund, from Available Amounts remaining (this amount being the "Excess Amount"), the amount necessary to cause the amount on deposit in that account to equal the Specified Reserve Fund Balance;
6. to the Certificateholders, the Certificateholders' Interest Distributable Amount, from Available Amounts;
7. after the class A-1 notes have been paid in full, to the Certificateholders, the Certificateholders' Principal Distributable Amount from Available Amounts;
8. to the Indenture Trustee, the Delaware Trustee and the Owner Trustee, any accrued and unpaid Trust Fees and Expenses, in each case to the extent such fees and expenses have not been previously paid by the Servicer; and

9. any Available Amounts remaining, to the Seller.

The Noteholders' Principal Distributable Amount will be allocated among the notes as described above under "The Notes — Payments of Principal."

For the purposes of this prospectus supplement, the following terms will have the following meanings:

The "Certificateholders' Distributable Amount" will mean, with respect to any Payment Date, the sum of the Certificateholders' Interest Distributable Amount and the Certificateholders' Principal Distributable Amount for that Payment Date.

The "Certificateholders' Interest Distributable Amount" will mean, with respect to any Payment Date, the sum of the Certificateholders' Monthly Interest Distributable Amount and the Certificateholders' Interest Carryover Shortfall for one or more prior Payment Dates.

The "Certificateholders' Interest Carryover Shortfall" will mean, with respect to any Payment Date, the excess, if any, of the sum of the Certificateholders' Monthly Interest Distributable Amount for that class for the preceding Payment Date plus any outstanding Certificateholders' Interest Carryover Shortfall on the preceding Payment Date, over the amount of interest that is actually paid on the certificates on the preceding Payment Date, plus, to the extent permitted by applicable law, interest on the Certificateholders' Interest Carryover Shortfall at the Pass Through Rate for the Interest Period.

The "Certificateholders' Monthly Interest Distributable Amount" will mean, with respect to any Payment Date, interest accrued for the related Interest Period at the Pass Through Rate on the Certificate Balance on the immediately preceding Payment Date, after giving effect to all payments of principal to Certificateholders on or prior to that Payment Date (or, in the case of the first Payment Date, on the Initial Certificate Balance).

The "Certificate Balance," for any Payment Date, will equal the Initial Certificate Balance, reduced by all amounts distributed on or prior to that Payment Date on the certificates and allocable to principal.

The "Certificateholders' Monthly Principal Distributable Amount" will mean, with respect to any Payment Date, the Certificateholders' Percentage of the Principal Distributable Amount for that Payment Date.

The "Certificateholders' Percentage" will mean the following:

1. for each Payment Date until the class A-1 notes have been paid in full, 0%;
2. thereafter, for each Payment Date to and including the Payment Date on which the principal amount of the class A-4 notes have been paid in full, the percentage equivalent of a fraction, the numerator of which is the initial aggregate principal amount of the certificates and the denominator of which is the sum of the initial aggregate principal amount of the class A-2, class A-3 and class A-4 notes and the initial aggregate principal amount of the certificates; and

3. thereafter, 100%.

The "Certificateholders' Principal Carryover Shortfall" will mean, with respect to any Payment Date, the excess of the Certificateholders' Monthly Principal Distributable Amount plus any outstanding Certificateholders' Principal Carryover Shortfall for the preceding Payment Date, over the amount in respect of principal that is actually distributed to the Certificateholders on that Payment Date.

The "Certificateholders' Principal Distributable Amount" will mean, with respect to any Payment Date, the sum of:

1. the Certificateholders' Monthly Principal Distributable Amount for that Payment Date; and
2. any outstanding Certificateholders' Principal Carryover Shortfall as of the close of the immediately preceding Payment Date.

"Interest Period" means (a) with respect to the class A-1 notes, the period from and including the most recent Payment Date on which interest has been paid (or, in the case of the first Payment Date, the Closing Date) to but excluding the next succeeding Payment Date and (b) with respect to the class A-2, class A-3 and class A-4 notes and the certificates, the period from and including the 18th day of the calendar month (or, in the case of the first Payment Date, from and including the Closing Date) to but excluding the 18th day of the next calendar month.

The "Noteholders' Distributable Amount" will mean, with respect to any Payment Date, the sum of the Noteholders' Interest Distributable Amount for all classes of notes plus the Noteholders' Principal Distributable Amount for that Payment Date.

The "Noteholders' Interest Carryover Shortfall" will mean, with respect to any Payment Date and a class of notes, the excess, if any, of the sum of the Noteholders' Monthly Interest Distributable Amount for that class for the preceding Payment Date plus any outstanding Noteholders' Interest Carryover Shortfall for that class on that preceding Payment Date, over the amount in respect of interest that is actually paid on the notes of that class on that preceding Payment Date, plus, to the extent permitted by applicable law, interest on the Noteholders' Interest Carryover Shortfall at the related Interest Rate for the related Interest Period.

The "Noteholders' Interest Distributable Amount" will mean, with respect to any Payment Date, the sum of the Noteholders' Monthly Interest Distributable Amount for all classes of notes and the Noteholders' Interest Carryover Shortfall for all classes of notes.

The "Noteholders' Monthly Interest Distributable Amount" will mean, with respect to any Payment Date and a class of notes, interest accrued for the related Interest Period at the related Interest Rate for that class on the outstanding principal amount of that class on the immediately preceding Payment Date, after giving effect to all payments of principal to Noteholders of that class on or prior to that Payment Date (or, in the case of the first Payment Date, on the original principal amount of that class).

The "Noteholders' Monthly Principal Distributable Amount" will mean, with respect to any Payment Date, the Noteholders' Percentage of the Principal Distributable Amount for that Payment Date.

The "Noteholders' Percentage" will mean:

1. for each Payment Date until the principal amounts of the class A-1 notes have been paid in full, 100%;
2. thereafter, for each Payment Date to and including the Payment Date on which the principal amount of the class A-4 notes have been paid in full, the percentage equivalent of a fraction, the numerator of which is the initial aggregate principal amount of the class A-2, class A-3, and class A-4, notes and the denominator of which is the sum of the initial aggregate principal amount of the class A-2, class A-3 and class A-4 notes and the initial aggregate principal amount of the certificates; and
3. thereafter, 0%.

The "Noteholders' Principal Carryover Shortfall" will mean, with respect to any Payment Date and a class of notes, the excess, if any, of the Noteholders' Monthly Principal Distributable Amount plus any outstanding Noteholders' Principal Carryover Shortfall for that class of notes for the preceding Payment Date over the amount in respect of principal that is actually paid as principal on that class on that Payment Date.

The "Noteholders' Principal Distributable Amount" will mean, with respect to any Payment Date and a class of notes, the sum of:

1. the Noteholders' Monthly Principal Distributable Amount;
2. any outstanding Noteholders' Principal Carryover Shortfall of that class as of the close of the immediately preceding Payment Date; and
3. on the Final Scheduled Payment Date for that class of notes, the amount necessary to reduce the outstanding principal amount of that class of notes to zero; provided, however, that the Noteholders' Principal Distributable Amount with respect to a class of notes shall not exceed the outstanding principal amount of that class.

The "Principal Distributable Amount" will mean, with respect to any Payment Date and the related Collection Period, the sum of the following amounts:

(1) (a) in the case of Precomputed Receivables, the principal portion of all scheduled payments due during the related Collection Period, computed in accordance with the actuarial method and (b) in the case of Simple Interest Receivables, the principal portion of all scheduled payments actually received during the related Collection Period, (2) the principal portion of all Prepayments received for the related Collection Period (to the extent such amounts are not included in clause (1) above), (3) the Principal Balance of each Receivable that the Servicer became obligated to purchase or the Seller became obligated

to repurchase (to the extent those amounts are not included in clauses (1) or (2) above) and (4) the Principal Balance of each Receivable that became a Defaulted Receivable during that Collection Period (to the extent those amounts are not included in clauses (1), (2) or (3) above).

CREDIT ENHANCEMENT

The protection afforded to the Noteholders will be effected both by the preferential right of the Noteholders to receive, to the extent described in this prospectus supplement, current distributions on the Receivables, the establishment of the Reserve Fund and the subordination of the Seller's right to receive excess interest.

SUBORDINATION

The rights of the Certificateholders to receive payments on the Receivables will be subordinated to the rights of the Noteholders and the maintenance of amounts on deposit in the Reserve Fund at the Specified Reserve Fund Balance to the extent described herein. The Seller is entitled to receive payments of interest collected on the Receivables which are not used by the trust to make other required payments. The Seller's right to receive this excess interest is subordinated to the payment of principal and interest on the notes, the funding of the Reserve Fund and the payment of principal and interest on the certificates.

RESERVE FUND

The Reserve Fund will be a segregated account in the name of the Indenture Trustee. The Reserve Fund will be created with an initial deposit by the Seller on the Closing Date of an amount equal to $7,886,388.29 (the "Reserve Fund Initial Deposit"). The Reserve Fund will thereafter be funded by the deposit therein of all Excess Amounts, if any, for each Payment Date to the extent necessary to restore or bring the amounts on deposit in the Reserve Fund to the Specified Reserve Fund Balance.

Amounts held from time to time in the Reserve Fund will continue to be held for the benefit of Noteholders and may be invested in Eligible Investments. Investment income on those investments (net of losses and expenses) will be paid to the Seller, upon the direction of the Servicer, to the extent that funds on deposit in the Reserve Fund exceed the Specified Reserve Fund Balance. If the amount on deposit in the Reserve Fund on any Payment Date (after giving effect to all deposits to and withdrawals from the Reserve Fund on that Payment Date) is greater than the Specified Reserve Fund Balance for that Payment Date, subject to limitations set forth in the Transfer and Servicing Agreements, the Indenture Trustee will include the amount of the excess in the amounts to be distributed to Certificateholders pursuant to clauses (6) and (7) in the first paragraph under "Payments on the Notes — Payment of Distributable Amounts" in this prospectus supplement. Any excess amounts remaining thereafter will be paid to the Seller. The Noteholders will not have any rights in, or claims to, amounts distributed to the Certificateholders or to the Seller.

The "Specified Reserve Fund Balance" with respect to any Payment Date will be equal to the greater of: (i) 0.50% of the initial aggregate principal balance of the Receivables as of the Cutoff Date and (ii) 0.75% of the aggregate principal amount of the Receivables as of the last day of the immediately preceding Collection Period; except that, if on any Payment Date (i) the average of the Charge-off Rates for the three preceding Collection Periods exceeds 2.25% or (ii) the average of the Delinquency Percentages for the three preceding Collection Periods exceeds 2.25%, then the Specified Reserve Fund Balance will be an amount equal to a specified percentage of the Pool Balance as of the last day of the immediately preceding Collection Period. Such percentage shall be determined by deducting from 8.00% the following fraction, expressed as a percentage: (a) one minus (b) a fraction, the numerator of which is the outstanding principal amount of the Notes with respect to such Payment Date and the denominator of which is the Pool Balance. Notwithstanding the foregoing, in no event will the Specified Reserve Fund Balance be more than the then outstanding principal amount of the Notes. As of any Payment Date, the amount of funds actually on deposit in the Reserve Fund may, in certain circumstances, be less than the Specified Reserve Fund Balance.

The "Charge-off Rate" with respect to a Collection Period will equal the Aggregate Net Losses with respect to the Receivables expressed, on an annualized basis, as a percentage of the average of (i) the Pool Balance on the last day of the immediately preceding Collection Period and (ii) the Pool Balance on the last day of such current Collection Period. "Aggregate Net Losses" with respect to a Collection Period will equal the Principal Balance of all Receivables newly designated during such Collection Period as Defaulted Receivables minus Net Liquidation Proceeds collected during such Collection Period with respect to all Defaulted Receivables. The "Delinquency Percentage" with respect to a Collection Period will equal the number of (a) Receivables 61 days or more delinquent (after taking into account permitted extensions) as of the last day of such Collection Period, determined in accordance with the Servicer's normal practices, plus (b) Receivables the related Financed Vehicles of which have been repossessed but have not been liquidated (to the extent the related Receivable is not otherwise reflected in clause (a) above or is not a Defaulted Receivable), expressed as a percentage of the aggregate number of Current Receivables on the last day of such Collection Period. A "Current Receivable" will be a Receivable that is not a Defaulted Receivable or a Liquidated Receivable. A "Liquidated Receivable" will be a Receivable that has been the subject of a Prepayment in full or otherwise has been paid in full or, in the case of a Defaulted Receivable, a Receivable as to which the Servicer has determined that the final amounts in respect thereof have been paid.

The Servicer may, from time to time after the date of this prospectus supplement, request each rating agency to approve a formula for determining the Specified Reserve Fund Balance that is different from those described above or change the manner by which the Reserve Fund is funded. If each rating agency delivers a letter to the Owner Trustee to the effect that the use of any new formula will not result in a qualification, reduction or withdrawal of its then-current rating of any class of the notes, then the Specified Reserve Fund Balance will be determined in accordance with the new formula. The Sale and Servicing Agreement will accordingly be amended, without the consent of any Noteholder, to reflect the new calculation.

Amounts held from time to time in the Reserve Fund will be held for the benefit of the Noteholders. On each Payment Date, funds will be withdrawn from the Reserve Fund to the extent that the amount on deposit in the Note Distribution Account with respect to such Payment Date is less than the sum of the Noteholders' Distributable Amount will be deposited in the Note Distribution Account for distribution to the Noteholders.

None of the Securityholders, the Indenture Trustee, the Owner Trustee or the Seller will be required to refund any amounts properly distributed or paid to them, whether or not there are sufficient funds on any subsequent Payment Date to make full distributions to the Securityholders.

The Reserve Fund and the subordination of the certificates are intended to enhance the likelihood of receipt by Noteholders of the full amount of principal and interest due them and to decrease the likelihood that the Noteholders will experience losses. However, the Reserve Fund could be depleted. If the amount required to be deposited into or required to be withdrawn from the Reserve Fund to cover shortfalls in collections on the Receivables exceeds the amount of available cash in the Reserve Fund, Noteholders could incur losses or suffer a temporary shortfall in the amounts distributed to the Noteholders.

DESCRIPTION OF THE TRANSFER AND SERVICING AGREEMENTS

THE TRANSFER AND SERVICING AGREEMENTS

The description of the terms of the Indenture, the Sale and Servicing Agreement, the Administration Agreement and the Trust Agreement (collectively, the "Transfer and Servicing Agreements") in this prospectus supplement does not purport to be complete and is subject to, and qualified in its entirety by reference to, all the provisions of the Transfer and Servicing Agreements. Forms of the Transfer and Servicing Agreements have been filed as exhibits to the Registration Statement. Copies of the final signed Transfer and Servicing Agreements will be filed with the SEC following the issuance of the securities. Any description of the Transfer and Servicing Agreements in this prospectus supplement supplements, and to the extent inconsistent replaces, the description of the general terms and provisions of the Transfer and Servicing Agreements set forth in the accompanying prospectus, to which description reference is hereby made.

SALE AND ASSIGNMENT OF RECEIVABLES

Information with respect to the conveyance of the Receivables from the Seller to the Trust on the Closing Date pursuant to the Sale and Servicing Agreement is set forth under "Description of the Transfer and Servicing Agreements — Sale and Assignment of Receivables" in the accompanying prospectus.

ACCOUNTS

In addition to the accounts referred to under "Description of the Transfer and Servicing Agreements — Accounts" in the accompanying prospectus, the Servicer will also establish and will maintain with the Indenture Trustee:

- the Reserve Fund in the name of the Indenture Trustee on behalf of the Noteholders; and
- the Yield Supplement Account in the name of the Indenture Trustee on behalf of the Noteholders and the Certificateholders.

COLLECTIONS

The Servicer will deposit all payments on Receivables received from Obligors and all proceeds of Receivables collected during each Collection Period into the Collection Account not later than two Business Days after receipt. However, so long as AHFC is the servicer, if each condition to making monthly deposits as may be required by the Sale and Servicing Agreement (including the satisfaction of specified ratings criteria by AHFC or AHFC obtaining a letter of credit or similar agreement and the absence of any Servicer Default) is satisfied, the Servicer may retain such amounts until the related Deposit Date. The Servicer or the Seller, as the case may be, will remit the aggregate Warranty Purchase Payments and Administrative Purchase Payments of Receivables to be purchased from the Trust into the Collection Account on or before each Deposit Date. The Servicer will be entitled to withhold, or to be reimbursed from amounts otherwise payable into or on deposit in the Collection Account, amounts previously deposited in the Collection Account but later determined to have resulted from mistaken deposits or postings. Except in certain circumstances described in the Sale and Servicing Agreement, pending deposit into the Collection Account, collections may be invested by the Servicer at its own risk and for its own benefit and will not be segregated from its own funds. We refer you to "Description of the Transfer and Servicing Agreements — Collections" in the accompanying prospectus.

"Eligible Investments" are specified in the Sale and Servicing Agreement and will be limited to investments which meet the criteria of each rating agency from time to time as being consistent with its then-current ratings of the securities.

Collections on or in respect of a Receivable made during a Collection Period (including Warranty Purchase Payments and Administrative Purchase Payments) will be applied first to interest accrued to date, second to principal until the principal balance is brought current, third to reduce the unpaid late charges as provided in the Receivable and finally to prepay principal of the Receivable. We refer you to "Description of the Transfer and Servicing Agreements — Collections" in the accompanying prospectus.

Collections on or in respect of a Receivable made during a Collection Period which are not late fees, prepayment charges, extension fees or certain other similar fees or charges will be applied first to any outstanding Advances made by the Servicer with respect to such Receivable, and then to the related Scheduled Payment. Any collections on or in respect of a Receivable remaining after such applications will be considered an "Excess Payment." Excess Payments constituting a prepayment in full of the related Receivable will be applied as a prepayment in full of such Receivable and all other Excess Payments on Precomputed Receivables will be held by the Servicer as a Payment Ahead (or if the Servicer has not satisfied particular requirements, deposit in the Payahead Account) and on Simple Interest Receivables will be applied as a partial prepayment (each, a "Prepayment").

On each Deposit Date, the Indenture Trustee will cause (1) Payments Ahead previously deposited in the Payahead Account or held by the Servicer in respect of the related Collection Period to be transferred to the Collection Account and (2) any Yield Supplement Withdrawal Amount to be deposited into the Collection Account.

ADVANCES

On or before the Business Day prior to each Payment Date (the "Deposit Date"), the Servicer will make a payment into the Collection Account for each Receivable of an amount equal to the product of the principal balance of the Receivable as of the first day of the related Collection Period and one-twelfth of its APR minus the amount of interest (and principal in the case of a Precomputed Receivable) actually received on the Receivable during the Collection Period (an "Advance"). If the calculation results in a negative number, an amount equal to the negative amount will be paid to the Servicer in reimbursement of outstanding Advances. In addition, if a Receivable becomes a Liquidated Receivable, the amount of accrued and unpaid interest on that Receivable (but not including interest for the current Collection Period) will, up to the amount of outstanding Advances in respect thereof, be withdrawn from the Collection Account and paid to the Servicer in reimbursement of the outstanding Advances. The Servicer will not be required to make any Advances (other than the Advance of an interest shortfall arising from a prepaid Receivable) to the extent that it does not expect to recoup the Advance from subsequent collections or recoveries. The Servicer will make all Advances by depositing into the Collection Account an amount equal to the aggregate of the Precomputed Advances and Simple Interest Advances in respect of a Collection Period on the Business Day immediately preceding the related Payment Date. We refer you to "Description of the Transfer and Servicing Agreements — Advances" in the accompanying prospectus.

SERVICING COMPENSATION

The servicing fee for the calendar month immediately preceding any Payment Date (a "Collection Period") will be one-twelfth of 1.00% (the "Servicing Rate") of the Pool Balance as of the first day of the related Collection Period or, in the case of the first Payment Date, the Pool Balance as of the Cutoff Date (the "Servicing Fee"). The Servicing Fee, together with any previously unpaid Servicing Fee, will be paid on each Payment Date solely to the extent of Available Amounts allocable to interest. The Servicer will be entitled to collect and retain as additional servicing compensation in respect of each Collection Period any late fees, prepayment charges and any other administrative fees and expenses or similar charges collected during that Collection Period, plus any investment earnings or interest earned during that Collection Period from the investment of monies on deposit in the Collection Account, the Payahead Account and the Note Distribution Account. We refer you to "Description of the Transfer and Servicing Agreements — Collections" in this prospectus supplement and "Description of the Transfer and Servicing Agreements — Servicing Compensation" in ths accompanying prospectus. The Servicer will be paid the Servicing Fee for each Collection Period on the following Payment Date related to that Collection Period. However, if it is acceptable to each rating agency without a reduction in the rating of each class of notes, the Servicing Fee in respect of a Collection Period (together with any portion of the Servicing Fee that remains unpaid from prior Payment Dates) will be paid at the beginning of that Collection Period out of collections of interest on the Receivables for that Collection Period. The Servicing Fee will be paid from Available Amounts allocable to interest prior to the payment of the Noteholders' Distributable Amounts or Certificateholders' Distributable Amounts.

YIELD SUPPLEMENT ACCOUNT

On or prior to the Closing Date, a yield supplement account will be established with the Indenture Trustee for the benefit of the Noteholders and the Certificateholders (the "Yield Supplement Account"). The Yield Supplement Account is designed solely to supplement the interest collections on those Receivables (the "Discount Receivables") that have APRs which are less than the sum of (a) the percentage equivalent of a fraction, the numerator of which is the sum for each note of the product of (1) the Interest Rate for the note, (2) the original principal balance of the note and (3) the expected weighted average life for the note at the pricing speed (assuming that the Servicer exercises its option to purchase the Receivables) and the denominator of which is the sum for each note of the product of (1) the original principal balance of the note and (2) the expected weighted average life for the note at the pricing speed (assuming that the Servicer exercises its option to purchase the Receivables) and (b) the Servicing Rate (the "Required Rate"). The Yield Supplement Account will be funded by the Seller on the Closing Date with an initial deposit in an amount of $267,720.61 (the "Yield Supplement Account Deposit").

On each Deposit Date, the Indenture Trustee shall withdraw from monies on deposit in the Yield Supplement Account and deposit into the Collection Account to be included in amounts distributed on the related Payment Date the lesser of the amount on deposit in the Yield Supplement Account and the sum of (a) the aggregate amount by which one month's interest on the Principal Balance as of the first day of the related Collection Period of each Discount Receivable (other than a Discount Receivable that is a Defaulted Receivable) at a rate equal to the Required Rate, exceeds one month's interest on such Principal Balance at the APR of each such Receivable (the "Yield Supplement Amount") and (b) after giving effect to the withdrawal of the amount described in clause (a) above, the amount by which the amount on deposit in the Yield Supplement Account exceeds the maximum amount required to be on deposit therein on the immediately succeeding Payment Date (together with the Yield Supplement Amount, the "Yield Supplement Withdrawal Amount").

On each Payment Date, the amount required to be on deposit in the Yield Supplement Account will decline and be equal to the sum of all Yield Supplement Amounts for all future Payment Dates, assuming that future scheduled payments on the Discount Receivables are made on the date on which they are scheduled as being due. The amount on deposit in the Yield Supplement Account will decrease as payments are made with respect to the Yield Supplement Amount and funds in excess of the maximum required balance are released as described above.

NET DEPOSITS

As an administrative convenience and as long as specified conditions are satisfied, for so long as AHFC is the Servicer, AHFC will be permitted to make the deposit of collections, aggregate Advances and amounts deposited in respect of purchases of Receivables by the Seller or the Servicer for or with respect to the related Collection Period net of payments to be made to the Servicer with respect to that Collection Period. The Servicer, however, will account to the Owner Trustee and to the Securityholders as if all of the foregoing deposits and payments were made individually. We refer you to "Description of the Transfer and Servicing Agreements — Net Deposits" in the accompanying prospectus.

OPTIONAL PURCHASE

The outstanding notes will be redeemed in whole, but not in part, on any Payment Date on which the Servicer or any successor to the Servicer exercises its option to purchase the Receivables. The Servicer or any successor to the Servicer may purchase the Receivables when the Pool Balance shall have declined to 10% or less of the Pool Balance as of the Cutoff Date, as described in the accompanying prospectus under "Description of the Transfer and Servicing Agreements — Termination." The "Redemption Price" for the outstanding notes will be equal to the unpaid principal amount of the outstanding notes plus accrued and unpaid interest on the notes and for the certificates will equal the Certificate Balance on the date of the optional purchase plus accrued and unpaid interest on the certificates.

REMOVAL OF SERVICER

The Indenture Trustee or Noteholders evidencing not less than 25% of the voting interests of the notes then outstanding (or if the notes have been paid in full and the Indenture has been discharged in accordance with its terms, by holders of certificates then outstanding evidencing not less than 25% of the voting interests thereof), may terminate the rights and obligations of the Servicer under the Sale and Servicing Agreement upon the following events ("Servicer Defaults"):

1. any failure by the Servicer to deliver to the applicable Trustee for deposit in any Account any required payment or to direct the Indenture Trustee to make the required payments therefrom and that failure continues unremedied for three Business Days after discovery thereof by the Servicer or after the giving of written notice of such failure to (a) the Servicer by the Owner Trustee or the Indenture Trustee, as applicable or (b) the Servicer and the Owner Trustee or the Indenture Trustee, as applicable, of written notice of the failure from not less than 25% of the outstanding amount of the notes;
2. any failure by the Servicer (or the Seller, as long as AHFC is the Servicer) to duly observe or perform in any material respect any other covenants or agreements in the Sale and Servicing Agreement, which failure materially and adversely affects the rights of the Securityholders, and which failure continues unremedied for 90 days after the giving of written notice of the failure to (a) the Servicer or the Seller, as the case may be, by the Owner Trustee or the Indenture Trustee, as applicable, or (b) the Servicer or the Seller, as the case may be, and the Owner Trustee or the Indenture Trustee by the holders of notes evidencing not less than 25% of the outstanding amount of the notes; and
3. the occurrence of an Insolvency Event (as defined in the attached prospectus) of the Servicer (or the Seller, as long as AHFC is the Servicer).

Under those circumstances, authority and power shall, without further action, pass to and be vested in the Indenture Trustee or a successor Servicer appointed by the Indenture Trustee under the Sale and Servicing Agreement. The Indenture Trustee or successor Servicer will succeed to all the responsibilities, duties and liabilities of the Servicer in its capacity under the Sale and Servicing Agreement and will be entitled to similar compensation arrangements. If, however, a bankruptcy trustee or similar official has been appointed for the Servicer, and no Servicer Default other than the appointment of a bankruptcy trustee or similar official has occurred, that trustee or official may have the power to prevent the Indenture Trustee or the Noteholders (or Certificateholders) from effecting a transfer of servicing. In the event that the Indenture Trustee is unwilling or unable so to act, it may appoint or petition a court of competent jurisdiction to appoint a successor with a net worth of at least $50,000,000 and whose regular business includes the servicing of motor vehicle receivables. The Indenture Trustee may make such arrangements for compensation to be paid, which in no event may be greater than the servicing compensation paid to the Servicer under the Sale and Servicing Agreement. Notwithstanding such termination, the Servicer shall be entitled to payment of certain amounts payable to it prior to such termination, for services rendered prior to such termination. Upon payment in full of the principal and interest on the notes, the Certificateholders will succeed to the rights of the Noteholders with respect to removal of the Servicer.

DUTIES OF THE OWNER TRUSTEE, THE DELAWARE TRUSTEE AND THE INDENTURE TRUSTEE

The Owner Trustee will make no representations as to the validity or sufficiency of the Trust Agreement, the certificates (other than the authentication of the certificates), the notes or of any Receivables or related documents and is not accountable for the use or application by the Seller or the Servicer of any funds paid to the Seller or the Servicer in respect of the notes, the certificates or the Receivables, or the investment of any monies by the Servicer before those monies are deposited into the Collection Account. The Owner Trustee will not independently verify the Receivables. The Owner Trustee is required to perform only those duties specifically required of it under the Trust Agreement. In addition to making distributions to the Certificateholders, those duties generally are limited to the receipt of the various certificates, reports or other instruments required to be furnished to the Owner Trustee under the Trust Agreement, in which case it will only be required to examine them to determine whether they conform to the requirements of the Trust Agreement. The Owner Trustee shall not be charged with knowledge of a failure by the Servicer to perform its duties under the Trust Agreement or the Sale and Servicing Agreement which failure constitutes a Servicer Default unless the Owner Trustee obtains actual knowledge of the failure as specified in the Trust Agreement.

The Owner Trustee will be under no obligation to exercise any of the rights or powers vested in it by the Trust Agreement or to make any investigation of matters arising under the Trust Agreement or to institute, conduct or defend any litigation under the Trust Agreement or in relation thereto at the request, order or direction of any of the Certificateholders, unless those Certificateholders have offered to the Owner Trustee security or indemnity reasonably satisfactory to the Owner Trustee against the costs, expenses and liabilities that may be incurred by the Owner Trustee in connection with the exercise of those rights.

The Delaware Trustee has been appointed solely for the purpose of complying with the requirement of the Delaware Statutory Trust Statute that the Trust have one trustee, which, in the case of a natural person, is a resident of the State of Delaware, or which in all other cases, has its principal place of business in the State of Delaware. The duties and responsibilities of the Delaware Trustee shall be limited solely to the execution and delivery of all documents and certificates to form and maintain the existence of the Trust under the Delaware Statutory Trust Statute. Except for the purpose of the foregoing sentence, the Delaware Trustee shall not be deemed a trustee and shall have no management responsibilities or owe any fiduciary duties to the Trust, the Seller or any beneficial owner.

The Indenture Trustee will make no representations as to the validity or sufficiency of the Indenture, the certificates, the notes (other than authentication of the notes) or of any Receivables or related documents, and is not accountable for the use or application by the Seller or the Servicer of any funds paid to the Seller or the Servicer in respect of the notes, the certificates or the Receivables, or the investment of any monies by the Servicer before those monies are deposited into the Collection Account. The Indenture Trustee will not independently verify the Receivables. If no Event of Default or Servicer Default has occurred, the Indenture Trustee is required to perform only those duties specifically required of it under the Indenture. In addition to making distributions to the Noteholders, those duties generally are limited to the receipt of the various certificates, reports or other instruments required to be furnished to the Indenture Trustee under the Indenture, in which case it will only be required to examine them to determine whether they conform to the requirements of the Indenture. The Indenture Trustee shall not be charged with knowledge of a failure by the Servicer to perform its duties under the Trust Agreement, the Sale and Servicing Agreement or the Administration Agreement which failure constitutes an Event of Default or Servicer Default unless the Indenture Trustee obtains actual knowledge of the failure as specified in the Indenture. The Indenture Trustee will be under no obligation to exercise any of the rights or powers vested in it by the Indenture or to make any investigation of matters arising under the Indenture or to institute, conduct or defend any litigation under the Indenture or in relation thereto at the request, order or direction of any of the Noteholders, unless those Noteholders have offered to the Indenture Trustee reasonable security or indemnity against the costs, expenses and liabilities that may be incurred by the Indenture Trustee in connection with the exercise of those rights. No Noteholder will have any right under the Indenture to institute any proceeding with respect to the Indenture, other than with respect to the failure by the Seller or the Servicer, as applicable, to remit payment, unless that Noteholder previously has given to the Indenture Trustee written notice of the Event of Default and (1) the Event of Default arises from the Servicer's failure to remit payments when due or (2) the holders of the notes evidencing not less than 25% of the voting interests of the notes, voting together as a single class, have made written request upon the Indenture Trustee to institute that proceeding in its own name as the Indenture Trustee under the Indenture and have offered to the Indenture Trustee reasonable indemnity and the Indenture Trustee for 60 days has neglected or refused to institute that proceeding.

THE OWNER TRUSTEE AND THE INDENTURE TRUSTEE

The Bank of New York will be the Owner Trustee under the Trust Agreement. As a matter of Delaware law, the Trust will be viewed as a separate legal entity, distinct from the Owner Trustee, and the Trust will be viewed as the issuer of the certificates. JPMorgan Chase Bank will be the Indenture Trustee under the Indenture. The Owner Trustee, the Indenture Trustee and any of their respective affiliates may hold certificates in their own names or as pledgees.

For the purpose of meeting the legal requirements of some jurisdictions, the Servicer and the Owner Trustee or the Servicer and the Indenture Trustee, in each case acting jointly (or in some instances, the Owner Trustee or the Indenture Trustee acting alone), will have the power to appoint co-trustees or separate trustees of all or any part of the Trust. In the event of an appointment of co-trustees or separate trustees, all rights, powers, duties and obligations conferred or imposed upon the Owner Trustee by the Sale and Servicing Agreement and the Trust Agreement or the Indenture Trustee by the Indenture will be conferred or imposed upon the Owner Trustee or the Indenture Trustee and each of their respective separate trustees or co-trustees jointly, or, in any jurisdiction in which the Owner Trustee or the Indenture Trustee will be incompetent or unqualified to perform specified acts, singly upon that separate trustee or co-trustee who will exercise and perform those rights, powers, duties and obligations solely at the direction of the Owner Trustee or the Indenture Trustee.

The Owner Trustee and the Indenture Trustee may resign at any time, in which event the Servicer will be obligated to appoint a successor thereto. The Servicer may also remove the Owner Trustee or the Indenture Trustee if either ceases to be eligible to continue as trustee under the Trust Agreement or the Indenture, as the case may be, becomes legally unable to act or becomes insolvent. In those circumstances, the Servicer will be obligated to appoint a successor Owner Trustee or Indenture Trustee, as applicable. Any resignation or removal of the Owner Trustee or the Indenture Trustee and appointment of a successor thereto will not become effective until acceptance of the appointment by the successor.

The Servicer will be obligated to pay the fees of the Owner Trustee, the Delaware Trustee and the Indenture Trustee in connection with their duties under the Trust Agreement and Indenture, respectively. The Owner Trustee, the Delaware Trustee and the Indenture Trustee will be entitled to indemnification by AHFC and the Seller for, and will be held harmless against, any loss, liability, fee, disbursement or expense incurred by the Owner Trustee, the Delaware Trustee or the Indenture Trustee not resulting from its own willful misfeasance, bad faith or negligence (in the case of the Owner Trustee or the Indenture Trustee) or gross negligence (in the case of the Delaware Trustee) (other than by reason of a breach of any of its representations or warranties set forth in the Trust Agreement or the Indenture, as the case may be). The Seller and the Servicer will be obligated to indemnify the Owner Trustee, the Delaware Trustee and the Indenture Trustee for specified taxes that may be asserted in connection with the transaction.

MATERIAL INCOME TAX CONSEQUENCES

The following is a general discussion of the material federal income tax and California tax considerations of the purchase, ownership and disposition of the notes. The discussion is based upon law, regulations, rulings and decisions now in effect, all of which are subject to change. The discussion below does not purport to deal with all federal tax and California tax considerations applicable to all categories of investors. It is recommended that investors consult their own tax advisors in determining the federal, state, local and any other tax consequences to them of the purchase, ownership and disposition of the notes. We refer you to "Material Income Tax Consequences — Tax Treatment of Owner Trusts" and " — Material State Tax Consequences With Respect to Owner Trusts" in the accompanying prospectus.

Under current law and assuming execution of, and compliance with, the Indenture and the Trust Agreement, in the opinion of Dewey Ballantine LLP, tax counsel to the Trust, (i) the notes will be characterized as debt for tax purposes, and (ii) the Trust will not be characterized as an association (or a publicly traded partnership) taxable as a corporation for federal income tax purposes.

TAX CHARACTERIZATION OF THE TRUST

The Seller and the Servicer will agree, and the beneficial owners of the certificates (the "Certificate Owners") will agree by their purchase of the certificates, to treat the Trust (i) as a partnership for purposes of federal and state income tax, franchise tax and any other tax measured in whole or in part by income, with the assets of the partnership being the assets held by the Trust, the partners of the partnership being the Certificate Owners, and the notes being debt of the partnership, or (ii) if a single beneficial owner owns all of the certificates and none of the notes are characterized as equity interests in the Trust, as disregarded as an entity separate from the Certificate Owner for purpose of federal and state income tax, franchise tax and any other tax measured in whole or in part by income, with the assets of the Trust and the notes treated as assets and indebtedness of the Certificate Owner. However, the proper characterization of the arrangement involving the Trust, the notes, the Seller and the Servicer is not clear because there is no authority on transactions closely comparable to the transaction described in this prospectus supplement.

If the Trust were taxable as a corporation for federal income tax purposes, it would be subject to corporate income tax on its taxable income. The Trust's taxable income would include all its income on the related Receivables, which may be reduced by its interest expense on some or all classes of the notes. Any such corporate income tax could materially reduce cash available to make payments on the notes and distributions on the certificates, and the Certificate Owners could be liable for any such tax that is unpaid by the Trust.

TREATMENT OF THE NOTES AS INDEBTEDNESS

The Seller, any Certificateholders and the Certificate Owners will agree, and the beneficial owners of the notes (the "Note Owners") will agree by their purchase of the notes, to treat the notes as debt for purposes of federal and state income tax, franchise tax and any other tax measured in whole or in part by income.

We do not anticipate issuing notes with any original issue discount, other than possibly original issue discount of a de minimis amount. We refer you to "Material Income Tax Consequences — Tax Treatment of Owner Trusts — Tax Consequences to Owners of the Notes — OID, Index Securities, Etc." and " —

Material State Tax Consequences with respect to Owner Trusts" in the accompanying prospectus. The prepayment assumption that will be used for purposes of computing original issue discount, if any, for federal income tax purposes is 1.5% ABS. We refer you to "Maturity and Prepayment Considerations" in this prospectus supplement.

CALIFORNIA INCOME TAX CONSEQUENCES

Under current law and assuming execution of, and compliance with, the Indenture and the Trust Agreement, in the opinion of Dewey Ballantine LLP, tax counsel to the Trust, (i) the notes will be characterized as debt for tax purposes, and (ii) the Trust will not be characterized as an association (or a publicly traded partnership) taxable as a corporation for California income and franchise tax purposes. Dewey Ballantine LLP will further render an opinion that Noteholders who are not residents of, or otherwise subject to tax in, California will not, solely by reason of their acquisition of an interest in any Class of Notes, be subject to California income, franchise, excise or similar taxes with respect to interest on any Class of Notes. We recommend that investors consult their own tax advisors to determine the state, local and other tax consequences to them of the purchase, ownership and disposition of the Notes.

TAX RETURN DISCLOSURE REQUIREMENTS

The U.S. Treasury Department recently issued temporary regulations directed at "tax shelters" that are quite broad and could be read to apply to transactions generally not considered to be tax shelters. These regulations require taxpayers that participate in a "reportable transaction" to disclose such transaction on their tax returns by attaching IRS Form 8886 and to retain information related to the transaction. Although the U.S. Treasury Department has announced it is considering how to narrow the breadth of these temporary regulations to exclude transactions for which disclosure is unnecessary, currently a transaction is a "reportable transaction" if it has one of several indicia. One or more of these indicia may be present with respect to the notes. You should consult your own tax advisor concerning any possible disclosure obligation with respect to your investment in and disposition of the notes.

ERISA CONSIDERATIONS

Section 406 of ERISA and Section 4975 of the Code prohibit pension, profit-sharing and other employee benefit plans, as well as individual retirement accounts and certain types of Keogh Plans (each, a "Benefit Plan"), from engaging in certain transactions with persons that are "parties in interest" under ERISA or "disqualified persons" under the Code with respect to such Benefit Plans. A violation of these "prohibited transaction" rules may result in an excise tax or other penalties and liabilities under ERISA and the Code for such persons. Title I of ERISA also requires that fiduciaries of a Benefit Plan subject to ERISA make investments that are prudent, diversified (except if prudent not to do so) and in accordance with governing, plan documents.

Certain transactions involving the trust might be deemed to constitute prohibited transactions under ERISA and the Code if assets of the trust were deemed to be assets of a Benefit Plan. Under a regulation issued by the United States Department of Labor (the "Plan Assets Regulation"), the assets of the trust would be treated as plan assets of a Benefit Plan for the purposes of ERISA and the Code only if the Benefit Plan acquired an "equity interest" in the trust and none of the exceptions contained in the Plan Assets Regulation were applicable. An equity interest is defined under the Plan Assets Regulation as an interest other than an instrument which is treated as indebtedness under applicable local law and which has no substantial equity features. Although there is little guidance on the subject, the notes should be treated as indebtedness without substantial equity features for purposes of the Plan Assets Regulation. This determination is based in part upon the traditional debt features of the notes, including the reasonable expectation of purchasers of notes that the notes will be repaid when due, as well as the absence of conversion rights, warrants and other typical equity features. The debt treatment of the notes for ERISA purposes could change if the trust incurred losses.

However, even if the notes are treated as debt for purposes of the Plan Assets Regulation, the acquisition or holding of notes by or on behalf of a Benefit Plan could be considered to give rise to a prohibited transaction if the trust or any of its affiliates is or becomes a party in interest or a disqualified person with respect to such Benefit Plan. In such case, certain exemptions from the prohibited transaction rules could be applicable depending on the type and circumstances of the plan fiduciary making the decision to acquire a note. Included among these exemptions are: Prohibited Transaction Class Exemption ("PTCE") 90 — 1, regarding investments by insurance company pooled separate accounts; PTCE 95-60, regarding investments by insurance company general accounts; PTCE 91-38, regarding investments by bank collective investment finds; PTCE 96-23, regarding transactions affected by "in-house asset managers"; and PTCE 84-14, regarding transactions effected by "qualified professional asset managers." Each investor using the assets of a Benefit Plan which acquires the notes, or to whom the notes are transferred, will be deemed to have represented that the acquisition and continued holding of the notes will be covered by one of the exemptions listed above or by another Department of Labor prohibited transaction class exemption.

Employee benefit plans that are governmental plans (as defined in Section 3(32) of ERISA) and certain church plans (as defined in Section 3(33) of ERISA) are not subject to ERISA requirements; however, such plans may be subject to comparable federal, state or local law restrictions.

A plan fiduciary considering the purchase of notes should consult its tax and/or legal advisors regarding whether the assets of the trust would be considered plan assets, the possibility of exemptive relief from the prohibited transaction rules and other related issues and their potential consequences.

The sale of notes to a Benefit Plan is in no respect a representation that this investment meets all relevant legal requirements with respect to investments by Benefit Plan generally or by a particular Benefit Plan, or that this investment is appropriate for Benefit Plans generally or any particular Benefit Plan.

UNDERWRITING

Subject to the terms and conditions set forth in an Underwriting Agreement (the "Underwriting Agreement"), the Seller has agreed to cause the Trust to sell to each of the underwriters named below (collectively, the "Underwriters"), and each of the Underwriters has severally but not jointly agreed to purchase, the principal amount of notes set forth opposite its name below:

UNDERWRITERS	CLASS A-1 NOTES	CLASS A-2 NOTES	CLASS A-3 NOTES	CLASS A-4 NOTES
Banc One Capital Markets, Inc.	$131,600,000	$161,700,000	$135,100,000	$111,250,000
Deutsche Bank Securities Inc.	131,600,000	161,700,000	135,100,000	111,250,000
Banc of America Securities LLC	28,200,000	34,650,000	28,950,000	23,800,000
Barclays Capital Inc.	28,200,000	34,650,000	28,950,000	23,800,000
Credit Suisse First Boston LLC	28,200,000	34,650,000	28,950,000	23,800,000
Salomon Smith Barney Inc.	28,200,000	34,650,000	28,950,000	23,800,000
Total	$376,000,000	$462,000,000	$386,000,000	$317,700,000

In the Underwriting Agreement, the Underwriters have agreed, subject to the terms and conditions set forth in the Underwriting Agreement, to purchase all of the notes if any of the notes are purchased. This obligation of the Underwriters is subject to specified conditions precedent set forth in the Underwriting Agreement.

The Seller has been advised by the Underwriters that they propose to offer the notes to the public initially at the prices set forth on the cover of this prospectus supplement, and to specified dealers at these prices less the concessions and reallowance discounts set forth below:

CLASS	SELLING CONCESSION	REALLOWANCE DISCOUNT
A-1	0.0875%	0.0700%
A-2	0.1225%	0.0980%
A-3	0.1540%	0.1232%
A-4	0.1750%	0.1400%

The Seller and AHFC have agreed to indemnify the Underwriters against specified liabilities, including liabilities under the Securities Act or to contribute to payments which the Underwriters may be required to make in respect thereof. However, in the opinion of the SEC, certain indemnification provisions for liability arising under the federal securities law are contrary to public policy and therefore unenforceable. In the ordinary course of their respective businesses, the Underwriters and their respective affiliates have engaged and may engage in investment banking and/or commercial banking transactions with AHFC and its affiliates. The notes are new issues of securities with no established trading market. The Seller has been advised by the Underwriters that they intend to make a market in the notes of each class as permitted by applicable laws and regulations. The Underwriters are not obligated, however, to make a market in the notes, and that market-making may be discontinued at any time without notice at the sole discretion of the Underwriters. Accordingly, no assurance can be given as to the liquidity of, or trading markets for, the notes of any class.

The Trust may, from time to time, invest funds in the Accounts in Eligible Investments acquired from the Underwriters.

The Underwriters have advised the Seller that, pursuant to Regulation M under the Securities Exchange Act of 1934, as amended, specified persons participating in this offering may engage in transactions, including stabilizing bids, syndicate covering transactions or the imposition of penalty bids, which may have the effect of stabilizing or maintaining the market price of the notes of any class at levels above those that might otherwise prevail in the open market. A "stabilizing bid" is a bid for or the purchase of the Securities of any class on behalf of the Underwriters for the purpose of fixing or maintaining the price of those Securities. A "syndicate covering transaction" is the bid for or the purchase of those notes of any class on behalf of the Underwriters to reduce a short position incurred by the Underwriters in connection with this offering. A "penalty bid" is an arrangement permitting one of the Underwriters to reclaim the selling concession otherwise accruing to another Underwriter or syndicate member in connection with this offering if the notes of any class originally sold by the other Underwriter or syndicate member are purchased by the reclaiming Underwriter in a syndicate covering transaction and has therefore not been effectively placed by the other Underwriter or syndicate member.

Stabilizing bids and syndicate covering transactions may have the effect of causing the price of the Securities of any class to be higher than it might be in the absence thereof, and the imposition of penalty bids might also have an effect on the price of any note to the extent that it discourages resale of that note. Neither the Seller nor the Underwriters makes any representation or prediction as to the direction or magnitude of any of that effect on the prices for the notes. Neither the Seller nor the Underwriters makes any representation that the Underwriters will engage in any of those transactions or that, once commenced, any of those transactions will not be discontinued without notice.

It is expected that delivery of the notes will be made against payment therefor on or about the Closing Date. Rule 15c6-1 of the Commission under the

Exchange Act of 1934 generally requires trades in the secondary market to settle in three business days, unless the parties to any such trade expressly agree otherwise. Accordingly, purchasers who wish to trade notes on the date hereof will be required, by virtue of the fact that the notes initially will settle five business days after the date hereof, to specify an alternate settlement cycle at the time of any such trade to prevent a failed settlement. It is suggested that purchasers of notes who wish to trade notes on the date hereof consult their own advisors.

Upon receipt of a request by an investor who has received an electronic prospectus from an Underwriter or a request by such investor's representative within the period during which there is an obligation to deliver a prospectus, AHFC, the Seller, or the Underwriters will promptly deliver, or cause to be delivered, without charge, a paper copy of the prospectus.

Each Underwriter will represent that (i) it has not offered or sold and, prior to the expiry of the period of six months from the closing date, will not offer or sell any Notes to persons in the United Kingdom except to persons whose ordinary activities involve them in acquiring, holding, managing or disposing of investments (as principal or agent) for the purposes of their businesses or who it is reasonable to expect will acquire, hold, manage or dispose of investments (as principal or agent) for the purposes of their businesses, or otherwise in circumstances that have not resulted and will not result in an offer to the public in the United Kingdom within the meaning of the Public Offers of Securities Regulations 1995, as amended; (ii) it has complied and will comply with all applicable provisions of the Financial Services and Markets Act 2000 ("the FSMA") with respect to anything done by it in relation to the Notes in, from or otherwise involving the United Kingdom; (iii) it is a person of a kind described in Articles 19 or 49 of the Financial Services and Markets Act 2000 (Financial Promotion) Order 2001, as amended (the "Financial Promotion Order"); and (iv) it has only communicated or caused to be communicated, and will only communicate or cause to be communicated, in the United Kingdom any document received by it in connection with the issue of the Notes to a person who is of a kind described in Articles 19 or 49 of the Financial Promotion Order or who is a person to whom such document may otherwise lawfully be communicated.

Neither this prospectus nor the notes have been, or will be, available to other categories of persons in the United Kingdom and no-one falling outside such categories is entitled to rely on, and must not act on, any information in this prospectus. The transmission of this prospectus to any person in the United Kingdom other than the categories stated above is unauthorized and may contravene FSMA.

NOTICE TO CANADIAN RESIDENTS

RESALE RESTRICTIONS

The distribution of the notes in Canada is being made only on a private placement basis exempt from the requirement that the Seller, on behalf of the Trust, prepare and file a prospectus with the securities regulatory authorities in each province where trades of notes are effected. Accordingly, any resale of the notes in Canada must be made in accordance with applicable securities laws which will vary depending on the relevant jurisdiction, and which may require resales to be made in accordance with available statutory exemptions or pursuant to a discretionary exemption granted by the applicable Canadian securities regulatory authority. Purchasers are advised to seek legal advice prior to any resale of the notes.

REPRESENTATIONS OF PURCHASERS

Each purchaser of notes in Canada who receives a purchase confirmation will be deemed to represent to the Seller, the Servicer, the related trustee, the Trust and the dealer from whom such purchase confirmation is received that (i) such purchaser is entitled under applicable provincial securities laws to purchase such notes without the benefit of a prospectus qualified under such securities laws, (ii) where required by law, that such purchaser is purchasing as principal and not as agent, and (iii) such purchaser has reviewed the text above under " — Resale Restrictions."

RIGHTS OF ACTION (ONTARIO PURCHASERS)

The securities being offered are those of a foreign issuer and Ontario purchasers will not receive the contractual right of action prescribed by Section 32 of the Regulation under the SECURITIES ACT (Ontario). As a result, Ontario purchasers must rely on other remedies that may be available, including common law rights of action for damages or rescission or rights of action under the civil liability provisions of the U.S. federal securities laws.

ENFORCEMENT OF LEGAL RIGHTS

All of the issuer's directors and officers as well as the experts named herein may be located outside of Canada and, as a result, it may not be possible for Canadian purchasers to effect service of process within Canada upon the issuer or such persons. All or a substantial portion of the assets of the issuer and such persons may be located outside of Canada and, as a result, it may not be possible to satisfy a judgment against the issuer or such persons in Canada or to enforce a judgment obtained in Canadian courts against such issuer or persons outside of Canada.

NOTICE TO BRITISH COLUMBIA RESIDENTS

A purchaser of notes to whom the Securities Act (British Columbia) applies is advised that such purchaser is required to file with the British Columbia Securities Commission a report within ten days of the sale of any notes acquired by such purchaser pursuant to this offering. Such report must be in the form attached to British Columbia Securities Commission Blanket Order BOR #95/17, a copy of which may be obtained from the Seller. Only one such report must be filed in respect of notes acquired on the same date and under the same prospectus exemption.

TAXATION AND ELIGIBILITY FOR INVESTMENT

Canadian purchasers of notes should consult their own legal and tax advisors with respect to the tax consequences of an investment in the notes in their particular circumstances and with respect to the eligibility of the notes for investment by the purchaser under relevant Canadian legislation.

LEGAL OPINIONS

In addition to the legal opinions described in the accompanying prospectus, legal matters relating to the notes and federal income tax and California state income tax and other matters will be passed upon for the Trust by Dewey Ballantine LLP. Certain legal matters will be passed upon for the Underwriters by McKee Nelson LLP. . . .

ANNEX A

GLOBAL CLEARANCE, SETTLEMENT AND TAX DOCUMENTATION PROCEDURES

Except in limited circumstances, the globally offered class A notes (the "Global Securities") will be available only in book-entry form. Investors in the Global Securities may hold the Global Securities through any of The Depository Trust Company ("DTC") or, upon request, through Clearstream Banking, societe anonyme ("Clearstream, Luxembourg") or the Euroclear System ("Euroclear"). The Global Securities will be tradable as home market instruments in both the European and U.S. domestic markets. Initial settlement and all secondary trades will settle in same-day funds.

Secondary market trading between investors holding Global Securities through Clearstream, Luxembourg and Euroclear will be conducted in the ordinary way in accordance with their normal rules and operating procedures and in accordance with conventional eurobond practice (i.e., seven calendar day settlement).

Secondary market trading between investors holding Global Securities through DTC will be conducted according to the rules and procedures applicable to U.S. corporate debt obligations and prior asset-backed securities issues.

Secondary cross-market trading between Clearstream, Luxembourg or Euroclear and DTC Participants holding securities will be effected on a delivery-against-payment basis through the respective depositaries of Clearstream, Luxembourg and Euroclear, in this capacity, and as DTC Participants.

Non-U.S. holders, as described below, of Global Securities will be subject to U.S. withholding taxes unless those holders meet particular requirements and deliver appropriate U.S. tax documents to the securities clearing organizations or their participants.

INITIAL SETTLEMENT

All Global Securities will be held in book-entry form by DTC in the name of Cede & Co. as nominee of DTC. Investors' interests in the Global Securities will be represented through financial institutions acting on their behalf as direct and indirect Participants in DTC. As a result, Clearstream, Luxembourg and Euroclear will hold positions on behalf of their participants through their respective depositaries, which in turn will hold the positions in accounts as DTC Participants.

Investors electing to hold their Global Securities through DTC will follow the settlement practices of prior asset-backed securities issues. Investor securities custody accounts will be credited with their holdings against payment in same-day funds on the settlement date.

Investors electing to hold their Global Securities through Clearstream, Luxembourg or Euroclear accounts will follow the settlement procedures applicable to conventional eurobonds, except that there will be no temporary global security and no "lock-up" or restricted period. Global Securities will be credited to the securities custody accounts on the settlement date against payment in same-day funds.

SECONDARY MARKET TRADING

Since the purchaser determines the place of delivery, it is important to establish at the time of the trade where both the purchaser's and seller's accounts are located to ensure that settlement can be made on the desired value date.

Trading between DTC Participants. Secondary market trading between DTC Participants will be settled using the procedures applicable to prior asset-backed securities issues in same-day funds.

Trading between Clearstream, Luxembourg and/or Euroclear Participants. Secondary market trading between Clearstream, Luxembourg Participants or Euroclear Participants will be settled using the procedures applicable to conventional eurobonds in same-day funds.

Trading between DTC Seller and Clearstream, Luxembourg or Euroclear Participants. When Global Securities are to be transferred from the account of a DTC Participant to the account of a Clearstream, Luxembourg Participant or a Euroclear Participant, the purchaser will send instructions to Clearstream, Luxembourg or Euroclear through a Clearstream, Luxembourg Participant or Euroclear Participant at least one business day prior to settlement. Clearstream, Luxembourg or Euroclear will instruct the respective Depositary, as the case may be, to receive the Global Securities against payment. Payment will include interest accrued on the Global Securities from and including the last coupon payment date to and excluding the settlement date, on the basis of a 360-day year of twelve 30-day months or a 360-day year and the actual number of days in the accrual period, as applicable. For transactions settling on the 31st of the month, payment will include interest accrued to and excluding the first day of the following month. Payment will then be made by the respective Depositary of the

DTC Participant's account against delivery of the Global Securities. After settlement has been completed, the Global Securities will be credited to the respective clearing system and by the clearing system, in accordance with its usual procedures, to the Clearstream, Luxembourg Participant's or Euroclear Participant's account. The securities credit will appear the next day (European time) and the cash debt will be back-valued to, and the interest on the Global Securities will accrue from, the value date, which would be the preceding day when settlement occurred in New York. If settlement is not completed on the intended value date, i.e., the trade fails, the Clearstream, Luxembourg or Euroclear cash debt will be valued instead as of the actual settlement date.

Clearstream, Luxembourg Participants and Euroclear Participants will need to make available to the respective clearing systems the funds necessary to process same-day funds settlement. The most direct means of doing so is to pre-position funds for settlement, either from cash on hand or existing lines of credit, as they would for any settlement occurring within Clearstream, Luxembourg or Euroclear. Under this approach, they may take on credit exposure to Clearstream, Luxembourg or Euroclear until the Global Securities are credited to their accounts one day later.

As an alternative, if Clearstream, Luxembourg or Euroclear has extended a line of credit to them, Clearstream, Luxembourg Participants or Euroclear Participants can elect not to pre-position funds and allow that credit line to be drawn upon to finance settlement. Under this procedure, Clearstream, Luxembourg Participants or Euroclear Participants purchasing Global Securities would incur overdraft charges for one day, assuming they cleared the overdraft when the Global Securities were credited to their accounts. However, interest on the Global Securities would accrue from the value date. Therefore, in many cases the investment income on the Global Securities earned during that one-day period may substantially reduce or offset the amount of the overdraft charges, although this result will depend on each Clearstream, Luxembourg Participant's or Euroclear Participant's particular cost of funds.

Since the settlement is taking place during New York business hours, DTC Participants can employ their usual procedures for sending Global Securities to the respective European Depositary for the benefit of Clearstream, Luxembourg Participants or Euroclear Participants. The sale proceeds will be available to the DTC seller on the settlement date. Thus, to the DTC Participants a cross-market transaction will settle no differently than a trade between two DTC Participants.

Trading between Clearstream, Luxembourg or Euroclear Seller and DTC Purchaser. Due to time zone differences in their favor, Clearstream, Luxembourg Participants and Euroclear Participants may employ their customary procedures for transactions in which Global Securities are to be transferred by the respective clearing system, through the respective Depositary, to a DTC Participant. The seller will send instructions to Clearstream, Luxembourg or Euroclear through a Clearstream, Luxembourg Participant or Euroclear Participant at least one business day prior to settlement. In these cases, Clearstream, Luxembourg or Euroclear will instruct the Relevant Depositary, as appropriate, to deliver the Global Securities to the DTC Participant's account against payment. Payment will include interest accrued on the Global Securities from and including the last coupon payment to and excluding the settlement date on the basis of a 360-day year of twelve 30-day months or a 360-day year and the actual number of days in the accrual period, as applicable. For transactions settling on the 31st of the month, payment will include interest accrued to and excluding the first day of the following month. The payment will then be reflected in the account of the Clearstream, Luxembourg Participant or Euroclear Participant the following day, and receipt of the cash proceeds in the Clearstream, Luxembourg Participant's or Euroclear Participant's account would be back-valued to the value date, which would be the preceding day, when settlement occurred in New York. Should the Clearstream, Luxembourg Participant or Euroclear Participant have a line of credit with its respective clearing system and elect to be in debt in anticipation of receipt of the sale proceeds in its account, the back valuation will extinguish any overdraft incurred over that one-day period. If settlement is not completed on the intended value date, i.e., the trade fails, receipt of the cash proceeds in the Clearstream, Luxembourg Participant's or Euroclear Participant's account would instead be valued as of the actual settlement date.

Finally, day traders that use Clearstream, Luxembourg or Euroclear and that purchase Global Securities from DTC Participants for delivery to Clearstream, Luxembourg Participants or Euroclear Participants should note that these trades would automatically fail on the sale side unless affirmative action were taken. At least three techniques should be readily available to eliminate this potential problem:

(1) borrowing through Clearstream, Luxembourg or Euroclear for one day, until the purchase side of the day trade is reflected in their Clearstream, Luxembourg or Euroclear accounts, in accordance with the clearing system's customary procedures;

(2) borrowing the Global Securities in the U.S. from a DTC Participant no later than one day prior to settlement, which would give the Global Securities sufficient time to be reflected in their Clearstream, Luxembourg or Euroclear account in order to settle the sale side of the trade; or

(3) staggering the value dates for the buy and sell sides of the trade so that the value date for the purchase from the DTC Participant is at least one day prior to the value date for the sale to the Clearstream, Luxembourg Participant or Euroclear Participant.

CERTAIN U.S. FEDERAL INCOME TAX DOCUMENTATION REQUIREMENTS

A beneficial owner of Global Securities holding securities through Clearstream, Luxembourg or Euroclear, or through DTC if the holder has an address outside the U.S., will be subject to the 30% U.S. withholding tax that generally applies to payments of interest, including original issue discount, on registered debt issued by U.S. Persons, unless:

(1) each clearing system, bank or other financial institution that holds customers' securities in the ordinary course of its trade or business in the chain of intermediaries between the beneficial owner and the U.S. entity required to withhold tax complies with applicable certification requirements and

(2) the beneficial owner takes one of the steps described below to obtain an exemption or reduced tax rate.

This summary does not deal with all aspects of U.S. federal income tax withholding that may be relevant to foreign holders of the Global Securities as well as the application of the withholding regulations. You should consult with your own tax advisors for specific advice regarding your holding and disposing of the Global Securities.

Exemption for Non-U.S. Persons — Form W-8 BEN. Beneficial owners of Global Securities that are Non-U.S. Persons, as defined below, can obtain a complete exemption from the withholding tax by filing a signed Form W-8BEN, Certificate of Foreign Status of Beneficial Owner for United States Tax Withholding. The W-8BEN is valid for a period of three years beginning on the date that the form is signed. If the information shown on form W-8BEN changes, a new Form W-8BEN must be filed within 30 days of the change.

Exemption for Non-U.S. Persons with effectively connected income — Form W-8ECI. A Non-U.S. Person may claim an exemption from U.S. withholding on income effectively connected with the conduct of a trade or business in the United States by filing Form W-8ECI, Certificate of Foreign Person's Claim for Exemption From Withholding on Income Effectively Connected With the Conduct of a Trade or Business in the United States. The Form W-8ECI is valid for a period of three years beginning on the date that the form is signed.

Exemption or reduced rate for Non-U.S. Persons resident in treaty countries — Form W-8BEN. A Non-U.S. Person may claim treaty benefits by filing Form W-8BEN, Certificate of Foreign Status of Beneficial Owner for United States Tax Withholding. The Form W-8BEN is valid for a period of three years beginning on the date that the form is signed.

Exemption for U.S. Persons — Form W-9. U.S. Persons can obtain a complete exemption from the withholding tax by filing Form W-9, Payer's Request for Taxpayer Identification Number and Certification.

A "U.S. Person" is:

(1) a citizen or resident of the United States;

(2) a corporation or partnership (including an entity treated as a corporation or partnership for United States federal income tax purpose) created or organized under the laws of the United States, any state thereof, or the District of Columbia;

(3) an estate that is subject to U.S. federal income tax regardless of the source of its income; or

(4) a trust if (a) a court within the U.S. is able to exercise primary supervision over the administration of the trust and one or more United States persons have authority to control all substantial decisions of the trust or (b) such trust was in existence on August 20, 1996 and is eligible to elect, and has made a valid election, to be treated as a U.S. Person despite not meeting the requirements of clause (a).

A "Non-U.S. Person" is any person who is not a U.S. Person.

ANNEX B

FINANCIAL STATEMENTS OF THE TRUST AND AUDIT LETTER

INDEPENDENT AUDITORS' REPORT

The Board of Directors of American Honda Receivables Corp.

as depositor for Honda Auto Receivables 2003-1 Owner Trust:

We have audited the accompanying balance sheet of Honda Auto Receivables 2003-1 Owner Trust, a wholly owned statutory trust of American Honda Receivables Corp., as of February 4, 2003. This financial statement is the responsibility of the Trust's management. Our responsibility is to express an opinion on this financial statement based on our audit.

We conducted our audit in accordance with auditing standards generally accepted in the United States of America. Those standards require that we plan and perform the audit to obtain reasonable assurance about whether the balance sheet is free of material misstatement. An audit of a balance sheet includes examining, on a test basis, evidence supporting the amounts and disclosures in that balance sheet. An audit of a balance sheet also includes assessing the accounting principles used and significant estimates made by management, as well as evaluating the overall balance sheet presentation. We believe that our audit of the balance sheet provides a reasonable basis for our opinion.

In our opinion, the balance sheet referred to above presents fairly, in all material respects, the financial position of Honda Auto Receivables 2003-1 Owner Trust as of February 4, 2003 in conformity with accounting principles generally accepted in the United States of America.

KPMG LLP

February 10, 2003

HONDA AUTO RECEIVABLES 2003-1 OWNER TRUST

Balance Sheet

February 4, 2003

ASSETS	
Cash	$1,000
Total assets	$1,000
UNDIVIDED INTERESTS IN TRUST	
Undivided interests in Trust	$1,000
Total undivided interests in Trust	$1,000

See accompanying notes to balance sheet.

HONDA AUTO RECEIVABLES 2003-1 OWNER TRUST

Notes to Balance Sheet

February 4, 2003

(1) ORGANIZATION AND SIGNIFICANT ACCOUNTING POLICIES

Honda Auto Receivables 2003-1 Owner Trust (the Trust) is a wholly owned statutory trust of American Honda Receivables Corp. (AHRC). AHRC is a wholly owned subsidiary of American Honda Finance Corporation (AHFC). AHFC is a wholly owned subsidiary of American Honda Motor Co., Inc. (AHM). AHM is a wholly owned subsidiary of Honda Motor Co., Ltd. (HML) and is the sole authorized distributor of Honda and Acura automobiles, motorcycles, power equipment, parts and accessories in the United States.

The Trust is a Delaware statutory trust that was formed on January 21, 2003. The sole purpose of the Trust is to conserve the Owner Trust estate and collect and disburse the periodic income therefrom for the use and benefit of the Trust Certificate holders and to engage in the following ministerial activities: (i) issue and sell notes and Trust certificates; (ii) with the proceeds from such sale, purchase certain receivables from AHRC; (iii) make payments on notes and certificates; and (iv) engage in other activities that are necessary, suitable or convenient to accomplish the foregoing.

(2) UNDIVIDED INTERESTS IN TRUST

Undivided interests in Trust represents the initial contribution made by the Depositor, AHRC, in exchange for 100% beneficial ownership interest in the Trust on January 21, 2003.

(3) INCOME TAXES

The Trust does not constitute a separate entity for federal income tax purposes or for state income or franchise purposes, as it is a mere nominee holder of legal titles of the Trust assets.

Appendix 6

Appendix 6

SECURITIES AND EXCHANGE COMMISSION
Washington, D.C. 20549

FORM 8-K CURRENT REPORT
PURSUANT TO SECTION 13 OR 15(D) OF THE SECURITIES EXCHANGE ACT OF 1934
DATE OF REPORT (DATE OF EARLIEST EVENT REPORTED):
February 25, 2003

HONDA AUTO RECEIVABLES 2003-1 OWNER TRUST
(Issuer with respect to Securities)
American Honda Receivables Corp.
(Exact name of registrant as specified in its charter)

California	333-71022	33-0526079
(State or other jurisdiction of incorporation)	(Commission File Number)	(IRS Employer Identification No.)

American Honda Receivables Corp.
700 Van Ness Avenue
Torrance, California 90501

(Address of principal executive offices) (Zip code)

Registrant's telephone number, including area code: (310) 781-4100

Item 2. Acquisition or Disposition of Assets

Description of the Securities and the Auto Loans

American Honda Receivables Corp. registered issuances of up to $10,000,000,000 principal amount of Asset Backed Notes and Asset Backed Certificates on a delayed or continuous basis pursuant to Rule 415 under the Securities Act of 1933, as amended (the "Act"), by the Registration Statements on Form S-3 (Registration File No. 333-71022) (the "Registration Statement"). Pursuant to the Registration Statement, Honda Auto Receivables 2003-1 Owner Trust (the "Issuer") issued $1,541,700,000 Class A-1 1.30% Asset Backed Notes (the "Class A-1 Notes"), Class A-2 1.46% Asset Backed Notes (the "Class A-2 Notes"), Class A-3 1.92% Asset Backed Notes (the "Class A-3 Notes") and Class A-4 2.48% Asset Backed Notes (the "Class A-4 Notes") (collectively the "Notes"), on February 25, 2003. This Current Report on Form 8-K is being filed to satisfy an undertaking to file copies of certain agreements executed in connection with the issuance of the Notes.

The Notes were issued pursuant to an Indenture (the "Indenture") attached hereto as Exhibit 4.1, dated as of February 1, 2003, between the Issuer and JPMorgan Chase Bank, as indenture trustee (the "Indenture Trustee"). The Notes represent non-recourse obligations of the Issuer, which obligations are secured by the pledge by the Issuer to the Indenture Trustee of auto loans and certain related property.

The Notes evidence indebtedness of the Issuer, the assets of which consist primarily of fixed rate motor vehicle retail installment sales contracts secured by automobiles financed thereby.

As of February 25, 2003, the receivables possessed the characteristics described in the Prospectus dated February 19, 2003 and the Prospectus Supplement dated February 19, 2003, filed pursuant to Rule 424(b)(5) of the Act on February 24, 2003.

Item 7. Financial Statements, Pro Forma Financial Information and Exhibits.

(a) Not applicable

(b) Not applicable

(c) Exhibit 1.1. Underwriting Agreement, dated February 19, 2003, among American Honda Receivables Corp. (the"Seller"), American Honda Finance Corporation (the "Servicer") and Deutsche Bank Securities Inc.

Exhibit 4.1. Indenture, dated as of February 1, 2003, between the Issuer and the Indenture Trustee.

Exhibit 4.2. Amended and Restated Trust Agreement, dated February 25, 2003, among American Honda Receivables Corp. (the "Depositor"), The Bank of New York (the "Owner Trustee") and The Bank of New York (Delaware) (the "Delaware Trustee").

Exhibit 4.3 Sale and Servicing Agreement, dated February 1, 2003, among the Seller, the Servicer and the Issuer.

Exhibit 4.4 Receivables Purchase Agreement, dated as of February 1, 2003, between American Honda Finance Corporation (the "Seller") and American Honda Receivables Corp. (the "Purchaser").

Exhibit 4.5 Administration Agreement, dated as of February 1, 2003, among the Issuer, American Honda Finance Corporation (the "Administrator"), the Depositor and the Indenture Trustee.

SIGNATURES

Pursuant to the requirements of the Securities Exchange Act of 1934, the registrant has duly caused this report to be signed on its behalf by the undersigned thereunto duly authorized.

Honda Auto Receivables 2003-1 Owner Trust
By: American Honda Receivables Corp.

By: /s/ Y. Takahashi

Name: Y. Takahashi

Title: President

Dated: February 25, 2003

EXHIBIT INDEX

Exhibit No.	Description
Exhibit 1.1.	Underwriting Agreement, dated February 19, 2003, among American Honda Receivables Corp. (the"Seller"), American Honda Finance Corporation (the "Servicer") and Deutsche Bank Securities Inc.
Exhibit 4.1.	Indenture, dated as of February 1, 2003, between the Issuer and the Indenture Trustee.
Exhibit 4.2.	Amended and Restated Trust Agreement, dated February 25, 2003, among American Honda Receivables Corp. (the "Depositor"), The Bank of New York (the "Owner Trustee") and The Bank of New York (Delaware) (the "Delaware Trustee").
Exhibit 4.3	Sale and Servicing Agreement, dated February 1, 2003, among the Seller, the Servicer and the Issuer.
Exhibit 4.4	Receivables Purchase Agreement, dated as of February 1, 2003, between American Honda Finance Corporation (the "Seller") and American Honda Receivables Corp. (the "Purchaser").
Exhibit 4.5	Administration Agreement, dated as of February 1, 2003, among the Issuer, American Honda Finance Corporation (the "Administrator"), the Depositor and the Indenture Trustee

Appendix 7

Appendix 7

EXECUTION COPY

$1,541,700,000

HONDA AUTO RECEIVABLES 2003-1 OWNER TRUST

$376,000,000 1.30% ASSET BACKED NOTES, CLASS A-1
$462,000,000 1.46% ASSET BACKED NOTES, CLASS A-2
$386,000,000 1.92% ASSET BACKED NOTES, CLASS A-3
$317,700,000 2.48% ASSET BACKED NOTES, CLASS A-4

AMERICAN HONDA RECEIVABLES CORP.

UNDERWRITING AGREEMENT
February 19, 2003

Deutsche Bank Securities Inc.,
as Representative of the Several Underwriters
31 West 52nd Street, 17th Floor
New York, New York 10019

Ladies and Gentlemen:

1. Introductory. American Honda Receivables Corp., a California corporation (the "Company"), proposes, subject to the terms and conditions stated herein, to cause the Honda Auto Receivables 2003-1 Owner Trust (the "Trust") to issue and sell $376,000,000 aggregate principal amount of 1.30% Asset Backed Notes, Class A-1 (the "Class A-1 Notes"), $462,000,000 aggregate principal amount of 1.46% Asset Backed Notes, Class A-2 (the "Class A-2 Notes"), $386,000,000 aggregate principal amount of 1.92% Asset Backed Notes, Class A-3 (the "Class A-3 Notes") and $317,700,000 aggregate principal amount of 2.48% Asset Backed Notes, Class A-4 (the "Class A-4 Notes" and together with the Class A-1 Notes, the Class A-2 Notes and the Class A-3 Notes, the "Notes"). The Notes will be issued pursuant to the Indenture, to be dated as of February 1, 2003 (the "Indenture"), between the Trust and JP Morgan Chase Bank (the "Indenture Trustee").

Concurrently with the issuance and sale of the Notes as contemplated herein, the Trust will issue $35,577,657.84 aggregate principal amount of certificates of beneficial interest (the "Certificates"), each representing an interest in the Owner Trust Estate. The Company will retain the Certificates. The Certificates will be issued pursuant to the Amended and Restated Trust Agreement, to be dated February 25, 2003 (the "Trust Agreement"), among the Company, Bank of New York, as owner trustee (the "Owner Trustee") and Bank of New York (Delaware), as Delaware Trustee (the "Delaware Trustee"). The Certificates are subordinated to the Notes.

The assets of the Trust will include, among other things, a pool of retail installment sale and conditional sale contracts secured by new and used Honda and Acura motor vehicles (the "Receivables"), with respect to Actuarial Receivables, certain monies due thereunder on or after February 1, 2003 (the "Cutoff Date"), and with respect to Simple Interest Receivables, certain monies due or received thereunder on or after the Cutoff Date, such Receivables to be sold to the Trust by the Company and to be serviced for the Trust by American Honda Finance Corporation ("AHFC" or, in its capacity as servicer, the "Servicer"). Capitalized terms used but not defined herein have the meanings ascribed thereto in the Sale and Servicing Agreement, to be dated as of February 1, 2003 (the "Sale and Servicing Agreement"), by and among the Trust, the Company and the Servicer or, if not defined therein, in the Indenture, the Trust Agreement or the Receivables Purchase Agreement, to be dated as of February 1, 2003 between AHFC and the Company (the "Receivables Purchase Agreement"), as the case may be. As used herein, "Basic Documents" shall have the meaning specified in the Sale and Servicing Agreement. The Company hereby agrees with the several Underwriters named in Schedule A hereto (collectively, the "Underwriters") as follows:

2. Representations and Warranties of the Company and AHFC. The Company and AHFC, jointly and severally, represent and warrant to, and agree with, the several Underwriters that:

(a) A registration statement on Form S-3 (No. 333-71022), including a prospectus, relating to the Notes has been filed with the Securities and Exchange Commission (the "Commission") and has become effective. Such registration statement, as amended as of the date of the Agreement is hereinafter referred to as the "Registration Statement," and the prospectus included in such Registration Statement, as supplemented to reflect the terms of the Notes as first filed with the Commission after the date of this Agreement pursuant to and in accordance with Rule 424(b) ("Rule 424(b)") under the Securities Act of 1933, as amended (the "Act"), including all material incorporated by reference therein, is hereinafter referred to as the "Prospectus."

(b) On the effective date of the Registration Statement relating to the Notes, such Registration Statement conformed in all respects to the requirements of the Act and the rules and regulations of the Commission promulgated under the Act (the "Rules and Regulations") and did not include any untrue statement of a material fact or omit to state any material fact required to be stated therein or necessary to make the statements therein not misleading, and on the date of this Agreement, the Registration Statement conforms, and at the time of the filing of the Prospectus in accordance with Rule 424(b), the Registration Statement and the Prospectus will conform in all respects to the requirements of the Act and the Rules and Regulations, and neither of such documents includes or will include any untrue statement of a material fact or omits or will omit to state any material fact required to be stated therein or necessary to make the statements therein not misleading. The preceding sentence does not apply to statements in or omissions from the Registration Statement or the Prospectus based upon written information furnished to the Company by any Underwriter through the Representative specifically for use therein, it being understood and agreed that the only such information is that described as such in Section 7(b).

(c) The Notes are "asset backed securities" within the meaning of, and satisfy the requirements for use of, Form S-3 under the Act.

(d) The documents incorporated by reference in the Registration Statement and Prospectus, at the time they were or hereafter are filed with the Commission, complied and will comply in all material respects with the requirements of the Securities Exchange Act of 1934, as amended (the "Exchange Act"), and the rules and regulations of the Commission thereunder.

(e) The Company has caused to be filed with the Commission on February 19, 2003 the Current Report on Form 8-K with respect to the Term Sheet dated February 18, 2003 relating to the Notes (the "Term Sheet").

(f) Each of the Company and AHFC has been duly incorporated and is an existing corporation in good standing under the laws of the State of California, with power and authority (corporate and other) to own its properties and conduct its business as described in the Prospectus; and each of the Company and AHFC is duly qualified to do business as a foreign corporation in good standing in all other jurisdictions in which its ownership or lease of property or the conduct of its business requires such qualification.

(g) No consent, approval, authorization or order of, or filing with, any governmental agency or body or any court is required to be obtained or made by the Company, AHFC or the Trust for the consummation of the transactions contemplated by this Agreement and the Basic Documents in connection with the issuance of the Notes and the Certificates and the sale by the Company of the Notes, except such as have been obtained and made under the Act, such as may be required under state securities laws and the filing of any financing statements required to perfect the Company's, the Trust's and the Indenture Trustee's interest in the Receivables, which financing statements will be filed in the appropriate offices prior to the Closing Date (as such term is defined in Section 3).

(h) Neither the Company nor AHFC is in violation of its Articles of Incorporation or By-laws or in default in the performance or observance of any obligation, agreement, covenant or condition contained in any agreement or instrument to which it is a party or by which it or its properties are bound which could have a material adverse effect on the transactions contemplated herein or in the Basic Documents. The execution, delivery and performance of this Agreement and the Basic Documents by the Company and AHFC, and the issuance of the Notes and the Certificates and the sale by the Company of the Notes and the compliance by the Company and AHFC with the terms and provisions hereof and thereof will not, subject to obtaining any consents or approvals as may be required under the securities or "blue sky" laws of various jurisdictions, result in a breach or violation of any of the terms and provisions of, or constitute a default under, any statute, rule, regulation or order of any governmental agency or body or any court, domestic or foreign, having jurisdiction over the Company or AHFC or any of their respective properties, or any agreement or instrument to which the Company or AHFC is a party or by which the Company or AHFC is bound or to which any of the properties of the Company or AHFC is subject, or the Articles of Incorporation or By-laws of the Company and AHFC, and the Company has full power and authority to authorize the issuance of the Notes and the Certificates and to sell the Notes as contemplated by this Agreement, the Indenture and the Trust Agreement, and each of the Company and AHFC has full power and authority to enter into this Agreement and the Basic Documents and to consummate the transactions contemplated hereby and thereby.

(i) On the Closing Date, the Company will have directed the Owner Trustee to authenticate and execute the Certificates and, when delivered and paid for pursuant to the Trust Agreement, the Certificates will have been duly issued and delivered and will constitute valid and legally binding obligations of the Trust, entitled to the benefits provided in the Trust Agreement and enforceable in accordance with their terms.

(j) Except as disclosed in the Prospectus, there are no pending actions, suits or proceedings against or affecting the Company or AHFC or any of their respective properties that, if determined adversely to the Company or AHFC, would individually or in the aggregate have a material adverse effect on the condition (financial or other), business or results of operations of the Company or AHFC, respectively, or would materially and adversely affect the ability of the Company or AHFC to perform its obligations under this Agreement or the other Basic Documents to which it is a party, or which are otherwise material in the context of the issuance and sale of the Notes or the issuance of the Certificates; and no such actions, suits or proceedings are threatened or, to the Company's or AHFC's knowledge, contemplated.

(k) As of the Closing Date, the representations and warranties of the Company and AHFC contained in the Basic Documents will be true and correct.

(l) This Agreement has been duly authorized, executed and delivered by each of the Company and AHFC.

(m) The Company has authorized the conveyance of the Receivables to the Trust, and, as of the Closing Date, the Company has directed the Trust to execute and issue the Notes and the Certificates and to sell the Notes.

(n) The Company's assignment and delivery of the Receivables to the Trust as of the Closing Date will vest in the Trust all of the Company's right, title and interest therein, subject to no prior lien, mortgage, security interest, pledge, adverse claim, charge or other encumbrance.

(o) The Trust's assignment of the Receivables to the Indenture Trustee pursuant to the Indenture will vest in the Indenture Trustee, for the benefit of the Noteholders, a first priority perfected security interest therein, subject to no prior lien, mortgage, security interest, pledge, adverse claim, charge or other encumbrance.

(p) The computer tape of the Receivables created as of February 1, 2003, and made available to the Representative by the Servicer was complete and accurate as of the date thereof and includes an identifying description of the Receivables that are listed on Schedule A to the Sale and Servicing Agreement.

(q) Any taxes, fees and other governmental charges in connection with the execution, delivery and performance of this Agreement, the Basic Documents, the Notes and the Certificates and any other agreements contemplated herein or therein shall have been paid or will be paid by the Company at or prior to the Closing Date to the extent then due.

(r) The consummation of the transactions contemplated by this Agreement and the Basic Documents, and the fulfillment of the terms hereof and thereof, will not conflict with or result in a breach of any of the terms or provisions of, or constitute a default under, or result in the creation of any lien, charge or encumbrance upon any of the property or assets of the Company or AHFC pursuant to the terms of, any indenture, mortgage, deed of trust, loan agreement, guarantee, lease financing agreement or similar agreement or instrument under which the Company or AHFC is a debtor or guarantor.

(s) The Company is not and, after giving effect to the issuance of the Certificates and the offering and sale of the Notes and the application of the proceeds thereof as described in the Prospectus, will not be required to be registered as an "investment company" as defined in the Investment Company Act of 1940, as amended (the "Investment Company Act").

(t) In connection with the offering of the Notes in the State of Florida, the Company and AHFC hereby certify that they have complied with all provisions of Section 517.075 of the Florida Securities and Investor Protection Act.

3. Purchase, Sale and Delivery of Notes. On the basis of the representations, warranties and agreements herein contained, but subject to the terms and conditions herein set forth, the Company agrees to sell to the Underwriters, and the Underwriters agree, severally and not jointly, to purchase from the Company, at a purchase price of, in the case of (i) the Class A-1 Notes, 99.87500% of the principal amount thereof; (ii) the Class A-2 Notes, 99.81927% of the principal amount thereof; (iii) the Class A-3 Notes, 99.77166% of the principal amount thereof; and (iv) the Class A-4 Notes, 99.73802% of the principal amount thereof, the respective principal amounts of each Class of the Notes set forth opposite the names of the Underwriters in Schedule A hereto.

The Company will deliver against payment of the purchase price, the Notes of each Class in the form of one or more permanent global securities in definitive form (the "Global Notes") deposited with the Indenture Trustee as custodian for The Depository Trust Company ("DTC") and registered in the name of Cede & Co., as nominee for DTC. Interests in any permanent Global Notes will be held only in book-entry form through DTC, except in the limited circumstances described in the Prospectus. Payment for the Notes shall be made by the Underwriters in Federal (same day) funds by official check or checks or wire transfer to an account in New York previously designated to the Representative by the Company at a bank acceptable to the Representative at the offices of Dewey Ballantine LLP, Los Angeles, California at 10:00 A.M., New York City time, on February 25, 2003, or at such other time not later than seven full business days thereafter as the Representative and the Company determine, such time being herein referred to as the "Closing Date", against delivery to the Indenture Trustee as custodian for DTC of the Global Notes representing all of the Notes. The Global Notes will be made available for checking at the above office of Dewey Ballantine LLP at least 24 hours prior to the Closing Date.

The Company will deliver the Certificates to the above office of Dewey Ballantine LLP on the Closing Date. The certificate for the Certificates so to be delivered will be in definitive form, in authorized denominations and registered in the name of the Company and will be made available for checking at the above office of Dewey Ballantine LLP at least 24 hours prior to the Closing Date.

Pursuant to Rule 15c6-1(d) under the Securities Exchange Act of 1934, as amended (the "Exchange Act"), the parties hereto have agreed that the Closing Date will be not later than February 25, 2003, unless otherwise agreed to as described above.

4. Offering by Underwriters. It is understood that, the several Underwriters propose to offer the Notes for sale to the public as set forth in the Prospectus, and each Underwriter represents, warrants and covenants, severally and not jointly, to the Company and AHFC that: (i) it has not offered or sold and, prior to the expiry of the period of six months from the Closing Date, will not offer or sell any Notes to persons in the United Kingdom except to persons whose ordinary activities involve them in acquiring, holding, managing or disposing of investments (as principal or agent) for the purposes of their businesses or who it is reasonable to expect will acquire, hold, manage or dispose of investments (as principal or agent) for the purposes of their businesses, or otherwise in circumstances that have not resulted and will not result in an offer to the public in the United Kingdom within the meaning of the Public Offers of Securities Regulations 1995, as amended, (ii) it has complied and will comply with all applicable provisions of the Financial Services and Markets Act 2000 with respect to anything done by it in relation to the Notes in, from or otherwise involving the United Kingdom, (iii) it is a person of a kind described in Articles 19 or 49 of the Financial Services and Markets Act 2000 (Financial Promotion) Order 2001, as amended (the "Financial Promotion Order") and (iv) it has only communicated or caused to be communicated, and will only communicate or

cause to be communicated, in the United Kingdom any document received by it in connection with the issue of the Notes to a person who is of a kind described in Articles 19 or 49 of the Financial Promotion Order or who is a person to whom such document may otherwise lawfully be communicated.

5. Certain Agreements of the Company. The Company agrees with the several Underwriters:

(a) The Company will file the Prospectus, properly completed, with the Commission pursuant to and in accordance with subparagraph (2) (or, if applicable and if consented to by the Representative, subparagraph (5)) of Rule 424(b) no later than the second business day following the date it is first used. The Company will advise the Representative promptly of any such filing pursuant to Rule 424(b).

(b) The Company will advise the Representative promptly, in writing, of any proposal to amend or supplement the Registration Statement or the Prospectus and will not effect such amendment or supplementation without the Representative's reasonable consent; and the Company will also advise the Representative promptly of any amendment or supplementation of the Registration Statement or the Prospectus and of the institution by the Commission of any stop order proceedings in respect of the Registration Statement and will use its best efforts to prevent the issuance of any such stop order and to obtain as soon as possible its lifting, if issued.

(c) If, at any time when a prospectus relating to the Notes is required to be delivered under the Act in connection with sales by any Underwriter or dealer, any event occurs as a result of which the Prospectus as then amended or supplemented would include an untrue statement of a material fact or omit to state any material fact necessary in order to make the statements therein, in the light of the circumstances under which they were made not misleading, or if it is necessary at any time to amend the Prospectus to comply with the Act, the Company will promptly notify the Representative of such event and will promptly prepare and file with the Commission (subject to the Representative's prior review pursuant to Section 5(b)), at its own expense, an amendment or supplement which will correct such statement or omission, or an amendment which will effect such compliance. Neither the Representative's consent to, nor the Underwriters delivery of, any such amendment or supplement shall constitute a waiver of any of the conditions set forth in Section 6.

(d) The Company will cause the Trust to make generally available to Noteholders, as soon as practicable, but no later than sixteen months after the date hereof, an earnings statement of the Trust covering a period of at least twelve consecutive months beginning after the later of (i) the effective date of the registration statement relating to the Notes and (ii) the effective date of the most recent post-effective amendment to the Registration Statement to become effective prior to the date of this Agreement and, in each case, satisfying the provisions of Section 11(a) of the Act (including Rule 158 promulgated thereunder).

(e) The Company will furnish to the Underwriters copies of the Prospectus, the Registration Statement and all amendments and supplements to such documents, in each case as soon as available and in such quantities as the Representative reasonably requests. The Prospectus shall be furnished on or prior to 3:00 P.M., New York time, on the business day following the execution and delivery of this Agreement. All other such documents shall be so furnished as soon as available. The Company will pay the expenses of printing and distributing to the Underwriters all such documents.

(f) The Company will arrange for the qualification of the Notes for offering and sale and the determination of their eligibility for investment under the laws of such jurisdictions as the Representative may reasonably designate and will continue such qualifications in effect so long as required for the distribution of the Notes; provided that in connection therewith the Company shall not be required to qualify as a foreign corporation to do business or to file a general consent to service of process in any such jurisdiction.

(g) For a period from the date of this Agreement until the retirement of the Notes (i) the Company will furnish to the Representative and, upon request, to each of the other Underwriters, copies of each certificate and the annual statements of compliance delivered to the Indenture Trustee pursuant to Section 3.09 of the Indenture and Sections 3.10 and 3.11 of the Sale and Servicing Agreement and the annual independent certified public accountant's servicing reports furnished to the Indenture Trustee pursuant to Section 3.12 of the Sale and Servicing Agreement, by first-class mail as soon as practicable after such statements and reports are furnished to the Indenture Trustee, and (ii) such other forms of periodic certificates or reports as may be delivered to the Indenture Trustee, the Owner Trustee or the Noteholders under the Indenture, the Sale and Servicing Agreement or the other Basic Documents.

(h) So long as any Note is outstanding, the Company will furnish to the Representative by first-class mail as soon as practicable, (i) all documents distributed, or caused to be distributed, by the Company to the Noteholders, (ii) all documents filed or caused to be filed by the Company with the Commission pursuant to the Exchange Act or any order of the Commission thereunder and (iii) such other information in the possession of the Company concerning the Trust as the Representative from time to time may reasonably request.

(i) Subject to the provisions of Section 9 hereof, the Company will pay all expenses incident to the performance of its obligations under this Agreement and will reimburse the Underwriters (if and to the extent incurred by them) for any filing fees and other expenses (including fees and disbursements of counsel) incurred by them in connection with qualification of the Notes for sale in jurisdictions that the Representative may designate pursuant to Section 5(f) hereof and determination of their eligibility for investment under the laws of such jurisdictions as the Representative reasonably designates and the printing of memoranda relating thereto, for any fees charged by investment rating agencies for the rating of the Notes, for any travel expenses of the officers and employees of the Underwriters and any other expenses of the Underwriters in connection with attending or hosting meetings with prospective purchasers of the Notes and for expenses incurred in distributing the Term Sheets and the Prospectus (including any amendments and supplements thereto).

(j) To the extent, if any, that the rating provided with respect to the Notes by Moody's Investors Service, Inc. ("Moody's"), Standard & Poor's, a division of The McGraw-Hill Companies, Inc. ("Standard & Poor's"), and Fitch, Inc. ("Fitch" and, together with Standard & Poor's and Moody's, the "Rating Agencies") is conditional upon the furnishing of documents or the taking of any other action by the Company, the Company shall furnish such documents and take any such other action.

(k) On or before the Closing Date, the Company and AHFC shall annotate and indicate unambiguously in the computer records of the Company and AHFC relating to the Receivables to show the Trust's absolute ownership of the Receivables, and from and after the Closing Date neither the Company nor AHFC shall take any action inconsistent with the Trust's ownership of such Receivables, other than as permitted by the Sale and Servicing Agreement.

6. Conditions of the Obligations of the Underwriters. The obligations of the several Underwriters to purchase and pay for the Notes on the Closing Date will be subject to the accuracy of the representations and warranties on the part of the Company and AHFC herein on the Closing Date, to the accuracy of the statements of Company and AHFC officers made pursuant to the provisions hereof, to the performance by the Company and AHFC of their respective obligations hereunder and to the following additional conditions precedent:

(a) The Representative shall have received a letter, dated the date hereof or the Closing Date, of KPMG LLP, in form and substance satisfactory to the Representative and counsel for the Underwriters, confirming that they are independent public accountants within the meaning of the Act and the applicable Rules and Regulations and stating in effect that (i) they have performed certain specified procedures as a result of which they determined that certain information of an accounting, financial or statistical nature (which is limited to accounting, financial or statistical information derived from the general accounting records of the Trust, AHFC and the Company) set forth in the Registration Statement, the Term Sheet and the Prospectus (and any supplements thereto), agrees with the accounting records of the Trust, AHFC and the Company, excluding any questions of legal interpretation, and (ii) they have performed certain specified procedures with respect to the Receivables.

(b) Prior to the Closing Date, no stop order suspending the effectiveness of the Registration Statement shall have been issued and no proceedings for that purpose shall have been instituted or, to the knowledge of the Company or the Representative, shall be contemplated by the Commission.

(c) Subsequent to the execution and delivery of this Agreement, there shall not have occurred (i) any change, or any development or event involving a prospective change, in or affecting particularly the business, properties, condition (financial or otherwise) or results of operations of the Company or AHFC which, in the judgment of a majority in interest of the Underwriters (including the Representative), materially impairs the investment quality of each Class of the Notes or makes it impractical or inadvisable to proceed with completion of the public offering or the sale of and payment for each Class of the Notes; (ii) any suspension or limitation of trading in securities generally on the New York Stock Exchange, or any setting of minimum prices for trading on such exchange; (iii) any banking moratorium declared by Federal, California or New York authorities; or (iv) any outbreak or escalation of major hostilities in which the United States is involved, any declaration of war by Congress or any substantial national or international calamity or emergency if, in the judgment of a majority in interest of the Underwriters (including the Representative), the effect of any such outbreak, escalation, declaration, calamity or emergency makes it impractical or inadvisable to proceed with completion of the public offering or the sale of and payment for each Class of the Notes.

(d) The Representative shall have received an opinion of Dewey Ballantine LLP, special counsel to the Company and AHFC, dated the Closing Date and satisfactory in form and substance to the Representative and counsel for the Underwriters, to the effect that:

(i) the Company has been duly incorporated and is an existing corporation in good standing under the laws of the State of California, with full corporate power and authority to own its properties and conduct its business as described in the Prospectus; the Company is duly qualified to do business and is in good standing in each jurisdiction in which its ownership or lease of property or the conduct of its business requires such qualification, except where the failure to be so qualified and in good standing would not have a material adverse effect on its obligations under the Basic Documents;

(ii) AHFC has been duly incorporated and is an existing corporation in good standing under the laws of the State of California, with corporate power and authority to own its properties and conduct its business as described in the Prospectus; AHFC is duly qualified to do business and is in good standing in each jurisdiction in which its ownership or lease of property or the conduct of its business requires such qualification, except where the failure to be so qualified and in good standing would not have a material adverse effect on its obligations under the Basic Documents;

(iii) each of the direction by the Company to the Indenture Trustee to authenticate the Notes and the direction by the Company to the Owner Trustee to execute the Notes has been duly authorized by the Company and, when the Notes have been duly executed and delivered by the Owner Trustee and, when authenticated by the Indenture Trustee in accordance with the terms of the Indenture and delivered to and paid for by the Underwriters pursuant to this Agreement, will be duly and validly issued and outstanding and will be entitled to the benefits of the Indenture;

(iv) the direction by the Company to the Owner Trustee to authenticate and execute the Certificates has been duly authorized by the Company;

(v) each Basic Document to which the Company or AHFC is a party has been duly authorized, executed and delivered by the Company and AHFC, respectively;

(vi) no consent, approval, authorization or order of, or filing with any governmental agency or body or any court is required for the execution, delivery and performance by the Company of this Agreement and the Basic Documents to which it is a party, for the execution, delivery and performance by AHFC of the Basic Documents to which it is a party or for the consummation of the transactions contemplated by this Agreement or the Basic Documents, except for (A) such as have been obtained and made under the Act, (B) such as may be required under state securities laws and (C) such authorizations, approvals or consents specified in such opinion as are in full force and effect as of the Effective Date and the Closing Date;

(vii) the execution, delivery and performance of this Agreement and the Basic Documents by the Company and the execution, delivery and performance of the Basic Documents by AHFC will not conflict with or result in a breach of any of the terms or provisions of, or constitute a default under, or result in the creation or imposition of any lien, charge or encumbrance upon any of the property or assets of AHFC or the Company pursuant to the terms of the Certificate of Incorporation or the By-Laws of AHFC or the Company or, to the best of such counsel's knowledge and information, any statute, rule, regulation or order of any governmental agency or body, or any court having jurisdiction over AHFC or the Company or their respective properties, or any agreement or instrument known to such counsel after due investigation to which AHFC or the Company is a party or by which AHFC or the Company or any of their respective properties is bound;

(viii) such counsel has no reason to believe that the Registration Statement or any amendment thereto, as of its effective date or as of such Closing Date, contained any untrue statement of a material fact or omitted to state any material fact required to be stated therein or necessary to make the statements therein not misleading, or that the Prospectus or any amendment or supplement thereto, as of its issue date or as of such Closing Date, contained any untrue statement of a material fact or omitted to state any material fact required to be stated therein or necessary in order to make the statements therein, in the light of the circumstances under which they were made, not misleading; the Registration Statement and the Prospectus complies in all material respects with the requirements of the Act and the rules and regulations promulgated thereunder; and such counsel does not know of any legal or governmental proceedings required to be described in the Registration Statement or the Prospectus which are not described as required or of any contracts or documents of a character required to be described in the Registration Statement or the Prospectus or to be filed as exhibits to the Registration Statement which are not described and filed as required; it being understood that such counsel need express no opinion as to the financial statements or other financial, numerical, statistical and quantitative information contained in the Registration Statement or the Prospectus;

(ix) the statements in the Registration Statement under the heading "CERTAIN LEGAL ASPECTS OF THE RECEIVABLES", to the extent they constitute statements of matters of law or legal conclusions with respect thereto, are correct in all material respects;

(x) such counsel is familiar with AHFC's standard operating procedures relating to AHFC's acquisition of a perfected first priority security interest in the vehicles financed by AHFC pursuant to retail installment sale contracts in the ordinary course of AHFC's business; assuming that AHFC's standard procedures are followed with respect to the perfection of security interests in the Financed Vehicles (and such counsel has no reason to believe that AHFC has not or will not continue to follow its standard procedures in connection with the perfection of security interests in the Financed Vehicles), AHFC has acquired or will acquire a perfected first priority security interest in the Financed Vehicles;

(xi) assuming that the Receivables are in substantially one of the forms attached to such opinion, the Receivables are "chattel paper" as defined in the UCC as in effect in the States of New York and California; and

(xii) immediately prior to the sale of Receivables by AHFC to the Company pursuant to the Receivables Purchase Agreement, AHFC was the sole owner of all right, title and interest in, to and under the Receivables and the other property to be transferred by it to the Company. AHFC has full power and authority to sell and assign the property to be sold and assigned to the Company pursuant to the Receivables Purchase Agreement and has duly authorized such sale and assignment to the Company by all necessary corporate action.

(e) The Representative shall have received an opinion of Dewey Ballantine LLP, special counsel to the Company and AHFC, dated the Closing Date and satisfactory in form and substance to the Representative and counsel for the Underwriters, to the effect that:

(i) the Receivables Purchase Agreement either (A) transfers an ownership interest in the Receivables and the proceeds thereof (subject to Section 9-315 of the UCC as in effect in the State of California (the "California UCC")) from AHFC to the Company or (B) creates a valid security interest in AHFC's rights in the Receivables and the proceeds thereof (subject to Section 9-315 of the California UCC) as security for the obligations of AHFC thereunder;

(ii) the Sale and Servicing Agreement either (A) transfers an ownership interest in the Receivables and the proceeds thereof (subject to Section 9-315 of the California UCC) from the Company to the Trust or (B) creates a valid security interest in the Company's rights in the Receivables and the proceeds thereof (subject to Section 9-315 of the California UCC) as security for the obligations of the Company thereunder;

(iii) the Indenture creates a valid security interest in the Trust's rights in the Receivables and the proceeds thereof (subject to Section 9-315 of the California UCC) as security for the obligations of the Trust thereunder;

(iv) the financing statement on Form UCC-1 naming AHFC as debtor is in appropriate form for filing in the relevant filing office under the California UCC. Upon the filing of such financing Statement in the relevant filing office, the security interest in favor of the Company in the Receivables and proceeds thereof will be perfected, and no other security interest of any other creditor of AHFC will be equal or prior to such security interest;

(v) the financing statement on Form UCC-1 naming the Company as debtor is in appropriate form for filing in the relevant filing office under the California UCC. Upon the filing of such financing statement in the relevant filing office, the security interest in favor of the Owner Trustee in the Receivables and proceeds thereof will be perfected, and no other security interest of any other creditor of the Company will be equal or prior to such security interest;

(vi) the provisions of the Indenture are effective to create in favor of the Indenture Trustee, a valid security interest (as such term is defined in Section 1-201 of the California UCC) in the Receivables and proceeds thereof to secure payment of the Notes;

(vii) the Trust Agreement is not required to be qualified under the Trust Indenture Act of 1939, as amended (the "Trust Indenture Act");

(viii) the Indenture has been duly qualified under the Trust Indenture Act;

(ix) the Registration Statement was declared effective under the Act as of the date specified in such opinion, the Prospectus either was filed with the Commission pursuant to the subparagraph of Rule 424(b) specified in such opinion on the date specified therein or was included in the Registration Statement, and, to the best of the knowledge of such counsel, no stop order suspending the effectiveness of the Registration Statement or any part thereof has been issued and no proceedings for that purpose have been instituted or are pending or contemplated under the Act, and the Registration Statement and the Prospectus, and each amendment or supplement thereof, as of their respective effective or issue dates, complies as to form in all material respects with the requirements of the Act and the Rules and Regulations;

(x) each of the Receivables Purchase Agreement, the Control Agreement, the Sale and Servicing Agreement and the Administration Agreement constitutes the legal, valid and binding agreement of the Company and AHFC, in each case as to those documents to which it is a party, enforceable against the Company and AHFC in accordance with their terms (subject to applicable bankruptcy, insolvency, fraudulent transfer, reorganization, moratorium and other similar laws affecting creditors' rights generally from time to time in effect, and subject, as to enforceability, to general principles of equity, regardless of whether such enforceability is considered in a proceeding in equity or at law) except, as applicable, that such counsel need not express an opinion with respect to indemnification or contribution provisions which may be deemed to be in violation of the public policy underlying any law or regulation;

(xi) assuming due authorization, execution and delivery by the Indenture Trustee and the Owner Trustee, the Indenture constitutes the legal, valid and binding agreement of the Trust, enforceable against the Trust in accordance with its terms (subject to applicable bankruptcy, insolvency, fraudulent transfer, reorganization, moratorium and other similar laws affecting creditors' rights generally from time to time in effect, and subject, as to enforceability, to general principles of equity, regardless of whether such enforceability is considered in a proceeding in equity or at law) except, as applicable, that such counsel need not express an opinion with respect to indemnification or contribution provisions which may be deemed to be in violation of the public policy underlying any law or regulation;

(xii) neither the Trust nor the Company is and, after giving effect to the issuance and sale of the Notes and the Certificates and the application of the proceeds thereof, as described in the Prospectus, neither the Trust nor the Company will be, an "investment company" as defined in the Investment Company Act; and

(xiii) this Agreement has been duly authorized, executed and delivered by the Company and AHFC.

(f) The Representative shall have received an opinion of Dewey Ballantine LLP, tax counsel for the Company, dated the Closing Date and satisfactory in form and substance to the Representative and counsel for the Underwriters, to the effect that for federal income tax purposes (i) the Notes will be characterized as indebtedness of the Trust that is secured by the Receivables, (ii) the Trust will not be classified as an association (or publicly traded partnership) taxable as a corporation and (iii) the statements set forth in the Prospectus under the headings "SUMMARY — ERISA Considerations", "ERISA

CONSIDERATIONS", "SUMMARY — Tax Status", "MATERIAL INCOME TAX CONSEQUENCES" and Annex A to the Prospectus, "Global Clearance, Settlement and Tax Documentation Procedures-Certain U.S. Federal Income Tax Documentation Requirements", to the extent such statements constitute matters of law or legal conclusions with respect thereto, are correct in all material respects.

(g) The Representative shall have received an opinion of Dewey Ballantine LLP, tax counsel for the Company, dated the Closing Date and satisfactory in form and substance to the Representative and counsel for the Underwriters, to the effect that for California state franchise and California state income tax purposes (i) the Notes will be characterized as debt and (ii) the Trust will not be classified as an association (or publicly traded partnership) taxable as a corporation.

(h) The Representative shall have received from McKee Nelson LLP, counsel for the Underwriters, such opinion or opinions, dated the Closing Date, with respect to the validity of the Notes, the Registration Statement, the Prospectus and other related matters as the Representative may require, and the Company shall have furnished to such counsel such documents as it may request for the purpose of enabling it to pass upon such matters.

(i) The Representative shall have received a certificate, dated the Closing Date, of the Chairman of the Board, the President or any Vice-President and a principal financial or accounting officer of each of the Company and AHFC in which such officers, to the best of their knowledge after reasonable investigation, shall state that: the representations and warranties of the Company and AHFC in this Agreement are true and correct in all material respects; the Company or AHFC, as applicable, has complied with all agreements and satisfied all conditions on its part to be performed or satisfied hereunder at or prior to the Closing Date in all material respects; the representations and warranties of the Company or AHFC, as applicable, in the Basic Documents are true and correct as of the dates specified in such agreements in all material respects; the Company or AHFC, as applicable, has complied with all agreements and satisfied all conditions on its part to be performed or satisfied under such agreements at or prior to the Closing Date; no stop order suspending the effectiveness of the Registration Statement has been issued and no proceedings for that purpose have been instituted or are contemplated by the Commission; and, subsequent to the date of the Prospectus, there has been no material adverse change, nor any development or event involving a prospective material adverse change, in the condition (financial or otherwise), business, properties or results of operations of the Company or AHFC or their respective businesses except as set forth in or contemplated by the Prospectus or as described in such certificate.

(j) The Representative shall have received an opinion of Thacher Proffitt & Wood, counsel to the Indenture Trustee, dated the Closing Date and satisfactory in form and substance to the Representative and counsel for the Underwriters, substantially to the effect that:

(i) the Indenture Trustee is a banking corporation validly existing under the laws of the State of New York;

(ii) the Indenture Trustee has the requisite power and authority to execute and deliver the Indenture, the Sale and Servicing Agreement, the Control Agreement and the Administration Agreement and perform its obligations under each of the Agreements, and has taken all necessary action to authorize the execution and delivery of the Indenture, the Sale and Servicing Agreement, the Control Agreement and the Administration Agreement and performance by it of each of the Agreements;

(iii) no approval, authorization or other action by or filing with any governmental authority of the United States of America, or of the State of New York, having jurisdiction over the banking or trust powers of the Indenture Trustee is required in connection with the execution and delivery by the Indenture Trustee of the Indenture, the Sale and Servicing Agreement, the Control Agreement and the Administration Agreement;

(iv) the execution and delivery of the Indenture, the Sale and Servicing Agreement, the Control Agreement and the Administration Agreement and the performance by the Indenture Trustee of the respective terms of the Agreements, do not conflict with or result in a violation of the Articles of Incorporation or By-Laws of the Indenture Trustee or the applicable federal laws of the United States of America or of the State of New York having jurisdiction over the banking or trust powers of the Indenture Trustee;

(v) each of the Indenture, the Sale and Servicing Agreement, the Control Agreement and the Administration Agreement has been duly executed and delivered by the Indenture Trustee and each of the Agreements constitutes a legal, valid and binding obligation of the Indenture Trustee, enforceable against the Indenture Trustee in accordance with its respective terms, except that certain of such obligations may be enforceable solely against the Trust Estate and except that such enforcement may be limited by bankruptcy, insolvency, reorganization, moratorium, liquidation, or other similar laws affecting the enforcement of creditors' rights generally, and by general principles of equity, including, without limitation, concepts of materiality, reasonableness, good faith and fair dealing (regardless of whether such enforceability is considered in a proceeding in equity or at law);

(vi) the Notes delivered on the date hereof have been duly authenticated by the Indenture Trustee in accordance with the terms of the Indenture.

(k) The Representative shall have received an opinion of Emmet, Marvin & Martin, LLP, counsel to the Owner Trustee, dated the Closing Date and satisfactory in form and substance to the Representative and counsel for the Underwriters, to the effect that:

(i) the Owner Trustee is a banking corporation validly existing under the laws of the State of New York;

(ii) the Owner Trustee has the power and authority to execute, deliver and perform its obligations under the Trust Agreement;

(iii) the Trust Agreement has been duly authorized, executed and delivered by the Owner Trustee and constitutes the legal, valid and binding obligation of the Owner Trustee, enforceable against the Owner Trustee in accordance with its terms (subject to applicable bankruptcy, insolvency, fraudulent transfer, reorganization, moratorium and other similar laws affecting creditors' rights generally from time to time in effect, and subject, as to enforceability, to general principles of equity, regardless of whether such enforceability is considered in a proceeding in equity or at law);

(iv) the execution and delivery by the Owner Trustee of the Trust Agreement and the performance by the Owner Trustee of its obligations thereunder do not conflict with, result in a breach or violation of, or constitute a default under the Articles of Association or By-laws of the Owner Trustee or of any law, governmental rule or regulation of the State of Delaware or of the United States of America governing the banking or trust powers of the Owner Trustee; and

(v) the execution, delivery and performance by the Owner Trustee of the Trust Agreement does not require any consent, approval or authorization of, or any registration or filing with, any Delaware or United States federal governmental authority having jurisdiction over the banking or trust powers of the Owner Trustee, other than those consents, approvals or authorizations as have been obtained and the filing of the Certificate of Trust with the Secretary of State of the State of Delaware, which have been duly filed.

(l) The Representative shall have received an opinion of Richards, Layton & Finger, P.A., counsel to the Delaware Trustee, dated the Closing Date and satisfactory in form and substance to the Representative and counsel for the Underwriters, to the effect that:

(i) the Delaware Trustee has been duly formed and is validly existing as a national banking association under the federal laws of the United States of America;

(ii) the Delaware Trustee has the power and authority to execute, deliver and perform its obligations under the Trust Agreement;

(iii) the Trust Agreement has been duly authorized, executed and delivered by the Delaware Trustee and constitutes the legal, valid and binding obligation of the Delaware Trustee, enforceable against the Delaware Trustee in accordance with its terms (subject to applicable bankruptcy, insolvency, fraudulent transfer, reorganization, moratorium and other similar laws affecting creditors' rights generally from time to time in effect, and subject, as to enforceability, to general principles of equity, regardless of whether such enforceability is considered in a proceeding in equity or at law);

(iv) neither the execution, delivery and performance by the Delaware Trustee of the Trust Agreement, nor the consummation of any of the transactions by the Delaware Trustee contemplated thereby, is in violation of the articles of organization or bylaws of the Delaware Trustee or of any law, governmental rule or regulation of the State of Delaware or of the United States of America governing the trust powers of the Delaware Trustee; and

(v) neither the execution, delivery and performance by the Delaware Trustee of the Trust Agreement, nor the consummation of any of the transactions by the Delaware Trustee contemplated thereby, requires the consent or approval of, the withholding of objection on the part of, the giving of notice to, the filing, registration or qualification with, or the taking of any other action in respect of, any governmental authority or agency under the laws of the State of Delaware or the federal laws of the United States of America governing the trust powers of the Delaware Trustee.

(m) The Representative shall have received one or more opinions of Richards, Layton & Finger, P.A., special Delaware counsel to the Trust, dated the Closing Date and satisfactory in form and substance to the Representative and counsel for the Underwriters, to the effect that:

(i) the Trust has been duly formed and is validly existing and in good standing as a statutory trust under the Delaware Statutory Trust Statute, 12 Del. C.(ss.)3801, et seq. (the "Delaware Act");

(ii) the Trust has the power and authority under the Delaware Act and the Trust Agreement to execute and deliver the Basic Documents to which the Trust is a party, to issue the Notes and the Certificates, to grant the Collateral (as such term is defined in the Indenture) to the Indenture Trustee as security for the Notes and to perform its obligations under each of said documents;

(iii) the Trust has duly authorized and executed the Certificates and the Notes, the Owner Trustee has duly authenticated the Certificates on behalf of the Trust, and when the Certificates are delivered upon the order of the Depositor in accordance with the Trust Agreement, the Certificates will be validly issued and entitled to the benefits of the Trust Agreement;

(iv) to the extent that Article 9 of the Uniform Commercial Code as in effect in the State of Delaware (the "Delaware UCC") is applicable (without regard to conflicts of laws principles), and assuming that the security interest created by the Indenture in the Collateral has been duly created and has attached, upon the filing of the financing statements set forth in such opinion (the "Delaware Financing Statements") with the Office of the Secretary of State (Uniform Commercial Code Division) (the "Division"), the Indenture Trustee will have a perfected security interest in the Trust's rights in that portion of the Collateral described in the Delaware Financing Statements that may be perfected by the filing of a UCC financing statement with the Division (the "Filing Collateral") and the proceeds thereof (as defined in Section 9-102(a)(64) of the Delaware UCC);

(v) the search report referenced in such opinion will set forth the proper filing office and the proper debtor necessary to identify those persons who under the Delaware UCC have on file financing statements against the Trust covering the Filing Collateral as of the Closing Date. Such search report identifies no secured party who has filed with the Division a financing statement naming the Trust as debtor, and describing the Filing Collateral prior to the Closing Date;

(vi) no refiling or other action is necessary under the Delaware UCC in order to maintain the perfection of such security interest except for the filing of continuation statements at five year intervals;

(vii) assuming for federal income tax purposes that the Trust will not be classified as an association or a publicly traded partnership taxable as a corporation, and that the Notes will be characterized as indebtedness for federal income tax purposes, then the Trust will not be subject to any franchise or income tax under the laws of the State of Delaware, and the Notes will also be characterized as indebtedness for Delaware tax purposes;

(viii) the Trust Agreement is the legal, valid and binding obligation of the parties thereto, enforceable against such parties, in accordance with its terms (subject to such exclusions and exceptions as are customary in opinions of this type);

(ix) under the Delaware Act, the Trust is a separate legal entity and, assuming that the Sale and Servicing Agreement conveys good title to the Trust property to the Trust as a true sale and not as a security arrangement, the Trust rather than the Certificateholders will hold whatever title to the Trust property as may be conveyed to it from time to time pursuant to the Sale and Servicing Agreement, except to the extent that the Trust has taken action to dispose of or otherwise transfer or encumber any part of the Trust property;

(x) under 3805(b) of the Delaware Act, no creditor of any Certificateholder (as defined in the Trust Agreement) shall have any right to obtain possession of, otherwise exercise legal or equitable remedies with respect to, the property of the Trust except in accordance with the terms of the Trust Agreement;

(xi) under 3805(c) of the Delaware Act, except to the extent otherwise provided in the Trust Agreement, a Certificateholder (including the Company in its capacity as Depositor under the Trust Agreement) has no interest in specific Receivables;

(xii) under 3808(a) and (b) of the Delaware Act, the Trust may not be terminated or revoked by any Certificateholder, and the dissolution, termination or bankruptcy of any Certificateholder shall not result in the termination or dissolution of the Trust, except to the extent otherwise provided in the Trust Agreement.

(n) The Representative shall have received an opinion of Dewey Ballantine LLP, counsel to the Company, dated the Closing Date and satisfactory in form and substance to the Representative and counsel for the Underwriters, (i) with respect to the characterization of the transfer of the Receivables by AHFC to the Company and (ii) to the effect that should AHFC become the debtor in a case under Title 11 of the United States Code (the "Bankruptcy Code") and the ___________ Company would not otherwise properly be a debtor in a case under the Bankruptcy Code, and if the matter were properly briefed and presented to a court exercising bankruptcy jurisdiction, the court, exercising reasonable judgment after full consideration of all relevant factors, should not order, over the objection of the Certificate holders or the Noteholders, the substantive consolidation of the assets and liabilities of the Company with those of AHFC and such opinion shall be in substantially the form previously discussed with the Representative and counsel for the Underwriters and in any event satisfactory in form and in substance to the Representative and counsel for the Underwriters.

(o) The Representative shall have received evidence satisfactory to it and its counsel that, on or before the Closing Date, UCC-1 financing statements have been or are being filed in the office of the Secretary of State of the state of (i) California reflecting the transfer of the interest of AHFC in the Receivables and the proceeds thereof to the Company and the transfer of the interest of the Company in the Receivables and the proceeds thereof to the Trust and (ii) Delaware reflecting the grant of the security interest by the Trust in the Receivables and the proceeds thereof to the Indenture Trustee.

(p) The Representative shall have received an opinion of Dewey Ballantine LLP, special counsel to the Company, dated the Closing Date and satisfactory in form and substance to the Representative and the counsel for the Underwriters to the effect that (i) the provisions of the Indenture are effective to create a valid security interest in favor of the Indenture Trustee, to secure payment of the Notes, in all "securities entitlements" (as defined in Section 8-102(a)(17) of the New York UCC) with respect to "financial assets" (as defined in Section 8-102(a)(9) of the New York UCC) now or hereafter credited to the Reserve Account (such securities entitlements, the "Securities Entitlements"), (ii) the provisions of the control agreement for purposes of Article 8 of the New York UCC are effective to perfect the security interest of the Indenture Trustee in the Securities Entitlements and (iii) no security interest of any other creditor of the Trust will be prior to the security interest of the Indenture Trustee in such Securities Entitlements.

(q) Each Class of the Notes shall have been rated in the highest rating category by each of Moody's, Fitch and Standard & Poor's.

(r) On or prior to the Closing Date, the Certificates shall have been issued to the Company.

(s) The Representative shall have received from Dewey Ballantine LLP and each other counsel for the Company, a letter dated the Closing Date to the effect that the Underwriters may rely upon each opinion rendered by such counsel to either Standard & Poor's, Moody's or Fitch in connection with the rating of any Class of the Notes, as if each such opinion were addressed to the Underwriters.

(t) The Representative shall have received an opinion of Scott Shea, Esq., counsel to the Company and AHFC, dated the Closing Date, to the effect that, to the best knowledge of such counsel after due inquiry, there are no actions, proceedings or investigations to which the Company or AHFC is a party or that are threatened before any court, administrative agency or other tribunal having jurisdiction over AHFC or the Company, (i) that are required to be disclosed in the Registration Statement, (ii) asserting the invalidity of this Agreement, any Basic Document, the Notes or the Certificates, (iii) seeking to prevent the issuance of the Notes or the Certificates or the consummation of any of the transactions contemplated by this Agreement or the Basic Documents, (iv) which might materially and adversely affect the performance by the Company or AHFC of its obligations under, or the validity or enforceability of, this Agreement, any Basic Document, the Notes or the Certificates or (v) seeking adversely to affect the federal income tax attributes of the Notes as described in the Prospectus under the heading "MATERIAL INCOME TAX CONSEQUENCES".

(u) As of the Closing Date, the representations and warranties of the Company and AHFC contained in the Basic Documents will be true and correct.

The Company will furnish the Representative with such conformed copies of such opinions, certificates, letters and documents as the Representative reasonably requests.

The Representative may, in its sole discretion, waive on behalf of the Underwriters compliance with any conditions to the obligations of the Underwriters hereunder.

7. Indemnification and Contribution.

(a) The Company and AHFC will, jointly and severally, indemnify and hold harmless each Underwriter against any losses, claims, damages or liabilities, joint or several, to which such underwriter may become subject, under the Act, or otherwise, insofar as such losses, claims, damages or liabilities (or actions in respect thereof) arise out of or are based upon any untrue statement or alleged untrue statement of any material fact contained or incorporated in the Registration Statement, the Term Sheet, the Prospectus, or any amendment or supplement thereto or arise out of or are based upon the omission or alleged omission to state therein a material fact required to be stated therein or necessary to make the statements therein not misleading and will reimburse each Underwriter for any legal or other expenses reasonably incurred by such Underwriter in connection with investigating or defending any such loss, claim, damage, liability or action as such expenses are incurred; provided, however, that neither the Company nor AHFC will be liable in any such case to the extent that any such loss, claim, damage or liability arises out of or is based upon an untrue statement or alleged untrue statement in or omission or alleged omission from any of such documents in reliance upon and in conformity with written information furnished to the Company or AHFC by any Underwriter through the Representative specifically for use therein, it being understood and agreed that the only such information furnished by any Underwriter consists of the information described as such in subsection (b) below; and provided, further that with respect to any untrue statement or omission or alleged untrue statement or omission made in the Term Sheet, the indemnity agreement contained in this subsection (a) shall not inure to the benefit of any Underwriter from whom the person asserting any such losses, claims, damages or liabilities purchased the Notes concerned, to the extent that the untrue statement or omission or alleged untrue statement or omission was eliminated or remedied in the Prospectus, which Prospectus was required to be delivered by such Underwriter under the Act to such person and was not so delivered if the Company or AHFC had previously furnished copies thereof to such Underwriter.

(b) Each Underwriter will severally and not jointly indemnify and hold harmless the Company and AHFC against any losses, claims, damages or liabilities to which the Company or AHFC may become subject, under the Act or otherwise, insofar as such losses, claims, damages or liabilities (or actions in respect thereof) arise out of or are based upon any untrue statement or alleged untrue statement of any material fact contained or incorporated in the Registration Statement, the Prospectus, or any amendment or supplement thereto, or arise out of or are based upon the omission or the alleged omission to state therein a material fact required to be stated therein or necessary to make the statements therein not misleading, in each case to the extent, but only to the extent, that such untrue statement or alleged untrue statement or omission or alleged omission was made in reliance upon and in conformity with written information furnished to the Company by such Underwriter through the Representative specifically for use therein, and will reimburse any legal or other expenses reasonably incurred by the Company or AHFC in connection with investigating or defending any such loss, claim, damage, liability or action as such expenses are incurred, it being understood and agreed that the only such information furnished by any Underwriter consists of the following information in the Prospectus furnished on behalf of each Underwriter: the concession and reallowance figures appearing in the third paragraph under the caption "Underwriting" and the information contained in the third paragraph, the second sentence of the fifth paragraph, and the seventh paragraph under the caption "Underwriting".

(c) Promptly after receipt by an indemnified party under this Section of notice of the commencement of any action, such indemnified party will, if a claim in respect thereof is to be made against the indemnifying party under subsection (a) or (b) above, notify the indemnifying party of the commencement thereof, but the omission so to notify the indemnifying party will not relieve it from any liability which it may have to any indemnified party otherwise than under subsection (a) or (b) above. In case any such action is brought against any indemnified party and it notifies the indemnifying party of the commencement thereof, the indemnifying party will be entitled to participate therein and, to the extent that it may wish, jointly with any other indemnifying party similarly notified, to assume the defense thereof, with counsel satisfactory to such indemnified party (who shall not, except with the consent of the indemnified party, be counsel to the indemnifying party), and after notice from the indemnifying party to such indemnified party of its election so to assume the defense thereof and after acceptance by the indemnified party of such counsel, the indemnifying party will not be liable to such indemnified party under this Section for any legal or other expenses subsequently incurred by such indemnified party in connection with the defense thereof other than reasonable costs of investigation. No indemnifying party shall, without the prior written consent of the indemnified party, effect any settlement of any pending or threatened action in respect of which any indemnified party is or could have been a party if indemnity could have been sought hereunder by such indemnified party unless such settlement includes an unconditional release of such indemnified party from all liability on any claims that are the subject matter of such action.

(d) If the indemnification provided for in this Section is unavailable or insufficient to hold harmless an indemnified party under subsection (a) or (b) above, then each indemnifying party shall contribute to the amount paid or payable by such indemnified party as a result of the losses, claims, damages or liabilities referred to in subsection (a) or (b) above (i) in such proportion as is appropriate to reflect the relative benefits received by the Company on the one hand and the Underwriters on the other from the offering of the Notes or (ii) if the allocation provided by clause (i) above is not permitted by applicable law, in such proportion as is appropriate to reflect not only the relative benefits referred to in clause (i) above but also the relative fault of the Company on the one hand and the Underwriters on the other in connection with the statements or omissions which resulted in such losses, claims, damages or liabilities as well as any other relevant equitable considerations. The relative benefits received by the Company on the one hand and the Underwriters on the other shall be deemed to be in the same proportion as the total net proceeds from the offering (before deducting expenses) received by the Company bear to the total underwriting discounts and commissions received by the Underwriters. The relative fault shall be determined by reference to, among other things, whether the untrue or alleged untrue statement of a material fact or the omission or alleged omission to state a material fact relates to information supplied by the Company or the Underwriters and the parties' relative intent, knowledge, access to information and opportunity to correct or prevent such untrue statement or omission. The amount paid by an indemnified party as a result of the losses, claims, damages or liabilities referred to in the first sentence of this subsection (d) shall be deemed to include any legal or other expenses reasonably incurred by such indemnified party in connection with investigating or defending any action or claim which is the subject of this subsection (d). Notwithstanding the provisions of this subsection (d), no Underwriter shall be required to contribute any amount in excess of the amount by which the total price at which the Notes underwritten by it and distributed to the public were offered to the public exceeds the amount of any damages which such Underwriter has otherwise been required to pay by reason of such untrue or alleged untrue statement or omission or alleged omission. No person guilty of fraudulent misrepresentation (within the meaning of Section 11(f) of the Act) shall be entitled to contribution from any person who was not guilty of such fraudulent misrepresentation. The Underwriters' obligations in this subsection (d) to contribute are several in proportion to their respective underwriting obligations and not joint.

(e) The obligations of the Company or AHFC under this Section shall be in addition to any liability which the Company or AHFC may otherwise have and shall extend, upon the same terms and conditions, to each person, if any, who controls any Underwriter within the meaning of the Act; and the obligations of the Underwriters under this Section shall be in addition to any liability which the respective Underwriters may otherwise have and shall extend, upon the same terms and conditions, to each director of the Company or AHFC, to each officer of the Company and AHFC who has signed the Registration Statement and to each person, if any, who controls the Company or AHFC within the meaning of the Act.

8. Default of Underwriters. If any Underwriter or Underwriters default in their obligations to purchase Notes hereunder on the Closing Date and the aggregate principal amount of Notes that such defaulting Underwriter or Underwriters agreed but failed to purchase does not exceed 10% of the total principal amount of Notes that the Underwriters are obligated to purchase on such Closing Date, the Representative may make arrangements satisfactory to the Company for the purchase of such Notes by other persons, including any of the Underwriters, but if no such arrangements are made by such Closing Date, the nondefaulting Underwriters shall be obligated severally, in proportion to their respective commitments hereunder, to purchase the Notes that such defaulting Underwriters agreed but failed to purchase on such Closing Date. If any Underwriter or Underwriters so default and the aggregate principal amount of Notes with respect to which such default or defaults occur exceeds 10% of the total principal mount of Notes that the Underwriters are obligated to purchase on such Closing Date and arrangements satisfactory to the Representative and the Company for the purchase of such Notes by other persons are not made within 36 hours after such default, this Agreement will terminate without liability on the part of any non-defaulting Underwriter or the Company, except as provided in Section 9. As used in this Agreement, the term "Underwriter" includes any person substituted for an Underwriter under this Section. Nothing herein will relieve a defaulting Underwriter from liability for its default.

9. Survival of Certain Representations and Obligations. The respective indemnities, agreements, representations, warranties and other statements of the Company or AHFC or their respective officers and of the several Underwriters set forth in or made pursuant to this Agreement will remain in full force and effect, regardless of any investigation, or statement as to the results thereof, made by or on behalf of any Underwriter or the Company or AHFC or any of their respective representatives, officers or directors or any controlling person, and will survive delivery of and payment for the Notes. If this Agreement is terminated pursuant to Section 8 or if for any reason the purchase of the Notes by the Underwriters is not consummated, the Company shall remain responsible for the expenses to be paid or reimbursed by it pursuant to Section 5 and the respective obligations of the Company, AHFC and the Underwriters pursuant to Section 7 shall remain in effect. If the purchase of the Notes by the Underwriters is not consummated for any reason other than solely because of the termination of this Agreement pursuant to Section 8 or the occurrence of any event specified in clause (ii), (iii) or (iv) of Section 6(c), the Company and AHFC, jointly and severally, will reimburse the Underwriters for all out — of pocket expenses (including fees and disbursements of counsel) reasonably incurred by them in connection with the offering of the Notes.

10. Notices. All communications hereunder will be in writing and, if sent to the Underwriters, will be mailed, delivered or sent by facsimile and confirmed to the Representative at 31 West 52nd Street, 17th Floor, New York, New York 10019, Attention: Global Structured Finance, (facsimile: (212) 469-7210), or, if sent to the Company, will be mailed, delivered or sent by facsimile transmission and confirmed to it at 700 Van Ness Avenue, Torrance, California 90501, Attention: John I. Weisickle, (facsimile: (310) 787-3910), and if to AHFC, will be mailed, delivered or sent by facsimile transmission and confirmed to it at 700 Van Ness Avenue, Torrance, California 90501, Attention: John I. Weisickle, (facsimile: (310) 787-3910); provided that any notice to an Underwriter pursuant to Section 7 will be mailed, delivered or telecopied and confirmed to such Underwriter.

11. No Bankruptcy Petition. Each Underwriter agrees that, prior to the date which is one year and one day after the payment in full of all securities issued by the Company or by a trust for which the Company was the depositor which securities were rated by any nationally recognized statistical rating organization, it will not institute against, or join any other person in instituting against, the Company any bankruptcy, reorganization, arrangement, insolvency or liquidation proceedings or other proceedings under any Federal or state bankruptcy or similar law.

12. Successors. This Agreement will inure to the benefit of and be binding upon the parties hereto and their respective successors and the officers and directors and controlling persons referred to in Section 9, and no other person will have any right or obligation hereunder.

13. Representation of Underwriters. The Representative will act for the several Underwriters in connection with this financing, and any action under this

Agreement taken by the Representative will be binding upon all the Underwriters.

14. Counterparts. This Agreement may be executed in any number of counterparts, each of which shall be deemed to be an original but all such counterparts shall together constitute one and the same Agreement.

15. Applicable Law; Submission to Jurisdiction.

(a) THIS AGREEMENT SHALL BE GOVERNED BY, AND CONSTRUED IN ACCORDANCE WITH, THE LAWS OF THE STATE OF NEW YORK.

(b) Each of the Company and AHFC hereby submits to the nonexclusive jurisdiction of the Federal and state courts in the Borough of Manhattan in The City of New York in any suit or proceeding arising out of or relating to this Agreement or the transactions contemplated hereby.

If the foregoing is in accordance with the Representative's understanding of our agreement, kindly sign and return to each of the Company and AHFC one of the counterparts hereof, hereupon it will become a binding agreement between the Company, AHFC and the several Underwriters in accordance with its terms.

Very truly yours,

AMERICAN HONDA RECEIVABLES CORP.

By: /s/ Y. Takahashi

____

Name: Y. Takahashi

Title: President

AMERICAN HONDA FINANCE CORPORATION

By: /s/ Y. Takahashi

____

Name: Y. Takahashi

Title: President

The foregoing Underwriting Agreement is hereby confirmed and accepted as of the date first above written:

Deutsche Bank securities inc., acting on behalf of itself and as the Representative of the several Underwriters

By: /s/ Richard V. Lawrence

Name: Richard V. Lawrence

Title: Director

By: /s/ Jay E. Steiner

Name: Jay E. Steiner

Title: Vice President

SCHEDULE A

UNDERWRITERS	AMOUNT OF CLASS A-1 NOTES	AMOUNT OF CLASS A-2 NOTES	AMOUNT OF CLASS A-3 NOTES	AMOUNT OF CLASS A-4 NOTES
Banc One Capital Markets, Inc.	$131,600,000	$161,700,000	$135,100,000	$111,250,000
Deutsche Bank Securities Inc.	131,600,000	161,700,000	135,100,000	111,250,000
Banc of America Securities LLC	28,200,000	34,650,000	28,950,000	23,800,000
Barclays Capital Inc.	28,200,000	34,650,000	28,950,000	23,800,000
Credit Suisse First Boston LLC	28,200,000	34,650,000	28,950,000	23,800,000
Salomon Smith Barney Inc.	28,200,000	34,650,000	28,950,000	23,800,000
Total	$376,000,000	$462,000,000	$386,000,000	$317,700,000

Appendix 8

Appendix 8

EXECUTION COPY

HONDA AUTO RECEIVABLES 2003-1 OWNER TRUST,
as Issuer,

and

JPMORGAN CHASE BANK,
as Indenture Trustee

INDENTURE

Dated as of February 1, 2003

CROSS REFERENCE TABLE*

TIA Section		Indenture Section
310	(a)(1)	6.11
	(a)(2)	6.11
	(a)(3)	6.10; 6.11
	(a)(4)	N.A.**
	(a)(5)	6.11
	(b)	6.08; 6.11
	(c)	N.A.
311	(a)	6.12
	(b)	6.12
	(c)	N.A.
312	(a)	7.01
	(b)	7.02
	(c)	7.02

* This Cross Reference Table shall not, for any purpose, be deemed to be part of this Indenture. [Eds. — The table provides cross-references between the Indenture and applicable sections of the Trust Indenture Act, 15 U.S.C. § 77aaa *et seq.*]

** N.A. means Not Applicable.

313	(a)	7.04
	(b)(1)	7.04
	(b)(2)	7.04
	(c)	7.04; 11.05
	(d)	7.04
314	(a)	7.03
	(b)	11.15
	(c)(1)	11.01
	(c)(2)	11.01
	(c)(3)	11.01
	(d)	11.01
	(e)	11.01
	(f)	11.01
315	(a)	6.01
	(b)	6.05; 11.01
	(c)	6.01
	(d)	6.01
	(e)	5.13
316	(a)	1.01
	(a)(1)(A)	5.11
	(a)(1)(B)	5.12
	(a)(2)	N.A.
	(b)	5.07
	(c)	N.A.
317	(a)(1)	5.03
	(a)(2)	5.03
	(b)	3.03
318	(a)	11.07

TABLE OF CONTENTS

ARTICLE ONE
DEFINITIONS AND INCORPORATION BY REFERENCE

*[Eds. — Page numbers added.]

ARTICLE FOUR

SATISFACTION AND DISCHARGE

ARTICLE FIVE

REMEDIES

ARTICLE SIX

THE INDENTURE TRUSTEE

ARTICLE SEVEN

NOTEHOLDERS' LISTS AND REPORTS

ARTICLE EIGHT

ACCOUNTS, DISBURSEMENTS AND RELEASES

ARTICLE NINE

SUPPLEMENTAL INDENTURES

ARTICLE TEN

REDEMPTION OF NOTES

ARTICLE ELEVEN

MISCELLANEOUS

SCHEDULES

EXHIBITS

This Indenture, dated as of February 1, 2003, is between Honda Auto Receivables 2003-1 Owner Trust, a Delaware statutory trust (the "Issuer"), and JPMorgan Chase Bank, as indenture trustee (the "Indenture Trustee").

Each party agrees as follows for the benefit of the other party and for the equal and ratable benefit of the holders of the Issuer's Class A-1 1.30% Asset Backed Notes (the "Class A-1 Notes"), Class A-2 1.46% Asset Backed Notes (the "Class A-2 Notes"), Class A-3 1.92% Asset Backed Notes (the "Class A-3 Notes") and Class A-4 2.48% Asset Backed Notes (the "Class A-4 Notes" and, together with the Class A-1 Notes, the Class A-2 Notes and the Class A-3 Notes, the "Notes"):

GRANTING CLAUSE

The Issuer hereby Grants to the Indenture Trustee at the Closing Date, on behalf of and for the benefit of the Holders of the Notes, without recourse, all of the Issuer's right, title and interest in, to and under (i) the Receivables and all monies due thereon and received thereon on and after February 1, 2003; (ii) the security interests in the Financed Vehicles; (iii) any proceeds of any physical damage insurance policies covering the Financed Vehicles and in any proceeds of any credit life or credit disability insurance policies relating to the Receivables or the Obligors; (iv) any proceeds of Dealer Recourse; (v) the right to realize upon any property (including the right to receive future Liquidation Proceeds) that shall have secured a Receivable and have been repossessed by or on behalf of the Issuer; (vi) all funds, and all investment property, from time to time carried in or credited to the Accounts, including the Reserve Fund Initial Deposit and the Yield Supplement Account Deposit and in all investment income and proceeds thereof; (vii) the rights of the Seller under the Receivables Purchase Agreement and the rights of the Issuer under the Sale and Servicing Agreement; (viii) any Servicer Letter of Credit; and (ix) all payments on or under and all proceeds of every kind and nature whatsoever in respect of any or all of the foregoing, including all proceeds of the conversion thereof, voluntary or involuntary, into cash or other liquid property, all cash proceeds, accounts, accounts receivable, notes, drafts, acceptances, chattel paper, checks, deposit accounts, insurance proceeds, condemnation awards, rights to payment of any and every kind and other forms of obligations and receivables, instruments and other property which at any time constitute all or part of or are included in the proceeds of any of the foregoing as each such term is defined in Section 1.01 (collectively, the "Collateral").

The foregoing Grant is made in trust to secure the payment of principal of and interest on, and any other amounts owing in respect of, the Notes, equally and ratably without prejudice, priority or distinction, and to secure compliance with the provisions of this Indenture, all as provided in this Indenture.

The Indenture Trustee, as Indenture Trustee on behalf of the Holders of the Notes, acknowledges such Grant, accepts the trusts under this Indenture in accordance with the provisions of this Indenture and agrees to perform its duties as required in this Indenture to the best of its ability to the end that the interests of the Holders of the Notes may be adequately and effectively protected.

ARTICLE ONE

DEFINITIONS AND INCORPORATION BY REFERENCE

Section 1.01. Definitions.

(a) Except as otherwise specified herein or as the context may otherwise require, the following terms have the respective meanings set forth below for all purposes of this Indenture.

"Act" shall have the meaning specified in Section 11.03(a).

"Administration Agreement" means the Administration Agreement, dated as of February 1, 2003, among the Administrator, the Issuer, the Depositor and the Indenture Trustee.

"Administrator" means AHFC or any successor Administrator under the Administration Agreement.

"AHFC" means American Honda Finance Corporation, and its successors.

"Authorized Officer" means, with respect to the Issuer, any officer of the Owner Trustee who is authorized to act for the Owner Trustee in matters relating to the Issuer and who is identified on the list of Authorized Officers delivered by the Owner Trustee to the Indenture Trustee on the Closing Date (as such list may be modified or supplemented from time to time thereafter) and, so long as the Administration Agreement is in effect, any Vice President or more senior officer of the Administrator who is authorized to act for the Administrator in matters relating to the Issuer and to be acted upon by the Administrator pursuant to the Administration Agreement and who is identified on the list of Authorized Officers delivered by the Administrator to the Indenture Trustee on the Closing Date (as such list may be modified or supplemented from time to time thereafter).

"Book-Entry Notes" means a beneficial interest in the Notes, ownership and transfers of which shall be made through book entries by a Clearing Agency as described in Section 2.09.

"Business Day" means any day other than a Saturday, a Sunday or a day on which banking institutions or trust companies in Los Angeles, California, Wilmington, Delaware or New York, New York are authorized or obligated by law, regulation, executive order or governmental decree to remain closed.

"Benefit Plan" means (a) an employee benefit plan (as defined in Section 3(3) of ERISA) that is subject to Title I of ERISA, (b) a plan (as defined in Section 4975(e)(1) of the Code) that is subject to Section 4975 of the Code, and (c) an entity whose underlying assets include assets of a plan described in (a) or (b) plan assets by reason of a plan's investment in such entities.

"Class" means all Notes whose form is identical except for variation in denomination, principal amount or owner.

"Class A-1 Final Payment Date" means March 18, 2004.

"Class A-1 Interest Rate" means 1.30% per annum (computed on the basis of the actual number of days in the related Interest Accrual Period divided by 360).

"Class A-1 Notes" means the Class A-1 1.30% Asset Backed Notes, substantially in the form of Exhibit A.

"Class A-2 Interest Rate" means 1.46% per annum (computed on the basis of a 360-day year consisting of twelve 30-day months).

"Class A-2 Notes" means the Class A-2 1.46% Asset Backed Notes, substantially in the form of Exhibit A.

"Class A-3 Interest Rate" means 1.92% per annum (computed on the basis of a 360-day year consisting of twelve 30-day months).

"Class A-3 Notes" means the Class A-3 1.92% Asset Backed Notes, substantially in the form of Exhibit A.

"Class A-4 Interest Rate" means 2.48% per annum (computed on the basis of a 360-day year consisting of twelve 30-day months).

"Class A-4 Notes" means the Class A-4 2.48% Asset Backed Notes, substantially in the form of Exhibit A.

"Clearing Agency" means an organization registered as a "clearing agency" pursuant to Section 17A of the Exchange Act, which initially shall be The Depository Trust Company.

"Clearing Agency Participant" means a broker, dealer, bank, other financial institution or other Person for whom from time to time a Clearing Agency effects book-entry transfers and pledges of securities deposited with the Clearing Agency.

"Closing Date" means February 25, 2003.

"Code" means the Internal Revenue Code of 1986, as amended from time to time, and Treasury Regulations promulgated thereunder.

"Collateral" has the meaning specified in the Granting Clause of this Indenture.

"Corporate Trust Office" means an office of the Indenture Trustee at which at any particular time its corporate trust business shall be administered, which office at the date of execution of this Indenture is located at 4 New York Plaza, 6th Floor, New York, New York 10004, Attention: Institutional Trust Services: Honda Auto Receivables 2003-1 Owner Trust, or at such other address as the Indenture Trustee may designate from time to time by notice to the Noteholders and the Issuer, or the principal corporate trust office of any successor Indenture Trustee at the address designated by such successor Indenture Trustee by notice to the Noteholders and the Issuer.

"Default" means any occurrence that is, or with notice or the lapse of time or both would become, an Event of Default.

"Definitive Notes" shall have the meaning specified in Section 2.11.

"ERISA" means the Employee Retirement Income Security Act of 1974, as amended.

"Event of Default" shall have the meaning specified in Section 5.01.

"Executive Officer" means, with respect to any corporation or depository institution, the Chief Executive Officer, Chief Operating Officer, Chief Financial Officer, President, Executive Vice President, any Vice President, the Secretary or the Treasurer of such corporation or depository institution; and with respect to any partnership, any general partner thereof.

"Grant" means mortgage, pledge, bargain, sell, warrant, alienate, remise, release, convey, assign, transfer, create and grant a lien upon and a security interest in and a right of set-off against, deposit, set over and confirm pursuant to this Indenture. A Grant of the Collateral or of any other agreement or instrument shall include all rights, powers and options (but none of the obligations) of the granting party thereunder, including the immediate and continuing right to claim for, collect, receive and give receipt for principal and interest payments in respect of the Collateral and all other monies payable thereunder, to give and receive notices and other communications, to make waivers or other agreements, to exercise all rights and options, to bring Proceedings in the name of the granting party or otherwise, and generally to do and receive anything that the granting party is or may be entitled to do or receive thereunder or with respect thereto.

"Holder" means the Person in whose name a Note is registered on the Note Register.

"Indenture" means this Indenture, as amended or supplemented from time to time.

"Indenture Trustee" means JPMorgan Chase Bank, a New York banking corporation, as Indenture Trustee under this Indenture, or any successor Indenture Trustee under this Indenture.

"Independent" means, when used with respect to any specified Person, that the Person (i) is in fact independent of the Issuer, any other obligor on the Notes, the Seller and any of their respective Affiliates, (ii) does not have any direct financial interest or any material indirect financial interest in the Issuer, any such other obligor, the Seller or any of their respective Affiliates and (iii) is not connected with the Issuer, any such other obligor, the Seller or any of their respective Affiliates as an officer, employee, promoter, underwriter, trustee, partner, director or person performing similar functions.

"Independent Certificate" means a certificate or opinion to be delivered to the Indenture Trustee under the circumstances described in, and otherwise complying with, the applicable requirements of Section 11.01, made by an Independent appraiser or other expert appointed by an Issuer Order and approved by the Indenture Trustee in the exercise of reasonable care, and such opinion or certificate shall state that the signer has read the definition of "Independent" in this Indenture and that the signer is Independent within the meaning thereof.

"Interest Accrual Period" means, subject to Section 11.12 hereof, with respect to any Payment Date and (i) the Class A-1 Notes, the period from and including the immediately preceding Payment Date (or, in the case of the first Payment Date, the Closing Date) to but excluding such Payment Date and (ii) the Class A-2 Notes, Class A-3 Notes and Class A-4 Notes, the period from and including the eighteenth day of the prior month (or, in the case of the first Payment Date, the Closing Date) to but excluding the eighteenth day of the month of such Payment Date.

"Interest Rate" means the Class A-1 Interest Rate, the Class A-2 Interest Rate, the Class A-3 Interest Rate or the Class A-4 Interest Rate, as applicable.

"Issuer" means Honda Auto Receivables 2003-1 Owner Trust until a successor replaces it and, thereafter, means the successor and, for purposes of any provision contained herein and required by the TIA, each other obligor on the Notes.

"Issuer Order" or "Issuer Request" means a written order or request signed in the name of the Issuer by any Authorized Officer and delivered to the Indenture Trustee.

"Note Depository Agreement" means the agreement dated February 25, 2003, among the Issuer, the Indenture Trustee and The Depository Trust Company, as the initial Clearing Agency, relating to the Notes, substantially in the form of Exhibit B hereto.

"Noteholder" or "Holder" means the Person in whose name a Note is registered on the Note Register.

"Note Owner" means, with respect to a Book-Entry Note, the Person who is the beneficial owner of such Book-Entry Note, as reflected on the books of the Clearing Agency or on the books of a Person maintaining an account with such Clearing Agency (directly as a Clearing Agency Participant or as an indirect participant, in each case in accordance with the rules of such Clearing Agency).

"Note Register" and "Note Registrar" shall have the respective meanings specified in Section 2.04.

"Notes" means the Class A-1 Notes, Class A-2 Notes, Class A-3 Notes and the Class A-4 Notes.

"Officer's Certificate" means a certificate signed by any Authorized Officer of the Issuer, under the circumstances described in, and otherwise complying with, the applicable requirements of Section 11.01, and delivered to the Indenture Trustee. Unless otherwise specified, any reference in this Indenture to an Officer's Certificate shall be to an Officer's Certificate of the Issuer.

"Opinion of Counsel" means one or more written opinions of counsel who may, except as otherwise expressly provided in this Indenture, be an employee of or counsel to the Issuer and who shall be satisfactory to the Indenture Trustee, and which opinion or opinions shall be addressed to the Indenture Trustee as Indenture Trustee, shall comply with any applicable requirements of Section 11.01 and shall be in form and substance satisfactory to the Indenture Trustee.

"Outstanding" means, as of the date of determination, all Notes theretofore authenticated and delivered under this Indenture except:

(i) Notes theretofore cancelled by the Note Registrar or delivered to the Note Registrar for cancellation;

(ii) Notes or portions thereof the payment for which money in the necessary amount has been theretofore deposited with the Indenture Trustee or any Paying Agent in trust for the Holders of such Notes (provided, however, that if such Notes are to be redeemed, notice of such redemption has been duly given pursuant to this Indenture or provision for such notice has been made, satisfactory to the Indenture Trustee); and

(iii) Notes in exchange for or in lieu of which other Notes have been authenticated and delivered pursuant to this Indenture unless proof satisfactory to the Indenture Trustee is presented that any such Notes are held by a bona fide Protected Purchaser;

provided, that in determining whether the Holders of the requisite Outstanding Amount have given any request, demand, authorization, direction, notice, consent or waiver hereunder or under any other Basic Document, Notes owned by the Issuer, any other obligor upon the Notes, the Seller or any of their respective Affiliates shall be disregarded and deemed not to be Outstanding, except that, in determining whether the Indenture Trustee shall be protected in relying upon any such request, demand, authorization, direction, notice, consent or waiver, only Notes that the Indenture Trustee knows to be so owned shall be so disregarded. Notes so owned that have been pledged in good faith may be regarded as Outstanding if the pledgee establishes to the satisfaction of the Indenture Trustee the pledgee's right so to act with respect to such Notes and that the pledgee is not the Issuer, any other obligor upon the Notes, the Seller or any Affiliate of any of their respective Affiliates.

"Outstanding Amount" means, except as otherwise indicated by the context, the aggregate principal amount of all Notes of all Classes Outstanding at the date of determination.

"Owner Trust Estate" means the Grant of the Collateral to the Indenture Trustee under this Indenture, including all proceeds thereof.

"Owner Trustee" means The Bank of New York, not in its individual capacity but solely as Owner Trustee under the Trust Agreement, or any successor Owner Trustee under the Trust Agreement.

"Paying Agent" means the Indenture Trustee or any other Person that meets the eligibility standards for the Indenture Trustee specified in Section 6.11 and is authorized by the Issuer to make payments to and distributions from the Collection Account and the Note Distribution Account, including payments of principal of or interest on the Notes on behalf of the Issuer.

"Payment Date" means the eighteenth calendar day of each month, commencing March 2003, or if such day is not a Business Day, then the next succeeding Business Day.

"Person" means any individual, corporation, partnership, joint venture, association, joint-stock company, trust, unincorporated organization or government or any agency or political subdivision thereof.

"Predecessor Note" means, with respect to any particular Note, every previous Note evidencing all or a portion of the same debt as that evidenced by such particular Note; and, for the purpose of this definition, any Note authenticated and delivered under Section 2.05 in lieu of a mutilated, lost, destroyed or stolen Note shall be deemed to evidence the same debt as the mutilated, lost, destroyed or stolen Note.

"Proceeding" means any suit in equity, action at law or other judicial or administrative proceeding.

"Protected Purchaser" shall have the meaning set forth in Article 8 of the UCC.

"Rating Agency Condition" means, with respect to any action, that each Rating Agency shall have been given ten days (or such shorter period as is acceptable to each Rating Agency) prior notice thereof and that each Rating Agency shall have notified the Seller, the Servicer, the Indenture Trustee and the Owner Trustee in writing that such action will not result in a qualification, reduction or withdrawal of the then current rating of the Notes.

"Record Date" means, with respect to a Payment Date or Redemption Date, the day immediately preceding such Payment Date or Redemption Date or, if Definitive Notes have been issued, the close of business on the last day of the month immediately preceding the month in which such Payment Date or Redemption Date occurs.

"Redemption Date" means, in the case of a redemption of the Notes pursuant to Section 10.01, the Payment Date specified by the Servicer or the Issuer pursuant to Section 10.01.

"Redemption Price" means, in the case of a redemption of the Notes pursuant to Section 10.01, an amount equal to the unpaid principal amount of the Notes redeemed plus accrued and unpaid interest thereon at the weighted average of the Interest Rates for each Class of Notes being so redeemed to but excluding the Redemption Date.

"Registered Holder" means the Person in whose name a Note is registered on the Note Register on the applicable Record Date.

"Sale and Servicing Agreement" means the Sale and Servicing Agreement, dated as of February 1, 2003, between the Issuer, the Seller and the Servicer.

"Schedule of Receivables" means the list of the Receivables set forth in Schedule A hereto.

"Securities Act" means the Securities Act of 1933, as amended.

"Servicer" means American Honda Finance Corporation, in its capacity as servicer under the Sale and Servicing Agreement, and any Successor Servicer thereunder.

"State" means any one of the 50 states of the United States or the District of Columbia.

"Seller" means American Honda Receivables Corp., in its capacity as seller under the Sale and Servicing Agreement, and its successors.

"Trust Indenture Act" or "TIA" means the Trust Indenture Act of 1939 as in force on the date hereof, unless otherwise specifically provided.

"UCC" means, unless the context otherwise requires, the Uniform Commercial Code, as in effect in the relevant jurisdiction, as amended from time to time.

"United States" means the United States of America.

(b) Except as otherwise specified herein or as the context may otherwise require, capitalized terms used herein that are not otherwise defined shall have the meanings ascribed thereto in the Sale and Servicing Agreement.

Section 1.02. Incorporation by Reference of Trust Indenture Act. Whenever this Indenture refers to a provision of the TIA, the provision is incorporated by reference in and made a part of this Indenture. The following TIA terms used in this Indenture have the following meanings:

"Commission" means the Securities and Exchange Commission.

"indenture securities" means the Notes.

"indenture security holder" means a Noteholder.

"indenture to be qualified" means this Indenture.

"indenture trustee" or "institutional trustee" means the Indenture Trustee.

"obligor" on the indenture securities means the Issuer and any other obligor on the indenture securities.

All other TIA terms used in this Indenture that are defined by the TIA, defined by TIA reference to another statute or defined by Commission rule have the meaning assigned to them by such definitions.

Section 1.03. Rules of Construction. Unless the context otherwise requires: (i) a term has the meaning assigned to it; (ii) an accounting term not otherwise defined has the meaning assigned to it in accordance with generally accepted accounting principles as in effect from time to time; (iii) "or" is not exclusive; (iv) "including" means including without limitation; (v) words in the singular include the plural and words in the plural include the singular; (vi) any agreement, instrument or statute defined or referred to herein or in any instrument or certificate delivered in connection herewith means such agreement, instrument or statute as from time to time amended, modified or supplemented and includes (in the case of agreements or instruments) references to all attachments thereto and instruments incorporated therein; (vii) references to a Person are also to its permitted successors and assigns; (viii) the words "hereof", "herein" and "hereunder" and words of similar import when used in this Indenture shall refer to this Indenture as a whole and not to any particular provision of this Indenture; (ix) the term "proceeds" shall have the meaning set forth in the applicable UCC;

and (x) Section, subsection and Schedule references contained in this Indenture are references to Sections, subsections and Schedules in or to this Indenture unless otherwise specified.

ARTICLE TWO

THE NOTES

Section 2.01. Form. The Class A-1 Notes, the Class A-2 Notes, the Class A-3 Notes and the Class A-4 Notes, in each case together with the Indenture Trustee's certificate of authentication, shall be in substantially the form set forth in Exhibit A, with such appropriate insertions, omissions, substitutions and other variations as are required or permitted by this Indenture, and may have such letters, numbers or other marks of identification and such legends or endorsements placed thereon as may, consistently herewith, be determined by the officers executing such Notes, as evidenced by their execution of the Notes. Any portion of the text of any Note may be set forth on the reverse thereof, with an appropriate reference thereto on the face of the Note.

Definitive Notes shall be typewritten, printed, lithographed or engraved or produced by any combination of these methods (with or without steel engraved borders), all as determined by the officers executing such Notes, as evidenced by their execution of such Notes.

Each Note shall be dated the date of its authentication. The terms of the Notes are the terms of this Indenture.

Section 2.02. Execution, Authentication and Delivery. The Notes shall be executed on behalf of the Issuer by any of its Authorized Officers. The signature of any such Authorized Officer on the Notes may be manual or facsimile. Notes bearing the manual or facsimile signature of individuals who were at any time Authorized Officers of the Issuer shall bind the Issuer, notwithstanding that such individuals or any of them have ceased to hold such offices prior to the authentication and delivery of such Notes or did not hold such offices at the date of such Notes.

The Indenture Trustee shall, upon Issuer Order, authenticate and deliver for original issue the following aggregate principal amount of Notes: (i) $376,000,000 of Class A-1 Notes, (ii) $462,000,000 of Class A-2 Notes, (iii) $386,000,000 of Class A-3 Notes and (iv) $317,700,000 of Class A-4 Notes. The aggregate principal amount of Class A-1 Notes, Class A-2 Notes, Class A-3 Notes and Class A-4 Notes outstanding at any time may not exceed such respective amounts except as provided in Section 2.05.

Each Note shall be dated the date of its authentication. The Notes shall be issuable as registered Notes in minimum denominations of $1,000 and in integral multiples of $1,000 in excess thereof.

No Note shall be entitled to any benefit under this Indenture or be valid or obligatory for any purpose, unless there appears on such Note a certificate of authentication substantially in the form provided for herein executed by the Indenture

Trustee by the manual signature of one of its authorized signatories, and such certificate upon any Note shall be conclusive evidence, and the only evidence, that such Note has been duly authenticated and delivered hereunder.

Section 2.03. Temporary Notes. Pending the preparation of Definitive Notes, the Issuer may execute, and upon receipt of an Issuer Order the Indenture Trustee shall authenticate and deliver, temporary Notes that are printed, lithographed, typewritten, mimeographed or otherwise produced, of the tenor of the Definitive Notes in lieu of which they are issued and with such variations not inconsistent with the terms of this Indenture as the officers executing such Notes may determine, as evidenced by their execution of such Notes.

If temporary Notes are issued, the Issuer shall cause Definitive Notes to be prepared without unreasonable delay. After the preparation of Definitive Notes, the temporary Notes shall be exchangeable for Definitive Notes upon surrender of the temporary Notes at the office or agency of the Issuer to be maintained as provided in Section 3.02, without charge to the related Holder. Upon surrender for cancellation of any one or more temporary Notes, the Issuer shall execute, and the Indenture Trustee shall authenticate and deliver in exchange therefor, a like tenor and principal amount of Definitive Notes of authorized denominations. Until so exchanged, the temporary Notes shall in all respects be entitled to the same benefits under this Indenture as Definitive Notes.

Section 2.04. Registration, Registration of Transfer and Exchange. The Issuer shall cause to be kept a register (the "Note Register") in which, subject to such reasonable regulations as it may prescribe, the Issuer shall provide for the registration of Notes and the registration of transfers of Notes. The Indenture Trustee initially shall be the "Note Registrar" for the purpose of registering Notes and transfers of Notes as herein provided. Upon any resignation of any Note Registrar, the Issuer shall promptly appoint a successor or, if it elects not to make such an appointment, assume the duties of Note Registrar.

If a Person other than the Indenture Trustee is appointed by the Issuer as Note Registrar, the Issuer will give the Indenture Trustee prompt written notice of the appointment of such Note Registrar and of the location, and any change in the location, of the Note Register, and the Indenture Trustee shall have the right to inspect the Note Register at all reasonable times and to obtain copies thereof, and the Indenture Trustee shall have the right to rely upon a certificate executed on behalf of the Note Registrar by an Executive Officer thereof as to the names and addresses of the Holders of the Notes and the principal amounts and number of such Notes.

Upon surrender for registration of transfer of any Note at the office or agency of the Issuer to be maintained as provided in Section 3.02, provided that the requirements of Section 8-401 of the UCC are met, the Issuer shall execute, and the Indenture Trustee shall authenticate and the Noteholder shall obtain from the Indenture Trustee, in the name of the designated transferee or transferees, one or more new Notes of the same Class in any authorized denominations, of a like aggregate principal amount.

At the option of the Holder, Notes may be exchanged for other Notes of the same Class in any authorized denominations, of a like aggregate principal amount, upon surrender of the Notes to be exchanged at such office or agency. Whenever any Notes are so surrendered for exchange, provided that the requirements of Section 8-401 of the UCC are met (as determined by the Issuer), the Issuer shall execute, and the Indenture Trustee shall authenticate and the Noteholder shall obtain from the Indenture Trustee, the Notes which the Noteholder making the exchange is entitled to receive.

All Notes issued upon any registration of transfer or exchange of Notes shall be the valid obligations of the Issuer, evidencing the same debt, and entitled to the same benefits under this Indenture, as the Notes surrendered upon such registration of transfer or exchange.

Every Note presented or surrendered for registration of transfer or exchange shall be duly endorsed by, or be accompanied by a written instrument of transfer in form satisfactory to the Indenture Trustee duly executed by, the Holder thereof or such Holder's attorney duly authorized in writing, with such signature guaranteed by an "eligible guarantor institution" meeting the requirements of the Note Registrar, which requirements include membership or participation in the Securities Transfer Agent's Medallion Program ("STAMP") or such other "signature guarantee program" as may be determined by the Note Registrar in addition to, or in substitution for, STAMP, all in accordance with the Exchange Act.

No service charge shall be made to a Holder for any registration of transfer or exchange of Notes, but the Issuer or the Indenture Trustee may require payment of a sum sufficient to cover any tax or other governmental charge that may be imposed in connection with any registration of transfer or exchange of Notes, other than exchanges pursuant to Section 2.03 or 9.06 not involving any transfer.

The preceding provisions of this Section notwithstanding, the Issuer shall not be required to make and the Note Registrar need not register transfers or exchanges of Notes selected for redemption or of any Note for a period of 15 days preceding the due date for any payment with respect to the Note.

Section 2.05. Mutilated, Destroyed, Lost or Stolen Notes. If (i) any mutilated Note is surrendered to the Indenture Trustee, or the Indenture Trustee receives evidence to its satisfaction of the destruction, loss or theft of any Note, (ii) there is delivered to the Indenture Trustee such security or indemnity as may be required by it to hold the Issuer and the Indenture Trustee harmless and (iii) the requirements of Section 8-405 of the UCC are met, then, in the absence of notice to the Issuer, the Note Registrar or the Indenture Trustee that such Note has been acquired by a Protected Purchaser, the Issuer shall execute, and upon its written request the Indenture Trustee shall authenticate and deliver, in exchange for or in lieu of any such mutilated, destroyed, lost or stolen Note, a replacement Note of the same Class; provided, however, that if any such destroyed, lost or stolen Note, but not a mutilated Note, shall have become or within seven days shall be due and payable, or shall have been called for redemption, instead of issuing a replacement Note, the Issuer may pay such destroyed, lost or stolen Note when so due or payable or upon the Redemption Date without surrender thereof. If, after the delivery of such replacement Note or payment of a destroyed, lost or stolen Note pursuant to the proviso to the preceding sentence, a Protected Purchaser of the original Note in lieu of which such replacement Note was issued presents for payment such original Note, the Issuer and the Indenture Trustee shall be entitled to recover such replacement Note (or such payment) from the Person to whom it was delivered or any Person taking such replacement Note from such Person to whom such replacement Note was delivered or any assignee of such Person, except a protected purchaser, and shall be entitled to recover upon the security or indemnity provided therefor to the extent of any loss, damage, cost or expense incurred by the Issuer or the Indenture Trustee in connection therewith.

Upon the issuance of any replacement Note under this Section, the Issuer or the Indenture Trustee may require the payment by the Holder of such Note of a sum sufficient to cover any tax or other governmental charge that may be imposed in relation thereto and any other reasonable expenses (including the fees and expenses of the Indenture Trustee or the Note Registrar) connected therewith.

Every replacement Note issued pursuant to this Section in replacement of any mutilated, destroyed, lost or stolen Note shall constitute an original additional contractual obligation of the Issuer, whether or not the mutilated, destroyed, lost or stolen Note shall be at any time enforceable by anyone, and shall be entitled to all the benefits of this Indenture equally and proportionately with any and all other Notes duly issued hereunder.

The provisions of this Section are exclusive and shall preclude (to the extent lawful) all other rights and remedies with respect to the replacement or payment of mutilated, destroyed, lost or stolen Notes.

Section 2.06. Persons Deemed Owner. Prior to due presentment for registration of transfer of any Note, the Issuer, the Indenture Trustee and any of their respective agents may treat the Person in whose name any Note is registered (as of the day of determination) as the owner of such Note for the purpose of receiving payments of principal of and interest, if any, on such Note and for all other purposes whatsoever, whether or not such Note be overdue, and none of the Issuer, the Indenture Trustee or any of their respective agents shall be affected by notice to the contrary.

Section 2.07. Payment of Principal and Interest, Defaulted Interest.

(a) Each Class of Notes shall accrue interest at the related Interest Rate, and such interest shall be due and payable on each Payment Date as specified therein, subject to Sections 3.01 and 11.12 hereof. Any installment of interest or principal, if any, payable on any Note that is punctually paid or duly provided for by the Issuer on the applicable Payment Date shall be paid to the Person in whose name such Note (or one or more Predecessor Notes) is registered on the Record Date by check mailed first-class postage prepaid to such Person's address as it appears on the Note Register on such Record Date, except that, unless

Definitive Notes have been issued pursuant to Section 2.11, with respect to Notes registered on the Record Date in the name of the nominee of the Clearing Agency (initially, such nominee to be Cede & Co.), payment will be made by wire transfer in immediately available funds to the account designated by such nominee and except for the final installment of principal payable with respect to such Note on a Payment Date, a Redemption Date or on the related Final Scheduled Payment Date, as the case may be (and except for the Redemption Price for any Note called for redemption pursuant to Section 10.01), which shall be payable as provided below. The funds represented by any such checks returned undelivered shall be held in accordance with Section 3.03.

(b) The principal of each Note shall be payable as provided in Section 8.02(d) hereof. Notwithstanding the foregoing, the entire unpaid principal amount of the Notes shall be due and payable, if not previously paid, on the related Final Payment Date or the date on which an Event of Default shall have occurred and be continuing, if the Indenture Trustee or Holders of the Notes representing not less than a majority of the Outstanding Amount have declared the Notes to be immediately due and payable in the manner provided in Section 5.02. All principal payments on each Class of Notes shall be made pro rata to the Noteholders of such Class entitled thereto. The Indenture Trustee shall notify the Person in whose name a Note is registered at the close of business 5 Business Days preceding the Payment Date on which the Issuer expects that the final installment of principal of and interest on such Note will be paid. Such notice shall be mailed or transmitted by facsimile prior to such final Payment Date and shall specify that such final installment will be payable only upon presentation and surrender of such Note and shall specify the place where such Note may be presented and surrendered for payment of such installment. Notices in connection with redemptions of Notes shall be mailed to Noteholders as provided in Section 10.02. In addition, the Administrator shall notify each Rating Agency upon the final payment of interest and principal of each Class of Notes, and upon the termination of the Trust, in each case pursuant to Section 1.02(a)(iii) of the Administration Agreement.

(c) If the Issuer defaults in a payment of interest on the Notes, the Issuer shall pay defaulted interest (plus interest on such defaulted interest to the extent lawful) at the applicable Interest Rate in any lawful manner. The Issuer may pay such defaulted interest to the Persons who are Noteholders on a subsequent special record date, which date shall be at least five Business Days prior to the next payment date. The Issuer shall fix or cause to be fixed any such special record date and related payment date, and, at least 15 days before any such special record date, the Issuer shall mail to each Noteholder a notice that states the special record date, the payment date and the amount of defaulted interest to be paid.

Section 2.08. Cancellation. All Notes surrendered for payment, registration of transfer, exchange or redemption shall, if surrendered to any Person other than the Indenture Trustee, be delivered to the Indenture Trustee and shall be promptly cancelled by the Indenture Trustee. The Issuer may at any time deliver to the Indenture Trustee for cancellation any Notes previously authenticated and delivered hereunder which the Issuer may have acquired in any manner whatsoever, and all Notes so delivered shall be promptly cancelled by the Indenture Trustee. No Notes shall be authenticated in lieu of or in exchange for any Notes cancelled as provided in this Section, except as expressly permitted by this Indenture. All cancelled Notes may be held or disposed of by the Indenture Trustee in accordance with its standard retention or disposal policy as in effect at the time unless the Issuer shall direct by an Issuer Order that they be destroyed or returned to it; provided, that such Issuer Order is timely and the Notes have not been previously disposed of by the Indenture Trustee.

Section 2.09. Book-Entry Notes. The Notes, upon original issuance, will be issued in the form of a typewritten Note or Notes representing the Book-Entry Notes, to be delivered to the Indenture Trustee, as agent for The Depository Trust Company, the initial Clearing Agency, by, or on behalf of, the Issuer. The Book-Entry Notes shall be registered initially on the Note Register in the name of Cede & Co., the nominee of the initial Clearing Agency, and no Note Owner will receive a definitive Note representing such Note Owner's interest in such Note, except as provided in Section 2.11. Unless and until definitive, fully registered Notes (the "Definitive Notes") have been issued to such Note Owners pursuant to Section 2.11:

(i) the provisions of this Section shall be in full force and effect;

(ii) the Note Registrar and the Indenture Trustee shall be entitled to deal with the Clearing Agency for all purposes of this Indenture (including the payment of principal of and interest on the Notes and the giving of instructions or directions hereunder) as the sole holder of the Notes, and shall have no obligation to the Note Owners;

(iii) to the extent that the provisions of this Section conflict with any other provisions of this Indenture, the provisions of this Section shall control;

(iv) the rights of Note Owners shall be exercised only through the Clearing Agency and shall be limited to those established by law and agreements between such Note Owners and the Clearing Agency and/or the Clearing Agency Participants. Pursuant to the Note Depository Agreement, unless and until Definitive Notes are issued pursuant to Section 2.11, the Clearing Agency will make book-entry transfers among the Clearing Agency Participants and receive and transmit payments of principal of and interest on the Notes to such Clearing Agency Participants; and

(v) whenever this Indenture requires or permits actions to be taken based upon instructions or directions of Holders of Notes evidencing a specified percentage of the Outstanding Amount, the Clearing Agency shall be deemed to represent such percentage only to the extent that it has received instructions to such effect from Note Owners and/or Clearing Agency Participants owning or representing, respectively, such required percentage of the beneficial interest in the Notes and has delivered such instructions to the Indenture Trustee.

Section 2.10. Notices to Clearing Agency. Whenever a notice or other communication to the Noteholders is required under this Indenture, unless and until Definitive Notes shall have been issued to such Note Owners pursuant to Section 2.11, the Indenture Trustee shall give all such notices and communications specified herein to be given to Holders of the Notes to the Clearing Agency, and shall have no obligation to such Note Owners.

Section 2.11. Definitive Notes. If (i)(A) the Administrator advises the Indenture Trustee in writing that the Clearing Agency is no longer willing or able to properly discharge its responsibilities with respect to the Book-Entry Notes and (B) neither the Indenture Trustee nor the Administrator is able to locate a qualified successor, (ii) the Administrator at its option advises the Indenture Trustee in writing that it elects to terminate the book-entry system through the Clearing Agency or (iii) after the occurrence of an Event of Default or a Servicer Default, Owners of Book-Entry Notes representing beneficial interests aggregating at least a majority of the Outstanding Amount of such Notes advise the Indenture Trustee and the Clearing Agency Participants through the Clearing Agency, in writing that the continuation of a book-entry system through the Clearing Agency is no longer in the best interests of such Note Owners, then, in each case, the Indenture Trustee shall notify all Note Owners of the related Class of Notes through the Clearing Agency of the occurrence of any such event and of the availability of Definitive Notes of the related Class of Notes to Note Owners requesting the same. Upon surrender to the Indenture Trustee of the Note or Notes representing the Book-Entry Notes by the Clearing Agency, accompanied by registration instructions, the Issuer shall execute and the Indenture Trustee shall authenticate the Definitive Notes in accordance with the instructions of the Clearing Agency. None of the Issuer, the Note Registrar or the Indenture Trustee shall be liable for any delay in delivery of such instructions and may conclusively rely on, and shall be protected in relying on, such instructions. Upon the issuance of Definitive Notes of a Class, the Indenture Trustee shall recognize the Holders of the Definitive Notes as Noteholders hereunder.

Section 2.12. Release of Collateral. Subject to Section 11.01 and the terms of the other Basic Documents, the Indenture Trustee shall release property from the lien of this Indenture only upon receipt of an Issuer Request accompanied by an Officer's Certificate, an Opinion of Counsel and Independent Certificates in accordance with TIA ss.ss. 314(c) and 314(d)(1) or an Opinion of Counsel in lieu of such Independent Certificates to the effect that the TIA does not require any such Independent Certificates.

Section 2.13. Tax Treatment. The Issuer has entered into this Indenture, and the Notes will be issued, with the intention that, for all purposes including federal, state and local income, single business and franchise tax purposes, the Notes will qualify as indebtedness of the Issuer secured by the Owner Trust Estate. The Issuer, by entering into this Indenture, and each Noteholder, by its acceptance of a Note (and each Note Owner by its acceptance of an interest in the applicable Book-Entry Note), agree to treat the Notes for all purposes including federal, state and local income, single business and franchise tax purposes as indebtedness of the Issuer.

Section 2.14. Employee Benefit Plans. The transfer of a Definitive Note shall not be registered unless the prospective transferee has represented in writing to the Indenture Trustee that either (i) it is not a Benefit Plan and is not acting on behalf of or investing the assets of a Benefit Plan or (ii) its acquisition and holding of the Definitive Note will be covered by a U.S. Department of Labor prohibited transaction class exemption. Any Person that acquires a beneficial interest in a Book-Entry Note with the assets of a Benefit Plan shall be deemed to represent that its acquisition and holding of such beneficial interest is covered by a U.S. Department of Labor prohibited transaction class exemption.

ARTICLE THREE
COVENANTS

Section 3.01. Payment of Principal and Interest. The Issuer will duly and punctually pay the principal of and interest, if any, on the Notes in accordance with the terms of the Notes and this Indenture. Without limiting the foregoing, subject to Section 8.02(c), the Issuer will cause to be distributed all amounts on deposit in the Note Distribution Account on a Payment Date deposited therein in accordance with Section 8.02(d). Amounts properly withheld under the Code by any Person from a payment to any Noteholder of interest and/or principal shall be considered as having been paid by the Issuer to such Noteholder for all purposes of this Indenture.

Section 3.02. Maintenance of Office or Agency. The Issuer will maintain in the Borough of Manhattan, The City of New York, an office or agency where Notes may be surrendered for registration of transfer or exchange, and where notices and demands to or upon the Issuer in respect of the Notes and this Indenture may be served. The Issuer hereby initially appoints the Indenture Trustee to serve as its agent for the foregoing purposes. The Issuer will give prompt written notice to the Indenture Trustee of the location, and of any change in the location, of any such office or agency. If at any time the Issuer shall fail to maintain any such office or agency or shall fail to furnish the Indenture Trustee with the address thereof, such surrenders, notices and demands may be made or served at the Corporate Trust Office, and the Issuer hereby appoints the Indenture Trustee as its agent to receive all such surrenders, notices and demands, provided that the Indenture Trustee shall not serve as an agent or office for the purpose of service of process on behalf of the Issuer.

Section 3.03. Money for Payments to be Held in Trust. As provided in Sections 5.04 and 8.02, all payments of amounts due and payable with respect to any Notes that are to be made from amounts withdrawn from the Collection Account and the Note Distribution Account pursuant to Section 8.02(c) shall be made on behalf of the Issuer by the Indenture Trustee or by another Paying Agent, and no amounts so withdrawn from the Collection Account and the Note Distribution Account for payments of Notes shall be paid over to the Issuer except as provided in this Section.

On or before the Business Day immediately preceding each Payment Date and Redemption Date, the Issuer shall deposit or cause to be deposited in the Collection Account (to be transferred to the Note Distribution Account on the related Payment Date) an aggregate sum sufficient to pay the amounts then becoming due under the Notes, such sum to be held in trust for the benefit of the Persons entitled thereto, and (unless the Paying Agent is the Indenture Trustee) shall promptly notify the Indenture Trustee in writing of its action or failure so to act.

The Issuer will cause each Paying Agent other than the Indenture Trustee to execute and deliver to the Indenture Trustee an instrument in which such Paying Agent shall agree with the Indenture Trustee (and if the Indenture Trustee acts as Paying Agent, it hereby so agrees), subject to the provisions of this Section, that such Paying Agent will:

(i) hold all sums held by it for the payment of amounts due with respect to the Notes in trust for the benefit of the Persons entitled thereto until such sums shall be paid to such Persons or otherwise disposed of as herein provided and pay such sums to such Persons as herein provided;

(ii) give the Indenture Trustee notice of any default by the Issuer (or any other obligor upon the Notes) of which it has actual knowledge in the making of any payment required to be made with respect to the Notes;

(iii) at any time during the continuance of any such default, upon the written request of the Indenture Trustee, forthwith pay to the Indenture Trustee all sums so held in trust by such Paying Agent;

(iv) immediately resign as a Paying Agent and forthwith pay to the Indenture Trustee all sums held by it in trust for the payment of Notes if at any time it ceases to meet the standards required to be met by a Paying Agent at the time of its appointment; and

(v) comply with all requirements of the Code with respect to the withholding from any payments made by it on any Notes of any applicable withholding taxes imposed thereon and with respect to any applicable reporting requirements in connection therewith.

The Issuer may at any time, for the purpose of obtaining the satisfaction and discharge of this Indenture or for any other purpose, by Issuer Order direct any Paying Agent to pay to the Indenture Trustee all sums held in trust by such Paying Agent, such sums to be held by the Indenture Trustee upon the same trusts as those upon which the sums were held by such Paying Agent; and upon such payment by any Paying Agent to the Indenture Trustee, such Paying Agent shall be released from all further liability with respect to such money.

Subject to applicable laws with respect to escheat of funds, any money held by the Indenture Trustee or any Paying Agent in trust for the payment of any amount due with respect to any Note and remaining unclaimed for two years after such amount has become due and payable shall be discharged from such trust and be paid to the Issuer on Issuer Request; and the Holder of such Note shall thereafter, as an unsecured general creditor, look only to the Issuer for payment thereof (but only to the extent of the amounts so paid to the Issuer), and all liability of the Indenture Trustee or such Paying Agent with respect to such trust money shall thereupon cease; provided, however, that the Indenture Trustee or such Paying Agent, before being required to make any such repayment, shall at the expense and written direction of the Issuer cause to be published once, in a newspaper published in the English language, customarily published on each Business Day and of general circulation in The City of New York, notice that such money remains unclaimed and that, after a date specified therein, which shall not be less than 30 days from the date of such publication, any unclaimed balance of such money then remaining will be repaid to or for the account of the Issuer. The Indenture Trustee shall also adopt and employ, at the expense and written direction of the Issuer, any other reasonable means of notification of such repayment (including, but not limited to, mailing notice of such repayment to Holders whose Notes have been called but have not been surrendered for redemption or whose right to or interest in monies due and payable but not claimed is determinable from the records of the Indenture Trustee or of any Paying Agent, at the last address of record for each such Holder).

Section 3.04. Existence. The Issuer will keep in full effect its existence, rights and franchises as a statutory trust under the laws of the State of Delaware (unless it becomes, or any successor Issuer hereunder is or becomes, organized under the laws of any other State or of the United States, in which case the Issuer will keep in full effect its existence, rights and franchises under the laws of such other jurisdiction) and will obtain and preserve its qualification to do business in each jurisdiction in which such qualification is or shall be necessary to protect the validity and enforceability of this Indenture, the Notes, the Collateral and each other instrument or agreement included in the Owner Trust Estate, including all licenses required under the Pennsylvania Motor Vehicle Sales Finance Act and MD. Fin. Inst. Code Ann., Title 11, Subtitle 4 in connection with this Agreement and the other Basic Documents and the transactions contemplated hereby and thereby until such time as the Issuer shall terminate in accordance with the terms hereof.

Section 3.05. Protection of Owner Trust Estate. The Issuer intends the security interest Granted pursuant to this Indenture in favor of the Indenture Trustee on behalf of the Noteholders to be prior to all other liens in respect of the Owner Trust Estate, and the Issuer shall take all actions necessary to obtain and maintain, for the benefit of the Indenture Trustee on behalf of the Noteholders, a first lien on and a first priority, perfected security interest in the Owner Trust Estate. The Issuer will from time to time execute and deliver all such supplements and amendments hereto and all such financing statements, continuation statements, instruments of further assurance and other instruments, all as prepared by the Administrator and delivered to the Issuer, and will take such other action necessary or advisable to:

(i) Grant more effectively any portion of the Owner Trust Estate;

(ii) maintain or preserve the lien and security interest (and the priority thereof) created by this Indenture or carry out more effectively the purposes hereof;

(iii) perfect, publish notice of or protect the validity of any Grant made or to be made by this Indenture;

(iv) enforce any of the Collateral;

(v) preserve and defend title to the Owner Trust Estate and the rights of the Indenture Trustee and the Noteholders in such Owner Trust Estate against the claims of all persons and parties; or

(vi) pay all taxes or assessments levied or assessed upon the Owner Trust Estate when due.

Section 3.06. Opinions as to Owner Trust Estate.

(a) Promptly after the execution and delivery of this Indenture, the Issuer shall furnish to the Indenture Trustee an Opinion of Counsel to the effect that, in the opinion of such counsel, either (i) all financing statements and continuation statements have been executed and filed that are necessary to create and continue the Indenture Trustee's first priority perfected security interest in the collateral for the benefit of the Noteholders, and reciting the details of such filings or referring to prior Opinions of Counsel in which such details are given, or (ii) no such action shall be necessary to perfect such security interest.

(b) Within 90 days after the beginning of each fiscal year of the Issuer beginning with the first fiscal year beginning more than three months after the Cutoff Date, the Issuer shall furnish to the Indenture Trustee an Opinion of Counsel, dated as of a date during such 90-day period, to the effect that, in the opinion of such counsel, either (i) all financing statements and continuation statements have been executed and filed that are necessary to create and continue the Indenture Trustee's first priority perfected security interest in the collateral for the benefit of the Noteholders, and reciting the details of such filings or referring to prior Opinions of Counsel in which such details are given, or (ii) no such action shall be necessary to perfect such security interest.

Section 3.07. Performance of Obligations; Servicing of Receivables.

(a) The Issuer will not take any action and will use its best efforts not to permit any action to be taken by others that would release any Person from any of such Person's material covenants or obligations under any instrument or agreement included in the Owner Trust Estate or that would result in the amendment, hypothecation, subordination, termination or discharge of, or impair the validity or effectiveness of, any such instrument or agreement, except as expressly provided in this Indenture, the other Basic Documents or such other instrument or agreement.

(b) The Issuer may contract with other Persons to assist it in performing its duties under this Indenture, and any performance of such duties by a Person identified to the Indenture Trustee in an Officer's Certificate of the Issuer shall be deemed to be action taken by the Issuer. Initially, the Issuer has contracted with the Servicer and the Administrator to assist the Issuer in performing its duties under this Indenture.

(c) The Issuer will and will cause the Administrator to, punctually perform and observe all of its obligations and agreements contained in this Indenture, the other Basic Documents and in the instruments and agreements included in the Owner Trust Estate, including but not limited to filing or causing to be filed all UCC financing statements and continuation statements required to be filed by the terms of this Indenture and the other Basic Documents in accordance with and within the time periods provided for herein and therein. Except as otherwise expressly provided therein, the Issuer shall not waive, amend, modify, supplement or terminate any Basic Document or any provision thereof without the written consent of the Indenture Trustee or the Holders of at least a majority of the Outstanding Amount or such greater percentage as may be specified in the particular provision.

(d) If the Issuer shall have knowledge of the occurrence of a Servicer Default, the Issuer shall promptly provide written notice to a Responsible Officer of the Indenture Trustee and to each Rating Agency thereof, and shall specify in such notice the action, if any, the Issuer is taking with respect of such default. If a Servicer Default shall arise from the failure of the Servicer to perform any of its duties or obligations under the Sale and Servicing Agreement with respect to the Receivables, the Issuer shall take all reasonable steps available to it to remedy such failure.

(e) As promptly as possible after the giving of notice of termination to the Servicer of the Servicer's rights and powers pursuant to Section 7.01 of the Sale and Servicing Agreement, the Indenture Trustee shall appoint a Successor Servicer, and such Successor Servicer shall accept its appointment by a written assumption in a form acceptable to the Indenture Trustee. In the event that a Successor Servicer has not been appointed and accepted its appointment at the time when the Servicer ceases to act as Servicer, the Indenture Trustee without further action shall automatically be appointed the Successor Servicer. The Indenture Trustee may resign as the Servicer by giving written notice of such resignation to the Issuer and in such event will be released from such duties and obligations, such release not to be effective until the date a new servicer enters into a servicing agreement as provided below. Upon delivery of any such notice to the Issuer, the Issuer shall obtain a new servicer as the Successor Servicer under the Sale and Servicing Agreement. Any Successor Servicer other than the Indenture Trustee shall (i) be an established financial institution having a net worth of not less than $50,000,000 and whose regular business includes the servicing of motor vehicle receivables and (ii) enter into a servicing agreement with the Issuer and the Seller having substantially the same provisions as the provisions of the Sale and Servicing Agreement applicable to the Servicer. If within 30 days after the delivery of the notice referred to above, the Issuer shall not have obtained such a new servicer, the Indenture Trustee may appoint, or may petition a court of competent jurisdiction to appoint, a Successor Servicer. In connection with any such appointment, the Issuer may make such arrangements for the compensation of such successor as it and such successor shall agree, subject to the limitations set forth below and in the Sale and Servicing Agreement, and in accordance with Section 7.02 of the Sale and Servicing Agreement, the Issuer and the Seller shall enter into an agreement with such successor for the servicing of the Receivables (such agreement to be in form and substance satisfactory to the Indenture Trustee). If the Indenture Trustee shall succeed to the Servicer's duties as servicer of the Receivables as provided herein, it shall do so in its individual capacity and not in its capacity as Indenture Trustee and, accordingly, the provisions of Article Six shall be inapplicable to the Indenture Trustee in its duties as the successor to the Servicer and the servicing of the Receivables. In case the Indenture Trustee shall become successor to the Servicer under the Sale and Servicing Agreement, the Indenture Trustee shall be entitled to appoint as Servicer any one of its Affiliates or agents, provided that it shall be fully liable for the actions and omissions of such Affiliate or agent in such capacity as Successor Servicer.

(f) Upon any termination of the Servicer's rights and powers pursuant to the Sale and Servicing Agreement, the Issuer shall promptly notify a Responsible Officer of the Indenture Trustee. As soon as a Successor Servicer is appointed, the Issuer shall notify the Indenture Trustee of such appointment, specifying in such notice the name and address of such Successor Servicer.

Section 3.08. Negative Covenants. So long as any Notes are Outstanding, the Issuer shall not:

(i) except as expressly permitted by Section 3.10(b) and the Basic Documents, sell, transfer, exchange or otherwise dispose of any of the properties or assets of the Issuer, including those included in the Owner Trust Estate, unless directed to do so by the Indenture Trustee;

(ii) claim any credit on, or make any deduction from the principal or interest payable in respect of, the Notes (other than amounts properly withheld from such payments under the Code or applicable state law) or assert any claim against any present or former Noteholder by reason of the payment of the taxes levied or assessed upon any part of the Owner Trust Estate;

(iii) (A) permit the validity or effectiveness of this Indenture to be impaired, or permit the lien created by this Indenture to be amended, hypothecated, subordinated, terminated or discharged, or permit any Person to be released from any covenants or obligations with respect to the Notes under this Indenture except as may be expressly permitted hereby, (B) permit any lien, charge, excise, claim, security interest, mortgage or other encumbrance (other than the lien of this Indenture) to be created on or extend to or otherwise arise upon or burden the Owner Trust Estate or any part thereof or any interest therein or the proceeds thereof (other than tax liens, mechanics' liens and other liens that arise by operation of law, in each case on any of the Financed Vehicles and arising solely as a result of an action or omission of the related Obligor) or (C) permit the lien created by this Indenture not to constitute a valid first priority (other than with respect to any such tax, mechanics' or other lien) security interest in the Owner Trust Estate; or

(iv) dissolve or liquidate in whole or in part.

Section 3.09. Annual Statement as to Compliance. The Issuer will deliver to the Indenture Trustee, within 120 days after the end of each fiscal year of the Issuer (commencing with the fiscal year ended March 2003), an Officer's Certificate stating, as to the Authorized Officer signing such Officer's Certificate, that:

(i) a review of the activities of the Issuer during such year and of its performance under this Indenture has been made under such Authorized Officer's supervision; and

(ii) to the best of such Authorized Officer's knowledge, based on such review, the Issuer has complied with all conditions and covenants under this Indenture throughout such year or, if there has been a default in its compliance with any such condition or covenant, specifying each such default known to such Authorized Officer and the nature and status thereof.

Section 3.10. Issuer May Consolidate, etc., Only on Certain Terms.

(a) The Issuer shall not consolidate or merge with or into any other Person, unless:

(i) the Person (if other than the Issuer) formed by or surviving such consolidation or merger shall be a Person organized and existing under the laws of the United States or any State and shall expressly assume, by an indenture supplemental hereto, executed and delivered to the Indenture Trustee, in form satisfactory to the Indenture Trustee, the due and punctual payment of the principal of and interest on all Notes and the performance or observance of every agreement and covenant of this Indenture, and each other Basic Document, on the part of the Issuer to be performed or observed;

(ii) immediately after giving effect to such transaction, no Default or Event of Default shall have occurred and be continuing;

(iii) the Rating Agency Condition shall have been satisfied with respect to such transaction;

(iv) the Issuer shall have received an Opinion of Counsel (and shall have delivered copies thereof to the Indenture Trustee) to the effect that such transaction will not have any material adverse tax consequence to the Issuer, any Noteholder or any Certificateholder;

(v) any action that is necessary to maintain the lien and security interest created by this Indenture shall have been taken; and

(vi) the Issuer shall have delivered to the Indenture Trustee an Officer's Certificate and an Opinion of Counsel (which shall describe the actions taken as required by clause (v) above or that no actions will be taken) each stating that such consolidation or merger comply with this Article and that all conditions precedent herein provided for relating to such transaction have been complied with (including any filing required by the Exchange Act).

(b) The Issuer shall not convey or transfer all or substantially all of its properties or assets, including those included in the Owner Trust Estate, to any Person (except as expressly permitted by the Basic Documents), unless:

(i) the Person that acquires by conveyance or transfer the properties or assets of the Issuer shall (A) be a United States citizen or a Person organized and existing under the laws of the United States or any State, (B) expressly assume, by an indenture supplemental hereto, executed and delivered to the Indenture Trustee, in form satisfactory to the Indenture Trustee, the due and punctual payment of the principal of and interest on all Notes and the performance or observance of every agreement and covenant of this Indenture and each other Basic Document on the part of the Issuer to be performed or observed, all as provided herein, (C) expressly agree by means of such supplemental indenture that all right, title and interest so conveyed or transferred shall be subject and subordinate to the rights of Holders of the Notes, (D) unless otherwise provided in such supplemental indenture, expressly agree to indemnify, defend and hold harmless the Issuer against and from any loss, liability or expense arising under or related to this Indenture and the Notes and (E) expressly agree by means of such supplemental indenture that such Person (or if a group of Persons, then one specified Person) shall make all filings with the Commission (and any other appropriate Person) required by the Exchange Act in connection with the Notes;

(ii) immediately after giving effect to such transaction, no Default or Event of Default shall have occurred and be continuing;

(iii) the Rating Agency Condition shall have been satisfied with respect to such transaction;

(iv) the Issuer shall have received an Opinion of Counsel (and shall have delivered copies thereof to the Indenture Trustee) to the effect that such transaction will not have any material adverse federal tax consequence to the Issuer, any Noteholder or any Certificateholder;

(v) any action that is necessary to maintain the lien and security interest created by this Indenture shall have been taken; and

(vi) the Issuer shall have delivered to the Indenture Trustee an Officer's Certificate and an Opinion of Counsel (which shall describe the actions taken as required by clause (v) above or that no actions will be taken) each stating that such conveyance or transfer and such supplemental indenture comply with this Article and that all conditions precedent herein provided for relating to such transaction have been complied with (including any filing required by the Exchange Act).

Section 3.11. Successor or Transferee.

(a) Upon any consolidation or merger of the Issuer in accordance with Section 310(a), the Person formed by or surviving such consolidation or merger (if other than the Issuer) shall succeed to, and be substituted for, and may exercise every right and power of, the Issuer under this Indenture with the same effect as if such Person had been named as the Issuer herein.

(b) Upon a conveyance or transfer of all of the properties or assets of the Issuer pursuant to Section 3.10(b), the Issuer will be released from every covenant and agreement of this Indenture to be observed or performed on the part of the Issuer with respect to the Notes immediately upon the delivery of written notice to the Indenture Trustee stating that the Issuer is to be so released.

Section 3.12. No Other Business. The Issuer shall not engage in any business other than financing, purchasing, owning, selling and managing the Receivables in the manner contemplated by this Indenture and the other Basic Documents and activities incidental thereto.

Section 3.13. No Borrowing. The Issuer shall not issue, incur, assume, guarantee or otherwise become liable, directly or indirectly, for any indebtedness except for (i) the Notes and (ii) any other indebtedness permitted by or arising under the other Basic Documents.

Section 3.14. Servicer's Obligations. The Issuer shall cause the Servicer to comply with Sections 3.10, 3.11, 3.12, 4.10 and Article Eight of the Sale and Servicing Agreement.

Section 3.15. Guarantees, Loans, Advances and Other Liabilities. Except as contemplated by the Basic Documents, the Issuer shall not make any loan or advance or credit to, or guarantee (directly or indirectly or by an instrument having the effect of assuring another's payment or performance on any obligation or capability of so doing or otherwise), endorse or otherwise become contingently liable, directly or indirectly, in connection with the obligations, stocks or dividends of, or own, purchase, repurchase or acquire (or agree contingently to do so) any stock, obligations, assets or securities of, or any other interest in, or make any capital contribution to, any other Person.

Section 3.16. Capital Expenditures. The Issuer shall not make any expenditure (by long-term or operating lease or otherwise) for capital assets (either realty or personalty).

Section 3.17. Removal of Administrator. So long as any Notes are Outstanding, the Issuer shall not remove the Administrator without cause unless the Rating Agency Condition shall have been satisfied in connection with such removal.

Section 3.18. Restricted Payments. Except as expressly permitted by the Basic Documents, the Issuer shall not, directly or indirectly, (i) pay any dividend or make any distribution (by reduction of capital or otherwise), whether in cash, property, securities or a combination thereof, to the Owner Trustee or any owner of a beneficial interest in the Issuer or otherwise with respect to any ownership or equity interest or security in or of the Issuer or to the Servicer, (ii) redeem, purchase, retire or otherwise acquire for value any such ownership or equity interest or security or (iii) set aside or otherwise segregate any amounts for any such purpose; provided, however, that the Issuer may make, or cause to be made, (a) distributions as contemplated by, and to the extent funds are available for such purpose under, the Sale and Servicing Agreement or the Trust Agreement and (b) payments to the Indenture Trustee pursuant to Section 1.02(b)(ii) of the Administration Agreement. The Issuer will not, directly or indirectly, make payments to or distributions from the Collection Account except in accordance with this Indenture and the Basic Documents.

Section 3.19. Notice of Events of Default. The Issuer shall give a Responsible Officer of the Indenture Trustee and each Rating Agency prompt written notice of each Event of Default hereunder and each default on the part of the Servicer or the Seller of its obligations under the Sale and Servicing Agreement.

Section 3.20. Further Instruments and Acts. Upon request of the Indenture Trustee, the Issuer will execute and deliver such further instruments and do such further acts as may be reasonably necessary or proper to carry out more effectively the purpose of this Indenture.

Section 3.21. Compliance with Laws. The Issuer shall comply with the requirements of all applicable laws, the non-compliance with which would, individually or in the aggregate, materially and adversely affect the ability of the Issuer to perform its obligations under the Notes, this Indenture or any Basic Document.

Section 3.22. Amendments of Sale and Servicing Agreement and Trust Agreement. The Issuer shall not agree to, any amendment to Section 9.01 of the Sale and Servicing Agreement or Section 11.01 of the Trust Agreement to eliminate the requirements thereunder that the Indenture Trustee or the Holders of the Notes consent to amendments thereto as provided therein.

ARTICLE FOUR

SATISFACTION AND DISCHARGE

Section 4.01. Satisfaction and Discharge of Indenture. This Indenture shall cease to be of further effect with respect to the Notes except as to (i) rights of registration of transfer and exchange, (ii) substitution of mutilated, destroyed, lost or stolen Notes, (iii) rights of Noteholders to receive payments of principal thereof and interest thereon, (iv) Sections 3.03, 3.04, 3.05, 3.08, 3.10, 3.12, 3.13, 3.20 and 3.22, (v) the rights, obligations and immunities of the Indenture Trustee hereunder (including the rights of the Indenture Trustee under Section 6.07 and the obligations of the Indenture Trustee under Section 4.02) and (vi) the rights of Noteholders as beneficiaries hereof with respect to the property so deposited with the Indenture Trustee payable to all or any of them, and the Indenture Trustee, on written demand of and at the expense of the Issuer, shall execute proper instruments acknowledging satisfaction and discharge of this Indenture with respect to the Notes, when

(i) either

(A) all Notes theretofore authenticated and delivered (other than (i) Notes that have been destroyed, lost or stolen and that have been replaced or paid as provided in Section 2.05 and (ii) Notes for whose payment money has theretofore been deposited in trust or segregated and held in trust by the Issuer and thereafter repaid to the Issuer or discharged from such trust, as provided in Section 3.03) have been delivered to the Indenture Trustee for cancellation; or

(B) all Notes not theretofore delivered to the Indenture Trustee for cancellation

(1) have become due and payable,

(2) will become due and payable at the Class A-4 Final Payment Date within one year, or

(3) are to be called for redemption within one year under arrangements satisfactory to the Indenture Trustee for the giving of notice of redemption by the Indenture Trustee in the name, and at the expense, of the Issuer,

and the Issuer, in the case of clauses (1), (2) or (3) above, has irrevocably deposited or caused to be irrevocably deposited with the Indenture Trustee cash or direct obligations of or obligations guaranteed by the United States (which will mature prior to the date such amounts are payable), in trust for such purpose, in an amount sufficient to pay and discharge the entire indebtedness on such Notes not theretofore delivered to the Indenture Trustee for cancellation when due to the related Final Payment Date or Redemption Date (if Notes shall have been called for redemption pursuant to Section 10.01), as the case may be;

(ii) the Issuer has paid or performed or caused to be paid or performed all amounts and obligations which the Issuer may owe to or on behalf of the Indenture Trustee for the benefit of the Noteholders under this Indenture or the Notes; and

(iii) the Issuer has delivered to the Indenture Trustee an Officer's Certificate, an Opinion of Counsel and (if required by the TIA or the Indenture Trustee) an Independent Certificate from a firm of certified public accountants, each meeting the applicable requirements of Section 11.01 (a) and, subject to Section 11.02, each stating that all conditions precedent herein provided for relating to the satisfaction and discharge of this Indenture have been complied with.

Section 4.02. Application of Trust Money. All monies deposited with the Indenture Trustee pursuant to Section 4.01 shall be held in trust in a segregated non-interest bearing account and applied by it, in accordance with the provisions of the Notes and this Indenture, to the payment, either directly or through any Paying Agent, as the Indenture Trustee may determine, to the Holders of the particular Notes for the payment or redemption of which such monies have been deposited with the Indenture Trustee, of all sums due and to become due thereon for principal and interest; but such monies need not be segregated from other funds of the Issuer except to the extent required herein or in the Sale and Servicing Agreement or required by law.

Section 4.03. Repayment of Monies Held by Paying Agent. In connection with the satisfaction and discharge of this Indenture with respect to the Notes, all monies then held by any Paying Agent other than the Indenture Trustee under the provisions of this Indenture with respect to such Notes shall, upon demand of the Issuer, be paid to the Indenture Trustee to be held and applied according to Section 3.03 and thereupon such Paying Agent shall be released from all further liability with respect to such monies.

ARTICLE FIVE

REMEDIES

Section 5.01. Events of Default. "Event of Default", wherever used herein, means any one of the following events (whatever the reason for such Event of Default and whether it shall be voluntary or involuntary or be effected by operation of law or pursuant to any judgment, decree or order of any court or any order, rule or regulation of any administrative or governmental body):

(i) default by the Issuer in the payment of any interest on any Note when the same becomes due and payable, and such default shall continue for a period of five days;

(ii) default by the Issuer in the payment of the principal of or any installment of the principal of any Note when the same becomes due and payable;

(iii) default in the observance or performance of any covenant or agreement of the Issuer made in this Indenture (other than a covenant or agreement, a default in the observance or performance of which is elsewhere in this Section specifically dealt with), or any representation or warranty of the Issuer made in this Indenture or in any certificate or other writing delivered pursuant hereto or in connection herewith proving to have been incorrect in any material respect as of the time when the same shall have been made, and such default shall continue or not be cured, or the circumstance or condition in respect of which such misrepresentation or warranty was incorrect shall not have been eliminated or otherwise cured, for a period of 30 days after there shall have been given, by registered or certified mail, to the Issuer by the Indenture Trustee or to the Issuer and the Indenture Trustee by the Holders of at least 25% of the Outstanding Amount, a written notice specifying such default or incorrect representation or warranty and requiring it to be remedied and stating that such notice is a "Notice of Default" hereunder;

(iv) the filing of a decree or order for relief by a court having jurisdiction in the premises in respect of the Issuer or any substantial part of the Owner Trust Estate in an involuntary case under any applicable federal or state bankruptcy, insolvency or other similar law now or hereafter in effect, or appointing a receiver, liquidator, assignee, custodian, trustee, sequestrator or similar official of the Issuer or for any substantial part of the Owner Trust Estate, or ordering the winding-up or liquidation of the Issuer's affairs, and such decree or order shall remain unstayed and in effect for a period of 60 consecutive days; or

(v) the commencement by the Issuer of a voluntary case under any applicable federal or state bankruptcy, insolvency or other similar law now or hereafter in effect, or the consent by the Issuer to the entry of an order for relief in an involuntary case under any such law, or the consent by the Issuer to the appointment or taking possession by a receiver, liquidator, assignee, custodian, trustee, sequestrator or similar official of the Issuer or for any substantial part of the Owner Trust Estate, or the making by the Issuer of any general assignment for the benefit of creditors, or the failure by the Issuer generally to pay its debts as such debts become due, or the taking of any action by the Issuer in furtherance of any of the foregoing.

The Issuer shall deliver to a Responsible Officer of the Indenture Trustee, within five days after the occurrence thereof, written notice in the form of an Officer's Certificate of any event which with the giving of notice and the lapse of time would become an Event of Default under clause (iii) above, its status and what action the Issuer is taking or proposes to take with respect thereto.

Section 5.02. Acceleration of Maturity, Rescission and Annulment.

(a) If an Event of Default should occur and be continuing, then and in every such case the Indenture Trustee or the Holders of Notes representing not less than a majority of the Outstanding Amount may declare all the Notes to be immediately due and payable, by a notice in writing to the Issuer (and to the Indenture Trustee if given by Noteholders), and upon any such declaration the unpaid principal amount of such Notes, together with accrued and unpaid interest thereon through the date of acceleration, shall become immediately due and payable.

(b) At any time after such declaration of acceleration of maturity has been made and before a judgment or decree for payment of the money due has been obtained by the Indenture Trustee as hereinafter in this Article provided, the Holders of Notes representing a majority of the Outstanding Amount, by written notice to the Issuer and the Indenture Trustee, may rescind and annul such declaration and its consequences if:

(i) the Issuer has paid or deposited with the Indenture Trustee a sum sufficient to pay:

(A) all payments of principal of and interest on all Notes and all other amounts that would then be due hereunder or upon such Notes if the Event of Default giving rise to such acceleration had not occurred; and

(B) all sums paid or advanced by the Indenture Trustee hereunder and the reasonable compensation, expenses, disbursements and advances of the Indenture Trustee and its agents and counsel; and

(ii) all Events of Default, other than the nonpayment of the principal of the Notes that has become due solely by such acceleration, have been cured or waived as provided in Section 5.12.

No such rescission shall affect any subsequent default or impair any right consequent thereto.

Section 5.03. Collection of Indebtedness and Suits for Enforcement by Indenture Trustee.

(a) The Issuer covenants that if the Notes are accelerated following the occurrence of an Event of Default, the Issuer will, upon demand of the Indenture Trustee, pay to it, for the benefit of the Holders of the Notes, the whole amount then due and payable on such Notes for principal and interest, with interest on the overdue principal and, to the extent payment at such rate of interest shall be legally enforceable, on overdue installments of interest at the related Interest Rate and, in addition thereto, such further amount as shall be sufficient to cover the costs and expenses of collection, including the reasonable compensation, expenses, disbursements and advances of the Indenture Trustee and its agents and counsel.

(b) In case the Issuer shall fail forthwith to pay such amounts upon such demand, the Indenture Trustee, in its own name and as trustee of an express trust, may institute a Proceeding for the collection of the sums so due and unpaid, and may prosecute such Proceeding to judgment or final decree and may enforce the same against the Issuer or other obligor upon such Notes and collect in the manner provided by law out of the property of the Issuer or other obligor upon such Notes, wherever situated, the monies adjudged or decreed to be payable.

(c) If an Event of Default occurs and is continuing, the Indenture Trustee may, as more particularly provided in Section 5.04, in its discretion, proceed to protect and enforce its rights and the rights of the Noteholders, by such appropriate Proceedings as the Indenture Trustee shall deem most effective to protect and enforce any such rights, whether for the specific enforcement of any covenant or agreement in this Indenture or in aid of the exercise of any power granted herein, or to enforce any other proper remedy or legal or equitable right vested in the Indenture Trustee by this Indenture or by law.

(d) In case there shall be pending, relative to the Issuer or any other obligor upon the Notes or any Person having or claiming an ownership interest in the Owner Trust Estate, Proceedings under Title 11 of the United States Code or any other applicable federal or state bankruptcy, insolvency or other similar law, or in case a receiver, assignee or trustee in bankruptcy or reorganization, or liquidator, sequestrator or similar official shall have been appointed for or taken possession of the Issuer or its property or such other obligor or Person, or in case of any other comparable judicial Proceedings relative to the Issuer or other obligor upon the Notes, or to the creditors or property of the Issuer or such other obligor, the Indenture Trustee, irrespective of whether the principal of any Notes shall then be due and payable as therein expressed or by declaration or otherwise and irrespective of whether the Indenture Trustee shall have made any demand pursuant to the provisions of this Section, shall be entitled and empowered, by intervention in such Proceedings or otherwise:

(i) to file and prove a claim or claims for the entire amount of principal and interest owing and unpaid in respect of the Notes and to file such other papers or documents as may be necessary or advisable in order to have the claims of the Indenture Trustee (including any claim for reasonable compensation to the Indenture Trustee and each predecessor Indenture Trustee, and their respective agents, attorneys and counsel, and for reimbursement of all expenses and liabilities incurred, and all advances made, by the Indenture Trustee and each predecessor Indenture Trustee, except as a result of negligence or bad faith) and of the Noteholders allowed in such Proceedings;

(ii) unless prohibited by applicable law and regulations, to vote on behalf of the Holders of Notes in any election of a trustee, a standby trustee or Person performing similar functions in any such Proceedings;

(iii) to collect and receive any monies or other property payable or deliverable on any such claims and to distribute all amounts received with respect to the claims of the Noteholders and of the Indenture Trustee on their behalf; and

(iv) to file such proofs of claim and other papers or documents as may be necessary or advisable in order to have the claims of the Indenture Trustee or the Holders of Notes allowed in any Proceedings relative to the Issuer, its creditors and its property;

and any trustee, receiver, liquidator, custodian or other similar official in any such Proceeding is hereby authorized by each of such Noteholders to make payments to the Indenture Trustee and, in the event that the Indenture Trustee shall consent to the making of payments directly to such Noteholders, to pay to the Indenture Trustee such amounts as shall be sufficient to cover reasonable compensation to the Indenture Trustee, each predecessor Indenture Trustee and their respective agents, attorneys and counsel, and all other expenses and liabilities incurred, and all advances made, by the Indenture Trustee and each predecessor Indenture Trustee except as a result of negligence or bad faith.

(e) Nothing herein contained shall be deemed to authorize the Indenture Trustee to authorize or consent to or vote for or accept or adopt on behalf of any Noteholder any plan of reorganization, arrangement, adjustment or composition affecting the Notes or the rights of any Holder thereof or to authorize the Indenture Trustee to vote in respect of the claim of any Noteholder in any such proceeding except, as aforesaid, to vote for the election of a trustee in bankruptcy or similar Person.

(f) All rights of action and of asserting claims under this Indenture, or under any of the Notes, may be enforced by the Indenture Trustee without the possession of any of the Notes or the production thereof in any trial or other Proceedings relative thereto, and any such action or Proceedings instituted by the Indenture Trustee shall be brought in its own name as trustee of an express trust, and any recovery of judgment, subject to the payment of the expenses, disbursements and compensation of the Indenture Trustee, each predecessor Indenture Trustee and their respective agents and attorneys, shall be for the ratable benefit of the Holders of the Notes.

(g) In any Proceedings brought by the Indenture Trustee (including any Proceedings involving the interpretation of any provision of this Indenture to which the Indenture Trustee shall be a party), the Indenture Trustee shall be held to represent all the Holders of the Notes, and it shall not be necessary to make any Noteholder a party to any such Proceedings.

Section 5.04. Remedies, Priorities.

(a) If an Event of Default shall have occurred and be continuing, the Indenture Trustee may do one or more of the following (subject to Sections 5.02 and 5.05):

(i) institute Proceedings in its own name and/or as trustee of an express trust for the collection of all amounts then payable on the Notes or under this Indenture with respect thereto, whether by declaration or otherwise, enforce any judgment obtained and collect from the Issuer and any other obligor upon such Notes monies adjudged due;

(ii) institute Proceedings from time to time for the complete or partial foreclosure of this Indenture with respect to the Owner Trust Estate;

(iii) exercise any remedies of a secured party under the UCC and any other remedy available to the Indenture Trustee and take any other appropriate action to protect and enforce the rights and remedies of the Indenture Trustee on behalf of the Noteholders under this Indenture; and

(iv) sell the Owner Trust Estate or any portion thereof or rights or interest therein, at one or more public or private sales called and conducted in any manner permitted by law; provided, however, that the Indenture Trustee may not sell or otherwise liquidate the Owner Trust Estate following an Event of Default, other than an Event of Default described in Section 5.01(i) or (ii), unless (A) the Holders of 100% of the Outstanding Amount consent thereto, (B) the proceeds of such sale or liquidation distributable to the Noteholders are sufficient to discharge in full all amounts then due and unpaid upon such Notes for principal and interest or (C) the Indenture Trustee determines that the Owner Trust Estate will not continue to provide sufficient funds for the payment of principal of and interest on the Notes as would have become due if the Notes had not been declared due and payable, and the Indenture Trustee obtains the consent of Holders of 66 2/3% of the Outstanding Amount. In determining such sufficiency or insufficiency with respect to clause (B) and (C) above, the Indenture Trustee may, but need not, obtain, at the expense of the Issuer, and rely upon an opinion of an Independent investment banking or accounting firm of national reputation as to the feasibility of such proposed action and as to the sufficiency of the Owner Trust Estate for such purpose.

(b) If the Indenture Trustee collects any money or property pursuant to this Article, it shall pay out the money or property in the following order and priority:

(i) to the Indenture Trustee and the Owner Trustee, any amounts due under the Trust Agreement or Section 6.07 hereof;

(ii) to the Servicer, for amounts due and unpaid in respect of Nonrecoverable Advances under the Sale and Servicing Agreement;

(iii) to the Servicer, for amounts due and unpaid in respect of the Total Servicing Fee under the Sale and Servicing Agreement;

(iv) to the Holders of the Notes of each Class, the Note Interest Distributable Amount ratably in proportion to the Note Interest Distributable Amount for each Class at their respective Interest Rates;

(v) to the Holders of Notes of all Classes, the outstanding principal amount of the Notes, pro rata in proportion to the Outstanding principal amount of each Class;

(vi) to the Holders of the Trust Certificates, the Certificate Interest Distributable Amount;

(vii) to the Holders of the Trust Certificates, the outstanding principal amount of the Trust Certificates; and

(viii) to the Seller, any remaining amount.

The Indenture Trustee may fix a record date and payment date for any payment to Noteholders pursuant to this Section. At least 15 days before such record date, the Issuer shall mail to each Noteholder and the Indenture Trustee a notice that states the record date, the payment date and the amount to be paid.

Section 5.05. Optional Preservation of the Receivables. If the Notes have been declared to be due and payable under Section 5.02 following an Event of Default and such declaration and its consequences have not been rescinded and annulled, the Indenture Trustee may, but need not, elect to maintain possession of the Owner Trust Estate. It is the desire of the parties hereto and the Noteholders that there be at all times sufficient funds for the payment of principal of and interest on the Notes, and the Indenture Trustee shall take such desire into account when determining whether or not to maintain possession of the Owner Trust Estate. In determining whether to maintain possession of the Owner Trust Estate, the Indenture Trustee may, but need not, obtain, at the expense of the Issuer, and rely upon an opinion of an Independent investment banking or accounting firm of national reputation as to the feasibility of such proposed action and as to the sufficiency of the Owner Trust Estate for such purpose.

Section 5.06. Limitation of Suits. No Holder of any Note shall have any right to institute any Proceeding, judicial or otherwise, with respect to this Indenture, or for the appointment of a receiver or trustee, or for any other remedy hereunder, unless:

(i) such Holder has previously given written notice to the Indenture Trustee of a continuing Event of Default;

(ii) the Holders of not less than 25% of the Outstanding Amount have made written request to the Indenture Trustee to institute such Proceeding in respect of such Event of Default in its own name as Indenture Trustee hereunder;

(iii) such Holder or Holders have offered to the Indenture Trustee reasonable indemnity against the costs, expenses and liabilities to be incurred in complying with such request;

(iv) the Indenture Trustee for 60 days after its receipt of such notice, request and offer of indemnity has failed to institute such Proceedings; and

(v) no direction inconsistent with such written request has been given to the Indenture Trustee during such 60-day period by the Holders of a majority of the Outstanding Amount.

It is understood and intended that no one or more Holders of Notes shall have any right in any manner whatever by virtue of, or by availing of, any provision of this Indenture to affect, disturb or prejudice the rights of any other Holders of Notes or to obtain or to seek to obtain priority or preference over any other Holders or to enforce any right under this Indenture, except in the manner herein provided.

In the event the Indenture Trustee shall receive conflicting or inconsistent requests and indemnity from two or more groups of Holders of Notes, each representing less than a majority of the Outstanding Amount, the Indenture Trustee in its sole discretion may determine what action, if any, shall be taken, notwithstanding any other provisions of this Indenture. The Indenture Trustee shall not be liable for any such determination made in good faith.

Section 5.07. Unconditional Rights of Noteholders to Receive Principal and Interest. Notwithstanding any other provisions in this Indenture, the Holder of any Note shall have the right, which is absolute and unconditional, to receive payment of the principal of and interest, if any, on such Note on or after the respective due dates thereof expressed in such Note or in this Indenture (or, in the case of redemption, on or after the Redemption Date) and to institute suit for the enforcement of any such payment, and such right shall not be impaired without the consent of such Holder.

Section 5.08. Restoration of Rights and Remedies. If the Indenture Trustee or any Noteholder has instituted any Proceeding to enforce any right or remedy under this Indenture and such Proceeding has been discontinued or abandoned for any reason or has been determined adversely to the Indenture Trustee or to such Noteholder, then and in every such case the Issuer, the Indenture Trustee and the Noteholders shall, subject to any determination in such Proceeding, be restored severally and respectively to their former positions hereunder, and thereafter all rights and remedies of the Indenture Trustee and the Noteholders shall continue as though no such Proceeding had been instituted.

Section 5.09. Rights and Remedies Cumulative. No right or remedy herein conferred upon or reserved to the Indenture Trustee or to the Noteholders is intended to be exclusive of any other right or remedy, and every right and remedy shall, to the extent permitted by law, be cumulative and in addition to every other right and remedy given hereunder or now or hereafter existing at law or in equity or otherwise. The assertion or employment of any right or remedy hereunder, or otherwise, shall not prevent the concurrent assertion or employment of any other appropriate right or remedy.

Section 5.10. Delay or Omission Not a Waiver. No delay or omission of the Indenture Trustee or any Holder of any Note to exercise any right or remedy accruing upon any Default or Event of Default shall impair any such right or remedy or constitute a waiver of any such Default or Event of Default or an acquiescence therein. Every right and remedy given by this Article or by law to the Indenture Trustee or to the Noteholders may be exercised from time to time, and as often as may be deemed expedient, by the Indenture Trustee or by the Noteholders, as the case may be.

Section 5.11. Control by Noteholders. The Holders of Notes representing a majority of the Outstanding Amount shall have the right to direct the time, method and place of conducting any Proceeding for any remedy available to the Indenture Trustee with respect to the Notes or exercising any trust or power conferred on the Indenture Trustee; provided that:

(i) such direction shall not be in conflict with any rule of law or with this Indenture;

(ii) subject to the terms of Section 5.04, any direction to the Indenture Trustee to sell or liquidate the Owner Trust Estate shall be by the Holders of Notes representing not less than 100% of the Outstanding Amount;

(iii) if the conditions set forth in Section 5.05 have been satisfied and the Indenture Trustee elects to retain the Owner Trust Estate pursuant to such Section, then any direction to the Indenture Trustee by the Holders of Notes representing less than 100% of the Outstanding Amount to sell or liquidate the Owner Trust Estate shall be of no force and effect; and

(iv) the Indenture Trustee may take any other action deemed proper by the Indenture Trustee that is not inconsistent with such direction.

Notwithstanding the rights of Noteholders set forth in this Section, subject to Section 6.01, the Indenture Trustee need not take any action for which it will not be adequately indemnified or might materially adversely affect the rights of any Noteholders not consenting to such action.

Section 5.12. Waiver of Past Defaults. Prior to the declaration of the acceleration of the maturity of the Notes as provided in Section 5.02, the Holders of Notes of not less than a majority of the Outstanding Amount may waive any past Default or Event of Default and its consequences except a Default (i) in payment of principal of or interest on any of the Notes or (ii) in respect of a covenant or provision hereof which cannot be modified or amended without the consent of the Holder of each Note. In the case of any such waiver, the Issuer, the Indenture Trustee and the Holders of the Notes shall respectively be restored to their former positions and rights hereunder; but no such waiver shall extend to any subsequent or other Default or Event of Default or impair any right consequent thereto. Upon any such waiver, such Default shall cease to exist and be deemed to have been cured and not to have occurred, and any Event of Default arising therefrom shall be deemed to have been cured and not to have occurred, for every purpose of this Indenture.

Section 5.13. Undertaking for Costs. All parties to this Indenture agree, and each Holder of any Note by such Holder's acceptance thereof shall be deemed to have agreed, that any court may in its discretion require, in any suit for the enforcement of any right or remedy under this Indenture, or in any suit against the Indenture Trustee for any action taken, suffered or omitted by it as Indenture Trustee, the filing by any party litigant in such suit of an undertaking to pay the costs of such suit, and that such court may in its discretion assess reasonable costs, including reasonable attorneys' fees, against any party litigant in such suit, having due regard to the merits and good faith of the claims or defenses made by such party litigant; but the provisions of this Section shall not apply to (i) any suit instituted by the Indenture Trustee, (ii) any suit instituted by any Noteholder, or group of Noteholders, in each case holding in the aggregate more than 10% of the Outstanding Amount or (iii) any suit instituted by any Noteholder for the enforcement of the payment of principal of or interest on any Note on or after the respective due dates expressed in such Note and in this Indenture (or, in the case of redemption, on or after the Redemption Date).

Section 5.14. Waiver of Stay or Extension Laws. The Issuer covenants (to the extent that it may lawfully do so) that it will not at any time insist upon, or plead or in any manner whatsoever claim or take the benefit or advantage of, any stay or extension law wherever enacted, now or at any time hereafter in force, that may affect the covenants or the performance of this Indenture; and the Issuer (to the extent that it may lawfully do so) hereby expressly waives all benefit or advantage of any such law, and covenants that it will not hinder, delay or impede the execution of any power herein granted to the Indenture Trustee, but will suffer and permit the execution of every such power as though no such law had been enacted.

Section 5.15. Action on Notes. The Indenture Trustee's right to seek and recover judgment on the Notes or under this Indenture shall not be affected by the seeking, obtaining or application of any other relief under or with respect to this Indenture. Neither the lien of this Indenture nor any rights or remedies of the Indenture Trustee or the Noteholders shall be impaired by the recovery of any judgment by the Indenture Trustee against the Issuer or by the levy of any execution under such judgment upon any portion of the Owner Trust Estate or upon any of the assets of the Issuer. Any money or property collected by the Indenture Trustee shall be applied in accordance with Section 5.04(b).

Section 5.16. Performance and Enforcement of Certain Obligations.

(a) Promptly following a request from the Indenture Trustee to do so and at the Administrator's expense, the Issuer shall take all such lawful action as the Indenture Trustee may request to compel or secure the performance and observance by the Seller or the Servicer, as applicable, of each of their obligations to the Issuer under or in connection with the Sale and Servicing Agreement in accordance with the terms thereof, and to exercise any and all rights, remedies, powers and privileges lawfully available to the Issuer under or in connection with the Sale and Servicing Agreement to the extent and in the manner directed by the Indenture Trustee, including the transmission of notices of default on the part of the Seller or the Servicer thereunder and the institution of legal or administrative actions or proceedings to compel or secure performance by the

Seller or the Servicer of each of their obligations under the Sale and Servicing Agreement.

(b) If an Event of Default has occurred and is continuing, the Indenture Trustee may, and at the direction (which direction shall be in writing) of the Holders of 66 2/3% of the Outstanding Amount shall, exercise all rights, remedies, powers, privileges and claims of the Issuer against the Seller or the Servicer under or in connection with the Sale and Servicing Agreement, including the right or power to take any action to compel or secure performance or observance by the Seller or the Servicer, of each of their obligations to the Issuer thereunder and to give any consent, request, notice, direction, approval, extension or waiver under the Sale and Servicing Agreement, and any right of the Issuer to take such action shall be suspended.

ARTICLE SIX
THE INDENTURE TRUSTEE

Section 6.01. Duties of Indenture Trustee.

(a) If an Event of Default has occurred and is continuing of which a Responsible Officer of the Indenture Trustee has actual knowledge, the Indenture Trustee shall exercise the rights and powers vested in it by this Indenture and use the same degree of care and skill in their exercise as a prudent person would exercise or use under the circumstances in the conduct of such person's own affairs; provided, however, that if the Indenture Trustee shall assume the duties of the Servicer pursuant to Section 3.07(e), the Indenture Trustee in performing such duties shall use the degree of care and skill customarily exercised by a prudent institutional servicer with respect to installment sale contracts that it services for itself or others.

(b) Except during the continuance of an Event of Default of which a Responsible Officer of the Indenture Trustee has actual knowledge:

(i) the Indenture Trustee shall undertake to perform such duties and only such duties as are specifically set forth in this Indenture and no implied covenants or obligations shall be read into this Indenture against the Indenture Trustee; and

(ii) in the absence of bad faith on its part, the Indenture Trustee may conclusively rely, as to the truth of the statements and the correctness of the opinions expressed therein, upon certificates or opinions furnished to the Indenture Trustee and conforming to the requirements of this Indenture; however, the Indenture Trustee shall examine the certificates and opinions to determine whether or not they conform to the requirements of this Indenture.

(c) The Indenture Trustee may not be relieved from liability for its own negligent action, its own negligent failure to act or its own willful misconduct, except that:

(i) this paragraph does not limit the effect of Section 6.01(b);

(ii) the Indenture Trustee shall not be liable for any error of judgment made in good faith by a Responsible Officer unless it is proved that the Indenture Trustee was negligent in ascertaining the pertinent facts; and

(iii) the Indenture Trustee shall not be liable with respect to any action it takes or omits to take in good faith in accordance with a direction received by it pursuant to Section 5.11.

(d) Every provision of this Indenture that in any way relates to the Indenture Trustee is subject to paragraphs (a), (b) and (c) of this Section.

(e) The Indenture Trustee shall not be liable for interest on any money received by it except as the Indenture Trustee may agree in writing with the Issuer.

(f) Money held in trust by the Indenture Trustee need not be segregated from other funds except to the extent required by law or the terms of this Indenture or the Sale and Servicing Agreement.

(g) No provision of this Indenture shall require the Indenture Trustee to expend or risk its own funds or otherwise incur financial liability in the performance of any of its duties hereunder or in the exercise of any of its rights or powers, if it shall have reasonable grounds to believe that repayment of such funds or adequate indemnity against such risk or liability is not reasonably assured to it.

(h) Every provision of this Indenture relating to the conduct or affecting the liability of or affording protection to the Indenture Trustee shall be subject to the provisions of this Section and to the provisions of the TIA.

(i) The Indenture Trustee shall not be charged with knowledge of any Event of Default unless either (i) a Responsible Officer shall have actual knowledge of such Event of Default or (ii) written notice of such Event of Default shall have been given to the Indenture Trustee in accordance with the provisions of this Indenture.

(j) The Indenture Trustee shall have no duty (A) to see to any recording, filing, or depositing of this Indenture or any agreement referred to herein or any financing statement or continuation statement evidencing a security interest, or to see to the maintenance of any such recording or filing or depositing or to any rerecording, refiling or redepositing of any thereof, (B) to see to any insurance, (C) to see to the payment or discharge of any tax, assessment, or other governmental charge or any lien or encumbrance of any kind owing with respect to, assessed or levied against, any part of the Owner Trust Estate, or (D) to confirm or verify the contents of any reports or certificates of the Servicer delivered to the Indenture Trustee pursuant to this Indenture believed by the Indenture Trustee to be genuine and to have been signed or presented by the proper party or parties.

Section 6.02. Rights of Indenture Trustee.

(a) Except as otherwise provided in the second succeeding sentence, the Indenture Trustee may conclusively rely on, and shall be protected in acting or refraining from acting upon, any resolution, Officer's Certificate, Opinion of Counsel, certificate of auditors, Independent Certificate or any other document believed by it to be genuine and to have been signed or presented by the proper person. The Indenture Trustee need not investigate any fact, calculation or matter stated in the document. Notwithstanding the foregoing, the Indenture Trustee, upon receipt of all resolutions, certificates, statements, opinions, reports, documents, orders or other instruments furnished to the Indenture Trustee that shall be specifically required to be furnished pursuant to any provision of this Indenture, shall examine them to determine whether they comply as to form to the requirements of this Indenture.

(b) Before the Indenture Trustee acts or refrains from acting, it may require an Officer's Certificate or an Opinion of Counsel. The Indenture Trustee shall not be liable for any action it takes or omits to take in good faith in reliance on an Officer's Certificate or Opinion of Counsel.

(c) The Indenture Trustee may execute any of the trusts or powers hereunder or perform any duties hereunder either directly or by or through agents or attorneys or a custodian or nominee, and the Indenture Trustee shall not be responsible for any misconduct or negligence on the part of, or for the supervision of, any such agent, attorney, custodian or nominee appointed with due care by it hereunder.

(d) The Indenture Trustee shall not be liable for any action it takes or omits to take in good faith which it believes to be authorized or within its rights or powers; provided, that the Indenture Trustee's conduct does not constitute willful misconduct, negligence or bad faith.

(e) The Indenture Trustee may consult with counsel, and the advice or opinion of counsel with respect to legal matters relating to this Indenture and the Notes shall be full and complete authorization and protection from liability in respect to any action taken, omitted or suffered by it hereunder in good faith and in accordance with the advice or opinion of such counsel.

(f) The Indenture Trustee shall be under no obligation to exercise any of the trusts or powers vested in it by this Indenture or to institute, conduct or defend any litigation hereunder or in relation hereto at the request, order or direction of any of the Noteholders, pursuant to the provisions of this Indenture, unless such Noteholders shall have offered to the Indenture Trustee security or indemnity reasonably satisfactory to the Indenture Trustee against the costs, expenses and liabilities which may be incurred therein or thereby; provided, however, nothing contained herein shall, however, relieve the Indenture Trustee of the obligation, upon the occurrence of an Event of Default of which a Responsible Officer of the Indenture Trustee shall have actual knowledge (which has not been cured), to exercise such of the rights and powers vested in it by this Indenture, and to use the same degree of care and skill in their exercise, as a prudent person would exercise or use under the circumstances in the conduct of such person's own affairs.

(g) The right of the Indenture Trustee to perform any discretionary act enumerated in this Indenture shall not be construed as a duty, and the Indenture

Trustee shall not be answerable in the performance of such act for other than its negligence or willful misconduct.

(h) The Indenture Trustee shall not be required to give any bond or surety in respect of the execution of the Owner Trust Estate created hereby or the powers granted hereunder.

(i) All rights of action and claims under this Indenture or the Note may be prosecuted and enforced by the Indenture Trustee without the possession of any of the Notes or the production thereof in any proceeding relating thereto, any such proceeding instituted by the Indenture Trustee shall be brought in its own name or in its capacity as Indenture Trustee. Any recovery of judgment shall, after provision for the payments to the Indenture Trustee provided for in Section 6.07, be for the ratable benefit of the Noteholders in respect of which such judgment has been recovered.

Section 6.03. Individual Rights of Indenture Trustee. The Indenture Trustee in its individual or any other capacity may become the owner or pledgee of Notes and may otherwise deal with the Issuer or its Affiliates with the same rights it would have if it were not Indenture Trustee. Any Paying Agent, Note Registrar, co-registrar or co-paying agent may do the same with like rights. However, the Indenture Trustee must comply with Sections 6.11 and 6.12.

Section 6.04. Indenture Trustee's Disclaimer. The Indenture Trustee shall not be responsible for and makes no representation as to the validity or adequacy of this Indenture, the Owner Trust Estate or the Notes, it shall not be accountable for the Issuer's use of the proceeds from the Notes, and it shall not be responsible for any statement of the Issuer in this Indenture or in any document issued in connection with the sale of the Notes or in the Notes other than the Indenture Trustee's certificate of authentication. The Indenture Trustee shall have no responsibility for filing any financing or continuation statement in any public office at any time or to otherwise perfect or maintain the perfection of any security interest or lien granted to it hereunder or to record this Indenture.

Section 6.05. Notice of Defaults. If a Default occurs and is continuing and if it is known to a Responsible Officer of the Indenture Trustee, the Indenture Trustee shall mail to each Noteholder notice of the Default within 90 days after it occurs. Except in the case of a Default in payment of principal of or interest on any Note (including payments pursuant to the mandatory redemption provisions of such Note), the Indenture Trustee may withhold the notice if and so long as a committee of its Responsible Officers in good faith determines that withholding the notice is in the interests of Noteholders.

Section 6.06. Reports by Indenture Trustee to Holders. The Indenture Trustee may make any statements which it is required to provide available to the applicable Noteholders, including, without limitation, all information as may be required to enable each Noteholder to prepare its respective federal and state income tax returns (and, at its option, any additional files containing the same information in an alternative format), via http://www.jpmorgan.com/absmbs. The Indenture Trustee shall have the right to change the way such statements are distributed in order to make such distribution more convenient and/or more accessible to the above parties and the Indenture Trustee shall provide timely and adequate notification to all above parties regarding any such changes; provided, however, that the Indenture Trustee will also mail copies of any such statements to any requesting Noteholders.

Section 6.07. Compensation and Indemnity. The Issuer shall, or shall cause the Administrator to, (i) pay to the Indenture Trustee from time to time reasonable compensation for its services, which compensation shall not be limited by any law on compensation of a trustee of an express trust, (ii) reimburse the Indenture Trustee for all reasonable out-of-pocket expenses incurred or made by it, including without limitation, costs of collection, in addition to the compensation for its services, which expenses shall include the reasonable compensation and expenses, disbursements and advances of the Indenture Trustee's agents, counsel, accountants and experts and (iii) indemnify the Indenture Trustee and its officers, directors, employees and agents against any and all loss, liability or expense (including reasonable attorneys' fees and expenses) incurred by it in connection with the administration of this trust and the performance of its duties hereunder not resulting from its own willful misconduct, negligence or bad faith. The Indenture Trustee shall notify the Issuer and the Administrator promptly of any claim for which it may seek indemnity. Failure by the Indenture Trustee to so notify the Issuer and the Administrator shall not relieve the Issuer or the Administrator of its obligations hereunder. The Issuer shall, or shall cause the Administrator to, defend any such claim, and the Indenture Trustee may have separate counsel and the Issuer shall, or shall cause the Administrator to, pay the fees and expenses of such counsel. Neither the Issuer nor the Administrator need reimburse any expense or indemnify against any loss, liability or expense incurred by the Indenture Trustee through the Indenture Trustee's own willful misconduct, negligence or bad faith.

The Issuer's payment obligations to the Indenture Trustee pursuant to this Section shall survive the discharge of this Indenture or the earlier resignation or discharge of the Indenture Trustee and shall extend to any co-trustee or separate trustee appointed pursuant to Section 6.10 hereunder. When the Indenture Trustee incurs expenses after the occurrence of a Default specified in Section 5.01 (iv) or (v) with respect to the Issuer, the expenses are intended to constitute expenses of administration under Title 11 of the United States Code or any other applicable federal or state bankruptcy, insolvency or similar law.

Anything in this Indenture to the contrary notwithstanding, in no event shall the Indenture Trustee be liable for special, indirect or consequential loss or damage of any kind whatsoever (including but not limited to lost profits, other than interest due but not paid on the Notes), even if the Indenture Trustee has been advised of the likelihood of such loss or damage and regardless of the form of action.

Section 6.08. Replacement of Indenture Trustee. No resignation or removal of the Indenture Trustee and no appointment of a successor Indenture Trustee shall become effective until the acceptance of appointment by the successor

Indenture Trustee pursuant to this Section. The Indenture Trustee may resign at any time by so notifying the Issuer. Noteholders representing a majority of the Outstanding Amount may remove the Indenture Trustee at any time and appoint a successor Indenture Trustee by so notifying the Indenture Trustee in writing. The Issuer shall remove the Indenture Trustee if:

(i) the Indenture Trustee fails to comply with Section 6.11;

(ii) a court having jurisdiction in the premises in respect of the Indenture Trustee in an involuntary case or proceeding under federal or state banking or bankruptcy laws, as now or hereafter constituted, or any other applicable federal or state bankruptcy, insolvency or other similar law, shall have entered a decree or order granting relief or appointing a receiver, liquidator, assignee, custodian, trustee, conservator, sequestrator (or similar official) for the Indenture Trustee or for any substantial part of the Indenture Trustee's property, or ordering the winding-up or liquidation of the Indenture Trustee's affairs, provided any such decree or order shall have continued unstayed and in effect for a period of 30 consecutive days;

(iii) the Indenture Trustee commences a voluntary case under any federal or state banking or bankruptcy laws, as now or hereafter constituted, or any other applicable federal or state bankruptcy, insolvency or other similar law, or consents to the appointment of or taking possession by a receiver, liquidator, assignee, custodian, trustee, conservator, sequestrator or other similar official for the Indenture Trustee or for any substantial part of the Indenture Trustee's property, or makes any assignment for the benefit of creditors or fails generally to pay its debts as such debts become due or takes any corporate action in furtherance of any of the foregoing; or

(iv) the Indenture Trustee otherwise becomes incapable of acting.

If the Indenture Trustee resigns or is removed or if a vacancy exists in the office of the Indenture Trustee for any reason (the Indenture Trustee in such event being referred to herein as the retiring Indenture Trustee), the Issuer shall promptly appoint a successor Indenture Trustee.

A successor Indenture Trustee shall deliver a written acceptance of its appointment to the retiring Indenture Trustee and to the Issuer. Thereupon the resignation or removal of the retiring Indenture Trustee shall become effective, and the successor Indenture Trustee shall have all the rights, powers and duties of the Indenture Trustee under this Indenture. The successor Indenture Trustee shall mail a notice of its succession to the Noteholders. The retiring Indenture Trustee shall promptly transfer all property held by it as Indenture Trustee to the successor Indenture Trustee.

If a successor Indenture Trustee does not take office within 60 days after the retiring Indenture Trustee resigns or is removed, the retiring Indenture Trustee, the Issuer or the Holders of a majority in Outstanding Amount may petition any court of competent jurisdiction for the appointment of a successor Indenture Trustee.

If the Indenture Trustee fails to comply with Section 6.11, any Noteholder may petition any court of competent jurisdiction for the removal of the Indenture Trustee and the appointment of a successor Indenture Trustee.

Any resignation or removal of the Indenture Trustee and appointment of a successor Indenture Trustee pursuant to the provisions of this Section shall not become effective until acceptance of appointment by the successor Indenture Trustee pursuant to this Section and payment of all fees and expenses owed to the outgoing Indenture Trustee. Notwithstanding the replacement of the Indenture Trustee pursuant to this Section, the Issuer's and the Administrator's obligations under Section 6.07 shall continue for the benefit of the retiring Indenture Trustee.

Section 6.09. Successor Indenture Trustee by Merger. If the Indenture Trustee consolidates or merges with, converts or transfers all or substantially all its corporate trust business or assets to, another corporation or banking association, the resulting, surviving or transferee corporation shall, without any further act, be the successor Indenture Trustee; provided, that such corporation or banking association shall be otherwise qualified and eligible under Section 6.11. The Indenture Trustee shall provide each Rating Agency prior written notice of any such transaction.

In case at the time such successor or successors by merger, conversion or consolidation to the Indenture Trustee shall succeed to the trusts created by this Indenture any of the Notes shall have been authenticated but not delivered, any such successor to the Indenture Trustee may adopt the certificate of authentication of any predecessor trustee and deliver such Notes so authenticated; and in case at that time any of the Notes shall not have been authenticated, any successor to the Indenture Trustee may authenticate such Notes either in the name of any predecessor hereunder or in the name of the successor to the Indenture Trustee; and in all such cases such certificates shall have the full force as is provided anywhere in the Notes or in this Indenture that the certificate of the Indenture Trustee shall have.

Section 6.10. Appointment of Co-Trustee or Separate Trustee.

(a) Notwithstanding any other provision of this Indenture, at any time, for the purpose of meeting any legal requirement of any jurisdiction in which any part of the Owner Trust Estate may at the time be located, the Indenture Trustee and the Administrator, acting jointly, shall have the power and may execute and deliver all instruments to appoint one or more Persons to act as a co-trustee or co-trustees, or separate trustee or separate trustees, of all or any part of the Trust, and to vest in such Person or Persons, in such capacity and for the benefit of the Noteholders, such title to the Owner Trust Estate or any part thereof, and, subject to the other provisions of this Section, such powers, duties, obligations, rights and trusts as the Indenture Trustee may consider necessary or desirable. If the Administrator shall not have joined in such appointment within 15 days after its receipt of a request to do so, the Indenture Trustee alone shall have the power to make such appointment. No co-trustee or separate trustee hereunder shall be required to meet the terms of eligibility as a successor trustee under Section 6.11 and no notice to Noteholders of the appointment of any co-trustee or separate trustee shall be required under Section 6.08.

(b) Every separate trustee and co-trustee shall, to the extent permitted by law, be appointed and act subject to the following provisions and conditions:

(i) all rights, powers, duties and obligations conferred or imposed upon the Indenture Trustee shall be conferred or imposed upon and exercised or performed by the Indenture Trustee and such separate trustee or co-trustee jointly (it being understood that such separate trustee or co-trustee is not authorized to act separately without the Indenture Trustee joining in such act), except to the extent that under any law of any jurisdiction in which any particular act or acts are to be performed the Indenture Trustee shall be incompetent or unqualified to perform such act or acts, in which event such rights, powers, duties and obligations (including the holding of title to the Owner Trust Estate or any portion thereof in any such jurisdiction) shall be exercised and performed singly by such separate trustee or co-trustee, but solely at the direction of the Indenture Trustee;

(ii) no trustee hereunder shall be personally liable by reason of any act or omission of any other trustee hereunder; and

(iii) the Indenture Trustee and the Administrator may at any time accept the resignation of or remove any separate trustee or co-trustee.

(c) Any notice, request or other writing given to the Indenture Trustee shall be deemed to have been given to each of the then separate trustees and co-trustees, as effectively as if given to each of them. Every instrument appointing any separate trustee or co-trustee shall refer to this Agreement and the conditions of this Article. Each separate trustee and co-trustee, upon its acceptance of the trusts conferred, shall be vested with the estates or property specified in its instrument of appointment, either jointly with the Indenture Trustee or separately, as may be provided therein, subject to all the provisions of this Indenture, specifically including every provision of this Indenture relating to the conduct of, affecting the liability of, or affording protection to, the Indenture Trustee. Every such instrument shall be filed with the Indenture Trustee and a copy thereof given to the Administrator.

(d) Any separate trustee or co-trustee may at any time constitute the Indenture Trustee, its agent or attorney-in-fact with full power and authority, to the extent not prohibited by law, to do any lawful act under or in respect of this Indenture on its behalf and in its name. If any separate trustee or co-trustee shall die, become incapable of acting, resign or be removed, all of its estates, properties, rights, remedies and trusts shall vest in and be exercised by the Indenture Trustee, to the extent permitted by law, without the appointment of a new or successor trustee.

Section 6.11. Eligibility, Disqualification. The Indenture Trustee shall at all times satisfy the requirements of TIA ss. 310(a). The Indenture Trustee shall have a combined capital and surplus of at least $50,000,000 as set forth in its most recent published annual report of condition, and the time deposits of the Indenture Trustee shall be rated at least A-1 by Standard & Poor's and P-1 by Moody's. The Indenture Trustee shall comply with TIA ss. 310(b); provided, however, that there shall be excluded from the operation of TIA ss. 310(b)(1) any indenture or indentures under which other securities of the Issuer are outstanding if the requirements for such exclusion set forth in TIA ss. 310(b)(1) are met.

In the event that, (A) the Indenture Trustee (i) or any of its directors or executive officers is an underwriter, or (ii) directly or indirectly, controls or is controlled by, or is in common control with, an underwriter; and (B) an Event of Default occurs, the Indenture Trustee shall comply with TIA ss. 310(b). For this purpose only and pursuant to TIA ss. 310(b), an "underwriter" means any person who, within one year prior to the occurrence of the Event of Default, was an underwriter of any of the notes outstanding at the time of such Event of Default.

Section 6.12. Preferential Collection of Claims Against Issuer. The Indenture Trustee shall comply with TIA ss. 311 (a), excluding any creditor relationship listed in TIA ss. 311(b). An Indenture Trustee who has resigned or been removed shall be subject to TIA ss. 311(a) to the extent indicated.

Section 6.13. Representations and Warranties of Indenture Trustee. The Indenture Trustee hereby makes the following representations and warranties on which the Issuer and Noteholders shall rely:

(i) it is a banking corporation duly organized, validly existing and in good standing under the laws of the State of New York;

(ii) it has full power, authority and legal right to execute, deliver, and perform this Indenture and shall have taken all necessary action to authorize the execution, delivery and performance by it of this Indenture;

(iii) assuming the necessary authorization, execution and delivery thereof by the other parties thereto, the duties and obligations of the Indenture Trustee under the Indenture constitute the valid, legal and binding obligations of the Indenture Trustee enforceable in accordance with its terms except as enforcement may be limited by bankruptcy, insolvency, reorganization or similar laws or equitable principles limiting creditors' rights generally, and provided that no representation is expressed as to the availability of equitable remedies;

(iv) that to the best knowledge of the Indenture Trustee, the Indenture Trustee is not in breach of or default under any law or administrative rule or regulation of the United States of America or any department, division, agency or instrumentality thereof, or any applicable court or administrative decree or order, and which would materially impair the ability of the Indenture Trustee to perform its obligations under the Indenture; and

(v) that to the best knowledge of the Indenture Trustee, no authorization, consent or other order of any state or federal government authority or agency having jurisdiction over the trust powers of the Indenture Trustee are required to be obtained by the Indenture Trustee for the valid authorization, execution and delivery by the Indenture Trustee of the Indenture or the authentication of the Notes.

ARTICLE SEVEN
NOTEHOLDERS' LISTS AND REPORTS

Section 7.01. Issuer to Furnish Indenture Trustee Names and Addresses of Noteholders. If Definitive Notes are issued, the Issuer will furnish or cause to be furnished to the Indenture Trustee (i) not more than five days after the earlier of (a) each Record Date and (b) three months after the last Record Date, a list, in such form as the Indenture Trustee may reasonably require, of the names and addresses of the Holders of Notes as of such Record Date, and (ii) at such other times as the Indenture Trustee may request in writing, within 30 days after receipt by the Issuer of any such request, a list of similar form and content as of a date not more than ten days prior to the time such list is furnished; provided, however, that so long as the Indenture Trustee is the Note Registrar, no such list shall be required to be furnished.

Section 7.02. Preservation of Information; Communications, Reports and Certain Documents to Noteholders.

(a) The Indenture Trustee shall preserve, in as current a form as is reasonably practicable, the names and addresses of the Holders of Notes contained in the most recent list furnished to the Indenture Trustee as provided in Section 7.01 and the names and addresses of Holders of Notes received by the Indenture Trustee in its capacity as Note Registrar. The Indenture Trustee may destroy any list furnished to it as provided in such Section 7.01 upon receipt of a new list so furnished.

(b) Noteholders may communicate pursuant to TIA ss. 312(b) with other Noteholders with respect to their rights under this Indenture or under the Notes.

(c) The Issuer, the Indenture Trustee and the Note Registrar shall have the protection of TIA ss. 312(c).

(d) The Indenture Trustee will provide to Securityholders the reports, certificates, opinions and documents specified in Section 3.15 of the Sale and Servicing Agreement, upon written request to the Indenture Trustee.

Section 7.03. Reports by Issuer.

(a) The Issuer shall:

(i) file with the Indenture Trustee, within 15 days after the Issuer is required to file the same with the Commission, copies of the annual reports and the information, documents and other reports (or copies of such portions of any of the foregoing as the Commission may from time to time by rules and regulations prescribe) that the Issuer may be required to file with the Commission pursuant to Section 13 or 15(d) of the Exchange Act;

(ii) file with the Indenture Trustee and the Commission in accordance with rules and regulations prescribed from time to time by the Commission such additional information, documents and reports with respect to compliance by the Issuer with the conditions and covenants of this Indenture as may be required from time to time by such rules and regulations; and

(iii) supply to the Indenture Trustee (and the Indenture Trustee shall transmit by mail to all Noteholders described in TIA ss. 313(c)) such summaries of any information, documents and reports required to be filed by the Issuer pursuant to clauses (i) and (ii) of this Section 7.03(a) and by rules and regulations prescribed from time to time by the Commission.

(b) Unless the Issuer otherwise determines, the fiscal year of the Issuer shall end on March 31 of each year.

Section 7.04. Reports by Indenture Trustee. If required by TIA ss. 313(a), within 60 days after each December 15 beginning with December 15, 2003, the Indenture Trustee shall mail to each Noteholder as required by TIA ss. 313(c) a brief report dated as of such date that complies with TIA ss. 313(a). The Indenture Trustee also shall comply with TIA ss. 313(b).

A copy of each report at the time of its mailing to Noteholders shall be filed by the Indenture Trustee with the Commission and each stock exchange, if any, on which the Notes are listed. The Issuer shall notify the Indenture Trustee in writing if and when the Notes are listed on any stock exchange.

ARTICLE EIGHT

ACCOUNTS, DISBURSEMENTS AND RELEASES

Section 8.01. Collection of Money. Except as otherwise expressly provided herein, the Indenture Trustee may demand payment or delivery of, and shall receive and collect, directly and without intervention or assistance of any fiscal agent or other intermediary, all money and other property payable to or receivable by the Indenture Trustee pursuant to this Indenture. The Indenture Trustee shall apply all such money received by it as provided in this Indenture. Except as otherwise expressly provided in this Indenture, if any default occurs in the making of any payment or performance under any agreement or instrument that is part of the Owner Trust Estate, the Indenture Trustee may take such action as may be appropriate to enforce such payment or performance, including the institution and prosecution of appropriate Proceedings. Any such action shall be without prejudice to any right to claim a Default or Event of Default under this Indenture and any right to proceed thereafter as provided in Article Five.

Section 8.02. Accounts.

(a) Pursuant to Section 4.01 of the Sale and Servicing Agreement, there has been established and there shall be maintained an Eligible Account (initially at JPMorgan Chase Bank) in the name, and under the sole dominion and control, of the Indenture Trustee until the Outstanding Amount has been reduced to zero, and thereafter, in the name, and under the sole dominion and control, of the Owner Trustee, which is designated as the Yield Supplement Account.

(b) On or prior to the Closing Date, the Issuer shall cause the Servicer to establish and maintain, in the name of the Indenture Trustee, Eligible Accounts for the benefit of the (i) Securityholders, the Collection Account, the Yield Supplement Account and the Payahead Account, and (ii) Noteholders, the Note Distribution Account and the Reserve Fund as provided in Section 4.01 of the Sale and Servicing Agreement.

(c) On or before each Payment Date, with respect to the preceding Collection Period, all amounts required to be deposited in the Collection Account will be deposited as provided in Sections 4.02 and 4.05 of the Sale and Servicing Agreement. On or before each Payment Date, all amounts required to be deposited in the Note Distribution Account with respect to the preceding Collection Period pursuant to Sections 4.06 and 4.07 of the Sale and Servicing Agreement will be transferred from the Collection Account, the Reserve Fund, the Payahead Account and/or the Yield Supplement Account to the Note Distribution Account.

(d) On each Payment Date and Redemption Date, the Indenture Trustee shall distribute all amounts on deposit in the Note Distribution Account to Noteholders in respect of the Notes to the extent of amounts due and unpaid on the Notes for principal and interest (including any premium) in the amounts and order as set forth in the Servicer's certificate which shall be in the following amounts and in the following order of priority (except as otherwise provided in Section 5.04(b)):

(i) the Note Interest Distributable Amount; provided, that if there are not sufficient funds in the Note Distribution Account to pay the allocable portion of the Note Interest Distribution Amount with respect to each Class of Notes, the amount in the Note Distribution Account shall be applied to the payment of such amount pro rata on the basis of the total Note Interest Distributable Amount due on the Notes;

(ii) the Note Principal Distributable Amount (first to the Class A-1 Notes until the Class A-1 Notes are paid in full, second to the Class A-2 Notes until paid in full, third to the Class A-3 Notes until paid in full, and fourth to the Class A-4 Notes until paid in full);

(iii) notwithstanding clause (ii) above, on each Payment Date after the Notes have been accelerated as provided in Section 5.02(a) following the occurrence of an Event of Default, until such time as the Notes have been paid in full, the Note Principal Distributable Amount shall be paid first to the Class A-1 Notes until the Class A-1 Notes are paid in full and then to the Class A-2, Class A-3 and Class A-4 Notes on a pro rata basis based on the Outstanding Amount of each such Class of Notes; and

(iv) in the event that there are insufficient funds in the Note Distribution Account, an amount will be withdrawn from the Reserve Fund pursuant to Section 4.07(b) of the Sale and Servicing Agreement.

Section 8.03. General Provisions Regarding Accounts.

(a) So long as no Default or Event of Default shall have occurred and be continuing, all or a portion of the funds in the Accounts shall be invested in Eligible Investments and reinvested by the Indenture Trustee upon the written direction of the Servicer, subject to the provisions of Section 4.01(b) of the Sale and Servicing Agreement. Except as otherwise provided in Section 4.01 (b) of the Sale and Servicing Agreement, all income or other gain from investments of monies deposited in the Accounts shall be paid to the Servicer, and any loss resulting from such investments shall be charged to the related Account.

(b) Subject to Section 6.01(c), the Indenture Trustee shall not in any way be held liable by reason of any insufficiency in any of the Accounts resulting from any loss on any Eligible Investment included therein except for losses attributable to the Indenture Trustee's failure to make payments on such Eligible Investments issued by the Indenture Trustee, in its commercial capacity as principal obligor and not as trustee, in accordance with their terms.

(c) If (i) the Servicer shall have failed to give investment directions for any funds on deposit in the Accounts to the Indenture Trustee by 2:00 P.M., New York Time (or such other time as may be agreed by the Issuer and the Indenture Trustee) on any Business Day or (ii) to the knowledge of a Responsible Officer of the Indenture Trustee a Default or Event of Default shall have occurred and be continuing with respect to the Notes but the Notes shall not have been declared due and payable pursuant to Section 5.02 or (iii) if such Notes shall have been declared due and payable following an Event of Default but amounts collected or receivable from the Owner Trust Estate are being applied in accordance with Section 5.05 as if there had not been such a declaration, then the Indenture Trustee upon actual knowledge by a Responsible Officer of such event shall, in the case of clause (i) above, maintain such funds in cash or, in the case of clauses (ii) or (iii) above, to the fullest extent practicable, invest and reinvest funds in the Accounts in the Eligible Investment listed in clause (vii) of the definition thereof.

Section 8.04. Release of Owner Trust Estate.

(a) Subject to the payment of its fees and expenses pursuant to Section 6.07, the Indenture Trustee may, and when required by the provisions of this Indenture shall, execute instruments to release property from the lien of this Indenture, or convey the Indenture Trustee's interest in the same, in a manner and under circumstances that are not inconsistent with the provisions of this Indenture. No party relying upon an instrument executed by the Indenture Trustee as provided in this Article shall be bound to ascertain the Indenture Trustee's authority, inquire into the satisfaction of any conditions precedent or see to the application of any monies.

(b) The Indenture Trustee shall, at such time as there are no Notes Outstanding and all sums due the Indenture Trustee pursuant to Section 6.07 have been paid, release any remaining portion of the Owner Trust Estate that secured the Notes from the lien of this Indenture and release to the Issuer or any other Person entitled thereto any funds then on deposit in the Accounts. The Indenture Trustee shall release property from the lien of this Indenture pursuant to this Section 8.04(b) only upon receipt of an Issuer Request accompanied by an Officer's Certificate, an Opinion of Counsel and (if required by the TIA) Independent Certificates in accordance with TIA ss.ss. 314(c) and 314(d)(1) meeting the applicable requirements of Section 11.01.

Section 8.05. Opinion of Counsel. The Indenture Trustee shall receive at least seven days written notice when requested by the Issuer to take any action pursuant to Section 8.04(a), accompanied by copies of any instruments involved, and the Indenture Trustee shall also require, as a condition to such action, an Opinion of Counsel, in form and substance satisfactory to the Indenture Trustee, stating the legal effect of any such action, outlining the steps required to complete the same, and concluding that all conditions precedent to the taking of such action have been complied with and such action will not materially and adversely impair the security for the Notes or the rights of the Noteholders in contravention of the provisions of this Indenture; provided, however, that such Opinion of Counsel shall not be required to express an opinion as to the fair value of the Owner Trust Estate. Counsel rendering any such opinion may rely, without independent investigation, on the accuracy and validity of any certificate or other instrument delivered to the Indenture Trustee in connection with any such action.

ARTICLE NINE
SUPPLEMENTAL INDENTURES

Section 9.01. Supplemental Indentures Without Consent of Noteholders.

(a) Without the consent of the Holders of any Notes but with prior notice to each Rating Agency, the Issuer and the Indenture Trustee, when authorized by an Issuer Order, at any time and from time to time, may enter into one or more indentures supplemental hereto (which shall conform to the provisions of the TIA as in force at the date of the execution thereof), in form satisfactory to the Indenture Trustee, for any of the following purposes:

(i) to correct or amplify the description of any property at any time subject to the lien of this Indenture, or better to assure, convey and confirm unto the Indenture Trustee any property subject or required to be subjected to the lien of this Indenture, or to subject additional property to the lien of this Indenture;

(ii) to evidence the succession, in compliance with the applicable provisions hereof, of another Person to the Issuer, and the assumption by any such successor of the covenants of the Issuer herein and in the Notes contained;

(iii) to add to the covenants of the Issuer, for the benefit of the Holder of any Notes, or to surrender any right or power herein conferred upon the Issuer;

(iv) to convey, transfer, assign, mortgage or pledge any property to or with the Indenture Trustee;

(v) to cure any ambiguity, to correct or supplement any provision herein or in any supplemental indenture that may be inconsistent with any other provision herein or in any supplemental indenture or the other Basic Documents or to make any other provisions with respect to matters or questions arising under this Indenture or in any supplemental indenture; provided, that such action shall not adversely affect the interests of the Holders of the Notes;

(vi) to evidence and provide for the acceptance of the appointment hereunder by a successor trustee with respect to the Notes and to add to or change any of the provisions of this Indenture as shall be necessary to facilitate the administration of the trusts hereunder by more than one trustee, pursuant to the requirements of Article Six; or

(vii) to modify, eliminate or add to the provisions of this Indenture to such extent as shall be necessary to effect the qualification of this Indenture under the TIA or under any similar federal statute hereafter enacted and to add to this Indenture such other provisions as may be expressly required by the TIA.

The Indenture Trustee is hereby authorized to join in the execution of any such supplemental indenture and to make any further appropriate agreements and stipulations that may be therein contained.

(b) The Issuer and the Indenture Trustee, when authorized by an Issuer Order, may, also without the consent of any of the Holders of the Notes but with prior notice to each Rating Agency, enter into an indenture or indentures supplemental hereto for the purpose of adding any provisions to, or changing in any manner or eliminating any of the provisions of, this Indenture or of modifying in any manner the rights of the Holders of the Notes under this Indenture; provided, however, that such action shall not, as evidenced by an Opinion of Counsel, adversely affect in any material respect the interests of any Noteholder.

Section 9.02. Supplemental Indentures With Consent of Noteholders. The Issuer and the Indenture Trustee, when authorized by an Issuer Order, also may, with prior notice to each Rating Agency and with the written consent of the Holders of not less than a majority of the Outstanding Amount, by Act of such Holders delivered to the Issuer and the Indenture Trustee, enter into an indenture or indentures supplemental hereto for the purpose of adding any provisions to, or changing in any manner or eliminating any of the provisions of, this Indenture or of modifying in any manner the rights of the Holders of the Notes under this Indenture; provided, however, that no such supplemental indenture shall, without the written consent of the Holder of each Outstanding Note affected thereby:

(i) change the date of payment of any installment of principal of or interest on any Note, or reduce the principal amount thereof, the Interest Rate thereon or the Redemption Price with respect thereto, change the provisions of this Indenture relating to the application of collections on, or the proceeds of the sale of, the Owner Trust Estate to payment of principal of or interest on the Notes, or change any place of payment where, or the coin or currency in which, any Note or the interest thereon is payable, or impair the right to institute suit for the enforcement of the provisions of this Indenture requiring the application of funds available therefor, as provided in Article Five, to the payment of any such amount due on the Notes on or after the respective due dates thereof (or, in the case of redemption, on or after the Redemption Date);

(ii) reduce the percentage of the Outstanding Amount, the consent of the Holders of which is required for any such supplemental indenture, or the consent of the Holders of which is required for any waiver of compliance with certain provisions of this Indenture or certain defaults hereunder and their consequences provided for in this Indenture;

(iii) modify or alter the provisions of the proviso to the definition of the term "Outstanding";

(iv) reduce the percentage of the Outstanding Amount required to direct the Indenture Trustee to direct the Issuer to sell or liquidate the Owner Trust Estate pursuant to Section 5.04 or amend the provisions of this Article which specify the percentage of the Outstanding Amount required to amend this Indenture or the other Basic Documents;

(v) modify any provision of this Section except to increase any percentage specified herein or provide that certain additional provisions of this Indenture or the Basic Documents cannot be modified or waived without the consent of the Holder of each Outstanding Note affected thereby;

(vi) modify any of the provisions of this Indenture in such manner as to affect the calculation of the amount of any payment of interest or principal due on any Note on any Payment Date (including the calculation of any of the individual components of such calculation) or affect the rights of the Holders of Notes to the benefit of any provisions for the mandatory redemption of the Notes contained herein; or

(vii) permit the creation of any lien ranking prior to or on a parity with the lien of this Indenture with respect to any part of the Owner Trust Estate or, except as otherwise permitted or contemplated herein, terminate the lien of this Indenture on any property at any time subject hereto or deprive the Holder of any Note of the security provided by the lien of this Indenture.

The Administrator shall certify to the Indenture Trustee whether or not any Notes would be affected by any supplemental indenture and any such certification shall be conclusive upon the Holders of all Notes, whether theretofore or thereafter authenticated and delivered hereunder.

It shall not be necessary for any Act of Noteholders under this Section to approve the particular form of any proposed supplemental indenture, but it shall be sufficient if such Act shall approve the substance thereof.

Promptly after the execution by the Issuer and the Indenture Trustee of any supplemental indenture pursuant to this Section, the Indenture Trustee shall mail to the Holders of the Notes to which such amendment or supplemental indenture relates a notice setting forth in general terms the substance of such supplemental indenture. Any failure of the Indenture Trustee to mail such notice, or any defect therein, shall not, however, in any way impair or affect the validity of any such supplemental indenture.

Section 9.03. Execution of Supplemental Indentures. In executing, or permitting the additional trusts created by, any supplemental indenture permitted by this Article or the modification thereby of the trusts created by this Indenture, the Indenture Trustee shall be entitled to receive, and subject to Sections 6.01 and 6.02, shall be fully protected in relying upon, an Opinion of Counsel stating that the execution of such supplemental indenture is authorized or permitted by this Indenture. The Indenture Trustee may, but shall not be obligated to, enter into any such supplemental indenture that affects the Indenture Trustee's own rights, duties, liabilities or immunities under this Indenture or otherwise.

Section 9.04. Effect of Supplemental Indenture. Upon the execution of any supplemental indenture pursuant to the provisions hereof, this Indenture shall be and shall be deemed to be modified and amended in accordance therewith with respect to the Notes affected thereby, and the respective rights, limitations of rights, obligations, duties, liabilities and immunities under this Indenture of the Indenture Trustee, the Issuer and the Holders of the Notes shall thereafter be determined, exercised and enforced hereunder subject in all respects to such modifications and amendments, and all the terms and conditions of any such supplemental indenture shall be and be deemed to be part of the terms and conditions of this Indenture for any and all purposes.

Section 9.05. Conformity with Trust Indenture Act. Every amendment of this Indenture and every supplemental indenture executed pursuant to this Article shall conform to the requirements of the TIA as then in effect so long as this Indenture shall then be qualified under the TIA.

Section 9.06. Reference in Notes to Supplemental Indentures. Notes authenticated and delivered after the execution of any supplemental indenture pursuant to this Article may, and if required by the Indenture Trustee shall, bear a notation in form approved by the Indenture Trustee as to any matter provided for in such supplemental indenture. If the Issuer or the Indenture Trustee shall so determine, new Notes so modified as to conform, in the opinion of the Indenture Trustee and the Issuer, to any such supplemental indenture may be prepared and executed by the Issuer and authenticated and delivered by the Indenture Trustee in exchange for Outstanding Notes.

ARTICLE TEN

REDEMPTION OF NOTES

Section 10.01. Redemption. The Outstanding Notes are subject to redemption in whole, but not in part, pursuant to Section 8.01 of the Sale and Servicing Agreement, on any Payment Date on which the Servicer exercises its option to purchase the Owner Trust Estate pursuant to said Section, for a purchase price equal to the Redemption Price; provided that the Issuer has available funds sufficient to pay the Redemption Price. The Servicer or the Issuer shall furnish each Rating Agency notice of such redemption. If the outstanding Notes are to be redeemed pursuant to this Section, the Servicer or the Issuer shall furnish written notice of such election to the Indenture Trustee not later than 20 days prior to the Redemption Date and the Issuer shall deposit by 8:00 A.M., Los Angeles time, on the Redemption Date with the Indenture Trustee in the Note Distribution Account the Redemption Price of the Notes to be redeemed, whereupon all such Notes shall be due and payable on the Redemption Date upon the furnishing of a notice complying with Section 10.02 to each Holder of the Notes.

Section 10.02. Form of Redemption Notice. Notice of redemption under Section 10.01 shall be given by the Indenture Trustee by first-class mail, postage prepaid, or by facsimile mailed or transmitted not later than ten days prior to the applicable Redemption Date to each Holder of Notes, as of the close of business on the Record Date preceding the applicable Redemption Date, at such Holder's address or facsimile number appearing in the Note Register.

All notices of redemption shall state:

(i) the Redemption Date;

(ii) the Redemption Price;

(iii) the place where such Notes are to be surrendered for payment of the Redemption Price (which shall be the office or agency of the Issuer to be maintained as provided in Section 3.02); and

(iv) that on the Redemption Date, the Redemption Price will become due and payable upon each Note and that interest thereon shall cease to accrue from and after the Redemption Date.

Notice of redemption of the Notes shall be given by the Indenture Trustee in the name and at the expense of the Issuer. Failure to give notice of redemption, or any defect therein, to any Holder of any Note shall not impair or affect the validity of the redemption of any other Note.

Section 10.03. Notes Payable on Redemption Date. The Notes or portions thereof to be redeemed shall, following notice of redemption as required by Section 10.02, on the Redemption Date become due and payable at the Redemption Price and (unless the Issuer shall default in the payment of the Redemption Price) no interest shall accrue on the Redemption Price for any period after the date to which accrued interest is calculated for purposes of calculating the Redemption Price.

ARTICLE ELEVEN

MISCELLANEOUS

Section 11.01. Compliance Certificates and Opinions, etc.

(a) Upon any application or request by the Issuer to the Indenture Trustee to take any action under any provision of this Indenture, the Issuer shall furnish to the Indenture Trustee (i) an Officer's Certificate stating that all conditions precedent, if any, provided for in this Indenture relating to the proposed action have been complied with, (ii) an Opinion of Counsel stating that in the opinion of such counsel all such conditions precedent, if any, have been complied with and (iii) (if required by the TIA) an Independent Certificate from a firm of certified public accountants meeting the applicable requirements of this Section, except that, in the case of any such application or request as to which the furnishing of such documents is specifically required by any provision of this Indenture, no additional certificate or opinion need be furnished.

Every certificate or opinion with respect to compliance with a condition or covenant provided for in this Indenture shall include:

(i) a statement that each signatory of such certificate or opinion has read or has caused to be read such covenant or condition and the definitions herein relating thereto;

(ii) a brief statement as to the nature and scope of the examination or investigation upon which the statements or opinions contained in such certificate or opinion are based;

(iii) a statement that, in the opinion of each such signatory, such signatory has made such examination or investigation as is necessary to enable such signatory to express an informed opinion as to whether or not such covenant or condition has been complied with; and

(iv) a statement as to whether, in the opinion of each such signatory, such condition or covenant has been complied with.

(b) (i) Prior to the deposit of any Collateral or other property or securities with the Indenture Trustee that is to be made the basis for the release of any property or securities subject to the lien of this Indenture, the Issuer shall, in addition to any obligation imposed in Section 11.01 (a) or elsewhere in this Indenture, furnish to the Indenture Trustee an Officer's Certificate certifying or stating the opinion of each person signing such certificate as to the fair value (within 90 days of such deposit) to the Issuer of the Collateral or other property or securities to be so deposited.

(ii) Whenever the Issuer is required to furnish to the Indenture Trustee an Officer's Certificate certifying or stating the opinion of any signer thereof as to the matters described in clause (i) above, the Issuer shall also deliver to the Indenture Trustee an Independent Certificate as to the same matters, if the fair value to the Issuer of the securities to be so deposited and of all other such securities made the basis of any such withdrawal or release since the commencement of the then-current fiscal year of the Issuer, as set forth in the certificates delivered pursuant to clause (i) above and this clause (ii), is 10% or more of the Outstanding Amount, but such a certificate need not be furnished with respect to any securities so deposited, if the fair value thereof to the Issuer as set forth in the related Officer's Certificate is less than $25,000 or less than one percent of the Outstanding Amount of the Notes.

(iii) Other than with respect to any release described in clause (A) or (B) of Section 11.01(b)(v), whenever any property or securities are to be released from the lien of this Indenture, the Issuer shall also furnish to the Indenture

Trustee an Officer's Certificate certifying or stating the opinion of each person signing such certificate as to the fair value (within 90 days of such release) of the property or securities proposed to be released and stating that in the opinion of such person the proposed release will not impair the security under this Indenture in contravention of the provisions hereof.

(iv) Whenever the Issuer is required to furnish to the Indenture Trustee an Officer's Certificate certifying or stating the opinion of any signer thereof as to the matters described in clause (iii) above, the Issuer shall also furnish to the Indenture Trustee an Independent Certificate as to the same matters if the fair value of the property or securities and of all other property (other than property described in clauses (A) or (B) of Section 11.01 (b)(v)) released from the lien of this Indenture since the commencement of the then-current calendar year, as set forth in the certificates required by clause (iii) above and this clause (iv), equals 10% or more of the Outstanding Amount, but such certificate need not be furnished in the case of any release of property or securities if the fair value thereof as set forth in the related Officer's Certificate is less than $25,000 or less than one percent of the then Outstanding Amount.

(v) Notwithstanding Section 2.10 or any other provision of this Section, the Issuer may, without compliance with the requirements of the other provisions of this Section, (A) collect, liquidate, sell or otherwise dispose of Receivables and Financed Vehicles as and to the extent permitted or required by the Basic Documents and (B) make cash payments out of the Accounts as and to the extent permitted or required by the Basic Documents, so long as the Issuer shall deliver to the Indenture Trustee every six months, commencing June 15, 2003 an Officer's Certificate of the Issuer stating that all the dispositions of Collateral described in clauses (A) and (B) above that occurred during the preceding six calendar months or, in the case of the first Officer's Certificate, the preceding four calendar months were in the ordinary course of the Issuer's business and that the proceeds thereof were applied in accordance with the Basic Documents.

Section 11.02. Form of Documents Delivered to Indenture Trustee. In any case where several matters are required to be certified by, or covered by an opinion of, any specified Person, it is not necessary that all such matters be certified by, or covered by the opinion of, only one such Person, or that they be so certified or covered by only one document, but one such Person may certify or give an opinion with respect to some matters and one or more other such Persons as to other matters, and any such Person may certify or give an opinion as to such matters in one or several documents.

Any certificate or opinion of an Authorized Officer of the Issuer may be based, insofar as it relates to legal matters, upon a certificate or opinion of, or representations by, counsel, unless such officer knows, or in the exercise of reasonable care should know, that the certificate or opinion or representations with respect to the matters upon which such officer's certificate or opinion is based are erroneous. Any such certificate of an Authorized Officer or Opinion of Counsel may be based, insofar as it relates to factual matters, upon a certificate or opinion of, or representations by, an officer or officers of the Servicer, the Seller, the Issuer or the Administrator, stating that the information with respect to such factual matters is in the possession of the Servicer, the Seller, the Issuer or the Administrator, unless such counsel knows, or in the exercise of reasonable care should know, that the certificate or opinion or representations with respect to such matters are erroneous.

Where any Person is required to make, give or execute two or more applications, requests, consents, certificates, statements, opinions or other instruments under this Indenture, they may, but need not, be consolidated and form one instrument.

Whenever in this Indenture, in connection with any application or certificate or report to the Indenture Trustee, it is provided that the Issuer shall deliver any document as a condition of the granting of such application, or as evidence of the Issuer's compliance with any term hereof, it is intended that the truth and accuracy, at the time of the granting of such application or at the effective date of such certificate or report (as the case may be), of the facts and opinions stated in such document shall in such case be conditions precedent to the right of the Issuer to have such application granted or to the sufficiency of such certificate or report. The foregoing shall not, however, be construed to affect the Indenture Trustee's right to rely upon the truth and accuracy of any statement or opinion contained in any such document as provided in Article Six.

Section 11.03. Acts of Noteholders.

(a) Any request, demand, authorization, direction, notice, consent, waiver or other action provided by this Indenture to be given or taken by Noteholders may be embodied in and evidenced by one or more instruments of substantially similar tenor signed by such Noteholders in person or by agents duly appointed in writing; and except as herein otherwise expressly provided such action shall become effective when such instrument or instruments are delivered to the Indenture Trustee and, where it is hereby expressly required, to the Issuer. Such instrument or instruments (and the action embodied therein and evidenced thereby) are herein sometimes referred to as the "Act" of the Noteholders signing such instrument or instruments. Proof of execution of any such instrument or of a writing appointing any such agent shall be sufficient for any purpose of this Indenture and (subject to Section 6.01) conclusive in favor of the Indenture Trustee and the Issuer, if made in the manner provided in this Section.

(b) The fact and date of the execution by any person of any such instrument or writing may be proved in any manner that the Indenture Trustee deems sufficient.

(c) The ownership of Notes shall be proved by the Note Register.

(d) Any request, demand, authorization, direction, notice, consent, waiver or other action by the Holder of any Notes shall bind the Holder of every Note issued upon the registration thereof or in exchange therefor or in lieu thereof, in respect of anything done, omitted or suffered to be done by the Indenture

Trustee or the Issuer in reliance thereon, whether or not notation of such action is made upon such Note.

Section 11.04. Notices, etc., to Indenture Trustee, Issuer and Rating Agencies. Any request, demand, authorization, direction, notice, consent, waiver or Act of Noteholders or other documents provided or permitted by this Indenture shall be in writing and if such request, demand, authorization, direction, notice, consent, waiver or Act of Noteholders is to be made upon, given or furnished to or filed with:

(i) the Indenture Trustee by any Noteholder or by the Issuer shall be sufficient for every purpose hereunder if made, given, furnished or filed in writing and mailed first-class, postage prepaid, overnight courier or facsimile (followed by original) to or with the Indenture Trustee at its Corporate Trust Office, or

(ii) the Issuer by the Indenture Trustee or by any Noteholder shall be sufficient for every purpose hereunder if in writing and mailed first-class, postage prepaid, overnight courier or facsimile (followed by original) to the Issuer addressed to: Honda Auto Receivables 2003-1 Owner Trust, in care of The Bank of New York, 101 Barclay Street, 8th Floor West, New York, New York 10286, Attention: Asset Backed Securities Unit — Honda 2003-1 or at any other address previously furnished in writing to the Indenture Trustee by the Issuer or the Administrator. The Issuer shall promptly transmit any notice received by it from the Noteholders to the Indenture Trustee.

Notices required to be given to each Rating Agency by the Issuer, the Indenture Trustee or the Owner Trustee shall be in writing, personally delivered, couriered or mailed by certified mail, return receipt requested, to (i) in the case of Fitch, at the following address: One State Street Plaza, New York, New York 10004, Attention: Asset Backed Surveillance Department, (ii) in the case of Moody's, at the following address: Moody's Investors Service, Inc., ABS Monitoring Department, 99 Church Street, New York, New York 10007 or (iii) in the case of Standard & Poor's, at the following address: Standard & Poor's Ratings Services, a division of The McGraw-Hill Companies, Inc., 55 Water Street, New York, New York 10041, Attention of Asset Backed Surveillance Department; or at such other address as shall be designated by written notice to the other parties.

Section 11.05. Notices to Noteholders; Waiver. Where this Indenture provides for notice to Noteholders of any event, such notice shall be sufficiently given (unless otherwise herein expressly provided) if in writing and mailed, first-class, postage prepaid to each Noteholder affected by such event, at such Holder's address as it appears on the Note Register, not later than the latest date, and not earlier than the earliest date, prescribed for the giving of such notice. In any case where notice to Noteholders is given by mail, neither the failure to mail such notice nor any defect in any notice so mailed to any particular Noteholder shall affect the sufficiency of such notice with respect to other Noteholders, and any notice that is mailed in the manner herein provided shall conclusively be presumed to have been duly given.

Where this Indenture provides for notice in any manner, such notice may be waived in writing by any Person entitled to receive such notice, either before or after the event, and such waiver shall be the equivalent of such notice. Waivers of notice by Noteholders shall be filed with the Indenture Trustee but such filing shall not be a condition precedent to the validity of any action taken in reliance upon such a waiver.

In case, by reason of the suspension of regular mail service as a result of a strike, work stoppage or similar activity, it shall be impractical to mail notice of any event to Noteholders when such notice is required to be given pursuant to any provision of this Indenture, then any manner of giving such notice as shall be satisfactory to the Indenture Trustee shall be deemed to be a sufficient giving of such notice.

Where this Indenture provides for notice to each Rating Agency, failure to give such notice shall not affect any other rights or obligations created hereunder, and shall not under any circumstance constitute a Default or Event of Default.

Section 11.06. Alternate Payment and Notice Provisions. Notwithstanding any provision of this Indenture or any of the Notes to the contrary, the Issuer may enter into any agreement with any Holder of a Note providing for a method of payment, or notice by the Indenture Trustee or any Paying Agent to such Holder, that is different from the methods provided for in this Indenture for such payments or notices. The Issuer will furnish to the Indenture Trustee a copy of each such agreement and the Indenture Trustee will cause payments to be made and notices to be given in accordance with such agreements.

Section 11.07. Conflict with Trust Indenture Act. If any provision hereof limits, qualifies or conflicts with another provision hereof that is required to be included in this Indenture by any of the provisions of the Trust Indenture Act, such required provision shall control.

The provisions of TIA Sections 310 through 317 that impose duties on any person (including the provisions automatically deemed included herein unless expressly excluded by this Indenture) are a part of and govern this Indenture, whether or not physically contained herein.

Section 11.08. Effect of Headings and Table of Contents. The Article and Section headings herein and the Table of Contents are for convenience only and shall not affect the construction hereof.

Section 11.09. Successors and Assigns. All covenants and agreements in this Indenture and the Notes by the Issuer shall bind its successors and assigns, whether so expressed or not. All agreements of the Indenture Trustee in this Indenture shall bind its successors, co-trustees and agents.

Section 11.10. Separability. In case any provision in this Indenture or in the Notes shall be invalid, illegal or unenforceable, the validity, legality and enforceability of the remaining provisions of this Indenture and the Notes shall not in any way be affected or impaired thereby.

Section 11.11. Benefits of Indenture. Nothing in this Indenture or in the Notes, express or implied, shall give to any Person, other than the parties hereto and their successors hereunder, and the Noteholders, and any other party secured hereunder, and any other Person with an ownership interest in any part of the Owner Trust Estate, any benefit or any legal or equitable right, remedy or claim under this Indenture.

Section 11.12. Legal Holidays. In any case where the date on which any payment is due shall not be a Business Day, then (notwithstanding any other provision of the Note's or this Indenture) payment need not be made on such date, but may be made on the next succeeding Business Day with the same force and effect as if made on the date on which nominally due, and no interest shall accrue for the period from and after any such nominal date.

Section 11.13. Governing Law. THIS INDENTURE SHALL BE CONSTRUED IN ACCORDANCE WITH THE LAWS OF THE STATE OF CALIFORNIA, WITHOUT REFERENCE TO ITS CONFLICT OF LAW PROVISIONS, AND THE OBLIGATIONS, RIGHTS AND REMEDIES OF THE PARTIES HEREUNDER SHALL BE DETERMINED IN ACCORDANCE WITH SUCH LAWS, EXCEPT THAT THE DUTIES, RIGHTS AND PROTECTIONS OF EACH OF THE OWNER TRUSTEE AND THE INDENTURE TRUSTEE SHALL BE GOVERNED BY THE LAWS OF THE STATE OF NEW YORK.

Section 11.14. Counterparts. This Indenture may be executed in any number of counterparts, each of which so executed shall be deemed to be an original, but all such counterparts shall together constitute but one and the same instrument.

Section 11.15. Recording of Indenture. If this Indenture is subject to recording in any appropriate public recording offices, such recording is to be effected by the Issuer and at its expense accompanied by an Opinion of Counsel (which may be counsel to the Indenture Trustee or any other counsel reasonably acceptable to the Indenture Trustee) to the effect that such recording is necessary either for the protection of the Noteholders or any other Person secured hereunder or for the enforcement of any right or remedy granted to the Indenture Trustee under this Indenture.

Section 11.16. Trust Obligation. No recourse may be taken, directly or indirectly, with respect to the obligations of the Issuer, the Owner Trustee or the Indenture Trustee on the Notes or under this Indenture or any certificate or other writing delivered in connection herewith or therewith, against (i) the Indenture Trustee or the Owner Trustee in its individual capacity, (ii) any owner of a beneficial interest in the Issuer or (iii) any partner, owner, beneficiary, agent, officer, director, employee or agent of the Indenture Trustee or the Owner Trustee in its individual capacity, any holder of a beneficial interest in the Issuer, the Owner Trustee or the Indenture Trustee or of any successor or assign of the Indenture Trustee or the Owner Trustee in its individual capacity, except as any such Person may have expressly agreed (it being understood that the Indenture Trustee and the Owner Trustee have no such obligations in their individual capacity) and except that any such partner, owner or beneficiary shall be fully liable, to the extent provided by applicable law, for any unpaid consideration for stock, unpaid capital contribution or failure to pay any installment or call owing to such entity. For all purposes of this Indenture, in the performance of any duties or obligations of the Issuer hereunder, the Owner Trustee shall be subject to, and entitled to the benefits of, the terms and provisions of Articles Six, Seven and Eight of the Trust Agreement.

Section 11.17. No Petition. The Indenture Trustee, by entering into this Indenture, and each Noteholder, by accepting a Note, hereby covenant and agree that they will not at any time institute against the Issuer, or join in any institution against the Issuer of, any bankruptcy, reorganization, arrangement, insolvency or liquidation proceedings, or other proceedings under any United States federal or state bankruptcy or similar law in connection with any obligations relating to the Notes, this Indenture or any of the other Basic Documents.

Section 11.18. Inspection. The Issuer agrees that, on reasonable prior notice, it will permit any representative of the Indenture Trustee, during the Issuer's normal business hours, to examine all the books of account, records, reports and other papers of the Issuer, to make copies and extracts therefrom, to cause such books to be audited by Independent certified public accountants, and to discuss the Issuer's affairs, finances and accounts with the Issuer's officers, employees and Independent certified public accountants, all at such reasonable times and as often as may be reasonably requested. Notwithstanding anything herein to the contrary, the foregoing shall not be construed to prohibit (i) the disclosure of any and all information that is or becomes publicly known, or information obtained by the Indenture Trustee from sources other than the Servicer or the Issuer, (ii) the disclosure of any and all information (A) if required to do so by any applicable law, rule or regulation, (B) to any government agency or regulatory body having or claiming authority to regulate or oversee any aspects of the Indenture Trustee's business or that of its affiliates, (C) pursuant to any subpoena, civil investigative demand or similar demand or request of any court, regulatory authority, arbitrator or arbitration to which the Indenture Trustee or any affiliate or an officer, director, employer or shareholder thereof is a party, (D) in any preliminary or final offering circular, registration statement or contract or other document pertaining to the transactions contemplated by the Agreement approved in advance by the Servicer or the Issuer or (E) to any affiliate, independent or internal auditor, agent, employee or attorney of the Indenture Trustee having a need to know the same, provided that the Indenture Trustee advises such recipient of the confidential nature of the information being disclosed, or (iii) any other disclosure authorized by the Servicer or the Issuer.

IN WITNESS WHEREOF, the parties hereto have caused this Indenture to be duly executed by their respective officers, thereunto duly authorized and duly attested, all as of the day and year first above written.

HONDA AUTO RECEIVABLES 2003-1 OWNER TRUST,

By: THE BANK OF NEW YORK, not in its individual capacity but solely as Owner Trustee on behalf of the Trust,

By: /s/ John Bobko

Name: John Bobko

Title: Assistant Vice President

JPMORGAN CHASE BANK,

not in its individual capacity but solely as Indenture Trustee,

By: /s/ Jennifer H. McCourt

Name: Jennifer H. McCourt

Title: Vice President

STATE OF New York)
) ss
COUNTY OF New York)

On February 21, 2003 before me, Deirdre Pierson, Notary Public, personally appeared John Bobko, Assistant Vice President of the Bank of New York

[X] personally known to me, or

[ ] proved to me on the basis of satisfactory evidence to be the person(s) whose name(s) is/are subscribed to the within instrument,

and acknowledged to me that she executed the same in her authorized capacity, and that by her signature on the instrument the person, or the entity upon behalf of which such person acted, executed the instrument.

WITNESS my hand and official seal.

Signature /s/ Deirdre Pierson [Seal]

____

STATE OF New York)
) ss
COUNTY OF New York)

On February 25, 2003 before me, Rosita Walters, Notary Public, personally appeared Jennifer H. McCourt, Vice President

[X] personally known to me, or

[ ] proved to me on the basis of satisfactory evidence to be the person(s) whose name(s) is/are subscribed to the within instrument,

and acknowledged to me that she executed the same in her authorized capacity, and that by her signature on the instrument the person, or the entity upon behalf of which such person acted, executed the instrument.

WITNESS my hand and official seal.

Signature /s/ Rosita Walters [Seal]

____

SCHEDULE A

SCHEDULE OF RECEIVABLES

Provided to the Owner Trustee at Closing

EXHIBIT A

FORM OF NOTE

UNLESS THIS NOTE IS PRESENTED BY AN AUTHORIZED REPRESENTATIVE OF THE DEPOSITORY TRUST COMPANY, A NEW YORK CORPORATION ("DTC"), TO THE ISSUER OR ITS AGENT FOR REGISTRATION OF TRANSFER, EXCHANGE OR PAYMENT, AND ANY NOTE ISSUED IS REGISTERED IN THE NAME OF CEDE & CO. OR IN SUCH OTHER NAME AS IS REQUESTED BY AN AUTHORIZED REPRESENTATIVE OF DTC (AND ANY PAYMENT IS MADE TO CEDE & CO. OR TO SUCH OTHER ENTITY AS IS REQUESTED BY AN AUTHORIZED REPRESENTATIVE OF DTC), ANY TRANSFER, PLEDGE OR OTHER USE HEREOF FOR VALUE OR OTHERWISE BY OR TO ANY PERSON IS WRONGFUL INASMUCH AS THE REGISTERED OWNER HEREOF, CEDE & CO., HAS AN INTEREST HEREIN.

THE PRINCIPAL OF THIS NOTE IS PAYABLE IN INSTALLMENTS AS SET FORTH HEREIN. ACCORDINGLY, THE OUTSTANDING PRINCIPAL AMOUNT OF THIS NOTE AT ANY TIME MAY BE LESS THAN THE AMOUNT SHOWN ON THE FACE HEREOF.

REGISTERED $__________

No. R-__

CUSIP NO. _______

HONDA AUTO RECEIVABLES 2003-1 OWNER TRUST

____% ASSET BACKED NOTES, CLASS [A-1] [A-2] [A-3] [A-4]

Honda Auto Receivables 2003-1 Owner Trust, a statutory trust organized and existing under the laws of the State of Delaware (the "Issuer"), for value received, hereby promises to pay to CEDE & CO., or registered assigns, the principal sum of ______________________ Dollars ($__________), payable to the extent described in the Indenture referred to on the reverse hereof on each Payment Date; provided, however, that the entire unpaid principal amount of this Note shall be payable on the earlier of ________________ ___, 20__ (the "Class [A-1] [A-2] [A-3] [A-4] Final Payment Date") and the Redemption Date, if any, selected pursuant to the Indenture.

The Issuer will pay interest on this Note at the rate per annum shown above on each Payment Date until the principal of this Note is paid or made available for payment, on the principal amount of this Note outstanding on the preceding Payment Date (after giving effect to all payments of principal made on the preceding Payment Date), or on the Closing Date in the case of the first Payment Date or if no interest has yet been paid, subject to certain limitations contained in the Indenture. [[Interest on this Class A-1 Note will accrue for each Payment Date from and including the immediately preceding Payment Date (or, in the case of the first Payment Date, the Closing Date), to but excluding such Payment Date]. [Interest on this [Class A-2,] [Class A-3,] [Class A-4] Note will accrue for each Payment Date from and including the eighteenth day of the prior month (or, in the case of the first Payment Date, the Closing Date) to but excluding the eighteenth day of the month of such Payment Date] and will be computed on the basis of [the actual number of days in the Interest Accrual Period with respect to the Class A-1 Notes divided by 360] [a 360-day year consisting of twelve 30-day months in the case of the Class A-2, Class A-3 and Class A-4 Notes]. Such principal of and interest on this Note shall be paid in the manner specified on the reverse hereof.

The principal of and interest on this Note are payable in such coin or currency of the United States of America as at the time of payment is legal tender for payment of public and private debts. All payments made by the Issuer with respect to this Note shall be applied first to interest due and payable on this Note as provided above and then to the unpaid principal of this Note.

Reference is made to the further provisions of this Note set forth on the reverse hereof, which shall have the same effect as though fully set forth on the face of this Note.

Unless the certificate of authentication hereon has been executed by the Indenture Trustee whose name appears below by manual signature, this Note shall not be entitled to any benefit under the Indenture, or be valid or obligatory for any purpose.

IN WITNESS WHEREOF, the Issuer has caused this instrument to be signed, manually or in facsimile, by its Authorized Officer, as of the date set forth below.

Date:

HONDA AUTO RECEIVABLES 2003-1 OWNER TRUST,

By: THE BANK OF NEW YORK, not in its individual capacity but solely as Owner Trustee on behalf of the Trust,

By:

____

Authorized Signatory

INDENTURE TRUSTEE'S CERTIFICATE OF AUTHENTICATION

This is one of the Notes designated above and referred to in the within-mentioned Indenture.

Date: JPMORGAN CHASE BANK, not in its individual capacity but solely as Indenture Trustee,

By:

____

Authorized Signatory

This Note is one of a duly authorized issue of Notes of the Issuer, designated as its ___% Asset Backed Notes, Class [A-1] [A-2] [A-3] [A-4] (the "Class [A-1] [A-2] [A-3] [A-4] Notes"), all issued under the Indenture, to which Indenture and all indentures supplemental thereto reference is hereby made for a statement of the respective rights and obligations thereunder of the Issuer, the Indenture Trustee and the Holders of the Notes. The Notes are subject to all terms of the Indenture. Capitalized terms used herein that are not otherwise defined shall have the meanings ascribed thereto in the Indenture.

The Class A-1 Notes, the Class A-2 Notes, the Class A-3 Notes and the Class A-4 Notes (collectively, the "Notes") are and will be equally and ratably secured by the collateral pledged as security therefor as provided in the Indenture.

Principal payable on the Notes will be paid on each Payment Date in the amount specified in the Indenture and in the Sale and Servicing Agreement. As described above, the entire unpaid principal amount of this Note will be payable on the earlier of the Class [A-1] [A-2] [A-3] [A-4] Final Payment Date and the Redemption Date, if any, selected pursuant to the Indenture. Notwithstanding the foregoing, under certain circumstances, the entire unpaid principal amount of the Class [A-1] [A-2] [A-3] [A-4] Notes shall be due and payable following the occurrence and continuance of an Event of Default, as described in the Indenture. All principal payments on the Class [A-1] [A-2] [A-3] [A-4] Notes shall be made pro rata to the Class [A-1] [A-2] [A-3] [A-4] Noteholders entitled thereto.

Payments of principal and interest on this Note due and payable on each Payment Date or Redemption Date shall be made by check mailed to the Person whose name appears as the registered Holder of this Note (or one or more Predecessor Notes) on the Note Register as of the close of business on the related Record Date, except that with respect to Notes registered on the Record Date in the name of the nominee of the Depository (initially, such nominee to be Cede & Co.), payments will be made by wire transfer in immediately available funds to the account designated by such nominee. Such checks shall be mailed to the Person entitled thereto at the address of such Person as it appears on the Note Register as of the applicable Record Date without requiring that this Note be submitted for notation of payment. Any reduction in the principal amount of this Note (or any one or more Predecessor Notes) affected by any payments made on any Payment Date or Redemption Date shall be binding upon all future Holders of this Note and of any Note issued upon the registration of transfer hereof or in exchange hereof or in lieu hereof, whether or not noted hereon. If funds are expected to be available, as provided in the Indenture, for payment in full of the remaining unpaid principal amount of this Note on a Payment Date or Redemption Date, then the Indenture Trustee, in the name of and on behalf of the Issuer, will notify the Person who was the registered Holder hereof as of the Record Date preceding such Payment Date or Redemption Date by notice mailed within five days of such Payment Date or Redemption Date and the amount then due and payable shall be payable only upon presentation and surrender of this Note at the Corporate Trust Office of the Indenture Trustee or at the office of the Indenture Trustee's agent appointed for such purposes located in The City of New York.

As provided in the Indenture and subject to the limitations set forth therein and on the face hereof, the transfer of this Note may be registered on the Note Register upon surrender of this Note for registration of transfer at the office or agency designated by the Issuer pursuant to the Indenture, duly endorsed by, or accompanied by a written instrument of transfer in form satisfactory to the Indenture Trustee duly executed by, the Holder hereof or such Holder's attorney duly authorized in writing, with such signature guaranteed by an "eligible guarantor institution" meeting the requirements of the Note Registrar, which requirements include membership or participation in the Securities Transfer Agent's Medallion Program ("STAMP") or such other "signature guarantee program" as may be determined by the Note Registrar in addition to, or in substitution for, STAMP, all in accordance with the Securities Exchange Act of 1934, as amended, and thereupon one or more new Notes of authorized denominations and in the same aggregate principal amount will be issued to the designated transferee or transferees. No service charge will be charged for any registration of transfer or exchange of this Note, but the transferor may be required to pay a sum sufficient to cover any tax or other governmental charge that may be imposed in connection with any such registration of transfer or exchange.

Each Noteholder or Note Owner, by acceptance of a Note or, in the case of a Note Owner, a beneficial interest in a Note, covenants and agrees that no recourse may be taken, directly or indirectly, with respect to the obligations of the Issuer, the Owner Trustee or the Indenture Trustee on the Notes or under the Indenture or any certificate or other writing delivered in connection therewith, against (i) the Indenture Trustee or the Owner Trustee in its individual capacity, (ii) any owner of a beneficial interest in the Issuer or (iii) any partner, owner, beneficiary, agent, officer, director or employee of the Indenture Trustee or the Owner Trustee in its individual capacity, any holder of a beneficial interest in the Issuer, the Owner Trustee or the Indenture Trustee or of any successor or assign of the Indenture Trustee or the Owner Trustee in its individual capacity, except as any such Person may have expressly agreed and except that any such partner, owner or beneficiary shall be fully liable, to the extent provided by applicable law, for any unpaid consideration for stock, unpaid capital contribution or failure to pay any installment or call owing to such entity.

Each Noteholder or Note Owner, by acceptance of a Note or, in the case of a Note Owner, a beneficial interest in a Note, covenants and agrees by accepting the benefits of the Indenture that such Noteholder or Note Owner will not at any time institute against the Seller or the Issuer, or join in any institution against the Seller or the Issuer of, any bankruptcy, reorganization, arrangement, insolvency or liquidation proceedings under any United States federal or state bankruptcy or similar law in connection with any obligations relating to the Notes, the Indenture or the other Basic Documents.

Any Person that acquires a beneficial interest in this Note with the assets of a Benefit Plan shall be deemed to represent that its acquisition and holding of such beneficial interest is covered by a U.S. Department of Labor prohibited transaction class exemption.

The Issuer has entered into the Indenture and this Note is issued with the intention that, for federal, state and local income, single business and franchise tax purposes, the Notes will qualify as indebtedness secured by the Owner Trust Estate. Each Noteholder, by acceptance of a Note (and each Note Owner by acceptance of a beneficial interest in a Note), agrees to treat the Notes for federal, state and local income, single business and franchise tax purposes as indebtedness of the Issuer.

Prior to the due presentment for registration of transfer of this Note, the Issuer, the Indenture Trustee and any agent of the Issuer or the Indenture Trustee may treat the Person in whose name this Note (as of the day of determination or as of such other date as may be specified in the Indenture) is registered as the owner hereof for all purposes, whether or not this Note be overdue, and none of the Issuer, the Indenture Trustee or any such agent shall be affected by notice to the contrary.

The Indenture permits, with certain exceptions as therein provided, the amendment thereof and the modification of the rights and obligations of the Issuer and the rights of the Holders of the Notes under the Indenture at any time by the Issuer with the consent of the Holders of Notes representing a majority of the Outstanding Amount of all Notes at the time Outstanding. The Indenture also contains provisions permitting the Holders of Notes representing specified percentages of the Outstanding Amount of the Notes, on behalf of the Holders of all the Notes, to waive compliance by the Issuer with certain provisions of the Indenture and certain past defaults under the Indenture and their consequences. Any such consent or waiver by the Holder of this Note (or any one or more Predecessor Notes) shall be conclusive and binding upon such Holder and upon all future Holders of this Note and of any Note issued upon the registration of transfer hereof or in exchange hereof or in lieu hereof whether or not notation of such consent or waiver is made upon this Note. The Indenture also permits the Indenture Trustee to amend or waive certain terms and conditions set forth in the Indenture without the consent of Holders of the Notes issued thereunder.

The Notes are issuable only in registered form in denominations as provided in the Indenture, subject to certain limitations therein set forth.

This Note and the Indenture shall be construed in accordance with the laws of the State of California, without reference to its conflict of law provisions, and the obligations, rights and remedies of the parties hereunder and thereunder shall be determined in accordance with such laws, except that the duties of the Indenture Trustee are governed by New York law.

No reference herein to the Indenture and no provision of this Note or of the Indenture shall alter or impair the obligation of the Issuer, which is absolute and unconditional, to pay the principal of and interest on this Note at the times, place and rate, and in the coin or currency herein prescribed.

ASSIGNMENT

Social Security or taxpayer I.D. or other identifying number of assignee:

FOR VALUE RECEIVED, the undersigned hereby sells, assigns and transfers unto: ____

(name and address of assignee)

the within Note and all rights thereunder, and hereby irrevocably constitutes and appoints ____

attorney, to transfer said Note on the books kept for registration thereof, with full power of substitution in the premises.

Dated: ________________ ______________________________

* Signature Guaranteed: *

* NOTICE: The signature to this assignment must correspond with the name of the registered owner as it appears on the face of the within Note in every particular, without alteration, enlargement or any change whatever. Such signature must be guaranteed by an "eligible guarantor institution" meeting the requirements of the Note Registrar, which requirements include membership or participation in STAMP or such other "signature guarantee program" as may be determined by the Note Registrar in addition to, or in substitution for, STAMP, all in accordance with the Securities Exchange Act of 1934, as amended.

EXHIBIT B

FORM OF NOTE DEPOSITORY AGREEMENT

[On File with Dewey Ballantine LLP]

Appendix 9

Appendix 9

EXECUTION COPY

AMERICAN HONDA RECEIVABLES CORP.,
as Depositor,

THE BANK OF NEW YORK,
as Owner Trustee

and

THE BANK OF NEW YORK (DELAWARE),
as Delaware Trustee

AMENDED AND RESTATED

TRUST AGREEMENT

Dated February 25, 2003

TABLE OF CONTENTS

ARTICLE ONE
DEFINITIONS

ARTICLE TWO
ORGANIZATION

ARTICLE THREE
TRUST CERTIFICATES AND TRANSFER OF INTERESTS

*[Eds. — Page numbers added.]

ARTICLE FOUR

ACTIONS BY OWNER TRUSTEE

ARTICLE FIVE

APPLICATION OF TRUST FUNDS; CERTAIN DUTIES

ARTICLE SIX

AUTHORITY AND DUTIES OF OWNER TRUSTEE

ARTICLE SEVEN

CONCERNING THE OWNER TRUSTEE AND THE DELAWARE TRUSTEE

ARTICLE EIGHT

COMPENSATION OF OWNER TRUSTEE AND THE DELWARE TRUSTEE

ARTICLE NINE

TERMINATION OF TRUST AGREEMENT

ARTICLE TEN

SUCCESSOR AND ADDITIONAL OWNER TRUSTEES

ARTICLE ELEVEN

MISCELLANEOUS

EXHIBITS

This Amended and Restated Trust Agreement, dated February 25, 2003, is among American Honda Receivables Corp., a California corporation, as depositor (the "Depositor"), The Bank of New York, as trustee (the "Owner Trustee"), and The Bank of New York (Delaware), as Delaware Trustee (the "Delaware Trustee").

WHEREAS, Honda Auto Receivables 2003-1 Owner Trust has been created pursuant to a trust agreement, dated as of January 21, 2003 between the Depositor and the Delaware Trustee (the "Initial Trust Agreement"); and

WHEREAS, the parties hereto are entering into this amended and restated trust agreement pursuant to which, among other things, the Initial Trust Agreement will be amended and restated and $1,541,700,000 aggregate principal amount of Asset Backed Certificates will be issued;

NOW, THEREFORE, in consideration of the mutual agreements herein contained, and of other good and valuable consideration, the receipt and adequacy of which are hereby acknowledged, the parties hereto agree as follows:

ARTICLE ONE

DEFINITIONS

Section 1.01. General Definitions. Whenever used herein, unless the context otherwise requires, the following words and phrases shall have the following meanings:

"Administration Agreement" means the administration agreement, dated as of February 1, 2003, among the Issuer, the Indenture Trustee, the Depositor and AHFC, as amended or supplemented from time to time.

"Administrator" means AHFC, as Administrator under the Administration Agreement, and its successors in such capacity.

"Agreement" means this Amended and Restated Trust Agreement, as the same may be amended and supplemented from time to time.

"AHFC" means American Honda Finance Corporation, and its successors.

"AHRC" means American Honda Receivables Corp., and its successors.

"Applicants" shall have the meaning specified in Section 3.07.

"Benefit Plan" means (i) an employee benefit plan (as such term is defined in Section 3(3) of ERISA) that is subject to the provisions of Title I of ERISA, (ii) a plan described in Section 4975(e)(1) of the Code or (iii) any entity whose underlying assets include plan assets by reason of a plan's investment in the entity.

"Certificate Balance" means, with respect to any Trust Certificate, the original certificate balance of such Trust Certificate minus all payments on such Trust Certificate with respect to principal.

"Certificate Distribution Account" means the account established and maintained as such pursuant to Section 5.01.

"Certificate of Trust" means the Certificate of Trust filed for the Issuer pursuant to Section 3810(a) of the Statutory Trust Statute, substantially in the form of Exhibit A to the Initial Trust Agreement.

"Certificate Rate" means 2.48% per annum calculated on the basis of a 360 day year of twelve 30 day months.

"Certificate Register" and "Certificate Registrar" means the register maintained and the registrar (or any successor thereto) appointed pursuant to Section 3.04.

"Certificateholder" or "Holder" means a Person in whose name a Trust Certificate is registered.

"Closing Date" means February 25, 2003.

"Code" means the Internal Revenue Code of 1986, as amended, and Treasury Regulations promulgated thereunder.

"Commission" means the Securities and Exchange Commission, and its successors.

"Corporate Trust Office" means, with respect to the Owner Trustee, the principal corporate trust office of the Owner Trustee located at 101 Barclay Street, 8th Floor West, New York, New York 10286, or at such other address as the Owner Trustee may designate by notice to the Owners and, the Depositor, or the principal corporate trust office of any successor Owner Trustee at the address designated by such successor Owner Trustee by notice to the Owners and the Depositor.

"Depositor" means AHRC in its capacity as depositor hereunder.

"Delaware Trustee" means The Bank of New York (Delaware), with its principal place of business in the State of Delaware, not in its individual capacity, but solely as Delaware Trustee under this Agreement, and any sucessor Delaware Trustee hereunder.

"DTC" means The Depository Trust Company, and its successors.

"ERISA" means the Employee Retirement Income Security Act of 1974, as amended.

"Exchange Act" means the Securities Exchange Act of 1934, as amended.

"Expenses" means all liabilities, obligations, losses, damages, taxes, claims, actions and suits, and any and all reasonable out of pocket costs, expenses and disbursements (including reasonable legal fees and expenses) of any kind and nature whatsoever.

"Indemnified Parties" means the Owner Trustee and its successors, assigns, agents and any co-trustee and the Delaware Trustee and its successors, assigns, agents and any co-trustee.

"Indenture" means the indenture dated as of February 1, 2003 between the Issuer and JPMorgan Chase Bank, as indenture trustee.

"Investment Letter" means a letter delivered in connection with the transfer of a Trust Certificate pursuant to Section 3.04(a), substantially in the form of Exhibit C.

"Issuer" means the Honda Auto Receivables 2003-1 Owner Trust, and its successors.

"Opinion of Counsel" means one or more written opinions of counsel, who may be an employee of or counsel to the Seller, the Depositor or the Servicer, which counsel shall be acceptable to the Indenture Trustee, the Owner Trustee or each Rating Agency, as applicable.

"Original Certificate Balance" means $35,577,657.84.

"Original Contribution Amount" means $1,000.00.

"Owner" means each Holder of a Trust Certificate.

"Owner Trust Estate" means all right, title and interest of the Issuer in and to the property and rights assigned to the Issuer pursuant to Article Two of the Sale and Servicing Agreement, all funds on deposit from time to time in the Accounts and the Certificate Distribution Account, all other property of the Issuer from time to time, including any rights of the Owner Trustee and the Issuer pursuant to the Sale and Servicing Agreement and the Administration Agreement and all proceeds of the foregoing.

"Owner Trustee" means The Bank of New York, not in its individual capacity but solely as owner trustee under this Agreement, and any successor Owner Trustee hereunder.

"Paying Agent" means any paying agent or co-paying agent appointed pursuant to Section 3.09.

"Payment Date" means the eighteenth calendar day of each month, commencing March 2003, or if such day is not a Business Day, then the next succeeding Business Day.

"Percentage Interest" means, as to any Trust Certificate, (i) the original certificate balance for such Trust Certificate, as specified on the face thereof, divided by (ii) the Original Certificate Balance; provided, that in determining whether the Holders of the requisite portion or percentage of the Trust Certificates have given any request, demand, authorization, direction, notice, consent or waiver hereunder or under any other Basic Document, Trust Certificates owned by the Issuer, any other obligor upon the Certificates, the Seller, the Servicer or any Affiliate of any of the foregoing Persons shall be disregarded and deemed to be excluded from the Certificate Balance (unless such Persons own 100% of the Trust Certificates), except that, in determining whether the Indenture Trustee and Owner Trustee shall be protected in relying on any such request, demand, authorization, direction, notice, consent or waiver, only Trust Certificates that the Indenture Trustee and the Owner Trustee have actual knowledge of being so owned shall be so disregarded. Trust Certificates so owned that have been pledged in good faith may be regarded as included in the Certificate Balance if the pledgee establishes to the satisfaction of the Indenture

Trustee or the Owner Trustee, as applicable, the pledgee's right so to act with respect to such Trust Certificates and that the pledgee is not the Issuer, any other obligor upon the Trust Certificates, the Seller or any Affiliate of any of their respective Affiliates. Neither the Indenture Trustee nor the Owner Trustee shall incur any liability to any person in determining whether a pledgee has the right to act with respect to such Trust Certificates.

"Record Date" means the day immediately preceding the Payment Date so long as the securities are in book-entry form, and the last day of the month preceding the Payment Date if the securities are issued in definitive form.

"Required Rating" means, with respect to any entity, that such entity (or the parent of such entity) has a rating of at least BBB — by Standard & Poor's and at least Baa3 by Moody's.

"Rule 144A Letter" means a letter delivered in connection with the transfer of a Trust Certificate pursuant to Section 3.04(a), substantially in the form attached hereto as Exhibit D.

"Sale and Servicing Agreement" means the sale and servicing agreement, dated as of February 25, 2003, among the Issuer, the Depositor and AHFC, as servicer, as amended or supplemented from time to time.

"Secretary of State" means the Secretary of State of the State of Delaware.

"Securities Act" means the Securities Act of 1933, as amended.

"Seller Certificate" means a certificate of transfer delivered in connection with the transfer of a Trust Certificate pursuant to Section 3.04(a), substantially in the form of Exhibit B.

"Statutory Trust Statute" means Chapter 38 of Title 12 of the Delaware Code, 12 Del.C. §§ 3801 et seq., as the same may be amended from time to time.

"Treasury Regulations" means regulations, including proposed or temporary regulations, promulgated under the Code. References herein to specific provisions of proposed or temporary regulations shall include analogous provisions of final Treasury Regulations or other successor Treasury Regulations.

"Trust Certificate" means a certificate evidencing the beneficial interest of an Owner in the Trust, substantially in the form of Exhibit A.

Section 1.02. Other Definitional Provisions.

(a) Capitalized terms used herein that are not otherwise defined have the meanings ascribed thereto in the Sale and Servicing Agreement or the Indenture, as the case may be.

(b) All terms defined in this Agreement shall have the defined meanings when used in any certificate or other document made or delivered pursuant hereto unless otherwise defined therein.

Section 1.03. Interpretive Provisions.

(a) For all purposes of this Agreement, except as otherwise expressly provided or unless the context otherwise requires, (i) terms used herein include, as appropriate, all genders and the plural as well as the singular, (ii) references to words such as "herein", "hereof" and the like shall refer to this Agreement as a whole and not to any particular part, article or section within this Agreement, (iii) references to a section such as "Section 1.01" and the like shall refer to the applicable Section of this Agreement, (iv) the term "include, and all variations thereof shall mean "include without limitation", (v) the term "or" shall include "and/or" and (vi) the term "proceeds" shall have the meaning set forth in the applicable UCC.

(b) As used in this Agreement and in any certificate or other document made or delivered pursuant hereto or thereto, accounting terms not defined in this Agreement or in any such certificate or other document, and accounting terms partly defined in this Agreement or in any such certificate or other document to the extent not defined, shall have the respective meanings given to them under generally accepted accounting principles. To the extent that the definitions of accounting terms in this Agreement or in any such certificate or other document are inconsistent with the meanings of such terms under generally accepted accounting principles, the definitions contained in this Agreement or in any such certificate or other document shall control.

ARTICLE TWO
ORGANIZATION

Section 2.01. Name. The trust created hereby shall be known as the "Honda Auto Receivables 2003-1 Owner Trust", in which name the Owner Trustee may conduct the business of the Issuer, make and execute contracts and other instruments and sue and be sued, to the extent herein provided.

Section 2.02. Office. The Delaware office of the Issuer shall be in care of the Delaware Trustee at White Clay Center Route 273, Newark, Delaware 19711, or at such other address in the State of Delaware as the Delaware Trustee may designate by written notice to the Owners and the Depositor. The New York, New York office of the Issuer shall be in care of the Owner Trustee at the Corporate Trust Office or at such other address in Delaware as the Owner Trustee may designate by written notice to the Owners and the Depositor.

Section 2.03. Purposes and Powers.

(a) The sole purpose of the Issuer is to conserve the Owner Trust Estate and collect and disburse the periodic income therefrom for the use and benefit of the Certificateholders, and in furtherance of such purpose to engage in the following ministerial activities:

(i) to issue the Notes pursuant to the Indenture and the Trust Certificates pursuant to this Agreement and to sell the Notes and the Trust Certificates;

(ii) with the proceeds of the sale of the Notes and the Trust Certificates, to purchase the Receivables, to fund the Reserve Fund and the Yield Supplement Account, to pay the organizational, start-up and transactional expenses of the

Trust and to pay the balance to the Depositor pursuant to the Sale and Servicing Agreement;

(iii) to assign, grant, transfer, pledge, mortgage and convey the Owner Trust Estate pursuant to the Indenture and to hold, manage and distribute to the Owners pursuant to the Sale and Servicing Agreement any portion of the Owner Trust Estate released from the Lien of, and remitted to the Trust pursuant to, the Indenture;

(iv) to enter into and perform its obligations under the Basic Documents to which it is to be a party;

(v) to engage in those activities, including entering into agreements, that are necessary to accomplish the foregoing or are incidental thereto or connected therewith; and

(vi) subject to compliance with the Basic Documents, to engage in such other activities as may be required in connection with conservation of the Owner Trust Estate and the making of distributions to the Owners and the Noteholders.

(b) The Issuer is hereby authorized to engage in the foregoing activities. The Issuer shall not engage in any activities other than in connection with the foregoing or other than as required or authorized by the terms of this Agreement or the other Basic Documents.

Section 2.04. Appointment of Owner Trustee and Delaware Trustee. The Depositor hereby appoints the Owner Trustee as trustee of the Issuer effective as of the date hereof, to have all the rights, powers and duties set forth herein, and the Owner Trustee hereby accepts such appointment. The Depositor hereby appoints the Delaware Trustee as a trustee of the Issuer effective as of the date hereof, for the sole purpose of satisfying Section 3807(a) of the Delaware Statutory Trust Statute, and the Delaware Trustee hereby accepts such appointment. The Owner Trustee may engage, in the name of the Issuer or in its own name on behalf of the Issuer, in the activities of the Issuer, make and execute contracts on behalf of the Issuer and sue on behalf of the Issuer.

Section 2.05. Initial Capital Contribution of Owner Trust Estate. The Depositor hereby reaffirms its sale, assignment, transfer and conveyance to the Owner Trustee, as of the date of the Initial Trust Agreement, the sum of $1,000.00 (the "Original Contribution Amount"). The Owner Trustee hereby reaffirms its receipt in trust from the Depositor, as of the date of the Initial Trust Agreement, of the Original Contribution Amount, which constituted the initial Owner Trust Estate and shall be on or before the date hereof deposited in the Certificate Distribution Account. On the date hereof the Owner Trustee is hereby directed to withdraw the Original Contribution Amount from the Certificate Distribution Account and transfer such sums to the Depositor via wire transfer to the Depositor's account from which the Original Contribution Amount was received. The Depositor shall pay organizational expenses of the Issuer as they may arise or shall, upon the request of the Owner Trustee, promptly reimburse the Owner Trustee for any such expenses paid by the Owner Trustee.

Section 2.06. Declaration of Trust. The Owner Trustee hereby declares that it will hold the Owner Trust Estate in trust upon and subject to the conditions set forth herein for the sole purpose of conserving the Owner Trust Estate and collecting and disbursing the periodic income therefrom for the use and benefit of the Owners, subject to the obligations of the Issuer under the Basic Documents. It is the intention of the parties hereto that the Issuer constitute a statutory trust under the Statutory Trust Statute and that this Agreement constitute the governing instrument of such statutory trust. It is the intention of the parties hereto that, solely for income and franchise tax purposes, (i) so long as there is a sole Owner, the Issuer shall be disregarded as an entity separate from the owner, with the assets of the Issuer being the Receivables and other assets held by the Issuer, the owner of the Receivables being the sole Owner and the Notes being non-recourse debt of the sole Owner and (ii) if there is more than one Owner, the Issuer shall be treated as a partnership for income and franchise tax purposes, with the assets of the partnership being the Receivables and other assets held by the Issuer and with the partners of the partnership being the Owners and the Notes being debt of the partnership. The parties agree that, unless otherwise required by appropriate tax authorities, the Issuer will file or cause to be filed annual or other necessary returns, reports and other forms consistent with the characterization of the Issuer as provided in the preceding sentence for such tax purposes. Effective as of the date hereof, the Owner Trustee and the Delaware Trustee, as applicable, shall have all rights, powers and duties set forth herein and in the Statutory Trust Statute for the sole purpose and to the extent necessary to accomplish the purpose of the Issuer as set forth in Section 2.03(a).

Section 2.07. Liability of Owners. The Owners shall be entitled to the same limitation of personal liability extended to stockholders of private corporations for profit organized under the general corporation law of the State of Delaware.

Section 2.08. Title to Trust Property. Legal title to the Owner Trust Estate shall be vested at all times in the Issuer as a separate legal entity except where applicable law in any jurisdiction requires title to any part of the Owner Trust Estate to be vested in a trustee or trustees, in which case title shall be deemed to be vested in the Owner Trustee, a co-trustee and/or a separate trustee, as the case may be.

Section 2.09. Situs of Issuer. The Issuer will be located in the State of Delaware. All bank accounts maintained by the Owner Trustee on behalf of the Issuer shall be located in the states of Delaware or New York. The Issuer shall not have any employees in any state other than Delaware; provided, however, that nothing herein shall restrict or prohibit the Owner Trustee from having employees within or without the State of Delaware. Payments will be received by the Issuer only in, and payments will be made by the Issuer only from, the states of Delaware or New York. The only office of the Issuer will be at the Corporate Trust Office.

Section 2.10. Representations and Warranties of the Depositor. The Depositor hereby represents and warrants to the Owner Trustee and the Delaware Trustee that:

(a) The Depositor has been duly organized and is validly existing as a corporation in good standing under the laws of the State of California, with power and authority to own its properties and to conduct its business as such properties are currently owned and such business is presently conducted, and had at all relevant times, and has, power, authority and legal right to acquire, own and sell the Receivables.

(b) The Depositor is duly qualified to do business as a foreign corporation in good standing, and has obtained all necessary licenses and approvals in all jurisdictions in which the ownership or lease of its property or the conduct of its business shall require such qualifications.

(c) The Depositor has the power and authority to execute and deliver this Agreement and to carry out its terms; the Depositor has full power and authority to sell and assign the property to be sold and assigned to and deposited with the Owner Trustee as part of the Owner Trust Estate and the Depositor has duly authorized such sale and assignment and deposit to the Issuer by all necessary corporate action; and the execution, delivery and performance of this Agreement have been duly authorized by the Depositor by all necessary corporate action.

(d) This Agreement constitutes a legal, valid and binding obligation of the Depositor, enforceable in accordance with its terms, except as such enforceability may be subject to or limited by bankruptcy, insolvency, reorganization, moratorium, liquidation, fraudulent conveyance or other similar laws affecting the enforcement of creditors' rights in general and by general principles of equity, regardless of whether such enforceability shall be considered in a proceeding in equity or in law.

(e) The execution, delivery and performance by the Depositor of this Agreement and the consummation of the transactions contemplated by this Agreement and the fulfillment of the terms hereof do not conflict with, result in any breach of any of the terms and provisions of, nor constitute (with or without notice or lapse of time) a default under, the articles of incorporation or bylaws of the Depositor, or conflict with or violate any of the material terms or provisions of, or constitute (with or without notice or lapse of time) a default under, any indenture, agreement or other instrument to which the Depositor is a party or by which it is bound; nor result in the creation or imposition of any Lien upon any of its properties pursuant to the terms of any such indenture, agreement or other instrument (other than pursuant to the Basic Documents); nor violate any law or, to the best of the Depositor's knowledge, any order, rule or regulation applicable to the Depositor of any court or of any federal or state regulatory body, administrative agency or other governmental instrumentality having jurisdiction over the Depositor or its properties; which breach, default, conflict, lien or violation would have a material adverse effect on the earnings, business affairs or business prospects of the Depositor.

(f) There are no proceedings or investigations pending or, to the Depositor's knowledge, threatened, before any court, regulatory body, administrative agency or other governmental instrumentality having jurisdiction over the Depositor or its properties: (i) asserting the invalidity of this Agreement, (ii) seeking to prevent the issuance of the Trust Certificates or the consummation of any of the transactions contemplated by this Agreement or (iii) seeking any determination or ruling that might materially and adversely affect the performance by the Depositor of its obligations under, or the validity or enforceability of, this Agreement.

ARTICLE THREE
TRUST CERTIFICATES AND TRANSFER OF INTERESTS

Section 3.01. Initial Ownership. Upon the formation of the Issuer by the contribution by the Depositor pursuant to Section 2.05 and until the issuance of the Trust Certificates, the Depositor shall be the sole beneficiary of the Issuer.

Section 3.02. The Trust Certificates. The Trust Certificates shall be issued in minimum denominations of $100,000 and integral multiples thereof; provided, however, that one Trust Certificate may be issued in such denomination as required to include any residual amount. The Trust Certificates shall be executed by the Owner Trustee on behalf of the Issuer by manual or facsimile signature of an authorized officer of the Owner Trustee and shall have deemed to have been validly issued when so executed and authenticated (as set forth in Section 3.03 below). Trust Certificates bearing the manual or facsimile signatures of individuals who were, at the time when such signatures were affixed, authorized to sign on behalf of the Owner Trustee, shall be validly issued and binding obligations of the Issuer and entitled to the benefit of this Agreement, notwithstanding that such individuals or any of them shall have ceased to be so authorized prior to the authentication and delivery of such Trust Certificates or did not hold such offices at the date of authentication and delivery of such Trust Certificates.

A transferee of a Trust Certificate shall become a Certificateholder and shall be entitled to the rights and subject to the obligations of a Certificateholder hereunder upon such transferee's acceptance of a Trust Certificate duly registered in such transferee's name pursuant to Section 3.04.

Section 3.03. Authentication and Delivery of Trust Certificates. On the Closing Date, the Owner Trustee shall cause to be authenticated and delivered upon the order of the Depositor, in exchange for the Receivables and the other assets of the Issuer, simultaneously with the sale, assignment and transfer to the Issuer of the Receivables, and the constructive delivery to the Issuer of the Receivable Files and the other assets of the Issuer, Trust Certificates duly authenticated by the Owner Trustee, in authorized denominations equaling in the aggregate the Original Certificate Balance and evidencing the entire ownership of the Issuer. No Trust Certificate shall entitle its Holder to any benefit under this Agreement, or be valid for any purpose, unless there shall appear on such Trust Certificate a certificate of authentication substantially in the form set forth in Exhibit A, executed by the Owner Trustee or its authenticating agent, by manual signature; and such authentication shall constitute conclusive evidence that such Trust Certificate shall have been duly authenticated and delivered hereunder. All Trust Certificates shall be dated the date of their authentication. Upon issuance, authentication and delivery pursuant to the terms hereof, the Trust Certificates will be entitled to the benefits of this Agreement. Whenever, in any Basic Document, a reference is made to authentication by the Owner Trustee, such reference shall include authentication by the Owner Trustee or its authenticating agent.

Section 3.04. Registration of Transfer and Exchange of Trust Certificates.

(a) The Certificate Registrar shall keep or cause to be kept, at the office or agency maintained pursuant to Section 3.08, a Certificate Register in which, subject to such reasonable regulations as it may prescribe, the Owner Trustee shall provide for the registration of Trust Certificates and of transfers and exchanges of Trust Certificates as herein provided. The Owner Trustee shall act as initial Certificate Registrar. The Owner Trustee may appoint an agent to act as Certificate Registrar. Upon any resignation of the Certificate Registrar, the Owner Trustee shall promptly appoint a successor thereto.

The Trust Certificates have not been registered under the Securities Act or listed on any securities exchange. No transfer of a Trust Certificate shall be made unless such transfer is made pursuant to an effective registration statement under the Securities Act and any applicable state securities laws or is exempt from the registration requirements under the Securities Act and such state securities laws. In the event that a transfer is to be made in reliance upon an exemption from the Securities Act and state securities laws, in order to assure compliance with the Securities Act and such laws, the Holder desiring to effect such transfer and such Holder's prospective transferee shall each certify to the Issuer in writing the facts surrounding the transfer in the form of a Seller Certificate and Investment Letter or a Rule 144A Letter. Except in the case of a transfer as to which the proposed transferee has provided a Rule 144A Letter, there shall also be delivered to the Issuer an Opinion of Counsel that such transfer may be made pursuant to an exemption from the Securities Act and an Opinion of Counsel or memorandum of law that such transfer may be made pursuant to an exemption from state securities laws, which Opinion(s) of Counsel and memorandum of law shall not be an expense of the Issuer or the Owner Trustee. The Depositor shall provide to any Holder of a Trust Certificate and any prospective transferee designated by any such Holder, information regarding the Trust Certificates and the Receivables and such other information as shall be necessary to satisfy the condition to eligibility set forth in Rule 144A(d)(4) for transfer of any such Trust Certificate without registration thereof under the Securities Act pursuant to the registration exemption provided by Rule 144A. Each Holder of a Trust Certificate desiring to effect such a transfer shall, and does hereby agree to, indemnify the Issuer, the Owner Trustee and the Depositor against any liability that may result if the transfer is not so exempt or is not made in accordance with federal and state securities laws. The Owner Trustee on behalf of the Issuer shall cause each Trust Certificate to contain a legend in the form set forth on the form of Trust Certificate attached hereto as Exhibit A.

(b) Upon surrender for registration of transfer of any Trust Certificate at the office of the Certificate Registrar and subject to the satisfaction of the preceding paragraph, the Owner Trustee shall execute, authenticate and deliver (or shall cause its authenticating agent to authenticate and deliver), in the name of the designated transferee or transferees, one or more new Trust Certificates in authorized denominations of a like aggregate original certificate balance dated the date of authentication by the Owner Trustee or any authenticating agent; provided that prior to such execution, authentication and delivery, the Owner Trustee shall have received an Opinion of Counsel to the effect that the proposed transfer will not cause the Issuer to be characterized, as an association (or a publicly traded partnership) taxable as a corporation or alter the tax characterization of the Notes for federal income tax purposes. At the option of a Holder, Trust Certificates may be exchanged for other Trust Certificates of authorized denominations of a like aggregate original certificate balance upon surrender of the Trust Certificates to be exchanged at the office or agency maintained pursuant to Section 3.08.

(c) At the option of a Certificateholder, Trust Certificates may be exchanged for other Trust Certificates in authorized denominations of a like aggregate original certificate balance upon surrender of the Trust Certificates to be exchanged at the office of the Certificate Registrar. Whenever any Trust Certificates are so surrendered for exchange, the Owner Trustee on behalf of the Issuer shall execute, authenticate and deliver (or shall cause its authenticating agent to authenticate and deliver) the Trust Certificates that the Certificateholder making the exchange is entitled to receive. Every Trust Certificate presented or surrendered for registration of transfer or exchange shall be accompanied by a written instrument of transfer in form satisfactory to the Owner Trustee and the Certificate Registrar duly executed by the Holder or such Holder's attorney duly authorized in writing.

(d) No service charge shall be made for any registration of transfer or exchange of Trust Certificates, but the Owner Trustee may require payment of a sum sufficient to cover any tax or governmental charge that may be imposed in connection with any transfer or exchange of Trust Certificates.

(e) The Trust Certificates may not be acquired by or for the account of a Benefit Plan. No transfer of a Trust Certificate shall be made unless the prospective transferee has certified to the Issuer in writing that it is not a Benefit Plan.

(f) All Trust Certificates surrendered for registration of transfer or exchange, if surrendered to the Issuer or any agent of the Owner Trustee or the Issuer under this Agreement, shall be delivered to the Owner Trustee and promptly cancelled by it, or, if surrendered to the Owner Trustee, shall be promptly cancelled by it, and no Trust Certificates shall be issued in lieu thereof except as expressly permitted by any of the provisions of this Agreement. The Owner Trustee shall dispose of cancelled Trust Certificates in accordance with its normal practice.

(g) The preceding provisions of this Section notwithstanding, the Owner Trustee shall not make, and the Certificate Registrar shall not register transfers or exchanges of, Trust Certificates for a period of 15 days preceding the due date for any payment with respect to the Trust Certificates.

Section 3.05. Mutilated, Destroyed, Lost or Stolen Trust Certificates. If (i) any mutilated Trust Certificate is surrendered to the Certificate Registrar, or the Certificate Registrar receives evidence to its satisfaction of the destruction, loss or theft of any Trust Certificate and (ii) there is delivered to the Certificate Registrar and the Owner Trustee such security or indemnity as may be required by them to save each of them harmless, then, in the absence of notice that such Trust Certificate has been acquired by a bona fide purchaser, the Owner Trustee on behalf of the Issuer shall execute and the Owner Trustee or its authenticating agent shall authenticate and deliver, in exchange for or in lieu of any such mutilated, destroyed, lost or stolen Trust Certificate, a new Trust Certificate in an authorized denomination and of a like original certificate balance. In connection with the issuance of any new Trust Certificate under this Section, the Owner Trustee may require the payment of a sum sufficient to cover any tax or other governmental charge that may be imposed in connection therewith. Any duplicate Trust Certificate issued pursuant to this Section shall constitute conclusive evidence of ownership in the Trust, as if originally issued, whether or not the lost, stolen or destroyed Trust Certificate shall be found at any time.

Section 3.06. Persons Deemed Owners. Prior to due presentation of a Trust Certificate for registration of transfer, the Owner Trustee, the Certificate Registrar, any Paying Agent and any of their respective agents may treat the Person in whose name any Trust Certificate is registered as the owner of such Trust Certificate for the purpose of receiving distributions pursuant to Section 5.02 and for all other purposes whatsoever, and none of the Owner Trustee, the Certificate Registrar, any Paying Agent or any of their respective agents shall be affected by any notice to the contrary.

Section 3.07. Access to List of Certificateholders' Names and Addresses. The Owner Trustee shall furnish or cause to be furnished to the Servicer and the Depositor, within 15 days after receipt by the Owner Trustee of a written request therefor from the Servicer or the Depositor, a list, in such form as the Servicer or the Depositor may reasonably require, of the names and addresses of the Certificateholders as of the most recent Record Date. If three or more Certificateholders, or one or more Certificateholders evidencing not less than 51% of the Percentage Interests of the Trust Certificates (hereinafter referred to as the "Applicants"), apply in writing to the Owner Trustee, and such application states that the Applicants desire to communicate with other Certificateholders with respect to their rights under this Agreement or under the Trust Certificates, then the Owner Trustee shall, within five Business Days after the receipt of such application, afford such Applicants access during normal business hours to the current list of Certificateholders. Each Holder, by receiving and holding a Trust Certificate, shall be deemed to have agreed not to hold any of the Depositor, the Certificate Registrar or the Owner Trustee accountable by reason of the disclosure of its name and address, regardless of the source from which such information was derived.

Section 3.08. Maintenance of Office or Agency. The Owner Trustee shall maintain in New York, New York, an office or offices or agency or agencies where Trust Certificates may be surrendered for registration of transfer or exchange and where notices and demands to or upon the Owner Trustee in respect of the Trust Certificates and the Basic Documents may be served. The Owner Trustee initially designates The Bank of New York, 101 Barclay Street, 8th Floor West, New York, New York 10286, Attention: Asset Backed Securities Unit — Honda 2003-1 as its office for such purposes. The Owner Trustee shall give prompt written notice to the Depositor and to the Certificateholders of any change in the location of the Certificate Register or any such office or agency.

Section 3.09. Appointment of Paying Agent. The Paying Agent shall make distributions to Certificateholders from the Certificate Distribution Account pursuant to Sections 5.02 and 5.03 and shall report the amounts of such distributions to the Owner Trustee. Any Paying Agent shall have the revocable power to withdraw funds from the Certificate Distribution Account for the purpose of making the distributions referred to above. The Owner Trustee may revoke such power and remove the Paying Agent if the Owner Trustee determines in its sole discretion that the Paying Agent shall have failed to perform its obligations under this Agreement in any material respect. The Owner Trustee initially appoints The Bank of New York as the Paying Agent and any co-paying agent chosen by the Paying Agent that is acceptable to the Owner Trustee. Each Paying Agent shall be permitted to resign as Paying Agent upon 30 days' written notice to the Owner Trustee. In the event that The Bank of New York shall no longer be the Paying Agent, the Owner Trustee shall appoint a successor to act as Paying Agent (which shall be a bank or trust company). The Owner Trustee shall cause such successor Paying Agent or any additional Paying Agent appointed by the Owner Trustee to execute and deliver to the Owner Trustee an instrument in which such successor Paying Agent or additional Paying Agent shall agree with the Owner Trustee that, as Paying Agent, such successor Paying Agent or additional Paying Agent will hold all sums, if any, held by it for payment to the Certificateholders in trust for the benefit of the Certificateholders entitled thereto until such sums shall be paid to such Certificateholders. The Paying Agent shall return all unclaimed funds to the Owner Trustee and upon removal of a Paying Agent such Paying Agent shall also return all funds in its possession to the Owner Trustee. The provisions of Sections 7.01, 7.03, 7.04, 8.01 and 8.02 shall apply to the Owner Trustee also in its role as Paying Agent, for so long as the Owner Trustee shall act as Paying Agent and, to the extent applicable, to any other paying agent appointed hereunder. Any reference in this Agreement to the Paying Agent shall include any co-paying agent unless the context requires otherwise.

Section 3.10. Definitive Trust Certificates. The Trust Certificates, upon original issuance, will be issued in definitive, fully registered form.

Section 3.11. Repayment of Trust Certificates. In the event of an optional purchase pursuant to Section 8.01 (a) of the Sale and Servicing Agreement, the Trust Certificates will be prepaid in whole, but not in part, at an aggregate prepayment price equal to the aggregate Certificate Balance of all the Trust Certificates plus accrued interest thereon at the Certificate Rate.

ARTICLE FOUR
ACTIONS BY OWNER TRUSTEE

Section 4.01. Prior Notice to Owners with Respect to Certain Matters. Subject to the provisions and limitations of Section 4.04, with respect to the following matters, the Owner Trustee shall not take action unless at least 30 days before the taking of such action, the Owner Trustee shall have notified the Certificateholders in writing of the proposed action and the Owners shall not have notified the Owner Trustee in writing prior to the 30th day after such notice is given that such Owners have withheld consent or provided alternative direction:

(a) the initiation of any claim or lawsuit by the Issuer (except claims or lawsuits brought in connection with the collection of the Receivables) and the compromise of any action, claim or lawsuit brought by or against the Issuer (except with respect to the aforementioned claims or lawsuits for collection of the Receivables);

(b) the election by the Issuer to file an amendment to the Certificate of Trust (unless such amendment is required to be filed under the Statutory Trust Statute);

(c) the amendment of the Indenture by a supplemental indenture in circumstances where the consent of any Noteholder is required;

(d) the amendment of the Indenture by a supplemental indenture in circumstances where the consent of any Noteholder is not required and such amendment materially adversely affects the interests of the Owners;

(e) the amendment, change or modification of the Administration Agreement, except to cure any ambiguity or to amend or supplement any provision in a manner or add any provision that would not materially adversely affect the interests of the Owners; or

(f) the appointment pursuant to the Indenture of a successor Note Registrar, paying agent for the Notes or Indenture Trustee or pursuant to this Agreement of a successor Certificate Registrar, or the consent to the assignment by the Note Registrar, Paying Agent, Indenture Trustee or Certificate Registrar of its obligations under the Indenture or this Agreement, as applicable.

Section 4.02. Action by Owners with Respect to Certain Matters. Subject to the provisions and limitations of Section 4.04, the Owner Trustee shall not have the power, except upon the direction of the Owners, to (i) remove the Administrator pursuant to Section 1.09 of the Administration Agreement, (ii) appoint a successor Administrator pursuant to Section 1.09 of the Administration Agreement, (iii) remove the Servicer pursuant to Section 7.02 of the Sale and Servicing Agreement, (iv) except as expressly provided in the Basic Documents, sell the Receivables after the termination of the Indenture, or (v) authorize the merger or consolidation of the Issuer with or into any other statutory trust or entity (other than in accordance with Section 3.10 of the Indenture). The Owner Trustee shall take the actions referred to in the preceding sentence only upon written instructions signed by the Owners.

Section 4.03. Action by Owners with Respect to Bankruptcy. The Owner Trustee shall not have the power to commence a voluntary proceeding in bankruptcy relating to the Issuer without the unanimous prior approval of all Owners (including the Depositor) and the delivery to the Owner Trustee by each such Owner of a certificate certifying that such Owner reasonably believes that the Issuer is insolvent.

Section 4.04. Restrictions on Owners' Power. The Owners shall not direct the Owner Trustee to take or to refrain from taking any action if such action or inaction would be contrary to any obligation of the Issuer or the Owner Trustee under this Agreement or any of the other Basic Documents or would be contrary to the purpose of the Issuer as set forth in Section 2.03, nor shall the Owner Trustee be obligated to follow any such direction, if given.

Section 4.05. Majority Control. Except as expressly provided herein, any action that may be taken by the Owners under this Agreement may be taken by the Holders of Trust Certificates evidencing not less than a majority of the Percentage Interests evidenced by the Trust Certificates. Except as expressly provided herein, any written notice of the Owners delivered pursuant to this Agreement shall be effective if signed by Holders of Trust Certificates evidencing not less than a majority of the Percentage Interests evidenced by the Trust Certificates at the time of the delivery of such notice.

ARTICLE FIVE

APPLICATION OF TRUST FUNDS; CERTAIN DUTIES

Section 5.01. Establishment of Trust Account. The Owner Trustee, for the benefit of the Certificateholders, shall establish and maintain (or shall cause to be established and maintained) in the name of the Issuer an Eligible Account (the "Certificate Distribution Account"), bearing a designation clearly indicating that the funds deposited therein are held for the benefit of the Certificateholders.

The Issuer shall possess all right, title and interest in funds on deposit from time to time in the Certificate Distribution Account and in the proceeds thereof. Except as otherwise expressly provided herein, the Certificate Distribution Account shall be under the sole dominion and control of the Owner Trustee for the benefit of the Certificateholders. If, at any time, the Certificate Distribution Account ceases to be an Eligible Account, the Owner Trustee (or the Depositor on behalf of the Owner Trustee, if the Certificate Distribution Account is not then held by the Owner Trustee or an Affiliate thereof) shall within ten Business

Days (or such longer period, not to exceed 30 calendar days, as to which each Rating Agency may consent) establish a new Certificate Distribution Account as an Eligible Account and shall transfer any cash and/or any investments to such new Certificate Distribution Account. Monies on deposit in the Certificate Distribution Account may be invested in Eligible Investments upon the terms set forth in Section 4.01 of the Sale and Servicing Agreement, as if the Certificate Distribution Account were an "Account". Earnings on investments of funds in the Certificate Distribution Account shall be paid to the Servicer as part of the Supplemental Servicing Fee and any losses and investment expenses shall be charged against the funds in such account.

Section 5.02. Application of Trust Funds.

(a) On each Payment Date, the Paying Agent will distribute to Certificateholders, on the basis of the Percentage Interest evidenced by their Trust Certificates, amounts deposited in the Certificate Distribution Account pursuant to Section 4.06 of the Sale and Servicing Agreement with respect to such Payment Date.

(b) On each Payment Date, the Paying Agent shall send to each Certificateholder the statement or statements provided to the Owner Trustee by the Servicer pursuant to Section 4.10 of the Sale and Servicing Agreement with respect to such Payment Date.

(c) In the event that any withholding tax is imposed on the Issuer's payment (or allocations of income) to an Owner, such tax shall reduce the amount otherwise distributable to the Owner in accordance with this Section. The Owner Trustee is hereby authorized and directed to retain from amounts otherwise distributable to the Owners sufficient funds for the payment of any tax that is legally owed by the Issuer (but such authorization shall not prevent the Owner Trustee from contesting any such tax in appropriate proceedings and withholding payment of such tax, if permitted by law, pending the outcome of such proceedings). The amount of any withholding tax imposed with respect to an Owner shall be treated as cash distributed to such Owner at the time it is withheld by the Issuer and remitted to the appropriate taxing authority. If there is a possibility that withholding tax is payable with respect to a distribution, the Owner Trustee may in its sole discretion withhold such amounts in accordance with this paragraph (c).

Section 5.03. Method of Payment. Subject to Section 9.01(c) respecting the final payment upon retirement of each Trust Certificate, distributions required to be made to Certificateholders on any Payment Date shall be made to each Certificateholder of record on the related Record Date by wire transfer, in immediately available funds, to the account of such Holder at a bank or other entity having appropriate facilities therefor, if such Certificateholder shall have provided to the Certificate Registrar appropriate written instructions at least five Business Days prior to such Payment Date, or, if not, by check mailed to such Certificateholder at the address of such Holder appearing in the Certificate Register.

Section 5.04. No Segregation of Monies; No Interest. Subject to Sections 5.01 and 5.02, monies received by the Owner Trustee hereunder need not be segregated in any manner except to the extent required by law or the Sale and Servicing Agreement and may be deposited under such general conditions as may be prescribed by law, and the Owner Trustee shall not be liable for any interest thereon.

Section 5.05. Accounting and Reports to Owners, Internal Revenue Service and Others. The Owner Trustee shall maintain (or cause to be maintained) the books of the Issuer on a fiscal year basis ending March 31 of each year and the accrual method of accounting. In addition, the Issuer shall deliver to each Owner such information, reports or statements as may be required by the Code and applicable Treasury Regulations and as may be required to enable each Owner to prepare its federal and state income tax returns. Consistent with the Issuer's characterization for tax purposes, as disregarded as an entity separate from the Owner, no federal income tax return shall be filed on behalf of the Issuer unless either (i) the Owner Trustee shall receive an Opinion of Counsel that, based on a change in applicable law occurring after the date hereof, the Code requires such a filing or (ii) the Internal Revenue Service shall determine that the Issuer is required to file such a return. Neither the Owner Trustee nor any Certificateholder will, under any circumstances, and at any time, make an election on IRS Form 8832 or otherwise, to classify the Trust as an association taxable as a corporation for federal, state or any other applicable tax purpose. In the event that the Issuer is required to file tax returns, the Owner Trustee shall prepare or shall cause to be prepared any tax returns required to be filed by the Issuer and shall remit such returns to the Depositor (or if the Depositor no longer owns any Certificates, the Owner designated for such purpose by the Depositor to the Owner Trustee in writing) at least five days before such returns are due to be filed. The Depositor (or such designee Owner, as applicable) shall promptly sign such returns and deliver such returns after signature to the Owner Trustee and such returns shall be filed by the Owner Trustee with the appropriate tax authorities. In no event shall the Owner Trustee or the Depositor (or such designee Owner, as applicable) be liable for any liabilities, costs or expenses of the Issuer or the Noteholders arising out of the application of any tax law, including federal, state, foreign or local income or excise taxes or any other tax imposed on or measured by income (or any interest, penalty or addition with respect thereto or arising from a failure to comply therewith) except for any such liability, cost or expense attributable to any act or omission by the Owner Trustee or the Depositor (or such designee Owner, as applicable), as the case may be, in breach of its obligations under this Agreement.

ARTICLE SIX

AUTHORITY AND DUTIES OF OWNER TRUSTEE

Section 6.01. General Authority. Subject to the provisions and limitations of Sections 2.03 and 2.06, the Owner Trustee is authorized and directed to execute and deliver the Basic Documents to which the Issuer is to be a party and each certificate or other document attached as an exhibit to or contemplated by the Basic Documents to which the Issuer is to be a party and any amendment or other agreement, as evidenced conclusively by the Owner Trustee's execution thereof. In addition to the foregoing, the Owner Trustee is authorized, but shall not be obligated, to take all actions required of the Issuer pursuant to the Basic Documents. The Owner Trustee is further authorized from time to time to take such action as the Administrator recommends with respect to the Basic Documents.

Section 6.02. General Duties. Subject to the provisions and limitations of Sections 2.03 and 2.06, it shall be the duty of the Owner Trustee to discharge (or cause to be discharged) all of its responsibilities pursuant to the terms of this Agreement and the other Basic Documents to which the Issuer is a party and to administer the Issuer in the interest of the Owners, subject to the Basic Documents and in accordance with the provisions of this Agreement. Notwithstanding the foregoing, the Owner Trustee shall be deemed to have discharged its duties and responsibilities hereunder and under the other Basic Documents to the extent the Administrator has agreed in the Administration Agreement to perform any act or to discharge any duty of the Owner Trustee hereunder or under any Basic Document, and the Owner Trustee shall not be held liable for the default or failure of the Administrator to carry out its obligations under the Administration Agreement.

Section 6.03. Action Upon Instruction.

(a) Subject to Article Four, in accordance with the terms of the Basic Documents, the Owners may by written instruction direct the Owner Trustee in the management of the Issuer. Such direction may be exercised at any time by written instruction of the Owners pursuant to Article Four.

(b) The Owner Trustee shall not be required to take any action hereunder or under any other Basic Document if the Owner Trustee shall have reasonably determined, or shall have been advised by counsel, that such action is likely to result in liability on the part of the Owner Trustee or is contrary to the terms hereof or of any other Basic Document or is otherwise contrary to law.

(c) Whenever the Owner Trustee is unable to decide between alternative courses of action permitted or required by the terms of this Agreement or under any other Basic Document, the Owner Trustee shall promptly give notice (in such form as shall be appropriate under the circumstances) to the Owners requesting instruction as to the course of action to be adopted, and to the extent the Owner Trustee acts in good faith in accordance with any written instruction of the Owners received, the Owner Trustee shall not be liable on account of such action to any Person. If the Owner Trustee shall not have received appropriate instruction within ten days of such notice (or within such shorter period of time as reasonably may be specified in such notice or may be necessary under the circumstances) it may, but shall be under no duty to, take or refrain from taking such action not inconsistent with this Agreement and the other Basic Documents, as it shall deem to be in the best interests of the Owners, and shall have no liability to any Person for such action or inaction.

(d) In the event that the Owner Trustee is unsure as to the application of any provision of this Agreement or any other Basic Document or any such provision is ambiguous as to its application, or is, or appears to be, in conflict with any other applicable provision, or in the event that this Agreement permits any determination by the Owner Trustee or is silent or is incomplete as to the course of action that the Owner Trustee is required to take with respect to a particular set of facts, the Owner Trustee may give notice (in such form as shall be appropriate under the circumstances) to the Owners requesting instruction and, to the extent that the Owner Trustee acts or refrains from acting in good faith in accordance with any such instruction received, the Owner Trustee shall not be liable, on account of such action or inaction, to any Person. If the Owner Trustee shall not have received appropriate instruction within ten days of such notice (or within such shorter period of time as reasonably may be specified in such notice or may be necessary under the circumstances) it may, but shall be under no duty to, take or refrain from taking such action not inconsistent with this Agreement or the other Basic Documents, as it shall deem to be in the best interests of the Owners, and shall have no liability to any Person for such action or inaction.

Section 6.04. No Duties Except as Specified in this Agreement or in Instructions. The Owner Trustee shall not have any duty or obligation to manage, make any payment with respect to, register, record, sell, dispose of, or otherwise deal with the Owner Trust Estate, or to otherwise take or refrain from taking any action under, or in connection with, any document contemplated hereby to which the Owner Trustee is a party, except as expressly provided by the terms of this Agreement or in any document or written instruction received by the Owner Trustee pursuant to Section 6.03; and no implied duties or obligations shall be read into this Agreement or any other Basic Document against the Owner Trustee. The Owner Trustee shall have no responsibility for filing any financing or continuation statement in any public office at any time or to otherwise perfect or maintain the perfection of any security interest or lien granted to it hereunder or to prepare or file any Commission filing for the Issuer or to record this Agreement or any other Basic Document. The Owner Trustee nevertheless agrees that it will, at its own cost and expense, promptly take all action as may be necessary to discharge any liens (other than the lien of the Indenture) on any part of the Owner Trust Estate that result from actions by, or claims against, the Owner Trustee that are not related to the ownership or the administration of the Owner Trust Estate.

Section 6.05. No Action Except Under Specified Documents or Instructions. The Owner Trustee shall not manage, control, use, sell, dispose of or otherwise deal with any part of the Owner Trust Estate except in accordance with (i) the powers granted to and the authority conferred upon the Owner Trustee pursuant to this Agreement, (ii) the Basic Documents and (iii) any document or instruction delivered to the Owner Trustee pursuant to Section 6.03.

Section 6.06. Restrictions. The Owner Trustee shall not take any action (i) that is inconsistent with the purposes of the Issuer set forth in Section 2.03 or (ii) that, to the actual knowledge of the Owner Trustee, would result in the Issuer's becoming taxable as a corporation for federal or state income tax purposes. The Owners shall not direct the Owner Trustee to take action that would violate the provisions of this Section.

ARTICLE SEVEN

CONCERNING THE OWNER TRUSTEE AND THE DELAWARE TRUSTEE

Section 7.01. Acceptance of Trusts and Duties. Each of the Owner Trustee and the Delaware Trustee accepts the trusts hereby created and each agrees to perform its duties hereunder with respect to such trusts, but only upon the terms of this Agreement. Each of the Owner Trustee and the Delaware Trustee also agrees to disburse all monies actually received by it constituting part of the Owner Trust Estate upon the terms of this Agreement and the other Basic Documents. Neither the Owner Trustee nor the Delaware Trustee shall be answerable or accountable hereunder or under any other Basic Document under any circumstances, except (i) for its own willful misconduct, bad faith or gross negligence or (ii) in the case of the inaccuracy of any representation or warranty contained in Section 7.03 expressly made by the Owner Trustee or the Delaware Trustee. In particular, but not by way of limitation (and subject to the exceptions set forth in the preceding sentence):

(a) neither the Owner Trustee nor the Delaware Trustee shall be liable for any error of judgment made in good faith by the Owner Trustee or the Delaware Trustee;

(b) neither the Owner Trustee nor the Delaware Trustee shall be liable with respect to any action taken or omitted to be taken by it in accordance with the instructions of the Administrator or any Owner or Owners;

(c) no provision of this Agreement or any other Basic Document shall require the Owner Trustee or the Delaware Trustee to expend or risk funds or otherwise incur any financial liability in the performance of any of its rights or powers hereunder or under any other Basic Document if the Owner Trustee or the Delaware Trustee shall have reasonable grounds for believing that repayment of such funds or adequate indemnity against such risk or liability is not reasonably assured or provided to it;

(d) under no circumstances shall the Owner Trustee or the Delaware Trustee be liable for indebtedness evidenced by or arising under any Basic Document, including the principal of and interest on the Notes or the Trust Certificates;

(e) neither the Owner Trustee nor the Delaware Trustee shall be responsible for or in respect of the validity or sufficiency of this Agreement or for the due execution hereof by the Depositor or for the form, character, genuineness, sufficiency, value or validity of any of the Owner Trust Estate, or for or in respect of the validity or sufficiency of the Basic Documents, other than the certificate of authentication on the Trust Certificates, and neither the Owner Trustee nor the Delaware Trustee shall in any event assume or incur any liability, duty or obligation to any Noteholder or to any Owner, other than as expressly provided for in the Basic Documents;

(f) neither the Owner Trustee nor the Delaware Trustee shall be liable for the default or misconduct of the Administrator, the Seller, the Depositor, the Indenture Trustee or the Servicer under any Basic Document or otherwise, and neither the Owner Trustee nor the Delaware Trustee shall have any obligation or liability to perform the obligations of the Issuer under this Agreement or the other Basic Documents that are required to be performed by the Administrator under the Administration Agreement, the Indenture Trustee under the Indenture or the Servicer or the Seller under the Sale and Servicing Agreement or any other Person under any of the Basic Documents; and

(g) neither the Owner Trustee nor the Delaware Trustee shall be under any obligation to exercise any of the rights or powers vested in it by this Agreement, or to institute, conduct or defend any litigation under this Agreement or otherwise or in relation to this Agreement or any other Basic Document, at the request, order or direction of any of the Owners, unless such Owners have offered to the Owner Trustee and the Delaware Trustee security or indemnity satisfactory to it against the costs, expenses and liabilities that may be incurred by the Owner Trustee and the Delaware Trustee therein or thereby; the right of the Owner Trustee and the Delaware Trustee to perform any discretionary act enumerated in this Agreement or in any other Basic Document shall not be construed as a duty, and neither the Owner Trustee nor the Delaware Trustee shall be answerable for other than its gross negligence, bad faith or willful misconduct in the performance of any such act.

Section 7.02. Furnishing of Documents.

The Owner Trustee shall furnish to the Owners, promptly upon receipt of a written request therefor, duplicates or copies of all reports, notices, requests, demands, certificates, financial statements and any other instruments furnished to the Owner Trustee under the Basic Documents.

Section 7.03. Representations and Warranties of the Owner Trustee and the Delaware Trustee.

(X) The Owner Trustee hereby represents and warrants to the Depositor and the Owners, that:

(a) it is a New York banking corporation duly organized and validly existing under the laws of the State of New York; it has all requisite corporate power and authority to execute, deliver and perform its obligations under this Agreement;

(b) it has taken all corporate action necessary to authorize the execution and delivery by it of this Agreement, and this Agreement will be executed and delivered by one of its officers who is duly authorized to execute and deliver this Agreement on its behalf; and

(c) neither the execution nor the delivery by it of this Agreement, nor the consummation by it of the transactions contemplated hereby, nor compliance by it with any of the terms or provisions hereof will contravene any federal, Delaware or New York law, governmental rule or regulation governing the banking or trust powers of the Owner Trustee or any judgment or order binding on it, or constitute any default under its charter documents or bylaws; and

(d) this Agreement constitutes a legal, valid and binding obligation of the Owner Trustee, enforceable against the Owner Trustee in accordance with its terms, except as such enforceability may be subject to or limited by bankruptcy, insolvency, reorganization, moratorium, liquidation, fraudulent conveyance or other similar laws affecting the enforcement of creditors' rights in general and by general principles of equity, regardless of whether such enforceability shall be considered in a proceeding in equity or in law; and

(e) the execution, delivery and performance by the Owner Trustee of this Agreement and the consummation of the transactions contemplated by this Agreement and the fulfillment of the terms hereof do not conflict with, result in any breach of any of the terms and provisions of, nor constitute (with or without notice or lapse of time) a default under, the charter documents or bylaws of the Owner Trustee; nor result in the creation or imposition of any Lien upon any of its properties pursuant to the terms of any such indenture, agreement or other instrument (other than pursuant to the Basic Documents); and

(f) there are no proceedings or investigations pending or, to the Owner Trustee's actual knowledge, threatened, before any court, regulatory body, administrative agency or other governmental instrumentality having jurisdiction over the Owner Trustee or its properties: (i) asserting the invalidity of this Agreement or (ii) seeking any determination or ruling that might materially and adversely affect the performance by the Owner Trustee of its obligations under, or the validity or enforceability of, this Agreement.

(Y) The Delaware Trustee hereby represents and warrants to the Depositor and the Owners, that:

(a) it is a Delaware banking corporation duly organized and validly existing under the laws of the State of Delaware; it has all requisite corporate power and authority to execute, deliver and perform its obligations under this Agreement;

(b) it has taken all corporate action necessary to authorize the execution and delivery by it of this Agreement, and this Agreement will be executed and delivered by one of its officers who is duly authorized to execute and deliver this Agreement on its behalf; and

(c) neither the execution nor the delivery by it of this Agreement, nor the consummation by it of the transactions contemplated hereby, nor compliance by it with any of the terms or provisions hereof will contravene any federal or Delaware law, governmental rule or regulation governing the banking or trust powers of the Delaware Trustee or any judgment or order binding on it, or constitute any default under its charter documents or bylaws; and

(d) this Agreement constitutes a legal, valid and binding obligation of the Delaware Trustee, enforceable against the Delaware Trustee in accordance with its terms, except as such enforceability may be subject to or limited by bankruptcy, insolvency, reorganization, moratorium, liquidation, fraudulent conveyance or other similar laws affecting the enforcement of creditors' rights in general and by general principles of equity, regardless of whether such enforceability shall be considered in a proceeding in equity or in law; and

(e) the execution, delivery and performance by the Delaware Trustee of this Agreement and the consummation of the transactions contemplated by this Agreement and the fulfillment of the terms hereof do not conflict with, result in any breach of any of the terms and provisions of, nor constitute (with or without notice or lapse of time) a default under, the charter documents or bylaws of the Delaware Trustee; nor result in the creation or imposition of any Lien upon any of its properties pursuant to the terms of any such indenture, agreement or other instrument (other than pursuant to the Basic Documents); and

(f) there are no proceedings or investigations pending or, to the Delaware Trustee's actual knowledge, threatened, before any court, regulatory body, administrative agency or other governmental instrumentality having jurisdiction over the Delaware Trustee or its properties: (i) asserting the invalidity of this Agreement or (ii) seeking any determination or ruling that might materially and adversely affect the performance by the Delaware Trustee of its obligations under, or the validity or enforceability of, this Agreement.

Section 7.04. Reliance, Advice of Counsel.

(a) The Owner Trustee and the Delaware Trustee shall incur no liability to anyone in acting upon any signature, instrument, notice, resolution, request, consent, order, certificate, report, opinion, bond or other document or paper believed by it to be genuine and believed by it to be signed by the proper party or parties. The Owner Trustee or the Delaware Trustee may accept a certified copy of a resolution of the board of directors or other governing body of any corporate party as conclusive evidence that such resolution has been duly adopted by such body and that the same is in full force and effect. As to any fact or matter the method of determination of which is not specifically prescribed herein, the Owner Trustee and the Delaware Trustee may for all purposes hereof rely on a certificate, signed by the president or any vice president or by the treasurer or other authorized officers of the relevant party, as to such fact or matter, and such certificate shall constitute full protection to the Owner Trustee or the Delaware Trustee, for any action taken or omitted to be taken by it in good faith in reliance thereon.

(b) In the exercise or administration of the trusts hereunder and in the performance of its duties and obligations under this Agreement and the other Basic Documents, the Owner Trustee and the Delaware Trustee (i) may act directly or through its agents or attorneys pursuant to agreements entered into with any of them, and the Owner Trustee and the Delaware Trustee shall not be liable for the conduct or misconduct of such agents or attorneys if such agents or attorneys shall have been selected by the Owner Trustee or the Delaware Trustee with reasonable care, and (ii) may consult with counsel, accountants and other skilled persons to be selected with reasonable care and employed by it. The Owner Trustee and the Delaware Trustee shall not be liable for anything done, suffered or omitted in good faith by it in accordance with the written opinion or advice of any such counsel, accountants or other such persons and not contrary to this Agreement or any other Basic Document.

Section 7.05. Not Acting in Individual Capacity. Except as otherwise provided in this Article, in accepting the trusts hereby created, The Bank of New York and The Bank of New York (Delaware), act solely as Owner Trustee and Delaware Trustee, respectively, hereunder and not in its individual capacity, and all Persons having any claim against the Owner Trustee or the Delaware Trustee by reason of the transactions contemplated by this Agreement or any other Basic Document shall look only to the Owner Trust Estate for payment or satisfaction thereof.

Section 7.06. Owner Trustee and Delaware Trustee Not Liable for Trust Certificates or Receivables. The recitals contained herein and in the Trust Certificates (other than the signature of the Owner Trustee and the certificate of authentication on the Trust Certificates) shall be taken as the statements of the Depositor, and the Owner Trustee and the Delaware Trustee assume no responsibility for the correctness thereof. The Owner Trustee and the Delaware Trustee make no representations as to the validity or sufficiency of this Agreement, any other Basic Document or the Trust Certificates (other than the signature of the Owner Trustee and the certificate of authentication on the Trust Certificates and the representations and warranties in Section 7.03) or the Notes, or of any Receivable or related documents. The Owner Trustee and the Delaware Trustee shall at no time have any responsibility or liability for or with respect to the legality, validity and enforceability of any Receivable, or the perfection and priority of any security interest created by any Receivable in any Financed Vehicle or the maintenance of any such perfection and priority, or for or with respect to the sufficiency of the Owner Trust Estate or its ability to generate the payments to be distributed to Certificateholders under this Agreement or the Noteholders under the Indenture, including, without limitation, the existence, condition and ownership of any Financed Vehicle; the existence and enforceability of any insurance thereon; the existence and contents of any Receivable on any computer or other record thereof; the validity of the assignment of any Receivable to the Issuer or of any intervening assignment; the completeness of any Receivable; the performance or enforcement of any Receivable; the compliance by the Depositor or the Servicer with any warranty or representation made under any Basic Document or in any related document or the accuracy of any such warranty or representation, or any action of the Administrator, the

Indenture Trustee or the Servicer or any subservicer taken in the name of the Owner Trustee.

Section 7.07. Owner Trustee and Delaware Trustee May Own Trust Certificates and Notes. The Owner Trustee or the Delaware Trustee in their individual or any other capacity may become the owner or pledgee of Trust Certificates or Notes and may deal with the Depositor, the Administrator, the Indenture Trustee and the Servicer in banking transactions with the same rights as it would have if it were not Owner Trustee or Delaware Trustee, respectively.

Section 7.08. Duties of the Delaware Trustee. The Delaware Trustee is appointed to serve as the trustee of the Trust in the State of Delaware for the sole purpose of satisfying the requirement of Section 3807(a) of the Delaware Act that the Trust have at least one trustee with a principal place of business in Delaware. It is understood and agreed by the parties hereto that the Delaware Trustee shall have none of the duties or liabilities of the Owner Trustee. The duties of the Delaware Trustee shall be limited to (a) accepting legal process served on the Trust in the State of Delaware and (b) the execution of any certificates required to be filed with the Secretary of State of the State of Delaware which the Delaware Trustee is required to execute under Section 3811 of the Delaware Act. To the extent that, at law or in equity, the Delaware Trustee has duties (including fiduciary duties) and liabilities relating thereto to the Trust, the beneficial owners thereof or any other person, it is hereby understood and agreed by the other parties hereto that such duties and liabilities are replaced by the duties and liabilities of the Delaware Trustee expressly set forth in this Section 7.08. The Delaware Trustee shall have all the rights, privileges and immunities of the Owner Trustee.

ARTICLE EIGHT

COMPENSATION OF OWNER TRUSTEE AND THE DELWARE TRUSTEE

Section 8.01. Owner Trustee's and Delaware Trustee's Fees and Expenses. The Owner Trustee and the Delaware Trustee shall receive as compensation for their services hereunder such fees as have been separately agreed upon before the date hereof among the Depositor and the Owner Trustee and the Delaware Trustee, and upon the formation of the Issuer, the Owner Trustee and the Delaware Trustee shall be entitled to be reimbursed by the Issuer for their other reasonable expenses hereunder, including the reasonable compensation, expenses and disbursements of such agents, representatives, experts and counsel as the Owner Trustee and the Delaware Trustee may employ in connection with the exercise and performance of its rights and its respective duties hereunder.

Section 8.02. Indemnification. The Issuer shall be liable as primary obligor for, and shall indemnify the Indemnified Parties from and against, any and all Expenses which may at any time be imposed on, incurred by, or asserted against the Owner Trustee, the Delaware Trustee or any other Indemnified Party in any way relating to or arising out of this Agreement, the other Basic Documents, the Owner Trust Estate, the administration of the Owner Trust Estate or the action or inaction of the Owner Trustee or any other Indemnified Party hereunder, except only that the Issuer shall not be liable for or required to indemnify an Indemnified Party from and against Expenses arising or resulting from any of the matters described in the third sentence of Section 7.01. The indemnities contained in this Section shall survive the resignation or termination of the Owner Trustee, the Delaware Trustee or the termination of this Agreement. In the event of any claim, action or proceeding for which indemnity will be sought pursuant to this Section, the Owner Trustee's or the Delaware Trustee's choice of legal counsel shall be subject to the approval of the Depositor (or if the Depositor is no longer an owner, the designee of the Depositor), which approval shall not be unreasonably withheld.

Section 8.03. Payments to the Owner Trustee and to the Delaware Trustee. Any amounts paid to the Owner Trustee and to the Delaware Trustee pursuant to this Article shall be deemed not to be a part of the Owner Trust Estate immediately after such payment. Any amounts owing to the Owner Trustee under this Agreement or the other Basic Documents shall constitute a claim against the Owner Trust Estate.

ARTICLE NINE

TERMINATION OF TRUST AGREEMENT

Section 9.01. Termination of Trust Agreement.

(a) This Agreement (other than Article Eight) and the Issuer shall terminate in accordance with Section 3808 of the Statutory Trust Statute and be of no further force or effect upon the earlier to occur of (i) the purchase on any Payment Date by the Servicer, or any successor Servicer, at its option, pursuant to Section 8.01(a) of the Sale and Servicing Agreement, of the Owner Trust Estate other than the Accounts and the Certificate Distribution Account, (ii) the final distribution by the Owner Trustee of all monies or other property or proceeds of the Owner Trust Estate in accordance with the terms of the Indenture, the Sale and Servicing Agreement and Article Five or (iii) the Payment Date next succeeding the month which is one year after the maturity or other liquidation of the last Receivable and the disposition of any amount received upon liquidation of any property remaining in the Owner Trust Estate. The bankruptcy, liquidation, dissolution, death or incapacity of any Owner shall not (i) operate to terminate this Agreement or the Issuer, (ii) entitle such Owner's legal representatives or heirs to claim an accounting or to take any action or proceeding in any court for a partition or winding up of all or any part of the Issuer or Owner Trust Estate or (iii) otherwise affect the rights, obligations and liabilities of the parties hereto.

(b) Except as provided in Section 9.01(a), neither of the Depositor nor any Owner shall be entitled to revoke or terminate the Issuer.

(c) The outstanding Trust Certificates are subject to redemption in whole, but not in part, pursuant to Section 8.01 of the Sale and Servicing Agreement; provided that the Issuer has available funds sufficient to pay the aggregate Certificate Balance of all the Trust Certificates, together with accrued interest at the Certificate Rate to but excluding the Payment Date. Notice of any termination of the Issuer, specifying the Payment Date upon which Certificateholders shall surrender their Trust Certificates to the Paying Agent for payment of the final distribution and cancellation, shall be given by the Owner Trustee by letter to Certificateholders mailed within five Business Days of receipt of notice of such termination from the Servicer given pursuant to Section 8.01(b) of the Sale and Servicing Agreement, stating (i) the Payment Date upon or with respect to which final payment of the Trust Certificates shall be made upon presentation and surrender of the Trust Certificates at the office of the Paying Agent therein designated, (ii) the amount of any such final payment and (iii) that the Record Date otherwise applicable to such Payment Date is not applicable, payments being made only upon presentation and surrender of the Trust Certificates at the office of the Paying Agent therein specified. The Owner Trustee shall give such notice to the Certificate Registrar (if other than the Owner Trustee) and the Paying Agent at the time such notice is given to Certificateholders. Upon presentation and surrender of the Trust Certificates, the Paying Agent shall cause to be distributed to Certificateholders amounts distributable on such Payment Date pursuant to Section 5.02. The Owner Trustee shall promptly notify each Rating Agency upon the final payment of the Trust Certificates.

(d) In the event that all of the Certificateholders shall not surrender their Trust Certificates for cancellation within six months after the date specified in the above mentioned written notice, the Owner Trustee shall give a second written notice to the remaining Certificateholders to surrender their Trust Certificates for cancellation and receive the final distribution with respect thereto. If within one year after the second notice all the Trust Certificates shall not have been surrendered for cancellation, the Owner Trustee may take appropriate steps, or may appoint an agent to take appropriate steps, to contact the remaining Certificateholders concerning surrender of their Trust Certificates, and the cost thereof shall be paid out of the funds and other assets that shall remain subject to this Agreement. Subject to applicable escheat laws, any funds remaining in the Issuer after exhaustion of such remedies shall be distributed by the Owner Trustee to the Depositor, in its capacities as Depositor and as Holder of such Certificate.

(e) Upon the winding up of the Issuer and its termination, the Owner Trustee shall cause the Certificate of Trust to be cancelled by filing a certificate of cancellation with the Secretary of State in accordance with Section 3810 of the Statutory Trust Statute.

ARTICLE TEN

SUCCESSOR AND ADDITIONAL OWNER TRUSTEES

Section 10.01. Eligibility Requirements for Owner Trustee and Delaware Trustee. The Delaware Trustee shall at all times be a corporation satisfying the provisions of Section 3807(a) of the Statutory Trust Statute. The Owner Trustee shall at all times (i) be authorized to exercise corporate trust powers, (ii) have a combined capital and surplus of at least $50,000,000, (iii) be subject to supervision or examination by federal or state authorities and (iv) have the Required Rating. If such corporation shall publish reports of condition at least annually pursuant to law or to the requirements of the aforesaid supervising or examining authority, then for the purpose of this Section, the combined capital and surplus of such corporation shall be deemed to be its combined capital and surplus as set forth in its most recent report of condition so published. In case at any time the Owner Trustee shall cease to be eligible in accordance with the provisions of this Section, the Owner Trustee shall resign immediately in the manner and with the effect specified in Section 10.02.

Section 10.02. Resignation or Removal of Owner Trustee. The Owner Trustee or Delaware Trustee may at any time resign and be discharged from the trusts hereby created by giving written notice thereof to the Administrator. Upon receiving such notice of resignation, the Administrator shall promptly appoint a successor Owner Trustee or Delaware Trustee, as applicable, by written instrument, in duplicate, one copy of which instrument shall be delivered to the resigning Owner Trustee or Delaware Trustee, as applicable, and one copy to the successor Owner Trustee or Delaware Trustee, as applicable. If no successor Owner Trustee or Delaware Trustee, as applicable, shall have been so appointed and have accepted appointment within 30 days after the giving of such notice of resignation, the resigning Owner Trustee may petition at the Issuer's expense any court of competent jurisdiction for the appointment of a successor Owner Trustee or Delaware Trustee, as applicable.

If at any time the Owner Trustee or Delaware Trustee, as applicable, shall cease to be eligible in accordance with Section 10.01 and shall fail to resign after written request therefor by the Administrator, or if at any time the Owner Trustee or Delaware Trustee, as applicable, shall be legally unable to act, or shall be adjudged bankrupt or insolvent, or a receiver of the Owner Trustee or Delaware Trustee, as applicable, or of either of their property shall be appointed, or any public officer shall take charge or control of the Owner Trustee or Delaware Trustee or of either of their property or affairs for the purpose of rehabilitation, conservation or liquidation, then the Administrator may remove the Owner Trustee or Delaware Trustee, as applicable. If the Administrator shall remove the Owner Trustee or Delaware Trustee, as applicable, under the authority of the immediately preceding sentence, the Administrator shall promptly appoint a successor Owner Trustee or Delaware Trustee, as applicable, by written instrument, in duplicate, one copy of which instrument shall be delivered to the outgoing Owner Trustee or Delaware Trustee, as applicable, so removed and one copy to the successor Owner Trustee or Delaware Trustee, as applicable, and shall pay all fees and expenses owed to the outgoing Owner Trustee or Delaware Trustee, as applicable.

Any resignation or removal of the Owner Trustee or Delaware Trustee, as applicable, and appointment of a successor Owner Trustee or Delaware Trustee, as applicable, pursuant to any of the provisions of this Section shall not become effective until acceptance of appointment by the successor Owner Trustee or Delaware Trustee, as applicable, pursuant to Section 10.03 and payment of all fees and expenses owed to the outgoing Owner Trustee or Delaware Trustee, as applicable. The Administrator shall provide notice of such resignation or removal of the Owner Trustee or Delaware Trustee, as applicable, to each Rating Agency.

Section 10.03. Successor Owner Trustee or Delaware Trustee. Any successor Owner Trustee or Delaware Trustee, as applicable, appointed pursuant to Section 10.02 shall execute, acknowledge and deliver to the Administrator and to its predecessor Owner Trustee or Delaware Trustee, as applicable, an instrument accepting such appointment under this Agreement, and thereupon the resignation or removal of the predecessor Owner Trustee or Delaware Trustee, as applicable, shall become effective, and such successor Owner Trustee or Delaware Trustee, as applicable, without any further act, deed or conveyance, shall become fully vested with all the rights, powers, duties and obligations of its predecessor under this Agreement, with like effect as if originally named as Owner Trustee or Delaware Trustee, as applicable. The predecessor Owner Trustee or Delaware Trustee, as applicable, shall upon payment of its fees and expenses deliver to the successor Owner Trustee or Delaware Trustee, as applicable, all documents and statements and monies held by it under this Agreement and the Administrator and the predecessor Owner Trustee or Delaware Trustee, as applicable, shall execute and deliver such instruments and do such other things as may reasonably be required for fully and certainly vesting and confirming in the successor Owner Trustee or Delaware Trustee, as applicable, all such rights, powers, duties and obligations.

No successor Owner Trustee or Delaware Trustee, as applicable, shall accept appointment as provided in this Section unless at the time of such acceptance such successor Owner Trustee or Delaware Trustee, as applicable, shall be eligible pursuant to Section 10.01.

Upon acceptance of appointment by a successor Owner Trustee or Delaware Trustee, as applicable, pursuant to this Section, the Administrator shall mail notice thereof to all Certificateholders, the Indenture Trustee, the Noteholders and each Rating Agency. If the Administrator shall fail to mail such notice within ten days after acceptance of such appointment by the successor Owner Trustee or Delaware Trustee, as applicable, the successor Owner Trustee or Delaware Trustee, as applicable, shall cause such notice to be mailed at the expense of the Administrator.

Section 10.04. Merger or Consolidation of Owner Trustee or Delaware Trustee. Any corporation into which the Owner Trustee or Delaware Trustee, as applicable, may be merged or converted or with which it may be consolidated, or any corporation resulting from any merger, conversion or consolidation to which the Owner Trustee or Delaware Trustee, as applicable, shall be a party, or any corporation succeeding to all or substantially all of the corporate trust business of the Owner Trustee or Delaware Trustee, as applicable, shall be the successor of the Owner Trustee or Delaware Trustee, as applicable, hereunder, without the execution or filing of any instrument or any further act on the part of any of the parties hereto, anything herein to the contrary notwithstanding; provided, that such corporation shall be eligible pursuant to Section 10.01 and, provided, further, that the Owner Trustee or Delaware Trustee, as applicable, shall mail notice of such merger or consolidation to each Rating Agency.

Section 10.05. Appointment of Co-Trustee or Separate Trustee. Notwithstanding any other provisions of this Agreement, at any time, for the purpose of meeting any legal requirements of any jurisdiction in which any part of the Owner Trust Estate or any Financed Vehicle may at the time be located, the Administrator and the Owner Trustee acting jointly shall have the power and shall execute and deliver all instruments to appoint one or more Persons approved by the Administrator and Owner Trustee to act as co-trustee, jointly with the Owner Trustee, or as separate trustee or separate trustees, of all or any part of the Owner Trust Estate, and to vest in such Person, in such capacity, such title to the Trust or any part thereof and, subject to the other provisions of this Section, such powers, duties, obligations, rights and trusts as the Administrator and the Owner Trustee may consider necessary or desirable. If the Administrator shall not have joined in such appointment within 15 days after the receipt by it of a request so to do, the Owner Trustee alone shall have the power to make such appointment. No co-trustee or separate trustee under this Agreement shall be required to meet the terms of eligibility as a successor Owner Trustee pursuant to Section 10.01, except that such co-trustee or successor trustee shall have the Required Rating, and no notice of the appointment of any co-trustee or separate trustee shall be required pursuant to Section 10.03.

Each separate trustee and co-trustee shall, to the extent permitted by law, be appointed and act subject to the following provisions and conditions:

(a) all rights, powers, duties and obligations conferred or imposed upon the Owner Trustee shall be conferred upon and exercised or performed by the Owner Trustee and such separate trustee or co-trustee jointly (it being understood that such separate trustee or co-trustee is not authorized to act separately without the Owner Trustee joining in such act), except to the extent that under any law of any jurisdiction in which any particular act or acts are to be performed, the Owner Trustee shall be incompetent or unqualified to perform such act or acts, in which event such rights, powers, duties and obligations (including the holding of title to the Owner Trust Estate or any portion thereof in any such jurisdiction) shall be exercised and performed singly by such separate trustee or co-trustee, but solely at the direction of the Owner Trustee;

(b) no trustee under this Agreement shall be personally liable by reason of any act or omission of any other trustee under this Agreement; and

(c) the Administrator and the Owner Trustee acting jointly may at any time accept the resignation of or remove any separate trustee or co-trustee.

Any notice, request or other writing given to the Owner Trustee shall be deemed to have been given to each of the then separate trustees and co-trustees, as effectively as if given to each of them. Every instrument appointing any separate trustee or co-trustee shall refer to this Agreement and the conditions of this Article. Each separate trustee and co-trustee, upon its acceptance of the trusts conferred, shall be vested with the estates or property specified in its instrument of appointment, either jointly with the Owner Trustee or separately, as may be provided therein, subject to all the provisions of this Agreement, specifically including every provision of this Agreement relating to the conduct of, affecting the liability of, or affording protection to, the Owner Trustee. Each such instrument shall be filed with the Owner Trustee and a copy thereof given to the Administrator.

Any separate trustee or co-trustee may at any time appoint the Owner Trustee as its agent or attorney-in-fact with full power and authority, to the extent not prohibited by law, to do any lawful act under or in respect of this Agreement on its behalf and in its name. If any separate trustee or co-trustee shall die, become incapable of acting, resign or be removed, all of its estates, properties, rights, remedies and trusts shall vest in and be exercised by the Owner Trustee, to the extent permitted by law, without the appointment of a new or successor co-trustee or separate trustee.

ARTICLE ELEVEN

MISCELLANEOUS

Section 11.01. Supplements and Amendments.

(a) This Agreement may be amended by the parties hereto with prior written notice to each Rating Agency, without the consent of any Securityholders, to cure any ambiguity, to correct or supplement any provisions in this Agreement or for the purpose of adding any provisions to or changing in any manner or eliminating any of the provisions in this Agreement or of modifying in any manner the rights of the Noteholders or the Certificateholders; provided, however, that such action shall not, as evidenced by an Opinion of Counsel, adversely affect in any material respect the interests of any Noteholder or Certificateholder.

(b) This Agreement may also be amended from time to time by the parties hereto, with prior written notice to each Rating Agency, with the consent of the Holders of Trust Certificates evidencing not less than a majority of the Percentage Interests evidenced by the Trust Certificates and, if such amendment materially and adversely affects the interests of the Noteholders, with the consent of Holders (as such term is defined in the Indenture) of Notes evidencing not less than a majority of the Outstanding Amount of the Notes, for the purpose of adding any provisions to or changing in any manner or eliminating any of the provisions of this Agreement or of modifying in any manner the rights of the Noteholders or the Certificateholders; provided, however, that no such amendment shall (i) increase or reduce in any manner the amount of, or accelerate or delay the timing of, collections of payments on Receivables or distributions that shall be required to be made for the benefit of the Noteholders or the Certificateholders, (ii) increase or reduce any Interest Rate or Certificate Rate or (iii) reduce the aforesaid percentage of the Outstanding Amount of the Notes or of the Percentage Interests evidenced by the Trust Certificates required to consent to any such amendment, without the consent of the Holders of all the outstanding Notes and Trust Certificates affected thereby.

(c) Prior to the execution of any such amendment or consent, the Owner Trustee shall furnish written notification of the substance of such amendment or consent to the Indenture Trustee, the Administrator and each Rating Agency.

(d) Promptly after the execution of any such amendment or consent, the Owner Trustee shall furnish written notification of the substance of such amendment or consent to each Certificateholder. It shall not be necessary for the consent of Certificateholders, Noteholders or the Indenture Trustee pursuant to this Section to approve the particular form of any proposed amendment or consent, but it shall be sufficient if such consent shall approve the substance thereof. The manner of obtaining such consents (and any other consents of Certificateholders provided for in this Agreement or in any other Basic Document) and of evidencing the authorization of the execution thereof by Certificateholders shall be subject to such reasonable requirements as the Owner Trustee may prescribe.

(e) Promptly after the execution of any amendment to the Certificate of Trust, the Owner Trustee shall cause the filing of such amendment with the Secretary of State.

(f) In connection with the execution of any amendment to this Agreement or any other basic Document to which the Issuer is a party and for which amendment the Owner Trustee's or Delaware Trustee's consent is sought, the Owner Trustee and the Delaware Trustee shall be entitled to receive and rely upon an Opinion of Counsel to the effect that the execution of such amendment is authorized or permitted by this Agreement or such other Basic Document, as the case may be, and that all conditions precedent in this Agreement or such other Basic Document, as the case may be, for the execution and delivery thereof by the Issuer or the Owner Trustee, as the case may be, have been satisfied. The Owner Trustee or Delaware Trustee may, but shall not be obligated to, enter into any such amendment that affects the Owner Trustee's or Delaware Trustee's own rights, duties or immunities under this Agreement or otherwise.

Section 11.02. No Legal Title to Owner Trust Estate in Owner. The Owner shall not have legal title to any part of the Owner Trust Estate. The Owners shall be entitled to receive distributions with respect to their undivided ownership interest therein only in accordance with Articles Five and Nine. No transfer, by operation of law or otherwise, of any right, title or interest of the Owners to and in their ownership interest in the Owner Trust Estate shall operate to terminate this Agreement or the trusts hereunder or entitle any transferee to an accounting or to the transfer to it of legal title to any part of the Owner Trust Estate.

Section 11.03. Limitations on Rights of Others. The provisions of this Agreement are solely for the benefit of the Owner Trustee, the Delaware Trustee, the Indemnified Parties, the Depositor, the Owners, the Administrator and, to the extent expressly provided herein, the Indenture Trustee and the Noteholders, and nothing in this Agreement, whether express or implied, shall be construed to give to any other Person any legal or equitable right, remedy or claim in the Owner Trust Estate or under or in respect of this Agreement or any covenants, conditions or provisions contained herein.

Section 11.04. Notices.

(a) Unless otherwise expressly specified or permitted by the terms hereof, all demands, notices and communications under this Agreement shall be in writing, personally delivered, mailed by certified mail, return receipt requested, or sent via facsimile transmission (followed by hard copy by overnight delivery) and shall be deemed to have been duly given upon receipt (i) in the case of the Owner Trustee, The Bank of New York, 101 Barclay Street, 8th Floor West, New York, New York 10286, Attention: Asset Backed Securities Unit — Honda 2003-1, (ii) in the case of the Delaware Trustee, The Bank of New York (Delaware), White Clay Center Route 273, Newark, Delaware 19711, Attention: Asset Backed Securities Unit — Honda 2003-1, (iii) in the case of the Depositor, to American Honda Receivables Corp., 700 Van Ness Avenue, Building 300, Torrance, California 90501, Attention: President or (iv) as to either party, at such other address as shall be designated by such party in a written notice to the other party.

(b) Any notice required or permitted to be given to a Certificateholder shall be given by first-class mail, postage prepaid, at the address of such Holder as shown in the Certificate Register. Any notice so mailed within the time prescribed in this Agreement shall be conclusively presumed to have been duly given, whether or not the Certificateholder receives such notice.

Section 11.05. Severability. If any one or more of the covenants, agreements, provisions or terms of this Agreement shall be for any reason whatsoever held invalid, then such covenants, agreements, provisions or terms shall be deemed severable from the remaining covenants, agreements, provisions or terms of this Agreement and shall in no way affect the validity or enforceability of the other covenants, agreements, provisions or terms of this Agreement or of the Trust Certificates or the rights of the Holders thereof.

Section 11.06. Separate Counterparts. This Agreement may be executed by the parties hereto in separate counterparts, each of which when so executed and delivered shall be an original, but all such counterparts shall together constitute but one and the same instrument.

Section 11.07. Successors and Assigns. All covenants and agreements contained herein shall be binding upon, and inure to the benefit of, each of the Depositor and its permitted assigns, the Owner Trustee and its successors, the Delaware Trustee and its successors and each Owner and its successors and permitted assigns, all as herein provided. Any request, notice, direction, consent, waiver or other instrument or action by an Owner shall bind the successors and assigns of such Owner.

Section 11.08. No Petition. The Owner Trustee and the Delaware Trustee, by entering into this Agreement, each Certificateholder, by accepting a Trust Certificate, and the Indenture Trustee and each Noteholder, by accepting the benefits of this Agreement, each hereby covenants and agrees that it will not at any time institute against the Depositor or the Issuer, or join in any institution against the Depositor or the Issuer of, any bankruptcy proceedings under any United States federal or state bankruptcy or similar law in connection with any obligations relating tot he Trust Certificates, the Notes, this Agreement or any other Basic Document.

Section 11.09. No Recourse. Each Certificateholder by accepting a Trust Certificate acknowledges that such Certificateholder's Trust Certificates represent beneficial interests in the Issuer only and do not represent interests in or obligations of the Depositor, the Seller, the Servicer, the Administrator, the Owner Trustee, the Delaware Trustee, the Indenture Trustee or any of their respective Affiliates and no recourse may be had against such parties or their assets, except as may be expressly set forth or contemplated in the Trust Certificates, this Agreement or any other Basic Document.

Section 11.10. Headings. The headings of the various Articles and Sections herein are for convenience of reference only and shall not define or limit any of the terms or provisions hereof.

Section 11.11. Governing Law. THIS AGREEMENT SHALL BE CONSTRUED IN ACCORDANCE WITH THE LAWS OF THE STATE OF DELAWARE, WITHOUT REFERENCE TO ITS CONFLICT OF LAW PROVISIONS, AND THE OBLIGATIONS, RIGHTS AND REMEDIES OF THE PARTIES HEREUNDER SHALL BE DETERMINED IN ACCORDANCE WITH SUCH LAWS.

Section 11.12. Trust Certificates Nonassessable and Fully Paid. Certificateholders shall not be personally liable for obligations of the Issuer. The interests represented by the Trust Certificates shall be nonassessable for any losses or expenses of the Issuer or for any reason whatsoever, and, upon the authentication thereof by the Owner Trustee pursuant to Section 3.03, 3.04 or 3.05, the Trust Certificates are and shall be deemed fully paid.

Section 11.13. Depositor Payment Obligation. The Depositor shall be responsible for payment of the Administrator's compensation under the Administration Agreement and shall reimburse the Administrator for all expenses and liabilities of the Administrator incurred thereunder. In addition, the Depositor shall be responsible for the payment of all fees and expenses of the Issuer and the Trustees paid by any of them in connection with any of their obligations under the Basic Documents to obtain or maintain any required license under the Pennsylvania Motor Vehicle Sales Finance Act and the Maryland Act (MD Fin. Inst. Code Ann., Title 11, Subtitle 4).

IN WITNESS WHEREOF, the parties hereto have caused this Amended and Restated Trust Agreement to be duly executed by their respective officers as of the day and year first above written.

AMERICAN HONDA RECEIVABLES CORP.,
as Depositor

By: /s/ Y. Takahashi

Name: Y. Takahashi

Title: President

THE BANK OF NEW YORK,
not in its individual capacity but solely as
Owner Trustee

By: /s/ John Bobko

Name: John Bobko

Title: Assistant Vice President

THE BANK OF NEW YORK (DELAWARE),
not in its individual capacity but solely as
Delaware Trustee

By: /s/ William T. Lewis

Name: William T. Lewis

Title: Senior Vice President

EXHIBIT A

FORM OF TRUST CERTIFICATE

THIS CERTIFICATE HAS NOT BEEN REGISTERED UNDER THE SECURITIES ACT OF 1933, AS AMENDED (THE "SECURITIES ACT"), OR ANY STATE SECURITIES LAWS, AND MAY NOT BE OFFERED, SOLD, PLEDGED OR OTHERWISE TRANSFERRED IN THE ABSENCE OF SUCH REGISTRATION OR AN EXEMPTION THEREFROM. IN ADDITION, THE TRANSFER OF THIS CERTIFICATE IS SUBJECT TO CERTAIN RESTRICTIONS AND CONDITIONS SET FORTH IN SECTION 3.04 OF THE TRUST AGREEMENT UNDER WHICH THIS CERTIFICATE ISSUED (A COPY OF WHICH TRUST AGREEMENT IS AVAILABLE FROM THE OWNER TRUSTEE UPON REQUEST), INCLUDING RECEIPT BY THE OWNER TRUSTEE OF AN INVESTMENT LETTER IN WHICH THE TRANSFEREE MAKES CERTAIN REPRESENTATIONS.

NUMBER: R-1 Initial Certificate Balance: $[ ]

HONDA AUTO RECEIVABLES 2003-1 OWNER TRUST

[ ]% ASSET BACKED CERTIFICATE

evidencing a fractional undivided interest in the Issuer, as defined below, the property of which includes a pool of retail installment sale or conditional sale contracts secured by new and used Honda and Acura motor vehicles.

(This Trust Certificate does not represent an interest in or obligation of American Honda Receivables Corp., American Honda Finance Corporation or any of their respective affiliates.)

THIS CERTIFIES THAT ____________________________ is the registered owner of a 100 PERCENT nonassessable, fully-paid, undivided interest in the Honda Auto Receivables 2003-1 Owner Trust (the "Issuer"), formed by American Honda Receivables Corp., a California corporation (the "Depositor").

The Issuer was created pursuant to a Trust Agreement dated as of January 21, 2003, as amended and restated by an Amended and Restated Trust Agreement dated February 25, 2003 (as amended or supplemented from time to time, the "Trust Agreement"), among the Depositor, The Bank of New York, as owner trustee (the "Owner Trustee"), and The Bank of New York (Delaware), as Delaware trustee (the "Delaware Trustee"), a summary of certain of the pertinent provisions of which is set forth below. Capitalized terms used herein that are not otherwise defined shall have the meanings ascribed thereto in the Trust Agreement.

This Trust Certificate is one of the duly authorized certificates designated as "Asset Backed Certificates" (the "Trust Certificates"). Issued under an Indenture dated as of February 1, 2003 (the "Indenture"), between the Issuer and JPMorgan Chase Bank, as indenture trustee, are four classes of Notes designated as "Class A-1 1.30% Asset Backed Notes," "Class A-2 1.46% Asset Backed Notes", "Class A-3 1.92% Asset Backed Notes" and "Class A-4 2.48% Asset Backed

Notes" (collectively, the "Notes"). This Trust Certificate is issued under and is subject to terms, provisions and conditions of the Trust Agreement, to which Trust Agreement the Holder of this Trust Certificate, by virtue of its acceptance thereof, assents and by which such Holder is bound. The property of the Issuer includes, among other things, a pool of retail installment sale or conditional sale contracts for new and used Honda and Acura motor vehicles (collectively, the "Receivables"), all monies received on or in respect of the Receivables on or after February 1, 2003, security interests in the vehicles financed thereby, certain bank accounts and the proceeds thereof, proceeds from claims on certain insurance policies and certain other rights under the Trust Agreement and the Sale and Servicing Agreement and all proceeds of the foregoing.

It is the intent of the Depositor, the Servicer and the Certificateholder that, solely for purposes of federal income, state and local income tax and any other income taxes, the Issuer will be treated as a disregarded entity not separate from the sole Certificateholder. The purchaser hereof, by acceptance of the Trust Certificates, agrees to treat, and to take no action inconsistent with the above treatment for so long as it is the sole Owner.

Solely in the event the Trust Certificates are held by more than a single Owner, it is the intent of the Depositor, the Servicer and the Certificateholders that, solely for purposes of federal income, state and local income and single business tax and any other income taxes, the Issuer will be treated as a partnership and the Certificateholders will be treated as partners in the partnership. The purchaser hereof and the other Certificateholders, by acceptance of a Trust Certificate, agree to treat, and to take no action inconsistent with the treatment of, the Trust Certificates for such tax purposes as partnership interests in the Issuer.

Each Certificateholder, by its acceptance of a Trust Certificate, covenants and agrees that such Certificateholder will not at any time institute against the Depositor, or join in any institution against the Depositor of, any bankruptcy, reorganization, arrangement, insolvency or liquidation proceedings , or other proceedings under any United States federal or state bankruptcy or similar law in connection with any obligations relating to the Trust Certificates, the Notes, the Trust Agreement or any other Basic Document.

Distributions on this Trust Certificate will be made as provided in the Trust Agreement by the Owner Trustee by wire transfer or check mailed to the Certificateholder of record in the Certificate Register without the presentation or surrender of this Trust Certificate or the making of any notation hereon. Except as otherwise provided in the Trust Agreement and notwithstanding the above, the final distribution on this Trust Certificate will be made after due notice by the Owner Trustee of the pendency of such distribution and only upon presentation and surrender of this Trust Certificate at the office or agency maintained for the purpose by the Owner Trustee.

Reference is hereby made to the further provisions of this Trust Certificate set forth on the reverse hereof, which further provisions shall for all purposes have the same effect as if set forth at this place.

Unless the certificate of authentication hereon shall have been executed by an authorized officer of the Owner Trustee, by manual signature, this Trust Certificate shall not entitle the Holder hereof to any benefit under the Trust Agreement or the Sale and Servicing Agreement or be valid for any purpose.

THIS TRUST CERTIFICATE SHALL BE CONSTRUED IN ACCORDANCE WITH THE LAWS OF THE STATE OF DELAWARE, WITHOUT REFERENCE TO ITS CONFLICT OF LAW PROVISIONS, AND THE OBLIGATIONS, RIGHTS AND REMEDIES OF THE PARTIES HEREUNDER SHALL BE DETERMINED IN ACCORDANCE WITH SUCH LAWS.

IN WITNESS WHEREOF, the Owner Trustee, on behalf of the Issuer and not in its individual capacity, has caused this Trust Certificate to be duly executed.

HONDA AUTO RECEIVABLES 2003-1 OWNER TRUST

By: THE BANK OF NEW YORK,
not in its individual capacity but solely as
Owner Trustee on behalf of the Trust

By:

____

Authorized Signatory

OWNER TRUSTEE'S CERTIFICATE OF AUTHENTICATION

This is one of the Trust Certificates referred to in the within-mentioned Trust Agreement.

THE BANK OF NEW YORK, OR
not in its individual capacity but
solely as Owner Trustee on behalf
of the Trust

By:

____

as Authenticating Agent

By:

____

Authorized Signatory

THE BANK OF NEW YORK,
not in its individual capacity but
solely as Owner Trustee on behalf
of the Trust

By:

____

Authorized Signatory

[REVERSE OF TRUST CERTIFICATE]

The Trust Certificates do not represent an obligations of, or an interest in, the Depositor, the Servicer, the Owner Trustee or any of their respective affiliates and no recourse may be had against such parties or their assets, except as expressly set forth or contemplated herein or in the Trust Agreement or the other Basic Documents. In addition, this Trust Certificate is not guaranteed by any governmental agency or instrumentality and is limited in right of payment to certain collections and recoveries with respect to the Receivables (and certain other amounts), all as more specifically set forth herein and in the Sale and Servicing Agreement. A copy of each of the Sale and Servicing Agreement and the Trust Agreement may be examined by any Certificateholder upon written request during normal business hours at the principal office of the Depositor and at such other places, if any, designated by the Depositor.

The Trust Agreement permits, with certain exceptions therein provided, the amendment thereof and the modification of the rights and obligations of the Depositor and the rights of the Certificateholders under the Trust Agreement at any time by the parties thereto with the consent of the Holders of the Trust Certificates and the Notes, each voting as a class, evidencing not less than a majority of the Percentage Interests evidenced by the outstanding Trust Certificates, or a majority of the outstanding principal balance of the Notes of each such class. Any such consent by the Holder of this Trust Certificate shall be conclusive and binding on such Holder and on all future Holders of this Trust Certificate and of any Trust Certificate issued upon the transfer hereof or in exchange herefor or in lieu hereof, whether or not notation of such consent is made upon this Trust Certificate. The Trust Agreement also permits the amendment thereof, in certain limited circumstances, without the consent of the Holders of any of the Trust Certificates.

As provided in the Trust Agreement and subject to certain limitations therein set forth, the transfer of this Trust Certificate is registrable in the Certificate Register upon surrender of this Trust Certificate for registration of transfer at the offices or agencies of the Certificate Registrar maintained by the Owner Trustee, accompanied by a written instrument of transfer in form satisfactory to the Owner Trustee and the Certificate Registrar duly executed by the Holder hereof or such Holder's attorney duly authorized in writing, and thereupon one or more new Trust Certificates evidencing the same original certificate balance in the Issuer will be issued to the designated transferee.

Except as provided in the Trust Agreement, the Trust Certificates are issuable only as registered Trust Certificates. As provided in the Trust Agreement and subject to certain limitations therein set forth, Trust Certificates are exchangeable for new Trust Certificates evidencing the same aggregate original certificate balance, as requested by the Holder surrendering the same. No service charge will be made for any such registration of transfer or exchange, but the Owner Trustee or the Certificate Registrar may require payment of a sum sufficient to cover any tax or governmental charge payable in connection therewith.

The Owner Trustee, the Certificate Registrar and any agent of the Owner Trustee or the Certificate Registrar may treat the Person in whose name this Trust Certificate is registered as the owner hereof for all purposes, and none of the Owner Trustee, the Certificate Registrar or any such agent shall be affected by any notice to the contrary.

The obligations and responsibilities created by the Trust Agreement and the Issuer created thereby shall terminate upon the payment to Certificateholders of all amounts required to be paid to them pursuant to the Trust Agreement and the Sale and Servicing Agreement and the disposition of all property held as part of the Owner Trust Estate. The Servicer of the Receivables may at its option purchase the Owner Trust Estate at a price specified in the Sale and Servicing Agreement, and such purchase of the Receivables and other property of the Issuer will effect early retirement of the Trust Certificates; provided, however, such right of purchase is exercisable only as of the last day of any Collection Period as of which the Pool Balance is less than or equal to 10% of the Original Pool Balance.

The Trust Certificates may not be acquired by a Benefit Plan. By accepting and holding this Trust Certificate, the Holder hereof shall be deemed to have represented and warranted that it is not a Benefit Plan.

ASSIGNMENT

FOR VALUE RECEIVED the undersigned hereby sells, assigns and transfers unto ______________________________

PLEASE INSERT SOCIAL SECURITY OR OTHER IDENTIFYING NUMBER OF ASSIGNEE

(Please print or type name and address, including postal zip code, of assignee) the within Trust Certificate, and all rights thereunder, any hereby irrevocably constitutes and appoints ________________ , attorney, to transfer said Trust Certificate on the books of the Certificate Registrar, with full power of substitution in the premises.

____

Signature Guaranteed:

NOTICE: The signature to this assignment must correspond with the name of the registered owner as it appears on the face of the within Trust Certificate in every particular, without alteration, enlargement or any change whatsoever. Such signature must be guaranteed by an "eligible guarantor institution" meeting the requirements of the Certificate Registrar, which requirements include membership or participation in STAMP or such other "signature guarantee program" as may be determined by the Certificate Registrar in addition to, or in substitution for, STAMP, all in accordance with the Securities Exchange Act of 1934, as amended.

EXHIBIT B
FORM OF TRANSFEROR CERTIFICATE

__________, ____

[Seller]

____

____

____

THE BANK OF NEW YORK
101 Barclay Street, 8th Floor West
New York, New York 10286

Re: Honda Auto Receivables 2003-1 Owner Trust Asset Backed Certificates

Dear Sirs:

In connection with our disposition of the above-referenced Asset Backed Certificates (the "Certificates") we certify that (i) we understand that the Certificates have not been registered under the Securities Act of 1933, as amended (the "Act"), and are being transferred by us in a transaction that is exempt from the registration requirements of the Act and (ii) we have not offered or sold any Certificates to, or solicited offers to buy any Certificates from, any person, or otherwise approached or negotiated with any person with respect thereto, in a manner that would be deemed, or taken any other action which would result in, a violation of Section 5 of the Act.

Very truly yours,

[NAME OF TRANSFEROR]

By

____

Authorized Officer

EXHIBIT C

FORM OF INVESTMENT LETTER

____________, ____

[Seller]

____

____

____

THE BANK OF NEW YORK
101 Barclay Street, 8th Floor West
New York, New York 10286

Re: Honda Auto Receivables 2003-1 Owner Trust Asset Backed Certificates

Dear Sirs:

In connection with our acquisition of the above-referenced Asset Backed Certificates (the "Certificates") we certify that (a) we understand that the Certificates are not being registered under the Securities Act of 1933, as amended (the "Act"), or any state securities laws and are being transferred to us in a transaction that is exempt from the registration requirements of the Act and any such laws, (b) we are an "accredited investor," as defined in Regulation D under the Act, and have such knowledge and experience in financial and business matters that we are capable of evaluating the merits and risks of investments in the Certificates, (c) we have had the opportunity to ask questions of and receive answers from the Seller concerning the purchase of the Certificates and all matters relating thereto or any additional information deemed necessary to our decision to purchase the Certificates, (d) we are acquiring the Certificates for investment for our own account and not with a view to any distribution of such Certificates (but without prejudice to our right at all times to sell or otherwise dispose of the Certificates in accordance with clause (f) below), (e) we have not offered or sold any Certificates to, or solicited offers to buy any Certificates from, any person, or otherwise approached or negotiated with any person with respect thereto, or taken any other action that would result in a violation of Section 5 of the Act or any state securities laws, (f) we are not a Benefit Plan and (g) we will not sell, or otherwise dispose of any Certificates unless (i) such sale, transfer or other disposition is made pursuant to an effective registration statement under the Act and in compliance with any state securities laws or is exempt from such registration requirements and, if requested, we will at our expense provide an Opinion of Counsel satisfactory to the addresses of this certificate that such sale, transfer or other disposition may be made pursuant to an exemption from the Act, (ii) the purchaser or transferee of such Certificate has executed and delivered to you a certificate to substantially the same effect as this certificate and (iii) the purchaser or transferee has otherwise complied with any conditions for transfer set forth in the Amended and Restated Trust Agreement dated as of

February 25, 2003, among American Honda Receivables Corp., The Bank of New York, as Owner Trustee, and The Bank of New York (Delaware), as Delaware Trustee.

Very truly yours,

[NAME OF TRANSFEROR]

By

____

Authorized Officer

EXHIBIT D

FORM OF RULE 144A LETTER

_________, ____

[Seller]

____

____

____

THE BANK OF NEW YORK
101 Barclay Street, 8th Floor
New York, New York 10286

Re: Honda Auto Receivables 2003-1 Owner Trust Asset Backed Certificates

Dear Sirs:

In connection with our acquisition of the above-referenced Asset Backed Certificates (the "Certificates") we certify that (a) we understand that the Certificates are not being registered under the Securities Act of 1933, as amended (the "Act"), or any state securities laws and are being transferred to us in a transaction that is exempt from the registration requirements of the Act and any such laws, (b) we have such knowledge and experience in financial and business matters that we are capable of evaluating the merits and risks of investments in the Certificates, (c) we have had the opportunity to ask questions of and receive answers from the Seller concerning the purchase of the Certificates and all matters relating thereto or any additional information deemed necessary to our decision to purchase the Certificates, (d) we have not, nor has anyone acting on our behalf, offered, transferred, pledged, sold or otherwise disposed of the Certificates or an interest in the Certificates, or solicited any offer to buy, transfer, pledge or otherwise dispose of the Certificates or any interest in the Certificates from any person in any manner or made any general solicitation by means of general advertising or in any other manner, taken any other action that would constitute a distribution of the Certificates under the Act or that would render the disposition of the Certificates a violation of Section 5 of the Act or any state securities laws or require registration pursuant thereto, and we will not act, or authorize any person to act, in such manner with respect to the Certificates, (e) we are not a Benefit Plan and (f) we are a "qualified institutional buyer" as that term is defined in Rule 144A under the Act. We are aware that the sale to us is being made in reliance on Rule 144A. We are acquiring the certificates for our own account or for resale pursuant to Rule 144A and understand that such certificates may be resold, pledged or transferred only (i) to a person reasonably believed to be a qualified institutional buyer that purchases for its own account or for the account of a qualified institutional buyer to whom notice is given that the resale, pledge or transfer is being made in reliance on Rule 144A or (ii) pursuant to another exemption from registration under the Act.

Very truly yours,

[NAME OF TRANSFEROR]

By

____

Authorized Officer

Appendix 10

Appendix 10

EXECUTION COPY

HONDA AUTO RECEIVABLES 2003-1 OWNER TRUST,
as Issuer,

AMERICAN HONDA RECEIVABLES CORP.,
as Seller,

And

AMERICAN HONDA FINANCE CORPORATION,
as Servicer

SALE AND SERVICING AGREEMENT

Dated as of February 1, 2003

TABLE OF CONTENTS

ARTICLE ONE

DEFINITIONS

Page*

*[Eds. — Page numbers added.]

ARTICLE THREE

ADMINISTRATION AND SERVICING OF RECEIVABLES

ARTICLE FOUR

DISTRIBUTIONS; RESERVE FUND; STATEMENTS TO SECURITYHOLDERS

ARTICLE FIVE

THE SELLER

ARTICLE SIX

THE SERVICER

ARTICLE SEVEN

SERVICER DEFAULTS

ARTICLE EIGHT

TERMINATION

ARTICLE NINE

MISCELLANEOUS

SCHEDULES

EXHIBITS

This Sale and Servicing Agreement, dated as of February 1, 2003, is among American Honda Receivables Corp., a California corporation ("AHRC" or, in its capacity as Seller, the "Seller"), American Honda Finance Corporation, a California corporation ("AHFC" or, in its capacity as Servicer, the "Servicer"), and Honda Auto Receivables 2003-1 Owner Trust, a Delaware statutory trust, as issuer (the "Issuer").

WHEREAS the Issuer desires to purchase from the Seller a portfolio of receivables arising in connection with retail installment sale or conditional sale contracts (the "Receivables") generated by AHFC in the ordinary course of its business, which Receivables have been sold by AHFC to AHRC;

WHEREAS, AHRC is willing to sell the Receivables to the Issuer pursuant to the terms hereof; and

WHEREAS, AHFC is willing to service the Receivables pursuant to the terms hereof;

NOW, THEREFORE, in consideration of the premises and the mutual covenants herein contained, the parties hereto agree as follows:

ARTICLE ONE

DEFINITIONS

Section 1.01. General Definitions. Whenever used in this Agreement, the following words and phrases, unless the context otherwise requires, shall have the following meanings:

"Absolute Prepayment Model" means a model calculating prepayment of receivables with respect to which the receivables prepay at a specified constant monthly prepayment rate.

"Accounts" means the Collection Account, the Note Distribution Account, the Payahead Account, the Yield Supplement Account and the Reserve Fund.

"Account Property" means, with respect to each Account, such Account, together with all cash, securities, financial assets and investments and other property from time to time deposited or credited to such Account and all proceeds thereof, including, with respect to the (i) Reserve Fund, the Reserve Fund Initial Deposit and (ii) Yield Supplement Account, the Yield Supplement Account Deposit.

"Actual Payment" means, with respect to a Receivable and a Collection Period, all payments received by the Servicer from or for the account of the related Obligor on such Receivable during such Collection Period, net of any Supplemental Servicing Fees attributable to such Receivable. Actual Payments do not include Applied Payments Ahead.

"Actuarial Receivable" means any Receivable which provides for the allocation of payments according to the "actuarial" method.

"Administration Agreement" means the Administration Agreement, dated as of February 1, 2003, among the Administrator, the Issuer, the Depositor and the Indenture Trustee.

"Administrator" means AHFC, or any successor Administrator under the Administration Agreement.

"Administrative Purchase Payment" means, with respect to a Payment Date and to an Administrative Receivable purchased by the Seller or the Servicer as of the end of the related Collection Period, which Receivable is (i) a Precomputed Receivable, (a) the sum of (1) all Scheduled Payments on such Receivable due after the last day of such Collection Period, (2) an amount equal to any reimbursement of Outstanding Advances made pursuant to the first sentence of Section 4.04(c) with respect to such Receivable, (3) all past due Scheduled Payments for which an Advance has not been made, minus (b) the sum of (1) all Payments Ahead in respect of such Administrative Receivable held by the Servicer or on deposit in the Payahead Account, (2) any Rebate and (3) any proceeds of the liquidation of such Receivable previously received (to the extent applied to reduce the Principal Balance of such Receivable) or (ii) a Simple Interest Receivable, the sum of (a) the unpaid principal balance owed by the related Obligor in respect of such Receivable and (b) interest on such unpaid principal balance at a rate equal to the APR of the related Receivable from the date of last payment by such Obligor to the last day of such Collection Period.

"Administrative Receivable" means a Receivable which the Servicer is required to purchase pursuant to Section 3.08 or which the Servicer has elected to purchase pursuant to Section 8.01.

"Advance" means a Precomputed Advance or a Simple Interest Advance.

"Affiliate" means, with respect to any specified Person, any other Person controlling or controlled by or under common control with such specified Person. For the purpose of this definition, "control", when used with respect to any specified Person, means the power to direct the management and policies of such Person, directly or indirectly, whether through the ownership of voting securities, by contract or otherwise; and the terms "controlling" and "controlled" have meanings correlative to the foregoing.

"Aggregate Net Losses" means, with respect to a Collection Period, an amount equal to the aggregate Principal Balance of all Receivables that became Defaulted Receivables during such Collection Period minus all Net Liquidation Proceeds collected during such Collection Period with respect to all Defaulted Receivables.

"Agreement" means this Sale and Servicing Agreement, and all amendments hereof and supplements hereto.

"AHFC" means American Honda Finance Corporation, and its successors.

"AHRC" means American Honda Receivables Corp., and its successors.

"Amount Financed" in respect of a Receivable means the aggregate amount advanced under such Receivable toward the purchase price of the related Financed Vehicle and any related costs, including but not limited to accessories, insurance premiums, service and warranty contracts and other items customarily financed as part of motor vehicle retail installment sale contracts.

"Annual Percentage Rate" or "APR" of a Receivable means the annual rate of finance charges stated in such Receivable.

"Applied Payment Ahead" means, with respect to a Precomputed Receivable and a Collection Period as to which (i) the Actual Payment is less than the Scheduled Payment and (ii) a Deferred Prepayment is on deposit in the Payahead Account or otherwise retained by the Servicer pursuant to Section 4.02(c), an amount equal to the lesser of (a) such Deferred Prepayment and (b) the amount by which the Scheduled Payment exceeds the Actual Payment.

"Available Amount" means, with respect to any Payment Date, the sum of Available Interest and Available Principal.

"Available Interest" means, with respect to any Payment Date, the total of the following amounts allocable to interest received by the Servicer on or in respect of the Receivables during the related Collection Period (computed, in the case of Precomputed Receivables, by the actuarial method and, in the case of Simple Interest Receivables, by the simple interest method): (i) the sum of the interest component of all (a) collections on or in respect of all Receivables other than Defaulted Receivables (including the interest portion of Applied Payments Ahead, but excluding Payments Ahead to be applied in one or more future Collections Periods), (b) Net Liquidation Proceeds, (c) Advances made by the Servicer, (d) Warranty Purchase Payments, (e) Administrative Purchase Payments and (f) the Yield Supplement Withdrawal Amount, if any, for the related Payment Date, less (ii) the sum of all (a) amounts received on or in respect of a particular Receivable (other than a Defaulted Receivable) to the extent of the aggregate Outstanding Interest Advances in respect of such Receivable and (b) Net Liquidation Proceeds with respect to a particular Receivable to the extent of the aggregate Outstanding Interest Advances in respect of such Receivable.

"Available Principal" means, with respect to any Payment Date, the total of the following amounts allocable to principal received by the Servicer on or in respect of the Receivables during the related Collection Period (computed, in the case of Precomputed Receivables, by the actuarial method and, in the case of Simple Interest Receivables, by the simple interest method): (i) the sum of the principal component of all (a) collections on or in respect of all Receivables other than Defaulted Receivables (including the principal portion of Applied Payments Ahead but excluding Payments Ahead), (b) Net Liquidation Proceeds, (c) Advances made by the Servicer, (d) Warranty Purchase Payments and (e) Administrative Purchase Payments, less (ii) an amount equal to all (a) amounts received on or in respect of a particular Receivable (other than a Defaulted Receivable) to the extent of the aggregate Outstanding Principal Advances in respect of such Receivable and (b) Net Liquidation Proceeds with respect to a particular Receivable to the extent of the aggregate Outstanding Principal Advances in respect of such Receivable.

"Basic Documents" means this Agreement, the Administration Agreement, the Indenture, the Note Depository Agreement, the Receivables Purchase Agreement, the Trust Agreement and the Control Agreement and any other documents or certificates delivered in connection therewith as the same may be amended, supplemented or otherwise modified and in effect.

"Basic Servicing Fee" means the fee payable pursuant to Section 3.09 to the Servicer on each Payment Date for services rendered during the related Collection Period, which shall be equal to one-twelfth of the Servicing Fee Rate multiplied by the Pool Balance as of the first day of the related Collection Period or, with respect to the first Payment Date, the Original Pool Balance.

"Business Day" means any day other than a Saturday, a Sunday or a day on which banking institutions in New York, New York, Los Angeles, California or Wilmington, Delaware are authorized or obligated by law, executive order or governmental decree to be closed.

"Certificate Balance" means, on any Payment Date, the Original Certificate Balance reduced by all distributions of principal previously made in respect of the Certificates.

"Certificate Distributable Amount" means, with respect to any Payment Date, the sum of the Certificate Interest Distributable Amount and the Certificate Principal Distributable Amount for such Payment Date.

"Certificate Distribution Account" has the meaning specified in the Trust Agreement.

"Certificate Interest Carryover Shortfall" means, with respect to any Payment Date, the excess, if any, of (x) the sum of (i) the Certificate Monthly Interest Distributable Amount and (ii) any outstanding Certificate Interest Carryover Shortfall for the preceding Payment Date, over (y) the amount in respect of interest on the Certificates that is actually paid as interest on the Certificates on such Payment Date, plus, to the extent permitted by applicable law, interest on the Certificate Interest Carryover Shortfall at the Certificate Rate for the Interest Accrual Period.

"Certificate Interest Distributable Amount" means, with respect to any Payment Date, the sum of the Certificate Monthly Interest Distributable Amount for such Payment Date and the Certificate Interest Carryover Shortfall for such Payment Date.

"Certificate Monthly Interest Distributable Amount" means, with respect to any Payment Date, interest accrued for the related Interest Accrual Period at the Certificate Rate on the Certificate Balance on the immediately preceding Payment Date after giving effect to all payments of principal to Certificateholders on or prior to such Payment Date (or, in the case of the first Payment Date, on the Original Certificate Balance).

"Certificate Monthly Principal Distributable Amount" means, with respect to any Payment Date, the Certificate Percentage of the Principal Distributable Amount for such Payment Date.

"Certificate Percentage" means (i) for each Payment Date until the principal amount of the Class A-1 Notes has been paid in full, 0%; (ii) after the principal amount of the Class A-1 Notes has been paid in full, for each Payment Date to and including the Payment Date on which the principal amount of the Class A-4 Notes has been paid in full, the percent equivalent of a fraction, the numerator of which is the initial principal amount of the Certificates and the denominator of which is the sum of the initial aggregate principal amount of the Class A-2, Class A-3 and Class A-4 Notes and the initial principal amount of the Certificates; and (iii) for each Payment Date after the Payment Date on which the principal amount of the Class A-4 Notes has been paid in full, 100%; notwithstanding the foregoing, for each Payment Date after the acceleration of the Notes following an Event of Default, the Certificate Percentage shall be 0% until the Notes have been paid in full.

"Certificate Pool Factor" means, with respect to the Certificates on any Payment Date, a seven-digit decimal figure equal to the outstanding principal balance of the Certificates on such Payment Date (after giving effect to any reductions thereof to be made on such Payment Date) divided by the Original Certificate Balance.

"Certificate Principal Carryover Shortfall" means, with respect to any Payment Date, the excess, if any, of (x) the sum of (i) the Certificate Monthly Principal Distributable Amount and (ii) any outstanding Certificate Principal Carryover Shortfall for the preceding Payment Date, over (y) the amount in respect of principal that is actually paid as principal on the Certificates on such Payment Date.

"Certificate Principal Distributable Amount" means, with respect to any Payment Date, the sum of the Certificate Monthly Principal Distributable Amount for each Payment Date and any outstanding Certificate Principal Carryover Shortfall as of the close of the immediately preceding Payment Date; provided, however, that the Certificate Principal Distributable Amount shall not exceed the Certificate Balance. In addition, on the Payment Date as of which all of the Receivables are to be purchased pursuant to Section 8.01, the principal required to be deposited into the Certificate Distribution Account will include the amount necessary to reduce the Certificate Balance to zero.

"Certificate Rate" means 2.48% per annum (computed on the basis of a 360 day year consisting of twelve 30-day months). "Certificateholders" has the meaning specified in the Trust Agreement.

"Charge-off Rate" with respect to a Collection Period will equal the Aggregate Net Losses with respect to the Receivables expressed, on an annualized basis, as a percentage of the average of the (i) Pool Balance on the last day of the immediately preceding Collection Period and (ii) Pool Balance on the last day of such current Collection Period.

"Class" means all Securities whose form is identical except for variation in denomination, principal amount or owner (i.e., each of Class A-1, Class A-2, Class A-3 and Class A-4).

"Class A-1 Final Payment Date" means the March 2004 Payment Date.

"Class A-1 Noteholder" means a Person in whose name a Class A-1 Note is Registered the Note Register.

"Class A-2 Final Payment Date" means the September 2005 Payment Date.

"Class A-2 Noteholder" means a Person in whose name a Class A-2 Note is registered in the Note Register.

"Class A-3 Final Payment Date" means the November 2006 Payment Date.

"Class A-3 Noteholder" means a Person in whose name a Class A-3 Note is registered in the Note Register.

"Class A-4 Final Payment Date" means the July 2008 Payment Date.

"Class A-4 Noteholder" means the Person in whose name a Class A-4 Note is registered in the Note Register.

"Closing Date" means February 25, 2003.

"Collection Account" means the account designated as such, and established and maintained pursuant to Section 4.01.

"Collection Period" means each calendar month during the term of this Agreement (or, in the case of the first Collection Period, the period of time since the Cutoff Date through the last day of the calendar month immediately preceding the month in which the first Payment Date occurs).

"Commission" means the Securities and Exchange Commission, and its successors.

"Control" shall have the meaning specified in Section 8-106 of the UCC.

"Control Agreement" means the control agreement, dated as of February 1, 2003, among AHRC, the Issuer, the Servicer, the Indenture Trustee and JPMorgan Chase Bank, as securities intermediary, as amended or supplemented from time to time.

"Corporate Trust Office" means the principal office of the Indenture Trustee at which at any particular time its corporate trust business shall be administered, which office at the date of the execution of this Agreement is located at 4 New York Plaza, 6th Floor, New York, New York 10004, Attention: Institutional Trust Services: Honda Auto Receivables 2003-1 Owner Trust, or at such other address as the Indenture Trustee may designate from time to time by notice to the Noteholders and the Seller, or the principal corporate trust office of any successor Indenture Trustee (of which address such successor Indenture Trustee will notify the Noteholders and the Seller).

"Current Receivable" means each Receivable that is not a Defaulted Receivable or a Liquidated Receivable.

"Cutoff Date" means February 1, 2003.

"Dealer" means the dealer of motor vehicles who sold a Financed Vehicle and who originated and assigned the Receivable relating to such Financed Vehicle to AHFC under an existing agreement between such dealer and AHFC.

"Dealer Recourse" means, with respect to a Receivable, all recourse rights against the Dealer which originated the Receivable, and any successor to such Dealer.

"Defaulted Receivable" means a Receivable (other than an Administrative Receivable or a Warranty Receivable as to which a Warranty Purchase Payment or an Administrative Purchase Payment has been made) as to which (i) all or any part of a Scheduled Payment is 120 or more days past due and the Servicer has not repossessed the related Financed Vehicle or (ii) the Servicer has, in accordance with its customary servicing procedures, determined that eventual payment in full is unlikely and either repossessed and liquidated the related Financed Vehicle or repossessed and held the related Financed Vehicle in its repossession inventory for 90 days, whichever occurs first.

"Deferred Prepayment" means, with respect to a Receivable and a Collection Period, the aggregate amount, if any, of Payments Ahead remitted to the Servicer in respect of such Receivable during one or more prior Collection Periods and currently held by the Servicer or in the Payahead Account.

"Delaware Trustee" means the Person acting as Delaware Trustee under the Trust Agreement, its successors in interest and permitted assigns, initially The Bank of New York (Delaware).

"Delinquency Percentage" means, with respect to a Collection Period, the percentage equivalent of a fraction, the numerator of which is the number of (i) Receivables 61 days or more delinquent (after taking into account permitted extensions) as of the last day of such Collection Period, determined in accordance with the Servicer's normal practices, plus (ii) Receivables the related Financed Vehicles of which have been repossessed but have not been liquidated (to the extent the related Receivable is not otherwise reflected in clause (i) above or is not a Defaulted Receivable), and the denominator of which is the aggregate number of Current Receivables on the last day of such Collection Period.

"Deposit Date" means, with respect to any Collection Period and Payment Date, the Business Day immediately preceding such Payment Date.

"Depositor " means the Seller in its capacity as Depositor under the Trust Agreement.

"Determination Date" means, with respect to any Payment Date, the thirteenth calendar day of the month in which such Payment Date occurs or, if such day is not a Business Day, the immediately succeeding Business Day.

"Discount Receivable" means any Receivable that has an APR which is less than the Required Rate.

"Eligible Account" means either (A) a segregated deposit account over which the applicable Trustee has sole signature authority, maintained with an Eligible Institution meeting the requirements of clause (i) thereof or (B) a segregated trust account maintained with an Eligible Institution meeting the requirements of clause (ii) thereof, in each case bearing a designation clearly indicating that the funds deposited therein are held for the benefit of the Securityholders, the Noteholders or the Certificateholders, as the case may be.

"Eligible Institution" means a depository institution or trust company, (i) the commercial paper or other short-term unsecured debt obligations of which have the Required Deposit Rating or (ii) having corporate trust powers and organized under the laws of the United States, any state thereof, the District of Columbia or the Commonwealth of Puerto Rico which has a long-term deposit rating from (A) Moody's of at least Baa3 or (B) Standard and Poor's of at least BBB — (or such lower rating as either Rating Agency shall approve in writing).

"Eligible Investments" means, at any time, any one or more of the following obligations and securities:

(i) obligations of, and obligations fully guaranteed as to timely payment of principal and interest by, the United States or any agency thereof, provided such obligations are backed by the full faith and credit of the United States;

(ii) general obligations of or obligations guaranteed by FNMA, any state of the United States, the District of Columbia or the Commonwealth of Puerto Rico then rated the highest available credit rating of each Rating Agency for such obligations;

(iii) securities bearing interest or sold at a discount issued by any corporation incorporated under the laws of the United States or any state thereof, the District of Columbia or the Commonwealth of Puerto Rico, so long as at the time of such investment or contractual commitment providing for such investment either the long-term unsecured debt of such corporation has the highest available credit rating from each Rating Agency for such obligations or the commercial paper or other short-term debt which is then rated has the highest available credit rating of each Rating Agency for such obligations;

(iv) certificates of deposit issued by any depository institution or trust company (including the Trustee) incorporated under the laws of the United States or any state thereof, the District of Columbia or the Commonwealth of Puerto Rico and subject to supervision and examination by banking authorities of one or more of such jurisdictions, provided that the short-term unsecured debt obligations of such depository institution or trust company has the highest available credit rating of each Rating Agency for such obligations;

(v) certificates of deposit issued by any bank, trust company, savings bank or other savings institution and fully insured by the FDIC;

(vi) repurchase obligations held by the Trustee that are acceptable to the Trustee with respect to any security described in clauses (i) or (ii) hereof or any other security issued or guaranteed by any other agency or instrumentality of the United States, in either case entered into with a federal agency or a depository institution or trust company (acting as principal) described in clause (iv) above;

(vii) any mutual fund, money market fund, common trust fund or other pooled investment vehicle having a rating, at the time of such investment, of no less than Aaa or its equivalent by Moody's, AAA or its equivalent by Standard & Poor's and AAA or its equivalent by Fitch, if rated by Fitch (including, but not limited to funds of which JPMorgan Chase Bank or an affiliate thereof is the manager or financial advisor);

(viii) such other investments acceptable to each Rating Agency in writing as will not result in the qualification, downgrading or withdrawal of the rating then assigned to any Rated Securities by such Rating Agency;

provided that each of the foregoing investments shall mature no later than the Deposit Date immediately following the date of purchase (other than in the case of the investment of monies in instruments of which the entity at which the related Account or the Certificate Distribution Account, as the case may be, is located is the obligor, which may mature on the related Payment Date), and shall be required to be held to such maturity.

Notwithstanding anything to the contrary contained in this definition, (a) no Eligible Investment may be purchased at a premium, and (b) no obligation or security is an "Eligible Investment" unless (i) the Trustee has Control over such obligation or security and (ii) at the time such obligation or security was delivered to the Trustee or the Trustee became the related Entitlement Holder, the Trustee did not have notice of any adverse claim with respect thereto within the meaning of Section 8-105 of the UCC.

For purposes of this definition, any reference to the highest available credit rating of an obligation shall mean the highest available credit rating for such obligation, or such lower credit rating (as approved in writing by each Rating Agency) as will not result in the qualification, downgrading or withdrawal of the rating then assigned to any Rated Securities by such Rating Agency.

"Entitlement Holder" shall have the meaning specified in Section 8-102 of the UCC.

"Entitlement Order" shall have the meaning specified in Section 8-102 of the UCC.

"Excess Payment" means, with respect to a Receivable and a Collection Period, the amount, if any, by which the Actual Payment exceeds the sum of (i) the Scheduled Payment and (ii) any Overdue Payment.

"Exchange Act" means the Securities Exchange Act of 1934, as amended.

"FDIC" means the Federal Deposit Insurance Corporation.

"FHLMC" means the Federal Home Loan Mortgage Corporation, and its successors.

"FNMA" means the Federal National Mortgage Association, and its successors.

"Final Payment Dates" means, collectively, the Class A-1 Final Payment Date, the Class A-2 Final Payment Date, the Class A-3 Final Payment Date and the Class A-4 Final Payment Date.

"Final Scheduled Maturity Date" means July 18, 2008.

"Financed Vehicle" means, with respect to any retail installment sale or conditional sale contract, the related new or used Honda or Acura motor vehicle, together with all accessions thereto, securing the related Obligor's indebtedness under such retail installment sale or conditional sale contract.

"Financial Asset" shall have the meaning specified in Section 8-102(a)(9) of the UCC.

"Fitch" means Fitch, Inc., or its successors.

"Indenture" means the indenture, dated as of February 1, 2003 between the Issuer and the Indenture Trustee.

"Indenture Trustee" means the Person acting as Indenture Trustee under the Indenture, its successors in interest and any successor trustee under the Indenture.

"Independent Director" means a director of the Seller who is not (i) a director, officer or employee of any Affiliate of the Seller, (ii) a natural person related to any director or officer of any Affiliate of the Seller, (iii) a holder (directly or indirectly) of more than 10% of any voting securities of any Affiliate of the Seller or (iv) a natural person related to a holder (directly or indirectly) of more than 10% of any voting securities of any Affiliate of the Seller.

"Insolvency Event" means, with respect to a specified Person, (i) the filing of a decree or order for relief by a court having jurisdiction in the premises in respect of such Person or any substantial part of its property in an involuntary case under any applicable federal or state bankruptcy, insolvency or other similar law now or hereafter in effect, or appointing a receiver, liquidator, assignee, custodian, trustee, sequestrator or similar official for such Person or for any substantial part of its property, or ordering the winding-up or liquidation of such Person's affairs, and such decree or order shall remain unstayed and in effect for a period of 90 consecutive days; or (ii) the commencement by such Person of a voluntary case under any applicable federal or state bankruptcy, insolvency or other similar law now or hereafter in effect, or the consent by such Person to the entry of an order for relief in an involuntary case under any such law, or the consent by such Person to the appointment of or taking possession by a receiver, liquidator, assignee, custodian, trustee, sequestrator or similar official for such Person or for any substantial part of its property, or the making by such Person of any general assignment for the benefit of creditors, or the failure by such Person generally to pay its debts as such debts become due, or the taking of action by such Person in furtherance of any of the foregoing.

"Insurance Policy" means, with respect to a Receivable, an insurance policy covering physical damage, credit life, credit disability, theft, mechanical breakdown or any similar event relating to the related Financed Vehicle or Obligor.

"Letter of Credit Bank" means any Person who has provided a Servicer Letter of Credit pursuant to Section 4.02(b).

"Lien" means any security interest, lien, charge, pledge, equity or encumbrance of any kind other than tax liens, mechanics' liens and any liens that attach to a Receivable or any property, as the context may require, by operation of law.

"Liquidated Receivable" means a Receivable that (i) has been the subject of a Prepayment in full, (ii) has otherwise been paid in full or (iii) the Servicer has determined that the final amounts in respect of such payment have been paid with respect to a Defaulted Receivable, regardless of whether all or any part of such payment has been made by the Obligor under such Receivable, the Seller pursuant to this Agreement, AHFC pursuant to the Receivables Purchase Agreement, the Servicer pursuant hereto, an insurer pursuant to an Insurance Policy or otherwise.

"Liquidation Expenses" means, with respect to a Defaulted Receivable, the amount charged by the Servicer, in accordance with its customary servicing procedures, to or for its account for repossessing, refurbishing and disposing of the related Financed Vehicle and other out-of-pocket costs related to such liquidation.

"Liquidation Proceeds" means, with respect to a Defaulted Receivable, all amounts realized with respect to such Receivable from whatever sources (including, without limitation, proceeds of any Insurance Policy), net of amounts that are required by law or such Receivable to be refunded to the related Obligor.

"Maximum Yield Supplement Amount" means with respect to any Collection Period and the related Deposit Date, after giving effect to the Yield Supplement Amount, the maximum amount required to be on deposit in the Yield Supplement Account on the immediately succeeding Payment Date, which is equal to the present value (using an interest rate of: 1.25%) of the sum of all Yield Supplement Amounts for all future Payment Dates, assuming that future Scheduled Payments on the Discount Receivables are made on the date on which they are scheduled as being due.

"Monthly Payment" means, with respect to any Receivable, the amount of each fixed monthly payment payable to the obligee under such Receivable in accordance with the terms thereof, net of any portion of such monthly payment that represents late payment charges, extension fees or collections allocable to payments to be made by Obligors for payment of insurance premiums, extended service contracts or similar items.

"Moody's" means Moody's Investors Service, Inc., or its successors.

"Motor Vehicle Receivables" shall have the meaning specified in Section 5.03(b)(ii)(A).

"Net Liquidation Proceeds" means, with respect to a Defaulted Receivable, Liquidation Proceeds less Liquidation Expenses.

"Nonrecoverable Advance" shall have the meaning specified in Section 4.04(c).

"Note Amount" means, with respect to any Payment Date, the aggregate outstanding principal amount of the Notes after giving effect to payments of principal made on the Notes on such Payment Date.

"Note Distributable Amount" means, with respect to any Payment Date, the sum of the Note Interest Distributable Amount and the Note Principal Distributable Amount for such Payment Date.

"Note Distribution Account" means the account designated as such, and established and maintained pursuant to Section 4.01.

"Note Interest Carryover Shortfall" means, with respect to any Payment Date and a Class of Notes, the excess, if any, of (x) the sum of (i) the Note Monthly Interest Distributable Amount for such Class for the preceding Payment Date and (ii) any outstanding Note Interest Carryover Shortfall for such Class on such preceding Payment Date, over (y) the amount of interest that is actually paid on the Notes on such preceding Payment Date, plus, to the extent permitted by law, interest on the Note Interest Carryover Shortfall at the related Interest Rate for the related Interest Accrual Period.

"Note Interest Distributable Amount" means, with respect to any Payment Date and a Class of Notes, the sum of the Note Monthly Interest Distributable Amount for such Payment Date and the Note Interest Carryover Shortfall for such Class of Notes. For all purposes of this Agreement and the other Basic Documents, interest with respect to the Class A-2, Class A-3 and Class A-4 Notes shall be computed on the basis of a 360-day year consisting of twelve 30-day months; and interest with respect to the Class A-1 Notes shall be computed on the basis of the actual number of days in each applicable Interest Accrual Period, divided by 360.

"Note Monthly Interest Distributable Amount" means, with respect to any Payment Date, interest accrued for the related Interest Accrual Period at the related Interest Rate for each Class of Notes on the Outstanding Amount of the Notes of each such Class on the immediately preceding Payment Date (or, in the case of the first Payment Date, the original principal amount of each such Class of Notes), after giving effect to all distributions of principal to the Noteholders of each such Class on or prior to such Payment Date.

"Note Monthly Principal Distributable Amount" means, with respect to any Payment Date, the Note Percentage of the Principal Distributable Amount for such Payment Date.

"Note Percentage" means (i) for each Payment Date until the principal amount of the Class A-1 Notes has been paid in full, 100%; (ii) for each Payment Date on or after the principal amount of the Class A-1 Notes has been paid in full to and including the Payment Date on which the principal amount of the Class A-4 Notes has been paid in full, the percent equivalent of a fraction, the numerator of which is the initial aggregate principal amount of the Class A-2, Class A-3 and Class A-4 Notes and the denominator of which is the sum of the initial aggregate principal amount of the Class A-2, Class A-3 and Class A-4 Notes and the initial principal amount of the Certificates; and (iii) for each Payment Date after the Payment Date on which the principal amount of the Class A-4 Notes has been paid in full, 0%; notwithstanding the foregoing, for each Payment

Date after the acceleration of the Notes following an Event of Default, the Note Percentage shall be 100% until the Notes have been paid in full.

"Note Pool Factor" means, with respect to each Class of Notes as of any Payment Date, a seven-digit decimal figure equal to the Outstanding Amount of such Class of Notes as of such Payment Date (after giving effect to any reductions thereof to be made on such Payment Date) divided by the original outstanding principal balance of such Class of Notes.

"Note Principal Carryover Shortfall" means, with respect to any Payment Date, the excess, if any, of the sum of the Note Monthly Principal Distributable Amount plus any outstanding Note Principal Carryover Shortfall for the preceding Payment Date, over the amount in respect of principal that is actually paid as principal on the Notes on such Payment Date.

"Note Principal Distributable Amount" means, with respect to any Payment Date, the sum of (i) the Note Monthly Principal Distributable Amount, (ii) any outstanding Note Principal Carryover Shortfall as of the close of the immediately preceding Payment Date and, (iii) on the Final Payment Date for a Class of Notes or the Payment Date as of which all of the Receivables are to be purchased pursuant to Section 8.01, the amount necessary (after giving effect to all amounts allocable to principal required to be deposited in the Note Distribution Account on such Payment Date) to reduce the Outstanding Amount of each related Class of Notes to zero; provided, however, that the Note Principal Distributable Amount with respect to a Class of Notes shall not exceed the Outstanding Amount of such Class of Notes.

"Notes" means the Class A-1 Notes, the Class A-2 Notes, the Class A-3 Notes and the Class A-4 Notes.

"Obligor" on a Receivable means the purchaser or co-purchasers of the related Financed Vehicle purchased in part or in whole by the execution and delivery of a retail installment contract or any other Person who owes or may be liable for payments under such retail installment contract.

"Offered Securities" shall have the meaning specified in Section 5.03(b)(ii)(B).

"Officers' Certificate" means a certificate signed by the president, any Vice President, the treasurer or the secretary of the Seller or the Servicer, as the case may be, and delivered to the Trustee.

"Opinion of Counsel" means a written opinion of counsel (who, in the case of counsel to the Seller or the Servicer, may be an employee of or outside counsel to the Seller or the Servicer), which counsel shall be acceptable to the Trustee.

"Original Certificate Balance" means $35,577,657.84.

"Original Pool Balance" means $1,577,277,657.84.

"Outstanding Advances" means, with respect to a Receivable and the last day of a Collection Period, the sum of all Advances made as of or prior to such date, minus (1) all payments or collections as of or prior to such date which are specified in Section 4.04(b) and (c) as applied to reimburse all unpaid Advances with respect to such Receivable and (2) all amounts for which the Servicer has deemed to have released all claims for reimbursement of Outstanding Advances pursuant to Section 3.08.

"Outstanding Amount" means the aggregate principal amount of all Notes, or if indicated by the context, all Notes of any class, outstanding at the date of the determination.

"Outstanding Interest Advances" means, as of the last day of a Collection Period with respect to a Receivable, the portion of Outstanding Advances allocable to interest.

"Outstanding Principal Advances" means, as of the last day of a Collection Period with respect to a Receivable, the portion of Outstanding Advances allocable to principal.

"Overdue Payment" shall have the meaning specified in Section 4.03(a).

"Owner Trust Estate" shall have the meaning specified in the Trust Agreement.

"Owner Trustee" means the Person acting as Owner Trustee under the Trust Agreement, its successors in interest and any successor owner trustee under the Trust Agreement.

"Payahead Account" means the account designated as such and established and maintained pursuant to Section 4.01.

"Payment Ahead" means, with respect to a Precomputed Receivable and a Collection Period, any Excess Payment (not representing, when added to any Deferred Prepayment with respect to such Precomputed Receivable, a prepayment in full of such Precomputed Receivable) which the Servicer, in accordance with its customary servicing practices, will apply towards the payment of Scheduled Payments due in one or more future Collection Periods.

"Payment Date" means, with respect to a Collection Period, the eighteenth calendar day of the next succeeding calendar month or, if such day is not a Business Day, the next succeeding Business Day, commencing March 2003.

"Percentage Interests" shall have the meaning specified in the Trust Agreement.

"Person" means any legal person, including any individual, corporation, partnership, joint venture, association, joint stock company, trust, unincorporated organization or government or any agency or political subdivision thereof.

"Pool Balance" means, as of any date, the aggregate Principal Balance of the Receivables (exclusive of all Administrative Receivables for which the Servicer has paid the Administrative Purchase Payment, Warranty Receivables for which the Seller has paid the Warranty Purchase Payment and Defaulted Receivables) as of the close of business on such date.

"Precomputed Advance" shall have the meaning specified in Section 4.04(a).

"Precomputed Receivable" means any Actuarial Receivable or Rule of 78s Receivable.

"Prepayment" means any Excess Payment with respect to a Receivable other than a Payment Ahead.

"Principal Balance" means, with respect to any Receivable as of any date, the Amount Financed minus the sum of the following amounts: (i) in the case of a Precomputed Receivable, that portion of all Scheduled Payments due on or prior to such date allocable to principal, computed in accordance with the actuarial method, (ii) in the case of a Simple Interest Receivable, that portion of all Scheduled Payments actually received on or prior to such date allocable to principal, computed in accordance with the simple interest method, (iii) any Warranty Purchase Payment or Administrative Purchase Payment with respect to such Receivable allocable to principal and (iv) any Prepayments or other payments applied to reduce the unpaid principal balance of such Receivable.

"Principal Distributable Amount" means, with respect to any Payment Date, the sum of the following amounts (i) in the case of (a) Precomputed Receivables, the principal portion of all Scheduled Payments due during the related Collection Period, computed in accordance with the actuarial method and (b) Simple Interest Receivables, the principal portion of all Scheduled Payments actually received during the related Collection Period, computed in accordance with the simple interest method, (ii) the principal portion of all Prepayments, received during such Collection Period (to the extent such amounts are not included in clause (i) above), (iii) the Principal Balance of each Receivable that became an Administrative Receivable or a Warranty Receivable during such Collection Period (to the extent such amounts are not included in clauses (i) or (ii) above) and (iv) the Principal Balance of each Receivable that became a Defaulted Receivable during such Collection Period (to the extent such amounts are not included in clauses (i), (ii) or (iii) above).

"Rated Securities" means each Class of Securities that has been rated by a Rating at the request of the Seller.

"Rating Agency" means Fitch, Moody's and Standard & Poor's.

"Rating Agency Condition" means, with respect to any action, that each Rating Agency shall have been given ten days' (or such shorter period as shall be acceptable to each Rating Agency) prior notice thereof and that each Rating Agency shall have notified the Seller, the Servicer and the Trustees in writing that such action will not result in a reduction or withdrawal of the then current rating of the Rated Securities.

"Rebate" means, with respect to a Precomputed Receivable and any date, the rebate, calculated in accordance with the actuarial method, under such Receivable that is or would be payable to the related Obligor for unearned finance charges or any other charges rebatable to the Obligor if such Obligor were to prepay such Receivable in full on such date.

"Receivable" means any retail installment sale contract executed by an Obligor in respect of a Financed Vehicle, and all proceeds thereof and payments thereunder, which Receivables shall be identified in a Schedule of Receivables.

"Receivable Files" means the documents specified in Section 2.02.

"Receivables Purchase Agreement" means the receivables purchase agreement, dated as of February 1, 2003, between AHFC and the Seller, as amended or supplemented from time to time.

"Released Administrative Amount" means, with respect to a Payment Date and to an Administrative Receivable, the Deferred Prepayment, if any, for such Administrative Receivable.

"Released Warranty Amount" means, with respect to a Payment Date and to a Warranty Receivable, the Deferred Prepayment, if any, for such Warranty Receivable.

"Required Rate" means the sum of (a) the percent equivalent of a fraction, the numerator of which is the sum for each Class of Notes of the product of (1) the Interest Rate for such Class of Notes, (2) the original principal balance of such Class of Notes and (3) the expected weighted average life for such Class of Notes at the prepayment speed of 1.5% under the Absolute Prepayment Model and the denominator of which is the sum for each such Class of Notes of the product of (1) the original principal balance of such Class of Notes and (2) the expected weighted average life for such Class of Notes at the prepayment speed of 1.5% under the Absolute Prepayment Model and (b) the Servicing Fee Rate.

"Required Deposit Rating" means the short-term credit rating of the related entity is at least equal to P-1 by Moody's, A-1+ by Standard & Poor's and F1 by Fitch.

"Required Servicer Rating" means, with respect to the Servicer, that the then short-term unsecured debt obligations of the Servicer are rated at least equal to P-1 by Moody's, and A-1 by Standard & Poor's.

"Reserve Fund" means the account designated as such, and established and maintained pursuant to Section 4.01.

"Reserve Fund Initial Deposit" means the initial deposit of cash in the amount of $7,886,388.29 made by or on behalf of the Seller into the Reserve Fund on the Closing Date.

"Reserve Fund Property" means, the Reserve Fund Initial Deposit and all proceeds thereof and all other amounts deposited in or credited to the Reserve Fund from time to time under this Agreement, all Eligible Investments made with amounts on deposit therein, all earnings and distributions thereon and proceeds thereof.

"Responsible Officer" means, in the case of the Indenture Trustee, any officer within the Corporate Trust Office of the Indenture Trustee, including any Managing Director, Vice President, assistant Vice President, assistant secretary or any other officer of the Indenture Trustee customarily performing functions similar to those performed by any of the above designated officers, in each case having direct responsibility for the administration of the Indenture and, with respect to the Owner Trustee, any officer in the Corporate Trust Administration Department of the Owner Trustee with direct responsibility for the administration of the Trust Agreement and the Basic Documents on behalf of the Owner Trustee.

"Retail installment contracts" means retail installment sale and conditional sale contracts.

"Rule of 78s Receivable" means any Receivable which provides for the allocation of payments according to the "sum of periodic balances" or "sum of monthly payments" method.

"Schedule of Receivables" means the schedule of Receivables attached as Schedule A to this Agreement, as it may be amended from time to time.

"Scheduled Payment" means, with respect to any Payment Date and to a Receivable, the payment set forth in such Receivable as due from the Obligor in the related Collection Period; provided, however, that in the case of the first Collection Period, the Scheduled Payment shall include all such payments due from the Obligor on or after the Cutoff Date.

"Securities" means the Notes and the Trust Certificates.

"Security Entitlement" shall have the meaning specified in Section 8-102(a)(17) of the UCC.

"Securityholders" means the Noteholders and the Certificateholders.

"Seller" means AHRC, in its capacity as Seller of the Receivables under this Agreement, and each successor thereto (in the same capacity) pursuant to Section 5.03.

"Servicer" means AHFC, in its capacity as servicer of the Receivables pursuant to this Agreement, and each successor thereto (in the same capacity) pursuant to Section 6.03.

"Servicer Default" shall have the meaning specified in Section 7.01.

"Servicer Letter of Credit" means, if the Servicer desires to remit collections on or in respect of the Receivables to the Collection Account on a monthly basis upon satisfaction of the conditions described in Section 4.02(b)(ii), (i) an irrevocable letter of credit, issued by a Letter of Credit Bank and naming the Indenture Trustee a beneficiary or (ii) a surety bond, insurance policy or deposit of cash or securities, which is satisfactory to each Rating Agency.

"Servicer's Certificate" means an Officers' Certificate of the Servicer delivered pursuant to Section 3.10, substantially in the form of Exhibit B.

"Servicing Fee Rate" means 1.00% per annum.

"Simple Interest Advance" shall have the meaning specified in Section 4.04(a).

"Simple Interest Receivable" means any Receivable which provides for the allocation of payments according to the "simple interest" method.

"Specified Reserve Fund Balance" means, on the Closing Date $7,886,388.29, and with respect to any Payment Date the greater of: (i) 0.50% of the Pool Balance as of the Cutoff Date and (ii) 0.75 % of the aggregate principal amount of the Receivables as of the immediately preceding Payment Date; except that, if on any Payment Date (i) the average of the Charge-off Rates for the three preceding Collection Periods exceeds 2.25% or (ii) the average of the Delinquency Percentages for the three preceding Collection Periods exceeds 2.25%, then the Specified Reserve Fund Balance will be an amount equal to a specified percentage of the Pool Balance as of the last day of the immediately preceding Collection Period. Such percentage shall be determined by deducting from 8.00% the following fraction, expressed as a percentage: (a) one minus (b) a fraction, the numerator of which is the outstanding principal amount of the Notes with respect to such Payment Date and the denominator of which is such Pool Balance. Notwithstanding the foregoing, in no event will the Specified Reserve Fund Balance be more than the outstanding principal amount of the Notes.

"Standard & Poor's" means Standard & Poor's Ratings Services, a division of The McGraw-Hill Companies, Inc., or its successors.

"Successor Servicer" means any entity appointed as a successor to the Servicer pursuant to Section 7.02.

"Supplemental Servicing Fee" means any interest earned on investment of the monies on deposit in the Accounts (other than the Yield Supplement Account and the Reserve Fund) during a Collection Period, net of any investment expenses and losses from such investments, plus all late fees, prepayment charges and other administrative fees and expenses or similar charges allowed by applicable law with respect to the Receivables, including, in the case of a Rule of 78s Receivable and that is prepaid in full, the difference between the Principal Balance of a Rule of 78s Receivable, minus the Principal Balance of such Receivable computed according to the actuarial method (plus accrued interest to the date of prepayment), received by the Servicer during such Collection Period.

"Total Servicing Fee" means the sum of the Basic Servicing Fee and the Supplemental Servicing Fee.

"Trust" means the Issuer.

"Trust Agreement" means the trust agreement, dated as of January 21, 2003, as amended and restated, on February 25, 2003, among the Depositor, the Owner Trustee and the Delaware Trustee.

"Trust Fees and Expenses" means all accrued and unpaid Trustees' fees, any amounts due to the Trustees for reimbursement of expenses or in respect of indemnification and other administrative fees of the Trust.

"Trustee" means either the Owner Trustee, the Indenture Trustee or the Delaware Trustee, as the context requires.

"Trustees" means the Owner Trustee, the Indenture Trustee and the Delaware Trustee.

"UCC" means the Uniform Commercial Code as in effect in the respective jurisdiction.

"United States" means the United States of America.

"Vice President" of any Person means any vice president of such Person, whether or not designated by a number or words before or after the title "Vice President", who is a duly elected officer of such Person.

"Warranty Purchase Payment" means, with respect to a Payment Date and to a Warranty Receivable repurchased by the Seller as of the end of the related Collection Period, which Receivable is (i) a Precomputed Receivable, (a) the sum of (1) all Scheduled Payments on such Receivable due after the last day of such Collection Period, (2) all past due Scheduled Payments for which an Advance has not been made, (3) all Outstanding Advances made in respect of such Receivable and (4) an amount equal to any reimbursement of Outstanding Advances made pursuant to the first sentence of Section 4.04(c) with respect to such Receivable minus (b) the sum of (1) all Payments Ahead in respect of such Warranty Receivable held by the Servicer or on deposit in the Payahead Account, (2) any Rebate and (3) any proceeds of the liquidation of such Receivable previously received (to the extent applied to reduce the Principal Balance of such Receivable) or (ii) a Simple Interest Receivable, the sum of (a) the unpaid principal balance owed by the related Obligor in respect of such Receivable and (b) interest on such unpaid principal balance at a rate equal to the APR of the related Receivable from the date of last payment by such Obligor to the last day of such Collection Period.

"Warranty Receivable" means a Receivable which the Seller is required to repurchase pursuant to Section 2.04.

"Yield Supplement Account" means the account designated as such, and established and maintained pursuant to Section 4.01.

"Yield Supplement Account Deposit" means the initial deposit of cash in the amount of $267,720.61 made by or on behalf of the Seller into the Yield Supplement Account on the Closing Date.

"Yield Supplement Amount" means, with respect to any Collection Period and the related Deposit Date, the aggregate amount by which one month's interest on the Principal Balance as of the first day of such Collection Period of each Discount Receivable (other than a Discount Receivable that is a Defaulted Receivable) at a rate equal to the Required Rate, exceeds one month's interest on such Principal Balance at the APR of each such Receivable.

"Yield Supplement Withdrawal Amount" means, with respect to any Collection Period and the related Deposit Date, the lesser of (a) the amount on deposit in the Yield Supplement Account and (b) the sum of (i) the Yield Supplement Amount and (ii) after giving effect to the withdrawal of the Yield Supplement Amount, the amount by which the amount on deposit in the Yield Supplement Account exceeds the Maximum Yield Supplement Amount.

Section 1.02. Other Definitional Provisions.

(a) Capitalized terms used herein that are not otherwise defined herein shall have the meanings ascribed thereto in the Indenture.

(b) All terms defined in this Agreement shall have the defined meanings when used in any certificate or other document made or delivered pursuant hereto unless otherwise defined therein.

Section 1.03. Interpretive Provisions.

(a) For all purposes of this Agreement, except as otherwise expressly provided or unless the context otherwise requires, (i) terms used herein include, as appropriate, all genders and the plural as well as the singular, (ii) references to words such as "herein", "hereof" and the like shall refer to this Agreement as a whole and not to any particular part, article or section within this Agreement, (iii) references to a section such as "Section 1.01" and the like shall refer to the applicable section of this Agreement, (iv) the term "include" and all variations thereof shall mean "include without limitation", (v) the term "or" shall include "and/or", and (vi) the term "proceeds" shall have the meaning set forth in the applicable UCC.

(b) As used in this Agreement and in any certificate or other document made or delivered pursuant hereto or thereto, accounting terms not defined in this Agreement or in any such certificate or other document, and accounting terms partly defined in this Agreement or in any such certificate or other document to the extent not defined, shall have the respective meanings given to them under generally accepted accounting principles. To the extent that the definitions of accounting terms in this Agreement or in any such certificate or other document are inconsistent with the meanings of such terms under generally accepted accounting principles, the definitions contained in this Agreement or in any such certificate or other document shall control.

ARTICLE TWO

CONVEYANCE OF RECEIVABLES; CUSTODY OF RECEIVABLES FILES

Section 2.01. Conveyance of Receivables.

(a) In consideration of the Issuer's delivery to or upon the order of the Seller of the Certificates and the net proceeds of the sale of the Notes, less an amount equal to the Reserve Fund Initial Deposit to be deposited to the Reserve Fund and the Yield Supplement Account Deposit to be deposited to the Yield Supplement Account, each on the Closing Date, the Seller does hereby sell, transfer, assign, set over and otherwise convey to the Issuer, without recourse (subject to the obligations of the Seller set forth herein), all right, title and interest of the Seller in, to and under:

(i) the Receivables and all monies due thereon or paid thereunder or in respect thereof (including proceeds of the repurchase of Receivables by the

Seller pursuant to Section 2.04 or the purchase of Receivables by the Servicer pursuant to Section 3.08 or 8.01) on or after the Cutoff Date;

(ii) the security interests in the Financed Vehicles;

(iii) any proceeds of any physical damage insurance policies covering the Financed Vehicles and in any proceeds of any credit life or credit disability insurance policies relating to the Receivables or the Obligors;

(iv) any proceeds of Dealer Recourse;

(v) the Receivables Purchase Agreement, but not the obligations of the Seller thereunder;

(vi) the right to realize upon any property (including the right to receive future Liquidation Proceeds) that shall have secured a Receivable and have been repossessed by or on behalf of the Issuer;

(vii) all funds on deposit from time to time in the Accounts, including the Reserve Fund Initial Deposit and the Yield Supplement Account Deposit, and in all investment income and proceeds thereof;

(viii) any Servicer Letter of Credit; and

(ix) the proceeds of any and all of the foregoing.

The Seller hereby confirms to the Issuer that, as of the Closing Date, the Seller shall have caused the portions of all related electronic records relating to the Receivables to be clearly and unambiguously marked, and shall have made the appropriate entries in its general accounting records, to indicate that such Receivables have been transferred and sold to the Issuer.

(b) The parties hereto intend that the conveyance hereunder be a sale. In the event that the conveyance hereunder is not for any reason considered a sale, the Seller hereby grants to the Issuer a first priority perfected security interest in all of its right, title and interest in, to and under the Receivables, and all other property conveyed hereunder and all proceeds of any of the foregoing. The parties hereto intend that this Agreement constitute a security agreement under applicable law. Such grant is made to secure the payment of all amounts payable hereunder.

Section 2.02. Custody of Receivable Files. To assure uniform quality in servicing the Receivables and to reduce administrative costs, the Issuer hereby revocably appoints the Servicer, and the Servicer accepts such appointment, to act for the benefit of the Issuer and the Indenture Trustee as custodian of the following documents or instruments which are hereby constructively delivered to the Indenture Trustee, as pledgee of the Issuer, as of the Closing Date with respect to each Receivable:

(a) the fully executed original of the Receivable;

(b) documents evidencing or related to any Insurance Policy;

(c) the original credit application of each Obligor, fully executed by such Obligor on AHFC's customary form, or on a form approved by AHFC for such application;

(d) the original certificate of title (or evidence that such certificate of title has been applied for) or such documents that the Servicer shall keep on file, in accordance with its customary procedures, evidencing the security interest in the related Financed Vehicle; and

(e) any and all other documents that the Seller or the Servicer, as the case may be, shall keep on file, in accordance with its customary procedures, relating to such Receivable or the related Obligor or Financed Vehicle.

Section 2.03. Representations and Warranties of Seller as to the Receivables. The Seller makes the following representations and warranties as to the Receivables on which the Issuer shall rely in acquiring the Receivables. Such representations and warranties speak as of the execution and delivery of this Agreement and as of the Closing Date, but shall survive the sale, transfer and assignment of the Receivables to the Issuer and the pledge thereof to the Indenture Trustee.

(a) Characteristics of Receivables. Each Receivable (i) shall have been originated in the United States by a Dealer for the retail sale of the related Financed Vehicle in the ordinary course of such Dealer's business, shall have been fully and properly executed by the parties thereto, shall have been purchased by AHFC from such Dealer under an existing agreement with AHFC, shall have been validly assigned by such Dealer to AHFC in accordance with the terms of such agreement and shall have been subsequently sold by AHFC to the Seller pursuant to the Receivables Purchase Agreement, (ii) shall have created or shall create a valid, continuing and enforceable first priority security interest in favor of AHFC in the related Financed Vehicle, which security interest has been assigned by AHFC to the Seller and shall be assignable, and shall be so assigned, by the Seller to the Owner Trustee, (iii) shall contain customary and enforceable provisions such that the rights and remedies of the holder thereof shall be adequate for realization against the collateral of the benefits of the security, (iv) shall, except as otherwise provided in this Agreement, provide for level Monthly Payments (provided that the payment in the first or last month in the life of the Receivable may be minimally different from the level payment) that fully amortize the Amount Financed over its original term and shall provide for a finance charge or shall yield interest at its APR, (v) shall provide for, in the event that such Receivable is prepaid, a prepayment that fully pays the Principal Balance and includes accrued but unpaid interest at least through the date of prepayment in an amount calculated by using an interest rate at least equal to its APR, (vi) shall have an Obligor that is not a federal, state or local governmental entity and (vii) is a retail installment contract.

(b) Schedule of Receivables. The information set forth in the Schedule of Receivables shall be true and correct in all material respects as of the opening of business on the Cutoff Date, and no selection procedures believed to be adverse to the Securityholders were utilized in selecting the Receivables from those motor vehicle receivables of AHFC which met the selection criteria set forth in this Agreement.

(c) Compliance with Law. Each Receivable and each sale of the related Financed Vehicle shall have complied at the time it was originated or made, and shall comply at the time of execution of this Agreement, in all material respects with all requirements of applicable federal, state and local laws, and regulations thereunder, including usury laws, the Federal Truth-in-Lending Act, the Equal Credit Opportunity Act, the Fair Credit Billing Act, the Fair Credit Reporting Act, the Fair Debt Collection Practices Act, the Federal Trade Commission Act, the Magnuson-Moss Warranty Act, Federal Reserve Board Regulations B , M and Z, state adaptations of the National Consumer Act and of the Uniform Consumer Credit Code and other consumer credit, equal credit opportunity and disclosure laws.

(d) Binding Obligation. Each Receivable shall constitute the genuine, legal, valid and binding payment obligation in writing of the related Obligor, enforceable by the holder thereof in accordance with its terms, except as enforceability may be subject to or limited by bankruptcy, insolvency, reorganization, moratorium, liquidation or other similar laws affecting the enforcement of creditors' rights in general and by general principles of equity, regardless of whether such enforceability shall be considered in a proceeding in equity or at law.

(e) No Bankrupt Obligors. According to the records of the Seller, as of the Cutoff Date, no Obligor is the subject of a bankruptcy proceeding.

(f) Security Interest in Financed Vehicles. According to the records of the Seller, as of the Cutoff Date, no Financed Vehicle has been repossessed and not reinstated and immediately prior to the sale, assignment and transfer thereof, all necessary steps shall be taken so that each Receivable shall be secured by a validly perfected first priority security interest in the related Financed Vehicle in favor of AHFC as secured party or all necessary and appropriate action with respect to such Receivable shall have been taken to perfect a first priority security interest in such Financed Vehicle in favor of AHFC as secured party.

(g) Receivables in Force. No Receivable shall have been satisfied, subordinated or rescinded, nor shall any Financed Vehicle have been released in whole or in part from the lien granted by the related Receivable.

(h) No Waivers. No provision of a Receivable shall have been waived in such a manner that such Receivable fails to meet all of the other representations and warranties made by the Seller herein with respect thereto.

(i) No Amendments. No Receivable shall have been amended or modified in such a manner that the total number of Scheduled Payments has been increased or that the related Amount Financed has been increased or that such Receivable fails to meet all of the other representations and warranties made by the Seller herein with respect thereto.

(j) No Defenses. No facts shall be known to the Seller which would give rise to any right of rescission, setoff, counterclaim or defense, nor shall the same have been asserted or threatened, with respect to any Receivable.

(k) No Liens. To the knowledge of the Seller, no liens or claims shall have been filed, including liens for work, labor or materials relating to a Financed Vehicle, that shall be liens prior to, or equal or coordinate with, the security interest in such Financed Vehicle granted by the related Receivable. To the knowledge of the Seller, there are no tax liens against the Seller, or against an Obligor affecting the related Receivable.

(l) No Defaults. Except for payment defaults that, as of the Cutoff Date, have been continuing for a period of not more than 30 days, no default, breach, violation or event permitting acceleration under the terms of any Receivable shall have occurred as of the Cutoff Date and no continuing condition that with notice or the lapse of time would constitute a default, breach, violation or event permitting acceleration under the terms of any Receivable shall have arisen; and the Seller shall not have waived any of the foregoing except as otherwise permitted hereunder.

(m) Insurance. Pursuant to the Receivables, each Obligor has been required to obtain physical damage insurance covering the related Financed Vehicle and the Obligor is required under the terms of the related Receivable to maintain such insurance.

(n) Title. It is the intention of the Seller that the transfer and assignment herein contemplated, taken as a whole, constitute a sale of the Receivables from the Seller to the Issuer and that the beneficial interest in and title to the Receivables not be part of the debtor's estate in the event of the filing of a bankruptcy petition by or against the Seller under any bankruptcy law. Other than (1) the sale by the Seller to the Issuer pursuant to this Agreement and (2) the security interest granted by the Issuer to the Indenture Trustee in the Indenture, no Receivable has been sold, transferred, assigned or pledged by the Seller to any Person other than the Issuer, and no Receivable has been sold, transferred, assigned or pledged by the Issuer to any Person other than the Indenture Trustee, and no provision of a Receivable shall have been waived, except as provided in clause (h) above; immediately prior to the transfer and assignment herein contemplated, the Seller had good and marketable title to each Receivable free and clear of all Liens and rights of any other Person and immediately prior to the pledge of security interest contemplated in the Indenture, the Issuer had good and marketable title to each Receivable free and clear of all Liens and rights of any other Person; immediately upon the transfer and assignment contemplated herein, the Issuer shall have good and marketable title to each Receivable, free and clear of all Liens and rights of any other Person and immediately upon the pledge of the security interest contemplated in the Indenture, the Indenture Trustee will have a valid and continuing security interest in the Receivables; and both the transfer and assignment herein contemplated and the pledge of security interest contemplated by the Indenture have been perfected under the applicable UCC.

(o) Lawful Assignment. No Receivable shall have been originated in, or shall be subject to the laws of, any jurisdiction under which the sale, transfer and assignment of such Receivable under this Agreement or pursuant to a transfer of the Securities shall be unlawful, void or voidable.

(p) All Filings Made. Both the Seller and the Issuer, respectively, have caused or will have caused, or have taken or will take, within ten days of the Closing Date, all steps necessary, including the filing of all appropriate financing statements (including UCC filings) necessary in the appropriate jurisdictions under the applicable law, to give the Issuer a first priority perfected security interest in the Receivables, and to give the Indenture Trustee a first priority perfected security interest therein, shall have been made. Except as contemplated hereby or in the Indenture, as applicable, neither the Seller or the Issuer has authorized the filing of nor is aware of any financing statements with respect to the Receivables, other than such financing statements that have been terminated on or prior to the Closing Date.

(q) One Original. There shall be only one original executed copy of each Receivable.

(r) Chattel Paper. Each Receivable constitutes "tangible chattel paper" as defined within the meaning of the applicable UCC.

(s) Maturity of Receivables. Each Receivable shall have an original maturity of not less than 12 months nor greater than 60 months and, as of the Cutoff Date, a remaining maturity of not less than 6 months nor greater than 59 months.

(t) Finance Charge. Each Receivable provides for the payment of a finance charge calculated on the basis of an APR ranging from 1.90% to 15.39%.

(u) Principal Balance. Each Receivable had an original principal balance of not less than $2,013.32 nor more than $81,062.46 and an average unpaid principal balance, as of the Cutoff Date, of $15,164.09.

(v) Origination. Each Receivable was originated on or after June 12, 1998 and on or before October 30, 2002.

(w) No Overdue Payments. No Receivable shall have a Scheduled Payment that is more than 30 days past due as of the Cutoff Date.

(x) Location of Receivable Files. Each Receivable File shall be kept at one of the locations listed in Schedule B hereto.

(y) Financed Vehicles. Each Financed Vehicle shall be a new or used Honda or Acura motor vehicle.

(z) Addresses of Obligors. The Obligor under each Receivable had a current billing address in the United States as of the Cutoff Date.

(aa) Security Interest. The Indenture creates a valid and continuing security interest (as defined in the applicable UCC) in the Receivables in favor of the Indenture Trustee, which security interest is prior to all other Liens, and is enforceable as such as against creditors of and purchasers from the Issuer.

(bb) Possession of Documents. The Servicer has in its possession all original copies of the agreements that constitute or evidence the Receivables. The agreements that constitute or evidence the Receivables do not have any marks or notations indicating that they have been pledged, assigned or otherwise conveyed to any Person other than the Indenture Trustee. All financing statements filed or to be filed against the Issuer in favor of the Indenture Trustee in connection herewith describing the Receivables contain a statement to the following effect: "A purchase of or security interest in any collateral described in this financing statement will violate the rights of the Indenture Trustee."

Section 2.04. Repurchase of Receivables Upon Breach. Upon discovery by the Seller, the Servicer or the Owner Trustee or upon the actual knowledge of a Responsible Officer of the Indenture Trustee of a breach of any of the representations and warranties of the Seller set forth in Section 2.03 that materially and adversely affects the interests of the Issuer, the Trustees or the Securityholders in any Receivable, the party discovering such breach shall give prompt written notice to the others. As of the last day of the second Collection Period following the Collection Period in which it discovers or receives notice of such breach (or, at the Seller's election, the last day of the first Collection Period following the Collection Period in which it discovers or receives notice of such breach), the Seller shall, unless such breach shall have been cured in all material respects, repurchase such Receivable, and, if necessary, the Seller shall enforce the obligation of AHFC under the Receivables Purchase Agreement to repurchase such Receivable from the Seller. This repurchase obligation shall apply to all representations and warranties of the Seller contained in Section 2.03 whether or not the Seller has knowledge of the breach at the time of the breach or at the time the representations and warranties were made. In consideration of the repurchase of any such Receivable, on the related Deposit Date, the Seller shall remit the Warranty Purchase Payment in respect of such Receivable to the Collection Account in the manner specified in Section 4.05 and shall be entitled to receive the Released Warranty Amount. In the event that, as of the date of execution and delivery of this Agreement, any Liens or claims shall have been filed, including Liens for work, labor or materials relating to a Financed Vehicle, that shall be prior to, or equal or coordinate with, the lien granted by the related Receivable, which Liens or claims shall not have been satisfied or otherwise released in full as of the Closing Date, and such breach materially and adversely affects the interests of the Issuer, the Trustees or the Securityholders in such Receivable, the Seller shall repurchase such Receivable on the terms and in the manner specified above. Upon any such repurchase, the Issuer shall, without further action, be deemed to transfer, assign, set-over and otherwise convey to the Seller, all right, title and interest of the Issuer in, to and under such repurchased Receivable, all monies due or to become due with respect thereto and all proceeds thereof. The Issuer and the Trustees shall execute such documents and instruments of transfer and assignment and take such other actions as shall be reasonably requested by the Seller to effect the conveyance of such Receivable pursuant to this Section. The sole remedy of the Issuer, the Trustees and the Securityholders with respect to a breach of the Seller's representations and warranties pursuant to Section 2.03 or with respect to the existence of any such Liens or claims shall be to require the Seller to repurchase the related Receivable pursuant to this Section and to enforce

AHFC's obligation to repurchase such Receivables from the Seller pursuant to the Receivables Purchase Agreement. Neither the Owner Trustee nor the Indenture Trustee shall have any duty to conduct an affirmative investigation as to the occurrence of any condition requiring the repurchase of any Receivable pursuant to Section 2.04 or the eligibility of any Receivables for purposes of this Agreement. In addition, no party to this agreement may waive a material breach of any of the representations and warranties contained in Section 2.03 above.

Section 2.05. Duties of Servicer as Custodian.

(a) Safekeeping. The Servicer, in its capacity as custodian, shall hold the Receivable Files for the benefit of the Issuer and maintain such accurate and complete accounts, records and computer systems pertaining to each Receivable File as shall enable the Issuer to comply with this Agreement. In performing its duties as custodian, the Servicer shall act with reasonable care, using that degree of skill and attention that it exercises with respect to the receivable files of comparable motor vehicle receivables that the Servicer services for itself or others. The Servicer shall conduct, or cause to be conducted, periodic examinations of the files of all receivables owned or serviced by it which shall include the Receivable Files held by it under this Agreement, and of the related accounts, records and computer systems, in such a manner as shall enable the Issuer or the Indenture Trustee to verify the accuracy of the Servicer's record keeping. The Servicer shall promptly report to the Issuer and the Indenture Trustee any failure on its part to hold the Receivable Files and maintain its accounts, records and computer systems as herein provided and promptly take appropriate action to remedy any such failure. Nothing herein shall be deemed to require an initial review or any periodic review of the Receivable Files by the Issuer or the Indenture Trustee.

(b) Maintenance of and Access to Records. The Servicer shall maintain each Receivable File solely in its capacity as Servicer at one of its offices specified in Schedule B hereto or at such other office as shall be specified to the Issuer and the Indenture Trustee by 30 days' prior written notice. The Servicer shall make available to the Issuer and the Indenture Trustee or its duly authorized representatives, attorneys or auditors the Receivable Files and the related accounts, records and computer systems maintained by the Servicer at such times as the Issuer and the Indenture Trustee shall reasonably instruct.

(c) Release of Documents. Upon instruction from the Indenture Trustee, the Servicer shall release any document in the Receivable Files to the Indenture Trustee or its agent or designee, as the case may be, at such place or places as the Indenture Trustee may designate, as soon as practicable. The Servicer shall not be responsible for any loss occasioned by the failure of the Indenture Trustee to return any document or any delay in doing so.

Section 2.06. Instructions; Authority to Act. The Servicer shall be deemed to have received proper instructions with respect to the Receivable Files upon its receipt of written instructions signed by a Responsible Officer of the Indenture

Trustee. A certified copy of a bylaw or of a resolution of the board of directors of the Indenture Trustee shall constitute conclusive evidence of the authority of any such Responsible Officer to act and shall be considered in full force and effect until receipt by the Servicer of written notice to the contrary given by the Indenture Trustee.

Section 2.07. Indemnification by Custodian. The Servicer, as custodian of the Receivable Files, shall fully indemnify and hold harmless the Issuer and the Trustees for any and all liabilities, obligations, losses, compensatory damages, payments, costs or expenses of any kind whatsoever that may be imposed on, incurred or asserted against the Issuer and the Trustees as the result of any improper act or omission in any way relating to the maintenance and custody of the Receivable Files by the Servicer, as custodian; provided, however, that the Servicer shall not be liable for any portion of any such amount resulting from the willful misfeasance, bad faith or negligence (in the case of the Owner Trustee or the Indenture Trustee) or gross negligence (in the case of the Delaware Trustee only).

Section 2.08. Effective Period and Termination. The Servicer's appointment as custodian of the Receivable Files shall become effective as of the Cutoff Date and shall continue in full force and effect until terminated pursuant to this Section. If the Servicer shall resign as Servicer pursuant to Section 6.05 or if all of the rights and obligations of the Servicer have been terminated pursuant to Section 7.02, the appointment of the Servicer as custodian of the Receivable Files shall be terminated without further action by the Indenture Trustee or by the Holders of Notes. The Indenture Trustee or, with the consent of the Indenture Trustee, the Owner Trustee may terminate the Servicer's appointment as custodian of the Receivable Files with cause at any time immediately upon written notification to the Servicer and, without cause, upon 30 days' prior written notification by the Servicer. As soon as practicable, but in no event later than 30 days immediately following the effective date of any termination of such appointment, the Servicer shall deliver the Receivable Files to the Indenture Trustee or its agent at such place or places as the Indenture Trustee may reasonably designate. Notwithstanding the termination of the Servicer as custodian of the Receivable Files, the Indenture Trustee agrees that upon any such termination, the Indenture Trustee shall provide, or cause its agent to provide, access to the Receivable Files to the Servicer for the purpose of carrying out its duties and responsibilities with respect to the servicing of the Receivables pursuant to this Agreement.

ARTICLE THREE

ADMINISTRATION AND SERVICING OF RECEIVABLES

Section 3.01. Duties of Servicer. The Servicer, for the benefit of the Issuer (to the extent provided herein), shall manage, service, administer and make collections on the Receivables (other than Administrative Receivables and Warranty Receivables) with reasonable care, using that degree of skill and attention that the Servicer exercises with respect to all comparable motor vehicle receivables that it services for itself or others. The Servicer's duties shall include collection and posting of all payments, responding to inquiries of Obligors or by federal, state or local government authorities with respect to the Receivables, investigating delinquencies, sending payment coupons to Obligors, reporting tax information to Obligors in accordance with its customary practices, policing the collateral, accounting for collections and furnishing monthly and annual statements to the Trustees with respect to distributions, generating federal income tax information, making Advances and performing the other duties specified herein. The Servicer shall follow its customary standards, policies and procedures and shall have full power and authority, acting alone, to do any and all things in connection with such managing, servicing, administration and collection that it may deem necessary or desirable. Without limiting the generality of the foregoing, the Servicer shall be authorized and empowered to execute and deliver, on behalf of itself, the Issuer, the Trustees, the Securityholders or any of them, any and all instruments of satisfaction or cancellation, or of partial or full release or discharge and all other comparable instruments, with respect to the Receivables and the Financed Vehicles. The Servicer is hereby authorized to commence, in its own name or in the name of the Issuer, a legal proceeding to enforce a Defaulted Receivable pursuant to Section 3.04 or to commence or participate in a legal proceeding (including without limitation a bankruptcy proceeding) relating to or involving a Receivable, including a Defaulted Receivable. If the Servicer commences or participates in such a legal proceeding in its own name, the Issuer shall thereupon be deemed to have automatically assigned, solely for the purpose of collection on behalf of the party retaining an interest in such Receivable, such Receivable and the other property conveyed to the Issuer pursuant to Section 2.01 with respect to such Receivable to the Servicer for purposes of commencing or participating in any such proceeding as a party or claimant, and the Servicer is authorized and empowered by the Issuer to execute and deliver in the Servicer's name any notices, demands, claims, complaints, responses, affidavits or other documents or instruments in connection with any such proceeding. If in any enforcement suit or legal proceeding it shall be held that the Servicer may not enforce a Receivable on the grounds that it shall not be a real party in interest or a holder entitled to enforce such Receivable, the Owner Trustee on behalf of the Issuer shall, at the Servicer's expense and written direction, take steps to enforce such Receivable, including bring suit in its name or the name of the Issuer, the Indenture Trustee, the Noteholders or the Certificateholders. The Owner Trustee on behalf of the Issuer shall furnish the Servicer with any powers of attorney and other documents and take any other steps which the Servicer may deem necessary or appropriate to enable the Servicer to carry out its servicing and administrative duties hereunder.

Section 3.02. Collection of Receivable Payments. The Servicer shall make reasonable efforts to collect all payments called for under the terms and provisions of the Receivables as and when the same shall become due, and shall follow such collection procedures as it follows with respect to all comparable motor vehicle receivables that it services for itself or others. The Servicer shall be authorized to grant extensions, rebates or adjustments on a Receivable without the prior consent of the Issuer. If, as a result of the extending of payments in accordance with the customary servicing standards of the Servicer, any Receivable will be outstanding later than the Final Scheduled Maturity Date occurs, the Servicer shall be obligated to repurchase such Receivable pursuant to Section 3.08. In addition, in the event that any such rescheduling or extension of a Receivable modifies the terms of such Receivable in such a manner as to constitute a cancellation of such Receivable and the creation of a new motor vehicle receivable that results in a deemed exchange thereof within the meaning of Section 1001 of the Code, the Servicer shall purchase such Receivable pursuant to Section 3.08, and the receivable created shall not be included in the Issuer. Notwithstanding the foregoing, extensions or modifications of the payment schedule of a Receivable can be made only in accordance with the customary servicing procedures of the Servicer, provided that the amount of any extension fee charged in connection with the extension of a Receivable is deposited into the Collection Account by the Servicer in accordance with Section 4.05(a). The Servicer may, in accordance with its customary servicing procedures, waive any prepayment charge, late payment charge or any other fees that may be collected in the ordinary course of servicing the Receivables.

Section 3.03. Rebates on Full Prepayments. In the event that the amount of a full Prepayment by an Obligor under a Precomputed Receivable, after adjustment for the applicable Rebate, is less than the amount that would be payable under the actuarial method if a full Prepayment were made at the end of the billing month under such Precomputed Receivable, either because the Rebate calculated under the terms of such Precomputed Receivable is greater than the amount calculable under the actuarial method or because the Servicer's customary servicing procedure is to credit a greater Rebate, the Servicer, as part of its servicing duties, shall remit such difference to the Trust by deposit into the Collection Account pursuant to Section 4.05(a).

Section 3.04. Realization Upon Receivables. On behalf of the Issuer, the Servicer shall use its best efforts, consistent with its customary servicing procedures, to repossess or otherwise comparably convert the ownership of any Financed Vehicle that it has reasonably determined should be repossessed or otherwise converted following a default under the Receivable secured by the Financed Vehicle (and shall specify such Receivables to the Trustees no later than the Determination Date following the end of the Collection Period in which the Servicer shall have made such determination). The Servicer shall follow such practices and procedures as it shall deem necessary or advisable and as shall be customary and usual in its servicing of motor vehicle receivables, which practices and procedures may include reasonable efforts to realize upon any Dealer Recourse, selling the related Financed Vehicle at public or private sale and other actions by the Servicer in order to realize upon such a Receivable. The Servicer shall be entitled to recover its reasonable Liquidation Expenses with respect to each Defaulted Receivable, which are not to exceed the related Net Liquidation Proceeds with respect to each such Defaulted Receivable. All Net Liquidation Proceeds realized in connection with any such action with respect to a Receivable shall be deposited by the Servicer in the Collection Account in the manner specified in Section 4.02(a). The foregoing is subject to the proviso that, in any case in which the Financed Vehicle shall have suffered damage, the Servicer shall not expend funds in connection with any repair or towards the repossession of such Financed Vehicle unless it shall determine in its discretion that such repair and/or repossession shall increase the Liquidation Proceeds of the related Receivable by an amount greater than the amount of such expenses.

Section 3.05. Maintenance of Physical Damage Insurance Policies. The Servicer shall, in accordance with its customary servicing procedures and underwriting standards, require that each Obligor shall have obtained physical damage insurance covering each Financed Vehicle as of the origination of the related Receivable.

Section 3.06. Maintenance of Security Interests in Financed Vehicles. The Servicer shall, in accordance with its customary servicing procedures and at its own expense, take such steps as are necessary to maintain perfection of the security interest created by each Receivable in the related Financed Vehicle. The Servicer is hereby authorized to take such steps as are necessary to reperfect such security interest on behalf of the Issuer in the event of the relocation of a Financed Vehicle or for any other reason. In the event that the assignment of a Receivable to the Issuer is insufficient, without a notation on the related Financed Vehicle's certificate of title, to grant to the Issuer a first priority perfected security interest in the related Financed Vehicle, the Servicer hereby agrees to serve as the agent of the Issuer for the purpose of perfecting the security interest of the Issuer in such Financed Vehicle and agrees that the Servicer's listing as the secured party on the certificate of title is solely in its capacity as agent of the Issuer.

Section 3.07. Covenants of Servicer. The Servicer makes the following covenants on which the Issuer shall rely in accepting the Receivables in trust pursuant to Section 2.01:

(a) Liens in Force. Except as otherwise contemplated by this Agreement, the Servicer shall not release in whole or in part any Financed Vehicle from the security interest securing the related Receivable.

(b) No Impairment. The Servicer shall do nothing to impair the rights of the Issuer in the Receivables.

(c) No Amendments. Subject to Section 3.02, the Servicer shall not amend or otherwise modify any Receivable such that the total number of Scheduled Payments is extended beyond the Final Scheduled Maturity Date, or either the Amount Financed or the APR is altered.

Section 3.08. Purchase of Receivables Upon Breach. Upon discovery by the Seller, the Servicer or the Issuer or upon the actual knowledge of a Responsible Officer of the Indenture Trustee or Owner Trustee of a breach of any of the covenants of the Servicer set forth in Section 3.07 that materially and adversely affects the interests of the Issuer, the Indenture Trustee or the Securityholders in any Receivable, or if an improper extension, rescheduling or modification of a Receivable is made by the Servicer as described in Section 3.02, the party discovering such breach shall give prompt written notice to the others. As of the last day of the second Collection Period following the Collection Period in which it discovers or receives notice of such breach (or, at the Servicer's election, the last day of the first Collection Period following the Collection Period in which it discovers or receives notice of such breach), the Servicer shall, unless such breach or impropriety shall have been cured in all material respects, purchase from the Issuer such Receivable. In consideration of the purchase of any such Receivable, on the related Deposit Date the Servicer shall remit the Administrative Purchase Payment to the Collection Account in the manner specified in Section 4.05, and shall be entitled to receive the Released Administrative Amount. Upon such deposit of the Administrative Purchase Payment, the Servicer shall for all purposes of this Agreement be deemed to have released all claims for reimbursement of Outstanding Advances made in respect of such Receivable. The sole remedy of the Issuer, the Trustees or the Securityholders against the Servicer with respect to a breach pursuant to Section 3.02 or 3.07 shall be to require the Servicer to purchase the related Receivables pursuant to this Section, except as otherwise provided in Section 6.02. Neither the Owner Trustee nor the Indenture Trustee shall have any duty to conduct any affirmative investigation as to the occurrence of any condition requiring the repurchase of any Receivable pursuant to this Section.

Section 3.09. Total Servicing Fee; Payment of Certain Expenses by Servicer. As compensation for the performance of its obligations hereunder, the Servicer shall be entitled to receive on each Payment Date the Total Servicing Fee. The Basic Servicing Fee in respect of a Collection Period shall be calculated based on a 360 day year comprised of twelve 30-day months. Except to the extent otherwise provided herein, the Servicer shall be required to pay all expenses incurred by it in connection with its activities under this Agreement (including fees and disbursements of the Trustees and independent accountants, taxes imposed on the Servicer, expenses incurred in connection with distributions and reports to Securityholders and all other fees and expenses not expressly stated under this Agreement to be for the account of the Securityholders).

Section 3.10. Servicer's Certificate. On or before each Determination Date, the Servicer shall deliver to the Trustees and each Rating Agency a Servicer's Certificate containing all information necessary to make the distributions required by Sections 4.06 and 4.07 in respect of the related Collection Period and all information necessary for the Trustees to send statements to Securityholders pursuant to Section 4.10. The Servicer shall also specify in writing to the Trustees, no later than the Determination Date following the last day of a Collection Period as of which the Seller shall be required to repurchase or the Servicer shall be required to purchase a Receivable, the identity of any such Receivable and the identity of any Receivable which the Servicer shall have determined to be a Defaulted Receivable during such Collection Period. Receivables purchased or to be purchased by the Servicer or the Seller and Receivables as to which the

Servicer has determined during such Collection Period to be Defaulted Receivables and with respect to which payment of the Administrative Purchase Payment or Warranty Purchase Payment has been provided from whatever source as of last day of such Collection Period shall be identified by the Seller's account number with respect to such Receivable (as specified in the Schedule of Receivables).

Section 3.11. Annual Statement as to Compliance; Notice of Default.

(a) The Servicer shall deliver to the Trustees and each Rating Agency, on or before 90 days after the end of each fiscal year, commencing with the fiscal year ended March 31, 2004, an Officer's Certificate of the Servicer, stating that (i) a review of the activities of the Servicer during the preceding 12-month period ended March 31 (or, if applicable, such shorter period in the case of the first such Officer's Certificate) and of its performance under this Agreement has been made under such officer's supervision, and (ii) to such officer's knowledge, based on such review, the Servicer has fulfilled all its obligations under this Agreement throughout such period, or, if there has been a default in the fulfillment of any such obligation, specifying each such default known to such officer and the nature and status thereof.

(b) The Servicer shall deliver to the Trustees and each Rating Agency, promptly after having obtained knowledge thereof, but in no event later than five Business Days thereafter, an Officer's Certificate specifying the nature and status of any event which with the giving of notice or lapse of time, or both, would become a Servicer Default.

Section 3.12. Annual Accountants' Report. The Servicer shall cause a firm of independent accountants (who may also render other services to the Servicer or to the Seller) to deliver to the Trustees on or before June 30 of each year, beginning with the June 30 that is at least six months after the Closing Date, a report with respect to the preceding 12-month period ended March 31 (or, if applicable, such shorter period in the case of the first such report) to the effect that such accountants have examined certain records and documents relating to the servicing of the Receivables under this Agreement (using procedures specified in such report, which procedures shall be substantially in compliance with generally accepted auditing standards and which procedure shall be specified to the Trustees by the Servicer in writing; in the event such firm of independent accountants requires any of the Trustees to agree to the procedures performed by such firm, the Servicer shall direct such Trustees in writing to so agree; it being understood and agreed that the Trustees will deliver such letters of agreement in conclusive reliance upon the direction of the Servicer, and none of the Trustees make any representation of warranty, independent inquiry or investigation as to, and shall have no obligation or liability in respect of, the sufficiency, validity or correctness of such procedures) and that nothing has come to their attention indicating that such servicing has not been conducted in compliance with the customary servicing procedures of the Servicer, including but not limited to the procedures set forth in this Agreement, except for (i) such exceptions as such firm shall believe to be immaterial and (ii) such other exceptions as shall be set forth in such report. Such report shall also indicate that the firm is independent with respect to the Seller and the Servicer within the meaning of the Code of Professional Ethics of the American Institute of Certified Public Accountants.

Section 3.13. Access to Certain Documentation and Information Regarding Receivables. The Servicer shall provide to the Trustees reasonable access to the documentation regarding the Receivables. The Servicer shall provide such access to any Securityholder only in such cases where a Securityholder is required by applicable statutes or regulations to review such documentation. In each case, such access shall be afforded without charge but only upon reasonable request and during normal business hours at the respective offices of the Servicer. Nothing in this Section shall derogate from the obligation of the Servicer to observe any applicable law prohibiting disclosure of information regarding the Obligors, and the failure of the Servicer to provide access as provided in this Section as a result of such obligation shall not constitute a breach of this Section.

Section 3.14. Amendments to Schedule of Receivables. If the Servicer, during a Collection Period, assigns to a Receivable an account number that differs from the original account number identifying such Receivable on the Schedule of Receivables, the Servicer shall deliver to the Seller and the Trustees on or before the Payment Date relating to such Collection Period an amendment to the Schedule of Receivables reporting the newly assigned account number, together with the old account number of each such Receivable. The first such delivery of amendments to the Schedule of Receivables shall include monthly amendments reporting account numbers appearing on the Schedule of Receivables with the new account numbers assigned to such Receivables during any prior Collection Period.

Section 3.15. Reports to Securityholders and Rating Agencies.

(a) At the expense of the Issuer, the Indenture Trustee shall provide to any Note Owner and the Owner Trustee shall provide to any Certificateholder who so requests in writing a copy of (i) any Servicer's Certificate, (ii) any annual statement as to compliance described in Section 3.1l(a), (iii) any annual accountants' report described in Section 3.12, (iv) any statement to Securityholder pursuant to Section 4.10, (v) the Trust Agreement, (vi) the Indenture or (vii) this Agreement (without Exhibits). The Indenture Trustee or the Owner Trustee, as applicable, may require such Securityholder or Note Owner to pay a reasonable sum to cover the cost of the Trustee's complying with such request.

(b) The Servicer shall forward to each Rating Agency a copy of each (i) Servicer's Certificate, (ii) annual statement as to compliance described in Section 3.11(a), (iii) Officer's Certificate of the Servicer described in Section 3.11(b), (iv) annual accountants' report pursuant to Section 3.12, (v) statement to Securityholders pursuant to Section 4.10 and (vi) other report it may receive pursuant to this Agreement, the Trust Agreement or the Indenture.

Section 3.16. Appointment of Subservicer. The Servicer may at any time appoint a subservicer to perform all or any portion of its obligations as Servicer hereunder if each Rating Agency and the Indenture Trustee has received 10 days prior written notice of the Servicer's intention to do so and has not notified the Servicer that such an appointment would or might result in the qualification, reduction or withdrawal of a rating then assigned by such Rating Agency to any Class of Notes; provided, however, that the Servicer shall remain obligated and be liable to the Issuer, the Owner Trustee, the Indenture Trustee, the Certificateholders and the Noteholders for the servicing and administering of the Receivables in accordance with the provisions hereof without diminution of such obligation and liability by virtue of the appointment of such subservicer and to the same extent and under the same terms and conditions as if the Servicer alone were servicing and administering the Receivables. The fees and expenses of the subservicer shall be as agreed between the Servicer and its subservicer from time to time, and none of the Issuer, the Owner Trustee, the Indenture Trustee, the Certificateholders or the Noteholders shall have any responsibility therefor.

ARTICLE FOUR

DISTRIBUTIONS; RESERVE FUND; STATEMENTS TO SECURITYHOLDERS

Section 4.01. Establishment of Accounts.

(a) The Servicer shall establish and maintain an Eligible Account with and in the name of the Indenture Trustee for the benefit of (i) the Securityholders (the "Collection Account"), (ii) the Noteholders (the "Note Distribution Account"), (iii) the Noteholders (the "Reserve Fund"), (iv) the Securityholders (the "Yield Supplement Account") and (v) the Securityholders (the "Payahead Account"), in each case, bearing a designation clearly indicating that the funds deposited therein are held for the benefit of the related Securityholders. Except as otherwise provided in this Agreement, in the event that the Indenture Trustee is no longer an Eligible Institution, the Servicer shall, with the assistance of the Indenture Trustee as necessary, cause the Accounts to be moved to an Eligible Institution.

(b) To the extent permitted by applicable laws, rules and regulations, all amounts held in (i) the Collection Account, the Note Distribution Account, the Reserve Fund and the Yield Supplement Account shall be either invested by the Indenture Trustee in Eligible Investments selected in writing by the Servicer or maintained in cash and (ii) the Payahead Account shall be either invested by the Indenture Trustee in investments defined in clause (vii) of the definition of the term "Eligible Investments" selected in writing by the Servicer or maintained in cash. Earnings on investment of funds in the Accounts (other than the Yield Supplement Account and the Reserve Fund) (net of losses and investment expenses) shall be paid to the Servicer as part of the Supplemental Servicing Fee and any losses and investment expenses shall be charged against the funds on deposit in the related Account.

(i) Except as otherwise provided in Section 4.01(b), the Indenture Trustee shall possess all right, title and interest in all funds on deposit from time to time in the Accounts and in all proceeds thereof (including all income thereon) and all such funds, investments, proceeds and income shall be part of the Owner Trust Estate. The Accounts shall be under the sole dominion and control of the Indenture Trustee for the benefit of the Noteholders or the Securityholders, as the case may be.

(ii) Notwithstanding anything else contained herein, the Servicer agrees that each Account and the Certificate Distribution Account will be established only with an Eligible Institution which agrees substantially as follows: (A) it will comply with Entitlement Orders related to such account issued by the Indenture Trustee without further consent by the Servicer; (B) until termination of this Agreement, it will not enter into any other agreement related to such account pursuant to which it agrees to comply with Entitlement Orders of any Person other than the Indenture Trustee; (C) all Account Property delivered or credited to it in connection with such account and all proceeds thereof will be promptly credited to such account; (D) it will treat all Account Property as Financial Assets; and (E) all Account Property will be physically delivered (accompanied by any required endorsements) to, or credited to an account in the name of, the Eligible Institution maintaining the related Account in accordance with such Eligible Institution's customary procedures such that such Eligible Institution establishes a Security Entitlement in favor of the Indenture Trustee with respect thereto over which the Indenture Trustee (or such other Eligible Institution) has Control.

(iii) The Servicer shall have the power, revocable by the Indenture Trustee or by the Owner Trustee with the consent of the Indenture Trustee, to instruct the Indenture Trustee to make withdrawals and payments from the Accounts for the purpose of permitting the Servicer or the Owner Trustee to carry out its respective duties hereunder or permitting the Indenture Trustee to carry out its duties under the Indenture.

Section 4.02. Collections.

(a) The Servicer shall remit daily to the Collection Account all payments received from or on behalf of the Obligors on or in respect of the Receivables (other than, in the case of Precomputed Receivables, payments constituting Payments Ahead) and all Net Liquidation Proceeds within two Business Days after receipt thereof.

(b) Notwithstanding the provisions of Section 4.02(a) and subject to the conditions set forth below, the Servicer may be permitted to make remittances of collections on a less frequent basis than that specified in Section 4.02(a) upon compliance with the specific terms and conditions set forth below in this Section and for so long as such terms and conditions are fulfilled. Accordingly, notwithstanding the provisions of Section 4.02(a), the Servicer will be permitted to remit such collections to the Collection Account in immediately available funds, on each Deposit Date but only for so long as (i)(A) the Servicer shall be AHFC,

(B) except as provided in clause (ii) below, the Required Servicer Rating is satisfied and (C) no Servicer Default shall have occurred and be continuing, provided, however, that immediately following the non-compliance with clause (B) above or in the event that an event of the nature specified in Section 7.01(c) has occurred (notwithstanding any period of grace contained in such clause), the Servicer shall remit such collections to the Collection Account on a daily basis within two Business Days of receipt thereof, or (ii)(A) if the conditions specified in clause (i)(A) and (C) above are satisfied, and (B) the Servicer shall have obtained (1) a Servicer Letter of Credit issued by a depository institution or insurance company, as the case may be, having a short-term credit rating at least equal to the Required Deposit Rating and providing that the Indenture Trustee may draw thereon in the event that the Servicer fails to deposit collections into the Collection Account on a monthly basis or (2) a surety bond, insurance policy or other deposit of cash or securities satisfactory to the Indenture Trustee and each Rating Agency; provided that in connection with clause (ii) above, the Servicer provides to the Indenture Trustee, from each Rating Agency for which the Servicer's then-current short-term credit rating is not at least equal to the Required Servicer Rating for such Rating Agency, a letter to the effect that the satisfaction of the conditions in clause (ii) above and allowing the Servicer to make monthly deposits will not result in a qualification, reduction or withdrawal of its then-current rating of any Class of Notes and, if applicable, an Officer's Certificate from the Servicer to the effect that the Servicer's then-current short-term credit rating is at least equal to the Required Servicer Rating from each other Rating Agency, if any; and, provided further, that if the Servicer shall have obtained a Servicer Letter of Credit in accordance with clause (ii) above, the Servicer shall be required to remit collections to the Collection Account on each Business Day to the extent that the aggregate amount of collections described in Section 4.02(a) and received during such Collection Period exceeds the Servicer Letter of Credit Amount. The Indenture Trustee shall not be deemed to have knowledge of any event or circumstance under clause (i)(C) above that would require daily remittance by the Servicer to the Collection Account unless a Responsible Officer has received notice of such event or circumstance from the Seller or the Servicer in an Officer's Certificate, from Securityholders as provided in Section 7.01 or from the Letter of Credit Bank. For purposes of this Article the phrase "payments made on behalf of Obligors" shall mean payments made by Persons other than the Seller, the Servicer or the Letter of Credit Bank, if any.

Any funds held by the Servicer which it determines are to be remitted (or any of its own funds which the Seller or the Servicer determines to pay to the Letter of Credit Bank) in respect of a failure previously to remit collections which failure resulted in a payment under the Servicer Letter of Credit, if any, shall not be remitted to the Collection Account, but shall instead be paid immediately and directly to the Letter of Credit Bank. Any such payment to the Letter of Credit Bank shall be accompanied by a copy of the Servicer's Certificate related to the previous failure to remit funds and an Officer's Certificate which includes a statement identifying, by reference to the items in such related Servicer's

Certificate, each shortfall in Servicer remittances to which such payment relates. The Servicer will also provide the Indenture Trustee with copies of each such Servicer's Certificate and Officer's Certificate delivered with any such payment to the Letter of Credit Bank.

(c) The Servicer shall deposit all Payments Ahead in the Payahead Account within two Business Days after receipt thereof, which Payments Ahead shall be transferred to the Collection Account pursuant to Section 4.06(a)(i). Notwithstanding the foregoing, so long as the Servicer is permitted to remit collections to the Collection Account on a monthly basis pursuant to Section 4.02(b), the Servicer will not be required to deposit Payments Ahead in the Payahead Account within two Business Days after receipt thereof but shall be entitled to retain such Payments Ahead, without segregation from its other funds, until such time as the Servicer shall be required to remit Applied Payments Ahead to the Collection Account pursuant to Section 4.06(a)(ii). Commencing with the first day of the first Collection Period that begins at least two Business Days after the day on which the Servicer is no longer permitted to remit collections to the Collection Account on a monthly basis pursuant to Section 4.02(b), and until such time as the Servicer is once again permitted by Section 4.02(b) to remit collections to the Collection Account on a monthly basis, all Payments Ahead then held by the Servicer shall be immediately deposited into the Payahead Account and all future Payments Ahead shall be remitted by the Servicer to the Payahead Account within two Business Days after receipt thereof.

Section 4.03. Application of Collections. On each Payment Date, all collections for the related Collection Period shall be applied by the Servicer as follows:

(a) With respect to each Receivable (other than an Administrative Receivable or a Warranty Receivable), payments made by or on behalf of the Obligor which are not Supplemental Servicing Fees shall be applied first to reimburse the Servicer for Outstanding Advances made with respect to such Receivable (each such payment, an "Overdue Payment"). Next, the amount of any payment in excess of Supplemental Servicing Fees and Outstanding Advances with respect to such Receivable shall be applied to the Scheduled Payment with respect to such Receivable. If the amount of such payment remaining after the applications described in the two preceding sentences (i) in the case of Precomputed Receivables equals (together with any Deferred Prepayment) the unpaid principal balance of such Receivable, it shall be applied to prepay the principal balance of such Receivable, or (ii) in the case of Simple Interest Receivables, it shall be applied to prepay the principal balance of such Receivable.

(b) With respect to each Administrative Receivable and Warranty Receivable, payments made by or on behalf of the Obligor shall be applied in the same manner, except that any Released Administrative Amount or Released Warranty Amount shall be remitted to the Servicer or the Seller, as applicable. A Warranty Purchase Payment shall be applied to reduce Outstanding Advances and such Warranty Purchase Payment or an Administrative Purchase Payment, as applicable, shall then be applied to the Scheduled Payment, in each case to the extent that the payments by the Obligor shall be insufficient, and then to prepay the unpaid principal balance of such Receivable in full.

Section 4.04. Advances.

(a) As of the close of business on the last day of a Collection Period, if the payments during such Collection Period by or on behalf of the Obligor on or in respect of a Receivable (other than an Administrative Receivable or a Warranty Receivable) after application under Section 4.03(a) shall be less than the Scheduled Payment, whether as a result of any extension granted to the Obligor or otherwise, then (i) in the case of a Precomputed Receivable, the Deferred Prepayment, if any, with respect to such Precomputed Receivable shall be applied by the Servicer to the extent of the shortfall, and such Deferred Prepayment shall be reduced accordingly and the Servicer shall advance to the Trust an amount equal to such shortfall (each, a "Precomputed Advance") and (ii) in the case of a Simple Interest Receivable, the Servicer shall advance to the Trust an amount equal to the product of the principal balance of such Receivable as of the first day of such Collection Period and one-twelfth of its APR minus the amount of interest actually received on such Receivable during such Collection Period (each, a "Simple Interest Advance"). If the calculation in clause (ii) above in respect of a Simple Interest Receivable results in a negative number, an amount equal to such negative amount shall be paid to the Servicer in reimbursement of any Outstanding Advances in respect of Simple Interest Receivables. In addition, in the event that a Simple Interest Receivable becomes a Liquidated Receivable, the amount of accrued and unpaid interest thereon (but not including interest for the current Collection Period) shall, up to the amount of Outstanding Advances in respect of Simple Interest Receivables in respect thereof, be withdrawn from the Collection Account and paid to the Servicer in reimbursement of such Outstanding Advances. No Advances will be made with respect to the Principal Balance of Simple Interest Receivables. Notwithstanding the foregoing, the Servicer shall not be required to make any Advance (other than a Simple Interest Advance in respect of an interest shortfall arising from the Prepayment of a Simple Interest Receivable) to the extent that the Servicer, in its sole discretion, shall determine that such Advance is unlikely to be recovered from subsequent payments made by or on behalf of the related Obligor, Liquidation Proceeds, by the Administrative Purchase Payment or by the Warranty Purchase Payment, in each case, with respect to such Receivable or otherwise. On each Deposit Date, the Servicer will deposit into the Collection Account an amount equal to all Advances to be made in respect of the related Collection Period. The Successor Servicer shall only be required to make Advances for payments on behalf of Obligors in respect of Receivables arising on or after the Collection Period in which the (i) Successor Servicer accepts its appointment or (ii) the Indenture Trustee is automatically appointed Successor Servicer.

(b) The Servicer shall be entitled to reimbursement for Outstanding Advances, without interest, with respect to a Receivable from the following sources with respect to such Receivable: (i) subsequent payments made by or on behalf of the related Obligor, (ii) Liquidation Proceeds, (iii) the Administrative Purchase Payment and (iv) the Warranty Purchase Payment.

(c) To the extent that during any Collection Period any funds described above in Section 4.04(b) with respect to a Receivable as to which the Servicer previously has made an unreimbursed Advance are received by the Issuer or the Servicer, and the Servicer determines that any Outstanding Advances (other than a Simple Interest Advance in respect of an interest shortfall arising from the Prepayment of a Simple Interest Receivable) with respect to such Receivable are unlikely to be recovered from payments made on or with respect to such Receivable (each, a "Nonrecoverable Advance"), then, on the related Payment Date, upon the Servicer providing the Seller and the Trustees with an Officer's Certificate setting forth the basis for its determination of any such Nonrecoverable Advance, the Indenture Trustee shall promptly remit to the Servicer from the Collection Account, (i) from Available Interest an amount equal to the portion of such Nonrecoverable Advance allocable to interest and (ii) from Available Principal an amount equal to the portion of such Nonrecoverable Advance allocable to principal, in each case without interest, in accordance with Section 4.06(c)(i). In lieu of causing the Indenture Trustee to remit any such amounts or the amounts described in clauses (i) through (iv) in Section 4.04(b), the Servicer may deduct such amounts from deposits otherwise to be made into the Collection Account in accordance with Section 4.09.

Section 4.05. Additional Deposits.

(a) The following additional deposits shall be made to the Collection Account one day prior to each Payment Date: (i) the Seller shall remit the aggregate Warranty Purchase Payments with respect to Warranty Receivables pursuant to Section 2.04 and (ii) the Servicer shall remit (A) any extension fee charged in connection with the extension of a Receivable pursuant to Section 3.02, (B) the amount required to be remitted in respect of certain full Prepayments pursuant to Section 3.03, (C) the aggregate Advances pursuant to Section 4.04(a), (D) the aggregate Administrative Purchase Payments with respect to Administrative Receivables pursuant to Section 3.08 and (E) the amount required upon the optional purchase of all Receivables by the Servicer or any successor to the Servicer pursuant to Section 8.01.

(b) All deposits required to be made in respect of a Collection Period pursuant to this Section by the Seller or the Servicer, as the case may be, may be made in the form of a single deposit and shall be made in immediately available funds, on the related Deposit Date.

Section 4.06. Distributions.

(a) On each Deposit Date, the Indenture Trustee shall cause to be made the following transfers and distributions in immediately available funds in the amounts set forth in the Servicer's Certificate for such Payment Date:

(i) from the Payahead Account (or directly from the Servicer in the case of Payments Ahead held by the Servicer pursuant to Section 4.02(b) or (c)) to the Collection Account, the aggregate Applied Payments Ahead;

(ii) if the Servicer is not permitted to hold Payments Ahead pursuant to Section 4.02(b) or (c), from the Collection Account to the Payahead Account, the aggregate Payments Ahead for the related Collection Period; and

(iii) from the Yield Supplement Account to the Collection Account, an amount equal to the Yield Supplement Withdrawal Amount, if any, for such Payment Date.

(b) On each Determination Date, the Servicer shall calculate all amounts required to be deposited in the Note Distribution Account and the Certificate Distribution Account and to make all distributions on the related Payment Date.

(c) On each Payment Date, the Servicer shall instruct the Indenture Trustee in writing (based on the information contained in the Servicer's Certificate delivered on the related Determination Date pursuant to Section 3.10) to make the following deposits and distributions for receipt by the Servicer or deposit in the applicable account, to the extent of the Available Amount, in the following order of priority:

(i) to the Servicer, Nonrecoverable Advances;

(ii) to the Servicer, the Total Servicing Fee (including any unpaid Total Servicing Fees from one or more prior Collection Periods);

(iii) to the Indenture Trustee, the Delaware Trustee and the Owner Trustee, any accrued and unpaid Trust Fees and Expenses, in each case to the extent such fees and expenses have not been previously paid by the Servicer, in its capacity as Administrator, until the Notes have been paid in full, the annual amount paid to the Trustees out of the Available Amount allocation as described in this clause (iii) shall not exceed $100,000.00;

(iv) to the Note Distribution Account, the Note Interest Distributable Amount to be distributed to the holders of the Notes at their respective Interest Rates;

(v) to the Note Distribution Account, the Note Principal Distributable Amount;

(vi) to the Reserve Fund, the amount, if any, necessary to reinstate the balance in the Reserve Fund up to the Specified Reserve Fund Balance;

(vii) after the Class A-1 Notes have been paid in full, to the Certificate Distribution Account, the Certificate Interest Distributable Amount to be distributed to Certificateholders;

(viii) after the Class A-1 Notes have been paid in full, to the Certificate Distribution Account, the Certificate Principal Distributable Amount;

(ix) to the Indenture Trustee, the Delaware Trustee and the Owner Trustee, any accrued and unpaid Trust Fees and Expenses remaining after application of the payments described in clause (iii) above; and

(x) to the Seller, any Available Amount remaining (after giving effect to the reduction in the Available Amount described in clauses (i) through (ix) above.

Notwithstanding that the Notes have been paid in full, the Indenture Trustee shall continue to maintain the Collection Account hereunder until the Pool Balance has been reduced to zero.

Section 4.07. Reserve Fund.

(a) On the Closing Date, the Seller will deposit the Reserve Fund Initial Deposit into the Reserve Fund from the net proceeds of the sale of the Notes. The Reserve Fund shall be the property of the Issuer subject to the rights of the Indenture Trustee in the Reserve Fund Property.

(b) In the event that the Note Distributable Amount exceeds the sum of the amounts deposited into the Note Distribution Account pursuant to Sections 4.06(c)(iv) and (v) on each Payment Date (or, if the Reserve Fund is not maintained by the Indenture Trustee, on the related Deposit Date), the Indenture Trustee shall cause an amount equal to the lesser of (A) the amount on deposit in the Reserve Fund and (B) the amount by which the Note Distributable Amount exceeds the sum of the amounts in the Note Distribution Account, to be deposited into the Note Distribution Account in immediately available funds in the amounts set forth in the Servicer's Certificate for such Payment Date; provided that such amount shall be applied first, to the payment of interest due on the Notes to the extent, if any, that the amount deposited pursuant to Section 4.06(c)(iv) is not sufficient to cover such payment of interest and, second, to the payment of principal of the Notes.

(c) On each Payment Date (or, if the Reserve Fund is not maintained by the Indenture Trustee, on the related Deposit Date), all interest and other income (net of losses and investment expenses) on funds on deposit in the Reserve Fund shall upon the written direction of the Servicer, be paid to the Seller to the extent that the funds therein exceed the Specified Reserve Fund Balance. Upon any distribution to the Seller of amounts in excess of the Specified Reserve Fund Balance, the Noteholders will not have any rights in, or claims to, such amounts.

Section 4.08. Yield Supplement Account. On the Closing Date, the Seller will deposit the Yield Supplement Account Deposit to the Yield Supplement Account from the net proceeds of the sale of the Notes. The Yield Supplement Account shall be the property of the Issuer subject to the rights of the Indenture Trustee for the benefit of the Securityholders.

Section 4.09. Net Deposits. For so long as AHFC shall be the Servicer and the Seller, the Servicer and the Indenture Trustee may make any remittances pursuant to this Article net of amounts to be distributed by the applicable recipient to such remitting party. Nonetheless, each such party shall account in writing for all of the above described remittances and distributions as if the amounts were deposited and/or transferred separately.

Section 4.10. Statements to Securityholders.

(a) On each Payment Date, the Servicer shall provide to the Owner Trustee to forward to each Certificateholder of record and to the Indenture Trustee to forward to each Noteholder of record a statement, based on the Servicer's Certificate furnished pursuant to Section 3.10, setting forth at least the following information as to the Securities, to the extent applicable:

(i) the amount of such distribution allocable to principal, as allocated to each Class of Notes and to the Certificates (stated separately for each Class of Notes and the Certificates);

(ii) the amount of such distribution allocable to interest, as allocated to each Class of Notes and to the Certificates (stated separately for each Class of Notes and the Certificates);

(iii) the Yield Supplement Amount, the Yield Supplement Withdrawal Amount and the amount on deposit in the Yield Supplement Account after giving effect to the distributions made on such Payment Date;

(iv) the Pool Balance as of the close of business on the last day of the related Collection Period, after giving effect to payments allocated to principal reported under clause (i) above;

(v) the Note Distributable Amount, the Certificate Distributable Amount and the Available Amount;

(vi) the Total Servicing Fee paid to the Servicer with respect to the related Collection Period;

(vii) the amount of non-recoverable Advances;

(viii) total Payments Ahead and the Applied Payments Ahead;

(ix) the amount of Trust Fees and Expenses;

(x) the amount of any Note Interest Carryover Shortfall and Note Principal Carryover Shortfall on such Payment Date and the change in such amounts from those with respect to the immediately preceding Payment Date;

(xi) the amount of any Certificate Interest Carryover Shortfall and Certificate Principal Carryover Shortfall on such Payment Date and the change in such amounts from those with respect to the immediately preceding Payment Date;

(xii) the Note Pool Factor for each Class of Notes and the Certificate Pool Factor, in each case as of such Payment Date;

(xiii) the balance on deposit in the Reserve Fund on such Payment Date, after giving effect to distributions made on the Payment Date, if any, and the change in such balance from the immediately preceding Payment Date; and

(xiv) the amount available under the Servicer Letter of Credit, if any, and such amount as a percentage of the Pool Balance as of the last day of such Collection Period.

Each amount set forth on the Payment Date statement under clauses (i), (ii), (vi), (x) and (xi) above shall be expressed as a dollar amount per $1,000 of original principal balance of a Note or the Original Certificate Balance of a Certificate, as the case may be.

(b) Within the prescribed period of time for tax reporting purposes after the end of each calendar year during the term of the Issuer, but not later than the latest date permitted by law, the related Trustee shall mail to each Person who at any time during such calendar year shall have been a Securityholder, a statement, prepared by the Servicer, containing certain information for such calendar year or, in the event such Person shall have been a Securityholder during a portion of such calendar year, for the applicable portion of such year, for the purposes of such Securityholder's preparation of federal income tax returns. In addition, the Servicer shall furnish to the Trustees for distribution to such Person at such time any other information necessary under applicable law for the preparation of such income tax returns.

ARTICLE FIVE

THE SELLER

Section 5.01. Representations of Seller. The Seller makes the following representations on which the Issuer is deemed to have relied in acquiring the Receivables. The representations speak as of the execution and delivery of this Agreement and as of the Closing Date, and shall survive the sale of the Receivables to the Issuer and the pledge thereof to the Indenture Trustee pursuant to the Indenture.

(a) Organization and Good Standing. The Seller has been duly organized and is validly existing as a corporation in good standing under the laws of the State of California, with power and authority to own its properties and to conduct its business as such properties are currently owned and such business is presently conducted, and had at all relevant times, and has, power, authority and legal right to acquire, own and sell the Receivables.

(b) Due Qualification. The Seller is duly qualified to do business as a foreign corporation in good standing, and has obtained all necessary licenses and approvals in all jurisdictions in which the ownership or lease of property or the conduct of its business shall require such qualifications.

(c) Power and Authority. The Seller has the power and authority to execute and deliver this Agreement and to carry out its terms, the Seller has full power and authority to sell and assign the property to be sold and assigned to and deposited with the Issuer and has duly authorized such sale and assignment by all necessary corporate action; and the execution, delivery and performance of this Agreement has been duly authorized by the Seller by all necessary corporate action.

(d) Valid Sale; Binding Obligation. This Agreement evidences a valid sale, transfer and assignment of the Receivables, enforceable against creditors of and purchasers from the Seller, and constitutes a legal, valid and binding obligation of the Seller enforceable in accordance with its terms, except as enforceability may be subject to or limited by bankruptcy, insolvency, reorganization, moratorium or other similar laws affecting the enforcement of creditors' rights in general and by general principles of equity, regardless of whether such enforceability shall be considered in a proceeding in equity or at law.

(e) No Violation. The execution, delivery and performance by the Seller of this Agreement and the consummation of the transactions contemplated by this Agreement and the fulfillment of the terms of this Agreement does not conflict with, result in any breach of any of the terms and provisions of, nor constitute (with or without notice or lapse of time) a default under, the articles of incorporation or bylaws of the Seller, or conflict with or violate any of the material terms or provisions of, or constitute (with or without notice or lapse of time) a default under, any indenture, agreement or other instrument to which the Seller is a party or by which it shall be bound; nor result in the creation or imposition of any Lien upon any of its properties pursuant to the terms of any such indenture, agreement or other instrument (other than this Agreement); nor violate any law or, to the Seller's knowledge, any order, rule or regulation applicable to the Seller of any court or of any federal or state regulatory body, administrative agency or other governmental instrumentality having jurisdiction over the Seller or its properties, which breach, default, conflict, lien or violation would have a material adverse effect on the earnings, business affairs or business prospects of the Seller.

(f) No Proceedings. There are no proceedings or investigations pending, or to the Seller's knowledge, threatened, before any court, regulatory body, administrative agency or other governmental instrumentality having jurisdiction over the Seller or its properties: (i) asserting the invalidity of this Agreement or any other Basic Document, (ii) seeking to prevent the issuance of the Securities or the consummation of any of the transactions contemplated by the Basic Documents, (iii) seeking any determination or ruling that might materially and adversely affect the performance by the Seller of its obligations under, or the validity or enforceability of, the Basic Documents or the Securities or (iv) relating to the Seller and which might adversely affect the federal income tax attributes of the Securities.

Section 5.02. Liability of Seller; Indemnities. The Seller shall be liable in accordance herewith only to the extent of the obligations specifically undertaken by the Seller under this Agreement, which obligations shall include the following:

(a) The Seller shall indemnify, defend and hold harmless the Issuer, the Trustees and the Servicer and any of the officers, directors, employees and agents of the Issuer, the Owner Trustee, the Delaware Trustee and the Indenture Trustee from and against any taxes that may at any time be asserted against any such Person with respect to the transactions contemplated herein and in the other Basic Documents, including any sales, gross receipts, general corporation, tangible personal property, privilege or license taxes (but, in the case of the Issuer, not including any taxes asserted with respect to, and as of the date of, the sale of the Receivables to the Issuer or the issuance and original sale of the Securities, or asserted with respect to ownership of the Receivables, or federal or other income taxes arising out of distributions on the Securities) and costs and expenses in defending against the same.

(b) The Seller shall indemnify, defend and hold harmless the Issuer, the Trustees and the Securityholders and any of the officers, directors, employees and agents of the Issuer, the Owner Trustee, the Delaware Trustee and the Indenture Trustee from and against any loss, liability or expense incurred by reason of (i) the Seller's willful misfeasance, bad faith or negligence in the performance of its duties under this Agreement, or by reason of reckless disregard of its obligations and duties under this Agreement and (ii) the Seller's or the Issuer's violation of federal or state securities laws in connection with the offering and sale of the Securities.

(c) The Seller shall indemnify, defend and hold harmless the Trustees and their respective officers, directors, employees and agents from and against all costs, expenses, losses, claims, damages and liabilities arising out of or incurred in connection with the acceptance or performance of the trusts and duties herein and contained in the Trust Agreement, in the case of the Owner Trustee and the Delaware Trustee, and contained in the Indenture, in the case of the Indenture Trustee, except to the extent that such cost, expense, loss, claim, damage or liability: (i) in the case of the Owner Trustee, shall be due to the willful misfeasance, bad faith or gross negligence (except for errors in judgment) of the Owner Trustee or shall arise from the breach by the Owner Trustee of any of its representations or warranties set forth in Section 7.03 of the Trust Agreement, (ii) in the case of the Indenture Trustee, shall be due to the willful misfeasance, bad faith or negligence of the Indenture Trustee, or (iii) in the case of the Delaware Trustee, shall be due to the willful misfeasance, bad faith or gross negligence of the Delaware Trustee (except for errors in judgment).

(d) The Seller shall pay any and all taxes levied or assessed upon all or any part of the Owner Trust Estate.

Indemnification under this Section shall survive the resignation or removal of the Owner Trustee, the Delaware Trustee or the Indenture Trustee, as the case may be, and the termination of this Agreement and shall include reasonable fees and expenses of counsel and expenses of litigation. If the Seller shall have made any indemnity payments pursuant to this Section and the Person to or on behalf of whom such payments are made thereafter shall collect any of such amounts from others, such Person shall promptly repay such amounts to the Seller, without interest.

Section 5.03. Merger, Consolidation or Assumption of the Obligations of Seller; Certain Limitations.

(a) Any corporation (i) into which the Seller may be merged or consolidated, (ii) which may result from any merger, conversion or consolidation to which the Seller shall be a party or (iii) which may succeed to all or substantially all of the business of the Seller, which corporation in any of the foregoing cases executes an agreement of assumption to perform every obligation of the Seller under this Agreement, shall be the successor to the Seller under this Agreement without the execution or filing of any document or any further act on the part of any of the parties to this Agreement, except that if the Seller in any of the foregoing cases is not the surviving entity, then the surviving entity shall execute an agreement of assumption to perform every obligation of the Seller hereunder. The Seller shall provide notice of any merger, consolidation or succession pursuant to this Section to each Rating Agency and shall receive from each Rating Agency a letter to the effect that such merger, consolidation or succession will not result in a qualification, downgrading or withdrawal of its then-current rating of any Class of Notes.

(b) (i) Subject to paragraph (ii) below, the purpose of the Seller shall be to engage in any lawful activity for which a corporation may be organized under the general corporation law of California other than the banking business, the trust company business or the practice of a profession permitted to be incorporated by the California Corporations Code.

(ii) Notwithstanding paragraph (b)(i) above, the purpose of the Seller shall be limited to the following purposes, and activities incident to and necessary or convenient to accomplish the following purposes: (A) to acquire, own, hold, sell, transfer, assign, pledge, finance, refinance and otherwise deal with, retail installment contracts or wholesale loans secured by, new and used Honda and Acura motor vehicles (the "Motor Vehicle Receivables"); (B) to authorize, issue, sell and deliver one or more series of obligations, consisting of one or more classes of certificates and/or notes or other evidence of indebtedness (the "Offered Securities") that are collateralized by or evidence an interest in Motor Vehicle Receivables; and (C) to negotiate, authorize, execute, deliver and assume the obligations or any agreement relating to the activities set forth in clauses (A) and (B) above, including but not limited to any pooling and servicing agreement, sale and servicing agreement, indenture, reimbursement agreement, credit support agreement, receivables purchase agreement or underwriting agreement and to engage in any lawful activity which is incidental to the activities contemplated by any such agreement. So long as any outstanding debt of the Seller or Offered Securities are rated by any nationally recognized statistical rating organization, the Seller shall not issue notes or otherwise borrow money unless (1) the Seller has made a written request to the related nationally recognized statistical rating organization to issue notes or incur borrowings, which notes or borrowings are rated by the related nationally recognized statistical rating organization the same as or higher than the rating afforded any outstanding rated debt or Offered Securities, or (2) such notes or borrowings (X) are fully subordinated (and which shall provide for payment only after payment in respect of all outstanding rated debt and/or Offered Securities) or are nonrecourse against any assets of the Seller other than the assets pledged to secure such notes or borrowings, (Y) do not constitute a claim against the Seller in the event such assets are insufficient to pay such notes or borrowings and (Z) where such notes or borrowings are secured by the rated debt or Offered Securities, are fully subordinated (and which shall provide for payment only after payment in respect of all outstanding rated debt and/or Offered Securities) to such rated debt or Offered Securities.

(c) Notwithstanding any other provision of this Section and any provision of law, the Seller shall not do any of the following:

(i) engage in any business or activity other than as set forth in clause (b) above;

(ii) without the affirmative vote of a majority of the members of the Board of Directors of the Seller (which must include the affirmative vote of all duly appointed Independent Directors, as required by the articles of incorporation and bylaws of the Seller), (A) dissolve or liquidate, in whole or in part, or institute proceedings to be adjudicated bankrupt or insolvent, (B) consent to the institution of bankruptcy or insolvency proceedings against it, (C) file a petition seeking or consent to reorganization or relief under any applicable federal or state law relating to bankruptcy, (D) consent to the appointment of a receiver, liquidator, assignee, trustee, sequestrator or other similar official of the corporation or a substantial part of its property, (E) make a general assignment for the benefit of creditors, (F) admit in writing its inability to pay its debts generally as they become due or (G) take any corporate action in furtherance of the actions set forth in clauses (A) through (F) above; provided, however, that no director may be required by any shareholder of the Seller to consent to the institution of bankruptcy or insolvency proceedings against the Seller so long as it is solvent; or

(iii) merge or consolidate with any other corporation, company or entity or sell all or substantially all of its assets or acquire all or substantially all of the assets or capital stock or other ownership interest of any other corporation, company or entity (except for the acquisition of Motor Vehicle Receivables of AHFC and the sale of Motor Vehicle Receivables to one or more trusts in accordance with the terms of clause (b)(ii) above, which shall not be otherwise restricted by this Section).

Section 5.04. Limitation on Liability of Seller and Others. The Seller and any director, officer, employee or agent of the Seller may rely in good faith on the advice of counsel or on any document of any kind, prima facie properly executed and submitted by any Person respecting any matters arising hereunder. The Seller shall not be under any obligation to appear in, prosecute or defend any legal action that shall not be incidental to its obligations under this Agreement, and that in its opinion may involve it in any expense or liability.

Section 5.05. Seller May Own Notes. The Seller and any Affiliate thereof may in its individual or any other capacity become the owner or pledgee of Notes with the same rights as it would have if it were not the Seller or an Affiliate thereof, except as expressly provided herein or in any other Basic Document.

ARTICLE SIX

THE SERVICER

Section 6.01. Representations of Servicer. The Servicer makes the following representations on which the Issuer is deemed to have relied in acquiring the Receivables. The representations speak as of the execution and delivery of this

Agreement and as of the Closing Date, and shall survive the sale of the Receivables to the Issuer and the pledge thereof to the Indenture Trustee pursuant to the Indenture:

(a) Organization and Good Standing. The Servicer has been duly organized and is validly existing as a corporation in good standing under the laws of the State of California, with power and authority to own its properties and to conduct its business as such properties are currently owned and such business is presently conducted, and had at all relevant times, and has, power, authority and legal right to acquire, own, sell and service the Receivables and to hold the Receivable Files as custodian on behalf of the Issuer.

(b) Due Qualification. The Servicer is duly qualified to do business as a foreign corporation in good standing, and has obtained all necessary licenses and approvals in all jurisdictions in which the ownership or lease of property or the conduct of its business (including the servicing of the Receivables as required by this Agreement) shall require such qualifications.

(c) Power and Authority. The Servicer has the power and authority to execute and deliver this Agreement and to carry out its terms; and the execution, delivery and performance of this Agreement has been duly authorized by the Servicer by all necessary corporate action.

(d) Binding Obligation. This Agreement constitutes a legal, valid and binding obligation of the Servicer enforceable in accordance with its terms, except as enforceability may be subject to or limited by bankruptcy, insolvency, reorganization, moratorium, liquidation or other similar laws affecting the enforcement of creditors' rights in general and by general principles of equity, regardless of whether such enforceability shall be considered in a proceeding in equity or in law.

(e) No Violation. The execution, delivery and performance by the Servicer of this Agreement and the execution, delivery and performance by the Seller of this Agreement and the consummation of the transactions contemplated by this Agreement and the fulfillment of the terms of this Agreement shall not conflict with, result in any breach of any of the terms and provisions of, nor constitute (with or without notice or lapse of time) a default under, the articles of incorporation or bylaws of the Servicer, or conflict with or breach any of the material terms or provisions of, or constitute (with or without notice or lapse of time) a default under, any indenture, agreement or other instrument to which the Servicer is a party or by which it shall be bound; nor result in the creation or imposition of any Lien upon any of its properties pursuant to the terms of any such indenture, agreement or other instrument (other than this Agreement); nor violate any law or, to the Servicer's knowledge, any order, rule or regulation applicable to the Servicer of any court or of any federal or state regulatory body, administrative agency or other governmental instrumentality having jurisdiction over the Servicer or its properties, which breach, default, conflict, lien or violation would have a material adverse effect on the earnings, business affairs or business prospects of the Servicer.

(f) No Proceedings. There are no proceedings or investigations pending, or to the Servicer's best knowledge, threatened, before any court, regulatory body, administrative agency or other governmental instrumentality having jurisdiction over the Servicer or its properties: (i) asserting the invalidity of this Agreement or any other Basic Document, (ii) seeking to prevent the issuance of the Securities or the consummation of any of the transactions contemplated by the Basic Documents, (iii) seeking any determination or ruling that might materially and adversely affect the performance by the Servicer of its obligations under, or the validity or enforceability of, the Basic Documents or the Securities or (iv) relating to the Servicer and which might adversely affect the federal income tax attributes of the Securities.

Section 6.02. Indemnities of Servicer.

(a) The Servicer shall be liable in accordance herewith only to the extent of the obligations specifically undertaken by the Servicer under this Agreement. In this regard, the Servicer shall indemnify, defend and hold harmless the Issuer, the Trustees, the Securityholders and the Seller and any of the officers, directors, employees and agents of the Issuer, the Owner Trustee, the Delaware Trustee and the Indenture Trustee from and against any and all costs, expenses, losses, damages, claims and liabilities (i) arising out of or resulting from the use, ownership or operation by the Servicer or any Affiliate thereof of a Financed Vehicle, and (ii) to the extent that such cost, expense, loss, claim, damage or liability arose out of, or was imposed upon any such Person through, the negligence, willful misfeasance or bad faith of the Servicer in the performance of its duties under this Agreement or by reason of reckless disregard of its obligations and duties under this Agreement.

For purposes of this Section, in the event of the termination of the rights and obligations of AHFC (or any successor thereto pursuant to Section 6.03) as Servicer pursuant to Section 7.01, or a resignation by such Servicer pursuant to this Agreement, such Servicer shall be deemed to be the Servicer pending appointment of a Successor Servicer (other than the Indenture Trustee) pursuant to Section 7.02. For the avoidance of doubt, AHFC shall not be liable for any claims described in the first sentence of this Section which relate to a date or period on or after the date on which AHFC is terminated or removed as the Servicer or which are cause by a successor servicer.

(b) Indemnification under this Section shall survive the resignation or removal of the Owner Trustee, the Delaware Trustee or the Indenture Trustee, as the case may be, or the termination of this Agreement and shall include reasonable fees and expenses of counsel and expenses of litigation. If the Servicer shall have made any indemnity payments pursuant to this Section and the Person to or on behalf of whom such payments are made thereafter collects any of such amounts from others, such Person shall promptly repay such amounts to the Servicer, without interest.

Section 6.03. Merger, Consolidation or Assumption of the Obligations of Servicer. Any corporation (i) into which the Servicer may be merged or consolidated, (ii) which may result from any merger, conversion or consolidation to which the Servicer shall be a party or (iii) which may succeed to all or substantially all of the business of the Servicer, which corporation in any of the foregoing cases executes an agreement of assumption to perform every obligation of the Servicer under this Agreement, shall be the successor to the Servicer under this Agreement without the execution or filing of any paper or any further act on the part of any of the parties to this Agreement. The Servicer shall provide notice of any merger, consolidation or succession pursuant to this Section to the Trustees and each Rating Agency.

Section 6.04. Limitation on Liability of Servicer and Others. Neither the Servicer nor any of the directors, officers, employees or agents of the Servicer shall be under any liability to the Issuer or any Securityholder, except as provided under this Agreement, for any action taken or for refraining from the taking of any action pursuant to this Agreement or for errors in judgment; provided, however, that this provision shall not protect the Servicer or any such person against any liability that would otherwise be imposed by reason of willful misfeasance, bad faith or negligence in the performance of duties or by reason of reckless disregard of obligations and duties under this Agreement. The Servicer and any director, officer, employee or agent of the Servicer may rely in good faith on any document of any kind prima facie properly executed and submitted by any Person respecting any matters arising under this Agreement.

Except as otherwise provided in this Agreement, the Servicer shall not be under any obligation to appear in, prosecute or defend any legal action that shall not be incidental to its duties to service the Receivables in accordance with this Agreement and that in its opinion may involve it in any expense or liability; provided, however, that the Servicer may undertake any reasonable action that it may deem necessary or desirable in respect of this Agreement and the other Basic Documents and the rights and duties of the parties to this Agreement and the other Basic Documents and the interests of the Certificateholders under this Agreement and the Noteholders under the Indenture. The legal expenses and costs of such action and any liability resulting therefrom will be expenses, costs and liabilities of the Issuer.

Section 6.05. AHFC Not to Resign as Servicer. Subject to the provisions of Section 6.03, AHFC shall not resign from the obligations and duties hereby imposed on it as Servicer under this Agreement except upon a determination that the performance of its duties under this Agreement shall no longer be permissible under applicable law. Notice of any such determination permitting the resignation of AHFC shall be communicated to the Trustees at the earliest practicable time (and, if such communication is not in writing, shall be confirmed in writing at the earliest practicable time) and any such determination shall be evidenced by an Opinion of Counsel to such effect delivered to the Trustees concurrently with or promptly after such notice. No such resignation shall become effective until the Indenture Trustee or a Successor Servicer shall have (i) assumed the responsibilities and obligations of AHFC in accordance with Section 7.02 and (ii) become the Administrator pursuant to Section 1.09 of the Administration Agreement.

ARTICLE SEVEN
SERVICER DEFAULTS

Section 7.01. Servicer Defaults. If any one of the following events (each, a "Servicer Default") shall occur and be continuing:

(a) any failure by the Servicer to deliver to the related Trustee for deposit in any of the Accounts or the Certificate Distribution Account any required payment or to direct the Indenture Trustee to make any required distributions therefrom, which failure continues unremedied for a period of three Business Days after discovery of such failure by an officer of the Servicer or after the date on which written notice of such failure, requiring the same to be remedied, shall have been given (i) to the Servicer by the related Trustee or (ii) to the Servicer and to the Trustees by the Holders of Notes, evidencing not less than 25% of the Outstanding Amount of the Notes;

(b) failure by the Servicer (or so long as the Servicer is AHFC, the Seller) duly to observe or to perform in any material respect any other covenants or agreements of the Servicer (or so long as the Servicer is AHFC, the Seller) set forth in this Agreement or any other Basic Document, which failure shall (i) materially and adversely affect the rights of Certificateholders or Noteholders and (ii) continue unremedied for a period of 90 days after the date on which written notice of such failure, requiring the same to be remedied, shall have been given (A) to the Servicer or the Seller (as the case may be) by the related Trustee or (B) to the Servicer or the Seller (as the case may be), and to the related Trustee by the Holders of Notes, evidencing not less than 25% of the Outstanding Amount of the Notes; or

(c) the occurrence of an Insolvency Event with respect to the Seller or the Servicer;

then, and in each and every case, so long as the Servicer Default shall not have been remedied, either the Indenture Trustee or the Holders of Notes evidencing not less than 25% of the Outstanding Amount of the Notes (or, if the Notes have been paid in full and the Indenture has been discharged in accordance with its terms, by holders of Certificates evidencing not less than 25% of the Percentage Interests) by notice then given in writing to the Servicer (and to the Indenture Trustee and the Owner Trustee if given by the Noteholders) may terminate all the rights and obligations (other than the obligations set forth in Section 6.02 that accrued on or prior to the effective date of the termination) of the Servicer under this Agreement. On or after the date specified in such written notice, all authority and power of the Servicer under this Agreement, whether with respect to the Notes, the Certificates or the Receivables or otherwise, shall, without further action, pass to and be vested in the Indenture Trustee or such Successor Servicer as may be appointed under Section 7.02; and, without limitation, the Indenture Trustee and the Owner Trustee are hereby authorized and empowered to execute and deliver, for the benefit of the predecessor Servicer, as attorney-in-fact or otherwise, any and all documents and other instruments, and to do or accomplish all other acts or things necessary or appropriate to effect the purposes of such notice of termination, whether to complete the transfer and endorsement of the Receivables and related documents, or otherwise. The predecessor Servicer shall cooperate with the Successor Servicer and the Trustees in effecting the termination of the responsibilities and rights of the predecessor Servicer under this Agreement, including the transfer to the Successor Servicer for administration by it of all cash amounts that shall at the time be held by the predecessor Servicer for deposit, or have been deposited by the predecessor Servicer, in the Accounts or the Certificate Distribution Account or thereafter received with respect to the Receivables and all Payments Ahead that shall at that time by held by the predecessor Servicer. All reasonable costs and expenses (including servicer conversion costs and attorneys' fees) incurred in connection with transferring the Receivable Files to the Successor Servicer and amending this Agreement to reflect such succession as Servicer pursuant to this Section shall be paid by the predecessor Servicer upon presentation of reasonable documentation of such costs and expenses. Any costs or expenses incurred in connection with a Servicer Default shall constitute an expense of administration under Title 11 of the United States Bankruptcy Code or any other applicable Federal or State bankruptcy laws. Upon receipt of notice of the occurrence of a Servicer Default, the Indenture Trustee shall give notice thereof to each Rating Agency.

Section 7.02. Appointment of Successor Servicer.

(a) Upon the Servicer's receipt of notice of termination pursuant to Section 7.01 or the Servicer's resignation pursuant to Section 6.05, the predecessor Servicer shall continue to perform its functions as Servicer under this Agreement, in the case of termination, only until the date specified in such termination notice or, if no such date is specified in a notice of termination, until receipt of such notice and, in the case of resignation, until the later of (i) the date 45 days from the delivery to the Trustees of written notice of such resignation (or written confirmation of such notice) in accordance with the terms of this Agreement and (ii) the date upon which the predecessor Servicer shall become unable to act as Servicer, as specified in the notice of resignation and accompanying Opinion of Counsel. In the event of the Servicer's termination hereunder, the Indenture Trustee shall appoint a Successor Servicer, and the Successor Servicer shall accept its appointment (including its appointment as Administrator under the Administration Agreement as set forth in Section 7.02(b)) by a written assumption in form acceptable to the Trustees. In the event that a Successor Servicer has not been appointed at the time when the predecessor Servicer has ceased to act as Servicer in accordance with this Section, the Indenture Trustee without further action shall automatically be appointed the Successor Servicer and the Indenture Trustee shall be entitled to receive the Total Servicing Fee. Notwithstanding the above, the Indenture Trustee shall, if it shall be legally unable or unwilling so to act, appoint or petition a court of competent jurisdiction to appoint any established institution, having a net worth of not less than $50,000,000 and whose regular business shall include the servicing of motor vehicle receivables, as the successor to the Servicer under this Agreement. In no event shall the Successor Servicer be liable for the acts or omissions of any predecessor Servicer.

(b) Upon appointment, the Successor Servicer (including the Indenture Trustee acting as Successor Servicer) shall (i) be the successor in all respects to the predecessor Servicer and shall be subject to all the responsibilities, duties and liabilities arising thereafter relating thereto placed on the predecessor Servicer and shall be entitled to the Total Servicing Fee and all the rights granted to the predecessor Servicer by the terms and provisions of this Agreement and (ii) become the Administrator pursuant to Section 1.09 of the Administration Agreement.

Section 7.03. Notification of Servicer Termination. Upon any termination of, or appointment of a successor to, the Servicer pursuant to this Article, the Owner Trustee shall give prompt written notice thereof to Certificateholders, and the Indenture Trustee shall give prompt written notice thereof to Noteholders and each Rating Agency.

Section 7.04. Waiver of Past Defaults. The Holders of Notes evidencing not less than a majority of the Outstanding Amount of the Notes or the Holders (as defined in the Trust Agreement) of Certificates evidencing not less than a majority of the Percentage Interests (in the case of a default by the Servicer that does not adversely affect the Indenture Trustee or the Noteholders or if all Notes have been paid in full and the Indenture Trustee has been discharged in accordance with its terms) may, on behalf of all Securityholders waive in writing any default by the Servicer in the performance of its obligations hereunder and its consequences, except a default in making any required deposits to or payments from any of the Accounts or the Certificate Distribution Account in accordance with this Agreement or in respect of a covenant or provision hereof that cannot be modified with the consent of each Securityholder. Upon any such waiver of a past default, such default shall cease to exist, and any Servicer Default arising therefrom shall be deemed to have been remedied for every purpose of this Agreement. No such waiver shall extend to any subsequent or other default or impair any right consequent thereto except to the extent expressly so waived.

Section 7.05. Repayment of Advances. If a Successor Servicer replaces the Servicer, the predecessor Servicer shall be entitled to receive reimbursement for all outstanding Advances made by the predecessor Servicer.

ARTICLE EIGHT

TERMINATION

Section 8.01. Optional Purchase of All Receivables.

(a) On the Payment Date following the last day of any Collection Period as of which the Pool Balance is 10% or less of the Original Pool Balance, the Servicer or any successor to the Servicer shall have the option to purchase the Owner

Trust Estate, other than the Accounts and the Certificate Distribution Account. To exercise such option, on the related Deposit Date the Servicer shall deposit pursuant to Section 4.05(a) in the Collection Account an amount equal to the aggregate Administrative Purchase Payments for the Receivables (including Defaulted Receivables), and shall succeed to all interests in and to the Issuer. Notwithstanding the foregoing, the Servicer or any successor to the Servicer shall not be permitted to exercise such option if the amount to be distributed to Securityholders on the related Payment Date would be less than the Note Distributable Amount and Certificate Distributable Amount.

(b) As described in Article Nine of the Trust Agreement, notice of any termination of the Trust shall be given by the Servicer to the Owner Trustee and the Indenture Trustee as soon as practicable after the Servicer has received notice thereof.

(c) Following the satisfaction and discharge of the Indenture and the payment in full of the principal of and interest on the Notes, the Certificateholders will succeed to the rights of the Noteholders hereunder and the Owner Trustee will succeed to the rights of the Indenture Trustee pursuant to this Agreement.

ARTICLE NINE
MISCELLANEOUS

Section 9.01. Amendment.

(a) This Agreement may be amended by the Seller, the Servicer and the Issuer, with the consent of the Indenture Trustee, but without the consent of any Securityholders, (i) to cure any ambiguity, to correct or supplement any provision in this Agreement which may be inconsistent with any other provision of this Agreement, to add, change or eliminate any other provision of this Agreement with respect to matters or questions arising under this Agreement that shall not be inconsistent with the provisions of this Agreement, (ii) to change the formula for determining the Specified Reserve Fund Balance or the manner in which the Reserve Fund is funded or to amend or modify any provisions of this Agreement relating to the remittance schedule with respect to collections deposited into the Collection Account or the Payahead Account pursuant to Section 4.02 or (iii) to amend or modify any provisions in this Agreement relating to the Servicer Letter of Credit, if any, or the acquisition thereof and including replacing the Servicer Letter of Credit with a surety bond, insurance policy or deposit of cash or securities satisfactory to the Indenture Trustee and each Rating Agency; provided, however, that in connection with any amendment pursuant to clause (i) above, any such action shall not, as evidenced by an Opinion of Counsel, adversely affect in any material respect the interests of any Securityholder and provided, further, that in connection with any amendment pursuant to clause (ii) or (iii) above, the Servicer shall deliver to the Trustees a letter from each Rating Agency to the effect that such amendment will not cause its then-current rating on the Rated Securities to be qualified, reduced or withdrawn.

(b) This Agreement may also be amended from time to time by the Seller, the Servicer and the Issuer, with the consent of the Indenture Trustee, the written consent of the Holders of Notes evidencing not less than a majority of the Outstanding Amount of the Notes and the Owner Trustee, consent of the Holders (as defined in the Trust Agreement) of outstanding Certificates evidencing not less than a majority of the Percentage Interests, for the purpose of adding any provisions to or changing in any manner or eliminating any of the provisions of this Agreement or of modifying in any manner the rights of the Securityholders; provided, however, that no such amendment shall (i) except as otherwise provided in Section 9.01 (a) increase or reduce in any manner the amount of, or accelerate or delay the timing of, collections of payments on Receivables or distributions that shall be required to be made for the benefit of the Securityholders or (ii) reduce the aforesaid percentage of the Outstanding Amount of the Notes and the Percentage Interests, the Holders of which are required to consent to any such amendment, without the written consent of all of the Securityholders.

(c) Promptly after the execution of any such amendment or consent, the Owner Trustee shall furnish written notification of the substance of such amendment or consent to each Certificateholder, the Indenture Trustee and each Rating Agency. It shall not be necessary for the consent of Securityholders pursuant to this Section to approve the particular form of any proposed amendment or consent, but it shall be sufficient if such consent shall approve the substance thereof. The manner of obtaining such consents and of evidencing the authorization of Certificateholders of the execution thereof shall be subject to such reasonable requirements as the Owner Trustee may require.

(d) Prior to the execution of any amendment to this Agreement, the Trustees shall be entitled to receive and rely upon an Opinion of Counsel stating that the execution of such amendment is authorized or permitted by this Agreement and the Opinion of Counsel referred to in Section 9.02(i)(1). The Trustees may, but shall not be obligated to, enter into any such amendment which affects the Owner Trustee's or the Indenture Trustee's, as applicable, own rights, duties or immunities under this Agreement or otherwise.

Section 9.02. Protection of Title to Trust.

(a) The Seller shall execute and file such financing statements and cause to be executed and filed such continuation statements, all in such manner and in such places as may be required by law fully to preserve, maintain and protect the interest of the Issuer and of the Indenture Trustee in the Receivables and in the proceeds thereof. The Seller shall deliver (or cause to be delivered) to the Trustees file-stamped copies of, or filing receipts for, any document filed as provided above, as soon as available following such filing.

(b) Neither the Seller nor the Servicer shall change its name, identity or corporate structure in any manner that would, could or might make any financing statement or continuation statement filed in accordance with Section 9.02(a) seriously misleading within the meaning of Section 9-507(c) of the UCC, unless it shall have given the Trustees at least 30 days' prior written notice thereof and shall, within 30 days of such change, execute and file the appropriate amendments to all previously filed financing statements or continuation statements.

(c) Each of the Seller and the Servicer shall give the Trustees at least 60 days' prior written notice of any relocation of its principal executive office if, as a result of such relocation, the applicable provisions of the UCC would require the filing of any amendment of any previously filed financing or continuation statement or of any new financing statement and shall promptly file any such amendment or new financing statement. The Servicer shall at all times maintain each office from which it shall service Receivables, and its principal executive office, within the United States.

(d) The Servicer shall maintain accounts and records as to each Receivable accurately and in sufficient detail to permit (i) the reader thereof to know at any time the status of such Receivable, including payments and recoveries made and payments owing (and the nature of each) and (ii) reconciliation between payments or recoveries on (or with respect to) each Receivable and the amounts from time to time deposited in the Accounts and any Payments Ahead held by the Servicer in respect of such Receivable.

(e) The Servicer shall maintain its computer systems so that, from and after the time of sale under this Agreement of the Receivables, the Servicer's master computer records (including any backup archives) that refer to a Receivable shall indicate clearly the interest of the Issuer and the Indenture Trustee in such Receivable and that such Receivable is owned by the Issuer and has been pledged to the Indenture Trustee. Indication of the Issuer's and the Indenture Trustee's interest in a Receivable shall be deleted from or modified on the Servicer's computer systems when, and only when, the related Receivable shall have been paid in full or repurchased.

(f) If at any time the Seller or the Servicer shall propose to sell, grant a security interest in, or otherwise transfer any interest in motor vehicle receivables to any prospective purchaser, lender or other transferee, the Servicer shall give to such prospective purchaser, lender or other transferee computer tapes, records or printouts (including any restored from backup archives) that, if they shall refer in any manner whatsoever to any Receivable, shall indicate clearly that such Receivable has been sold and is owned by the Issuer and has been pledged to the Indenture Trustee.

(g) The Servicer shall permit the Indenture Trustee and its agents at any time during normal business hours to inspect, audit and make copies of and abstracts from the Servicer's records regarding any Receivable.

(h) Upon request, the Servicer shall furnish to the Owner Trustee or to the Indenture Trustee, within five Business Days, a list of all Receivables (by contract number and name of Obligor) then held as part of the Issuer, together with a reconciliation of such list to the Schedule of Receivables and to each of the Servicer's Certificates furnished before such request indicating removal of Receivables from the Issuer.

(i) The Servicer shall deliver to the Trustees:

(1) promptly after the execution and delivery of this Agreement and of each amendment hereto, an Opinion of Counsel stating that, in the opinion of such counsel, either (A) all financing statements and continuation statements have been executed and filed that are necessary fully to preserve and protect the interest of the Trustees in the Receivables, and reciting the details of such filings or referring to prior Opinions of Counsel in which such details are given, or (B) no such action shall be necessary to preserve and protect such interest; and

(2) within 90 days after the beginning of each fiscal year of the Issuer beginning with the first fiscal year beginning more than three months after the Cutoff Date, an Opinion of Counsel, dated as of a date during such 90-day period, stating that, in the opinion of such counsel, either (A) all financing statements and continuation statements have been executed and filed that are necessary fully to preserve and protect the interest of the Trustees in the Receivables, and reciting the details of such filings or referring to prior Opinions of Counsel in which such details are given, or (B) no such action shall be necessary to preserve and protect such interest.

Each Opinion of Counsel referred to in clause (1) or (2) above shall specify any action necessary (as of the date of such opinion) to be taken in the following year to preserve and protect such interest.

(j) The Seller shall, to the extent required by applicable law, cause the Notes to be registered with the Commission pursuant to Section 12(b) or Section 12(g) of the Exchange Act within the time periods specified in such sections.

Section 9.03. Notices. All demands, notices and communications under this Agreement shall be in writing, personally delivered or mailed by certified mail, return receipt requested, and shall be deemed to have been duly given upon receipt (i) in the case of the Seller, to CT Corp., 818 West 7th Street, Second Floor, Los Angeles, California 90017, (ii) in the case of the Servicer, to American Honda Finance Corporation, 700 Van Ness Avenue, Building 300, Torrance, CA 90501, Attention: President, (iii) in the case of the Issuer or the Owner Trustee, at the Corporate Trust Office (as such term is defined in the Trust Agreement), (iv) in the case of the Indenture Trustee, at the Corporate Trust Office (as such term is herein defined), (v) in the case of Moody's, to Moody's Investors Service, Inc., ABS Monitoring Department, 99 Church Street, New York, New York 10007, (vi) in the case of Standard & Poor's, to Standard & Poor's Ratings Services, a division of The McGraw-Hill Companies, Inc., 55 Water Street, New York, New York 10041, Attention: Asset Backed Surveillance Department, (vii) in the case of Fitch, to Fitch, Inc., One State Street Plaza, New York, New York 10004, Attention: Asset Backed Surveillance Department or (viii) as to each of the foregoing, at such other address as shall be designated by written notice to the other parties.

Section 9.04. Assignment.

(a) Notwithstanding anything to the contrary contained herein, except as provided in the remainder of this Section, as provided in Sections 5.03, 6.03 and 6.05, this Agreement may not be assigned by the Seller or the Servicer without the prior written consent of Holders of Notes evidencing not less than a majority of the Outstanding Amount of the Notes and Holders (as such term is defined in the Trust Agreement) of Certificates evidencing not less than a majority of the Percentage Interests. And as provided in the provisions of this Agreement concerning the resignation of the Servicer, this Agreement may not be assigned by the Seller or the Servicer.

(b) The Seller hereby acknowledges and consents to the mortgage, pledge, assignment and grant of a security interest by the Issuer to the Indenture Trustee pursuant to the Indenture for the benefit of the Noteholders of all right, title and interest of the Issuer in, to and under the Receivables and/or the assignment of any or all of the Issuer's rights and obligations hereunder to the Indenture Trustee.

Section 9.05. Limitations on Rights of Others. The provisions of this Agreement are solely for the benefit of the Seller, the Servicer, the Issuer, the Owner Trustee, the Certificateholders, the Indenture Trustee and the Noteholders, and nothing in this Agreement, whether express or implied, shall be construed to give to any other Person any legal or equitable right, remedy or claim in the Owner Trust Estate or under or in respect of this Agreement or any covenants, conditions or provisions contained herein. The Owner Trustee and the Delaware Trustee are third-party beneficiaries of Sections 2.07, 5.02 and 6.02 of this Agreement and is entitled to the rights and benefits thereof and may enforce the provisions as if it were a party hereto.

Section 9.06. Severability. If any one or more of the covenants, agreements, provisions or terms of this Agreement shall be for any reason whatsoever held invalid, then such covenants, agreements, provisions or terms shall be deemed severable from the remaining covenants, agreements, provisions or terms of this Agreement and shall in no way affect the validity or enforceability of the other covenants, agreements, provisions or terms of this Agreement.

Section 9.07. Separate Counterparts. This Agreement may be executed by the parties hereto in separate counterparts, each of which when so executed and delivered shall be an original, but all such counterparts shall together constitute but one and the same instrument.

Section 9.08. Headings. The headings of the various Articles and Sections herein are for convenience of reference only and shall not define or limit any of the terms or provisions hereof.

Section 9.09. Governing Law. THIS AGREEMENT SHALL BE CONSTRUED IN ACCORDANCE WITH THE LAWS OF THE STATE OF CALIFORNIA, WITHOUT REFERENCE TO ITS CONFLICT OF LAW PROVISIONS, AND THE OBLIGATIONS, RIGHTS AND REMEDIES OF THE PARTIES HEREUNDER SHALL BE DETERMINED IN ACCORDANCE WITH SUCH LAWS,

EXCEPT THAT THE DUTIES, RIGHTS AND PROTECTIONS OF EACH OF THE OWNER TRUSTEE AND THE INDENTURE TRUSTEE SHALL BE GOVERNED BY THE LAWS OF THE STATE OF NEW YORK.

Section 9.10. Nonpetition Covenants.

(a) Notwithstanding any prior termination of this Agreement, the Servicer and the Seller shall not, prior to the date which is one year and one day after the termination of this Agreement with respect to the Issuer, acquiesce, petition or otherwise invoke or cause the Issuer to invoke the process of any court or government authority for the purpose of commencing or sustaining a case against the Issuer under any federal or state bankruptcy, insolvency or similar law, or appointing a receiver, liquidator, assignee, trustee, custodian, sequestrator or other similar official of the Issuer or any substantial part of its property, or ordering the winding up or liquidation of the affairs of the Issuer.

(b) Notwithstanding any prior termination of this Agreement, the Servicer shall not, prior to the date which is one year and one day after the termination of this Agreement with respect to the Seller, acquiesce, petition or otherwise invoke or cause the Seller to invoke the process of any court or government authority for the purpose of commencing or sustaining a case against the Seller under any federal or state bankruptcy, insolvency or similar law, or appointing a receiver, liquidator, assignee, trustee, custodian, sequestrator or other similar official of the Seller or any substantial part of its property, or ordering the winding up or liquidation of the affairs of the Seller.

Section 9.11. Limitation of Liability of Owner Trustee and Indenture Trustee.

(a) Notwithstanding anything contained herein to the contrary, this Agreement has been countersigned by The Bank of New York, not in its individual capacity but solely in its capacity as Owner Trustee of the Issuer and in no event shall The Bank of New York, in its individual capacity or, except as expressly provided in the Trust Agreement, The Bank of New York, as Owner Trustee of the Issuer have any liability for the representations, warranties, covenants, agreements or other obligations of the Issuer hereunder or in any of the certificates, notices or agreements delivered pursuant hereto, as to all of which recourse shall be had solely to the assets of the Issuer. For all purposes of this Agreement, in the performance of its duties or obligations hereunder or in the performance of any duties or obligations of the Issuer hereunder, the Owner Trustee shall be subject to, and entitled to the benefits of, the terms and provisions of Articles Six, Seven and Eight of the Trust Agreement.

(b) Notwithstanding anything contained herein to the contrary, this Agreement has been accepted by JPMorgan Chase Bank, not in its individual capacity but solely as Indenture Trustee and in no event shall JPMorgan Chase Bank have any liability for the representations, warranties, covenants, agreements or other obligations of the Issuer hereunder or in any of the certificates, notices or agreements delivered pursuant hereto, as to all of which recourse shall be had solely to the assets of the Issuer.

IN WITNESS WHEREOF, the parties hereto have caused this Sale and Servicing Agreement to be duly executed by their respective officers as of the day and year first above written.

HONDA AUTO RECEIVABLES 2003-1 OWNER TRUST

By: THE BANK OF NEW YORK, not in its individual capacity but solely as Owner Trustee on behalf of the Trust

By: /s/ John Bobko

Name: John Bobko

Title: Assistant Vice President

AMERICAN HONDA RECEIVABLES CORP., as Seller

By: /s/ Y. Takahashi

Name: Y. Takahashi

Title: President

AMERICAN HONDA FINANCE CORPORATION, as Servicer

By: /s/ Y. Takahashi

Name: Y. Takahashi

Title: President

Acknowledged and accepted as of the day and year first above written:
JPMORGAN CHASE BANK, not in its individual capacity but solely as Indenture Trustee

By: /s/ Jennifer H. McCourt

Name: Jennifer H. McCourt

Title: Vice President

SCHEDULE A

SCHEDULE OF RECEIVABLES

Delivered to the Owner Trustee and Indenture Trustee at Closing.

SCHEDULE B

LOCATION OF RECEIVABLE FILES

American Honda Finance Corporation
6261 Katella Avenue
Suite 1A
Cypress, California 90630

American Honda Finance Corporation
1335 Northmeadow Parkway, Suite 100
Roswell, Georgia 30076

American Honda Finance Corporation
3625 West Royal Lane
Suite 100
Irving, Texas 75063

American Honda Finance Corporation
470 Granby Road, Suite 2
S. Hadley, Massachusetts 01075

American Honda Finance Corporation
2170 Point Blvd.
Suite 100
Elgin, Illinois 60123

American Honda Finance Corporation
2420 Camino Ramon
Suite 350
San Ramon, California 94583

American Honda Finance Corporation
8601 McAlpine Park Drive, #230
Charlotte, North Carolina 28211

American Honda Finance Corporation
121 Continental Drive
Suite 308
Newark, Delaware 19713

American Honda Finance Corporation
700 Van Ness Avenue, Building 300
Torrance, California 90501

EXHIBIT A

FORM OF DISTRIBUTION STATEMENT TO SECURITYHOLDERS

Honda Auto Receivables 2003-1 Owner Trust

NOTE PRINCIPAL DISTRIBUTABLE AMOUNT $____________

Class A-1 Notes: ($______ per $1,000 original principal amount)
Class A-2 Notes: ($______ per $1,000 original principal amount)
Class A-3 Notes: ($______ per $1,000 original principal amount)
Class A-4 Notes: ($______ per $1,000 original principal amount)

NOTE INTEREST DISTRIBUTABLE AMOUNT $____________

Class A-1 Notes: ($______ per $1,000 original principal amount)
Class A-2 Notes: ($______ per $1,000 original principal amount)
Class A-3 Notes: ($______ per $1,000 original principal amount)
Class A-4 Notes: ($______ per $1,000 original principal amount)

NOTE PRINCIPAL CARRYOVER SHORTFALL $____________
change from immediately preceding Payment Date

Class A-1 Notes: ($______ per $1,000 original principal amount)
Class A-2 Notes: ($______ per $1,000 original principal amount)
Class A-3 Notes: ($______ per $1,000 original principal amount)
Class A-4 Notes: ($______ per $1,000 original principal amount)

NOTE INTEREST CARRYOVER SHORTFALL $____________
change from immediately preceding Payment Date $____________

Class A-1 Notes: ($______ per $1,000 original principal amount)
Class A-2 Notes: ($______ per $1,000 original principal amount)
Class A-3 Notes: ($______ per $1,000 original principal amount)
Class A-4 Notes: ($______ per $1,000 original principal amount)

AVAILABLE AMOUNT $____________

Available Interest $____________

Available Principal $____________

CERTIFICATE INTEREST DISTRIBUTABLE AMOUNT $____________

($______ per 1,000 original principal amount)

CERTIFICATE PRINCIPAL DISTRIBUTABLE AMOUNT $____________

($______ per 1,000 original principal amount)

NOTE DISTRIBUTABLE AMOUNT $____________

CERTIFICATE DISTRIBUTABLE AMOUNT	$____________
CERTIFICATE PRINCIPAL CARRYOVER SHORTFALL	$____________
change from immediately preceding Payment Date	$____________
CERTIFICATE INTEREST CARRYOVER SHORTFALL	$____________
change from immediately preceding Payment Date	$____________
POOL BALANCE	$____________
NOTE POOL FACTOR	$____________
Class A-1 Notes	$____________
Class A-2 Notes	$____________
Class A-3 Notes	$____________
Class A-4 Notes	$____________
CERTIFICATE POOL FACTOR	$____________
RESERVE FUND BALANCE	$____________
change from immediately preceding Payment Date	$____________
PAYMENTS AHEAD	$____________
APPLIED PAYMENTS AHEAD	$____________
TOTAL SERVICING FEE	$____________
($______ per 1,000 original principal amount)	
NONRECOVERABLE ADVANCES	$____________
YIELD SUPPLEMENT WITHDRAWAL AMOUNT	$____________
YIELD SUPPLEMENT AMOUNT	$____________
AMOUNT ON DEPOSIT IN YIELD SUPPLEMENT ACCOUNT	$____________
TRUST FEES AND EXPENSES	$____________
PRINCIPAL PAYMENT AMOUNT	$____________

EXHIBIT B

FORM OF SERVICER'S CERTIFICATE

[On File with Dewey Ballantine LLP]

Appendix 11

Appendix 11

EXECUTION COPY

AMERICAN HONDA FINANCE CORPORATION,

as Seller,

and

AMERICAN HONDA RECEIVABLES CORP.,

as Purchaser

RECEIVABLES PURCHASE AGREEMENT

Dated as of February 1, 2003

TABLE OF CONTENTS

ARTICLE ONE

DEFINITIONS

Page*

ARTICLE TWO

CONVEYANCE OF RECEIVABLES

ARTICLE THREE

PAYMENT OF RECEIVABLES PURCHASE PRICE

*[Eds. — Page numbers added.]

ARTICLE FOUR

TERMINATION

ARTICLE FIVE

MISCELLANEOUS PROVISIONS

SCHEDULES

This Receivables Purchase Agreement, dated as of February 1, 2003, is between American Honda Finance Corporation, a California corporation, as seller, and American Honda Receivables Corp., a California corporation, as purchaser.

In consideration of the premises and mutual agreements herein contained, each party agrees as follows for the benefit of the other party and for the benefit of the Owner Trustee:

ARTICLE ONE
DEFINITIONS

Section 1.01. Definitions. Whenever used in this Agreement, the following words and phrases shall have the following meanings:

"Agreement" means this Receivables Purchase Agreement and all amendments hereof and supplements hereto.

"Closing Date" means February 25, 2003.

"Cutoff Date" means February 1, 2003.

"Delaware Trustee" means The Bank of New York (Delaware), as Delaware Trustee under the Trust Agreement.

"Indenture" means the Indenture, dated as of February 1, 2003, between the Issuer and the Indenture Trustee.

"Indenture Trustee" means JPMorgan Chase Bank, a New York banking corporation, as indenture trustee under the Indenture.

"Issuer" means Honda Auto Receivables 2003-1 Owner Trust, a Delaware statutory trust.

"Owner Trustee" means The Bank of New York, as owner trustee under the Trust Agreement.

"Purchaser" means American Honda Receivables Corp., in its capacity as purchaser of the Receivables under this Agreement, and its successors and assigns.

"Receivables Purchase Price" means $1,541,603,274.54 less agreed upon securitization-related fees, costs and expenses.

"Sale and Servicing Agreement" means the Sale and Servicing Agreement, dated as of February 1, 2003, among American Honda Receivables Corp., as seller, American Honda Finance Corporation, as servicer, and the Issuer.

"Schedule of Receivables" means the schedule of receivables attached as Schedule A hereto.

"Seller" means American Honda Finance Corporation, in its capacity as seller of the Receivables under this Agreement, and its successors and assigns.

"Servicer" means American Honda Finance Corporation in its capacity as servicer under the Sale and Servicing Agreement and its successors and assigns.

"Trust Agreement" means the trust agreement dated January 21, 2003, as amended and restated on February 25, 2003 among American Honda Receivables Corp., as depositor, the Owner Trustee and the Delaware Trustee.

"Trustees" means the Delaware Trustee, the Indenture Trustee and the Owner Trustee.

"Warranty Receivable" means a Receivable purchased by the Seller pursuant to Section 2.03(c).

Section 1.02. Other Definitional Provisions.

(a) All capitalized terms not otherwise defined in this Agreement shall have the defined meanings used in the Sale and Servicing Agreement.

(b) The words "hereof," "herein" and "hereunder" and words of similar import when used in this Agreement shall refer to this Agreement as a whole and not to any particular provision of this Agreement; Section, subsection and Schedule references contained in this Agreement are references to Sections, subsections and Schedules in or to this Agreement unless otherwise specified; the term "proceeds" shall have the meaning set forth in the applicable UCC; and the word "including" means including without limitation.

ARTICLE TWO
CONVEYANCE OF RECEIVABLES

Section 2.01. Conveyance of Receivables.

(a) The Seller hereby sells, transfers, assigns, sets over and otherwise conveys to the Purchaser, and the Purchaser hereby purchases from the Seller, without recourse (subject to the Seller's obligations hereunder), all of the right, title and interest of the Seller in, to and under the following:

(i) the Receivables listed in the Schedule of Receivables and all monies due thereon or paid thereunder or in respect thereof (including proceeds of the repurchase of Receivables by the Seller pursuant to Section 2.03(c)) on or after the Cutoff Date;

(ii) the security interests in the Financed Vehicles;

(iii) any proceeds of any physical damage insurance policies covering the Financed Vehicles and in any proceeds of any credit life or credit disability insurance policies relating to the Receivables or the Obligors;

(iv) any proceeds of Dealer Recourse;

(v) the right to realize upon any property (including the right to receive future Liquidation Proceeds) that shall have secured a Receivable and have been repossessed by or on behalf of the Issuer; and

(vi) the proceeds of any and all of the foregoing.

(b) In connection with the foregoing conveyance, the Seller agrees to record and file, at its own expense, one or more financing statements with respect to the Receivables now existing and hereafter created for the sale of chattel paper (as defined in Section 9-102 of the UCC as in effect in the State of California) meeting the requirements of applicable state law in such manner as is necessary to perfect the sale of the Receivables to the Purchaser, and the proceeds thereof (and any continuation statements as are required by applicable state law), and to deliver a file-stamped copy to the Indenture Trustee of each such financing statement (or continuation statement) or other evidence of such filings (which may, for purposes of this Section, consist of telephone confirmation of such filings with the file stamped copy of each such filings to be provided to the Purchaser in due course), as soon as is practicable after receipt by the Seller thereof.

In connection with the foregoing conveyance, the Seller further agrees, at its own expense, on or prior to the Closing Date (i) to annotate and indicate in its computer files that the Receivables have been transferred to the Purchaser pursuant to this Agreement, (ii) to deliver to the Purchaser a computer file or printed or microfiche list containing a true and complete list of all such Receivables, identified by account number and by the Principal Balance of each Receivable as of the Cutoff Date, which file or list shall be marked as Schedule A to this Agreement and is hereby incorporated into and made a part of this Agreement and (iii) to deliver the Receivable Files to or upon the order of the Purchaser.

The parties hereto intend that the conveyance hereunder be a sale. In the event that the conveyance hereunder is not for any reason considered a sale, the Seller hereby grants to the Purchaser a first priority perfected security interest in all of its right, title and interest in, to and under the Receivables, and all other property conveyed hereunder and listed in this Section and all proceeds of any of the foregoing. The parties intend that this Agreement constitute a security agreement under applicable law. Such grant is made to secure the payment of all amounts payable hereunder, including, without limitation, the Receivables Purchase Price.

Section 2.02. Representations and Warranties of the Seller and the Purchaser.

(a) The Seller hereby represents and warrants to the Purchaser as of the date of this Agreement and the Closing Date that:

(i) Organization and Good Standing. The Seller is a corporation duly organized, validly existing and in good standing under the laws of the State of California, and has power and authority to own its properties and to conduct its business as such properties are currently owned and such business is presently conducted, and had at all relevant times, and shall have, power, authority and legal right to acquire, own and sell the Receivables.

(ii) Due Qualification. The Seller is duly qualified to do business as a foreign corporation in good standing, and has obtained all necessary licenses and approvals in all jurisdictions in which the ownership or lease of property or the conduct of its business (including the servicing of the Receivables as required by the Sale and Servicing Agreement) shall require such qualifications.

(iii) Power and Authority. The Seller shall have the power and authority to execute and deliver this Agreement and to carry out its terms; and the execution, delivery and performance of this Agreement shall have been duly authorized by the Seller by all necessary corporate action.

(iv) Binding Obligation. This Agreement constitutes a legal, valid and binding obligation of the Seller, enforceable against it in accordance with its terms, except as enforceability may be subject to or limited by bankruptcy, insolvency, reorganization, moratorium, liquidation or other similar laws affecting the enforcement of creditors' rights in general and by general principles of equity, regardless of whether such enforceability shall be considered in a proceeding in equity or at law.

(v) No Violation. The execution, delivery and performance by the Seller of this Agreement and the consummation of the transactions contemplated by this Agreement and the fulfillment of the terms hereof shall not conflict with, result in any breach of any of the terms and provisions of, nor constitute (with or without notice or lapse of time) a default under, the articles of incorporation or bylaws of the Seller, or conflict with or breach any of the material terms or provisions of, or constitute (with or without notice or lapse of time) a default under, any indenture, agreement or other instrument to which the Seller is a party or by which it may be bound or any of its properties are subject; nor result in the creation or imposition of any lien upon any of its properties pursuant to the terms of any such indenture, agreement or other instrument (other than this Agreement); nor violate any law or, to the knowledge of the Seller, any order, rule or regulation applicable to it or its properties of any court or of any federal or state regulatory body, administrative agency or other governmental instrumentality having jurisdiction over the Seller or any of its properties.

(vi) No Proceedings. There are no proceedings or investigations pending or, to the knowledge of the Seller, threatened against the Seller, before any court, regulatory body, administrative agency or other tribunal or governmental instrumentality (i) asserting the invalidity of this Agreement, (ii) seeking to prevent the consummation of any of the transactions contemplated by this Agreement or (iii) seeking any determination or ruling that, in the reasonable judgment of the Seller, would materially and adversely affect the performance by the Seller of its obligations under this Agreement.

(b) The Purchaser hereby represents and warrants to the Seller as of the date of this Agreement and the Closing Date that:

(i) Organization and Good Standing. The Purchaser is a corporation duly organized, validly existing and in good standing under the laws of the State of California, and has power and authority to own its properties and to conduct its business as such properties are currently owned and such business is presently conducted, and had at all relevant times, and shall have, power, authority and legal right to acquire, own and sell the Receivables.

(ii) Due Qualification. The Purchaser is duly qualified to do business as a foreign corporation in good standing, and has obtained all necessary licenses and approvals in all jurisdictions in which the ownership or lease of property or the conduct of its business shall require such qualifications.

(iii) Power and Authority. The Purchaser shall have the power and authority to execute and deliver this Agreement and to carry out its terms; and the execution, delivery and performance of this Agreement shall have been duly authorized by the Purchaser by all necessary corporate action.

(iv) Binding Obligation. This Agreement constitutes a legal, valid and binding obligation of the Purchaser, enforceable against it in accordance with its terms, except as enforceability may be subject to or limited by bankruptcy, insolvency, reorganization, moratorium, liquidation or other similar laws affecting the enforcement of creditors' rights in general and by general principles of equity, regardless of whether such enforceability shall be considered in a proceeding in equity or at law.

(v) No Violation. The execution, delivery and performance of this Agreement and the consummation of the transactions contemplated by this Agreement and the fulfillment of the terms hereof shall not conflict with, result in any breach of any of the terms and provisions of, nor constitute (with or without notice or lapse of time) a default under, the articles of incorporation or bylaws of the Purchaser, or conflict with or breach any of the material terms or provisions of, or constitute (with or without notice or lapse of time) a default under, any indenture, agreement or other instrument to which the Purchaser is a party or by which it may be bound or any of its properties are subject; nor result in the creation or imposition of any lien upon any of its properties pursuant to the terms of any such indenture, agreement or other instrument (other than this Agreement); nor violate any law or, to the knowledge of the Purchaser, any order, rule or regulation applicable to it or its properties of any court or of any federal or state regulatory body, administrative agency or other governmental instrumentality having jurisdiction over the Purchaser or any of its properties.

(vi) No Proceedings. There are no proceedings or investigations pending or, to the knowledge of the Purchaser, threatened against the Purchaser, before any court, regulatory body, administrative agency or other tribunal or governmental instrumentality (i) asserting the invalidity of this Agreement, (ii) seeking to prevent the consummation of any of the transactions contemplated by this Agreement or (iii) seeking any determination or ruling that, in the reasonable judgment of the Purchaser, would materially and adversely affect the performance by the Purchaser of its obligations under this Agreement.

(c) The representations and warranties set forth in this Section shall survive the sale of the Receivables by the Seller to the Purchaser and the sale of the Receivables by the Purchaser to the Issuer. Upon discovery by the Seller or the Purchaser of a breach of any of the foregoing representations and warranties, the party discovering such breach shall give prompt written notice to the others.

Section 2.03. Representations and Warranties as to the Receivables.

(a) Eligibility of Receivables. The Seller hereby represents and warrants to the Purchaser as of the Cutoff Date that:

(i) Characteristics of Receivables. Each Receivable (A) shall have been originated in the United States by a Dealer for the retail sale of the related Financed Vehicle in the ordinary course of such Dealer's business, shall have been fully and properly executed by the parties thereto, shall have been purchased by the Seller from such Dealer under an existing agreement with the Seller and shall have been validly assigned by such Dealer to the Seller in accordance with its terms, (B) shall have created or shall create a valid, subsisting and enforceable first priority security interest in favor of the Seller in the related Financed Vehicle, (C) shall contain customary and enforceable provisions such that the rights and remedies of the holder thereof shall be adequate for realization against the collateral of the benefits of the security, (D) shall provide for level Monthly Payments (provided that the payment in the first or last month in the life of the Receivable may be minimally different from the level payment) that fully amortize the Amount Financed over its original term and shall provide for a finance charge or shall yield interest at its APR, (E) shall provide for, in the event that such Receivable is prepaid, a prepayment that fully pays the Principal Balance and includes accrued but unpaid interest at least through the date of prepayment in an amount calculated by using an interest rate at least equal to its APR, (F) shall have an Obligor that is not a federal, state or local governmental entity and (G) is a retail installment contract.

(ii) Schedule of Receivables. The information set forth in the Schedule of Receivables shall be true and correct in all material respects as of the opening of business on the Cutoff Date, and no selection procedures believed to be adverse to the Securityholders were utilized in selecting the Receivables from those motor vehicle receivables of the Seller which met the selection criteria set forth in this Agreement.

(iii) Compliance with Law. Each Receivable and each sale of the related Financed Vehicle shall have complied at the time it was originated or made, and shall comply at the time of execution of this Agreement in all material respects with all requirements of applicable federal, state and local laws, and regulations thereunder, including usury laws, the Federal Truth-in-Lending Act, the Equal Credit Opportunity Act, the Fair Credit Billing Act, the Fair Credit Reporting Act, the Fair Debt Collection Practices Act, the Federal Trade Commission Act, the Magnuson-Moss Warranty Act, Federal Reserve Board Regulations B and Z, state adaptations of the National Consumer Act and of the Uniform Consumer Credit Code and other consumer credit, equal credit opportunity and disclosure laws.

(iv) Binding Obligation. Each Receivable shall constitute the genuine, legal, valid and binding payment obligation in writing of the related Obligor, enforceable by the holder thereof in accordance with its terms, except as enforceability may be subject to or limited by bankruptcy, insolvency, reorganization, moratorium, liquidation or other similar laws affecting the enforcement of creditors' rights in general and by general principles of equity, regardless of whether such enforceability shall be considered in a proceeding in equity or at law.

(v) No Bankrupt Obligors. According to the records of the Seller, as of the Cutoff Date, no Obligor is the subject of a bankruptcy proceeding.

(vi) Security Interest in Financed Vehicles. According to the records of the Seller, as of the Cutoff Date, no Financed Vehicle has been repossessed and not reinstated and immediately prior to the sale, assignment and transfer thereof, all necessary steps shall be taken so that each Receivable shall be secured by a validly perfected first priority security interest in the related Financed Vehicle in favor of the Seller as secured party or all necessary and appropriate action with respect to such Receivable shall have been taken to perfect a first priority security interest in such Financed Vehicle in favor of the Seller as secured party.

(vii) Receivables in Force. No Receivable shall have been satisfied, subordinated or rescinded, nor shall any Financed Vehicle have been released in whole or in part from the lien granted by the related Receivable.

(viii) No Waivers. No provision of a Receivable shall have been waived in such a manner that such Receivable fails to meet all of the other representations and warranties made by the Seller herein with respect thereto.

(ix) No Amendments. No Receivable shall have been amended in such a manner that the number of Scheduled Payments has been increased or that the related Amount Financed has been increased or such Receivable fails to meet all of the other representations and warranties made by the Seller herein with respect thereto.

(x) No Defenses. No facts shall be known to the Seller which would give rise to any right of rescission, setoff, counterclaim or defense, nor shall the same have been asserted or threatened, with respect to any Receivable.

(xi) No Liens. To the knowledge of the Seller, no liens or claims shall have been filed, including liens for work, labor or materials relating to a Financed Vehicle, that shall be liens prior to, or equal or coordinate with, the security interest in such Financed Vehicle granted by the related Receivable.

(xii) No Defaults. Except for payment defaults continuing for a period of not more than 30 days as of the Cutoff Date, no default, breach, violation or event permitting acceleration under the terms of any Receivable shall have occurred and no continuing condition that with notice or the lapse of time would constitute a default, breach, violation or event permitting acceleration under the terms of any Receivable shall have arisen; and the Seller shall not have waived any of the foregoing except as otherwise permitted hereunder.

(xiii) Insurance. Pursuant to the Receivables, each Obligor has been required to obtain physical damage insurance covering the related Financed Vehicle and the Obligor is required under the terms of the related Receivable to maintain such insurance.

(xiv) Good Title. It is the intention of the Seller that the transfer and assignment herein contemplated, taken as a whole, constitute a sale of the Receivables from the Seller to the Purchaser and that the beneficial interest in and title to the Receivables not be part of the debtor's estate in the event of the filing of a bankruptcy petition by or against the Seller under any bankruptcy law. No Receivable has been sold, transferred, assigned or pledged by the Seller to any Person other than the Purchaser, and no provision of a Receivable shall have been waived, except as provided in clause (viii) above; immediately prior to the transfer and assignment herein contemplated, the Seller had good and marketable title to each Receivable, free and clear of all Liens and rights of others; immediately upon the transfer and assignment thereof, the Purchaser shall have good and marketable title to each Receivable, free and clear of all Liens and rights of others; and the transfer and assignment herein contemplated has been perfected under the applicable UCC.

(xv) Lawful Assignment. No Receivable shall have been originated in, or shall be subject to the laws of, any jurisdiction under which the sale, transfer and assignment of such Receivable under this Agreement or pursuant to the transfer of the Securities shall be unlawful, void or voidable.

(xvi) All Filings Made. Both the Seller and the Purchaser, respectively, have caused or will have caused, within ten days of the Closing Date, the filing of all appropriate financing statements (including UCC filings) necessary in the appropriate jurisdictions under the applicable law the Indenture Trustee a first priority perfected ownership interest in the Receivables shall have been made.

(xvii) One Original. There shall be only one original executed copy of each Receivable.

(xviii) Chattel Paper. Each Receivable constitutes "tangible chattel paper" as defined within the meaning of the applicable UCC.

(xix) Additional Representations and Warranties. (A) Each Receivable shall have an original maturity of at least 12 months and not more than 60 months and, as of the Cutoff Date, a remaining maturity of not less than 6 months nor greater than 59 months; (B) each Receivable shall provide for payment of a finance charge or shall yield interest calculated on the basis of an APR ranging from 1.90% to 15.39%; (C) each Receivable shall have had an original principal balance of not less than $2,013.32 nor more than $81,062.46 and, as of the Cutoff Date, an average unpaid principal balance of $15,164.09; (D) each Receivable was originated on or after June 12, 1998 and on or prior to October 30, 2002; (E) each Financed Vehicle shall be a new or used Honda or Acura motor vehicle; (F) the Obligor under each Receivable had a current billing address in the United States as of the Cutoff Date; and (G) no Receivable shall have a Scheduled Payment that is more than 30 days past due as of the Cutoff Date.

(xx) Possession of Documents. The Servicer has in its possession all original copies of the agreements that constitute or evidence the Receivables. The agreements that constitute or evidence the Receivables do not have any marks or notations indicating that they have been pledged, assigned or otherwise conveyed to any Person other than the Indenture Trustee (pursuant to and as provided in the Sale and Servicing Agreement and the Indenture). All financing statements filed or to be filed against the Seller in favor of Purchaser and assigned to the Indenture Trustee in connection herewith describing the Receivables contain a statement to the following effect: "A purchase of or security interest in any collateral described in this financing statement will violate the rights of the Indenture Trustee."

(b) Notice of Breach. The representations and warranties set forth in this Section shall speak as of the execution and delivery of this Agreement, but shall survive the sale, transfer and assignment of the Receivables to the Purchaser and any subsequent assignment or transfer pursuant to the Sale and Servicing Agreement. The Purchaser, the Seller, the Issuer, the Owner Trustee, the Delaware Trustee or the Indenture Trustee, as the case may be, shall inform the other parties promptly, in writing, upon discovery of any breach of the Seller's representations and warranties pursuant to this Section which materially and adversely affects the interests of the Noteholders in any Receivable.

(c) Repurchase of Receivables. In the event of a breach of any representation or warranty set forth in Section 2.03(a) which materially and adversely affects the interests of the Noteholders in any Receivable and unless the breach shall have been cured by the last day of the second Collection Period following the Collection Period in which the discovery of the breach is made or notice is received, as the case may be (or, at the option of the Seller, the last day in the first Collection Period following the Collection Period in which such discovery is made), the Seller shall repurchase such Receivable. In consideration of the purchase of any such Receivable, the Seller shall remit an amount equal to the Warranty Purchase Payment in respect of such Receivable to the Purchaser and shall be entitled to receive the Released Warranty Amount. In the event that, as of the date of execution and delivery of this Agreement, any Liens or claims shall have been filed, including Liens for work, labor or materials relating to a Financed Vehicle, that shall be prior to, or equal or coordinate with, the lien granted by the related Receivable (whether or not the Seller has knowledge thereof), and such breach materially and adversely affects the interests of the Noteholders in such Receivable, the Seller shall repurchase such Receivable on the terms and in the manner specified above. Upon any such repurchase, the Purchaser shall, without further action, be deemed to transfer, assign, set-over and otherwise convey to the Seller, without recourse, representation or warranty, all the right, title and interest of the Purchaser in, to and under such repurchased Receivable, all monies due or to become due with respect thereto and all proceeds thereof. The Purchaser, the Issuer, the Owner Trustee, the Delaware Trustee or the Indenture Trustee, as applicable, shall execute such documents and instruments of transfer or assignment and take such other actions as shall reasonably be requested by the Seller to effect the conveyance of such Receivable pursuant to this Section. The sole remedy of the Purchaser, the Issuer, the Trustees or the Securityholders with respect to a breach of the Seller's representations and warranties pursuant to Section 2.03(a) or with respect to the existence of any such Liens or claims shall be to require the Seller to repurchase the related Receivables pursuant to this Section.

Section 2.04. Covenants of the Seller. The Seller hereby covenants that:

(a) Security Interests. Except for the conveyances hereunder, the Seller will not sell, pledge, assign or transfer to any other Person, or grant, create, incur, assume or suffer to exist any Lien on any Receivable, whether now existing or hereafter created, or any interest therein; the Seller will immediately notify the Purchaser of the existence of any Lien on any Receivable and, in the event that the interests of the Noteholders in such Receivable are materially and adversely affected, such Receivable shall be repurchased from the Purchaser by the Seller in the manner and with the effect specified in Section 2.03(c), and the Seller shall defend the right, title and interest of the Purchaser in, to and under the Receivables, whether now existing or hereafter created, against all claims of third parties claiming through or under the Seller; provided, however, that nothing in this subsection shall prevent or be deemed to prohibit the Seller from suffering to exist upon a Receivable any Lien for municipal or other local taxes if such taxes shall not at the time be due and payable or if the Seller shall currently be contesting the validity of such taxes in good faith by appropriate proceedings and shall have set aside on its books adequate reserves with respect thereto.

(b) Delivery of Payments. The Seller agrees to deliver in kind upon receipt to the Servicer under the Sale and Servicing Agreement (if other than the Seller) all payments received by the Seller in respect of the Receivables as soon as practicable after receipt thereof by the Seller.

(c) No Impairment. The Seller shall take no action, nor omit to take any action, which would impair the rights of the Purchaser in any Receivable, nor shall it, except as otherwise provided in this Agreement or the Sale and Servicing Agreement, reschedule, revise or defer payments due on any Receivable.

ARTICLE THREE

PAYMENT OF RECEIVABLES PURCHASE PRICE

Section 3.01. Payment of Receivables Purchase Price. In consideration of the sale of the Receivables from the Seller to the Purchaser as provided in Section 2.01, on the Closing Date the Purchaser agrees to pay the Seller an amount equal to the Receivables Purchase Price. The Receivables Purchase Price shall be paid in the form of (i) $1,530,527,215.64, the net cash proceeds from the public offering by the Purchaser of the Notes and (ii) $8,154,108.90, being deemed paid and returned to the Purchaser as a capital contribution.

ARTICLE FOUR
TERMINATION

Section 4.01. Termination. The respective obligations and responsibilities of the Seller and the Purchaser created hereby shall terminate, except for the indemnity obligations of the Seller as provided herein, upon the termination of the Issuer as provided in the Trust Agreement.

ARTICLE FIVE
MISCELLANEOUS PROVISIONS

Section 5.01. Amendment.

(a) This Agreement may be amended from time to time by the Purchaser and the Seller, without the consent of the Securityholders, to cure any ambiguity, to correct or supplement any provision herein which may be inconsistent with any other provision herein or to add any other provision with respect to matters or questions arising under this Agreement which shall not be inconsistent with the provisions of this Agreement or the Sale and Servicing Agreement; provided, however, that such action shall not, as evidenced by an Opinion of Counsel to the Purchaser delivered to the Indenture Trustee, adversely affect in any material respect the interests of the Securityholders.

(b) This Agreement may also be amended from time to time by the Purchaser and the Seller with the consent of the Indenture Trustee, the consent of the Holders of Notes evidencing at least a majority of the Outstanding Amount of the Notes and the consent of the Holders (as such term is defined in the Trust Agreement) of Certificates evidencing at least a majority of all the percentage interests evidenced by the Certificates, for the purpose of adding any provisions to or changing in any manner or eliminating any of the provisions of this Agreement.

Section 5.02. Protection of Right, Title and Interest to Receivables.

(a) The Seller, at its expense, shall cause this Agreement and/or all financing statements and continuation statements and any other necessary documents covering the Purchaser's right, title and interest to the Receivables and other property conveyed by the Seller to the Purchaser hereunder to be promptly recorded, registered and filed, and at all times to be kept recorded, registered and filed, all in such manner and in such places as may be required by law fully to preserve and protect the right, title and interest of the Purchaser hereunder to all of the Receivables and such other property. The Seller shall deliver to the Purchaser file-stamped copies of, or filing receipts for, any document recorded, registered or filed as provided above, as soon as available following such recording, registration or filing. The Purchaser shall cooperate fully with the Seller in connection with the obligations set forth above and will execute any and all documents reasonably required to fulfill the intent of this subsection.

(b) In the event that the Seller makes any change in its name, identity or corporate structure which would make any financing statement or continuation statement filed in accordance with Section 5.02(a) seriously misleading within the meaning of Section 9-507(c) of the UCC as in effect in the applicable state, the Seller shall give the Purchaser not less than 5 days prior written notice of any such change and shall, within 30 days of such change, execute and file such financing statements or amendments as may be necessary to continue the perfection of the Purchaser's security interest in the Receivables and the proceeds thereof.

(c) The Seller will give the Purchaser prompt written notice of any relocation of any office from which the Seller keeps records concerning the Receivables or of its principal executive office and whether, as a result of such relocation, the applicable provisions of the UCC would require the filing of any amendment of any previously filed financing or continuation statement or of any new financing statement and shall execute and file such financing statements or amendments as may be necessary to continue the perfection of the interest of the Purchaser in the Receivables and the proceeds thereof.

Section 5.03. Governing Law. THIS AGREEMENT SHALL BE CONSTRUED IN ACCORDANCE WITH THE LAWS OF THE STATE OF CALIFORNIA, AND THE OBLIGATIONS, RIGHTS AND REMEDIES OF THE PARTIES HEREUNDER SHALL BE DETERMINED IN ACCORDANCE WITH SUCH LAWS.

Section 5.04 Notices. All demands, notices and communications hereunder shall be in writing and shall be deemed to have been duly given if personally delivered at or mailed by registered mail, return receipt requested, in the case of (i) the Purchaser, to American Honda Receivables Corp., 700 Van Ness Avenue, Building 300, Torrance, California 90501, Attention: President; (ii) the Seller, to American Honda Finance Corporation, 700 Van Ness Avenue, Building 300, Torrance, California 90501, Attention: President; and (iii) the Indenture Trustee, to JPMorgan Chase Bank, 4 New York Plaza, 6th Floor, New York, New York 10004, Attention: Corporate Trust Services; or, as to any of such Persons, at such other address as shall be designated by such Person in a written notice to the other Persons.

Section 5.05. Severability of Provisions. If any one or more of the covenants, agreements, provisions or terms of this Agreement shall for any reason whatsoever be held invalid, then such covenants, agreements, provisions or terms shall be deemed severable from the remaining covenants, agreements, provisions and terms of this Agreement and shall in no way affect the validity or enforceability of the other covenants, agreements, provisions or terms of this Agreement or any amendment or supplement hereto.

Section 5.06. Assignment. This Agreement may not be assigned by the Purchaser or the Seller except as contemplated by this Section and the Sale and Servicing Agreement; provided, however, that simultaneously with the execution and delivery of this Agreement, the Purchaser shall assign all of its right, title and interest herein to the Issuer, which in turn, will pledge its rights to the Indenture Trustee for the benefit of the Noteholders as provided in Section 2.01 of the Sale and Servicing Agreement, to which the Seller hereby expressly consents. The Seller agrees to perform its obligations hereunder for the benefit of the Issuer and that the Indenture Trustee may enforce the provisions of this Agreement, exercise the rights of the Purchaser and enforce the obligations of the Seller hereunder without the consent of the Purchaser.

Section 5.07. Further Assurances. The Seller and the Purchaser agree to do and perform, from time to time, any and all acts and to execute any and all further instruments required or reasonably requested by the other party hereto or by the Issuer or the Indenture Trustee more fully to effect the purposes of this Agreement, including, without limitation, the execution of any financing statements, amendments, continuation statements or releases relating to the Receivables for filing under the provisions of the UCC or other law of any applicable jurisdiction.

Section 5.08. No Waiver; Cumulative Remedies. No failure to exercise and no delay in exercising, on the part of the Purchaser, the Issuer or the Seller, any right, remedy, power or privilege hereunder shall operate as a waiver thereof; nor shall any single or partial exercise of any right, remedy, power or privilege hereunder preclude any other or further exercise thereof or the exercise of any other right, remedy, power or privilege. The rights, remedies, powers and privileges herein provided are cumulative and not exhaustive of any rights, remedies, powers and privileges provided by law.

Section 5.09. Counterparts. This Agreement may be executed in two or more counterparts, (and by different parties on separate counterparts), each of which shall be an original, but all of which together shall constitute one and the same instrument.

Section 5.10. Third-Party Beneficiaries. This Agreement will inure to the benefit of and be binding upon the parties hereto, the Issuer and the Indenture Trustee for the benefit of the Noteholders, both of which shall be considered to be third-party beneficiaries hereof. Except as otherwise provided in this Agreement, no other Person will have any right or obligation hereunder.

Section 5.11. Headings. The headings herein are for purposes of reference only and shall not otherwise affect the meaning or interpretation of any provision hereof.

Section 5.12. Seller Indemnification.

(a) Purchaser, Issuer and Securityholders. The Seller shall indemnify and hold harmless the Purchaser, the Issuer and the Securityholders from and against any loss, liability, expense or damage suffered or sustained by reason of any acts, omissions or alleged acts or omissions arising out of activities of the Seller pursuant to this Agreement or as a result of the transactions contemplated hereby, including, but not limited to, any judgment, award, settlement, reasonable attorneys' fees and other costs or expenses incurred in connection with the defense of any actual or threatened action, proceeding or claim; provided, however, that the Seller shall not indemnify the Purchaser, the Issuer or the Securityholders if such acts, omissions or alleged acts or omissions constitute negligence or willful misconduct by the Purchaser, the Issuer or the Securityholders.

(b) Trustees. The Seller shall indemnify, defend and hold harmless the Trustees from and against any and all costs, expenses, losses, claims, damages and liabilities to the extent that such cost, expense, loss, claim, damage or liability arose out of, and was imposed upon the Trustees through the negligence, willful misfeasance or bad faith of the Seller in the performance of its duties under this Agreement or by reason of reckless disregard of its obligations and duties under this Agreement.

Section 5.13. Merger, Consolidation or Assumption of the Obligations of the Seller.

(a) The Seller shall not consolidate with or merge into any other corporation or convey or transfer its properties and assets substantially as an entirety to any Person, unless:

(i) the corporation formed by such consolidation or into which the Seller is merged or the Person which acquires by conveyance or transfer the properties and assets of the Seller substantially as an entirety shall be organized and existing under the laws of the United States, any state thereof or the District of Columbia, and, if the Seller is not the surviving entity, shall expressly assume, by an agreement supplemental hereto, executed and delivered to the Purchaser and the Indenture Trustee, in form satisfactory to the Purchaser and the Indenture Trustee, the performance of every covenant and obligation of the Seller hereunder and shall benefit from all the rights granted to the Seller hereunder; and

(ii) the Seller shall have delivered to the Purchaser and the Indenture Trustee an Officer's Certificate of the Seller and an Opinion of Counsel each stating that such consolidation, merger, conveyance or transfer and such supplemental agreement comply with this Section and that all conditions precedent herein provided for relating to such transaction have been complied with.

(b) The obligations of the Seller hereunder shall not be assignable nor shall any Person succeed to the obligations of the Seller hereunder except in each case in accordance with the provisions of Section 5.06 and this Section.

IN WITNESS WHEREOF, the parties hereto have caused this Agreement to be duly executed by their respective officers as of the day and year first above written.

AMERICAN HONDA FINANCE CORPORATION,
as Seller

By: /s/ Y. Takahashi

Name: Y. Takahashi
Title: President

AMERICAN HONDA RECEIVABLES CORP.,
as Purchaser

By: /s/ Y. Takahashi

Name: Y. Takahashi
Title: President

SCHEDULE A

SCHEDULE OF RECEIVABLES

Omitted — originals on file at the offices of the Seller, the Purchaser and the Indenture Trustee

Appendix 12

Appendix 12

EXECUTION COPY

HONDA AUTO RECEIVABLES 2003-1 OWNER TRUST,
as Issuer,

AMERICAN HONDA FINANCE CORPORATION,
as Administrator,

AMERICAN HONDA RECEIVABLES CORP.,
as Depositor,

and

JPMORGAN CHASE BANK,

as Indenture Trustee

ADMINISTRATION AGREEMENT

Dated as of February 1, 2003

TABLE OF CONTENTS

*[Eds. — Page numbers added.]

EXHIBITS

This Administration Agreement, dated as of February 1, 2003 (the "Agreement"), is among Honda Auto Receivables 2003-1 Owner Trust, as issuer (the "Issuer"), American Honda Finance Corporation ("AHFC"), as administrator (in such capacity, the "Administrator"), American Honda Receivables Corp. ("AHRC"), as depositor (in such capacity, the "Depositor"), and JPMorgan Chase Bank, as indenture trustee (the "Indenture Trustee").

WHEREAS, the Issuer was created pursuant to the Amended and Restated Trust Agreement, dated as of February 25, 2003 (the "Trust Agreement"), among the Depositor, The Bank of New York, as owner trustee (the "Owner Trustee") and The Bank of New York (Delaware), as Delaware trustee (the "Delaware Trustee");

WHEREAS, the Issuer is issuing 1.30% Asset Backed Notes, Class A-1, 1.46% Asset Backed Notes, Class A-2, 1.92% Asset Backed Notes, Class A-3 and 2.48% Asset Backed Notes, Class A-4 (collectively, the "Notes") pursuant to an Indenture, dated as of the date hereof (the "Indenture"), between the Issuer and the Indenture Trustee;

WHEREAS, the Issuer has entered into certain agreements in connection with the issuance of the Notes and of certain beneficial ownership interests of the Issuer, including (i) the Indenture, (ii) a Sale and Servicing Agreement, dated as of the date hereof (the "Sale and Servicing Agreement"), among the Issuer, AHRC, as transferor (in such capacity, the "Seller"), and AHFC, as servicer (in such capacity, the "Servicer"), and (iii) a Letter of Representations, dated February 25, 2003 (the "Note Depository Agreement" and, together with this Agreement, the Indenture, the Sale and Servicing Agreement, the Control Agreement and the Trust Agreement, the "Related Documents"), among the Issuer, the Indenture Trustee and The Depository Trust Company;

WHEREAS, pursuant to the Related Documents, the Issuer and the Owner Trustee are required to perform certain duties in connection with (i) the Notes and the collateral therefor pledged pursuant to the Indenture (the "Collateral") and (ii) the beneficial ownership interests in the Issuer (the registered holders of such interests being referred to herein as the "Owners");

WHEREAS, the Issuer and the Owner Trustee desire to have the Administrator perform certain of the duties of the Issuer and the Owner Trustee referred to in the preceding clause and to provide such additional services consistent with the terms of this Agreement and the other Related Documents as the Issuer and the Owner Trustee may from time to time request; and

WHEREAS, the Administrator has the capacity to provide the services required hereby and is willing to perform such services for the Issuer and the Owner Trustee on the terms set forth herein;

NOW, THEREFORE, in consideration of the mutual agreements herein contained, and of other good and valuable consideration, the receipt and adequacy of which are hereby acknowledged, the parties hereto agree as follows:

Section 1.01. Capitalized Terms; Interpretive Provisions.

(a) Capitalized terms used herein that are not otherwise defined shall have the meanings ascribed thereto or incorporated by reference in the Sale and Servicing Agreement, the Trust Agreement or the Indenture, as the case may be. Whenever used herein, unless the context otherwise requires, the following words and phrases shall have the following meanings:

"Agreement" means this Administration Agreement, as amended, supplemented or modified from time to time.

"Related Documents" has the meaning set forth in the Preamble.

(b) For all purposes of this Agreement, except as otherwise expressly provided or unless the context otherwise requires, (i) terms used in this Agreement include, as appropriate, all genders and the plural as well as the singular, (ii) references to this Agreement include all Exhibits hereto, (iii) references to words such as "herein", "hereof" and the like shall refer to this Agreement as a whole and not to any particular part, Article or Section within this Agreement, (iv) the term "include" and all variations thereof shall mean "include without limitation", (v) the term "or" shall include "and/or" and (vi) the term "proceeds" shall have the meaning ascribed to such term in the UCC.

Section 1.02. Duties of the Administrator.

(a) The Administrator agrees to perform all its duties as Administrator and, except as specifically excluded herein, agrees to perform all the duties of the Issuer and the Owner Trustee under the Related Documents. In addition, the Administrator shall consult with the Owner Trustee regarding the duties of the Issuer or the Owner Trustee under the Related Documents. The Administrator shall monitor the performance of the Issuer and shall advise the Owner Trustee when action is necessary to comply with the respective duties of the Issuer and the Owner Trustee under the Related Documents. The Administrator shall prepare for execution by the Issuer or the Owner Trustee, or shall cause the preparation by other appropriate persons of, all such documents, reports, notices, filings, instruments, certificates and opinions that it shall be the duty of the Issuer or the Owner Trustee to prepare, file or deliver pursuant to the Related Documents. In furtherance of the foregoing, the Administrator shall take (or, in the case of the immediately preceding sentence, cause to be taken) all appropriate action that the Issuer or the Owner Trustee is required to take pursuant to the Indenture including, without limitation, such of the foregoing as are required with respect to the following matters under the Indenture (references are to Sections of the Indenture):

(i) the preparation of or obtaining of the documents and instruments required for execution and authentication of the Notes and delivery of the same to the Indenture Trustee (Section 2.02);

(ii) the duty to cause the Note Register to be kept and to give the Indenture Trustee notice of any appointment of a new Note Registrar and the location, or change in location, of the Note Register (Section 2.04);

(iii) the notification of Noteholders and the Rating Agencies of the final principal payment on the Notes (Section 2.07(b));

(iv) the fixing or causing to be fixed of any special record date and the notification of the Indenture Trustee and Noteholders with respect to special payment dates, if any (Section 2.07(c));

(v) the preparation of Definitive Notes in accordance with the instructions of the Clearing Agency (Section 2.11);

(vi) the preparation, obtaining or filing of the instruments, opinions and certificates and other documents required for the release of collateral (Section 2.12);

(vii) the duty to cause newly appointed Paying Agents, if any, to deliver to the Indenture Trustee the instrument specified in the Indenture regarding funds held in trust (Section 3.03);

(viii) the direction to the Indenture Trustee to deposit monies with Paying Agents, if any, other than the Indenture Trustee (Section 3.03);

(ix) the obtaining and preservation of the Issuer's qualifications to do business, including under the Pennsylvania Motor Vehicle Sale Finance Act and MD. Fin. Inst. Code Ann., Title 11, Subtitle 4 (Section 3.04);

(x) the preparation of all supplements and amendments to the Indenture and all financing statements, continuation statements, instruments of further assurance and other instruments and the taking of such other action as are necessary or advisable to protect the Owner Trust Estate (Section 3.05);

(xi) the delivery of the Opinion of Counsel on the Closing Date and the annual delivery of Opinions of Counsel as to the Owner Trust Estate, and the annual delivery of the Officer's Certificate and certain other statements as to compliance with the Indenture (Sections 3.06 and 3.09);

(xii) the identification to the Indenture Trustee in an Officer's Certificate of a Person with whom the Issuer has contracted to perform its duties under the Indenture (Section 3.07(b));

(xiii) the notification of the Indenture Trustee and the Rating Agencies of each Servicer Default and, if such Servicer Default arises from the failure of the Servicer to perform any of its duties or obligations under the Servicing Agreement with respect to the Receivables, the taking of all reasonable steps available to remedy such failure (Section 3.07(d));

(xiv) the preparation and obtaining of documents and instruments required for the release of the Issuer from its obligations upon the merger or consolidation of the Issuer under the Indenture and the obtaining of the Opinion of Counsel and the Officer's Certificate relating thereto (Section 3.10);

(xv) the duty to cause the Servicer to comply with Sections 3.10, 3.11, 3.12, 4.10 and Article Eight of the Sale and Servicing Agreement (Section 3.14);

(xvi) the delivery of written notice to the Indenture Trustee and each Rating Agency of each Event of Default and each default by the Servicer or the Seller under the Sale and Servicing Agreement (Section 3.19);

(xvii) the monitoring of the Issuer's obligations as to the satisfaction and discharge of the Indenture and the preparation of an Officer's Certificate and the obtaining of the Opinion of Counsel and the Independent Certificate relating thereto (Section 4.01);

(xviii) the compliance with Section 5.04 of the Indenture with respect to the sale of the Owner Trust Estate in a commercially reasonable manner if an Event of Default shall have occurred and be continuing (Section 5.04);

(xix) the preparation and delivery of notice to Noteholders of the removal of the Indenture Trustee and the appointment of a successor Indenture Trustee (Section 6.08);

(xx) the preparation and delivery to each Noteholder such information as may be required to enable such holder to prepare its federal and state income tax returns (Section 6.06);

(xxi) the preparation of any written instruments required to confirm more fully the authority of any co-trustee or separate trustee and any written instruments necessary in connection with the resignation or removal of the Indenture Trustee or any co-trustee or separate trustee (Sections 6.08 and 6.10);

(xxii) the furnishing of the Indenture Trustee with the names and addresses of Noteholders during any period when the Indenture Trustee is not the Note Registrar (Section 7.01);

(xxiii) the preparation and, after execution by the Issuer, the filing with the Commission, any applicable state agencies and the Indenture Trustee of documents required to be filed on a periodic basis with, and summaries thereof as may be required by rules and regulations prescribed by, the Commission and any applicable state agencies and the transmission of such summaries, as necessary, to the Noteholders (Section 7.03);

(xxiv) the opening of one or more accounts in the Issuer's name and the taking of all other actions necessary with respect to investment and reinvestment of funds in the Accounts (Sections 8.02 and 8.03);

(xxv) the preparation of an Issuer Request and Officer's Certificate and the obtaining of an Opinion of Counsel and Independent Certificates, if necessary, for the release of the Owner Trust Estate (Sections 8.04 and 8.05);

(xxvi) the preparation of Issuer Requests, the obtaining of Opinions of Counsel and the certification to the Indenture Trustee with respect to the execution of supplemental indentures and the mailing to the Noteholders of notices with respect to such supplemental indentures (Sections 9.01 and 9.02);

(xxvii) the execution and delivery of new Notes conforming to any supplemental indenture (Section 9.06);

(xxviii) the duty to notify Noteholders and the Rating Agencies of redemption of the Notes or to cause the Indenture Trustee to provide such notification (Sections 10.01 and 10.02);

(xxix) the preparation and delivery of all Officer's Certificates, Opinions of Counsel and Independent Certificates with respect to any requests by the Issuer to the Indenture Trustee to take any action under the Indenture (Section 11.01(a));

(xxx) the preparation and delivery of Officer's Certificates and the obtaining of Independent Certificates, if necessary, for the release of property from the Lien of the Indenture (Section 11.01(b));

(xxxi) the notification of each Rating Agency, upon the failure of the Issuer, the Owner Trustee or the Indenture Trustee to give such notification, of the information required pursuant to Section 11.04 of the Indenture (Section 11.04); and

(xxxii) the recording of the Indenture, if applicable (Section 11.15).

(b) The Administrator shall:

(i) pay from time to time reasonable compensation to (A) the Indenture Trustee for all services rendered by the Indenture Trustee under the Basic Documents and (B) the Owner Trustee for all services rendered under the Trust Agreement (in each case which compensation shall not be limited by any provision of law in regard to the compensation of a trustee of an express trust);

(ii) except as otherwise expressly provided in the Indenture, reimburse the Indenture Trustee upon its request for all reasonable expenses, disbursements and advances incurred or made by the Indenture Trustee in accordance with any provision of the Basic Documents (including the reasonable compensation, expenses and disbursements of its agents and counsel), except any such expense, disbursement or advance as may be attributable to its willful misconduct, negligence or bad faith;

(iii) except as otherwise expressly provided in the third sentence of Section 7.01 of the Trust Agreement, reimburse the Owner Trustee and the Delaware Trustee upon its request for all reasonable expenses, disbursements and advances incurred or made by the Owner Trustee and the Delaware Trustee in accordance with any provision of the Trust Agreement (including reasonable compensation, expenses and disbursements of its agents and counsel), except any such expense, disbursement or advance as may be attributable to its willful misconduct, gross negligence or bad faith; and

(iv) indemnify the Indenture Trustee, the Delaware Trustee, the Owner Trustee and their respective agents for, and hold them harmless against, any loss, liability or expense incurred without negligence (or, in the case of the Owner Trustee only, gross negligence), willful misconduct or bad faith on their part, arising out of or in connection with the acceptance or administration of the transactions contemplated by the Basic Documents, as the case may be, including the reasonable costs and expenses of defending themselves against any claim or liability in connection with the exercise or performance of any of their powers or duties thereunder.

The obligations of the Administrator under this Section 1.02(b) shall survive the termination of this agreement.

(c) In addition to the duties set forth in Sections 1.02(a) and (b), the Administrator shall perform such calculations and shall prepare or shall cause the preparation by other appropriate Persons of, and shall execute on behalf of the Issuer or the Owner Trustee, all such documents, notices, reports, filings, instruments, certificates and opinions that the Issuer or the Owner Trustee are required to prepare, file or deliver pursuant to the Related Documents, and at the request of the Owner Trustee shall take all appropriate action that the Issuer or the Owner Trustee are required to take pursuant to the Related Documents. In furtherance thereof, the Owner Trustee shall, on behalf of itself and of the Issuer, execute and deliver to the Administrator and to each successor Administrator appointed pursuant to the terms hereof, one or more powers of attorney substantially in the form of Exhibit A hereto, appointing the Administrator the attorney-in-fact of the Owner Trustee and the Issuer for the purpose of executing on behalf of the Owner Trustee and the Issuer all such documents, reports, filings, instruments, certificates and opinions. Subject to Section 1.06, and in accordance with the directions of the Owner Trustee, the Administrator shall administer, perform or supervise the performance of such other activities in connection with the Collateral (including the Related Documents) as are not covered by any of the foregoing provisions and as are expressly requested by the Owner Trustee and are reasonably within the capability of the Administrator.

(d) Notwithstanding anything in this Agreement or the Related Documents to the contrary, the Administrator shall be responsible for promptly notifying the Owner Trustee in the event that any withholding tax is imposed on the Issuer's payments (or allocations of income) to a Trust Certificateholder as contemplated in Section 5.02(c) of the Trust Agreement. Any such notice shall specify the amount of any withholding tax required to be withheld by the Owner Trustee pursuant to such provision.

(e) Notwithstanding anything in this Agreement or the Related Documents to the contrary, the Administrator shall be responsible for performance of the duties of the Owner Trustee set forth in Section 5.05 of the Trust Agreement with respect to, among other things, accounting and reports to Owners; provided, however, that the Owner Trustee shall retain responsibility for the distribution of the Schedule K-1's, necessary to enable each Owner to prepare its federal and state income tax returns.

(f) The Administrator shall perform any duties expressly required to be performed by the Administrator under the Trust Agreement or the Indenture.

(g) In carrying out the foregoing duties or any of its other obligations under this Agreement, the Administrator may enter into transactions or otherwise deal with any of its Affiliates; provided, however, that the terms of any such transactions or dealings shall be in accordance with any directions received from the Issuer and shall be, in the Administrator's opinion, no less favorable to the Issuer than would be available from unaffiliated parties.

(h) With respect to matters that in the reasonable judgment of the Administrator are non-ministerial, the Administrator shall not take any action unless within a reasonable time before the taking of such action, the Administrator shall have notified the Owner Trustee of the proposed action and the Owner Trustee shall not have withheld consent or provided an alternative direction. For the purpose of the preceding sentence, "non-ministerial matters" shall include:

(i) the amendment of or any supplement to the Indenture;

(ii) the initiation of any claim or lawsuit by the Issuer and the compromise of any action, claim or lawsuit brought by or against the Issuer (other than in connection with the collection of the Receivables);

(iii) the amendment, change or modification of the Basic Documents;

(iv) the appointment of successor Note Registrars, successor Paying Agents and successor Indenture Trustees pursuant to the Indenture or the appointment of successor Administrators or successor Servicers, or the consent to the assignment by the Note Registrar, any Paying Agent or Indenture Trustee of its obligations under the Indenture; and

(v) the removal of the Indenture Trustee.

(i) Notwithstanding anything to the contrary in this Agreement, the Administrator shall not be obligated to, and shall not, (i) make any payments to the Noteholders under the Related Documents, (ii) sell the Owner Trust Estate pursuant to Section 5.04 of the Indenture, (iii) take any other action that the Issuer directs the Administrator not to take on its behalf or (iv) take any other action which may be construed as having the effect of varying the investment of the Trust Certificateholders.

Section 1.03. Records. The Administrator shall maintain appropriate books of account and records relating to services performed hereunder, which books of account and records shall be accessible for inspection by the Issuer and the Depositor at any time during normal business hours.

Section 1.04. Compensation. As compensation for the performance of the Administrator's obligations under this Agreement and as reimbursement for its expenses related thereto, the Administrator shall be entitled to an annual payment of compensation which shall be solely an obligation of the Depositor.

Section 1.05. Additional Information to be Furnished to the Issuer. The Administrator shall furnish to the Issuer from time to time such additional information regarding the Collateral as the Issuer shall reasonably request.

Section 1.06. Independence of the Administrator. For all purposes of this Agreement, the Administrator shall be an independent contractor and shall not be subject to the supervision of the Issuer or the Owner Trustee with respect to the manner in which it accomplishes the performance of its obligations hereunder.

Unless expressly authorized by the Issuer, the Administrator shall have no authority to act for or represent the Issuer or the Owner Trustee in any way and shall not otherwise be deemed an agent of the Issuer or the Owner Trustee.

Section 1.07. No Joint Venture. Nothing contained in this Agreement (i) shall constitute the Administrator and either the Issuer or the Owner Trustee as members of any partnership, joint venture, association, syndicate, unincorporated business or other separate entity, (ii) shall be construed to impose any liability as such on any of them or (iii) shall be deemed to confer on any of them any express, implied or apparent authority to incur any obligation or liability on behalf of the others.

Section 1.08. Other Activities of Administrator. Nothing herein shall prevent the Administrator or its Affiliates from engaging in other businesses or, in its sole discretion, from acting in a similar capacity as an administrator for any other Person or entity, even though such person or entity may engage in business activities similar to those of the Issuer, the Owner Trustee or the Indenture Trustee.

Section 1.09. Term of Agreement; Resignation and Removal of Administrator. This Agreement shall continue in force until the dissolution of the Issuer, upon which event this Agreement shall automatically terminate.

(a) Subject to Sections 1.09(d) and 1.09(e), the Administrator may resign its duties hereunder by providing the Issuer with at least 60 days' prior written notice.

(b) Subject to Sections 1.09(d) and 1.09(e), the Issuer may remove the Administrator without cause by providing the Administrator with at least 60 days' prior written notice.

(c) Subject to Sections 1.09(d) and 1.09(e), at the sole option of the Issuer, the Administrator may be removed immediately upon written notice of termination from the Issuer to the Administrator if any of the following events shall occur:

(i) the Administrator shall default in the performance of any of its duties under this Agreement and, after notice of such default, shall not cure such default within ten days (or, if such default cannot be cured in such time, shall not give within ten days such assurance of cure as shall be reasonably satisfactory to the Issuer);

(ii) the existence of any proceeding or action, or the entry of a decree or order for relief by a court or regulatory authority having jurisdiction over the Administrator in an involuntary case under the federal bankruptcy laws, as now or hereafter in effect, or appointing a receiver, liquidator, assignee, trustee, custodian, sequestrator or other similar official of the Administrator or of any substantial part of its property, or ordering the winding up or liquidation of the affairs of the Administrator and the continuance of any such action, proceeding, decree or order unstayed and, in the case of any such order or decree, in effect for a period of 90 consecutive days; or

(iii) the commencement by the Administrator of a voluntary case under the federal bankruptcy laws, as now or hereafter in effect, or the consent by the Administrator to the appointment of or taking of possession by a receiver, liquidator, assignee, trustee, custodian, sequestrator or other similar official of the Administrator or of any substantial part of its property or the making by the Administrator of an assignment for the benefit of creditors or the failure by the Administrator generally to pay its debts as such debts become due or the taking of corporate action by the Administrator in furtherance of any of the foregoing.

The Administrator agrees that if any of the events specified in clauses (ii) or (iii) above shall occur, it shall give written notice thereof to the Issuer and the Indenture Trustee within seven days after the occurrence of such event.

(d) No resignation or removal of the Administrator pursuant to this Section shall be effective until (i) a successor Administrator shall have been appointed by the Issuer and (ii) such successor Administrator shall have agreed in writing to be bound by the terms of this Agreement in the same manner as the Administrator is bound hereunder.

(e) The appointment of any successor Administrator shall be effective only after satisfaction of the Rating Agency Condition with respect to the proposed appointment.

(f) Subject to Sections 1.09(d) and 1.09(e), the Administrator acknowledges that upon the appointment of a successor Servicer pursuant to the Sale and Servicing Agreement, the Administrator shall immediately resign and such successor Servicer shall automatically become the Administrator under this Agreement.

Section 1.10. Action Upon Termination, Resignation or Removal. Promptly upon the effective date of termination of this Agreement pursuant to the first sentence of Section 1.09 or the resignation or removal of the Administrator pursuant to Section 1.09(a), (b) or (c), respectively, the Administrator shall be entitled to be paid all fees and reimbursable expenses accruing to it to the date of such termination, resignation or removal. The Administrator shall forthwith upon such termination pursuant to the first sentence of Section 1.09 deliver to the Issuer all property and documents of or relating to the Collateral then in the custody of the Administrator. In the event of the resignation or removal of the Administrator pursuant to Section 1.09(a), (b) or (c), respectively, the Administrator shall cooperate with the Issuer and take all reasonable steps requested to assist the Issuer in making an orderly transfer of the duties of the Administrator.

Section 1.11. Notices. All demands, notices and communications hereunder shall be in writing and shall be delivered or mailed by registered or certified first-class United States mail, postage prepaid, hand delivery, prepaid courier service, or by telecopier (followed by hard copy by overnight delivery), and addressed in each case as follows: (a) if to the Issuer or the Owner Trustee, to: The Bank of New York, 101 Barclay Street, 8th Floor West, New York, New York 10286, Attention: Asset Backed Securities Unit — Honda 2003-1; (b) if to the Administrator, to: American Honda Finance Corporation, 700 Van Ness Avenue,

Building 300, Torrance, California 90501, Attention: President; (c) if to the Depositor, to: American Honda Receivables Corp., 700 Van Ness Avenue, Building 300, Torrance, California 90501, Attention: President; and (d) if to the Indenture Trustee, to: JPMorgan Chase Bank, 4 New York Plaza, 6th Floor, New York, New York 10004, Attention: Institutional Trust Services: Honda Auto Receivables 2003-1 Owner Trust; or to such other address as any party shall have provided to the other parties in writing. Any notice required to be in writing hereunder shall be deemed given if such notice is mailed by certified mail, postage prepaid, or hand-delivered to the address of such party as provided above.

Section 1.12. Amendments. This Agreement may be amended from time to time by a written amendment duly executed and delivered by the parties hereto, with the written consent of the Owner Trustee but without the consent of the Noteholders or the Certificateholders, for the purpose of adding any provisions to or changing in any manner or eliminating any of the provisions of this Agreement or of modifying in any manner the rights of the Noteholders or the Certificateholders; provided, that such amendment will not, in the Opinion of Counsel satisfactory to the Indenture Trustee, materially and adversely affect the interest of any of the Noteholders or the Certificateholders. This Agreement may also be amended by the parties hereto with the written consent of the Owner Trustee and the Holders of Notes evidencing at least a majority of the Outstanding Amount and the Holders of Trust Certificates evidencing at least a majority of the Percentage Interests evidenced by the Trust Certificates for the purpose of adding any provisions to or changing in any manner or eliminating any of the provisions of this Agreement or of modifying in any manner the rights of the Noteholders or the Certificateholders; provided, however, that no such amendment may (i) increase or reduce in any manner the amount of, or accelerate or delay the timing of, collections of payments on the Receivables or distributions that are required to be made for the benefit of the Noteholders or the Certificateholders or (ii) reduce the aforesaid percentage of the Holders of Notes and Trust Certificates which are required to consent to any such amendment, without the written consent of the Holders of all outstanding Notes and Trust Certificates. Notwithstanding the foregoing, the Administrator may not amend this Agreement without the permission of the Depositor, which permission shall not be unreasonably withheld.

Section 1.13. Successors and Assigns. This Agreement may not be assigned by the Administrator unless such assignment is previously consented to in writing by the Issuer and the Owner Trustee and subject to the satisfaction of the Rating Agency Condition in respect thereof. An assignment with such consent and satisfaction, if accepted by the assignee, shall bind the assignee hereunder in the same manner as the Administrator is bound hereunder. Notwithstanding the foregoing, this Agreement may be assigned by the Administrator without the consent of the Issuer or the Owner Trustee to a corporation or other organization that is a successor (by merger, consolidation or purchase of assets) to the Administrator; provided, that such successor organization executes and delivers to the Issuer, the Owner Trustee and the Indenture Trustee an agreement, in form and substance reasonably satisfactory to the Owner Trustee and the Indenture Trustee, in which such corporation or other organization agrees to be bound hereunder by the terms of said assignment in the same manner as the Administrator is bound hereunder. Subject to the foregoing, this Agreement shall bind any successors or assigns of the parties hereto.

Section 1.14. Governing Law. THIS AGREEMENT SHALL BE CONSTRUED IN ACCORDANCE WITH THE LAWS OF THE STATE OF CALIFORNIA, WITHOUT REFERENCE TO ITS CONFLICT OF LAW PROVISIONS, AND THE OBLIGATIONS, RIGHTS AND REMEDIES OF THE PARTIES HEREUNDER SHALL BE DETERMINED IN ACCORDANCE WITH SUCH LAWS, EXCEPT THAT THE DUTIES, RIGHTS AND PROTECTIONS OF EACH OF THE OWNER TRUSTEE AND THE INDENTURE TRUSTEE SHALL BE GOVERNED BY THE LAWS OF THE STATE OF NEW YORK.

Section 1.15. Headings. The headings of the various Sections herein are for convenience of reference only and shall not define or limit any of the terms or provisions hereof.

Section 1.16. Counterparts. This Agreement may be executed by the parties hereto in separate counterparts, each of which when so executed and delivered shall be an original, but all such counterparts shall together constitute but one and the same instrument.

Section 1.17. Severability. Any provision of this Agreement that is prohibited or unenforceable in any jurisdiction shall, as to such jurisdiction, be ineffective to the extent of such prohibition or unenforceability without invalidating the remaining provisions hereof, and any such prohibition or unenforceability in any jurisdiction shall not invalidate or render unenforceable such provision in any other jurisdiction.

Section 1.18. Limitation of Liability of Owner Trustee and Indenture Trustee.

(a) Notwithstanding anything contained herein to the contrary, this instrument has been countersigned by The Bank of New York, in its capacity as Owner Trustee of the Issuer and in no event shall The Bank of New York, in its individual capacity or any beneficial owner of the Issuer have any liability for the representations, warranties, covenants, agreements or other obligations of the Issuer hereunder, as to all of which recourse shall be had solely to the assets of the Issuer. For all purposes of this Agreement, in the performance of any duties or obligations of the Issuer hereunder, the Owner Trustee shall be subject to, and entitled to the benefits of, the terms and provisions of Articles Six, Seven and Eight of the Trust Agreement.

(b) Notwithstanding anything contained herein to the contrary, this Agreement has been executed by JPMorgan Chase Bank in its capacity as Indenture Trustee under the Indenture and in no event shall JPMorgan Chase Bank in its individual capacity have any liability for the representations, warranties, covenants, agreements or other obligations of the Issuer hereunder or in any of the certificates, notices or agreements delivered pursuant hereto, as to all of which recourse shall be had solely to the assets of the Issuer.

Section 1.19. Third-Party Beneficiary. The Owner Trustee and the Delaware Trustee are third-party beneficiaries to this Agreement and are entitled to the rights and benefits hereunder and may enforce the provisions hereof as if they were a party hereto.

Section 1.20. Rights of the Indenture Trustee. The Indenture Trustee shall be afforded the same rights, protections, immunities and indemnities set forth in the Indenture as if specifically set forth herein.

IN WITNESS WHEREOF, the parties hereto have caused this Agreement to be duly executed and delivered as of the day and year first above written.

HONDA AUTO RECEIVABLES 2003-1 OWNER TRUST,

as Issuer

By: THE BANK OF NEW YORK,
not in its individual capacity
but solely as Owner Trustee

/s/ John Bobko

By: ______________________________

Name: John Bobko

Title: Assistant Vice President

AMERICAN HONDA RECEIVABLES CORP.,

as Depositor

/s/ Y. Takahashi

By: ______________________________

Name: Y. Takahashi

Title: President

JPMORGAN CHASE BANK,
not in its individual capacity but solely as
Indenture Trustee

/s/ Jennifer McCourt

By: ______________________________

Name: Jennifer McCourt

Title: Vice President

AMERICAN HONDA FINANCE CORPORATION,

as Administrator

/s/ Y. Takahashi

By: ______________________________

Name: Y. Takahashi

Title: President

EXHIBIT A

POWER OF ATTORNEY PURSUANT TO SECTION 1.02(c) OF ADMINISTRATION AGREEMENT

KNOW ALL MEN BY THESE PRESENTS, that The Bank of New York (the "Grantor"), located at 101 Barclay Street, 8th Floor West, New York, New York 10286, as owner trustee of Honda Auto Receivables 2003-1 Owner Trust, a Delaware statutory trust (the "Issuer"), does hereby appoint American Honda Finance Corporation, a California corporation (the "Grantee"), located at 700 Van Ness Avenue, Building 300, Torrance, California 90501, as its attorney-in-fact with full power of substitution and hereby authorizes and empowers the Grantee, in the name of and on behalf of the Grantor or the Issuer, to take the following actions from time to time with respect to the duties of the Administrator under the Administration Agreement, dated as of February 1, 2003 (the "Administration Agreement"), among the Issuer, the Administrator, American Honda Receivables Corp., as depositor and JPMorgan Chase Bank, as indenture trustee, for the purpose of executing on behalf of the Grantor or the Issuer all such documents, reports, filings, instruments, certificates and opinions required pursuant to the Related Documents:

The Grantee is hereby empowered to do any and all lawful acts necessary or desirable to effect the performance of the duties under the Administration Agreement and the Grantor hereby ratifies and confirms any and all lawful acts the Grantee shall undertake pursuant to and in conformity with this Power of Attorney.

This Power of Attorney is revocable in whole or in part as to the powers herein granted upon notice by the Grantor. If not earlier revoked, this Power of Attorney shall expire completely or, if so indicated, in part, upon the earlier of (i) the termination of the amended and restated trust agreement, dated February 25, 2003 (the "Trust Agreement"), between American Honda Receivables Corp., as depositor and the Grantor, as owner trustee, or (ii) the termination of the Administration Agreement, as each may be amended, restated or supplemented from time to time. Capitalized terms used herein that are not otherwise defined shall have the meanings ascribed thereto in the Trust Agreement or the Administration Agreement, as the case may be.

THIS POWER OF ATTORNEY SHALL BE CREATED UNDER AND GOVERNED AND CONSTRUED UNDER THE INTERNAL LAWS OF THE STATE OF NEW YORK.

The Grantor executes this Power of Attorney with the intent to be legally bound hereby, and with the intent that such execution shall have the full dignity afforded by the accompanying witnessing and notarization and all lesser dignity resulting from the absence of such witnessing and notarization or any combination thereof.

Dated this ____ day of February, 2003.

[Seal] THE BANK OF NEW YORK,
not in its individual capacity but solely as Owner
Trustee of the Honda Auto Receivables 2003-1
Owner Trust

By ____________________________________
Name:
Title:
Signed and delivered in the presence of.

____

Address: ________________________________

[Unofficial Witness]

Table of Cases

(Principal cases are in all caps; references are to pages.)

Table of Statutes

(References are to pages.)

FEDERAL LAW

Internal Revenue Code

United States Code

Treasury Regulations

Code of Federal Regulations

UNIFORM ACTS

Uniform Commercial Code

Uniform Fraudulent Conveyance Act

Uniform Fraudulent Transfer Act

STATE STATUTES

Alabama

Delaware

Louisiana

North Carolina

New Jersey

Ohio

South Dakota

Texas

INTERNATIONAL

Convention on Contract for the International Sale of Goods (UNCITRAL)

English Statutes

INDEX

[References are to pages.]

A

B

[References are to pages.]

[References are to pages.]

[References are to pages.]